A Great and Terrible King

A Great and Terrible King

EDWARD I AND THE FORGING OF BRITAIN

MARC MORRIS

PEGASUS BOOKS
NEW YORK LONDON

A GREAT AND TERRIBLE KING

Pegasus Books, Ltd.
148 West 37th Street, 13th Floor
New York, NY 10018

First Pegasus Books paperback edition June 2016
First Pegasus Books hardcover edition March 2015

ISBN: 978-1-68177-133-5

10 9 8 7 6

Printed in the United States of America
Distributed by Simon & Schuster
www.pegasusbooks.com

In memory of Rees Davies

Countries are not laid up in heaven; they are shaped and reshaped here on earth by the stratagems of men and the victories of the fortuitous.

R. R. Davies, *The First English Empire* (2000)

Like Alexander, he would speedily subdue the whole world, if Fortune's moving wheel would stand still forever.

The Song of Lewes, on Edward I (1264)

Contents

Illustrations ix

Preface xi

1 A Saint in Name 1
2 The Family Feud 31
3 Civil Peace and Holy War 70
4 The Return of the King 103
5 The Disobedient Prince 131
6 Arthur's Crown 159
7 Peaceful Endeavours 194
8 The Great Cause 229
9 The Struggle for Mastery 262
10 Uniting the Kingdom? 301
11 A Lasting Vengeance 345
12 A Great and Terrible King 363

Abbreviations 379
Notes 383
Bibliography 421
Family Trees 435
Index 439

Illustrations

Photo Insert

A possible portrait of Edward I. *Copyright Dean and Chapter of Westminster.*
Conwy Castle. *Cadw, Welsh Government (Crown Copyright)*
Harlech Castle. *Cadw, Welsh Government (Crown Copyright)*
Caernarfon Castle. *Cadw, Welsh Government (Crown Copyright)*
Beaumaris Castle. *Cadw, Welsh Government (Crown Copyright)*
The Eleanor Cross at Geddington. *Copyright Marc Morris*
The tomb of Eleanor of Castile. *Copyright Westminster Abbey, London, UK/The Bridgeman Art Library.*
The Coronation Chair. *Copyright Dean and Chapter of Westminster.*
Monpazier. *Copyright Philippe Dufour*
Edward I's chamber at the Tower of London (St. Thomas's Tower). *Copyright Historic Royal Palaces/newstream.co.uk*
Caerlaverock Castle, Scotland. *Copyright Marc Morris*
Lanercost Priory, Cumbria. *Copyright Marc Morris*
Edward I in his open tomb. *Copyright Society of Antiquaries of London.*
The tomb of Edward I at Westminster Abbey. *Copyright Dean and Chapter of Westminster.*

Maps

England   p. xvii
Wales   p. 30
Gascony   p. 206
Scotland   p. 238

Preface

On learning that I was writing a book about Edward I, my non-historian friends and neighbours have asked me, almost invariably, the same two questions. 'Was he Edward the Confessor?' has been by far the most common. No, I would always answer, he was not; but he was named *after* him. In many cases this only served to provoke a subsidiary, more vexed inquiry. If my subject was named *after* one of his forebears, then how on earth could he possibly be 'the First'? The answer, of course, is that he couldn't, and that, strictly speaking, he wasn't. For those who would care to know precisely how this confusing situation came about, I have added a short note of explanation at the end of this Preface.

The second question that has usually been put to me concerns the nature of the evidence for writing the biography of a medieval king, and specifically its quantity. In general, people tend to presume that there can't be very much, and imagine that I must spend my days poking around in castle muniment rooms, looking for previously undiscovered scraps of parchment. Sadly, they are mistaken. The answer I always give to the question of how much evidence is: more than one person could look at in a lifetime. From the early twelfth century, the kings of England began to keep written accounts of their annual expenditure, and by the end of the century they were keeping a written record of almost every aspect of royal government. Each time a royal document was issued, be it a grand charter or a routine writ, a copy was dutifully entered on to a large parchment roll. Meanwhile, in the provinces, the king's justices kept similar rolls to record the proceedings of the cases that came before his courts. Miraculously, the great majority of these documents have survived, and are now preserved in the National Archives at Kew near London. Some of them, when unrolled, extend to twenty or thirty feet. And their number is legion:

for the thirteenth century alone, it runs to tens of thousands. Mercifully for the medieval historian, the most important have been transcribed and published, but even this printed matter would be enough to line the walls of an average-sized front room with books. Moreover, the quantity is increased by the inclusion of non-royal material. Others besides the king were keeping records during Edward I's day. Noblemen also drew up financial accounts, issued charters and wrote letters; monks did the same, only in their case the chances of such material surviving was much improved by their membership of an institution. Monks, in addition, continued to do as they had always done, and kept chronicles, and these too provide plenty to keep the historian busy. To take just the most obvious example from the thirteenth century, the monk of St Albans called Matthew Paris composed a chronicle, the original parts of which cover the quarter century from 1234 to 1259. In its modern edition it runs to seven volumes.

I say all this merely to demonstrate how much there is to know about our medieval ancestors, and not to pretend that I have in some way managed to scale this mountain all by myself. For the most part I have not even had to approach the mountain at all, for this book is grounded on the scholarly work of others. Nevertheless, even the secondary material for a study of Edward I presents a daunting prospect. At a conservative estimate, well over a thousand books and articles have been published in the last hundred years that deal with one aspect or another of the king's reign. For scholarly works on the thirteenth century as a whole, that figure would have to be multiplied many times over.

By this stage, anyone who had quizzed me about the making of this book – assuming they were still listening – must have had a third question forming in their minds, though they were all too polite to pose it. That question, I imagine, was 'why bother?' Why devote a sizeable chunk of one's own life to re-examining the deeds of a man who has been dead for seven centuries? The answer, as I hope the finished product will make clear, is that the reign of Edward I matters. Not for nothing did I settle on a subtitle that includes the phrase 'the forging of Britain'. This period was one of the most pivotal in the whole of British history, a moment when the destinies of England, Wales, Scotland and Ireland were decided. It was also one of the most dramatic. Edward summoned the biggest armies and the largest parliaments seen in Britain during the Middle Ages; he built the greatest chain of castles in Europe; he expelled the Jews, conquered the Welsh and very nearly succeeded in conquering the Scots. We are often told these days that we ought to have a greater sense of what it means to be British. I hope that this book goes some small way towards fulfilling that need.

Naturally, this is not the first attempt to broach the subject (nor, I predict, will it be the last). In the twentieth century Edward I was examined at length by two eminent medieval historians, Maurice Powicke and Michael Prestwich. As the notes at the end of this book make clear, my debt to both is very great. During several years of writing and research I have turned to their books constantly and repeatedly, and have always been struck by insights that would not have occurred to me from the original evidence. And even when I have looked at the evidence and reached different conclusions, their work has always provided me with an invaluable starting point. The main way in which my work differs from theirs is in its construction. Both Powicke and Prestwich chose to approach Edward thematically, devoting whole chapters to his lawmaking, his diplomacy, and so on. I have opted for a chronological treatment, which gives the following pages some claim to originality. No one has attempted to tell Edward's story from beginning to end since before the First World War, which effectively means that no one has told his story in this way since the invention of medieval history as a modern academic discipline. Of course, such a chronological approach has certain inherent drawbacks. Some academic readers may be disappointed that there is not more here on Edward's statutes or his governmental inquiries. I can only offer the excuse that the discussion of such topics would have been hard to incorporate into an already complicated narrative without the whole thing grinding to a halt, and that, in any case, these topics have been well covered elsewhere. I also take some comfort from recent research which suggests that the 'English Justinian' probably had no hand, and perhaps little interest, in drawing up the laws that were issued in his name. On a more positive note, the task of putting the events of Edward's life in their correct order has led me to question existing orthodoxies more frequently than I had imagined might be necessary. I hope that the new interpretations I have offered in their place will be found convincing, or at least stimulating, by other medievalists.

Mention of other medievalists leads me to a long list of acknowledgements; as I have already said, this volume rests in no small measure on the researches of others. Chapter Eight, for example, draws heavily on the recent work of Archie Duncan, who was kind enough to send me a draft of his latest thoughts on Edward's activities at Norham, and also to lend me his translation of the sections of Walter of Guisborough that relate to events in Scotland. Paul Brand and Henry Summerson were equally kind in allowing me to read their recent unpublished papers, Huw Ridgeway and Bob Stacey responded helpfully to emails requesting clarification of certain aspects of Henry III's reign, and David

D'Avray and George Garnett patiently answered my telephone inquiries about the mysteries of the English coronation. I received similar help, in one form or another, from Jeremy Ashbee, Paul Binski, Robert Bartlett, Nicola Coldstream, Beth Hartland, Jess Nelson, Michael Prestwich, John Pryor, Matthew Reeve, Robin Studd, Mark Vaughn and Fiona Watson. Others have provided useful critical feedback and moral support: in particular, I should like to thank Adrian Jobson, Michael Ray and Andrew Spencer, and also Richard Huscroft, who offered me the additional treat of a tour of the tombs at Westminster Abbey. On another visit to the Abbey I was well received by Richard Mortimer, while Jane Spooner, Chris Gidlow and their colleagues were similarly welcoming at the Tower of London. My special thanks to Guilhem Pépin for his considerable assistance with the map of Gascony, and to Philippe Dufour for the aerial photograph of Monpazier. I must also thank Gillian Suttie for her hospitality during a tour of Scotland, and Mark Slater and Jo Topping for the gracious use of their house in France which lies conveniently close to some of Edward's bastides. Martin Allen at the Fitzwilliam Museum in Cambridge provided last-minute help with coins, and Jeff Cottenden took a rather splendid picture for the front cover. My estimable agent, Julian Alexander, had great faith in this project from the first, and introduced me to Hutchinson, where I have been well looked after by my editor Tony Whittome, his colleague James Nightingale, and the others at Random House.

The biggest debts, as usual, I have left until last. Once again I have to thank my former supervisors in London and Oxford, David Carpenter and John Maddicott, for their invaluable support and advice. As well as fielding email inquiries and phone calls, both read the entire book in draft, made many useful suggestions and saved me from innumerable errors. The same thanks go to my partner, Catherine, who has probably suffered more than any other person in recent years on account of Edward I. Not only did she read every word of every draft; she has also stoically endured Edward's tendency to crop up in almost every conversation, and uncomplainingly allowed him to dictate her holiday destinations for the past three years. I hope at least some of it was fun, and promise that the sequel will be set in New York, Japan or Australia.

My final words of thanks, though, are reserved for Rees Davies. When I arrived in Oxford ten years ago to begin my doctorate, I knew little about English medieval history, but even less about the histories of Wales, Ireland and Scotland. It is chiefly down to Rees's teaching and writing that this imbalance was corrected. He was never my teacher in any strict sense, but during my time in Oxford he offered advice and support without which I would never have completed my thesis.

Although he had few positive things to say about Edward I, he was supportive of my intention of writing a book about him and unstinting in his encouragement while I was in the early stages of research. In intellectual terms, the finished product owes more to Rees than to any other individual, and if it encourages others to seek out and discover his works for themselves, then for that reason alone it will have been a book worth writing.

Edward the First, or Edward the Fourth?

Before the reign of the king we call Edward I, England had been ruled by several other kings who shared his name; the trouble was that, even from a thirteenth-century standpoint, they had all lived a very long time in the past. At the time of Edward's accession in 1272, even his most recent royal namesake, Edward the Confessor, had been dead for more than two centuries. Everyone in the thirteenth century remembered the Confessor, for by then he had become the patron saint of the English royal family. But when it came to the other King Edwards, people were altogether more hazy. Towards the end of Edward I's reign, for example, some of his subjects felt compelled to chronicle his remarkable deeds, and decided that they needed to distinguish the king by giving him a number. Unfortunately, they miscounted, including in their tallies the Confessor (who ruled from 1042 to 1066), and also the celebrated tenth-century king, Edward the Elder (899–924), but overlooking entirely the short and unmemorable reign of Edward the Martyr (975–78). For this reason, at least two thirteenth-century writers referred to Edward I as 'Edward the Third'. Had they counted correctly, they would have called him 'Edward the Fourth'.

Fortunately for us, such early and inaccurate numbering schemes did not endure. In general, when his contemporaries wished to distinguish Edward, they called him 'King Edward, son of King Henry'. The need for numbers arose only after his death, when he was succeeded by a son, and then a grandson, both of whom bore his illustrious name. By the middle of the fourteenth century, Englishmen found themselves having to differentiate between three consecutive, identically named kings, and so unsurprisingly they started referring to them as the First, Second and Third. Anyone troubled by the recollection that once upon a time there had been other kings called Edward could salve their historical conscience by adding 'since the Conquest'. Thus the Norman Conquest became the official starting point for the numbering of English kings. But it was only necessary to have such a starting point in the first place because of Henry III's idiosyncratic decision to resurrect the name of a long-dead Anglo-Saxon royal saint and bestow it on his eldest son.

A Note on Money

For those readers who, like me, were born after the English currency was decimalised, it is worth pointing out that sterling used to be measured in pounds, shillings and pence: twelve pennies made a shilling, and twenty shillings made a pound. This was as true in the thirteenth century as it was before 1971, though in the Middle Ages the pennies went a good deal further. In Edward I's day an unskilled labourer could earn one or two pence for a day's work, while a skilled craftsmen might earn double that sum. A man who took home £20 a year would have been considered very well off, and even the greatest individuals in English society – the earls – rarely enjoyed incomes in excess of £5,000. Only Edward himself had a five-figure income, receiving around £27,000 a year from ordinary royal revenues, which he spent running his household and, by extension, the kingdom as a whole. Caernarfon Castle, although never completed, ended up costing roughly the same amount. The only type of coin in widespread circulation was the silver penny, so a pound was a weighty bag of coins, and even a small-sounding sum like £5 had to be counted out as 1,200 silver pennies. Money was also reckoned in marks, which were equivalent to 160 pennies, or two-thirds of a pound.

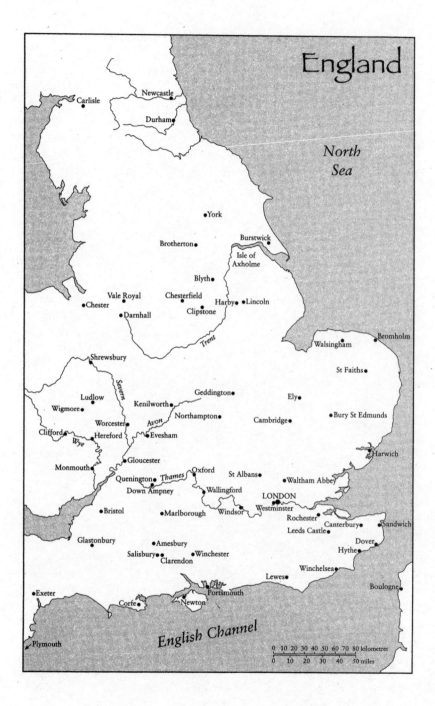

1

A Saint in Name

This story begins in the year 1239 with a girl called Eleanor.
Eleanor lives in England, a peaceful and prosperous kingdom,
much the same size then as it is now. Eleanor herself, however,
is not English. She was bred and brought up in Provence, an independent county in the south of what is now modern France. The reason
Eleanor is living in England in 1239 is because, three and a half years
earlier, she had been married to the king of England, Henry III. At the
time of their wedding, Henry was twenty-eight. Eleanor was twelve.

Eleanor is now sixteen years old, or very nearly so, and reportedly
a great beauty: graceful, charming and elegant. Henry is very much in
love with her, and she with him, but she has yet to win the hearts of
his subjects. In the thirteenth century the English did not take to
foreigners with the same easy readiness they do today. We may take as
our witness a monk of St Albans by the name of Matthew Paris, who,
as well as being a thorough-going xenophobe, also happens to be one
of the most gossipy, prolific and best-informed chroniclers of the entire
Middle Ages. Brother Matthew and his contemporaries had observed
the effects of Eleanor's arrival and seen the thing they most feared: an
influx of foreigners, surrounding their king, separating him from his
'natural' subjects and advising him – so the English believed – badly.
Rather ridiculously, Paris tried to pin the blame for this on Eleanor.
Foreigners were pulling the kingdom to pieces, he said, and Henry,
'being under the influence of his wife', was letting them.

It was also apparently held against Eleanor that, three years into her
marriage, she had not produced any children. 'It was feared the queen
was barren,' said Matthew Paris, with the sympathy of a professional
celibate. Again, this was quite ridiculous, given Eleanor's tender years.
What is much more likely is that Henry III, a kind and considerate
man, had been exercising a bit of self-restraint. Twelve was the minimum

age at which the medieval Church would permit girls to marry, and Henry and Eleanor had probably had sex soon after their wedding, but this would have been for political reasons, to ensure that their union was valid and binding. Common sense and compassion suggested that twelve was too young for regular marital relations and to run the risk that Eleanor might become pregnant.

By the time Matthew Paris made this comment, however, Eleanor was fifteen, Henry was thirty-one, and they were definitely sleeping together. We know this because on 9 September 1238, in the middle of the night, a knife-wielding madman broke into Henry's bedchamber with the intention of killing the king. He failed because, as Matthew Paris himself tells us, Henry was not in his room at the time. Luckily, he was with the queen.

And now, a little over nine months on from that dramatic evening, the queen is about to confound her critics and silence the rumour-mongers. It is June 1239, just a few days short of midsummer, and Eleanor is lodged in Henry's palace at Westminster, by the side of the River Thames, on the site where the modern Houses of Parliament stand. And there, during the night of 17–18 June, in a room presumably lit by lanterns and candles, she gives birth to her first child. Her delivery is successful, the baby is healthy, and – best of all – it is a boy. In the most important aspect of her role as queen, Eleanor has triumphed. She has provided Henry, and England, with an heir to the throne.[1]

There was immediate celebration in the Palace of Westminster. At Henry's command the clerks of the royal chapel sang the triumphant anthem *Christus Vincit, Christus Regnat, Christus Imperat* (Christ conquers, Christ reigns, Christ rules), and messengers were sent speeding off in all directions to spread the good news. In nearby London, a walled city of some 50,000 souls, the citizens went wild, dancing through the streets with lanterns, drums and tambourines. Soon the royal messengers were returning, laden with costly gifts from the king's greatest subjects. In some cases Henry apparently felt that these presents were not costly enough and sent their bearers back to get better ones. According to Matthew Paris, this provoked some wag at court to quip, 'God has given us this child, but the king is selling him to us!' Paris himself, striking a more serious tone, thought that Henry's ingratitude had 'deeply clouded his magnificence', and the episode, while not very significant, does provide something of a character note for the king. Henry, as other contemporaries observed, was a *vir simplex*: charitably, a 'straightforward' chap; more obviously, a simpleton. Consequently, he tended to act in inept ways such as this. Even when fortune handed him a silk purse, Henry could generally be relied upon to make a pig's ear out of it.[2]

A much more important indicator of the king's personality is provided by the name he chose for his newborn son. Henry, although king of England, was ancestrally and culturally French. He and his family were direct descendants of William the Conqueror, the Norman duke who had snatched England's throne some 170 years earlier. Similarly, his leading subjects were all directly descended from the Conqueror's Norman companions. When they talked to each other they spoke French (or at least a slightly anglicised, Norman version of it), and, when they came to christen their children, they gave them French names. William (Guillaume), for example, was still a popular name, for obvious reasons. So too was Richard (Ricard), because it evoked the memory of Henry's famous uncle, Richard the Lionheart. And Henry (Henri) itself was perfectly respectable and commonplace. Henry III might have been rather limited in his abilities, but his two namesake predecessors had both been fearsome and successful warrior kings, worthy of commemoration and emulation.

All these options, however, Henry rejected. He had no desire to father conquerors, or for that matter crusaders. Thanks to his own father, the notorious King John, he had grown up surrounded by uncertainty and conflict. John had died in the midst of a self-inflicted civil war, bequeathing to his son a kingdom scarred and divided. What Henry craved above all for himself and his subjects was peace, harmony and stability. And it was a reflection of this ambition that he decided to call his son Edward.

Edward was a deeply unfashionable name in 1239 – no king or nobleman had been lumbered with it since the Norman Conquest, because it belonged to the side that had lost. Edward was an Old English name, and it sounded as odd and outlandish to Norman ears after 1066 as other Old English names – Egbert, Æthelred, Egfrith – still sound to us today. To call a boy such a name after the Conquest was to invite ridicule; he was bound to be mocked by the Williams, Richards and Henrys who were his peers.

But Henry III had good reason for foisting this unfashionable name on his firstborn son. After his father's death, his mother had abandoned him – Isabella of Angoulême left England for her homeland in France, remarried and never returned. Effectively orphaned from the age of nine, the young king had found substitute father figures among the elderly men who had helped him govern his kingdom. But these men too, Henry ultimately decided, had failed him, and by 1234 he found himself alone once more. It was at this point, though, that the king

3

discovered a new mentor, a man who would never, ever let him down – largely because he had already been dead for the best part of two centuries.

Henry's new patron was Edward the Confessor, the penultimate king of Anglo-Saxon England. Like Henry himself, Edward had not been a very successful ruler: his death in January 1066 had sparked the succession crisis that led to the Norman Conquest nine months later. Posthumously, however, Edward had acquired a reputation as a man of great goodness – so much so that, a century after his death, he had been officially recognised as a saint. Thereafter his reign had acquired the retrospective glow of a golden age: men spoke with great reverence about his good and just laws (even though, in reality, he never made any). Of course, the fact that Edward was not a great warrior had made him an unlikely exemplar for the conquering dynasty of kings who came after him. But to a man like Henry III, who was entirely lacking in military skill, the Confessor seemed the perfect role model. There were, moreover, other similarities between their two lives that must have struck Henry as highly significant. Edward had lost his father and been abandoned by his mother at a young age; he had grown up with war and wished to cultivate peace; he had been misled by treacherous ministers. Above all, Edward, like Henry, was famed for his piety. Edward was the king who established the royal palace at Westminster, in order to be near the great abbey (minster) that he spent the last years of his life rebuilding. In due course he was buried in the abbey church, and his tomb there became a pilgrim shrine. It was the greatest testament to Henry III's love and reverence for the Confessor that, from 1245, he would spend vast sums rebuilding the abbey for a second time, replacing the old Romanesque church with the massive Gothic building that stands today.

It was no surprise to anyone, therefore, that Henry should choose to call his son Edward in honour of his idol. Nor, probably, was it a coincidence that the boy happened to be born in Westminster. Henry spent plenty of time in his palace there, partly to be near the abbey, and partly because Westminster was a centre for some branches of royal government. But the king had lots of other palaces and castles all over England, and to govern his realm properly he was obliged to travel around them. It seems likely that Henry had deliberately arranged it so that he and Eleanor were in Westminster as the end of her term approached, so that they would be in the closest possible proximity to the Confessor's shrine. Being born in Westminster also meant that Edward could be baptised there. A few days after his birth, the new baby became the first king of England to be christened in the abbey, surrounded by

4

a great crowd of bishops, noblemen and ladies, no fewer than twelve of whom became his godparents. Henry was evidently determined from the first that his son would have all the affection and guidance in childhood that he himself had lacked.[3]

Westminster's spiritual and governmental advantages made it a busy place, unsuitable for the raising of children. A few weeks after Edward's birth the court left the palace and travelled fifty miles up the Thames (twenty miles as the crow flies) to the royal castle at Windsor.[4] It was here, in the quiet Berkshire countryside, that Henry and Eleanor intended their son should grow up. Soon after their wedding in 1236 Henry had begun a major rebuilding programme to update the venerable fortress – Windsor had been established by William the Conqueror – in line with contemporary standards of luxury and his own exacting tastes. A brand-new chamber had already been constructed for the queen and, just a few weeks after his birth, work began on an adjacent courtyard for her son. Henry went on to build a wholly new suite of rooms at Windsor for himself and Eleanor, with an especially grand chapel. Altogether the king spent well over £10,000 on these improvements – enough to have built an entirely new castle from scratch.

Almost nothing of these buildings survives today. The fragments that remain, however (such as the doors to the chapel), and the detailed orders that Henry sent to his designers, are enough to establish the quality of the life that they afforded. Chambers were fashioned expensively in stone, with fireplaces and en-suite toilets. They were linked by covered walkways and lit by large windows, glazed with glass of many colours. Interior decor was sumptuous: floors were exquisitely tiled, pillars were sculpted from Purbeck marble, walls were painted with colourful patterns or hung with tapestries. Henry's favourite decorative scheme, it seems, was for green walls spangled with gold stars. Outside, in the courtyards, gardens were planted with herbs and flowers.[5]

Nor was this level of luxury confined to Windsor. At all his palaces and castles, even ones he hardly ever visited, Henry delighted in commissioning new building work, improving the plumbing or the wainscoting, or ordering new wall-paintings (favourite subject: Edward the Confessor). It made him something of a target for satirical comment. 'White bread, chambers and tapestries,' mocked one observer, 'to ride like a dean on a docile mount: the king likes better all that than to put on a coat of mail.' But it also meant that Henry and his young family enjoyed a level of comfort that is the antithesis of what most people today imagine as 'medieval'. Even as a small child Edward ate off silver plate, and drank fine wine, imported from the south of France. By his parents' command, he was dressed in expensive silks, robes of scarlet trimmed with fur, and cloth of gold.[6]

As the orders for these items imply, Henry was an attentive and doting father, and his itinerary suggests that he spent as much time as he could at Windsor. Nevertheless, the fact that such orders had to be committed to writing indicates that, for most of the time, the business of government meant that the king had to be elsewhere. So too, on some occasions, did Eleanor – her most notable absence being a seventeen-month visit to France with Henry in 1242–43. In general, however, the queen was at Windsor far more often than her husband. Such evidence as survives suggests that she probably resided at the castle for well over half of all the weeks in any one year.[7]

This was without doubt because she wanted to spend as much time as possible with her growing brood of children. In the autumn of 1240 Edward had been joined at Windsor by a little sister, delivered at the castle on 29 September and christened Margaret in honour of a maternal aunt. A few years later, in 1243, came Beatrice, born in Bordeaux during her parents' trip to France and named in this instance after Eleanor's mother. When a second son arrived at the start of 1245 it was Henry's turn to do the naming, and once again he defied convention in order to honour another Old English royal saint. Baby Edmund was soon installed in what had become a veritable royal nursery. As well as his younger siblings, Edward by this stage was keeping company with his cousin Henry and a number of other noble children.[8]

Needless to say, the queen had plenty of help in raising them all. Her foremost assistants were Hugh and Sybil Giffard, a husband and wife team who were entrusted with Edward's custody from the moment of his birth. Sybil, indeed, had helped to deliver Edward and was later well rewarded by Henry for having acted as midwife. There were also several other ladies on hand to assist in the practicalities of child-raising. As an infant Edward had two nurses, Alice and Sarah, whose responsibilities would have extended to suckling him.[9]

Eleanor was also supported, in a less immediate but nevertheless crucially important way, by certain members of her own family. On her mother's side, the queen had no fewer than six clever and ambitious uncles. These men, who hailed from the Alpine province of Savoy, saw in their niece's marriage the opportunity for self-advancement, and she in return looked to them for help and advice. One of these uncles, William of Savoy, had accompanied Eleanor to England in 1236 (and, until his death in 1239, had been the principal cause of English discontent). A few years later Boniface of Savoy arrived, having been elected, at

Henry's urging, as archbishop of Canterbury. But between these two brothers, and more important than either, came Peter of Savoy. He appeared in England soon after Christmas 1240 and immediately established himself as one of the king's closest advisers. (Among the many properties that Henry later rewarded him with was a house on the Strand, which became the Savoy Palace and, latterly, the Savoy Hotel.) An exceptionally smooth operator – even Matthew Paris had to admit that he was 'discreet and circumspect' – Peter understood from the start that his influence depended on Eleanor, and that her importance flowed from her position as the mother of the heir to the throne. Peter therefore also became his niece's principal confidant and collaborator, and took steps to ensure that together they maintained the tightest possible control over her son. Even before Peter's arrival, a Savoyard clerk had been made responsible for controlling access to Edward and, within a year of his coming, the old constable of Windsor was replaced by Bernard of Savoy, who may have been Peter's bastard brother. No aspect of Edward's welfare, no matter how unglamorous, escaped Savoyard attention. Just months after his arrival, presumably because of the health risk they posed, Peter advised Henry to clear all the horses out of Windsor Castle, along with their dung.[10]

Little is known of Edward's education, but we may make some general observations. Hugh Giffard, husband of Sybil, was described by Matthew Paris as the boy's teacher (*pedagogus*), and it is entirely possible that Hugh was responsible for giving Edward some of his earliest lessons, though these were more likely of a basic social nature rather than an overtly scholarly one. Hugh died before Edward's seventh birthday, which was the stage at which most medieval thinkers reckoned that infancy ended and the more rigorous training associated with boyhood ought to begin. Up to that point, the care and education of children was considered to be principally a female concern.[11]

It was therefore more likely Sybil Giffard, the nurses Alice and Sarah, and, indeed, the queen herself who began one of the most important aspects of Edward's education, namely teaching him to read. Although there were a number of male clerks in the boy's household, their tasks were probably administrative in nature and connected with the performance of religious services. It was, as one thirteenth-century poem put it, 'woman [that] teacheth child the book'. Learning to read was perfectly normal for aristocrats in the thirteenth century, as indeed it was for most other ranks of society. By the time Edward was king, for example, it was a legal requirement that even serfs (unfree peasants) should own a seal with which to authenticate documents. Writing, on the other hand was a more specialised technical skill, and because it was rather messy many nobles no doubt considered it somewhat beneath them, especially since they employed plenty of dedicated clerical staff in their households. Edward, therefore, was certainly a reader, but probably not a writer.[12]

One of the things that had made literacy easier and more appealing for the English aristocracy by the thirteenth century was the increasing quantity of literature being translated into their everyday tongue. The Bible, prayer books and psalters were all available in French translation, and, since religious devotion was the primary spur to reading, these were probably the first kind of books that Edward would have encountered. Nevertheless, despite the increasing availability of such material and the increasing use of French in letters, both public and private, it was important for a boy who was being groomed as a future king to obtain at least a basic level of literacy in Latin (here his clerks may have been more help to him than his mother). Latin remained the principal written language of royal government, and the only *lingua franca* suitable for corresponding with other European rulers, particularly the pope. Lastly, Edward would also have learned English from an early age, probably from the mouths of his native-born guardians, Hugh and Sybil Giffard, and perhaps his nurses, rather than from his Provençal mother. Such knowledge would offer him no great social benefits – hardly anything of value was committed to writing in English, nor was English spoken in the sophisticated court circles in which Edward generally moved – yet there would have been advantages later in life for a king who could communicate in the tongue used by the vast majority of his subjects.[13]

What kind of things would Edward have learned about? There was no curriculum as such, but there were nevertheless a wide range of subjects that were considered suitable for study. A knowledge of history was desirable, chiefly because it furnished examples of worthy individuals whose successful behaviour could be emulated, as well as losers whose mistakes ought to be avoided. To this end Edward probably learned a good deal of the history of his own family, which provided ready-made heroes, such as Richard the Lionheart (Edward's great-uncle), as well as less laudable figures, such his grandfather, King John. The unavoidable exemplar, however, was Edward the Confessor. Henry III filled his palaces with images of his favourite royal saint, and never failed to celebrate his two annual festivals (usually at Westminster). Henry had been particularly keen that his wife should join him in appreciation of the Confessor's all-round wonderfulness from the moment she arrived in England, and commissioned none other than Matthew Paris to write for her, in French, a history of the saintly king's reign. Eleanor dutifully obliged her husband by imitating his hero-worship, and must surely have shared her new-found knowledge with her eldest son: Edward also became a devoted follower of his namesake's cult, albeit not to the same excessive extent as his father.[14]

If Eleanor had a personal hand in the development of her son's historical awareness, it may have been to teach him about the more distant, legendary past of the country she had come to regard as home. To judge from her book purchases, the queen was a great reader of medieval romances – that is, stirring tales of chivalry, rather than love stories in the modern sense. Her enthusiasm for such literature was probably formed during her youth in Provence – the fashion for romances had originated in southern France in the half century before her birth. The stories they recounted were set in a variety of historic epochs, including Ancient Greece and Rome (the Romance of Alexander) and early medieval France (the Romance of Charlemagne). By far the most popular romances of all, however, not just in England and with Eleanor, but in every part of Europe, were those set in Ancient Britain – the tales of King Arthur, and his knights of the Round Table.[15]

Such stories were read, or listened to, for fun and amusement. They were typically full of action, often violent and bloody, and placed a high value on sheer physical accomplishment. Heroes were praised for their prowess in tournaments and their body count on the battlefield. But, at the same time, romances also had a didactic purpose, to the extent that they celebrated a wider set of virtues that society – especially secular, aristocratic society – held dear. Those who heard tell of Arthur and his knightly companions knew that they should be courageous, not cowardly; loyal, not treacherous; generous, not greedy; frank and open in their dealings, not sly and deceptive.[16]

When it came to learning about geography there was no substitute for venturing out into the wider world. While it made sense not to expose young children to too much travel, they were moved on special occasions. Henry III, for example, typically celebrated Christmas at Winchester or Westminster, and we can be fairly certain that he would have wanted his family with him for the festivities. Similarly, Eleanor had places she liked to stay apart from Windsor: the royal palace at Woodstock, near Oxford, and the palaces at Clarendon and Marlborough in Wiltshire, were among her favourite destinations. Her children must have been brought to her from time to time – as infants both Edward and Margaret had special saddles made to allow them to ride with an adult – or have travelled with their mother in her carriage. Leaving the safety of the nursery inevitably brought risks: on his seventh birthday

in 1246 Edward was with his parents on the Hampshire coast, celebrating the dedication of Beaulieu Abbey, when he suddenly fell so
seriously ill that he was unable to be moved for three weeks. By the
same token, illness could strike anywhere: Edward was also reportedly
sick as a child in the more familiar surroundings of Westminster and
Windsor.[17]

Risk had to be balanced against the importance of allowing a growing
boy to experience the world beyond the palace walls, and to practise
the kind of activities that would allow him to develop a more robust
physique. Seven was precisely the age when it was thought that such
training should begin. Following the death of his first mentor, Hugh
Giffard, in 1246, Edward was committed to the care of Bartholomew
Pecche, a knight formerly responsible for little Margaret's welfare. It
must have been under Bartholomew's watchful eye that his new charge
first began to acquire the skills and enthusiasms that he demonstrated
in later life: how to gallop a horse; how to train and track hawks; how
to hunt. Henry III, almost uniquely among medieval monarchs, does
not seem to have engaged in such pursuits, and clearly did not relish
them. But in 1247, a year after Pecche's appointment, the king granted
his son permission to hunt in Windsor Forest. This assumes that Edward
was becoming familiar with weapons, learning how to handle knives,
bows and swords. It cannot have been much later that he found the
strength to lift a lance, and began to hone the ability of hitting a target.[18]

As Edward left his infancy behind, therefore, he grew fitter, stronger,
more accomplished, and more aware of the world around him: not only
the hills and woods around Windsor and a number of other royal residences, but also the landscape of southern England as a whole, seen
first from the windows of his mother's carriage, and increasingly standing
in the stirrups of his own horse. By today's standards, this landscape
would seem thinly populated and underproductive: in the thirteenth
century, only around 3 to 4 million people lived in England, the vast
majority of them dwelling in small villages, and obliged (either to their
lords, or for their own sakes) to till the soil in order to survive. Yet by
medieval standards this was a densely populated country with a dynamic
and expanding economy. The population was growing rapidly, which
meant that more and more land was being brought under the plough.
A kingdom that to us would have seemed almost empty must have
seemed bustling to Edward. Everywhere he looked, there were ancient
forests being felled, new towns being founded, and peasants on their
way to market to sell their surplus produce.[19]

And what of the world beyond? Except for what he saw with his own
eyes, Edward would have had only a limited concept of geography.

Accurate maps of the kind that we today take for granted were in his day entirely unknown. The extent of cartographical science as it stood in the thirteenth century is best summed up by the large sheet of parchment that now hangs in Hereford Cathedral, and that is generally referred to as the *Mappa Mundi* (although other medieval maps also go by the same name, which means 'cloth of the world'). Edward may never have seen this particular map – it was created towards the end of his life, probably in Lincolnshire. He would, however, have seen other examples drawn to an identical scheme, for they were quite popular among those able to afford them. In the 1230s Henry III commissioned two such world maps for the royal residences at Winchester and Westminster, and miniature versions were sometimes copied into prayer books. It would have been quite likely that Edward owned one himself.

It is a popular misconception that in the Middle Ages people believed that the world was flat. They didn't – this is a patronising but sadly pervasive modern myth. Astronomical observation and ancient authorities told medieval man that his world was spherical. A true understanding of the Earth's surface, however, eluded him, due to the limited extent of his geographical knowledge. In an age before Columbus, Europeans knew of only three continents: Africa, Asia, and Europe itself. These, they believed, were entirely concentrated in the northern hemisphere, for the equator was held to be an impassibly hot barrier, beyond which no life could exist. This, therefore, is what the Hereford *Mappa Mundi* endeavours to show: the northern half of a spherical world, and the many wonders within it.

In this global scheme the British Isles are extremely peripheral, squeezed against the edge of the bottom left-hand quadrant. Yet, in spite of the very limited amount of space that this affords, the result is surprisingly detailed: over thirty towns and cities are crammed in, as well as mountain ranges and major rivers. The map's designer, however, was concerned to record more than the merely topographic. The further he ventured beyond western Europe and the hazier his geographical knowledge became, the more he felt able to include material of a mythological nature. The map's southern edge is populated by strange human creatures: hermaphrodites, people with four eyes, men with their faces in their stomachs. Africa teems with monsters and beasts, among them the cyclops, the fawn and the unicorn. In the Mediterranean, too, there is a heavy emphasis on ancient legend: the Golden Fleece, the Labyrinth and the Scylla and Charybdis all jostle for space.

And yet, in spite of the wealth of classical and fantastical material that the *Mappa Mundi* includes, its view of the world is unmistakably a

Christian one. Scenes from the Bible, including Noah's Ark and the Tower of Babel, dominate the depiction of the Holy Land. At the top edge of the parchment, above the Earth itself, sits God, surrounded by angels, and below him stands the Virgin Mary. But it is to the middle of the map that the viewer's eye is inevitably drawn. At the centre of the circle – directly over the marks made by the artist's compass as he drew the outline of the world – is the city of Jerusalem.[20]

To regard Jerusalem as the centre of the world was obviously another consequence of possessing a Christian perspective: immediately above his picture of the Holy City, the *Mappa Mundi* artist drew a picture of the crucified Christ. More than this, though, it was to see the world through the eyes of a crusader. By the middle of the thirteenth century, the Christians of western Europe had been engaged for 150 years in a struggle to wrest control of Jerusalem from the Islamic rulers of the Middle East. At the end of the eleventh century, when the first crusaders had departed, the idea had been a revolutionary one; by Edward's day it was a central and universally accepted fact of life. A journey to the East to fight the infidel had become a major part of what it meant to be a knight, as fundamental as owning a horse or knowing how to hold a lance. To wear the sign of the cross and to fight in defence of the Holy City was the highest of all knightly endeavours. Nor was it just the concern of the military classes: all ranks of society were exhorted to support crusaders, morally and financially. Rarely would a year go by without a new preaching initiative, intended to drum up prayers and funds for a new expedition.[21]

Edward's understanding of the history of crusading would have been limited to what he heard in popular tales. From these he would have known, for example, how the knights of the First Crusade had travelled thousands of miles, overcome unimaginable hardships, and eventually succeeded in liberating Jerusalem. Likewise he would have heard the equally famous stories of the Third Crusade, the attempt to retake Jerusalem after its fall in 1187 – an ultimately unsuccessful mission, but one redeemed by the heroic exploits of Richard the Lionheart. King Richard, of course, provided a family connection with crusading, being the uncle of Henry III, but by Edward's day he had been dead for almost half a century. An altogether more vital link with crusading existed, however, in the form of Edward's own Uncle Richard, Henry's younger brother.

Richard, earl of Cornwall (or Richard of Cornwall, as he is usually known) had left England on crusade in the summer of 1240, before Edward's first birthday. It was, in fact, thanks to Edward's arrival that the earl's departure had become a feasible proposition, because before that moment he had been first in line to the throne. Alas, when it came to fighting, Richard had more in common with his older brother than his illustrious namesake, and as a consequence there was no military action of any consequence in the course of his expedition. But Richard was far more intelligent than Henry, and was especially skilled at negotiation. Indeed, such was his diplomatic ability that, during his brief stay in the Holy Land, the earl negotiated the return of Jerusalem. The deal proved short lived – the city fell again four years later – but at the time it secured Richard an international reputation for statesmanship, and he returned to England in 1242 garlanded with laurels and convinced of his own triumphant success. Moreover, he returned full of the wonders he had seen: bands of musicians riding on the back of elephants, Saracen girls who danced on balls. The earl told these tales to Matthew Paris, who wrote them down, and we can be fairly certain he would have shared them with his nephew as well: Richard, as well as being Edward's uncle, was one of the more important of his many godparents, and the two of them became very close.[22]

Henry III was predictably more muted in his enthusiasm for crusaders and crusading than his brother and most of his other subjects. He possessed the requisite piety in abundance, but lacked the necessary penchant for violence. In the late 1240s, however, in the wake of Jerusalem's recent fall, the pressure on him to participate was becoming irresistible. Many English noblemen were ready to go east under their own banners, or even to join the expedition of Louis IX, king of France, who set sail for the Holy Land in 1248. This last, in particular, really threw down the gauntlet to Henry, for the French king was his great rival. Would he, the king of England, stand idly by while King Louis took all the glory? With national and dynastic pride at stake, Henry eventually decided that the answer was no. In March 1250, in a grand public ceremony, the king surprised his subjects and took the cross. Many other nobles and knights also took their vows at the same time, and crusade fever soon took hold of the whole court. Within a few weeks, Queen Eleanor had borrowed a copy of *The Song of Antioch*, a romance history of the First Crusade. The following year Henry began to commission new wall-paintings in many of his castles and palaces, featuring scenes from the same story, or episodes from the life of Richard the Lionheart. Wherever an impressionable eleven-year-old looked or listened, there was an exhortation to go on crusade.

Having taken his vow, Henry III could not depart at once. A crusade was not a whimsical jaunt; on the contrary, it was the undertaking of a lifetime, and required many months, running into years, of careful preparation. Crusaders had to be sure, above all, of two things. First, that they had enough money to fund their expedition. To this end, Henry made economies in his expenditure, and began to save up a gold treasure (gold having greater currency in the East than the silver coinage used in the West). Second, a crusader needed to ensure that his lands would be safe and secure during his absence. Here Henry had less success, and soon found himself running into deep difficulties. These difficulties, however, even as they cast the king's crusade into doubt, were the making of his eldest son.[23]

Henry III was first and foremost king of England, but he was also lord of other lands besides. In Ireland, for example, English adventurers had carved out new domains in the last decades of the twelfth century, and Henry's grandfather, Henry II, had intervened to ensure that the English Crown had the whip hand. In Wales too, the English had made considerable inroads in the course of the twelfth century, with the result that large parts of the south and east of the country were ruled by English lords or royal officials. Neither of these 'British' zones, however, was a cause for concern in 1250; they, like England, seemed secure. The problem that loomed in 1250 lay across the Channel with Henry's ancestral lands on the Continent.[24]

Ever since 1066, when Duke William of Normandy had seized the throne of England, English kings had held extensive lands in what is now France. In the course of the twelfth century they had expanded their empire further and further south, until eventually their power reached the Pyrenees. Henry II, the chief architect of this expansion, had ended up with more lands in France than the king of France himself, and this, naturally, was the main cause of Anglo-French antagonism. The balance of power, however, had been dramatically reversed in the next generation. Henry II's son, the incompetent King John, had lost almost all the lands his father had assembled. Within a decade of John's death in 1216, and before his son – Henry III – had come of age, all that remained of a once great family inheritance was the south-western corner of France, known as Aquitaine, or Gascony.[25]

Seen in this light, Gascony was a much diminished rump, but regarded on its own the duchy was an extensive possession, stretching over 150 miles from north to south and around half that distance from east to west. Henry III jealously guarded this last remnant of his Continental inheritance, and sought anxiously to protect it by extending his influence elsewhere in the region. It had been for this reason, and to keep up the continuing competition with France, that the king had sought a wife from Provence: eighteen months before Henry had married Eleanor, King Louis had married her elder sister, Margaret. One day,

Henry hoped, he would regain the territories his father had lost. It was with this ambition that he had set out for France during Edward's infancy – a disastrous adventure that had served only to underline his reputation as a military bungler. In the meantime, what mattered most was conserving Gascony. This was a particular priority for Eleanor and her advising uncle, Peter of Savoy, for they had long determined that the duchy should one day go to Edward. Almost from the moment of his birth they had seen off other would-be claimants – principally Richard of Cornwall – and, soon after his tenth birthday, their labours were rewarded: in September 1249, Henry III made a formal grant of Gascony to his eldest son. But by the time the king took the cross some six months later, affairs in the duchy were spinning out of control. Rebellion was beginning to rage, imperilling both Edward's inheritance and Henry's crusade. Its cause was Simon de Montfort.[26]

Simon de Montfort, earl of Leicester, was Henry III's brother-in-law (the king's sister, another Eleanor, was Simon's wife). He was also everything that Henry was not: quick-witted, silver-tongued and, in the words of Matthew Paris, 'famous and experienced in warfare'. His personality and accomplishments had recommended him, particularly to Eleanor of Provence, as the best man for the job of safeguarding Gascony until Edward's coming of age. In the summer of 1248, largely at the queen's behest, Montfort had been appointed by Henry as the royal lieutenant in the duchy.[27]

It was a bad decision. Tough and clever Montfort may have been, but he was also uncommonly egotistical and inflexibly self-righteous. These qualities, which arose in part from his religious fanaticism, made the earl an ideal crusader – he had already been east once and had vowed to go again – but they rendered him altogether unsuitable for the business of governing Gascony. The lieutenant's authority and resources were limited: local towns and lords, when they grew fractious, needed gentle conciliation. Montfort's method was to fight fire with fire, and very soon the whole duchy was ablaze. Even as Henry III took the cross in March 1250, his brother-in-law was writing to him, explaining how certain Gascons were using guerrilla warfare to cripple his government.[28]

Henry's initial response was to back Montfort: throughout 1250 the earl was given thousands of pounds to spend on mercenaries and castle-building. But, as the tide of complaints from Gascony swelled, and the rebellion continued to intensify, Henry started to change his mind. Eventually, much to Montfort's anger, the king cut his funding and, at Christmas 1251, the two men had a furious public row. The earl was told to stand down, but returned to the duchy in defiance and wreaked more havoc.[29]

The escalating crisis in Gascony had grave implications for Henry's crusade, and alarmed those of his subjects who had sworn to go east. In April 1252 their worst fears were confirmed, ironically, by Henry's botched efforts to allay them. At that point the king let it be known that he would definitely be departing, and that to this end he had fixed a firm date. But the date was midsummer 1256, a further four years into the future. The long delay was necessary because, having sent investigators to Gascony, Henry now believed that the only way that the province could be stabilised was with a military expedition led by himself.[30]

Here too, however, the king ran into extreme difficulty. The fundamental problem was money. War was an expensive business, and Henry III was not a rich king. His private financial resources, which amounted to the rents and sales from his own lands, were by no means great. He could demand extra money from his subjects, but the methods for obtaining it were old fashioned, punitive and unfair. Essentially, the king was reliant on revenues and fines raised by his local officials – foresters, justices and sheriffs – and the more funds that were needed, the more oppressive and unscrupulous these officials had to be. It says a lot that the stories of Robin Hood, in which such men are the villains, originated in Henry's reign.[31]

The obvious solution was to impose a general levy on everyone – a tax – and Henry's immediate predecessors had on occasion done just that. King Richard and King John had found that they could raise huge sums in this way – England, it bears repeating, was a rich and prosperous country – but such taxes proved highly unpopular, and were regarded as tantamount to robbery. It soon became impossible to impose them without first obtaining a much broader degree of consent than was customary for other political decisions. The solution suggested in King John's reign, that the king should consult with all those who held lands directly from him, proved impracticable. It fell to Henry's ministers to devise a new way of obtaining approval, and, at some point in the period 1237–54, they decided to summon representatives from the counties and towns of England. Around the same time, a new word was coined to describe such assemblies: parliament.[32]

To his surprise and frustration, however, Henry found that when parliaments were summoned they were not nearly as compliant nor as automatically obliging as he would have liked. Knights of the shires and burgesses from the towns had plenty to say about the oppressiveness of his government, and linked his demands for money to the redress of their grievances. On the issue of Gascony, moreover, they were loath to pay any money at all. The kings of England might have been deeply attached to the duchy, but their English subjects felt no similar affection – to them it was merely an expensive burden. When, in the autumn of 1252, Henry asked for a tax to fund his intended expedition, parliament refused (and, to add insult to injury, pointed out his shortcomings as a warrior). The king was left hamstrung. Caught between rebellion in Gascony on the one hand, and political opposition in England on the other, Henry did what he did best, and dithered.[33]

Perhaps the only person who could have viewed the king's procrastination with something approaching equanimity was his eldest son. The crisis in Gascony pulled Edward onto the political stage for the first time (Matthew Paris, for example, now begins to notice him properly). In April 1252, as part of his strategy of appeasement, Henry publicly renewed his earlier grant of the duchy to Edward. Those Gascons then in England were summoned to London, and Edward was presented to them as their new lord. He went through the conventional performance expected in such circumstances – receiving oaths of loyalty from the Gascon lords who knelt before him, and distributing valuable gifts as a token of the benefits that his lordship would bring. Edward was twelve going on thirteen at the time; too young, perhaps, to play his role with total conviction, but only just. With every month that Henry delayed, his son grew taller and stronger, more convincing and more politically conscious. When, in the summer of 1252, Henry promised to intervene in Gascony, he was able to envisage an alternative scenario, acceptable to himself as well as to the Gascons, in which Edward would be sent in his stead. Edward may even have been privately pleased that the summer of 1256 was still four years away; it was not beyond the bounds of possibility for seventeen-year-olds to go on crusade.[34]

Any immediate hopes that Edward entertained of a larger role as a result of the Gascon crisis, however, were dashed by its rapid escalation in the spring of 1253. Castile, the greatest of the several kingdoms that made up medieval Spain, had for decades been a friendly neighbour on Gascony's southern border. But now it had acquired a new king in the shape of Alfonso X, who had entered into his inheritance the previous year determined to make his mark not only in Spain but also on the wider European stage. With a tenuous claim of his own to Gascony, and almost certainly tempted by invitations from the Gascon rebels, Alfonso found the prospect of extending his power across the Pyrenees impossible to resist. In the spring of 1253 a new rebellion was launched with his backing, and he made it clear that his intention was to invade. Castles and towns fell swiftly in the face of this new assault; in April the people of Bordeaux, Gascony's principal city, wrote a panicked letter to Henry III. If he did not act immediately, they assured him, the duchy would be lost forever. It was a prospect terrifying enough to shake the king into action. Still unable to secure a consensual tax, he resorted to a prerogative to which all lords were entitled and demanded a levy to pay for the knighting of his eldest son. If this gave Edward cause to imagine that this meant the beginning of his military career, however, he was mistaken. When Henry and his hastily assembled army sailed from Portsmouth in August, he left Edward behind, in the care of his mother, who remained in England as regent. 'The boy,' says Matthew Paris, 'stood crying and sobbing on the shore, and would not depart as long as he could see the swelling sails of the ships.'[35]

When it finally came down to it, Edward, now fourteen, was still considered a child by his parents; the role they envisaged for him was not knight but pawn. Even as the king sailed to war, his advisers were labouring to make peace. They correctly divined that Alfonso's backing for the Gascon rebels was opportunistic and speculative, and worked throughout the summer and autumn to convince him that his best interests lay in a diplomatic solution. The Spanish king was a slippery customer, repeatedly stalling in the hope of establishing the best terms he could get, but Henry III had considerable success in putting down the Gascon rebels, and by the start of 1254 Alfonso was ready to settle. He was prepared to drop his support for the rebellion and his claim to Gascony in return for a marriage alliance. His young half-sister – yet another Eleanor – would marry Henry's eldest son.[36]

Henry had, in fact, envisaged such an alliance from the off. 'Friendship between princes can be obtained in no more fitting manner than by the link of conjugal troth,' he had declared, rather loftily, in the spring of the previous year when commissioning his ambassadors. What he had not anticipated was that such friendship would have to be bought at such a high price. Before he would agree to the marriage, Alfonso demanded that Edward be endowed with lands worth £10,000 a year. This was almost certainly more than Henry had ever intended to give, but, short of other options, he duly consented. On 14 February, still in Gascony, the English king issued a charter that created for his son a great appanage. Its principal component was, of course, Gascony itself, as had long been intended. But, to meet Alfonso's stipulated value, it now also comprised (with certain exceptions) all the royal lands in Ireland and Wales and, in England, the lapsed earldom of Chester, the castle of Bristol and a number of important manors in the Midlands. Nor was this the end of the Spanish king's conditions. Alfonso was also determined to meet his future brother-in-law before the wedding took place, and demanded the privilege of knighting him. Consequently,

Edward found his position dramatically transformed. At a single stroke he had become the richest landowner in Henry III's realm after the king himself. Moreover, the prospect of overseas adventure, denied to him just nine months before, had been reopened. On 29 May he and his mother took ship at Portsmouth and set sail for Gascony.[37]

The summer of 1254, during which he celebrated his fifteenth birthday, was therefore one of many new experiences for Edward: his first sea voyage, which lasted almost a fortnight and placed him, as never before, at God's mercy; his first glimpse of warfare, for he joined his father on what remained of the frontline, and participated – at least to the extent that he was present – in the reduction of the last rebel strongholds. But what must surely have loomed largest in the young man's mind during these weeks was the thought of his impending marriage. It was, of course, an arranged match, dictated to the greatest possible degree by the exigencies of foreign policy. Nevertheless, it was not a forced arrangement. Constraining couples to marry against their will had been forbidden by the Church since the late twelfth century, a fact to which Edward alluded in July, when the final documents for his betrothal were drawn up. Anxious to prove he was his own man and that no parental arm-twisting had occurred, he affirmed that he had agreed 'willingly and spontaneously' to marry Eleanor, adding, with a chivalrous flourish, 'of whose prudence and beauty we have heard by general report'.[38]

In late September, having spent several weeks in Bordeaux, Edward set out for Spain. He went without his parents. Henry had already spent too much time and too much money on the pacification of his restless duchy. It was time for him and the queen to return to England, which they duly did a few weeks later. This did not mean, however, that their son travelled unaccompanied. A retinue of lords, the best that could be assembled at short notice, rode with him. Some persons of importance came from England, others from Gascony. Several, by design, were also young men, yet to be knighted, and this was the second matter that would have impinged on Edward: his impending graduation into the ranks of knighthood. Significantly, he travelled to Spain with his tutor-in-arms, Bartholomew Pecche, and two of Bartholomew's sons, who were also due to be dubbed by the Spanish king.

On 18 October the Anglo-Gascon riding party arrived in Burgos, a city that had until recently prided itself on being the principal residence of Castile's kings, and that still boasted strong attachments to the royal house. Their arrival was too late for any of the planned festivities to coincide with the feast of the translation of Edward the Confessor (13 October), as Henry III had hoped might be the case. Frustratingly, thanks to the silence of Spanish sources, we know almost nothing of what happened next – not even the dates of the ceremonies were registered by local chroniclers. Edward and his companions were in all probability knighted on 1 November, in the monastery of Las Huelgas, outside the city walls, where the kings of Castile were buried. On the same day, and in the same place (but, again, with the same caveats about probability) Edward met Eleanor for the first time and they were married. Like Edward, we are almost entirely ignorant of any details about Eleanor beyond the general report of her prudence and beauty. We do know that she was a few weeks short of her thirteenth birthday.[39]

Edward, his new wife and their companions did not tarry for long in Castile after the wedding – no more than a week at most. By 21 November they were back in Gascony, at which point their progress deliberately slowed. With the essential diplomacy of the marriage completed and the threat of Castilian interference finally removed, Edward had no need to rush anywhere. On the contrary, the departure of his parents a few weeks before meant that he was now in charge of the duchy in his own right, and it was therefore important for him to visit its most important towns and impress himself on his people. 'Edward, firstborn son of the illustrious king of England, now ruling in Gascony as prince and lord' – the opening line of the very first document he issued after his return from Spain seems to catch the duchy's new young master in an exultant mood.[40]

But soon into the new year the spirit of festivity faded, and the serious business of restoring order began. Finding Gascony's finances in a dire state, Edward elected to levy a tax, the pretext (as earlier in England) being his recent elevation to knighthood. By itself this would have been bad enough from the Gascons' point of view; as it was, Edward's demand coincided with another imposed by Henry III to fund his crusade, and the combined burden was enough to spark a fresh round of dissension in the duchy. By the spring of 1255 Edward had been forced on to the defensive: seizing towns, fortifying castles, ordering the construction of ships, and bringing in supplies of material, money and grain from his other new lordship of Ireland. In England, his father was panicked into sending reinforcements of pre-paid knights, even cancelling a tournament in view of what he saw as his son's desperate need for manpower in an hour of peril.[41]

For such parental assistance – assuming it ever arrived – Edward would presumably have been grateful. By the summer he had quelled the new disturbances and was expanding his authority by dealing with the older rivalries among the Gascons themselves. Not all Henry III's interventions, however, can have been so welcome to him. Indeed, the difficulties Edward faced in asserting his authority in Gascony had as much to do with its limited nature as it did to any Gascon resistance. With most of the duchy's officials having been put in place by the king before his departure, little was left to his son's initiative. On the rare occasions when Edward did take independent action, moreover, Henry would intervene from afar and modify his decisions. In the main rebel town of La Réole, for instance, the rebels had held out in the church, and for this reason Edward ordered that the building be razed to the ground. His father, however, immediately overruled him, and submitted the decision on the church to the arbitration of two bishops, with the inevitable result that most of its fabric was spared.[42]

Commenting on the amount of land that Henry III had granted to his son, Matthew Paris had been typically withering. Henry, he said, had left himself 'a mutilated little king'. In fact, Henry had been quite canny. While the grant was unquestionably large, it was composed almost entirely of outlying territories where his own authority was debatable; even the castles and manors granted to Edward in England were recent acquisitions to which the king's right was far from unimpeachable. More importantly, Henry had not resigned his position as the chief lord of any of these lands, and had retained the titles – lord of Ireland, duke of Aquitaine – that went with them. Edward's initial, one-off assertion that he was 'the firstborn son of the illustrious king of England, now ruling in Gascony as prince and lord' may have been jubilant, but its self-evident awkwardness betrayed the fact that he had no new title of his own. Indeed, it underlined the fact that his authority was entirely derived from that of his father, who could interfere and overrule at any time. Just like Simon de Montfort before him, Edward was really no more than Henry's lieutenant.[43]

The way the relationship was supposed to work was spelt out in a letter that the king sent to his son on 17 August 1255. On his way home from Gascony Henry had visited Paris to renew his truce with the king of France, and now that a new three-year ceasefire was in place, Henry felt it was time that Edward moved on. He should go to Ireland, where he could spend the winter reforming and ordering his other new overseas lordship. Gascony could be left in the hands of a lieutenant – indeed, Henry had already appointed a suitable candidate. All this was done at the suggestion of Peter of Savoy, the great-uncle who had micro-managed Edward's affairs since his early infancy. In fact, the letter concluded, all being well, Peter would probably arrive in Gascony in a few weeks' time to help Edward make the necessary arrangements for his departure.[44]

Although nothing was said in Henry's letter, it must have been communicated to Edward privately that the king expected him to go to Ireland on his own – that is, without his new wife. Just days after writing to his son, the king began to make preparations for the reception of Eleanor of Castile in England. This decision is not unduly surprising: Ireland was a wild place, only half tamed, and therefore perhaps regarded as an unsuitable destination for a Spanish princess. There was, however, another and perhaps more likely reason for wishing to keep the couple apart. At the end of May, Eleanor, who was thirteen and a half, had almost certainly given birth to a premature daughter.[45] She, it seems, had not been as fortunate as her namesake in avoiding the risks that went with early consummation. The sad news would have reached England later in the summer, and Edward's parents would doubtless have felt the strong urge to advise and protect. A period of abstinence after their own example must have seemed a good idea, but could not be instituted with any effectiveness until Edward and Eleanor were back in England. In the meantime, a six-month separation would be a good start. Such thinking on the part of the king and queen would be understandable, even sensible. But given the young couple's strong attachment, as witnessed by their almost total inseparability in later years, Edward can only have regarded this as yet another unnecessary instance of parental interference, and a further mockery of his supposed independence. He certainly decided to resist it.

In accordance with the wishes of Henry III, Eleanor of Castile was dispatched to England, probably in late September – she arrived safe and sound at Dover on 9 October. Her departure must have coincided with the arrival in Gascony, as promised, of Peter of Savoy, who for the next month proceeded to help Edward finalise the arrangements for his own exit.[46] Peter, however, had not seen his great-nephew for at least a year, and may have been surprised by the picture with which he was now presented. At sixteen years old, Edward had probably attained the physical attributes for which he was later famous. He was broad browed and broad chested, blond haired and handsome, despite having inherited a drooping eyelid from his father. Beyond all this, though, he had grown to be mightily tall. Edward, said one contemporary, 'towered head and shoulders above the average', and an eighteenth-century exhumation of his body confirmed that he was, in fact, six foot two inches tall – hence, of course, his (apparently) popular nickname, Longshanks. In terms of appearance, it is even possible that Edward, left to his own devices, had begun to dress differently: as an adult, he reportedly eschewed the kind of rich and ostentatious garments that his parents had provided for him as a child.[47] It must have quickly become clear to Peter of Savoy that his protégé had developed in all kinds of directions and could no longer be manipulated with the same ease. Edward left Gascony at the end of October, but not for Ireland as his parents and Peter had planned. Instead, he travelled northwards through France, and from there he crossed to England. By the end of November he was in London, where the citizens received him with the same pomp that had greeted the arrival of his wife just six weeks before.[48]

In spite of his best-laid plans, therefore, Henry III found himself celebrating Christmas not only with his new daughter-in-law, but also in the company of his firstborn son, who was seemingly determined to test the limits of his independence. That Christmas their first recorded quarrel arose. Its cue was a row between the merchants of Gascony, who complained – to Edward – that royal customs officers were seizing their goods without payment. The officers responded by seeking out their employer – Henry – before whom they denied the accusations, while at the same time reminding him that 'there is only one king in England who has the power to administer justice'. The heart of the matter, in short, was the scope of Edward's own authority, and the extent to which it was subordinate to that of his father. When Edward raised the issue in person with Henry, the king theatrically recalled the misfortunes of his grandfather Henry II, whose sons had famously rebelled against him. Edward, of course, was nowhere near rebellion, and very soon the affair was calmed. But he remained chafing at his restraints, anxious to play a more visible role, and to exercise greater power. According to Matthew Paris, who took it as a bad omen, Edward increased the size of his own retinue at this time, and now rode accompanied by 200 horsemen.[49]

Paris was seeing bad omens everywhere in England that winter. Recording the reception of Eleanor of Castile in October, the dyspeptic monk had noted that the Londoners had laughed derisively at the fashions of her Spanish entourage (their installation of carpets in her chambers being especially worthy of scorn). Wiser heads, said Paris – by which he meant himself – were more troubled by the wider problem of which Eleanor's advent was merely the latest regrettable symptom, namely, the king's preference for surrounding himself with undesirable foreigners. First there had been Henry's own queen, whose arrival twenty years earlier had occasioned an influx of Savoyards – not only great men like Peter of Savoy and Archbishop Boniface, but dozens of other lesser individuals who had come to England in search of advantageous marriages, pensions and positions at court. Now, it seemed, a similar invasion of Spaniards was imminent.[50]

Far more harmful to the kingdom's health than either of these groups, however, were the foreigners who had arrived in the interim. In the spring of 1247 Henry III had been pleased to welcome into England some of the children of his mother's second marriage. Isabella of Angoulême, having abandoned Henry and his siblings thirty years earlier, had nevertheless gone on to have more sons and daughters by her second husband – nine more, to be precise – and these young men and women faced poor prospects in their native Poitou, diminished as it was by French expansion. Henry had shown no hesitation in inviting five of their number to cross the Channel and enjoy all the bounty he was able to bestow. To his half-brothers Aymer and William de Valence, the king was especially generous: Aymer, at Henry's insistence, was elected as bishop of Winchester (the opposition was stiff because Aymer was neither well-educated nor yet out of his teens); William, meanwhile, the king promoted into the upper echelons of secular society, granting him lands, pensions, and the marriage of a rich heiress. Pensions were also promised to two other half-brothers, Guy and Geoffrey de Lusignan, and Henry's half-sister, Alice, was granted the future earl of Surrey as her husband.[51]

By promoting the Lusignans (as his half-siblings are collectively known) in this way, Henry was storing up for himself a world of trouble. It was not simply that the king's open-handed generosity was excessive; the problem with such profligacy was that it placed Henry's family in direct competition for patronage with the family of his queen, and sparked a bitter rivalry between them that the king could neither comprehend nor control. It had already led to a notorious incident in 1252 when Aymer and his brothers had sought to settle a row with Archbishop Boniface by attacking two of his manors and roughing up several of his servants. The resort to violence was all too typical of the Lusignans, and so too was the king's readiness to excuse it. Henry regarded all his relatives with a simple, blind affection, but he was particularly indulgent of his half-brothers. They, more than anyone, had helped him to crush the rebellion in Gascony, and as a consequence the king had returned to England more determined than ever to see them raised and rewarded.[52]

Edward, for this reason, remained extremely wary of the Lusignans, seeing in their hunger for land a major threat to his own newly created network of lordships.[53] Nevertheless, the young lord with the large retinue of horsemen was evidently attracted by the glamorous aura of violence of the kind his half-uncles projected. The next occasion on which we catch up with Edward is in June 1256, a fortnight before his seventeenth birthday, at which point we find him participating in his first tournament.

The event, which took place at Blyth in Nottinghamshire, had been specially arranged on his behalf, and was probably given the go-ahead only after a certain amount of special pleading: in general Henry III disapproved of tournaments, and almost always took steps to ban them. According to Matthew Paris, the meeting at Blyth was intended as an introduction to the 'laws of chivalry'. Edward must already have been an accomplished horseman and proficient in the use of weapons. What he needed, and what a tournament offered, was the opportunity to put these skills into practice, to demonstrate his capacity for prowess and courage, and to learn the strategic arts of war. Thirteenth-century tournaments had little in common with those of the later Middle Ages, where the emphasis was on entertainment and individual jousting. Such spectacles were becoming more popular in Edward's day, but tournaments were still for the most part what they had always been – mock battles. Over a wide area, two teams would set about trying to outwit and capture each other, just as they would in a genuine engagement. To this extent, tournaments approximated today's militaristic team-building exercises, but they differed in being far more dangerous. Even though participants wore armour and used blunted weapons, there was still ample scope for serious injury or worse. Edward appears to have escaped unscathed from his debut at Blyth (deference to the heir to the throne no doubt played its part), but others were not so lucky. Paris reports that many of the participants were very badly wounded, and noted that by Christmas several of them were dead.[54]

From Nottinghamshire the newly blooded knight and his companions rode north to continue their adventures in Scotland. Edward had no territorial interests to look to there, as he did in Ireland and in Wales. Scotland was a kingdom in its own right, and recognised as such by the kings of England. This was not so much a diplomatic visit, however, as a social call. Five years earlier Edward's younger sister, Margaret, had been married to Alexander III, king of Scots. At that time they had all been children – the groom aged ten, the bride aged eleven and her older brother aged twelve – and so were all in their mid-teens at the time of Edward's trip. Although we cannot say for sure, it seems likely that Edward would have taken Eleanor with him on this northern jaunt and that one of his main reasons for visiting his sister was to introduce her to his own wife. The trip lasted only a few weeks, and next to nothing is known about their activities, but Edward's appearance at Whithorn in south-western Scotland is suggestive. He can only have been drawn there by the shrine of St Ninian, so the possibility exists that the two young couples had embarked on a pilgrimage together.[55]

Short and obscure though it is, this northern excursion serves to emphasise an important point, namely that the kingdoms of Scotland and England rubbed along quite well in the thirteenth century. The English did not regard their northern neighbours as equals, nor were they. Scotland was a much poorer and less populous country than England, its kings far less powerful. Henry III, in giving his daughter away in 1251, had hammered this point home by organising a wedding ceremony at York of unparalleled magnificence. Preparations had begun six months in advance, with supplies ordered from all over England as well as from the Continent. (Edward had been part of the spectacle that day, dressed, like his knightly attendants, from head to toe in gold.)[56] Henry at that time was still hoping to go on crusade and intended before his departure to impress upon his new ten-year-old son-in-law, albeit benevolently, the supreme power of the English Crown. Nonetheless, the very fact of the marriage proved that the kings of Scots were regarded as part of the civilised club of European rulers. They and their nobles demonstrated their credentials for membership by speaking French. In the towns of Scotland, especially in the Lowlands, most Scots spoke English. In ways that were crucially important, Scotland was very alike to England.[57]

By contrast, the next stop on Edward's itinerary in 1256 was very different. From Whithorn Edward travelled south, arriving at his lordship of Chester by mid-July, from where he moved into Wales. Geographically, of course, there were similarities between Wales and Scotland that a first-time visitor would have readily appreciated, and this meant that economically, too, they had certain similarities – Wales, like Scotland, was poor in comparison with England. Culturally, however, Wales was very different from both its near neighbours. Perhaps most obviously, the Welsh spoke Welsh, even at the highest social levels. This was a source of pride to the Welsh themselves, but to the French-speaking kings and nobles of England and Scotland it sounded like so much incomprehensible babble.[58]

More perplexing still for English and Scottish onlookers, and far more problematic, were Welsh social attitudes, which stood in sharp opposition to their own. Take, for instance, the rules governing inheritance. In England and Scotland, and indeed almost everywhere else in western Europe, the rule was primogeniture: firstborn sons inherited estates in their entirety. This was hard on any younger brothers or sisters, but had the great advantage of keeping a family's lands intact from one generation to the next. In Wales, by contrast, the rule was 'partibility': every male member of the family – not just sons and brothers, but uncles and nephews too – expected his portion of the spoils, and rules of precedence were only loosely defined. This meant that the death of a Welsh landowner was almost always followed by a violent, sometimes fratricidal struggle, as each male kinsman strove to claim the lion's share.[59]

The result of this idiosyncratic approach to inheritance was that Welsh politics were wont to be tumultuous. The fact that partibility applied at the highest levels was one of the main reasons why there was no single political authority in Wales as there was in England and Scotland. Welsh poets spoke of their country as if it were neatly divided into three kingdoms, but this was a broad simplification; the reality was a complex patchwork of petty lordships. Occasionally one ruler might, through force of arms, diplomacy or sheer good luck, contrive to establish something greater. But such constructs were always temporary. When a successful Welsh ruler died, his work was swiftly undone by the general carve-up that inevitably followed.[60]

Such cultural and political differences meant that the English found it difficult to do business with the Welsh as they did with the Scots. Inherent instability meant that amicable relations were hard to sustain. The king of England could marry his daughter to the king of Scots, safe in the knowledge that her rights would be guaranteed; but he would not give her away to a Welsh ruler, no matter how great, for who knew how long his greatness might last?[61]

And yet, if the English found the practice of partibility baffling, they were far more troubled when the Welsh showed any signs of abandoning it. From the start of the thirteenth century, up until the time of Edward's birth, there had been a worrying (from the English point of view) movement in the direction of pan-Welsh political unity. Gwynedd, the most remote and traditional of Wales's three ancient 'kingdoms', had extended its power from the mountains of Snowdonia to cover much of the rest of the country. When, therefore, the architect of this expansion, Llywelyn the Great, had died in 1240, Henry III had been quick to intervene and undo his work. In the years that followed, Gwynedd was torn down to size, and its pretensions to leadership were crushed. Llywelyn's descendants were forcibly persuaded to follow traditional Welsh practice and share power among themselves. Lesser Welsh rulers who had formerly acknowledged Llywelyn's mastery were disabused, and obliged to recognise that their proper overlord was, in actual fact, the king of England. Most contentiously, Henry confiscated and kept for himself a large and comparatively prosperous area of north Wales. Known as *Perfeddwlad* (middle country) to the Welsh, and as the Four Cantrefs to the English, this region between the rivers Dee and Conwy had been contested by both sides for hundreds of years, but Henry was determined that from that point on the English would retain it for good. The Four Cantrefs, he declared, were an inseparable part of the Crown of England, and to give force to this assertion he built two new royal castles there, one at Dyserth, the other at Deganwy. At the same time, lordship in the region was made more exacting. From their base at Chester, royal officials introduced English customs and practices, including more punitive financial demands. By 1254, when the Four Cantrefs (or 'the king's new conquest in Wales', as they were now also being termed) were handed over to Edward as part of his endowment, the castles were complete, and the process of anglicisation well advanced. At the time of Edward's visit two years later, his officials there were in a supremely confident mood. According to chronicle reports, his chief steward boasted openly before the king and queen that he had the Welsh in the palm of his hand.[62]

Edward's stay in Wales, like his stay in Scotland, was brief: by early August he was back in Chester, and by the end of summer he was back in London. His father was also there at that time, together with many other great lords. The city, says Matthew Paris, had been ornamented in honour of their coming. On 29 August a great feast was thrown in Westminster. The king and queen were in attendance, along with all their children: even Margaret and her husband, King Alexander, were present, at the end of a short visit to England. The royal family, when occasion demanded, was still able to present a united front.[63]

But the tensions among them were many, serious and multiplying. Between Edward and Henry the struggle for authority went on unabated. Behind the king's back, for example, Edward had begun to interfere in the municipal politics of Bordeaux. Within a fortnight of the Westminster feast, he had struck a secret deal favouring one city faction above the other, undermining his father's efforts to reconcile the rival parties. The tussle between father and son, moreover, was leading to wider problems in England. Edward's hunger for power was driving him to irresponsible excesses and creating scandal in the country at large. Matthew Paris tells one tale, much cited in modern histories, of how Edward, out riding one day with his gang of thuggish followers, encountered another young man and ordered his gratuitous mutilation. The story looks vague – no names or places are given – and we might charitably interpret it as exaggerated gossip. But there are plenty of other stories about the bad behaviour of Edward's household at this time that are all too credible, and that are corroborated by administrative accounts of the damage they caused.[64]

Henry, meanwhile, continued to exhibit his own brand of irresponsibility by failing to take action where it was needed most. Naturally, he failed to curb his son's excesses, just as he failed to correct the bad behaviour of his Lusignan half-brothers. But that was not all. It was now over six years since the king had vowed to go on crusade, and over four years since he had assured more committed crusaders that they would be leaving at midsummer 1256. Here, too, therefore, Henry was seen to have failed. The departure date had passed, and no preparations for an expedition were in place: such gold treasure as the king had amassed for the East had been spent saving Gascony. Not that this deterred Henry, whose inability to take appropriate action was exceeded only by his propensity for embarking on preposterous personal initiatives. In spite of his insolvency, the king was now pursuing a new scheme to install his younger son, Edmund, on the throne of Sicily. The pope, who had suggested the project, had assured Henry that it was a perfectly acceptable alternative to fighting in the Holy Land. The king's subjects in England, however, begged to differ: when parliament was asked to fund the ludicrous adventure the response was a flat refusal. Unable to obtain money by consensual means, Henry demanded more and more fines from his sheriffs, justices and foresters. With each day that passed, throughout the whole kingdom, his government became ever more oppressive and unpopular.[65]

Then, lastly, there was the queen. Eleanor of Provence was now thirty-three years old, poised precisely between her teenaged son and a husband approaching his fiftieth year. More mature than Edward, more vigorous than Henry, Eleanor was in many respects no less irresponsible than either. A harsh and exacting landlord, she showed no sympathy for the English in their suffering, reciprocating the lack of affection they had shown her since the start. The slip of a girl from those days was gone: in her place stood a grown woman, and behind her a powerful network of expatriate Savoyards. To these people – her own people – the queen did feel responsible, and in recent developments she saw great danger to their position. Her husband favoured his hateful half-brothers, and her son was running out of control. Edward, from the moment of his birth, had been the source of all her power and influence. The more he began to pull away from her, the more she prepared to tighten her embrace.[66]

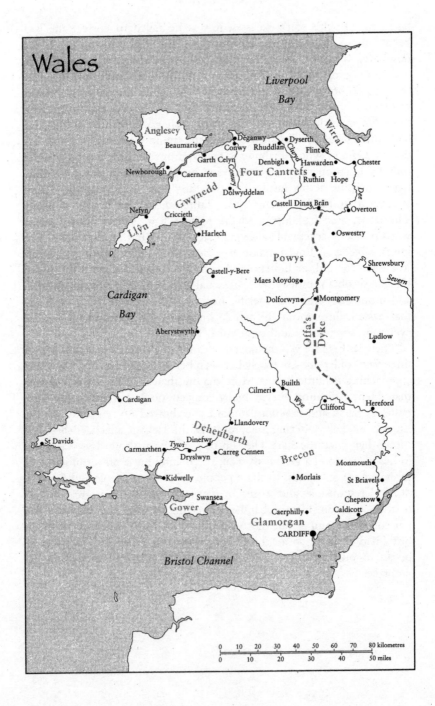

2

The Family Feud

The trouble began in Wales. The view expressed in 1256 by Edward's chief steward that everything there was progressing according to plan and that the Welsh were in the palm of his hands was, of course, the view of an insensitive and complacent Englishman. To the Welsh of the Four Cantrefs it seemed rather that they were under the heel of the oppressor's boot. For the past decade, ever since Henry III had confiscated their homeland, they had been complaining of the unjust behaviour of royal officials, yet nothing had been done to alleviate their distress. Once the region had been transferred to Edward's control, matters had, if anything, become worse, and it may well be that his visit in the summer of 1256 was the final straw. Until that moment the Welsh might have hoped, like the Gascons, that a new young lord would bring a turn-around in their desperate circumstances. If so, they must have been sadly disillusioned by the arrogant swagger of Edward and his gang of unruly followers. Expectations had been raised, only to be dashed. The people of the Perfeddwlad realised that they would have to look elsewhere in their search for a saviour.[1]

The obvious candidate was not far to seek. Across the River Conwy, the people of Gwynedd had acquired a new, dynamic and undisputed leader. Llywelyn ap Gruffudd, grandson of Llywelyn the Great, had also suffered the experience of being brought low by the English. In 1247, following Henry III's military intervention, he had been obliged to share what little remained of his grandfather's power with his older brother, Owain. Since that time, however, he had worked secretly and assiduously to revive the fortunes of his dynasty. Supremacy in Gwynedd itself had been assured in the summer of 1255 when Llywelyn, then in his early thirties, had defeated Owain in battle and had him cast into prison. Yet victory in arms had not solved all his problems. He

31

still had other, younger brothers to provide for, and only a diminished patrimony that he was unwilling to divide. Llywelyn and his family needed more land, just as surely as the men and women of the Four Cantrefs needed better lordship. The result was not hard to foresee. At the start of November 1256 Llywelyn led his army across the Conwy and swept east through the area of English occupation. Within a matter of days the region was completely in his hands. Only the new English castles at Dyserth and Deganwy held out.[2]

The English court was at Windsor when the news broke. Henry III favoured a diplomatic response and wrote to Llywelyn expressing his surprise and disappointment. As for his son's reaction, we have the testimony of Matthew Paris: 'Edward was determined to check the impetuous rashness of the Welsh, to punish their presumption, and to wage war against them to their extermination.' Such intentions, though, were frustrated by the onset of foul weather. 'The whole winter that year,' Paris explained, 'was so wet and stormy that the entire country of Wales . . . was utterly inaccessible to the English, and thus Edward's labour and expenditure of money were fruitless and of no avail.'[3]

Money was, in fact, the truly insurmountable problem. Edward had immediately recognised that his own financial resources would be insufficient for a war in Wales. His first instinct had been to rush to his uncle, Richard of Cornwall, who had furnished him with a loan of 4,000 marks (£2,666). But by December it was all was gone, and Richard had no more money to give, so Edward turned to his parents for aid. Their money, however, was tied up in the disastrous scheme to obtain the throne of Sicily for Edward's younger brother. The grandeur of his folly in embarking on this project was starting to dawn on Henry, in line with the mounting criticism it was attracting from his subjects. In January 1257, for example, his latest request for funds was rejected by a specially convened assembly of Cistercian abbots. In such circumstances, the king would have already been ill disposed to hear his eldest son's appeal for assistance. As it was, given their recent tussles over authority, and Edward's express desire for greater independence, he was also able to relish the irony of the situation. When, in February, Edward again beseeched his father for assistance in Wales, Henry could not resist the obvious rejoinder. 'What is it to me?' he reportedly demanded. 'The land is yours by my gift.' The rebellion, he advised, was an opportunity to be seized; Edward should make a name for himself, so that his enemies might fear him in the future. 'As for me,' the king concluded, 'I am concerned with other business.' Edward, in short, was on his own.[4]

Llywelyn, meanwhile, was winning lots of new friends. Other dispossessed Welsh lords were flocking to his banner, and he was restoring them to their lands, 'keeping nothing for himself but fame and honour', in the words of a Welsh chronicler. Having driven the English out of north Wales, Llywelyn was now pushing south. In December and January he had marched his forces into Deheubarth and Powys, the two other ancient 'kingdoms' of Wales. By February their success was such that they were able to launch attacks on the English lordships along the south Welsh coast. In Kidwelly and in Gower the foreigners were thrown onto the defensive, and the castle at Swansea was burned to the ground. Llywelyn's power and fame were growing daily. 'The Welsh followed him,' said one English writer, 'as if they were glued to him.'[5]

His drive into south Wales brought Llywelyn into a new arena of contention with his principal adversary. Edward's endowment had also included a number of lordships and castles in the south, and it was from these positions – principally his castles at Carmarthen and Cardigan – that the king's son elected to strike back. Cardigan, in particular, located on the west coast, had the advantage that it could be supplied from Ireland, and this process was already under way when the English counteroffensive was launched at the end of May. Edward himself was still in Westminster at the time, and just as well, for the result was an unmitigated disaster. No sooner had his troops set out from Carmarthen than they came under heavy attack from the Welsh, and when, on 2 June, the two sides met in open battle, Edward's army, including its commander, was completely wiped out.[6]

The killing of so many Englishmen, especially ones of rank, meant that the war in Wales was no longer something that Henry III could reasonably ignore. The king now accepted that he would have to intervene in person, and to this end a royal army was ordered to muster at Chester in August. In the middle of that month both father and son advanced into north Wales at the head of these forces, intending to strike at the heart of Llywelyn's power. Here too, however, the English response failed as a result of its undue haste. Although the king's host quickly regained control of the Four Cantrefs, raising the sieges of Dyserth and Deganwy in the process, it lacked the supplies to progress any further. Ships that should have arrived from Ireland failed to appear. After vainly scanning the horizon at Deganwy for a week, Henry announced that he was giving up. Less than a month after they had set out from Chester, his army began their retreat, harassed all the while by attacks from the Welsh. By October the king was back in Westminster.[7]

The failure of the English assault left Llywelyn stronger than ever. As the royal armies withdrew, the Welsh leader was able to reoccupy the Four Cantrefs and resume his attacks on their two castles. More than this, however, he could now plausibly maintain that his power was irresistible. Those Welsh lords who had until this point regarded themselves merely as his allies were persuaded – no doubt forcibly in some cases – that Llywelyn was, in fact, their rightful superior. Throughout the winter of 1257–58, Llywelyn concentrated on eliciting such admissions, seeking to transform his military triumph into something greater still – an acknowledged political supremacy. By March his purpose was achieved, and he was trying out a new title to match his enhanced status. No longer simply 'lord of Snowdon', he was now, in addition, 'prince of Wales'.

During those same winter months, Edward was also redefining himself and his relationship with those around him. The fiasco in Wales had made one thing abundantly clear: his parents, and especially his mother, had failed him, and not only on the issue of money. Eleanor and her Savoyard circle had controlled Edward's affairs since the day he was born. His administration and estates, including those in Wales now lost to Llywelyn, had from the first been administered by men of his mother's choosing. Edward was now determined that this would no longer be the case. As he prepared for a renewed offensive in the spring, he began to reshape his entourage along lines of his own devising, introducing men who possessed the kind of talents that he personally prized. Henry of Almain, son of Richard of Cornwall, the cousin with whom Edward had grown up at Windsor, was one such. But there were also brand-new associates with whom Edward had come into contact only by virtue of the outbreak of war. These men were the lords of the March of Wales.[7]

The March of Wales was a term applied to the numerous lordships spread along the south Welsh coast and the country's eastern border with England. Carved out in the wake of the Norman Conquest, and aggressively expanded whenever subsequent opportunity allowed, these lordships were by their nature opposed to the polities of native Wales. At the same time, however, they formed no part of England. Having conquered their lands without royal assistance, the lords of the March had developed the theory that they were not answerable to the English Crown. 'In the March of Wales,' so their maxim went, 'the king's writ does not run.' The March, as a consequence, was literally a law unto itself: its lordships were governed like little, self-contained kingdoms, and relations between them and their Welsh neighbours were regulated according to Marcher rules. Most often this meant that matters were decided by force, and Marcher lords therefore tended to be an anachronistic breed. Such men kept their castles in good repair at all times, and their swords within easy reach.[10]

Llywelyn, in his exuberance, had not only reversed the conquests of Henry III; he had also intruded himself into the March, and thereby provoked the Marchers' wrath. This made them natural allies for Edward, and before Christmas 1257 several of their number had joined his inner circle. Roger Clifford, for example, was the latest in a long line of lords who took their name from Clifford Castle in Herefordshire, and who took their position as Marchers seriously (one of his relatives once famously forced the bearer of a royal writ to eat it – parchment, wax seal and all). In November 1257 Edward sent Clifford to Carmarthen in order to restock its castle, ready for the renewal of war.[11]

In these developments there was plenty to alarm the queen and her advisers, who had already been given cause to worry in recent years by the independent direction in which Edward's activities had been leading him. Not until too late, however, did they perceive the logical outcome of his increasing fraternisation with the violent men of the March and his continuing need for ready cash. Only in the spring of 1258 did it become apparent, when Edward, in return for substantial loans, mortgaged several of his English manors to the Marcher lord of Pembroke and his brother, the bishop-elect of Winchester. Which is to say, when he struck a deal with William and Aymer de Valence, his notorious Lusignan half-uncles. The queen's worst enemies had become her son's principal allies.

This was a moment of crisis for Eleanor and her Savoyard circle. They had of late been losing the struggle against the Lusignans for Henry III's affections. If they lost their long-established control of Edward to their rivals they stood to be permanently undone. The danger hardly required further emphasis, but this was provided anyway, when on 1 April Aymer de Valence sent an armed gang to attack the property of one of the queen's closest advisers – an act of lawlessness reminiscent of his earlier assault against her uncle Boniface, but worse in that on this occasion one of the defenders died.[12]

By the time parliament met in Westminster a week later, the Savoyards had decided to take action against the Lusignans. To put their plan into effect they sought additional support among the other aristocrats in attendance and found no shortage of willing and powerful allies. Since their first arrival in England Henry III's half-brothers had by their arrogant and lawless behaviour made many enemies among the great men of his court. Even while parliament was in session, William de Valence began to quarrel violently with other English lords, openly accusing them of failing to prosecute the war in Wales with sufficient vigour, and going so far as to accuse them of colluding treasonably with the Welsh. Ironically, the men he accused *were* in collusion by this point – but only with each other, and in a plot to remove their accuser and his brothers from England for good.

As the conspiracy around the queen closed ranks, however, she and her Savoyard supporters were evidently advised by their new aristocratic allies that assistance came at a price. Appalling as the Lusignans were, everyone accepted that the responsibility for correcting their behaviour had ultimately rested with the king. Yet for years Henry had failed to curb his half-brothers' excesses, turning a blind eye to even the gravest of misdemeanours. At the start of the present parliament, when a complaint had been laid before him about Aymer de Valence's most recent murderous attack, the king had simply brushed the matter aside and tried to make light of the offence.

Moreover, his indulgence of the Lusignans was just one aspect of Henry's ineptitude. Parliament had been summoned, after all, to discuss how to address the disaster that was still unfolding in Wales, and also the ludicrous business involving Sicily. It was the latter, above all, that really marked Henry down as a *vir simplex*, a man severely lacking in sound judgement. Not only was the scheme inherently unfeasible; the king's failure to obtain a tax to fund it had led him to demand unreasonably large sums from his local officials. Across the country, sheriffs, foresters and justices were extorting excessive sums; the whole kingdom was paying the price for Henry's woeful lack of common sense. If, therefore, the king was to be compelled to sort out his half-brothers, he must also be compelled to attend to counsels beyond those of his wife and her uncles, the other architects of the Sicilian scheme. It was a deal that the Savoyards were ready to strike. To preserve their power over Henry and Edward, they were willing to see them both constrained.[13]

It was the last day of April, and the Easter parliament was drawing to a close. Two days before, the king, still focused on the Sicilian business, had asked for a new tax. Today he would receive his answer. At around nine in the morning Henry was seated in the Great Hall of the Palace of Westminster, when suddenly a multitude of knights and barons appeared before him. They were armed – that is, they were wearing their armour; their swords, as a mark of respect, they had left at the door. The threat of force, though, remained abundantly clear. 'What is this, my lords?' asked the trembling king. 'Am I your captive?'

'No, my lord, no,' replied Roger Bigod, the earl of Norfolk, who stood at the front of the crowd. What they wanted, he explained, was the removal of the 'wretched and intolerable' Lusignans, and a promise from the king that in future he would attend to the counsels of the company now confronting him.

And the company was formidable. Besides Bigod, two other earls had joined the Savoyard conspiracy. Richard de Clare, earl of Gloucester, was one; Simon de Montfort, earl of Leicester, was the other. Their status was significant: earls were the only noblemen of rank in thirteenth-century England (there were no dukes or marquises above them), and in total they numbered only about a dozen. But what really mattered in this instance was the raw power on display. Bigod, Clare and Montfort all had extensive estates and, as a consequence, massive incomes, which in turn gave them the wherewithal to recruit and reward others. In addition, Bigod and Montfort had reputations as fearsome warriors. Together, the three earls and their followers formed an irresistible force. Henry saw that he had no choice but to comply with their demands, and swore on the gospels that he would accept their counsels.[14]

So too did his son. Edward is not identified specifically in the chroniclers' accounts of the confrontation in Westminster Hall, though he was almost certainly present. Frustratingly, at this crucial time, he has a tendency to shrink from view. What is not in doubt is the strength of his opposition to what was happening. We are specifically told that he swore his oath unwillingly, and his unwillingness must be one of the main reasons that the earls' plan faltered at its first step. Another was the inherent contradiction between the forceful opening remarks of Roger Bigod and the moderate scheme he and his allies went on to propose. Their plan, it transpired, was to create a committee of twenty-four men that would undertake the reform of the realm, and it was generously conceded that Henry should select half of its members. But in response, the king included the Lusignans among his nominees, thereby making an instant mockery of Bigod's demand for the brothers' banishment. 'The nobles,' said Matthew Paris, 'had not yet learned what knot to bind their Proteus with (for it was an arduous and difficult matter).' Within days talks had broken down entirely, with nothing agreed except that they should reassemble in Oxford in one month's time.[15]

The revolution looked to have been botched. Henry went to his birthplace at Winchester, the magnates to their own parts, and each side attempted to muster their strength. All parties were able to maintain the fiction that that they were raising troops for a campaign in Wales, but everyone realised that what was really looming was a civil war. The mood across the whole country was tense. The earls sought to close all the seaports, fearing that the king would try to bring in foreign mercenaries; in London, the city gates were fastened at night with better bars; a week before the Oxford parliament was due to meet, Bigod drew up a new will, naming Clare and Montfort as his executors.[16]

In the event, however, swords remained sheathed. When the Oxford parliament assembled, around 11 June, it was huge. Local knights had ridden there from all over England, partly in response to the summons to fight in Wales, but also because the word was out – reform of Henry's unjust and oppressive regime was finally under way. The knights were all in favour; parliament buzzed with petitions for far-reaching change. The king's party were hopelessly outnumbered, and their opponents buoyed by popular support. Riding the crest of this wave, the earls acted decisively to complete the take-over of royal government that had stalled the previous month. A new, far more radical scheme was proposed, which became known as the Provisions of Oxford. On 22 June a new royal council was created, and almost all of its fifteen members were strong supporters of the original coup. On the same day all royal castles, which were naturally in the hands of the king's supporters, were transferred to the keeping of what one eyewitness called 'reliable Englishmen' – that is, supporters of the earls. Next the new council set out to recover all the lands and castles that Henry had lately granted away as gifts. Ostensibly this was a measure to improve royal finances, but its real aim was to break the power of the Lusignans, who in recent years had been the principal beneficiaries of the king's bounty. The brothers understood the threat to their position only too well, and swore 'by the death and wounds of Christ' that they would not comply, leaving Simon de Montfort to spell out the alternative in stark terms. 'Make no mistake about it,' the earl told William de Valence, 'either you lose your castles, or you lose your head.'[17]

The only awkward and embarrassing detail in all of this was that the Lusignans still had the backing of the heir to the throne. Far from driving them apart, adversity had pulled Edward and his half-uncles closer together, and together they were determined to resist the revolution that was taking place. As the council moved to strip the brothers of their power, Edward, in what can only be read as a deliberately provocative act, began to appoint them to positions of authority in his own lands. Guy de Lusignan he made keeper of Oléron, an island off the coast of Gascony, while Geoffrey de Lusignan he placed in charge of the duchy as a whole. This was discovered by the council, who took steps to reverse it, but probably not before a fresh twist which further underlined the strength of the bond between the king's half-brothers and his eldest son. Towards the end of June Edward and the Lusignans stole out of Oxford and fled south. The earls raced after them, fearing that if the brothers reached the coast they might succeed in landing foreign troops. As it was, the fugitives shut themselves up in Wolvesey Castle, Aymer's episcopal residence in Winchester, and there, in the first week of July, a final stand-off took place. Now offered only imprisonment or banishment, the Lusignans opted for the latter. On the day of their surrender Edward swore an oath to abide by the new scheme of government prescribed by the Provisions of Oxford. Four days later, having been escorted to Dover, his half-uncles sailed across the channel and into exile. The April plot had finally succeeded. The Lusignans were gone, and the king and his son were shackled.[18]

What had happened at Oxford in June 1258 had been truly revolutionary. Nothing like it had ever been attempted before, and nothing similar would be tried again for another four centuries. The new council imposed on Henry III had assumed almost all of the king's executive power. From now on the earls and their allies would rule on such crucial matters as the distribution of royal lands and the custody of royal castles. Royal policy would not be concocted by the king and a narrow clique of advisers; it would be decided by the council, in consultation with the rest of the realm in parliament: one of the most important of the Provisions of Oxford laid down that parliament had to meet three times a year for this purpose. Nothing was left to Henry's initiative except the most routine aspects of government. The king of England had effectively been reduced to a rubber stamp.[19]

All this affected Edward as well. Like his father, he too was obliged to accept the rule of an advisory committee: a separate body of four men, answerable to the main council, had been created to regulate his affairs. The real worry for Edward, though, was the envisaged duration of the new arrangements, which threatened to remain in place far into the future. The Provisions of Oxford stated that the council would appoint the keepers of royal castles for the next twelve years, a stipulation that would continue to apply even if Henry III died in the meantime. In such circumstances Edward would simply take over his father's role as the council's cipher.[20]

Nevertheless, there were limits to conciliar control. The earls and their allies sought to restrain and redirect the monarchy, not to replace it. Henry and Edward, for this reason, had considerable freedom in their personal movement and – the banishment of the Lusignans apart – freedom of association. For a man of Henry's non-martial nature, this offered little opportunity for self-help. The king chose to place his faith in God, and to this end embarked in the autumn of 1258 on a tour of East Anglian shrines. Edward, by contrast, saw in his freedom the opportunity to improve his circumstances. His overriding aim, revealed in a private agreement with the earl of Gloucester in March 1259, was 'that he may speedily have his castles and lands in his hand and in his power'.[21]

The situation in Wales gave him a good degree of cover, and justified his continued association with his tough, warlike friends from the March. In the summer of 1258 the new council had concluded a truce with Llywelyn ap Gruffudd, but by the autumn it had already been breached, and Edward was therefore able to maintain that he was 'going to Wales'. Where there was no war, moreover, it could be simulated. It is striking that in the spring and summer of 1259 Edward attended at least three tournaments, even crossing to France for one of them. This was a tried and tested way for a lord to recruit violent young men to his banner and to train them covertly in readiness for the real business of war. The suspicion has to be that this was Edward's ulterior motive. If 1258 had shown anything, it was that matters were ultimately decided by force.[22]

But the revolution had also shown that, in the long run, ideas could matter more. Edward, his father and the Lusignans had lost in 1258 because they were perceived, not without reason, to be the villains of the piece. By the same token, the earls had succeeded because their manifesto was popular. For years the cry in the country had been for more responsible, less oppressive government, and that was what the Provisions of Oxford promised. Reform was in train, and not just of an irresponsible royal regime: lordship of every kind was coming under scrutiny, and offenders stood to be shamed and punished.

Edward took all of this on board, perceiving how the charges applied in his own case. His behaviour of late, and that of his friends and officials, if not in the same league as that of the Lusignans, had nevertheless been far from exemplary. To regain his independence, he would have to do more than simply confront the new council; he would also have to rebuild his damaged public image and align himself with the forces calling for reform. His conversion was swift but verifiably sincere. In a private letter to his chief official in Chester, Edward decreed that it was essential for good government to be maintained at all times. 'If . . . common justice is denied to anyone of our subjects by us or our bailiffs,' he said, 'we lose the favour of God and man, and our lordship is belittled.'

The letter was written on 21 August 1259, while Edward was at Warwick, participating in the last of his three known tournaments that year.[23] As the summer drew to a close and the autumn approached, he was ready to resume the fight for real.

★   ★   ★

By this point the revolutionary regime was running into grave difficulties. The earls and their allies had dealt with the king's oppressive
government; it remained to correct the endemic abuses in private
administrations across the country. But on this issue fundamental
differences had arisen between leading members of the council. Roger
Bigod, for example, was all for pushing ahead with the process. His
younger brother, Hugh, had been sent at the start of the revolution on
a countrywide judicial tour to correct all manner of wrongdoings.
Together, the two of them represented the more idealistic aspects of
reform. By contrast, Richard de Clare had set his teeth against further
progress. He had joined the original conspiracy because he had favoured
getting rid of the Lusignans, but, in terms of reputation, there was little
to distinguish him from the exiled brothers. Clare was particularly
resistant to the idea of opening up his own administration to public
scrutiny, knowing that the findings were bound to be damning.[24]

Between the idealism of the Bigods and the self-interest of Clare
stood Simon de Montfort, who managed to maintain an improbable
mix of both positions. In his own mind at least, Montfort was not a
man to compromise. Like the others, he had sworn a sacred oath to
uphold the Provisions of Oxford, and being a religious fanatic he took
it very seriously. At the same time, the earl had possessed reasons of his
own for participating in the coup. His disputes with the king's half-
brothers had been bitter, but they were nothing compared to his deep-
seated grievances against Henry himself. Partly because of his unpaid
expenses in Gascony, but mainly because of a long-standing dispute
about the size of his wife's estate, Montfort maintained that his royal
brother-in-law owed him massive amounts of land and money. Like
the Bigod brothers, the earl wanted reform and was impatient to see it
carried through. But more than this he wanted his private claims settled
– so much so that, like Richard de Clare, he was ready to frustrate
reform if it suited his own ends.[25]

All these factors, evident from the first, came into sharper focus in the
autumn parliament of 1259. Because of the disagreements among the
major earls, the much talked about reforms of baronial administration had
still not taken place. As a result, parliament opened with a protest by a
mysterious group of men, described by one chronicler as 'the community of the bachelors of England'. The most interesting thing about their
protest is that, as well as being directed at the council, it was directed at
Edward – and it was Edward who swore immediately to support the
bachelors 'to the death' in fighting for the community of England and
the commonweal. The term 'bachelors' was often used to describe young
men at tournaments, which raises the possibility that at least some of the

protesters were the same men with whom Edward had been mixing throughout the spring and summer, and rouses the suspicion that his immediate pledge of support for their cause was not quite as spontaneous as it might first appear. This was his first opportunity to demonstrate his own power and new-found sense of social responsibility, and it was effective. The council, moved by the threat of force, finally proceeded to pass the long-promised reforms, which became known as the Provisions of Westminster.[26]

One person, above all, took note of Edward's stand, and that was Simon de Montfort. The earl was one of Edward's godparents, though that hardly made him unique, and up to this point there is little to suggest that they were in any way close. From this moment on, however, mutual self-interest and a new-found reciprocal esteem drew them together. Each must have been impressed by the other's zeal for reform and preparedness to threaten force. With the support of Edward and his bachelor friends, Montfort could push for the settlement of his personal claims; with Montfort's backing on the council, Edward could perhaps regain control of his lands and castles. By the middle of October a deal had been struck, and the two men had sworn a secret agreement to aid and counsel each other. Its terms and its aims are not altogether clear, but one fact above all is striking. In pursuit of their objectives, godfather and godson were prepared to wage war.[27]

This private pact between two of the principal players, hitherto in opposing camps, prompts an important general observation. For a long time, historians regarded the politics of the years immediately after 1258 in terms of a monolithic struggle – a clash between a group of idealistic barons on the one hand and a royalist party bent on resisting reform on the other.[28] As we have already seen, however, it was not nearly that simple: profound divisions existed among both the royal family and the reforming magnates. There *was* a lot of idealism in the air in 1258, and intense debate about how England ought to be governed. But, at the same time, the people engaged in these debates had emotions every bit as complicated as our own, private grievances and ambitions, and competing, often conflicting calls on their loyalty: their love for their families and their friends, their hatred for their enemies. Indeed, what was arguably more important during these years than any clash of principle was the series of bitter feuds at the heart of the royal family: between the Savoyards and the Lusignans, between Montfort and Henry III, between Edward and his mother. To follow the shifts in these feuds can be a complicated business, but it is the surest guide to what was really happening in England as the revolution of 1258 started to unravel.

Consider, for example, the historic peace that was being brokered between England and France in the autumn of 1259. With some regret and reluctance, Henry III was finally about to drop his ancestral claims to Normandy, Anjou, Poitou and Maine in exchange for French recognition of his right to hold Gascony. It was sound policy, and had almost universal political support, but not from Edward and Montfort (indeed, their opposition to the proposed treaty was another factor that had served to pull them together). Edward's disapproval, arguably misplaced, was at least sincere – he seems to have feared that too much was being conceded; Montfort's objections, by contrast, were almost entirely cynical. The terms of the draft treaty – terms that Montfort himself had helped to negotiate – required the renunciation of rights in France from an unusually large section of Henry III's family: not just the king and his sons, but his siblings too. This meant a quitclaim was required from Eleanor, Henry's sister, but could not be obtained, for she also happened to be Montfort's wife. To the fury of both the king and the council, the Montforts stubbornly refused to drop Eleanor's claim until they received satisfaction on all their personal grievances.

For months the Montforts played this card, but by the end of the year they were forced to cede it. In November Henry III took part of his court across the Channel in order to finalise the peace. Under sustained pressure from both kings, the Montforts were forced to give up their veto in return for the promise of a later settlement with Henry. On 4 December the historic peace, known as the Treaty of Paris, was sealed, and Montfort's leverage evaporated.[29] In the New Year he returned to England, disappointed, bitter, and in search of new ways to put pressure on his brother-in-law.

He did not have to look for long, for in his absence his godson had been busy. The finalisation of the French peace had heralded the end of Montfort's strategy of obstruction, but it had presented Edward with his greatest opportunity since 1258. The departure of his father to France had also meant the departure of his mother, still the principal check on his independence, as well as her main supporters, Richard de Clare and Peter of Savoy. England had been left in the hands of a diminished group of councillors, headed by the Bigod brothers, both moderate men. Edward saw his chance and seized it with both hands. As soon as the royal party sailed he made his move, ousting the men appointed to keep his castles and replacing them with custodians of his own choosing. (His marcher friend Roger Clifford, for example, was handed control of three castles in south Wales.) In early December Edward installed himself in Bristol Castle, the centre of his administration, where he and his supporters spent a defiant Christmas. But by the end of

January they were loitering on the Sussex coast, probably in order to meet Montfort, and in early February the earl and his nephew arrived in London, ready to push their own agenda.[30]

Ostensibly, they came to uphold reform. It was a central requirement of the Provisions of Oxford that three parliaments should be held every year, and it was now time for the February session. But with Henry still abroad, the other councillors in Westminster balked: could a parliament assemble in the absence of the king? Henry had already written from France telling the council in no uncertain terms that the answer was no. So which mattered more: obeying the king or obeying the Provisions? Montfort, Edward and their partisans could argue for the integrity of reform, but there was clearly much more at stake besides. Edward's self-proclaimed independence, Montfort's ability to obtain personal redress – these too would be decided by the outcome of this new clash of wills.[31]

Edward, at least, made some attempt to reach an accommodation. Later in February, he sent letters to his father – now hovering close to the Channel at St Omer – and Henry wrote back, 'pleased and rejoiced' at his son's words. But the king was much influenced by the queen and her allies, who were already recruiting mercenary troops, and were certainly not about to be sweet-talked into accepting Edward's recent self-enfranchisement as a fait accompli. Henry therefore concluded his reply by saying he would send someone back 'to see if deeds matched words', and in the event he sent Richard de Clare, whose arrival in England caused an immediate escalation. There was a deep personal animosity between the earl of Gloucester and Edward, its principal cause being their rival claims to Bristol Castle.[32] As a result, the earl was as determined as the queen to see her son put back in his box. When he discovered that Edward and Montfort were attempting to hold a parliament in spite of the king's prohibition, he responded by raising forces of his own. London was sent into panic by the prospect of hostile forces gathering within its walls. On the other side of the Channel, too, there was now great alarm: malicious rumours, almost certainly started by Gloucester, told Henry that his errant son was about to seize the throne.

It took the intervention of another earl to pull matters back from the brink. In early April, Richard of Cornwall, having played no discernible part in English politics for over a year, arrived in Westminster to back the beleaguered council and stiffen London's resolve. Under his direction, all the city's gates were closed and guarded, and every male over the age of fifteen was issued with arms. Consequently, as the date of the controversial parliament (25 April) drew near, the contending forces found themselves shut out. Gloucester and his supporters made their camp in Southwark, while Edward and Montfort took up residence in the hospital of St John in Clerkenwell. A state of high tension continued until, at last, the king himself returned. Henry entered London on the last day of the month, escorted by a hundred foreign knights.[33]

The king's return meant that matters could no longer be decided by force. To cross swords with Gloucester would be one thing, but for Edward and Montfort to move on London now would constitute open rebellion. Negotiation was the only way forward, though the path was far from easy. 'Let not my son Edward appear before me,' Henry is reported to have said, afraid his fatherly love would compromise his kingly anger. 'If I see him, I shall not restrain myself from embracing him.' Edward's own anger was directed less at his father than his mother. 'She was said to be the cause of all the malice,' said the same chronicler, no doubt reflecting the view from Clerkenwell. With emotions running high on both sides, it took two weeks of further mediation by Richard of Cornwall before Edward and his parents were brought face to face in a specially convened assembly of magnates in St Paul's Cathedral. Before this company Edward denied his recent actions had been intended to injure his father, at the same time proudly asserting that only his father, together with his uncle, could judge him. Henry and Eleanor in due course gave their son the kiss of peace, but in the queen's case this was clearly an empty show. The price of reconciliation for Edward was a return to subjugation. It was immediately followed by the removal of his men from his castles and the installation of new appointees.[34]

For Montfort, meanwhile, there was to be no reconciliation at all. Henry and Eleanor were by this time heartily sick of their brother-in-law, who in the past year had almost derailed the French peace and then seduced their son from the path of obedience, even to the point of rebellion. They were determined to put the earl on trial, and proceedings against him began in parliament in July. An extraordinarily detailed record preserves both Henry's accusations and Montfort's denials, the latter sarcastic in tone and reflecting Montfort's reputation as a silver-tongued speaker. But, in spite of his sparkling performance, Montfort was in a tight spot, short of options and allies. As well as incurring the wrath of the king and queen, he had forfeited the support of moderate councillors such as the Bigods, to whom he had tried to dictate during the recent crisis. The only figure of real consequence who continued to stand beside him was Edward, but he could do little following his return to a state of tutelage. It was, in short, hard to see how either of their situations could be reversed or improved.[35]

Their unlooked-for saviour was Llywelyn ap Gruffudd. Ever since his stunning victories of 1257 and the revolution in England the following year, the self-proclaimed prince of Wales had been resting on his laurels and restraining his hand. Llywelyn had conquered enough territory for the time being; what he wanted from the English now was the admission of his right to hold it. To his frustration, however, no such recognition had been forthcoming – all the council in England had been prepared to grant him was a series of temporary truces, which suggested that in the fullness of time they expected to challenge his supremacy. By the beginning of 1260 the prince had decided that he could wait no longer, and brought new pressure to bear on the situation by besieging the royal castle at Builth. For six whole months the garrison there had held out, but suddenly in the middle of Montfort's trial, messengers arrived in Westminster. Builth had fallen, and Llywelyn had razed it to the ground.[36]

News of this fresh disaster in Wales caused chaos in Westminster. Henry's orders show him buffeted by conflicting advice, one day commanding harsh retaliation against Llywelyn, the next countenancing the prince's further appeasement. Undoubtedly the chief advocate of a strong military response was Edward. Builth had been his castle, but – thanks to the restrictions imposed upon him – not under his own control. Furious at its loss, he refused to absolve its keeper, and by extension the council, from blame. A month after the castle's fall, Edward was in his lordship of Cheshire, preparing to lead an assault into Llywelyn's territory. Others, meanwhile, raced to renew the truce. In the event, the appeasers won the day. A new two-year ceasefire was agreed and, on 1 September, one week before a royal army was due to muster in Chester, Henry III called off the attack.[37]

For all Edward's righteous anger at the loss of Builth (and his presumed anger at being prevented from avenging it), the distraction had been timely. Montfort's trial had been derailed as soon as news of the crisis had broken. Partly this was because Montfort himself would have been needed in Wales had any war of retaliation taken place. More generally, the crisis had divided the council not only in their opinions but also in their persons. Those councillors with lands in the March had rushed to their defence, while others must have returned to their own parts to raise troops. It was only a temporary diaspora, but it gave Edward and Montfort a crucial respite, and room to manoeuvre.[38]

The key to their recovery, they realised, was an alliance with the earl of Gloucester. On the face of it this was an astonishing proposition, given that just a few months earlier he had been their chief adversary. There was enough mutual self-interest, however, to recommend a rapprochement. Much as they may have personally disliked Gloucester, both Edward and Montfort recognised that his enormous wealth and power made him an essential ally. If Edward was to regain his independence, and Montfort was to make his temporary reprieve permanent, some form of understanding would have to be reached. Gloucester, for his part, also had good reasons for adopting this new, rather awkward embrace. He had, for one thing, been uneasy about Montfort's trial since its inception, fearing that it would expose his own dubious and provocative role during the Easter rising. In more general terms, Gloucester found that he was still part of a council intent on pushing ahead with reform, outnumbered by men who remained determined to investigate and correct abuses committed by great lords in the running of their own estates. Here too Gloucester had much to worry about. Having opposed this policy from the start, he now made its emasculation his price for supporting Edward and Montfort. Together they agreed that great lords like themselves should be allowed to correct their own failings, and not have to submit their administrations to any independent scrutiny. It was a shabby compromise, but it worked where a stand on principle had failed. When a new parliament assembled in October, the three improbable allies arrived in Westminster and took over the government.[39]

Henry III and the other councillors were taken completely off guard by this swift and bloodless coup, and were powerless to prevent it. Committed reformers like the Bigod brothers were ejected from the council or persuaded to bow out; other key figures, such as the treasurer and the chancellor, were replaced by men chosen by Edward and Montfort. The changes were so swift and so silent that they passed almost unnoticed by contemporary chroniclers. All that registered was the spectacle as the new junta brazenly advertised its success. In the course of the parliament Edward publicly knighted Montfort's two eldest sons, Henry and Simon, respectively a year older and a year younger than Edward himself. As for Henry III, he was simultaneously furious and incredulous. The council that had been foisted upon him two years previously may have been unwanted, but hitherto it had at least had the virtue of being dominated by moderate men; now it was controlled by his principal antagonist. In a few short months his mercurial brother-in-law and his headstrong son had succeeded in completely turning the tables.[40]

Edward was once again free to decide his own future, and he wasted no time in doing so. Immediately after the October parliament he crossed the Channel. He left with a large entourage of young knights, the two Montfort boys included among his existing cohort of friends. Together they travelled through France as far south as Lyon, participating in tournaments and being honourably received wherever they went. To this extent, the trip was simply a continuation of the chivalric celebrations that had begun at Westminster. But Edward also crossed to France with an express political purpose. Within a month of his departure, while paused in Paris, he was reunited with all four of his exiled Lusignan uncles. Nothing in the past two years had lessened his determination to renew his earlier association with the notorious brothers; quite the reverse. His parents had proved that they were still bent on controlling his behaviour, so he continued to make a special point of defying their wishes. Soon after reaching Gascony, where he and his entourage spent Christmas, Edward appointed Guy de Lusignan his lieutenant in the duchy. There could be no clearer signal, especially to the queen, that her son was determined to control his own destiny.[41]

Edward remained in Gascony until March, at which point he must have learned of dramatic developments in England. In his absence, Montfort and Gloucester had become complacent, rather assuming that Henry and Eleanor would placidly accept their recent coup. But the king was genuinely incensed by the new state of affairs, as were the queen and her Savoyard supporters. When the time had come for the regular February parliament, it was their turn to seize the initiative. Forsaking the comforts of the Palace of Westminster, they rushed instead to the Tower of London. Henry generally had little use for the great fortress on the city's eastern edge, established by his more warlike ancestor William the Conqueror almost two centuries before. Indeed, during the two decades prior to this point, there is no record of his having visited the Tower at all. In 1261, however, he was grateful for its mighty walls. Safely ensconced within them, he fulminated against Montfort and Gloucester, accusing them, among other things, of exceeding their authority as councillors, of appointing ministers against his wishes, and of causing Edward to withdraw from his father's friendship. Negotiation followed, but no resolution. All that was agreed was that the two sides would hold talks at Easter, which fell on 24 April. It may even have been agreed to defer further discussion until Edward's arrival. In any case, when news reached him of this fresh stand-off, Edward hurried home.[42]

He returned in the same spirit of determined defiance in which he had left, bringing with him William de Valence, now the most notorious of the Lusignan brothers, Aymer de Valence, equally notorious, having died in December. This alarmed those in the Tower with the king: it was, after all, the queen and her Savoyard circle who had been the chief architects of the Lusignans' exile. In late March, reflecting the anxieties of those about him, Henry wrote to his son forbidding him to return

48

with Valence by his side. The king's opponents, by contrast, appear to have been less worried by this prospect. Soon after forging his alliance with Edward, Montfort had contrived to repair his relationship with the Lusignans, and had long been ready to acquiesce in Edward's wish to see them reinstated. The earl appears to have been convinced that, since Edward himself was still firmly attached to his side, Valence's loyalty could be similarly retained. It was with the assent of the opposition that both men arrived in England shortly before Easter, and Valence immediately swore the oath to uphold the Provisions of Oxford.

Here, however, Montfort badly miscalculated, reckoning without the independent will of the king, the pragmatism of the queen and, above all, the motives of Valence himself. Henry had never had any quarrel with his half-brother and was delighted by the prospect of his return. Eleanor and her circle, although altogether less elated, now accepted that there was an urgent need for reconciliation. Valence, of course, had returned to England not to fight for any cause other than the restoration of his own estates. It was an easy decision to make. Within days he had crossed over and joined the king's party.[43]

The defection of a man who remained deeply unpopular in England was not in itself problematic for the king's opponents, but it was highly dangerous in creating a conflict of loyalties for their greatest asset. Edward's long-standing desire to be reunited with Valence, the uncle who encouraged his independence before 1258, was now at odds with his more recent attachment to Montfort, the uncle who had supported his subsequent bids for freedom. There was, of course, still the question of reform, but here too the issue no longer seemed as clear cut as had once been the case. By the time of Edward's return to England, both sides were claiming to be adhering to the programme that had been set out at Oxford. (His parents had apparently moderated their stance.) It was with some justification that Henry could accuse Montfort and Clare of having exceeded the letter of these reforms, and Edward, as a party to their recent coup, knew that Montfort was not above amending the reform programme to suit his own ends.[44] Where, then, should his loyalty lie: with one uncle or the other? With one profession of integrity or another?

In making this difficult choice, Edward could not help but be swayed, like William de Valence, by his own self-interest. For over two years he had sought to recruit other vigorous young knights to his banner, and the process of rewarding them had imposed a serious drain on his finances. According to one chronicler, 'the tongue could scarcely convey' the sums Edward had spent during the crisis of the previous Easter. His recent tour of the international tournament circuit would have demanded similar lavish expenditure and may have dealt a final and fatal blow. Whatever the precise cause, Edward stood on the brink of bankruptcy in the spring of 1261, and knew that solvency could proceed from only one source. Towards the end of May his decision was made. Following Valence's example, Edward rejoined his parents' side.[45]

For his parents, their son's defection could not have been more timely. It was at precisely this moment that Henry also welcomed the return of a messenger he had secretly sent abroad at the start of the year. A few days later, the court moved from London to Winchester, and there, on 12 June, the king revealed his true colours. He now held in his hands a letter from the pope, absolving him from his oath to the Provisions of Oxford, and annulling all the initiatives introduced since 1258. The repeated professions of respect for the reform programme made throughout the spring had been entirely duplicitous. Henry declared that he would rule his kingdom as of old, without his council, as he alone saw fit.[46]

The close coincidence begs an important question: did Edward know of his parents' dishonest intention before his decision to switch sides or learn of it only afterwards? One chronicler has it that he was disgusted by their conduct and, on discovering that he too had been absolved from obeying the Provisions by the pope's letter, promptly re-swore his oath to uphold them. Unfortunately, however, this particular writer was rather confused, especially when it came to chronology, and presents the episode as if it occurred before Edward's defection.[47] Another annalist says that Edward was won over by his mother's flattery, which might also be taken to suggest that he was deceived. Other individuals close to the king were, for certain, taken in by his stance during the spring. Hugh Bigod, brother of the earl of Norfolk, was one such. But as soon as Henry showed his hand at Winchester, such men showed their disgust by rejoining Montfort and Clare. Edward did not do so. Instead, as civil war threatened, he left the country.[48]

His decision to go abroad at this moment would seem to be the best indication that Edward did indeed feel duped. He could not rejoin the opposition; some of his reasons for deserting them still stood, and he also had to maintain what was left of his pride. At the same time, he was not prepared to assist his parents by fighting against his former allies. As the summer of 1261 progressed, and news of the king's duplicity spread, the opposition became more potent and more popular. Montfort orchestrated widespread resistance to the king's government, installing his own supporters in the counties to challenge the king's sheriffs, and attempting to summon a parliament in defiance of royal authority. Henry and Eleanor responded by planning to bring in forces from overseas; foreign knights were expected to land at Dover in the first week of November. In all of this, though, Edward took no part. As the crisis in England deepened, he went to Gascony and busied himself with the duchy's internal problems. There is no sign that he raised any troops for his parents. When November arrived he was still far away, attending to a dispute on the foothills of the Pyrenees. As the crisis at home approached its climax, Edward's continued absence suggests that he had washed his hands of the whole affair.[49]

In the event there was no fighting in England. War was avoided when the earl of Gloucester, whose alliance with Montfort had seemed improbable from the start, reverted to type and rejoined the king – thanks, it was said, to bribes promised him by the queen. This final desertion compromised the opposition to the extent that further resistance became useless. Those men who remained with Montfort sought terms with the king, drawn in by Henry's promise of arbitration on the issue of the reform. Montfort himself, however, refused to submit. He had tried arbitration in the past and got nowhere. To obtain satisfaction of his personal grievances against Henry, the earl had to win power over him. That had not happened; the latest round had gone to the king. Deeply disappointed, and accusing his erstwhile allies of breaking their oaths, Montfort left for France, leaving an uneasy peace to settle on Henry's kingdom.[50]

And so 1261 drew to a close. For Henry and Eleanor it had been a year of great triumph. By guile and cunning, they had outmanoeuvred their opponents and overturned all the restrictions placed on royal authority. For Montfort, by contrast, the wheel had turned full circle. His refusal (on this occasion) to compromise may have bolstered his image in the country at large, and indeed his image of himself, but it had left him bereft of allies and facing a possibly permanent exile.[51]

If Montfort felt isolated by the end of 1261, so too did his former protégé. One of the most galling developments in the past twelve months for Edward had been the very small number of his supporters that had been prepared to join him in desertion. His closest friends – Henry of Almain, for example – had remained in opposition. The same was true of the Marcher lords, such as Roger Clifford, who had joined his household in 1257 and contributed much to its martial reputation. That winter, as Edward celebrated Christmas and the New Year in Bordeaux, he must have contrasted the festivities with those of the previous year, when he and his friends had stopped in the city midway through their tour of the tournament fields. In spite of the collapse of Montfort's party and the peace made between the opposition and the king, there had as yet been no rapprochement between Edward and his former supporters.[52]

Nor was any rapprochement likely to occur, thanks to the vigorous scrutiny to which his parents had been subjecting his affairs in his absence. In the autumn of 1261 Henry and Eleanor began an audit of Edward's finances, and attributed the disarray they uncovered to profligacy and peculation on the part of his erstwhile acquaintances. Roger Clifford was one of the men who stood accused. Another was Roger Leybourne, who until the summer had been the steward of Edward's estates. Leybourne, in particular, was marked out as the chief culprit and charged with repaying the very heavy sum of £1,820. There was more to this than simply righting Edward's finances after a period of heavy and (quite possibly) irresponsible expenditure. The queen, especially, had never approved of the violent and unruly element in her son's household; men who (as she saw it) had encouraged him not only in squandering his money but also in his general disobedience. Having succeeded in dividing Edward from their company in 1261, she was now determined to keep them apart by driving further wedges between them. One well-informed chronicler blamed Eleanor for inciting her son against Leybourne and, if this was the case, by the spring of 1262 she had succeeded. In April Edward himself revoked a grant of land that he had made to his former steward some eighteen months before, a sure sign that the esteem that the gift had originally symbolised was now lost.[53]

Edward by this time was back in England, having returned towards the end of February. His primary concern seems to have been his parents' ongoing re-arrangement of his lands and finances. Henry and Eleanor, although they did not try to impose the same strict controls on their son as before, nonetheless took steps that were clearly intended to limit his ability for independent action, at least in the immediate future. In June 1262, for example, they contrived to reduce the size of his landed estate. Edward was persuaded to surrender, for three years, sizeable parts of his endowment, in return for which he was compensated with a slice of royal revenue. Significantly, the major losses were all in England and Wales. His territories in Gascony and Ireland were unaffected, and the intention may well have been to try and confine Edward's political ambitions to these overseas dominions. England was only recently pacified; his continued presence there might serve as a rallying point for further trouble. As it was, he had little incentive to stay. Immediately after this new deal had been agreed, he returned to France.[54]

Estranged from his friends, deprived of his lands, and lacking any obvious political purpose, in the summer of 1262 Edward entered one of the most listless stages of his adult life. He did at least find some new companions with whom to share it. Since the winter of 1260 there had been a number of French knights in his household. Edward now increased their number, to the point where new recruits from Burgundy, Champagne and Flanders became the dominant element.[55] With this new entourage, he once again took to the tournament field. According to one hostile English chronicler, the new tour began badly, with Edward himself being beaten and gravely wounded soon after his arrival in France. Nothing points to a concern with any more serious pursuits – there is no evidence, for example, to suggest that on this occasion Edward paid a visit to Gascony to attend in person to the duchy's affairs. It would be unfair to describe his activities as frivolous, but he does appear directionless, cut adrift. Much of the summer and autumn he spent in Paris, to where his parents had travelled in pursuance of their feud with Simon de Montfort. Inevitably the arbitration proposed between the earl and his in-laws failed, collapsing in a blizzard of mutual recrimination. In December Henry and Eleanor returned to England, leaving Montfort angry and unreconciled in his political isolation. Their son, however, did not go with them. He too lingered on the Continent, saying he would come back at a later date. The reasons for Edward's self-imposed exile also remained in place: he saw no urgent need to hurry home.[56]

But then he had not heard the latest of Llywelyn ap Gruffudd. The prince, already impatient for a permanent peace with England, had concluded by the autumn of 1262 that he had been wasting his time. The English had not respected the truces they had granted him; the Marcher lords were attacking his lands. It is even possible that Llywelyn had learned of Henry III's opinion, expressed in a letter during the summer, that the recent Welsh conquests were illegitimate and must be reversed. Either way, the prince was now angry enough to throw off all restraint. At the end of November he and his army overran the whole of the middle March, raiding and burning into Herefordshire. The Welsh war against England had been resumed on the fullest scale.[57]

Henry III received this bad news as soon as he landed in England, a few days before Christmas. Already in an ill-humour – an epidemic in Paris had nearly killed him, and had carried off scores of his friends and servants – the king immediately dispatched a petulant letter to his eldest son, chiding him for his complacency in remaining abroad while his lands in Wales burned. This was hardly fair, but then Henry's barbs hardly mattered: all Edward saw was the opportunity he had been waiting for, a chance to win renown and respect in an arena where he had once been humiliated. On 24 February he landed at Dover, and by the start of April he had arrived in the March.[58]

But his return had unseen and far-reaching side effects. As in Wales, so too in England: everywhere there was deep dissatisfaction with Henry III's rule. The king, in restoring himself to power the previous year, had gone too far. Overthrowing his council was one thing; but Henry had also swept away all the good work of reform – the aspect of the Provisions that had proved so very popular from the first. By the summer of 1262 men had begun openly to denounce the royal regime, prompting a government crackdown in response. Henry himself was an obvious target for public reproach, but in his subjects' eyes the real villains were his foreign advisers. It was Queen Eleanor and her Savoyard circle who were correctly perceived as the principal architects of the king's return to unfettered power.[59]

In this general atmosphere of hostility, nobody harboured greater resentment against the government than Edward's former friends. Roger Clifford, Roger Leybourne and their companions were still incensed at the way they had been parted from their former leader and harassed on the orders of his mother. By the second half of 1262 they were already demonstrating signs of being dangerously disaffected, going about in arms and holding unlicensed tournaments. The country as a whole was combustible, but these desperadoes were the explosive charge.[60]

Edward's return lit the fuse. A new war with Wales had given his former friends cause to hope for reconciliation, confident in the expectation that he would need their military services, as of old. But Edward, when he returned, came accompanied by his new associates – the French knights with whom he had taken up during his months of exile. This proved too much for the likes of Clifford and Leybourne to stomach – yet more foreigners coming into the kingdom, reaping the rewards and the favours that should rightfully have been their own. Desperation drove them into direct action. A ready-made banner was to hand in the form of the Provisions of Oxford – a scheme concocted in part to rid the land of undesirable foreigners. All they lacked was a leader, but the obvious candidate was not far to seek. On 25 April, in response to their call, Simon de Montfort returned to England.[61]

In early May, therefore, as Edward was struggling to bring relief to his besieged castles in north Wales, Montfort was mustering armed opposition in the heart of Henry III's kingdom. With his instinctive grasp for good publicity, the earl rallied his new army of malcontents at Oxford, where the reform programme had been launched almost five years before, and where they now renewed their oaths to uphold the Provisions. A letter was immediately dispatched to the king demanding that he denounce as mortal enemies all those who refused to do the same. The equally swift refusal this elicited provided the necessary pretext. In the first week of June, under Montfort's direction, Clifford, Leybourne and their companions unleashed a series of devastating attacks on the lands of the queen and her supporters. In time-honoured medieval fashion, they burned crops and buildings, reducing to ashes their enemies' economic assets. Hostages were also taken: the opening attack saw the Savoyard bishop of Hereford dragged from his cathedral and carried off to imprisonment at one of Clifford's castles.[62]

This new and ferocious firestorm caught the royal family completely off guard. Edward, for his part, responded swiftly, abandoning the war in Wales and racing south-east. His first thought was to secure the loyalty of the Channel ports and thus keep open the way for further foreign aid. Obtaining reinforcements, however, would take time, and this, like other commodities, was fast running out. When Edward rejoined his parents in London a few days later, he found a desperate situation. Henry and Eleanor had fled to the Tower, but it was not a well-planned move of the kind they had made two years before. Then the Tower had been well stocked and well garrisoned; now it was empty of both food and soldiers. Money, too, was in short supply, and without it even the existing foreign mercenaries that Edward had with him could not be retained for much longer. Ordinarily, the royal family could have turned to the rich citizens of London for support. But, at this moment, according to one chronicler, 'there was no one in the city who would give them a halfpennyworth of credit'. London's ruling oligarchy, although instinctively royalist, correctly surmised that this attitude placed them out of step with the rest of their fellow citizens. In the streets of the capital, as across the country as a whole, anti-royal and anti-foreign feeling was running high, especially after Edward's arrival with his mercenary army of Frenchmen.[63]

It was London, rather than its unwelcome royal residents, that received an ultimatum from Montfort in the last week of June. Were they for or against the Provisions of Oxford? The city's rulers decided that they were indeed in favour, and sent a delegation to the Tower to persuade the king that he should do likewise, at the same time urging him to get rid of his son's foreign knights. Henry was inclined to agree. By this stage the raids on royalist property were no longer confined to the west of England. Now there was plundering and devastation of royalist property in East Anglia too. With no provisions and no money, submission to the demands of Montfort and his allies seemed to be the only way out of the spiralling crisis.[64]

Before the king could make his decision, however, his eldest son had determined on independent action. On 29 June Edward and his followers rode to the New Temple, which lay to the west of the city just outside its walls. The chief headquarters in England of the famous crusading order of the Templars, the Temple was also favoured by the wealthy as a place of deposit for their riches. This, indeed, gave Edward his argument for admission. Finding the doors locked on his arrival, he obtained the keys by claiming he had come to view his mother's jewels. It was a lie. Once inside, Edward's men used iron hammers to smash open the chests, and seized, by one estimate, almost a thousand pounds. They then sped with their loot to Windsor Castle, which they proceeded to stock by similar methods, raiding the surrounding countryside for supplies. By resorting to deceit and robbery, Edward had obtained what his father in London lacked: the wherewithal – so he hoped – to resist Montfort.[65]

But Montfort was too good a general to have his fire drawn by this distraction. Moving south, the earl and his cohorts skirted Windsor and made instead for Kent, where they took all the ports except Dover – the mighty castle and its royalist garrison held out. In London, meanwhile, the situation had descended into total chaos. The raid on the Temple, an outrageous act of royal presumption, had triggered the feared revolution. Within hours of Edward's departure the lesser citizens had taken to the streets and begun attacking and looting the properties of prominent royalists and foreigners. On 4 July, still trapped in the Tower, Henry III agreed to submit to the demands of his enemies. These had now expanded in line with Montfort's estimation of his own success and the virulence of the xenophobia he had unleashed. Having begun their protest by demanding that the realm should be governed only by 'native-born men', the opposition now insisted on nothing less than the total expulsion of all foreigners, 'never to return'.[66]

The king might meekly accept this new provision; his Provençal queen could never do so. In any case, she was made of sterner stuff than her husband. Even as Montfort's forces advanced on the capital, Eleanor of Provence decided she would rather take a stand with her eldest son. On 13 July she and a small number of attendants set out from the Tower by boat, intent on following the Thames upstream to Windsor. But word of her departure travelled more quickly than the queen herself. By the time she reached London Bridge, a hostile crowd was waiting, and, as her the barge tried to pass beneath, they let fly with insults, eggs and stones. Realising that her life was in danger, the queen abandoned her voyage and took refuge in the palace of the bishop of London.[67]

The royal family was beaten. Two days later Montfort and his forces entered London, and Henry and Eleanor submitted. Within a week, acting on Henry's orders, the garrison at Dover Castle had also surrendered. Only Edward, with his army of French knights at Windsor, continued to resist, though with an increasing awareness that resistance might prove useless. Their desperate attempt to take Bristol a few days before London's fall had failed in the face of opposition from the town's angry citizens. News of the loss of Dover, which ended all hope of aid from abroad, must have coincided with news of Montfort's advance: the earl and his army, now marching under royal banners, left London on 24 July, intending to besiege Windsor. There was no choice but to agree to terms. The demand for the expulsion of all foreigners had been devised chiefly with this moment in mind. As Edward himself rejoined his parents, his army of French knights were escorted to the coast, having sworn 'never to return'.[68]

Montfort was now effectively in charge of the kingdom. In a few short months, through a skilful combination of violence and xenophobic rabble-rousing, he had achieved the mastery over Henry III that had eluded him for the past two years. Flushed with success, he began reordering government along lines of his own choosing, promoting his friends to high office and granting them custody of key royal castles. Faced with this monopoly of force, the best that the king and his family could manage was a secret appeal for help to the king of France. This, too, however, proved futile. King Louis obligingly summoned Henry and his family to Boulogne, along with Montfort and his supporters, only to surprise everyone by ruling that the July settlement should stand. The royalist attempt to discredit Montfort had actually succeeded in granting his government a measure of international legitimacy.[69]

Back home, however, support for the earl's regime was already evaporating. The blitzkrieg of the summer may have been devastatingly effective in military terms, but it had left a bitter legacy of recrimination in its wake. Those whose lands and property had been despoiled wanted compensation, but the new government was insufficiently organised to provide redress. A specially convened parliament at the start of September had found no way forward. At the start of October the archbishop of Canterbury – a Savoyard himself, and hence a victim of the attacks – ordered the excommunication of those who had taken part in the raids, including Montfort, whom he named as the chief culprit. In simple terms, Montfort was unable to sort out the mess his coup had caused.[70]

More dangerous still to the earl was the internal collapse of his own party. The men who had invited him back to England – Roger Clifford, Roger Leybourne and their ilk – did not care in the slightest for the Provisions of Oxford, nor, for that matter, for any of their leader's private grievances. Their sole ambition had been to revenge themselves on the queen and to restore their relationship with her eldest son. With the exile of the foreign knights from Windsor, the way for reconciliation became clear. Once again, Montfort had failed to foresee the logical conclusion of his actions. Within weeks of his surrender Edward had settled his difference with Clifford, Leybourne and the rest. In an agreement on 18 August, they swore 'to be his friends in all his affairs'.[71]

This was apparently kept secret from Montfort. By this stage, reconciliation between Edward and his uncle was no longer an option. It was over two years since the spring of 1261, when their close alliance had been ended by Edward's defection. Perhaps the earl regarded his godson as an ungrateful turncoat from that moment onwards. If so, there is no evidence of reciprocal hostility: Edward had continued to act as if conflicted, and had showed no sign of sympathy for his parents in their struggle against his uncle. It was only in 1263 that we can be certain that his neutrality came to an end. That summer Montfort had revealed a whole new dimension to his malevolence and opportunism. In pursuit of his private feud with Henry III, the earl had seen fit to exploit Edward's difficulties in Wales as well as his rift with his friends. As a consequence, the English position in north Wales was now entirely lost – late in the summer, Llywelyn had finally achieved his long-sought supremacy in the Four Cantrefs by destroying the castles at Dyserth and Deganwy. Montfort had also, by his willingness to provoke more widespread hostility to royal authority, endangered the life of the queen: the episode at London Bridge had a profound impact on Edward, and he would never forgive those responsible. Aside from its obvious psychological effect, an attack on an anointed queen was something that Edward, as a future king, could not allow to pass. Montfort had not only usurped the power of the Crown; he had also besmirched its dignity. For this reason, above all, he had to be stopped.[72]

In mid-October, as a new parliament assembled in Westminster, Edward put his plan into action. He moved with sly circumspection: Montfort, attended by large numbers of armed Londoners, still had the monopoly of force. Claiming, therefore, that he wanted to see his wife, Edward made his way to Windsor. Very soon he was joined by the friends he had won back in the summer, and by Henry III, who left Westminster the next morning. Then the floodgates burst. Almost all the magnates who had come to parliament came over to the king's side. Few of them can have been taken in by Henry's declaration that he intended to uphold the Provisions of Oxford, and some of them, it was said, had been bribed by Edward with promises of land. Most of those who now rallied to Windsor, however, were attracted by neither idealism nor greed but by a desire to end the chaos Montfort had created. The need now was for stable and properly constituted government which only a king could provide.[73]

From a military point of view this new royalist party looked unstoppable. In November Henry and Edward took Oxford and Winchester, and by December they were threatening Dover and London itself. Montfort had been outmanoeuvred and also left massively outnumbered. Apart from his own sons and a handful of long-standing friends, the men who continued to stand by him were for the most part ideologues: radical churchmen and hot-headed young knights who believed in the Provisions as a just and holy cause. Staring defeat in the face, Montfort now in his turn pushed for a new arbitration by the king of France. His wish was granted, and early in the new year Henry, Edward and the numerous royalist party crossed the Channel to argue their case against the much smaller band of Montfortians. Alas for the latter group, Louis IX had changed his mind. Since his earlier intervention, the French king had been lobbied by the royalists who had remained resident at his court during the autumn – Eleanor of Provence, after her close encounter with the London mob, must have been particularly persuasive. Accordingly, judgement went in favour of Henry III: kings should rule unfettered, Louis declared, and as such the Provisions should be quashed entirely. The decision – the so-called 'Mise of Amiens' – was not quite a total disaster for Montfort: to some extent it helped the earl by confirming him as the only hope for those who truly believed in reform. After its publication more men joined his side, a few even returning from the royalist camp. In general terms, however, the verdict *was* disastrous. Its uncompromising severity left Montfort and his acolytes with no option but to go to war.[74]

The fighting began at once in a predetermined theatre. Immediately before his departure for France, Henry III had set out to distract Montfort by striking hard at his personal interests. The king's well-chosen instrument for this task was Roger Mortimer, one of the most significant of the new royalists recruited the previous autumn. Mortimer was a Marcher lord – indeed, *the* Marcher lord par excellence, a man with a fearsome reputation in arms. As such he might have been expected to have joined Edward's circle at an earlier date, but personal grievances, first with Henry, later with Edward himself, had served to keep him in the opposition camp. All that had been quickly forgotten in

December, however, when Henry had given Mortimer permission to seize three valuable royal manors in Herefordshire. It was a doubly astute move, for the manors in question had previously been granted to Montfort. At a stroke, the king had cemented the support of one redoubtable warrior and simultaneously set him against another. The clash was as swift as it was inevitable. Within days of the decision at Amiens, Montfort struck back, sending his sons to attack Mortimer's other estates and castles. Other royalists and Montfortians quickly piled into the fray. Before Henry III had returned from Amiens, the March was already in flames, with near disastrous consequences. Edward, having rushed home ahead of his father, came close to being captured at Gloucester. Trapped in the castle, he escaped only because of the naive chivalry of his assailants, who granted him a truce and withdrew.[75]

From that moment on, however, the royalists contrived to win almost every trick. Henry summoned an army to Oxford in March and, with Edward once again by his side, wrested back Montfort's early gains in the Midlands. On 5 April they won a considerable victory at Northampton, capturing around eighty of the earl's knightly supporters, including his son, Simon. In response Montfort tried to make new gains in Kent, laying siege to Rochester Castle, but without success. Henry and Edward appeared in the south sooner than he expected, and sent him scurrying back to London.[76]

Siege and counter-siege, raid and counter-raid: such was the normal method of medieval warfare. Skilled commanders moved their troops like pieces on a chessboard, taking individual castles and knights as part of a developing strategy. Attrition and retaliation were the name of the game; direct confrontation was to be avoided at all costs. No matter how daring a general might be, he would almost never commit to battle because of the enormous risk involved. In the noise and confusion of a battle everything could be lost in a few short hours. As a consequence, they were rare events: in the spring of 1264, there had been no battle in England for almost half a century. Montfort, a renowned warrior well into his mid-fifties, had never fought in one.

And yet it was battle that Montfort now sought. In recent weeks his range of options had diminished rapidly. After his retreat to London they had never seemed so limited or so bleak. Dover Castle, his only other significant asset, was now threatened by the arrival in the south of the royal army; once it fell, Montfort would be trapped. In strategic terms it was almost checkmate, but the earl was not a man readily to concede defeat. On 6 May, like a cornered animal, he came out fighting, marching his forces out of London in search of his enemies.[77]

Henry and Edward were in Sussex when they received news of

Montfort's warlike approach, and quickly moved to nearby Lewes, where both the town walls and the castle offered a strong defensive advantage. When their enemy drew up his forces a few miles to the north, however, it seemed they had been unduly cautious. Montfort's army, as contemporary chroniclers attest, was tiny; modern estimates suggest that his cavalry may have been outnumbered by their royalist counterparts by as many as three to one. Unsurprisingly, therefore, there was little mood for negotiation in the king's camp. Henry III himself was apparently ready to talk, but his son was bullishly dismissive: the Montfortians could have peace, Edward assured them, if they presented themselves with halters round their necks, ready for hanging. Exchanges between the two camps concluded on 13 May with the exchange of formal letters of defiance. 'From this time forth,' wrote Edward and the royalists, 'we will do our utmost to inflict injury upon your persons and possessions.'[78]

Montfort was eager to fight at once, hoping to hasten his enemies into handing him an advantage. Lewes nestles in a gap in the South Downs, and the road to the north runs through a narrow defile. If the royalists could be lured in this direction, Montfort's inferior numbers would matter less. Henry and Edward, however, refused to be rushed. The surrounding hills, as much as the town and the castle, were their protection. They would engage the earl on their own terms in the morning, assuming he was still there. In the meantime they went to bed.

They woke at dawn to discover Montfort and his army staring down at them. During the night, the earl had used the woods to the west of Lewes and the enveloping darkness to march his men, undetected, to the top of the Downs. He now had command of the high ground, and his troops were already ranged ready for battle. Formed into three divisions, their frontline stretched over half a mile.[79]

After a swift council of war the royalists drew up their army in a similar formation, with three divisions arrayed according to the immediate position of their commanders. Henry III, lodged in the priory to the south of Lewes, led the division on the left; Edward, quartered in the castle to the north of the town, the one on the right. A third division, led by Henry's brother, Richard of Cornwall, formed in the middle. This deployment, arrived at seemingly by chance, would determine the outcome of the battle.[80]

The cavalry, at the front of each contingent, were first to engage, thundering towards each other and meeting in a clash of wood and steel. It is hard to imagine either Henry or his brother leading such an assault, but Edward knew his moment had come. 'He was not slow to attack in the strongest places, fearing the onslaught of none,' wrote one eyewitness (and a Montfortian one at that) immediately after the event. All those long hours in the saddle since boyhood and the more recent practice on the tournament field now stood Edward in good stead. He and his friends defeated the horsemen on Montfort's left flank with their first charge, capturing them or putting them to flight. That left only the infantry to the rear, and they too had begun to flee from the oncoming swords and lances.[81]

Edward, however, was not about to let these foot soldiers escape unscathed. By chance, the contingent facing his own had been chiefly comprised of Londoners – the same rabble that had attacked and abused his mother the previous year. Edward was now in a position to exact bloody revenge. Exhilarated by his initial success, he and his knights rode after the fugitives, pursuing them to the north for several miles, slaughtering as they went.

It was a fatal error. By the time they regrouped and returned to Lewes – probably around mid-morning – all was lost. Edward's departure had given Montfort the essential opening he needed, with disastrous consequences for the royalists. Richard of Cornwall had been captured having taken refuge in a windmill (a cause of much amusement for his captors). Henry III, badly beaten, had escaped back in the direction of the town, but he too was trapped: Montfort's forces were closing in on Lewes from all directions. And now it was Edward's turn to suffer defeat. At his approach, a force of Montfortians rode out and attacked him, putting many of his followers to flight. Edward himself evaded capture and began searching for his father. He found the king, together with the remnant of his army, holed up in the priory.[82]

The Battle of Lewes was clearly over, and Simon de Montfort was indisputably the victor. Against all odds, his small force of inexperienced young knights – many of them ennobled only on the eve of the conflict – had triumphed over the superior might of the royal army. It was, as contemporaries were quick to conclude, nothing short of miraculous: proof that the earl's cause was just, and a sure sign that he and his followers were favoured by God.[83]

And yet outright victory remained elusive. Until Montfort had custody of the king and his son, he could not translate triumph on the battlefield into the political settlement that was his ultimate goal. Nor would getting hold of the pair be easy. To begin with, the royalists were far from being an entirely spent force. Henry had retreated into Lewes Priory with some of his contingent, and Edward still had his redoubtable Marcher friends by his side. It was enough, according to one chronicler, for Edward at least to consider making a sortie. Montfort almost certainly had the strength to take the priory by storm, but that posed an altogether more awkward problem. The Battle of Lewes would make a song worthy of remembrance; the Siege of Lewes Priory would not. Attacking a house of God would compromise the earl's credibility as a holy warrior and undermine the righteousness of his cause. For similar reasons, there was no real question of executing royalist prisoners like Richard of Cornwall, although Montfort did apparently make the threat. Aristocrats could kill their non-noble inferiors with impunity, as the case of the unfortunate Londoners had shown, but they did not kill or mutilate each other, even in battle. Capture, imprisonment, ransom and release – these were the long-established conventions of thirteenth-century warfare. It was almost two hundred years since the last English earl had been executed, and not even Montfort, ruthless as he was, would dare to break such a taboo.[84]

Both sides, therefore, recognised that a negotiated surrender by the royalists was the only way forward: terms were agreed that evening. Montfort's superior position is evident from the fact that, on most points, he got his way. The restoration of the Provisions of Oxford had been the earl's cry to arms, so it was no surprise that the reforms were now resurrected in their entirety. Henry III was once again obliged to accept the tutelage of a council that would rule on his behalf. Montfort's only concession on this matter was a promise to review the arrangement at a later date, but such promises he could easily contrive to ignore. On another front, however, the earl was forced to make a major concession that betrays the limits of his bargaining power. In return for the surrender of the king and his son, Montfort agreed to let the Marchers go free. This was a serious gamble, for these were dangerous men, whose number included not only Edward's bellicose friends Roger Clifford and Roger Leybourne, but also Roger Mortimer, the man who had recently become Montfort's hated rival. Accordingly, the earl imposed all manner of conditions and oaths on them, and sought further to guarantee their good behaviour by retaining two high-ranking hostages. Henry of Almain, the eldest son of Richard of Cornwall, was one. Edward was the other.[85]

From this moment on, therefore, the king and his son were once again in Montfort's power. For all the constitutional and conciliar structures that Montfort erected, this was now effectively his kingdom. Henry, of course, remained king in name and it was necessary to maintain the fiction that he was still in charge of government. He was kept comfortably in London, theoretically at liberty but under the watchful eyes of a new set of household officers. Edward, on the other hand, was officially a prisoner and could therefore be kept in much stricter custody. There would be no opportunities, of the kind he had exploited in the past, for sneaking off to renew the struggle. After a brief spell of incarceration at Dover, he and Henry of Almain were transferred to Richard of Cornwall's castle at Wallingford in Berkshire. Soon they were joined by Earl Richard himself, who was also being detained at Montfort's pleasure.[86]

Hope of deliverance lay in two directions. In the west the Marchers remained at large and unpacified, refusing from the first to co-operate with Montfort's new regime. Across the Channel, meanwhile, royalist exiles were being rallied by Eleanor of Provence. Drawing on all the political and financial credit she could muster, the queen had begun to build an army and a fleet with the intention of winning back her husband's kingdom. The seriousness of this threat is attested by the scale of the English response. Playing on the xenophobia he had become so adept at exploiting, Montfort assembled a massive peasant army in Kent, ready to resist the planned invasion. In the event, however, the earl's great experimental horde was never put to the test. As summer turned to autumn, Eleanor's expedition started to stall, and by November her mercenary forces had disbanded. That left Montfort a free hand to deal with the Marchers, who were brought to new terms in December, and promised to go into exile in Ireland. As their options narrowed, the royalists became increasingly desperate. November witnessed a daring attempt by some of the knights of Edward's household to spring their lord and his co-detainees from their captivity at Wallingford, but this, too, was unsuccessful. The would-be rescuers were forced to depart empty-handed when the defenders threatened to liberate Edward themselves with the aid of a trebuchet.[87]

The new regime, however, was vulnerable from within as much as from without. Montfort may have been a natural autocrat, surrounded by councillors of his own creation, but there was still one individual in the winter of 1264 whose wishes and opinions he was obliged to respect. Gilbert de Clare (or Gilbert the Red, as he was sometimes known, on account of his ginger hair) was by far the most important of the angry young men who had fought alongside the earl at Lewes. His particular grievance against Henry III was the king's maladroit handling of his inheritance, and his inheritance – the earldom of Gloucester – was the key to his importance. The eldest son of the late, not especially lamented Richard de Clare, Gilbert had succeeded – eventually – to his father's massive estates and wealth, and this meant that his political affiliation mattered. After their victory in battle, Montfort had unhesitatingly accorded Gilbert a role in government that, in theory at least, was equal to his own. In terms of real power, however, the new earl of Gloucester was soon left feeling short changed, resenting the way his older ally monopolised the spoils or lavished them on his own overbearing sons. In terms of policy, too, a gulf began to appear between the two men. Gloucester began, in particular, to develop serious qualms about the continued detention of the heir to the throne. This was part conscience, part self-interest, for a day would surely come when Edward would wear his father's crown, and would call to account those responsible for his incarceration.[88]

Gloucester must have been relieved, therefore, when, at the start of 1265, Montfort yielded to pressure and agreed to release his principal prisoner. On 11 March, in a grand ceremony in Westminster Hall, Edward was handed over to his father. By that date, however, it had become apparent that Montfort was prepared to countenance this measure only because he had developed an alternative vision of England's future. In return for his liberty, Edward was obliged to hand over to the earl and his sons almost all of his lands. It was an ominous move, for these had long been declared an inalienable part of the royal estate. An additional provision that Edward would be disinherited should he ever attempt to bring foreign troops into the realm further underlined the alarming direction in which Montfort's thoughts were moving. If not for himself, then for his sons, the earl was considering a bid for the crown.[89]

The ceremony in Westminster Hall was an empty show – Edward was allowed no more liberty after his release from captivity than his closely supervised father – but it was probably responsible for pushing Gloucester into decisive action. Around this moment he quit the court and went west to his own estates in Wales. Montfort was alive to the danger – this was the same region where the Marchers, having reneged on their promise to go to Ireland, were continuing to cause trouble. Within a few weeks the old earl took his private army of followers, along with Henry III and Edward, and went west in pursuit of his erstwhile ally. His hope was a peaceful reconciliation, and for a brief moment in early May talks with Gloucester seemed to promise such a prospect. But then came the news that a force of royalist exiles, led by William de Valence, had landed in Pembrokeshire – a region under Gloucester's control. Immediately, the scales fell from Montfort's eyes. His enemies were clearly in collusion, and a new plot to restore Henry III was already under way.[90]

Montfort perceived all of this quickly, and moved to Hereford, where he began to make preparations for the expected military action. What he failed to see developing, however, was the most important element of the royalist plan. Perhaps fearing his chances in a fight, the earl seems to have continued to hope for a compromise with Gloucester, and to have further imagined that this might be brokered with the help of his godson. In the last week of May Edward was permitted to receive a string of visitors, including his friends Clifford and Leybourne, as well as Gloucester's younger brother, Thomas. The extent to which Montfort's optimism was in this respect misplaced was revealed on 28 May, when Edward and Thomas were permitted to ride out from Hereford in order to exercise their horses. They proceeded to ride each animal, including those of their guards, until all were exhausted. All that is, except one, which Edward promptly mounted and galloped away from his captors. 'Lordings, I bid you good day!' he reportedly shouted. 'Greet my father well, and tell him I hope to see him soon, to release him from custody!' It was clearly a precisely planned escape. In woods outside the city Edward found Roger Mortimer lying in wait, and together they sped north to Ludlow, where they met Gloucester. There a new alliance was struck. The earl would help recover the kingdom if Edward would swear to uphold its established laws, banish aliens and rule only through natives. Edward readily assented. The manifesto, while crude, preserved the popular demands of the reformers without placing any serious constraints on the power of a future king.[91]

Montfort was left reeling by his catastrophic error, and watched helplessly as his various royalist enemies – the recently returned exiles, the recalcitrant Marchers – now rushed to join Edward, Mortimer and Gloucester. Against such a formidable coalition, the earl and his small force in Hereford could do nothing. To survive, they needed to move back east, where Montfort could muster more support. Their opponents, however, acted swiftly to prevent such a plan. In June Edward and his allies mounted a lightning campaign to seize control of the River Severn: every bridge was broken and every boat beached on the eastern shore. By the end of the month they had their quarry trapped behind an impassable north–south line, and in July they moved in for the kill. Montfort had no option but to retreat. In the weeks that followed he was reduced to moving his tiny army, and the reluctant Henry III, around south Wales, pursued all the while by Edward and his companions.[92]

The endgame took place in the opening days of August. The start of the month found Montfort back at Hereford, still trapped, but now hopeful of deliverance. The cavalry was coming. The earl's namesake son, Simon, had received his father's call for help and was advancing westwards with reinforcements. Already their approach had forced Edward to move back to Worcester, and the line of the Severn, in anticipation of this new threat.[93]

Alas, Montfort had not counted on the inexperience of his offspring and the daring of his enemies. On 1 August news reached Edward that young Simon had arrived at Kenilworth, his father's great fortress in the Midlands, but had failed to ensconce himself safely within its walls:

confident that conflict was still a day's ride away, the intended relief force
had camped in the town and were availing themselves of its comfortable beds and baths. This was too good an opportunity for the royalists
to waste. Setting off at once with only a cavalry force, Edward and his
allies rode through the night from Worcester to Kenilworth – a distance
of some thirty-five miles – and fell upon the sleeping Montfortian army
at dawn. The rout was not quite total: young Simon saved his own skin
by rowing, naked, across the castle's moat, and others must have had
similar lucky escapes. Nevertheless, the raid was a striking success: a
great many Montfortian knights were caught napping, and Edward
returned to Worcester on 2 August with numerous high-ranking captives.[94]

But by this time Montfort had crossed the Severn. Having seized
the opportunity presented by his enemies' temporary absence, the earl
was now camped on the river's eastern shore. He was, in fact, only a
few miles south of Worcester, but Edward, after his exhausting dash
through the night, was unable to contemplate pushing himself or his
forces any further. Both armies therefore spent an uneasy twenty-four
hours resting in close proximity. During this time, Montfort heard the
news from Kenilworth, and not all of it was bad. In spite of its losses,
his son's army was still intact. The hope of uniting their two forces
therefore remained undimmed, and with this end in mind the earl
began to move his army on the evening of 3 August. Marching under
cover of darkness, he aimed to give his enemies the slip for a final time.
At dawn the next day, which broke around 5 a.m., his forces arrived
in Evesham, and there they paused for breakfast.[95]

Three hours later, their spirits suddenly soared: on the horizon
were spotted the advancing banners of young Simon's army. Their
stealthy night-time manoeuvres, it seemed, had been a success. With
these reinforcements, they would stand a fighting chance. But then,
with equal suddenness, all hope evaporated. From the top of the tower
of Evesham Abbey, the lookout called down to Montfort in despair.
'We are all dead men, for it is not your son, as you believed.'[96]

It was Edward. The royalist army had not been given the slip at all.
On the contrary, they had silently shadowed their opponents throughout
the night, all the while remaining undetected. Playing the advantage
of surprise for all it was worth, they had advanced the last few miles
under the banners captured at Kenilworth two days before. Now, at
last, the lengthy game of cat-and-mouse of the past two months was
over: Montfort was trapped. Evesham lies in a loop of the River Avon,
closed in from every direction except the north, and it was here, at the
top of the hill, that Edward and Gloucester lined up their army.[97]

The old sorcerer had been out-generalled by both his former

apprentices, and he knew it. 'How skilfully they are advancing,' he exclaimed, before adding, with characteristic arrogance, 'They learned that from me!' His only possible escape route was the bridge at the southern end of the town, but there was not nearly enough time to get a whole army across it. The earl and his cavalry might flee and leave the others to their fate, but the loss of prestige would spell the end of his career. In any case, flight was hardly Montfort's style. Instead, he rallied his forces for a final time and marched north out of Evesham, up the hill, to face his foes. The sky darkened and a thunderstorm broke.[98]

Montfort's chances at Evesham were terrible. The element of surprise and the command of the high ground, both so useful to him at Lewes, had this time been seized by his enemies. Once again, his forces were outnumbered three to one. When the two sides engaged, the wide royalist frontline quickly absorbed and enveloped the smaller Montfortian force. Defeat was inevitable.[99]

So too was death. Well before the first blow had been struck, Edward had let it be known that, on this occasion, the normal rules of chivalric warfare were to be suspended. No quarter was to be given, no surrender accepted. Consequently, as the royalists closed in, the killing began. Montfort's young knights were dragged from their horses, stripped of their armour and stabbed. At least thirty of them perished in this way, an orgy of blood-letting not seen for centuries. Montfort himself, meanwhile, had received the special honour of a dedicated death-squad – a dozen men, 'the strongest and most intrepid in arms', chosen by Edward and Gloucester on the eve of battle, whose sole task was to find the earl and kill him. Yet in the end it was Roger Mortimer, the pugnacious Marcher lord with the personal grudge, who struck the killer blow, running Montfort through the neck with his lance. Others then fell on the earl's lifeless body, hacking off his hands, feet and head. In a final piece of grotesque savagery, his genitals were cut off and placed in his mouth, and the severed head was dispatched to Mortimer's wife as a grisly token of her husband's triumph.[100]

Amid such brutal carnage, there were few survivors. One man dressed in Montfortian armour had a miraculous escape, but not before he had been wounded in the shoulder. 'I am Henry of Winchester, your king!' he cried. 'Do not kill me!' Roger Leybourne immediately intervened and saved the stricken monarch, but it was Edward himself who led his father away from the battlefield.[101]

Meanwhile, all around them, the killing continued to rage. Those fleeing across the fields were cut down as they ran. In the town, too, the streets were thick with the slaughtered. Even those who sought sanctuary in the abbey church were not spared. 'The choir, the walls, the cross, the statues and the altars were sprayed with the blood of the wounded and the dead,' wrote one horrified eyewitness. 'From the bodies around the high altar, a stream of blood ran right down into the crypts.'

'The murder of Evesham,' wrote another, 'for battle it was none.'[102]

3

Civil Peace and Holy War

The quantity and the quality of blood spilt at Evesham rendered it a decisive victory; the dead can neither negotiate nor stage a comeback. Montfort's ghost would haunt his killers for some time to come, but his gory end meant that he could trouble them only in the improbable guise of a popular saint. Likewise, the simultaneous dispatch of so many of the earl's diehard supporters seemed to herald a new political dawn. Edward's triumph in battle ensured that his father, though physically traumatised, was restored to full and unfettered power. The schemes to limit the king's authority, begun in 1258 and repeatedly challenged, modified and reinstated thereafter, had also perished. Whatever future the idea of reform might have, it would not be imposed on the Crown by force. God had granted victory to the royalists. Henceforth the monopoly of might lay with Henry and his son.[1]

It should have been a relatively straightforward matter to transform this military supremacy into a lasting peace. In the end, Montfort had been a man more feared than loved. Even before Evesham his regime had been close to the point of collapse, hamstrung by a lack of genuinely loyal support. When news of the earl's death broke, men who had been biding their time during his rule came swiftly back to the king's side. At Windsor Castle the garrison surrendered at once, as did the troops holding the Tower of London. Only at Kenilworth Castle, to which Simon de Montfort junior had retreated, was stronger resistance expected, and even here there was hope for the royalists in the depth of their enemies' despair. Young Simon had arrived at Evesham too late, but still in time to witness his father's head being paraded on the point of a spear – a sight, it was said, that left him unable to eat or drink for days.[2]

The mercy that Montfort had been denied in his final encounter would be the essential ingredient in making a firm peace. If at that instant

70

chivalry had been suspended for the sake of political convenience, it was now imperative that it be revived for the same reason. Edward seems to have been well aware of this. For him, the killing at Evesham, as well as being a means to an end, had also been a cathartic moment. He may not have mourned the passing of his uncle, but he is said to have wept openly for the loss of so many others, including his sometime friend Henry de Montfort, who had died fighting alongside his father. Accordingly, in the aftermath of battle, Edward was minded to be merciful. When several leading Montfortians, including the earl's former steward, approached him just three days later, he promised them his protection, and assured them that neither they nor their goods would be harmed. They duly agreed to submit, and thus the surrender of two more garrisons – those at Berkhamsted and Wallingford – was secured.[3]

For such men, the fact that Edward's concessionary attitude extended not only to their persons but also to their property was crucially important. Disinheritance, more so even than death, was the rebel's greatest fear, for it entailed lasting shame and the end of his family's fortune. Consequently it was also the offended overlord's greatest threat, and one that in 1265 Henry III was in a strong position to invoke. In the immediate wake of Evesham the king had authorised the seizure of all lands held by his enemies. Royalists had rushed from the battlefield to occupy the manors of those who were known, or even merely believed, to be Montfortians. The reappropriation was startlingly swift. In a matter of weeks more than a thousand properties were confiscated.[4]

Edward, who had hurried to Chester in order to superintend the recovery of his own estates, appears to have assumed that this nationwide land-grab was a prelude to a bargaining process. During this time, for example, he had letters sent to the garrison at Kenilworth, promising them death and disinheritance unless they agreed to an immediate surrender. The threat was dire, but the corollary was also clear. Those who did submit, by implication, would be spared such terrible penalties.[5]

But by the time Edward had returned south, his father had decided on a different course of action. In the middle of September, during a specially convened parliament at Winchester, Henry proclaimed his peace. Then, the following day, he dropped a political bombshell. The lands lately seized by his faithful subjects, he announced, would not in any circumstances be returned to their former owners; all those who had stood with Montfort to whatever degree were to remain disinherited forever.

As the wiser men in attendance were quick to observe, this was a poisonous prescription. Richard of Cornwall was a man with more reason than most to harbour thoughts of vengeance towards the

Montfortians, having only just been released from captivity at Kenilworth, where he had been kept in chains. Yet he was still shrewd enough to appreciate that his brother's policy could lead only to further conflict, for if former rebels had no hope of recovering their lands, they had no reason to lay down their arms. Along with a few other magnates, the earl washed his hands of the whole sorry business and withdrew from court in protest.[6]

His nephew, however, did not accompany him. Despite his instinctive understanding of the need for settlement, Edward went along with the royalist majority that was bent on revenge. It may be that he felt unable to resist the demands of his own powerful supporters. Roger Mortimer, in the words of one writer, was 'greedy for spoils'. Whatever the case, Edward took his place among the seventy or so individuals close to the king who were rewarded with a share of the loot. The trouble was that more than four times that number had been deprived of their stake in society.[7]

The next target for the royalists' vengeance was London. Henry felt particularly venomous towards the capital and its citizens, whom he regarded as Montfort's willing collaborators. During the earl's rule, the mayor of London, called upon to swear fealty to his sovereign, had actually dared to couch his oath in conditional terms. 'We will be faithful and duteous to you,' the wretched man had said, 'so long as you will be a good lord and king.' Henry now set out to deliver London a lesson of his own by way of return. From Winchester he moved to Windsor, to where he summoned an army, and let it be known that he intended to besiege the city.[8]

This news sent London into a panic. A small band of committed Montfortians wanted to man the walls and resist, but the majority agreed that the only sensible course was to throw themselves on the king's mercy. To this end, the mayor and some forty of the more eminent citizens set out for Windsor in early October in the hope of allaying the royal wrath. They were only partially successful. The planned siege was called off, but the delegates themselves, in spite of the safe-conducts they had received, were cast into prison. Henry then proceeded to enter London unopposed, and celebrated the feast of the Confessor on 13 October in Westminster Abbey, ceremoniously wearing his crown to emphasise his majesty. Meanwhile, in the city itself the indiscriminate redistribution of property continued, and again Edward willingly accepted his share of the spoils. Several of his friends were rewarded with confiscated houses, and he himself was given custody of the mayor and certain other prominent prisoners.[9]

The hostility that the king and his son harboured towards London, of course, arose to a large extent as a result of the attack on the queen in the summer of 1263. Eleanor of Provence had crossed to France soon after that notorious incident and had remained there ever since, masterminding her husband's return to power. Now, at last, she was expected home, and the court moved into Kent in anticipation of her arrival. On 29 October Edward met his mother off the boat at Dover, and two days later she was reunited with Henry at Canterbury. It had been almost two years since the royal couple had seen each other, and the disagreements that had arisen between them during the struggle with Montfort had long since been forgotten; if anything their affection for each other had deepened. In a letter to Louis IX written some time later, Henry spoke fondly of Eleanor, saying he was 'cheered by the sight of her, and by talking to her'.[10]

Such amiable companionship had also been denied to Edward, but shortly before his mother's return he was reunited with his own wife. Eleanor of Castile appears to have been kept with the king during her husband's year of confinement, and subjected to the same close supervision. Montfort's rule must have been a deeply distressing time for the young couple, with each of them left for long periods uncertain of the other's fate. Nor was their misery during these months to be measured solely by the stress of captivity and conflict; family life had also been disastrous. Their daughter Katherine, born at some point after 1261, and at that date their only child, had died in September 1264. Another daughter, born in January 1265 and christened Joan, was dead within eight months (and thus perhaps never seen alive by her father). The benefits of peace, therefore, were anticipated in personal as well as political terms. By the time of the queen's return in October, her daughter-in-law was once again pregnant.[11]

Also returning to England at this moment, probably with his mother, was Edward's younger brother, Edmund. Although his youth had precluded him from playing any major role in the tumultuous years leading up to Evesham, Edmund was nevertheless to become the greatest beneficiary of the controversial peace. While the court was still at Canterbury, he received from his father all the lands once held by Simon de Montfort, and in due course he received the late earl's title too. The counterpart to his elevation, and adding to the general joy among the royal family at their reunion, was the departure of Henry's sister, Eleanor de Montfort. The widowed countess, who had been holed up at Dover since her husband's death, had surrendered to Edward just days before the queen's return, and crossed the Channel into permanent exile.[12]

Amid the comings and goings of familiar faces, there was one individual who stood out as an obvious newcomer. Ottobuono de Fieschi was an Italian by birth, a lawyer by training and, since 1252, a cardinal. Now, in the autumn of 1265, he had arrived in England in his new capacity as a legate *a latere* – that is, he had been sent from the pope's side with extensive powers to act in the pope's name. At the time of his appointment Montfort had still been in power, and Ottobuono had therefore been authorised, if necessary, to invade England with the assistance of the king of France. Evesham, however, had removed this unhappy prospect, and the legate was able to land peaceably at Dover in the company of the queen. He would, of course, still have much work to do, punishing and pardoning on the pope's behalf, and helping to rebuild the authority of both the Crown and the Church. But the earl's death and the collapse of his regime must have given Ottobuono reason to imagine that his task would be an easier one than he and his master in Rome had originally envisaged.[13]

If so, he was soon disappointed. The vengeful policy of disinheritance proclaimed at Winchester was already working its pernicious effect. Montfortians who had been deprived of their lands by the king's decision were taking to the woods and the fens, and preparing to resist his government like so many desperate Robin Hoods. In December the court moved to Northampton in readiness to tackle the rebel garrison at Kenilworth, but the planned assault had to be postponed because of the local risings that were breaking out in other parts of the country. Simon de Montfort junior, the royalists discovered, had already left his father's castle and gone into Lincolnshire, where other disinherited men were rallying to his banner. The marshy and inaccessible region known as the Isle of Axholme provided them with a natural fortress.

The royalists were therefore obliged to divide their forces, and while Henry remained at Northampton, his eldest son set out to subdue the new rebel base. Left to his own devices, Edward felt free to pursue a more conciliatory line, and he soon brokered a deal with his adversaries. In return for a guarantee of life, limb and liberty, they agreed to submit to the king's judgement at Easter. Young Simon came to Northampton to stand trial immediately, and was sentenced to a year's exile.

With equal suddenness, however, these initiatives broke down. Simon took fright, fearing he would not be allowed to leave the country after all, and fled abroad in February. (A few months later, he was followed by his younger brother Guy.) The problem for the royalists, it was becoming clear, was not merely military; they were also struggling against the belief among their enemies that their promises counted for nothing.[14]

What was true in general applied to Edward in particular. In retrospect, one tends to admire Edward's cunning and courage in the years leading up to Evesham, and indeed in many of his actions contemporaries would have found nothing remiss. To some extent chivalry endorsed guile and deception. The advance into battle with borrowed Montfortian banners, for instance, would have been seen by most as nothing more than a clever ruse. Yet there had been other occasions during the war where Edward's actions had amounted to perfidy – his escape from the city of Gloucester in early 1264 being especially notorious. On the strength of that episode, the author of *The Song of Lewes* had famously compared Edward to a leopard (*leopardus* in Latin, which rhymed with *Edwardus*). If we divide the word, he explained, it becomes *leo* (lion) and *pardus* (panther). To be a lion was good; they were commendably ferocious. Panthers, on the other hand, were apparently shifty and untrustworthy creatures, and that, averred the poet, was Edward's problem. 'A lion by pride and fierceness, he is by inconstancy and changeableness a panther, changing his word and promise, cloaking himself in pleasant speech. When he is in tight spot he promises whatever you wish, but as soon as he has escaped, his promise is forgotten.'[15]

Saddled with such a reputation, all Edward could do was continue with his conciliatory stance and hope thereby to disprove his opponents' negative assumptions. His first notable success in this regard came in mid-March, at which point he joined forces with his old friend Roger Leybourne. At the start of the year Leybourne had been charged with the task of securing the coastal towns of Kent and Sussex. The Cinque Ports, as they are still corporately known, had become a refuge for pirates and Montfortian sympathisers – it had been via the port of Winchelsea that Simon junior had made good his escape. Leybourne had set about reducing them to obedience with his usual flair for military operations, and had already succeeded in taking Sandwich by storm.[16]

What ultimately won over Winchelsea, however, was not simply the combined land–sea assault that Edward and Leybourne proceeded to unleash, but the generosity of the concessions that the former now brought to the table. In return for their submission, the defenders were guaranteed all their lands and liberties, and freely pardoned all their recent crimes. The leniency of these terms seemed most unfair to the London chronicler who recorded them; just two months earlier Henry III had imposed a massive 20,000 mark fine on the capital in return for having a similar pardon. But the calculated clemency of the king's son was soon seen to be paying dividends. The Cinque Ports remained conspicuously loyal thereafter, and Edward – in his new capacity as their warden – derived a personal profit from the peace he had imposed.[17]

Nevertheless, this success was but a single swallow, not the sudden advent of summer. The royalist plan for April had been to resume the assault on Kenilworth, but the weeks after Easter witnessed a new wave of violence as the king's opponents – the Disinherited, as they had now been popularly dubbed – failed to keep to the terms of their earlier surrender and instead went on the rampage. One group laid waste to the counties of East Anglia; others began to create similar havoc in the Midlands and in Hampshire. Rumour had it that the sons of Montfort had raised troops overseas and were poised to return. Once again, the royalists were forced to disperse to deal with the hydra that Henry III had ill-advisedly created.[18]

At length, they began to obtain the upper hand. In mid-May Edward's cousin and companion in captivity, Henry of Almain, scored a signal victory over one band of rebels at Chesterfield in Derbyshire, capturing some of the leaders and putting the rest to flight. A few days later Edward himself defeated another group that had been terrorising the people of Hampshire from their camp in Alton Wood. This encounter, which saw the heir to the throne engaged in hand-to-hand combat with the rebels' leader, Adam Gurdon, soon became the stuff of legend. Edward was said to have been so impressed with the skill of his adversary that he allowed him generous terms of surrender. The reality was not quite so romantic: although Gurdon was spared, he was afterwards taken to Windsor for imprisonment. Nevertheless, the story shows how Edward's reputation was beginning to improve. Far from being the duplicitous and bloodthirsty leopard, he was now spoken of as a model of chivalrous clemency.[19]

By midsummer the royalists were again ready to resume their assault on Kenilworth, where the garrison was still determined to resist. The great stone fortress, modified and improved by Montfort, presented a formidable challenge, not least because of the great artificial lake that obstructed its western approaches. Reducing the castle would depend to a large extent on the skill of the king's engineers, and thus, despite the use of barges from his own lordship of Chester, there was little for Edward himself to do. Command in this instance lay with his younger brother, Edmund, who had commenced the siege some weeks earlier and who, as Montfort's successor, was also Kenilworth's new lord.[20]

This lull in Edward's workload was timely, however, for his wife was approaching the end of her term, and the gap in his known itinerary suggests that he probably went to join her at Windsor. There, on the night of 13–14 July, Eleanor was safely delivered of a healthy baby, which to general rejoicing was a boy. The citizens of London demonstrated their delight by awarding themselves the following day off work, and danced through the streets as they had on the occasion of Edward's birth twenty-seven years earlier. No doubt the father himself was equally pleased and proud, but the most noteworthy aspect of his response was the decision to call the new child John. At a time of continuing baronial rebellion, it seems remarkably bold, not to say brash, of Edward to have resurrected the name of his notorious grandfather, and to have bestowed it on the son who might one day succeed him.[21]

The rebellion still showed no signs of diminishing. Soon after Edward's return to Kenilworth – he reappears there in early August – news came of yet another outbreak in East Anglia. John Deyville, a committed Montfortian who had repeatedly evaded capture, had marshalled his fellow malcontents and seized the city of Ely. As with their earlier stand at Axholme, the Disinherited had found themselves another isolated fastness in the Fens, from which they were able to mount devastating raids against neighbouring towns and villages.[22]

The prospect of seemingly ceaseless insurgency reinforced the argument for offering the rebels more lenient terms, and in August a parliament assembled at Kenilworth to determine precisely what these terms should be. Edward, to judge from his own generosity in the preceding months, is likely to have endorsed the moderate view, but, as at the start of the siege, he seems to have maintained a low profile during the discussions, perhaps deliberately. As it was, the final decision, announced at the end of October, was seen to be the work of Cardinal Ottobuono and Henry of Almain, who had jointly headed the debating committee. In the teeth of opposition from hard-liners such as Roger Mortimer, it was agreed that the rebels would be allowed to recover their lost lands in return for substantial fines – several times the annual rent of the properties concerned, the scale varying according to the degree of each individual's offence. Since the fines raised from these manors would be paid to their royalist occupiers, nobody stood to lose out entirely. The rebels would eventually redeem their inheritances, and the royalists would still feel that they had been adequately rewarded.[23]

The Dictum of Kenilworth, as this scheme became known, was a major step in the right direction. It induced many minor offenders, whose fines had been fixed at twice their annual incomes, to lay down their arms and accept the king's peace. But the hardcore Montfortians at Kenilworth and Ely, expected to forego five years' rent in return for forgiveness, rejected the deal as still too harsh and vowed to fight on.

In the case of the Kenilworth garrison this constituted an act of considerable bravado, for their ability to resist was fading fast. In the end, after six months under siege, the prospect of imminent starvation induced them to surrender in the days immediately before Christmas.[24]

At the start of the new year of 1267, therefore, it remained only to deal with the rebels ensconced at Ely, and in February the royalists reassembled at nearby Bury St Edmunds to begin the task. An exchange of messengers between the two camps confirmed that there was no hope of further compromise. Deyville and his colleagues were true disciples of Montfort, convinced of the righteousness of their cause. To Henry's observation that he would be fully justified in retaining their lands forever, they replied that his redemption scheme was tantamount to disinheritance anyway. Military action was evidently the only option; Edward's appearance at several coastal towns in January suggests that he was probably mustering the necessary naval support for an attack on the island city.[25]

Yet again, however, as the royalists closed in to suppress what seemed to be the last centre of resistance, another sprang up. News now came from the north of a rising led by John de Vescy, a young and devoted acolyte of the late earl of Leicester (legend has it that he saved Montfort's severed foot at Evesham and took it home to venerate). Although he had accepted the Dictum of Kenilworth, Vescy had latterly come to regret his decision; for him and others; the sight of their former opponents occupying their ancestral estates had evidently proved too much to stomach. Together they had formed a solemn league, forcibly reoccupied their lands and castles, and vowed to defend them.[26]

On learning of this latest upset, Edward assembled a host of knights and sped north, arriving at Vescy's castle of Alnwick around the end of March. As in similar confrontations of the previous year, it seems that some serious fighting ensued, and Alnwick was retaken by force. Once again, however, what struck contemporaries was Edward's magnanimity in victory. 'Pious and merciful', enthused one London chronicler, 'he not only put off vengeance, but offered his pardon to the offender'. It probably helped in this instance that Vescy, although an idealistic adherent of Montfort, had also grown up in the royal household, and it is fair to point out that after his surrender he still remained saddled with a substantial fine. Nevertheless, the swiftness with which Edward had quelled the northern rising was impressive, and neither Vescy nor his neighbours created any trouble thereafter. Indeed, as the same chronicler correctly noted, the young lord of Alnwick became one of Edward's closest friends.[27]

The king, by contrast, had enjoyed far less success against the stalwart defenders of Ely and was castigated for his inactivity on this score. Having decamped from Bury to Cambridge in order to begin his military operations, Henry had attempted to invade the island with a fleet of boats, but his attempt had ended in failure, and the royalists had been repulsed with heavy losses.[28]

This setback, however, was the least of the king's worries. Far worse was the alarming split that had arisen within his own ranks. Gilbert de Clare, the young earl of Gloucester, whose role in Montfort's downfall had proved so crucial, had belatedly come out in support of the remaining rebels. In early April he had led a great number of his own troops to London, and Cardinal Ottobuono, charged with holding the city in the king's name, had naively (and in spite of the concern expressed by the Londoners themselves) allowed his army to enter. The citizens fears were quickly realised. Once inside the walls Gloucester's men had seized control, and were soon joined by some of the Disinherited from Ely, including John Deyville. The London mob, quiet since the previous year, had also declared in favour of this new alliance. The legate had fled to the Tower, which in consequence had been placed under siege. Meanwhile, across the rest of the capital, the rebels readied themselves for a final showdown. Great ditches were dug and earthworks raised around the city, as well as around the neighbouring borough of Southwark. This time, London would be ready to resist.[29]

With Gloucester's backing and the capital's reoccupation, there was a real chance that sporadic insurgency could escalate into a new civil war. Towards the end of April Edward rejoined his father at Cambridge, bringing with him a large army he had recruited in northern England (and possibly even from the Lowlands of Scotland). Thus reinforced, the royalists marched towards London in early May. At the same moment the redoubtable Roger Leybourne was sent overseas to engage the services of foreign mercenaries, and Eleanor of Provence was stationed at Dover ready to receive them. Local levies and siege equipment were demanded from neighbouring counties in expectation of taking the capital by force.[30]

Ultimately, however, reason and moderation averted the need for further bloodshed. Cardinal Ottobuono, having negotiated his way out of the Tower, played a major role, persuading the English clergy to contribute to a relief fund for the Disinherited. But the real heroes of the hour were Richard of Cornwall and the other moderate magnates who had condemned the harsh treatment of the rebels over eighteen months earlier. Under their auspices, a new agreement was reached, which saw a crucial amendment to the Dictum of Kenilworth. Henceforth, it was announced, rebels who agreed to redeem their lands would obtain repossession immediately, rather than (as had formerly been the case) at the end of their term of repayment. This had been Gloucester's chief demand, and having obtained it he agreed to stand down his men. In mid-June the earl withdrew from London, allowing Henry III to enter a few days later and proclaim his peace. It remained only to bring the rump of rebels at Ely to heel, a task that fell to Edward, and that he accomplished the following month.[31]

At long last, the disturbances of the past decade had come to an end. They would, of course, have ended far sooner had the victors of Evesham not embarked on their understandable but ill-judged policy of retribution. Instead, the battle had been followed by two more years of unnecessary violence and destruction. England, already in a terrible state of confusion at the time of Montfort's death, had been reduced to total chaos. In almost every corner of the kingdom lordship and landholding were in dispute, and nowhere had escaped the repeated waves of destruction. During the recent occupation of London, even Henry III's precious Palace of Westminster had been sacked, the looters making off with windows, doors and fireplaces.

But the work of reconstruction and regeneration could now finally begin, and the heavens themselves seemed to be in sympathy. Back in 1258, when the revolution had broken, the weather had been appalling, and in consequence a terrible famine had stalked the land. In 1267, by contrast, the bad times had clearly passed, and the air was filled with hope. One Londoner writing that summer noted with satisfaction the richness of the woods and the spinneys, the gardens and the cornfields, and concluded 'this year was more fruitful than any in times past'.

'Moreover,' added another of the capital's contented inhabitants, 'an enormous amount of Gascon wine was imported.'[32]

In these days of renewed optimism, there was no greater cause for hope than the character of the heir to the throne. More than any other individual, Edward had been transformed by the tumultuous events of the past ten years. The swaggering youth whose irresponsible excesses had been lamented by the late Matthew Paris was gone; in his place was a man who, at twenty-eight, had proved his ability on almost every relevant score. The civil war, culminating in the two great battles of Lewes and Evesham, had shown that he possessed a general's skill and a lion's courage. The hard-won peace that had eventually followed had allowed him to demonstrate his flair for persuasion and to repair his associated reputation for panther-like duplicity. Without question, Edward had emerged as the most powerful figure in English politics. More than ever before, he looked like a king in waiting.

And yet who knew how long he would have to wait? Henry III, at almost sixty, was old but hardly ancient; despite his tendency to complain of ill-health, he might soldier on for several years to come. In such a scenario, Edward would have to assume a much more subdued role than the one he had been playing of late. He could, of course, assist his father in the business of government, but for the next few years government promised to be a tedious business of settling land disputes. Equally, he could attend to his own estates, but here too there was little prospect of genuine excitement. The one arena that would have presented a challenge was Wales, but Edward's concerns there had lately been ceded to others. His lands in south Wales had been transferred to his younger brother in 1265; those in the north had been lost to Llywelyn ap Gruffudd in the summer of 1263, when the castles of Dyserth and Deganwy had finally fallen, and there was no question, given England's exhaustion and instability, of recovering them at any point soon. Accordingly, in the late summer of 1267, Henry and his sons travelled to the Welsh border and granted Llywelyn a permanent peace.[33]

What Edward and his friends craved was fresh adventure. Their desire for further opportunities to prove their martial prowess is clear from the numerous tournaments they organised in the autumn of 1267. But counterfeit combat was no substitute for the real thing, to which recent events had made them accustomed; these young but experienced warriors now required an altogether larger stage for their ambitions. The answer to their predicament was therefore obvious – the natural next step for knights in search of renown. Edward and his friends should go on crusade.[34]

The idea of an English crusade had hung fire since the mid-1250s, at which point Henry III's half-baked plan of leading an expedition had finally collapsed. To some extent the king's dalliance in this highly emotive area of foreign policy had been the cause of his domestic crisis. Having initially vowed to fight in the Holy Land, he had subsequently fallen in with the pope's suggestion that the kingdom of Sicily would make an equally legitimate target. Alas for Henry, his subjects had begged to differ, and ultimately overcome his bull-headed intransigence on this and other issues by depriving him of power. As a result, the only holy war that Englishmen had experienced had been a kind of ironic parody. In 1263 Montfort and his youthful devotees had decided that their cause was so righteous that it constituted a crusade; a little later the papacy had thrown its weight behind the royalists and conferred crusade status on their struggle to overthrow Montfort. Both sides, it seems, had ridden into battle at Evesham with crosses stitched to their surcoats.[35]

By this time, however, the papacy had reverted to its original tune and placed the Holy Land back at the top of its military agenda. In 1263 a new call to arms had been issued to the princes of Europe, exhorting them to go east. Needless to say, it had fallen on deaf ears in war-torn England, but the subsequent coming of peace had encouraged the pope to renew his efforts. Promoting the new crusade was a major part of Cardinal Ottobuono's remit as papal legate; with the help of the English clergy, he had begun a propaganda drive soon after his arrival. To some extent, it sat well with his other aim of bringing reconciliation. From the time of the First Crusade onwards, preachers of the cross had urged Christians to stop sinfully fighting against each other, and to head east instead, so that they could righteously slaughter the infidel.[36]

But in the fraught atmosphere after Evesham, not everyone was convinced. In February 1267 the rebels in Ely had responded with scorn to the suggestion that they should leave the country at the pope's say-so. To them Ottobuono's presence was simply a reminder of the disreputable schemes concocted by the Crown and the papacy a decade earlier; his message was clearly a cynical plot to remove Englishmen from England so that their lands might be given to foreigners. Even once peace had been restored, such attitudes proved hard to dispel. The cardinal preached the cross in London immediately after Henry III had re-occupied the city, but few of those who responded to his call were former rebels.[37]

Among royalists, by contrast, the response was rather more encouraging. Those receiving the redemption fines imposed after the peace were obviously in a better financial position to go on crusade than those obliged to pay them. Moreover, apart from sheer kicks, there were two additional factors that gave the king's supporters greater motivation. First, and most obviously, there was a strong religious imperative. The victors of Evesham would have felt a great debt of gratitude to God, as well as the need to atone for the exceptional level of bloodshed. Secondly, and probably no less importantly, there was once again the matter of Anglo-French rivalry. In March 1267 Louis IX had announced his intention of taking the cross for the second time. This had been the essential breakthrough as far as the papacy was concerned, but for the English royal family, their friends and relatives, it merely drew attention to the unfulfilled vows they had sworn in 1250. To hesitate again could only magnify their existing embarrassment on this score.[38]

What made sense to royalists in general, however, seemed altogether less sensible in the case of the heir to the throne. Edward was the best guarantor of stability and guardian of the Crown's interests; were he removed, even for a short time, the kingdom might again descend into chaos. Henry III, for all his religious conviction, was clearly appalled at the prospect of losing his eldest son, and many others must have shared in his concern. Representations were evidently made to the pope, who responded in early 1268 by reiterating them in a letter to Edward and urging him not to go. A little later, recognising that Henry remained anxious to have his venerable vow fulfilled by proxy, the pope suggested that his second son, Edmund, would make a more suitable substitute.[39]

But Edward was undeterred by such objections. In his mind it was an equally unconscionable thought that his friends should go without him. His household, although composed for the most part of Englishmen, still contained some high-ranking French knights, several of whom had travelled to the East with Louis IX a generation before and who must have been particularly influential. The same was true of Louis himself, who had become close to Edward, his nephew, as a consequence of their frequent contact during the 1260s. The French king's encouragement and the example of his countrymen evidently counted for more than the admonitions of Henry III and the pope. By the end of 1267, if not before, Edward had resolved to go.[40]

At length, the objectors in England were won over. Cardinal Ottobuono was soon convinced that an English crusade would go ahead only if Edward was its leader, and Henry III was eventually talked round in the early months of 1268. By the start of the summer the stage was set, and a special parliament was summoned to Northampton – a location almost certainly selected because of its spectacular church of the Holy Sepulchre, built by a knight of the First Crusade in imitation of the original he had seen in Jerusalem. There, on Sunday, 24 June 1268 – the feast of St John the Baptist – Ottobuono preached the pope's message, and Edward, his brother Edmund and their cousin Henry of Almain all responded by taking the cross. Hundreds of others followed their example. For the most part they were royalists, such as Roger Clifford, Roger Leybourne and William de Valence, but a handful of former rebels also joined their company. John de Vescy, the rehabilitated lord of Alnwick, was one. Gilbert de Clare, earl of Gloucester, was another, and by far the most important in terms of portraying the crusade as a pathway to reconciliation. The carefully co-ordinated ceremony was clearly a breakthrough moment, and represented the culmination of Cardinal Ottobuono's efforts. His mission in England completed, the legate left for home the following month.[41]

With regard to the ceremony at Northampton, two other important points deserve to be noted. First, the exultation that day followed on directly from the joyous scenes of the previous month, when Edward and Eleanor had celebrated the birth of their second son, whom they named Henry in honour of his grandfather. Second, the fact that she was now a mother to two small children in no way deterred Eleanor from taking the cross herself. Women were in general discouraged from going on crusade, but by the thirteenth century it had become quite common for ladies of the highest rank to accompany their husbands eastward. Eleanor de Montfort, for example, had done so in the 1240s, as had Queen Margaret of France. On this occasion the French queen was happily staying behind, but her son Philip was planning to take his wife, Isabel, and Edward's youngest sister, Beatrice, intended to travel with her husband, the son of the duke of Brittany. Given this context, Eleanor of Castile was almost bound to participate. Indeed, given her closeness to Edward, her well-attested fondness for chivalric pursuits, and also the fact that she was the daughter of Ferdinand III, one of Spain's greatest crusading heroes, it would have been altogether more surprising had Eleanor elected to remain at home.[42]

As for Henry III in the 1250s, so too now for his son, the question became one of preparation and, more specifically, money. To go on crusade had always been an extremely costly undertaking. From the time of the First Crusade onwards, knights had been forced to mortgage or sell their estates in order to raise the necessary funds to maintain themselves and their dependants during the many months, often running into years, that an expedition might last.[43]

Such personal economies were still in order in 1268, but there were also some alternative sources of funding available. By the thirteenth century, crusading had become a well-organised, centrally managed institution under the direction of the pope. The papacy, in fact, had pioneered many of the fund-raising techniques still employed by international charities today. Collection boxes were placed in churches; people were prompted to leave bequests in their wills. The papacy had even hit upon the neat idea of encouraging the non-military members of society to take the cross, then allowing them to redeem their vows in exchange for a cash payment. Using all the money raised by such methods, the Church was able to subsidise the kind of crusaders that were really wanted – warriors with the appropriate experience and equipment.[44]

In theory, therefore, Edward should have been able to lay his hands on such funds. The problem was that, because of his father's earlier opposition, his initial application for a grant had been declined. Following Henry's subsequent volte-face, Ottobuono had endeavoured to reverse this decision, commending Edward to the pope as a doughty leader worthy of financial support. Alas, however, the pope died before he could be prevailed upon to change his mind, and the college of cardinals fell into a protracted argument over who should be his successor. Thus, for the foreseeable future, Edward was unable to count on obtaining funds from what should have been the most obvious source.[45]

Denied money by the Church, Edward determined to raise it instead from the laity. In the autumn of 1268 plans were laid to convince parliament to finance a crusade by means of a national tax. This was nothing if not ambitious. To begin with, the country had only recently emerged from years of devastating civil war. More to the point, that war had been provoked, in part, by the excessive financial demands of the Crown. By the time of the famous Oxford parliament of 1258, the knights of the shire had become so fed up with Henry III's oppressive government that they had been willing to support its overthrow. Some of them, for the same reason, had subsequently gone on to support Simon de Montfort. The revolution might now have been reversed, and Montfort might have been dead and buried, but the grievances that had given force to both remained very much alive. It had been over thirty years since parliament had agreed to approve a royal request for tax. Unless the complaints of local society were answered, it was a situation that was unlikely to change.

Edward thus faced a seemingly impossible situation. To persuade men to vote him money, he would have to address their grievances, yet to address their grievances, he would have to ease their financial burden. It was similar to the vicious circle that had defeated his father. Unable to obtain parliament's consent to taxation, Henry had ordered his sheriffs, foresters and justices to raise more revenues. This, in turn, only made the men of the localities feel even more oppressed, and thus rendered them even less likely to vote the king a tax the next time he summoned a parliament.

Any attempt to conciliate local opinion therefore had to be carefully judged; it would have made no sense to cede the right to any regular form of revenue in the vague hope that this might engender enough goodwill to permit the collection of a one-off tax. What was needed was a targeted concession: something that would ease the demands, not on everyone's pockets, but specifically on those of the knights in parliament. For this reason, Edward proposed legislation against the Jews.[46]

As the popularity of crusading implies, thirteenth-century England was an aggressively Christian country, and it would not be incorrect to say that Christianity dominated the lives of each and every one of its 3 to

4 million inhabitants. It would be incorrect, however, to claim that the kingdom was entirely uniform in its religious observance, for amid this massive Christian majority lived a tiny number of non-believers. The Jews had first arrived in England shortly after the Norman Conquest, at which point they had established a small community in London. Two centuries later they could be found dwelling in most of the country's major towns and cities, yet collectively they still accounted for no more than 5,000 people.[47]

As a minority population, marked out as different by their faith and rituals (and to some extent their appearance and dress), the Jews were always liable to be marginalised and persecuted. In one respect, however, difference had given them a distinct advantage. In the late twelfth century the pope had forbidden Christians from practising usury, or lending money at interest. In so doing he effectively created a Jewish moneylending monopoly. From that moment on, any Christian wishing to obtain financial credit, from the humblest local landowner to the king of England himself, had to look to the Jews to provide it.[48]

Needless to say, while being moneylenders made the Jews necessary, it hardly made them any more popular, and they would not have survived for long had they not been protected by the English Crown. Unfortunately, such protection came at a price, and that price was systematic exploitation. Almost as soon as their monopoly of the credit market had been established, it was decided that the Jews were, in effect, the king's property, much as if they had been unfree peasants living on one of his manors. As such, the king could tax them at will, imposing a so-called 'tallage' whenever he felt the need. It also meant that when a Jew died, all his assets went to the Crown, including any outstanding loans he had made that had yet to be collected.[49]

To contemporary Christians, none of this seemed in any way unreasonable: the Jews, it was felt, should be kept in their place, just as unfree peasants were. If anything, the Crown's treatment was regarded in many quarters – Rome, for instance – as rather too lenient. Put crudely, if the king wanted his Jews to turn a profit, it behoved him to keep his demands moderate, and allow the Jewish community to prosper. For the first part of the thirteenth century, this was by and large what had happened. By the time of Edward's birth in 1239, thanks to their special relationship with the Crown, England's Jews were probably the most prosperous in Europe.[50]

But thereafter Henry III, with characteristic incompetence, had contrived to wreck the system. Unable to obtain taxation from parliament to fund his misguided European adventures, Henry had turned to the Jews and tallaged them without mercy. In the two decades after

1240, the king had unthinkingly extorted a total of nearly 100,000 marks, taking twice the annual average that had been customary before this point. As a result, by the early 1260s, the prosperity of the Jewish community had been broken beyond repair.[51]

The financial persecution of a small, infidel minority might have elicited no more than a general shrug of indifference had that minority not also been moneylenders. As it was, Henry's rapacious harrying of the Jews had knock-on effects that were equally disastrous for many of his Christian subjects. Inevitably, once their own savings had been exhausted, Jewish creditors looked to recover the monies they had loaned to others. It was similarly inevitable, however, that their clients could not offer immediate repayment. Thus, in order to meet the king's pressing demands for cash, the Jews were forced to take the extreme step of selling their loans on to others at a heavy discount. A debt of £100, for example, might be sold for £50, or even far less, if the need for quick capital was sufficiently desperate.

So far, so uncontroversial: it hardly mattered to Christians if a few Jewish moneylenders went to the wall in this way. The problem for Christians lay in the motives of those who were the purchasers in this new market. Discounted Jewish debts were typically snapped up by the richest individuals at Henry III's court – William de Valence and Richard of Cornwall were two of the most prominent pioneers in the field. Such men were not concerned to recover the principal of a loan, nor even (as the Jews themselves were) the considerable interest that would accumulate on it. The target on which their acquisitive eyes were fixed was the property against which the loan had been secured. Having obtained a debt, there was nothing to stop an unscrupulous Christian speculator from demanding immediate repayment of the entire sum – repayment that, naturally, the unfortunate debtor would not be able to produce. This being the case, the speculator could simply foreclose on the debt and seize whatever lands had been put up as collateral. A modern analogy would be a bank suddenly deciding to sell its mortgages to an individual who refused to respect the repayment terms, and who began repossessing the properties on which the mortgages had been secured.[52]

Thus the effects of Henry III's punitive taxation of the Jews had been felt far beyond the Jewish community itself. For a few very wealthy courtiers with capital to spare, it had created a new and easy way to obtain lands. For the majority of lesser landowners, by contrast, it had created nothing but misery and distress. Some, having done nothing more than take on perfectly serviceable debts from the only available source, had found themselves partially or totally disinherited. Others –

anyone else who still owed money to the Jews – had in consequence become extremely anxious lest the same should happen to them. Reform had been demanded in 1258, but nothing had been done. In 1260, at the time of Edward and Montfort's Easter rising, the Jewish exchequer, where records of debt were kept, had been raided and robbed of its rolls. Finally, during the years of civil war violence, attacks on the Jews themselves had begun. Between 1263 and 1267 there were massacres in, among other places, London, Canterbury, Winchester, Lincoln, Bristol, Nottingham and Worcester. Angry, fearful Montfortian knights, already encouraged to be anti-Semitic by their Christian religion, struck down their creditors in the hope of erasing the evidence of their indebtedness. The restoration of peace had brought an end to these attacks, but the problems associated with Jewish credit remained.[53]

It was these problems that Edward proposed to remedy in the hope that he could thereby appease the knightly class, and thus obtain the tax for his crusade. At the start of 1269 he and Henry of Almain pushed for a raft of legal restrictions on Jewish moneylending aimed at curtailing its abuse by rich Christians. Debts to Jews, they suggested, should not be sold to Christians without prior permission from the king; those that were ought not to gather interest. In addition, they advocated doing away altogether with so-called 'rentcharges' – a novel device whereby a debtor made annual payments from his property in return for his loan, and another means by which predatory magnates were wont to snap up encumbered estates.

But when these measures were published in the Easter parliament of 1269 they failed to have the desired effect. The knights of the shires had witnessed plenty of well-intentioned but toothless legislation passed in the previous decade; it may well have been that they insisted on seeing these new measures enforced before they would consider the question of money. This, in turn, may have provoked opposition from those great men in attendance who had a vested interest in the existing operation of Jewish credit and who no doubt hoped that the new laws would simply be left to gather dust. Whatever the case, no effort was subsequently made to enforce the restrictions, and no consent was obtained for a grant of taxation.[54]

Edward was running out of options. If neither the clergy nor the laity would grant him financial aid, his crusade was doomed to fail. In the relentless search for funds a certain desperation was already apparent. In the early months of 1269 his father had handed him the custody (and hence the revenues) of seven royal castles, eight counties and the city of London. Later, in April, his brother Edmund was married to a rich heiress, Avelina de Forz, who stood to inherit the earldoms of

Devon and Aumale, the Isle of Wight and extensive lands in Yorkshire. Lastly, in May, there was an exceedingly shabby episode whereby both brothers and several of their powerful friends – Henry of Almain and William de Valence chief among them – conspired to deprive the earl of Derby, Robert de Ferrers, of all his property. A former Montfortian, Ferrers was also a foolish young man who had clashed several times with Edward during the course of the war. He should nonetheless have been allowed to stand, like other rebels, to the Dictum of Kenilworth and recover his estates by redemption. That he was not is testimony to the personal animosity Ferrers aroused in both Edward and his fellow crusaders, but above all it underlines their greed: the earl's estates and titles, extorted from him under duress, were duly transferred to Edmund.[55]

While the magnates of England floundered in their struggle to raise money, in France the crusade was gaining an unstoppable momentum. Louis IX, in his capacity as the expedition's undisputed captain, had summoned a final council of war to Paris that summer, which Edward dutifully attended in August. The meeting was not without its benefits. The French king took pity on his hard-up nephew and furnished him with a loan of £17,000 (the sum to be repaid over twelve years from the customs revenues of Bordeaux). Although not nearly enough to cover all costs, this was at least a sizeable step in the right direction. In other ways, however, the Paris summit compounded the pressure on Edward. During their debates Louis and the other leaders fixed a firm date for their departure. The crusade would leave from southern France, it was agreed, in one year's time – whether the English were ready or not.[56]

Part of Edward's problem was the attitude of his father. Although Henry III continued to pay lip-service to the idea of going on crusade and had dropped his objection to his eldest son's involvement, his overriding ambition lay in a different (and to some extent opposing) direction. Whereas Edward intended to thank God for his victory at Evesham by going east, Henry wished to celebrate his divine deliverance at home, on his doorstep. The new church at Westminster Abbey, begun in 1245, was still a long way from completion (the east end and the transepts were finished, but the nave was only half-built). Nevertheless, enough had been done for the king to prepare for the reburial of Edward the Confessor, his hero, whose tomb had been removed when construction work had started. Henry's hopes had evidently been pinned for some time on a dedication service in 1269: that year's liturgical calendar was a rare, exact match with the calendar of 1163, when the Confessor's body had last been translated. Ever since his restoration to power, the king had urged on the works relentlessly, ploughing whatever spare cash he could find into finishing the abbey's ceremonial sections. Everything had to be ready by the feast of St Edward on 13 October; Henry intended it to be the climactic moment of his long and troubled reign.[57]

Edward returned from France in good time to participate. Viewed optimistically, there was a chance that his father's day of triumph might occasion a breakthrough for the crusade. To witness his supreme moment, Henry had summoned an especially large parliament. If its lesser members were sufficiently dazzled by the spiritual experience, they might well condescend to approve the much-needed tax grant.

Alas, the great day did not go quite as planned. The dedication went ahead, and the saint's body was reverently moved to its new, not-quite-finished shrine: Henry, Richard of Cornwall, Edward and Edmund carried the Confessor's coffin in a solemn procession around the church themselves. But before the ceremony there were arguments over precedence between the officiating archbishop of York and the rest of the clergy, and a similar row arose between the citizens of London and Winchester ahead of the feast that followed. Moreover, while the new church was undeniably awesome, and the king's hospitality excited 'the admiration and wonder of all', neither was enough to alter the mood of the knights in parliament. Asked once again to sanction the collection of tax, they once again refused.[58]

Nor was that the only problem. Notably absent from the dedication of the new abbey was Gilbert de Clare, the easily displeased earl of Gloucester. Although he had taken the cross at Northampton the previous year, Gilbert had subsequently become irritated on a number of scores with both Edward and Henry (he had been particularly irked by concessions made in the March of Wales to Llywelyn ap Gruffudd, which hurt his own interests in the region). Isolated incidents seemed like a concerted campaign to get him; the contemptible treatment of his one-time ally Robert de Ferrers cannot have done much to allay his fears. According to one chronicler, the earl now professed to be staying away from court in the autumn of 1269 because he believed that Edward was plotting to capture him.[59]

Far from uniting men in common purpose, the crusade appeared to be deepening the divisions between them. The knights of the shires, still aggrieved with the king's government, refused to subsidise the adventure. Former Montfortians, burdened by their redemption fines, had mostly declined to take part. From the first the expedition had threatened to drive a new wedge between Edward and his father, and to some extent Henry's support remained equivocal. Now the earl of

Gloucester, the single greatest participant after Edward himself, seemed disaffected to a point that might jeopardise the realm's fragile peace. None of this boded well for a departure in ten months' time. And yet, at the same time, the crusade could not be abandoned. Financially, because of his agreement with Louis IX, and spiritually, because of his vow at Northampton, Edward was bound to go.

Even the spiritual obligations were more complicated and onerous than might have been wished. Some four years prior to taking the cross, Edward had made another solemn promise before God. The occasion had been one of his several sea crossings in the winter of 1263–64, a voyage that apparently became so perilous that the passengers had feared for their lives. There was a strong tradition among medieval aristocrats, when faced with such circumstances, of swearing to found a religious house in the event of their deliverance, and at the time Edward had shown no hesitation in upholding it. As a consequence, he had not one but two vows to honour, and he could hardly consider embarking on a crusade (which would entail, among manifold other dangers, more sea voyages) until the earlier one had been fulfilled. It was probably for this reason that he left Westminster at the end of 1269 and travelled to his own lordship of Chester. He had already determined that his religious house, a Cistercian abbey, should be situated at Darnhall, near Winsford, but he may have wished to inspect the sight for himself and perhaps also, in view of his financial straits, to moderate the scale of its endowment.[60]

Edward thus spent both Christmas and New Year in the north-west, but he had few other reasons to celebrate. If he was to join the crusade he would have to leave England in six months' time, yet the obstacles in his path still seemed insurmountable. In February, at which point he returned south, there was hope that his breach with Gilbert de Clare could be healed by the intervention of Louis IX. This plan, however, came to nothing. According to a Kentish chronicler, the earl crossed the Channel to Paris, but paid no heed to the French king's counsels.[61]

When parliament reassembled after Easter, therefore, it represented Edward's last chance both to settle with Clare and to obtain the crucial tax. Fortunately, in the case of the former, matters got off to an encouraging start. The earl soon agreed to the suggestion that his quarrel with Edward should be put to arbitration, and Richard of Cornwall, that seasoned settler of disputes, was drafted in to devise a suitable compromise. Meanwhile, Edward and the other crusaders must have set about persuading the knights of the shire to vote in favour of a subsidy. Records of parliament at this date are virtually non-existent, so one can only imagine how much hard bargaining, arm twisting and bribery took place between the session's opening and the crucial vote a fortnight later. One of the chief demands of the shire knights must have been a confirmation of Magna Carta (on which more later), for Henry in due course obliged them on just this score. The key concession, however, is likely to have been a firm commitment to enforce the restrictions on Jewish moneylending, introduced but seemingly stifled the previous year. When, on 14 May, the king instructed the exchequer to enforce the legislation with immediate effect, thereby relieving a large section of the local landowners in parliament of the burden of the Jewish debts, it was a clear quid pro quo. Two days earlier, the crusade tax had finally been approved.[62]

Suddenly everything was possible. Henry III was so thrilled by this last-minute breakthrough that a week later he announced his intention of joining the expedition (a fit of enthusiasm that was mercifully short lived). Another week on and Richard of Cornwall succeeded in resolving Edward's dispute with Gilbert de Clare. It took a further month to hammer out the precise terms, but on 27 May it was agreed that neither man would wage war on the lands of the other, and that Gilbert would set out for the East a year after Edward's departure.[63]

That departure now had to follow very fast if the English were to make the French deadline; the weeks of waiting while the first fruits of the tax were gathered must have been hugely frustrating. During this time Edward drew up formal contracts with the men who would be serving under him, which reveal that his force numbered 225 knights. Every crusader, however, would have travelled with a number of attendants: Eleanor of Castile, for example, was taking her steward, her valet, her tailor and two of her clerks. In total, therefore, the English army probably numbered around a thousand people.[64]

At last, all was ready, and the court moved to Winchester for a final round of preparations. On 2 August Edward appointed a committee of five men, headed by Richard of Cornwall, to supervise his lands and affairs during his absence. The earl was also nominated as the guardian of his godson's three children – John, now four, and Henry, two, had recently been joined by baby Eleanor. The same day, Edward issued the foundation charter for his abbey at Darnhall, and two days later he was formally made his father's proxy when Henry III at last resigned his twenty-year-old vow. The crusaders then moved to Portsmouth, where the fleet that would convey them across the Channel was waiting, but contrary winds and the death of the archbishop of Canterbury meant they had to wait a further fortnight. It was not until 20 August, having first been diverted to Dover, that Edward, Eleanor and their companions finally set sail for France.[65]

★ ★ ★

They had already been cutting it fine; now they were officially late. Louis IX and the other crusaders had resolved to set out from southern France no later than 18 August. Edward's original intention had been to travel via Gascony, in order to provide for the duchy's security and to collect more men and supplies. This plan now had to be abandoned. In an attempt to make up lost time, the English army passed directly through France, covering more than 600 miles in the space of a month. By the end of September they had reached the appointed rendezvous, Aigues Mortes, a port on the Mediterranean coast, developed by Louis at the time of his first crusading adventure.[66]

It must have been disappointing, if not altogether surprising, to discover that the French king and his companions were already long gone. Perhaps aware of Edward's delay, and no doubt unwilling to watch an idle army consume his carefully stockpiled supplies, Louis had peremptorily set out at the beginning of July. The surprise lay not in his premature departure but in his direction of travel. The French fleet had not sailed east, as expected, but south. Astonishingly, in spite of the years of planning and the pressing needs of the Holy Land, Louis had made a last-minute alteration to his itinerary, and decided to lead his army to North Africa.[67]

The instigator of this unexpected and seemingly perverse decision was the king's youngest brother, Charles of Anjou. An adventurous and fiercely ambitious man, Charles had recently succeeded where Henry III had so conspicuously failed, and established himself as king of Sicily. Invested by the pope in 1266, he had subsequently cemented his rule by conquering the island and beheading his German rival. Now he wished to carve out a wider Mediterranean empire and was targeting Tunis on the African coast. Of old the emirs there had paid a gold tribute to Sicily's kings, but latterly this custom had lapsed, and Tunis had become a refuge for Charles's enemies. The new king was determined to reverse the situation, and saw in his elder brother's crusade the perfect instrument. Somehow he persuaded Louis that the Holy Land's interests would be best served by a strike on Tunis; a rumour that the emir was ready to convert to Christianity may have helped him argue his case.[68]

One can only wonder at the reaction of Edward and his companions on being told that the crusade for which they had saved and struggled for so long had been redirected in such an apparently whimsical fashion. (And, one is bound to wonder, had they arrived sooner, would they have been able to prevent its redirection?) As it was, they saw little option but to follow where the main French army had led. In early October they set out from Aigues Mortes in Louis's wake, clearly unaware that any hope of uniting with the French king were already in vain.[69]

For Louis was already dead. He had died on 25 August, just days after Edward had left England, carried off by a plague that had struck the French army soon after its arrival in Africa. Several hundred other Frenchmen had also succumbed, and the survivors had concluded that the best way forward was a negotiated retreat. Charles of Anjou, whom providence had deigned to spare, had succeeded in obtaining the promises he needed from the Tunisian emir, and saw no reason to prolong hostilities. Thus, by the time the English arrived on 9 November, the African adventure was over. Edward was reportedly appalled to discover that a peace deal had already been reached and that the French had already begun their withdrawal. Faced for a second time with a fait accompli, and perhaps wondering whether they would get to do any fighting at all, the English crusaders agreed to Charles's suggestion that they should sail to Sicily before deciding how to proceed.[70]

In the event the decision was made for them. On reaching Sicily, the French fleet put in at Trapani, a town on the island's western tip, only to be smashed to pieces by a great storm. More men and horses were lost, as well as a great deal of treasure and supplies. It was enough to persuade Louis's son and successor, Philip III, who was no doubt still reeling from the loss of his father and a younger brother, that the crusade was a doomed enterprise. In January 1271 he departed back in the direction of France, taking the overland route through Italy, leading what had essentially become a great funeral procession.[71]

The storm was no less decisive for the English, but pointed them in a different direction. Edward's ships had found an alternative anchorage – possibly Palermo – and had been spared destruction. This was taken as a sign of divine approval: God had protected them and clearly intended them to continue. There were evidently some voices in the English camp urging caution, perhaps fearful that France, after Louis's death, would prove an unstable neighbour. Edward, in response, detached Henry of Almain from his side and sent him north with the retreating French army, intending that his cousin should bolster the governments of England and Gascony. But beyond this, the thoughts of the English that winter were focused on completing the mission to which they were sworn. Fresh ships were hired and fresh supplies gathered, and when Edward put to sea once more in the spring, his course was set firmly for the East.[72]

More specifically, it was set for Outremer – the Christian lands 'beyond the sea'. Some 170 years earlier, in their quest to capture Jerusalem, the first crusaders had conquered a broad swathe of territory along the eastern Mediterranean coast. At Antioch, Tripoli and Edessa, these pioneers had established themselves as counts and princes, while in the Holy City itself they had set themselves up as kings.

And, for a time, their dominions had flourished. Settlers came from the West, building castles, cathedrals, towns and villages. Pious knights vowed to defend the new colonies, banding together in brotherhood to form revolutionary new organisations – the military orders of the Hospital and the Temple. At its greatest extent, Outremer stretched over a hundred miles inland, and as far south as the shores of the Red Sea.[73]

This age of expansion, however, had not lasted for long. In the generations that followed, the Muslim world recovered its composure and retaliated. By the end of the twelfth century the kingdom of Jerusalem had been reduced to a narrow coastal strip, and its kings, having lost the Holy City itself in 1187, were reduced to ruling from the port of Acre (modern-day Akko).

After these upheavals came half a century of comparative stability. In spite of fresh crusades and Muslim counteroffensives, the territorial status quo was preserved. Such significant alterations as did take place – the brief Christian reoccupation of Jerusalem, for example, negotiated by Richard of Cornwall – owed more to a prevailing spirit of practical accommodation that to the periodic outbursts of militancy.[74]

But in the interval between Cornwall's crusade and the coming of his nephew the political landscape of the Holy Land had again been radically transformed, and militancy was once more in the ascendant. The obliging Islamic rulers with whom the earl had treated were gone, swept away by revolution; the Mamluks, their former soldier-slaves, were now the masters of the Muslim state, and they were altogether less inclined to do deals with the infidel. From 1260, under the leadership of the short but ferocious Sultan al-Zahir Baybars, they had switched to the offensive, and soon the castles and cities of Outremer had begun to fall like ripe fruit. Caeserea, fortified at great expense by Louis IX, was taken in 1265; Antioch, the city of song and legend, fell just three years later. When, in the spring of 1271, Crac des Chevaliers, the greatest of all the crusader castles, surrendered after a prolonged siege, it seemed as if these were the end days for Christian rule in the East.[75]

Thus, for the citizens of Acre, the sight of an English fleet sailing into their harbour just a few weeks later could hardly have been more timely or more welcome. Prior to that point, as one chronicler credibly reported, they had been completely demoralised, and contemplating the unhappy prospect of having to surrender to the sultan's forces. But, the same writer continued, the coming of Edward and his companions in the second week of May gave them fresh hope, and encouraged them to believe that they might weather the impending storm.[76]

Baybars, when he heard of Edward's arrival, also experienced a change of heart. At that moment he was over a hundred miles to the north, still engaged in his military campaign, and advancing with what a Muslim chronicler called 'resolute determination' towards the Christian city of Tripoli. On hearing the news from Acre, however, 'his resolution weakened somewhat'. Tripoli was granted a ten-year truce, and the sultan moved south to deal with the source of his distraction.[77]

He came, no doubt, partly to size up his new foe, but mostly to demonstrate the extent of his own might. In early June he arrived in the vicinity of Acre, but made no immediate move against the city itself. Instead, he attacked the nearby castle of Montfort, which succumbed after a short siege. Only then did Baybars complete his advance, taking with him the castle's captured garrison, which he proceeded to release right in front of Acre's walls.[78]

For those inside the city, especially the newcomers, this calculated display of magnanimity was a deeply dispiriting sight. The English, as we have seen, numbered no more than a few hundred knights, plus their lesser attendants. Mamluk armies, by contrast, were typically reckoned in thousands, and sometimes tens of thousands. The disparity in this instance was not lost on the leader of the new crusade as he looked out from Acre's battlements. 'When Edward saw the sultan's host, and his great power,' said one local chronicler, 'he knew well that he did not have enough men to fight him.' Baybars' message was clear: the English, like Outremer's other Christian inhabitants, were there at his sufferance. The following morning, once it was evident that no one was going to contest this assertion, he withdrew his forces.[79]

Unfortunately for the English, this was not to be their only lesson in the harsh realities of life in the Holy Land. The following month, ignoring the sultan's warning, Edward led a retributive raid into Muslim territory. His target was the castle at St Georges Lebeyne (modern al-Bi'na), some twelve miles east of Acre, and by all accounts his troops did plenty of damage, seizing some crops, destroying others, and killing many unfortunate Muslims. But, as the same accounts attest, there were also numerous casualties among the crusaders; July, the English discovered, is not the best time to don a mail shirt in the Middle East. So great was the heat that many of them died of thirst, their departure apparently hastened by an unfamiliar diet of fruit, raisins and honey.[80]

It thus became evident to Edward that if he was to have any hope of beating Baybars he must do two things. First, he must wait for it to cool down a bit. Second, he must find himself some allies. The men of Acre, including the Knights Templar and the Knights Hospitaller, could clearly be counted on, for they had participated in the raid on St Georges. So too could the titular king of Jerusalem, Hugh de Lusignan. He had already aided the English once before, inasmuch as he was also the king of Cyprus, and the crusaders had briefly stopped on the island during the last stage of the voyage. The hope now became that he could help them again in the same capacity. His Cypriot subjects took some convincing – it is 150 miles from Cyprus to Acre – but at length (and after Edward's personal intervention) they also agreed to provide military service. And so, as the summer days grew shorter, the list of allies lengthened. In September it received a further boost when Edward's brother Edmund belatedly arrived, bringing more reinforcements from England.[81]

By themselves, such efforts might seem a futile waste of time – mere wishful thinking on the part of a man who been told too many stories about his Lionhearted ancestor. Trying to defend a beleaguered city was one thing; dreaming of defeating Baybars was quite another. The first might be construed as a noble cause; the second seemed more like suicide. It did not matter how many men came out of the West: no amount of co-operation among Christians was going to produce a force capable of beating the Mamluks in battle.

The fact was, however, that the Christians were not by themselves, for the revolution that had brought Baybars and his brethren to power was not the only shock wave to have rocked the Middle East in recent times. It was not to the West, but to the North, that the crusaders now looked in the hope of the greatest aid. As soon as Edward had arrived in Acre, he had dispatched three members of his household on a dangerous mission. They had gone to seek an alliance with Abagha Khan, ruler of the Mongols.[82]

The rise of the Mongols had been, without question, the single most astonishing event of Edward's age; it still remains one of the most remarkable occurrences in the whole of human history. Around the start of the thirteenth century, the horsemen of the Central Asian steppes had ceased fighting each other, begun fighting their neighbours and, in the space of just seven decades, carved out the second most extensive empire the world has ever seen (only the British Empire exceeded it and then by only a narrow margin). From China in the east, across southern Russia and even unto the fringes of Europe itself, the Mongols, led at first by the mighty Ghengis Khan and later by his sons, had conquered and slaughtered everything in their path.[83]

Accordingly, there had been much initial consternation among the princes and peoples of Christendom about the speed of their advance. But in the 1250s the threat to Europe had receded as the Mongols had begun to invade the Middle East, and suddenly the ferocious heathens of yesteryear had started to look like potential partners in the struggle against the Mamluks. In 1265 Abagha, great-grandson of Ghengis and ruler of the il-Khanate (the Persian province of the Mongol Empire) was married to a daughter of the Christian emperor of Constantinople; there was even talk in some quarters (quite inaccurate, as it turned out) that he himself might convert. Regardless of his religious orientation, however, the il-khan was united with the Christians in regarding Baybars and the Mamluks as his enemies, and that was reason enough to hope for an alliance.[84]

It evidently took Edward's ambassadors several months to deliver his message, and one can only imagine the perils and hardships they must have endured in order to do so: Abagha's reply, when it arrived, was dated at Marāgheh, a city over 700 miles from Acre (not far from Tabriz in modern Iran). Nevertheless, the reply was highly encouraging. While the il-khan could not come himself – he was at that instant dealing with other enemies – he indicated that lieutenants would shortly be invading the Holy Land in order to engage with Baybars. A combined offensive, it seemed, was on.

And with immediate effect. Abagha's letter can hardly have reached Acre before the news that thousands of Mongol horsemen were indeed pouring southwards. By October they were just 200 miles away and had already driven the Mamluks out of the ancient city of Aleppo. Baybars rose to the bait. He and his men did not fear the il-khan's forces. They had beaten them once already, eleven years earlier, at the celebrated battle of Ain Julat (a rare setback in the otherwise relentless Mongol advance). This new invasion would be similarly repulsed. In November the sultan and his army rode north.[85]

Now was the moment for the Christian coalition to strike. On 23 November Edward, his brother and the English crusaders, King Hugh and the barons of Cyprus, the Templars, the Hospitallers and the knights of Acre all rode out. Their target this time was Qaqun, a castle some forty miles to the south. Recently redeveloped by Baybars as a centre for governing the surrounding lordships, Qaqun represented a valuable prize in its own right. More important for the crusaders, however, was the castle's strategic significance, for it lay halfway between Acre and Jerusalem, and guarded the road that ran between them. If the English were to have any chance of retaking the Holy City, they would have to take Qaqun first.[86]

It must therefore have been a bitter disappointment to Edward and his friends that in this last respect their mission failed. As before, they succeeded in slaughtering many local herdsmen and seizing large numbers of animals; indeed, to read the enthusiastic reports of local Christian chroniclers, one might almost imagine that cattle-rustling had been the principal objective. The castle at Qaqun, however, held out. It was, as one writer explained, 'very strong, surrounded by ditches full of water'. The crusaders would undoubtedly have taken it, he continued, had not a Muslim relief force approached (and, added a Muslim writer, chased them back in the direction of Acre).[87]

Nor was this the only disappointment. On their return the Christians discovered that the clash they had been counting on in the north had not taken place. On learning of Baybars' advance, the Mongols had withdrawn from their positions and retreated. By early December the sultan had reoccupied the city of Aleppo, where he was in due course informed of the unsuccessful attack on Qaqun. 'If so many men cannot take a house,' he observed witheringly, 'it seems unlikely that they will conquer the kingdom of Jerusalem.'[88]

It was Baybars' initial intention to punish the crusaders for their presumption; he was already halfway to Acre with his army before foul weather forced him to abandon his plans. Just how serious his assault would have been remains an open question. Retaliation was no doubt on the sultan's mind, but it is highly unlikely that he would have wished to reduce the city to rubble. The fact of the matter was that Acre was a great mercantile hub, and Baybars needed it to continue functioning as such. His recent conquests against the Christians had given him control of the north–south routes through the Holy Land, and these would be crucial in countering the more serious threat presented by the Mongols. But Acre also had a role to play in this greater struggle, for the prosperity of the Mamluk Empire was to some extent dependent on trade with the Christian capital. Moreover, as this implies, there were also many Christians living in Acre who were equally dependent on the same commercial links. The merchants of Venice, masters of the Mediterranean market, had an especially large stake in the city. Such considerations and vested interests provided a powerful argument for mutual toleration, and the preservation of the status quo.[89]

As such, of course, they were anathema to a committed crusader who had been conditioned from birth to see this part of the world in black-and-white terms. When he arrived in Acre Edward had been appalled to find Christians trading with Muslims, and had endeavoured to implement a ban (without success: the Venetians had simply responded by waving the royal charter that guaranteed their commercial privileges). If his refusal to engage with such practical politics seems lamentable, one can well understand his frustration. He and his companions had travelled thousands of miles and spent impossible sums to reach the Holy Land. They were tantalisingly close to their goal – Jerusalem lies just seventy miles from Acre – and could not lightly abandon the hope of attaining it. At some point during their stay, Eleanor of Castile presented her husband with a specially commissioned copy of *De re militari* (Concerning Matters Military), a celebrated tract on warfare by the Roman writer Vegetius; it is tempting to imagine Edward leafing through its pages in search of inspiration. He certainly remained focused on military matters. It was probably during the winter of 1271–72, confined within Acre, that he began to build a new tower in the city walls. His hope was clearly that the struggle with Baybars would continue, and it must therefore have been a galling blow when, in April 1272, a ten-year truce was agreed with the sultan. 'He was not pleased when the peace was made,' wrote one Muslim commentator, 'and did not become a party to it.'[90]

Being the only significant non-signatory to a ceasefire made Edward a dangerous loose cannon. Even some of those who had cheered his arrival the previous year would now no doubt have happily waved him back onto a boat. It was Baybars, however, who took active steps to hasten the Englishman's departure. Accounts of what happened are almost hopelessly confused in their detail. According to Muslim sources, who would seem best placed to know the background, the sultan instructed one of his lieutenants to pretend to be ready to betray his own side. It was a simple ruse, but it was also the first positive news that the English had received in months, so Edward (no stranger to employing deception in his own dealings) allowed himself to be taken in. When Muslim messengers arrived at his court – bearing gifts, in the best enemy-tricking tradition – they were welcomed and allowed to stay for some time. It was not until 17 June (which happened to be Edward's birthday) that they put their plan into action. With the promise of news concerning Baybars, one of their number secured a private audience and, finding himself alone with Edward and his interpreter, revealed his true purpose by drawing a dagger. According to English sources – better placed to know the details of the attack – Edward succeeded in killing his would-be assassin but not before sustaining a serious injury himself. He had been stabbed, with a blade that was feared to be poisoned.[91]

It as at this point, famously, that legend has Eleanor of Castile intervening to save her stricken husband; in one version of events she proves her love (and mettle) by sucking the poison from his wound. Sadly, this is almost certainly a retrospective romanticisation. It was first reported half a century later by an Italian writer, and even he was careful to preface his account with the medieval chronicler's time-honoured disclaimer 'they say that . . .'. Other accounts of the scene have Eleanor being led away weeping by John de Vescy, and suggest that it was another of Edward's close friends, Otto de Grandson, who attempted the sucking operation.[92]

Whatever the case, there was nothing at all fanciful about the degree to which Edward's life had been placed in peril. The day after the assault he drew up his will in anticipation of the worst, and for a time it seemed that the worst would happen. The greatest danger from such injuries was that they would turn gangrenous, and infection would spread to the rest of the body, slowly killing the victim. This apparently started to happen to Edward's wound, and it seems he was saved only by having the blackened flesh around it cut away. Such a procedure was in itself highly risky – the patient in this instance would have been well aware that, in similar circumstances, a careless surgeon had hastened the demise of his great-uncle Richard. It is arresting to think that, had he not had ready access to the skilled doctors of Acre, Edward would have quite likely died there and then, and the future history of the British Isles, if not of the Middle East, might have been profoundly different.[93]

Although his enemy refused to die, Baybars had otherwise achieved his objective. Edward's injury meant that the English crusade had now definitely reached its end. In truth this was a conclusion that had been apparent ever since the sealing of the truce. Edmund had left for home the following month, and later in the summer other English commanders began to follow suit. Their leader delayed a little while longer. Prevailing headwinds in the eastern Mediterranean meant that the journey home usually took twice as long as the outward voyage – anything up to eight weeks – and Edward would have needed to convalesce for as long as possible before subjecting himself to such an ordeal. Eleanor, too, having recently given birth to a baby daughter, Joan, would have been in no immediate hurry to leave.

As a summer turned to autumn, however, and a seasonal easterly wind began to blow, the couple finally bade farewell to the Holy Land. In late September they sailed from Acre, and by the start of November they were back in Sicily, where they were again welcomed by Charles of Anjou. Unable to travel quickly because of his wound, and doubtless already starting to enjoy the celebrity status conferred by his miraculous survival, Edward spent Christmas in Charles's company on the Italian mainland. He was still there early in the new year when messengers arrived from England, and hailed him as their king.[94]

4

The Return of the King

Henry III had suffered several bouts of ill health in the two years since the departure of his sons, and in consequence had rarely ventured far beyond his palace at Westminster. It was there, in the early days of November, that his final illness took hold. Confined to his chamber for almost a fortnight, he died in the evening of Wednesday 16 November 1272. He was sixty-five years old, and had reigned for fifty-six years. Since his death was not sudden, we may suppose with some confidence that his beloved wife, Queen Eleanor, was with him at the end.[1]

The funeral took place the following Sunday in Westminster Abbey, the building upon which Henry had lavished so much money and attention for over a quarter of a century. He had long intended to be buried in the church, and had latterly decided that his final resting place should be the tomb once occupied by Edward the Confessor and recently left vacant by the saint's translation. In contrast to the rather inglorious scenes that had marred that occasion, Henry's funeral passed without a hitch. All the leading magnates of the realm were present. The ceremony was magnificent. The king's body, carried on an open bier, was dressed in robes of red samite, decorated with gold embroidery and precious stones. 'He shone more gloriously in death than he did in life,' said one perceptive chronicler.[2]

Edward had known that his father was ill. In the spring of 1271 letters had been sent after him by the council in England, urging him to return home. It is highly unlikely, however, that this news reached him before his arrival in the Holy Land, and in due course he would have heard of Henry's recovery. When, therefore, he landed in Sicily on his return journey, Edward had every reason for hoping to see his father again, and consequently it came as a galling blow in January when he received the news of Henry's death. According to one chronicler, he wept for his irreplaceable loss, and in a letter written immediately afterwards Edward himself spoke of his 'bitter sadness'.[3] Despite the disagreements that had occasionally arisen between them, and the marked difference in their tastes and abilities, father and son had been very close, and the bond between them had been very strong. For all his faults as a king, Henry had been a doting and affectionate parent. Indeed, blind affection for his family was one of the main factors that had compromised his kingship.

While Edward's grief is therefore not surprising, his reaction to his father's death was, in one respect, highly unusual. A normal response would have been to drop everything and hurry in the direction of Westminster Abbey. By long tradition, the abbey was England's coronation church: every king since the Norman Conquest, beginning with the Conqueror himself, had been crowned there. The argument for haste was simple: convention also decreed that it was the coronation that made a man a king. Indeed, no king of England had ever been regarded as such until he had gone through with the ceremony. The all-time record for reaching Westminster was set in 1100 by Henry I, who was crowned just three days after the death of his brother, William II. But all would-be kings tended to spur their horses that bit harder when news reached them that the position had become vacant.[4]

Until 1272, that is. When Henry III died this ancient tradition was broken. The decision to break it was evidently deliberate and premeditated, and arose as a direct consequence of Edward's decision to go on crusade. When a king died, his authority died with him. Once Henry III was dead, all government in his name ceased. It would clearly have been intolerable for England to have remained without royal government until Edward's return (or, for that matter, to assume that he would be returning). Consequently, the matter was decided (although there is no record of it) before the crusaders' departure. Edward would not have to wait for his coronation; his reign would commence immediately after his father's death.

For this is exactly what happened. The day after Henry's death, Edward's peace was proclaimed in Westminster Hall. Three days later, in the course of the funeral in Westminster Abbey, the assembled magnates swore allegiance to Edward as their new king. They did this, as they explained in a letter to Edward, before his father's tomb had been sealed: an interesting point of detail that shows they were already thinking in terms that future generations would reduce to the famous maxim, 'the king is dead; long live the king'.[5]

Similarly, Edward, from the moment he received this letter, understood that his world had changed. He had no crown to wear, nor for that matter any of the other trappings of kingship. Indeed, in his response to the news from England, Edward had to apologise for using Charles of Anjou's seal to authenticate his letters. But those letters were his first royal act, and began with the words 'Edward, by the grace of God, king of England'.[6]

For the first time, therefore, there was no overriding need for haste. There could be no challenge to Edward's accession. Not only had his right been formally accepted by the great men of the realm at Westminster. Careful forethought had also ensured that the instruments of royal power were already in his hands. A few months before his son's departure, Henry III had taken the remarkable step of transferring all the royal castles and counties in England to keepers of Edward's choosing. As a consequence Edward's grip on England was quite secure.[7]

Nevertheless, a kingdom could not cope without its king forever, especially when it had suffered so many other misfortunes. Henry III was only the leading loss of the last two years. While Edward had cheated death in the Holy Land, the family he left behind had not been so lucky. His eldest son, John, had not survived the summer of 1271, dying soon after his fifth birthday. More serious in the short term, the committee of five men that Edward had left to superintend his affairs had been reduced to three, the chief casualty being its senior member, Richard of Cornwall. Having shouldered much of the burden of government during his brother's incapacity in 1271, Richard himself had suffered a stroke at the end of the year, and had died the following spring. As a consequence, although Edward's grip on the provinces was secure, the direction of his affairs at the centre was altogether less robust. In their letter to Edward the remaining regents urged him to make haste, and Edward, in response, promised to hurry.[8]

While he was on the Continent, however, it made sense to sort out Continental business, and the first item on his agenda was another fatality. In this case, death was not only an occasion for grief on Edward's part, but also for anger. His father, his uncle and his son had at least died of natural causes. His cousin, Henry of Almain, had been murdered.

It had happened in the spring of 1271, soon after Edward had sent Henry from his side in the course of their outward voyage. Henry's mission, as we have seen, was to superintend affairs in Gascony and, eventually, in England – an additional precaution that was probably deemed necessary in light of the new and uncertain conditions arising from the death of Louis IX and the early return of the French crusaders.[9] It is also likely, however, that part of his remit was to deal with the sons of Simon de Montfort, Simon and Guy, last seen fleeing from

England in the early months of 1266. In the time since their escape the two brothers had done remarkably well for themselves, carving out new careers in the service of none other than Charles of Anjou, who had found their warlike qualities useful and rewarded them well as a result. Guy, for example, had been appointed as governor of Tuscany, where he had also received generous grants of land, and married a rich heiress.

When, therefore, Edward in due course had found himself obliged to rely on Charles's generosity, and his crusading plans to some extent dependent upon his host's goodwill, the case for a rapprochement with the Montforts had become quite compelling. Later, as king, Edward claimed that the reason he had sent Henry of Almain north was to effect a reconciliation on his behalf. Henry seemed well suited for the task: he was, like Edward himself, a cousin to the two brothers.

Events, however, had taken a very different turn when the two parties met in Viterbo, not far from Rome, just a few weeks later. Guy de Montfort had come there to meet his lord, Charles of Anjou, who was also travelling with the French court. But when he learned that Henry was also present in the city, Guy sought him out and, finding his cousin hearing mass in the church of St Silvester, stabbed him to death. It was an unpremeditated act of retribution: a hot-blooded response to the cold-blooded killing of his father and brother at Evesham six years before. The victim, unlike the murderer, had not been present at the battle; Henry was simply a convenient royalist target for Guy's terrible wrath. 'I have taken my vengeance,' he said, as he left his cousin dying in the church, before returning to drag the body out into the street, where it received the same mutilation that had been inflicted on his father's corpse.

Two years on, and it was Edward who burned with a desire for revenge. The murder had scandalised all of Europe, and both Montforts had once again become fugitives from justice. Simon, the older brother, who was apparently complicit in the murder, had himself died in 1271 ('like Cain, cursed by God,' said one English chronicler). Guy, on the other hand, was still at large in Italy, being sheltered by the powerful family of his wife. As Edward set out northwards at the start of 1273, his first thoughts were of laying hands on the killer. Attempts to muster local support for a military campaign, however, came to nothing: the citizens of central Italy were understandably keener that a negotiated solution be found. Edward therefore looked to the help of the papacy, now fully functional once again after the recent election of Gregory X. The new pope was Edward's friend – he had accompanied Cardinal Ottobuono to England, and preceded the crusaders to Acre – and he received the new king in the city of Orvieto with great ceremony. But in the course of a stay that lasted over two months, nothing could be done to induce Guy's surrender. Eventually, Edward realised he would have to depart empty handed, and had to content himself with the knowledge that his intended quarry had at least been excommunicated. He would have been less pleased with the later intelligence that the sentence had been lifted and, later still, to learn that Guy had regained his liberty after a number of years in prison. It would, however, surely have gratified him to know that the notoriety of his cousin's killer would be everlasting. At the time of Almain's murder, Dante Alighieri was only a small boy living in Florence. But when he later came to write his *Divine Comedy*, he condemned Guy de Montfort to the seventh circle of Hell, steeped to the neck in a river of boiling blood.[10]

Although he had tarried for many weeks in his quest for justice, Edward left Italy in no great hurry. All along his route crowds flocked to see him, and every city through which he passed – Bologna, Parma and Milan being the major ones – feted him as a hero. As a result, when he eventually crossed the Alps in early June, he encountered a delegation of bishops and nobles from England, who had been expecting to meet their new king in Paris and eventually gone to seek him out. There was clearly considerable anxiety to have Edward back home. The men who met him would have been able to convey some positive news – a parliament had been held in his absence, and the knights and burgesses present had sworn their allegiance – but they would also have brought less glad tidings: magnates feuding with each other, risings in distant parts of the country, and a general increase in lawlessness. The absence of a king was keenly felt.[11]

By this stage, however, Edward had already decided that his first priority lay in a different direction. Now that his father was dead, he was not only king of England, he was also – at last! – duke of Aquitaine. Almost twenty years on from his first visit, Edward finally had the title and authority to deal decisively with his French dominions, which were at least as needful of his attention as England, and arguably more so. In any case, it made good sense to attend to them while he was this side of the Channel. Gascony, therefore, was to be Edward's next stop; England would have to wait a little longer.[12]

The first and most crucial matter to attend to in respect of Gascony was its relationship with the neighbouring kingdom of France. Accordingly, having left Eleanor (who was again pregnant) to go straight on to the duchy, Edward headed north to Paris, where towards the end of July he was welcomed by the new French king, Philip III. Some fourteen years earlier their late fathers had met in the same city and agreed a historic peace: a deal by which, as we have seen, Henry III had surrendered his ancestral claims to Normandy, Maine, Anjou and Poitou in return for recognition of his right to hold Gascony from Louis IX. On that occasion, as part of the same agreement, Henry had done homage to Louis. Which is to say, both men had participated in an ancient ritual, practised for centuries in every corner of Europe, by which one individual acknowledged that he or she was in some way subservient to another. On that day – 4 December 1259 – Henry had knelt before Louis, placed his hands within Louis's hands, and declared that, as far as Gascony was concerned, he was Louis's man.[13]

But what precisely did this mean? Homage could signify as little or as much as either party wanted it to. Neither Henry nor Louis seems to have felt that they had done anything especially novel; both took it as self-evident that the king of France was, or at least ought to be, the overlord of the duke of Gascony.[14] And yet, as the treaty they drew up makes manifestly clear, neither had much clue as to what this might entail in practice. When, for example, having promised to do homage to Louis, Henry had tried to specify what services he would render as a result, words had failed him. 'We will do appropriate services,' he had declared vaguely, 'until it be found what services are due for these things.' 'Then we shall be bound to do them,' he had added, helpfully, 'just as they have been found.'

Such was the general tenor of the Treaty of Paris – well-intentioned but mired for the most part in clauses that were hopelessly imprecise or that looked to some later date for their resolution. The latter was especially true of the treaty's opening section, which endeavoured to answer perhaps the most fundamental question of all: what, territorially speaking, was Gascony? For more than a century its border with France had been debated with swords rather than words. While it was noble of Henry and Louis to have preferred to pick up their pens, it meant that clause after clause began with a hesitant 'if'. Possession of one disputable district after another was declared to be contingent upon the future decision of this court, the outcome of that inquiry, or (in one particular case) whether the owners in 1259 ended up having children or not.[15]

Fourteen years on, and almost nothing had been done to resolve these problems. Henry III had sealed the treaty only to be distracted for a decade by domestic politics in England. While, therefore, there was no question of either Edward or Philip refusing to abide by the deal – both of them had been signatories in 1259 – it did mean that they had an immense amount of fine detail to work out, and therein the devil lurked. Accordingly, when Edward came to Paris to repeat his father's performance, he chose his words with care. 'Lord king,' he said to Philip, 'I do homage to you for all the lands I ought to hold from you.'[16]

It was with the intention of beginning the process of clarification that Edward left Paris for Gascony in August. Just as he had done homage to Philip as his king, he now required his subjects within the duchy to do the same to him as their duke. He also let it be known that he wanted to create a written record of the services they owed. 'By voice of herald and by sound of trumpet', his tenants were advised to assemble at his coming and furnish him with the requisite information. Having passed through Bordeaux – where, as well as accepting the homages of the citizenry, he was presumably received with some pomp – Edward proceeded further south to the town of St Sever, where he received the same acknowledgement from the leading lords of the duchy, and where the laborious process of registering their obligations began.[17]

At this point, however, his plans were rudely interrupted by the rebellion of the greatest lord in Gascony (after Edward himself, that is). Gaston de Béarn, whose lands lay in the hills along the duchy's southern border, had a history of causing trouble. He had been, for example, the chief ringleader of local resistance during the unpopular rule of Simon de Montfort. The reason for his recalcitrance in 1273 is altogether less certain, but it seems to have stemmed from an escalating disagreement with the duchy's abrasive new seneschal, Luke de Tany. (Before his departure on crusade, Edward had appointed his old friend Roger Leybourne as lieutenant in Gascony, but Leybourne had been another of the many unexpected casualties during Edward's absence, dying in the autumn of 1271.) Whatever the precise cause, Gaston refused to appear before Edward, forcing the new duke to break off his administrative business and embark on a punitive military expedition.

This took a long time. Although Gaston was initially brought to heel within a matter of weeks, he immediately broke the terms of his surrender and retreated to his castles in the foothills of the Pyrenees. Flushing him out involved a series of sieges that kept Edward occupied throughout the autumn and into the winter. It was not until the beginning of 1274 that the rebellious vicomte was finally cornered and once again forced to submit.

Nor was that the end of the matter. After his second surrender, Gaston immediately appealed to Philip III, and the French king obliged him by revoking his dispute with Edward to Paris. In this way, Gaston exposed and exploited the great chink in Edward's armour: namely, the non-absolute nature of his authority. Here was the most pernicious effect of the Treaty of Paris. If the duke of Gascony was properly subordinate to the king of France, it followed that any Gascon who was disgruntled by a ducal decision could appeal to the higher judgement of the French king's court. Edward could do all he might to limit this tendency, but he could not deny the fundamental principal. In 1274, therefore, much to his chagrin, he had no option but to abandon his attempt to discipline Gaston de Béarn and leave the matter in the hands of his lawyers.[18]

It was time to move on. With the winter now wasted by his fruitless pursuit of Gaston, Edward had to abandon his intention of returning to England by Easter. Instead he spent the spring completing the interrupted survey of his ducal rights, which culminated in March with a parliament in Bordeaux. In April he and Eleanor left Gascony, but on their way north there was more delay in Limoges, a once debatable area of ducal authority, where the oppressed citizens were keen to acknowledge Edward as their lord, but the oppressive local viscountess would have none of it. The result was yet another appeal to Philip III, who must have been pleased at the frequency with which opportunities to display his superiority were accumulating. It was not until the end of July that Edward reached the French coast and took ship to England.[19]

His year in France had not been a complete waste of time. During his stay in the south Edward had taken the opportunity to cultivate good relations with his neighbours, the kings of Navarre and Aragon, and had concluded alliances with both. Eleanor, meanwhile, had been pleased to meet up with her half-brother, Alfonso X of Castile, for the first time in twenty years. The Spanish king had travelled to meet her at Bayonne, where he had become the godfather to her newly delivered third son: Alfonso junior had been sent back to England ahead of his parents in June.[20] In overall terms, however, the visit to Gascony had been a frustrating one. Edward had made a start on consolidating his authority within the duchy, but there was still much work to be done. Moreover, with regard to the all-important issue of his relationship with the king of France, things seemed more complicated than ever, and the questions of territory and authority remained to be satisfactorily answered.

When Edward landed at Dover on 2 August 1274 it was clearly to a tremendous sense of popular excitement. 'Behold, he shines like a new Richard!' enthused one Londoner in a song written shortly before the new king's arrival. But it was not merely the fact that Englishmen now had not one but two crusading heroes to boast about; nor was it that, after almost four years of absence, Edward had kept his public in England waiting for such a very long time. It was probably not even the palpable sense of relief at his safe return, and the prospect of better royal rule that only a resident king could provide. Important though all these factors were, they must for the moment have taken second place to the sheer visceral thrill that accompanied the knowledge that the country was about to witness a coronation.[21]

Coronations were by their nature rare events, but in this particular instance the wait had been quite exceptional. Almost four decades had elapsed since the ceremony staged in 1236 for Eleanor of Provence, and Eleanor had only been a queen consort. To recollect the coronation of a reigning monarch would have been a feat beyond the memories of most Englishmen, for it was well over half a century since the young Henry III had been transformed from a boy of nine into a king.

Edward, of course, by virtue of the groundbreaking decision taken before his departure, was considered a king already. This did not mean, however, that in his case a coronation was in any way redundant or unnecessary: quite the contrary. The royal title may have passed to him, as his writs proclaimed, 'by the grace of God', but it still remained to call upon the Almighty to bless his rule, and for that the ancient, mystical rite of a coronation remained essential. Moreover, the fact that there was no longer the need to rush matters meant that those responsible for orchestrating the ceremony had months rather than days to make their preparations, and this in turn meant that the scale of the celebrations could be truly majestic. If there was a quantum leap in the history of the coronation as a royal spectacle, this was it.

On Saturday, 18 August Edward and his entourage rode into London. The mayor and citizens had adorned their city 'without consideration of cost' with silks and cloth of gold. Not just the citizens themselves, we are told, but all the magnates of the kingdom, both clerks and laymen, had gathered in the capital to cheer the arrival of their new king. Unfortunately, only one chronicler set these events down in any detail, and he was evidently somewhat overwhelmed by the spectacle, declaring that 'neither tongue nor pen' would suffice to describe it. He does, however, mention the 'multifarious inventions' that had been prepared in Edward's honour, which sound a lot like the kind of pageants that are generally held to be the preserve of later coronations.

The fact that Edward had entered London on a Saturday was also highly significant. Very likely what our tongue-tied correspondent was witnessing was the birth of the custom whereby a new king would ride from the Tower of London to Westminster on the day before his coronation. The king's ministers had certainly taken the trouble to spruce up the Tower in advance of his arrival, and, at Edward's express request, the mayor had cleared the clutter from Cheapside – London's main market, and the east–west thoroughfare along which later 'vigil processions' would pass. This being the case, Edward would seem to have begun another new tradition in 1274; one that would last until the seventeenth century.[22]

In processing ceremoniously through London, Edward was following a fashion laid down by his father, who had loved to indulge in such showy excesses – spectacle being one of the few things that Henry III could usually be relied upon to get right, and a way of compensating for his political failures. On several important occasions during his reign – the reception of Eleanor of Castile in 1255, for example – the late king had staged similarly elaborate parades through the capital. Henry's contribution, moreover, went beyond the provision of general precedents. In fact, much of the detailed long-term planning for Edward's coronation can be traced back to his father's initiative.[23]

As an example, consider where and how Edward spent the night before his coronation. When the procession ended, the king and his household would have installed themselves in the Palace of Westminster, where Edward would have prepared himself for a solemn spiritual exercise akin to the one he had performed in Burgos some twenty years before. Just like a young man about to be knighted, so too with a king about to crowned: he was expected to spend the night before the ceremony in quiet contemplation, reflecting on the responsibilities that went with the awesome status about to be conferred upon him.

The location for this time-honoured tradition would have been the king's bedchamber in the palace – later known, for reasons that will become apparent, as the Painted Chamber. It was here that Henry III had died, and in 1274 his spirit still hung about the walls. Some ten years earlier, the old king had caused the room to be redecorated. A disastrous fire that had ripped through the palace in 1263 had provided the excuse, and Henry's life-threatening illness the same year had suggested a suitable theme. On the wall directly behind the royal bed, the king's painters had created a coronation scene. The subject, naturally, was Edward the Confessor, being crowned by a crowd of bishops. On either side, outside of the curtains that closed around the bed, King Solomon's guards stood watch. Henry's aim, we must assume, was to provide his son with appropriate images on which to reflect during his vigil. Edward was to ponder the example of the Confessor, and the wisdom of Solomon.[24]

★ ★ ★

On Sunday, 19 August, the day itself dawned. Regrettably, we have no detailed eyewitness accounts of the kind that survive for some other medieval coronations. Past precedent and later example indicate that Edward, accompanied by Eleanor, led by the clergy and the magnates, would have processed the short distance from the palace to the abbey. The new abbey, of course, was Henry III's greatest legacy, and Edward was the first king to be crowned in it. Henry and his architect had been acutely conscious of Westminster's long-standing role as the coronation church, and had tailored the new building accordingly. Its ornate north portal was sufficiently huge to admit with ease those processing from the palace; the galleries around its transepts allowed spectators to view the proceedings from on high. The crossing of the church, where much of the ceremony would be acted out, seems to have been rendered deliberately massive for this reason. On the day of Edward's coronation, as on later occasions, it was very likely filled with a giant wooden stage. This was elevated so that those standing in the nave could observe the king, and – most remarkably – of sufficient height that those earls, barons and knights among the congregation could *ride* underneath it. In seeking to picture Edward's coronation, we must imagine the north and south transepts of the abbey filled with aristocrats who were not merely elaborately dressed, but apparently mounted on their horses too.[25]

Once the procession from the palace had passed inside the abbey, the ceremony itself began. In keeping with the grandeur of the setting and the splendid array of the participants, it was a magnificent piece of religious drama. Solemn prayers were intoned, censers were swung, torches and candles burned, glorious anthems rang out. If this all sounds slightly vague, it is because, once again, we cannot say precisely what took place. Indeed, contemporaries would have struggled to do so. The long years from one king's inauguration to the next gave ample scope for old practices to be forgotten and new ones to be introduced. In the case of Edward's coronation, one senses that Henry III, as well as designing the theatre, must also have contributed many details to the script. Later medieval kings, for example, would begin by making an offering at the altar of two gold figurines, one of Edward the Confessor, the other of St John the Evangelist – a 'tradition' almost certainly introduced in 1274 on the posthumous instructions of the Confessor's most avid devotee.[26]

Nevertheless, at the heart the proceedings lay strong strands of continuity. In its bare essentials, the English coronation service had changed (and has changed) very little across the centuries. The coronation oath, for example – Edward's next significant act after making his offering at the altar – had been a central part of the service since it was first devised in the tenth century. By this long-established convention, the new king made three basic promises: to protect the Church, to do good justice, and to suppress evil laws and customs. A fourth promise, to protect the rights of the Crown, had been added in the mid-twelfth century. This was, of course, a much more self-interested pledge as far the king was concerned, and one to which Edward would attach much importance later in his reign.[27]

The next part of the service, the unction, was of similar long standing. Edward would have descended from the stage towards the altar and disrobed down to his undershirt, in order that the archbishop of Canterbury could anoint various bits of his body with holy oil. The most mystical part of the whole ceremony, it took place on a suitably mystical pavement of multicoloured marble mosaic, the work of Italian craftsmen, and another finishing touch supplied by Henry III. The unction was the point where medieval practice drew on biblical precedent: the Old Testament kings, David and Solomon, had been anointed in this way, and, for this reason, the choir in Westminster Abbey sang the anthem *Unxerunt Salomonem* (They Anointed Solomon) while the act was performed. Traditionally this had been the critical part of the service – the religious ritual that transformed a mere man into a king – and Edward, although king in name already, must nevertheless have regarded it as the supreme spiritual moment. At this moment his rule became blessed, and the gifts of the Holy Spirit were bestowed upon him. In more practical terms, it meant that, in addition to the holy oil that had been applied to his breast, shoulders and elbows, Edward also had chrism – an even holier oil – poured over his head, where custom decreed that it must remain for a full seven days.[28]

Lastly came the investiture: the part of the ceremony where the king was re-dressed in the most elaborate royal fashion and adorned with all manner of symbolic baubles (collectively known as the regalia). These had tended to multiply over the years, with the result that by the thirteenth century the new king was weighed down with glittering ornament. Edward was vested in a golden tunic, girded with a sword, and robed with a mantle woven with gold. A gold ring was placed on his finger, and golden spurs were attached to his heels. Once he was wearing his special coronation gloves, a golden rod and a golden sceptre were placed in his hands. These items had for the most part been wrought in the early thirteenth century but, thanks to the enthusiasm and credulity of Henry III, by 1274 each was believed to have been an original first used by Edward the Confessor himself. When, therefore, Edward was invested with the greatest item of all – described in a later account as 'a great crown of gold . . . with precious jewellery of great stones, rubies and emeralds', he understood this to be the same object once worn by his sainted namesake.[29]

Edward's coronation, therefore, for all that it took place in a magnificent new church, and despite the manifold small details of staging introduced by Henry III, was essentially traditional in format and stuck to a time-honoured script. There was, however, one genuine moment of novelty in the proceedings, a deviation so striking that several chroniclers saw fit to record it, even though they recorded nothing else. It was supplied by the king himself, at what was literally the crowning moment. Once the great gold crown had been placed on his head, Edward immediately removed it and set it aside, saying (according to one chronicler) 'he would never take it up again until he had recovered the lands given away by his father to the earls, barons and knights of England, and to aliens'.[30]

By this deliberately dramatic act, Edward revealed the policy that would preoccupy him during his first years of government, and to some extent for the rest of his reign: namely, the recovery of things that he believed his father had lost. The chronicler's implication that the king was concerned only with lands is probably slightly skewed, perhaps through misreporting, perhaps through oversimplification. Henry III, it is true, had granted away plenty of property, both to Englishmen and foreigners: the greatest beneficiaries had been those closest to him, such as Richard of Cornwall, William de Valence and Simon de Montfort. It would have been politically unthinkable, however, for Edward to have taken back these lands from such men or their descendants, and even more inconceivable for him to have implemented what in the fifteenth century would have been called an Act of Resumption, demanding at a stroke the return of all the lands alienated by his father. Edward did have the sense that the Crown could use more land, but he preferred to act privately, and wrangle it out of softer targets.[31]

What Edward was determined to recover – and what he more likely declared he would recover – were his rights. Chroniclers were apt to confuse lands and rights, since the two often went together.[32] In the Middle Ages, landowners might claim all manner of rights and privileges: the right to hold a court, for example, or to take a toll, even the right to do justice on red-handed thieves with their own private gallows. Rights could also be expressed negatively, as the right not to have to do something. Some landowners would claim that they and their tenants did not have to attend the king's court, or to answer the summons of his officials. Either way, in asserting and maintaining such rights or liberties, there was financial advantage to be had. Holding your own court, for example, meant you received the profits it raised in fines; not attending a royal court meant you avoided paying similar fines to the king.

Such rights and privileges could be very ancient and legitimate; they might also be officially sanctioned by the king. Henry III, when he found it difficult to obtain the support of his greatest subjects, was wont to appease them by granting just such exemptions. Often as not, however, rights and privileges were simply assumed by landowners who sensed that they could get away with it, and this had been the case during much of Henry's lax rule. Great men in particular had taken excessive liberties, shutting out the king's agents – his sheriffs, justices and bailiffs – and creating what amounted to their own private fiefdoms.[33]

Edward was determined not only to halt this tendency (thereby upholding his coronation oath to protect the rights of the Crown), but also to throw it into reverse (hence his vow to recover his father's losses). He was, of course, well-qualified for the task, by virtue of being a more masterful man than Henry. In the course of the struggle with Simon de Montfort he had fought hard to earn the personal authority that his father had so visibly lacked. There was, as a result, little chance of anyone scaring or dominating Edward in the way that Montfort had scared and dominated Henry. Similarly, Edward's crusade had further enhanced his standing, cementing his relationships with a powerful circle of friends of the kind his father had never known. The crusaders returned from the East as brothers-in-arms, their loyalties to each other, and above all to their new king, heightened by a sense of having been tested together in a great adventure. With such men to support him, Edward would have no need to resort to his father's policy of appeasement in order to get his own way.

In the short term, however, Edward's crusade had exacerbated the problems in England. His four-year absence, and the absence of many other powerful individuals, had deprived royal government of valuable support at a time when such support was most necessary. In his last years, politically as well as physically, Henry III had become weaker than ever. The regency government that succeeded him was weaker still, its authority severely dented by the unfortunate deaths of Richard of Cornwall and his intended replacement, Henry of Almain. As a consequence, the situation in England had continued to worsen. Those magnates who had remained in England – a majority that included all the earls – had usurped more power and appropriated more privileges. In some cases they had begun feuding with each other for local dominance. This, and Edward's continued absence, had led to another serious problem: a general rise in lawlessness. Murders and robberies had

increased, sheriffs had turned a blind eye, the courts had failed to maintain order. Here too, the new king realised, something must be done,
and done at once. Hence, according to one chronicler, another royal
announcement was made at the coronation. Justice, said Edward, should
be maintained everywhere; the guilty, even knights and great men,
should be hanged, and justices, bailiffs and sheriffs should take no
bribes.[34]

To help him achieve these aims – restoring justice and royal rights
– Edward looked above all to the man who, more than any other, had
run the country in his absence. Robert Burnell was a man of modest
social origins but great ability and seemingly limitless ambition. A clerk
– that is, a man in holy orders – he had joined Edward's household in
the mid-1250s and gradually established himself as its most indispen-
sable administrative member. By 1270, such was his standing that he
was considered (by Edward, at least) as the obvious candidate to replace
the late archbishop of Canterbury. The monks of Canterbury, alas, had
disagreed. Burnell may have been an administrative genius and a
charming man to boot, but his charms had in the past worked rather
too well on the ladies. At least one mistress and as many as five bastard
children were a standing argument against his promotion to England's
highest spiritual office.[35]

The summer of 1270 had nevertheless been a decisive turning point.
Up to that moment Edward had intended to take Burnell with him
on crusade; after the Canterbury vacancy he decided that his trusted
friend should stay at home. At the very last moment, the young clerk
– he was probably not very much older than his master – was appointed
as one of the five men responsible for superintending Edward's affairs
during his absence. Before long he was calling the shots for the other
members of the committee. Once death had reduced their number to
three, Burnell emerged as the natural leader and, when Henry III had
subsequently succumbed, the humble clerk from Shropshire effectively
replaced him. Official documents thereafter speak of Burnell as 'occupying the king's place in England'.[36]

With Edward back in his kingdom, the obvious role for Burnell was
chancellor; a month after the coronation he was appointed to the post.
We tend to assume – because the chancellor was later styled Lord
Chancellor – that the role was judicial in origin; in fact the remit of
the medieval chancellor was far wider than that of his latter-day successors. Originally the job was more akin to that of a modern prime
minister. The chancellor was so called because he ran the chancery, or
royal writing office. In this capacity he controlled the great seal, the
stamp with which the most important royal orders were authenticated.

Charters, letters and treaties, as well as writs initiating legal actions originated from within his department, which employed around a hundred lesser clerks, so great was its workload. Put simply, the chancery was the instrument by which the king's will was articulated. It was essential, therefore, that the chancellor was somebody in whom the king could have absolute trust, and whom other people would find accessible and approachable. Burnell was all these things. Although not faultless in his private life, he was extremely conscientious in his work, particularly when it came to ensuring government was just and fair. Chancellors by tradition were also bishops, so Burnell was in line for further promotion. When the bishop of Bath and Wells died in early December, the new chancellor was speedily elected as his replacement.[37]

By then the business of reforming England's government had already begun. In the middle of October, within weeks of Burnell's appointment, orders had gone out for the removal and replacement of all England's sheriffs. The sheriffs, as the king's chief agents in the counties (shire-reeves), were responsible for executing royal orders and accounting for the profits of royal lands. They were also responsible for enforcing the law and doing justice, and to that extent their role is comparable with that of their more recent and familiar Hollywood counterparts. Like the sheriffs of the Wild West, the sheriffs of medieval England exercised great power in their localities; good ones were always in demand, bad ones a perennial cause for complaint. By beginning his reign, therefore, with a clean sweep of the board, Edward sent out a clear signal that major change was under way.[38]

Shuffling the sheriffs, however, was only the first part of a much grander project. That same autumn, Edward and Burnell launched a great inquiry. In November, specially appointed commissioners began travelling in pairs around the country, assembling juries of local people, and requiring them to answer a long list of questions – as many as fifty in some cases. Certain questions demonstrated the same basic concern that Edward had shown in Gascony – that is, they asked how much land the king held in each county and what services he could expect in consequence. In general, however, this inquest went much further than its Gascon predecessor. Edward also wanted information, as he explained in his instructions to the commissioners, 'concerning the deeds and behaviour of all our sheriffs and bailiffs'. This, in other words, was not merely an investigation into rights and liberties; it was also an exercise in uncovering their abuse. Hence the need for the sheriffs to be switched in advance: folk would be far more likely to come forward and complain of corruption or oppression once their chief oppressor was gone. Nor was it just royal officials who were under the spotlight.

Local people were also asked 'whether lords, or their stewards, or bailiffs of any kind' had committed transgressions or crimes against the king and the community.[39]

The main point of the exercise, to judge from the weighting of the questions, was to discover where and by whom the king's rights had been usurped – the recovery of lost rights being Edward's main pre-occupation. And yet, by virtue of asking questions about the conduct of local officials, both royal and baronial, it was seen at the time as being a much more laudable and less self-interested exercise. Indeed, the chroniclers who commented on the inquiry saw it exclusively as a crackdown by the king on the corrupt, and a step in keeping with his promise to improve law and order. It was, in short, a cleverly handled initiative on the government's part, contrived with the intention not only of recovering royal rights and correcting official abuse, but also of winning popular acclaim for the new king and his government.

To this extent, the survey was a great success. In every district visited by the commissioners, men and women came forward in great numbers to give their evidence. It helped that there were no cumbersome legal procedures involved; people could just turn up and complain orally. The commissioners held their inquiries, not at a county level, but at the level of the now-redundant subdivision of the county known as the hundred (depending on size and density of population, a county could have as few as four hundreds or as many as forty). Consequently, their findings, once written up, formed what are now known as the Hundred Rolls. Working at great speed throughout the winter of 1274–75, Edward's commissioners conducted the single greatest survey of England since the Domesday Book some two centuries before.[40]

Domesday, however, was a dusty and fundamentally dissimilar precedent. The immediate ancestor of the initiatives that Edward introduced at the start of his reign was the reform programme that had been foisted on his father in 1258. Edward, of course, had strenuously resisted the attempt to limit the king's authority by means of a baronial council, but, this important difference apart, he had otherwise admired the ideals espoused by the reformers. Montfort and his co-conspirators had taught him in a matter of months a lesson that Henry III had spent a life-time failing to grasp, namely that royal power depended not merely on the support of a few great men at court, but ultimately on the good-will of many hundreds of lesser men across the rest of the country. The first steps taken by the revolutionary council in 1258 had been to replace all the sheriffs and address the grievances of local society – precisely the steps that Edward sought to replicate after his accession. Such reforms had not failed the first time round because they were inherently unworkable; on the contrary, many of them were eminently sensible and practical, the product of much serious and conscientious thought on the part of their authors. What they would require to work – and what Edward was now able to provide – was firm application. The new king was ready to put his house in order himself.[41]

As in 1258, so too in Edward's reign, the process of inquiry culminated in the drafting of new legislation. By March 1275 the Hundred Rolls commissioners had completed their work, and their findings were returned to the king, who used them to compile a comprehensive set of remedies. The result was a great statute, published at Westminster soon after Easter. It began by stating its intention boldly. 'Our lord the king greatly wills and desires to set to rights the state of the kingdom in the things in which there is need of amendment.' No fewer than fifty-one separate articles followed (more than double the number set down by the statute's spiritual predecessor, the Provisions of Westminster drafted by the reformers in 1259). Most set out to address Edward's two main policy aims – restoring royal rights and improving law and order. The latter intention, in particular, was emphasised from the start, where the statute lamented that 'the peace has been less kept than it ought to be, the laws abused, and wrongdoers less punished than they ought to be'. 'People are less afraid to do wrong,' it continued, and for this reason many of the proposed solutions involved the introduction of stiffer penalties: mandatory minimum sentences and heavy fines. But steps were also taken to try to improve matters by other means. All men, for instance, were reminded of their duty to be armed and ready to accompany the sheriff when he needed to raise a posse (Latin, *posse comitatus*, the power of the county) for the pursuit and arrest of criminals.[42]

Not all of this giant piece of legislation can have been concocted as a direct response to the Hundred Rolls inquiry. The commissioners had assembled a vast amount of information – far too much for even the most dedicated team of ministers to process in the short time that elapsed before the Statute of Westminster was published. As the targeted questions given to the investigators show, the king's ministers had been aware from the start of the nature of the problems they faced. This was especially true in the case of Robert Burnell. The man who had steered the ship during Edward's absence must have been one of the key figures in drafting the new statute, along with other ministers, senior judges and lawyers.[43]

Nevertheless, some parts of the statute were clearly informed by the inquiry's findings. In particular, those clauses that sought to alleviate the burden of local government seem to respond directly to the most common complaints recorded in the rolls. And being seen to respond was the essential point of the exercise. The inquiry had taken the country's pulse. Each new roll, as it was received, must have sharpened awareness of the legislators, either confirming their earlier diagnoses or suggesting new ones. The Statute of Westminster is steeped in a sense of its own worth; designed, in its own words, 'for the common good and for the relief of those who are oppressed'. It begins and ends with a reminder that this was Edward's first act 'after his coronation', and in this respect it resembles the 'coronation charters' issued by earlier kings – promises of good government made at the start of their reigns in order to win popularity. Edward's statute went much further than any of these earlier manifestos. Prepared over many months, during which there was unprecedented public consultation, it was the most thorough-going and extensive coronation charter ever issued.

This was reflected in the correspondingly elaborate efforts taken to publicise the finished statute. On the king's instructions, it was read aloud in local courts, in the marketplaces of towns and cities, and in other places besides. Copies were given not only to sheriffs and royal bailiffs (to impress upon them their responsibilities) but also, as an additional safeguard, to several local knights in every county (the probable intention being that they should watch for infringements). The most impressive part of the publicity process, however, was the initial fanfare. Publication of the statute was timed to coincide with the first parliament of Edward's reign, which was, for this reason, enormous in its size. As many as 800 representatives were summoned, both knights from the shires and, especially, burgesses from the towns. Together with the usual turnout of earls, barons, bishops and abbots, they constituted not only the largest audience imaginable, but also the biggest parliament assembled in England in the Middle Ages.[44]

The confident assurance with which Edward and his ministers handled public opinion and legislation at the start of his reign is further reflected in the sure-footed way they managed parliament. As we have seen, parliament had experienced a quantum leap during the early part of Henry III's reign. The word itself is first used in an official context around the time that the king, as well as summoning the great men with whom English monarchs had long been wont to discuss important matters of state, had taken the innovative step of summoning representatives from the shires and boroughs. But Henry, having fathered this new child, failed to nurture it, with the result that parliament became ever more argumentative and obstructive. The king wanted the knights and burgesses he summoned to approve his requests for money. They, in turn, demanded redress of their grievances with his government. Henry responded to such criticism by jamming his fingers in his ears; parliament retaliated by withholding its consent to taxation. From one assembly to the next, for year after year, this predictable pantomime was re-enacted. The king and his people would meet to parlay, only to talk at cross purposes.[45]

With Edward's accession, however, the relationship was reinvented, and the dialogue became meaningful and productive. Rather than ignore his subjects' criticisms, the new king actively solicited them. The evidence suggests that those knights and burgesses summoned to his first parliament at Easter 1275 were encouraged to bring their complaints for consideration. Those that did so must have been moderately surprised to receive swift redress, either in the course of the meeting itself, or soon afterwards, by special commissioners who were sent out 'to hear and determine' (*oyer et terminer*) the plaintiff's case. This was, therefore, an exercise in consultation in keeping with the spirit of the Hundred Rolls inquiry. The difference was that it was not intended to be a one-off. Parliaments were henceforward to be regular events, just as the reformers in 1258 had insisted they should be, and Edward continued to invite complaints, or 'petitions', as they became known. The initiative was, in fact, so popular that dealing with petitions quickly became one of parliament's principal functions (later in the reign, restrictions on petitioning had to be introduced, to ensure there was still sufficient time to discuss more important matters of state). At a stroke, Edward had transformed the malfunctioning institution he had inherited from his father into a forum where the king and his people could come together for their mutual benefit.[46]

In order to preserve this new spirit of bonhomie, Edward knew that it would be essential to avoid his father's tendency of demanding money from parliament. Apart from antagonising his subjects, taxation was a dangerously unstable base on which to found the Crown's finances. In all of his endeavours, Henry III had been repeatedly hamstrung by parliament's refusal to grant him funds. If Edward was to avoid the same unpopularity and embarrassment, he had to find another, more reliable form of income.

The solution was to tap trade. Thirteenth-century England was a rich country with a rapidly expanding economy. The evidence was everywhere: markets and fairs were being established at a rapid rate; forests were being felled to create new arable land and pasture; more and more silver coinage was being minted and put into circulation. Nowhere, however, was this prosperity more apparent than in the ever-increasing numbers of sheep. Wool had long been England's main export, sold to the textile manufacturers of Flanders. By the thirteenth century the business was booming. Great monasteries and lay magnates built up massive flocks on their estates, then sold their fleeces on to an increasingly prosperous class of merchants. If there was one sector of the economy that could afford to contribute to the royal coffers, the wool market was it.[47]

What Edward therefore proposed in 1275 was the introduction of customs duties on wool. This had been tried on a couple of occasions in the past, but with no great success. On this occasion, however, the circumstances were more propitious. In the first place, Edward to some extent had the mercantile community over a barrel. During his absence on crusade a trade dispute between England and Flanders had prompted the regency government to impose an embargo on the export of wool. It had not been terribly effective – Edward at one stage complained that the number of contraband fleeces being smuggled out of England was making him a laughing stock on the Continent – but in the end this initial period of laxity worked to the king's advantage. It meant that, when Edward returned, not only was the ban enforced with much greater stringency; he was also able to threaten the punishment of those who had contrived to evade it. Anxious to avoid Edward's wrath, and desirous to have the restrictions lifted, the wool merchants were predisposed to lend a favourable ear to his new customs scheme. In the course of the Easter parliament they agreed that the Crown should collect half a mark (a third of a pound) on every sack of wool exported. Since a sack held around 250 fleeces and sold for about £10, the new duty only amounted to about 3 per cent.[48]

The real key to Edward's success, however, lay in privatisation. During his crusade he had come to rely on the services of a company of Italian bankers known as the Riccardi of Lucca; on his return journey, in particular, their loans had helped to keep him solvent. This, like the use of customs, was not a wholly novel departure. Edward's predecessors had been turning to such banking societies for the occasional loan since the twelfth century, when the Italians had cornered the market in international finance. Where Edward innovated was in transforming an occasional relationship into a permanent one. Earlier kings of England – Henry III, as always, furnishes a good example – had obtained loans from the Italians without giving much thought as to how they might be repaid. Edward, by contrast, struck a new deal, whereby the Riccardi agreed to provide him with credit on demand, and he, in return, handed them the entire operation of his new customs. It was a simple yet brilliant arrangement: Edward, even in a financial emergency, would always have sufficient cash, and the Riccardi had the security of knowing that, in time, they could recover their money from the steady profit (on average, around £11,000 a year) that the customs brought in. It was not a cheap system as far as the Crown was concerned – the Riccardi probably charged interest at something like 33 per cent – but for the guarantee of liquidity it was worth every penny. By knitting together two existing ideas – customs and Italian loans – Edward had solved the problem of hand-to-mouth finance that had blighted his father's reign.[49]

But there was still one major and inescapable problem. Edward had returned from his crusade with colossal debts. This might seem surprising, given the sizeable sums that he had secured to finance the expedition in advance of its departure. In addition to the £17,500 Edward had raised by mortgaging the customs of Bordeaux to Louis IX, the hard-won tax he had wrung from parliament in 1270 had (eventually) yielded an impressive total of £31,500. All this money, however, had been proved quite inadequate to the task. Louis's loan had been almost entirely absorbed by the initial contract payments to Edward's followers, and those contracts had been set to run for one year only. The cost of repeatedly renewing them over the next three years would by itself have been enough to soak up the proceeds of the parliamentary subsidy. Besides this, of course, Edward had had plenty of other expenses to meet: the transportation of men and horses by ship (a contractual obligation); the purchase of fresh horses in the Holy Land; the construction of his tower in Acre. Above all, there had been the day-to-day cost of running his extensive household – a royal household from January 1273 – while it was overseas. Borrowing had begun while Edward was still in Acre and had increased dramatically during his return; debts to the Riccardi alone amounted to some £22,500. It helped that the new pope, Gregory X, agreed to a retrospective tax on the English Church that generated a yield almost equivalent to this sum. But Edward was still left owing numerous creditors, and the Riccardi in particular, what were, in the words of one chronicler, 'inestimable sums'.[50]

The only solution was to seek the thing that, in general, Edward hoped to avoid – a tax. This was a tricky proposition, for it ran counter to the policy of conciliation he had pursued during the early months of his rule. Obtaining consent to the imposition of customs had been one thing – the merchant class, compromised by contraband, had needed to strike a deal with the king. Obtaining consent to a general subsidy was, by contrast, a challenge of quite a different order, for it required the consent of the knights of the shire, and they felt no corresponding obligation to make concessions. It is true that, like the merchants, the knights had been summoned en masse to the first parliament of the reign, and, like the rest of the king's subjects, they must have been gladdened by the contents of the Statute of Westminster. By themselves, however, the new laws were evidently not enough to secure support for grant of taxation. Indeed, it is not impossible that Edward sought the knights' consent during his first parliament, only to be rebuffed. In spite of all the consultation and legislation, nothing had been done on the matter that still troubled these men most. The Statute of Westminster, for all its breadth, had been silent on the subject of England's Jews.[51]

This, of course, was by no means a new issue. It had been by introducing measures intended to limit the burden of Jewish moneylending that Edward had obtained his first crusade tax in 1270. The trouble was, however, that these provisions – and also certain subsequent ones made during Edward's absence – had not gone to the heart of the problem. The pernicious aspect of Jewish credit was not the business itself, but the dubious trade by which rich Christian speculators snapped up the estates of the indebted. The measures applied in 1270, while they had offered relief to some individuals by cancelling their debts, had imposed hardly any restriction on the illicit market; Jewish bonds continued to be bought and sold much as before, and small landowners continued to go under as result. Edward, in short, had raised expectations of relief, and charged handsomely for doing so, but his remedy had not worked. The knights of the shire had good reason to feel that in 1270 they had been sold a dud. Consequently, five years on, their complaint was more vociferous and to the point. If Edward wanted another vote of funds from parliament, he would have to provide a more effective solution to the Jewish problem.[52]

The king's answer, when it came, was certainly bold. In October 1275, under the terms of a brand-new statute, Jewish moneylending was banned altogether. 'The usuries of the Jews,' Edward declared in the statute's opening sentence, had led to 'many evils, and instances of the disinheriting of the good men of his land.' This was a move, in other words, intended in the first instance to win over the knights of the shire, and to this extent the new law was a great success. Published in the course of a parliament that assembled in October, the Statute of the Jewry was the essential concession that enabled Edward to levy his much-needed tax. With an assessment rate set at a fifteenth (6.6 per cent), the receipts were impressive. All told, it raised over £80,000 – enough to clear Edward's crusade debts and leave him comfortably in credit.[53]

The losers, of course, were the Jews. The new statute outlawed the practice that had been their economic mainstay since their first arrival in England some two centuries before. Without moneylending the Jewish community could not hope to survive for long. Edward and his advisers were not oblivious to this; indeed, they had given considerable thought to providing a remedy. Henceforth, the statute declared,

Jews were to live 'by lawful trade, and by their labour' – that is, they were permitted to set themselves up as merchants who might buy and sell with their Christian neighbours. There was nothing insincere in this ambitious attempt at social engineering: as far as Edward was concerned, he was being very conscientious about the whole business. Acknowledging that 'he and his ancestors have always received great benefit from the Jewish people in the past', the king took the Jews into his protection and granted them his peace. It was his will, he declared, 'that they may be safely preserved and defended by his sheriffs and other bailiffs and faithful men', and he further ordered 'that none shall do them harm or damage or wrong, in their bodies or in their goods'.[54]

To this extent, the statute recognised and tried to limit the effects of anti-Semitism, which was not merely universal in thirteenth-century England but increasing in its intensity. This was a society in which conscientious Christians strove to keep pace with the bigoted teaching of their religious leaders. Simon de Montfort, a well-known fanatic, may have gone beyond what was lawful in encouraging his supporters to attack and kill Jews in the 1260s, but his virulent hatred was otherwise a matter for praise. When, for example, at the start of his career in England, he had expelled the Jews from Leicester, it was an act expressly intended to save his and his family's souls, and carried out with the blessing of Robert Grosseteste, later bishop of Lincoln, and one of the greatest Christian theologians of his age. Moreover, it was far from being an exceptional initiative. Edward's mother, Eleanor of Provence, although happy enough to have extensive contact with the Jews in her financial dealings, nevertheless requested royal permission to expel them from her dower lands in 1275 – permission that was duly granted. Henry III and Louis IX, both outstandingly devoted sons of the Church, were both pioneering anti-Semites as a result. Louis has the distinction of being the first European king to ban the Jews from lending money (an act of 1235). Henry, meanwhile, was the first king of England to endorse (in 1255) the pernicious myth, English in its origin, that the Jews ritually murdered Christian children.[55]

And yet, even as it tacitly acknowledged this rampant hatred, the Statute of Jewry took steps that reinforced it. Conscious of the fact that by exhorting the Jews to do business with Christians he might be seen as encouraging exactly the kind of close relations that the Church so roundly condemned, Edward endeavoured to restrict such inter-action to a bare minimum. From now on, the new statute decreed, Jews were to live only in the king's towns and cities; no Christians were to live among them. And, so that there should be no confusion whatsoever on this score, every Jew above the age of seven was to wear 'a distinguishing mark on his outer garment' – a badge of yellow felt three inches by six inches, shaped like the two tablets of the Mosaic Law. Such badges had been a key recommendation of the Church for more than half a century.[56]

It was, therefore, highly unlikely that any Jews would survive, let alone prosper, 'by lawful trade' with their Christian neighbours. No one was more acutely aware of this than the Jews themselves. Shortly after its publication, they collectively petitioned Edward about the new law, pointing out the many disadvantages they would face in trying to compete with Christian traders, and beseeching him to allow them to live as they had before, 'in the time of his ancestors'. Their protest, however, was in vain. The statute stood, unmodified, in all its points. 'The good men of his land' had paid their king too high a price for it to be otherwise.[57]

When the autumn parliament of 1275 had ended, Edward left Westminster to spend a week at the Tower of London, where the direct correlation between the Crown's power and its newly re-established wealth was already making itself manifest. On the king's orders, the ancient fortress was being transformed in line with the latest developments in military thinking. This meant, above all, a massive expansion in the size of the site. Edward's intention was to give the Tower a 'concentric' design, creating multiple lines of defence, one inside the other. That summer hundreds of men – their wages for that year alone came to £2,500 – had begun filling the existing moat and digging its replacement, the giant trench that surrounds the Tower today. Interestingly, the building accounts reveal that the individual in charge was 'Brother John of the Order of St Thomas of Acre', an engineer evidently recruited in the Holy Land and perhaps the man responsible for Edward's building endeavours there. The moat, moreover, was only the first part of a major programme of redevelopment. Other experts were engaged in the more complicated business of completing the southern section of the new circuit, a task that involved extending the Tower's site out into the River Thames. To the west, meanwhile, construction had started on a series of gatehouses that together would form a new main entrance. And, amid all this military engineering, domestic concerns were not being neglected. Also under way from the summer of 1275 were a new set of royal apartments, St Thomas's Tower, which still survive more or less unaltered.[58]

If there was a target audience for this massive restatement of royal power, it was the citizens of London themselves, the restless rabble who had dared to challenge the Crown on several occasions during the previous reign. To them Edward evidently wished to send a clear message from the start. Elsewhere in England the new king may have chosen to present a conciliatory face, but when it came to the capital his aspect was deliberately one of intimidation. The enlarged Tower stood as a permanent warning to the Londoners that their recent behaviour was not to be repeated. As such, the new works there, like Edward's treatment of the Jews, introduced a discordant note of domination and intolerance to the otherwise harmonious fanfare that heralded the start of his reign.

It also signalled a dramatic shift in priorities. While the diggers and ditchers were beginning their noisy business on the eastern edge of the city, back in Westminster the stonemasons' hammers had fallen silent. The abandonment of Henry III's half-built abbey was yet another reminder that this was not simply a new reign, but a new political era.[59]

The early days of this new era did not pass without disappointment or distress. Not long after their return to England, Edward and Eleanor's eldest surviving son, Henry, had fallen seriously ill, and neither prayers nor medication had been sufficient to save him. He died in October 1274, leaving only one younger brother – Alfonso, not yet passed his first birthday – to take the place of heir apparent. Probably more distressing still for Edward was the sudden passing, in the early months of 1275, of both his sisters. Margaret and Beatrice, respectively queen of Scots and wife of the future duke of Brittany, were, in the words of one chronicler, 'women of great fame and in the flower of youth'. Both had been present with their husbands at the coronation, and their subsequent deaths, said the chronicler, converted the great joy of that occasion into great sadness.[60]

Nevertheless, these early days had been in every other respect quite astonishingly successful. Not for centuries had a king of England begun his reign so peacefully or auspiciously. This success was in large part down to Edward himself. By taking swift but well-considered action on a number of fronts – widespread public consultation, wide-ranging legislation, innovative financial reform – he had won the backing and the respect of his subjects. Or, as one chronicler put it at the time, 'bound the hearts of his people to him with an inestimable love'. Even the citizens of London, in spite of past differences, had welcomed their new king with much pomp on the eve of his coronation, and thrown a well-lubricated party on the day itself (the water conduit in Cheapside reportedly ran with red and white wine). Back in Westminster, meanwhile, the coronation ceremony had been followed by the coronation banquet, preparations for which had been under way for months. Royal orders for victuals reveal a feast of Solomonic proportions: dozens of peacocks, cranes and swans; hundreds of pigs, boar and oxen; thousands of chickens, rabbits, eels and lampreys. The Palace of Westminster had been especially extended and redecorated for the occasion at a cost of over £1,000, with temporary accommodation for the thousands of guests, and temporary kitchens to feed them.[61]

Anyone attending this feast would have been struck by more than just the splendour; equally striking was the extent to which the world had moved on. It was not just that one king had replaced another; the whole court had been renewed in recent years. Henry III lay in the abbey next door; Richard of Cornwall was interred at his own foundation at Hailes in Gloucestershire; the butchered remains of Simon de Montfort were buried in the abbey church at Evesham. Peter of Savoy, one of the dominant figures of the previous reign, had died in 1268; his brother, Boniface, the longest serving archbishop of Canterbury since the tenth century, in 1270. The only survivors of note from the old days were Eleanor of Provence and William de Valence, but neither was set to resume the controversial roles they had played earlier in their careers.[62]

As the old generation had passed away, a new one had risen to take its place. Edward himself, at thirty-five, was in his prime; Eleanor, at thirty-three, still fair and once again pregnant. Robert Burnell, the king's closest adviser, was probably around the same age, perhaps a little older. And as for the rest of the court, they were all similarly youthful. Of the ten earls then living in England, four were also in the mid-thirties, and four more in their twenties. The septuagenarian earl of Hereford would shortly be succeeded by his twentysomething grandson, which left the earl of Surrey feeling very old at forty-three.[63]

Edward and his companions had reached the point in their lives were they had ample experience – of politics, of war, of government, of life in general – yet at the same time they retained the vigour and energy to tackle the huge challenges that lay ahead. Their corporate character is captured perfectly by a tale (told somewhat later and therefore perhaps slightly improved with age) about the post-coronation celebrations. During the feast, we are assured, King Alexander of Scotland presented a little diversion of his own devising. A hundred of his knights appeared, alighted from their mounts, and then – to general delight – released them, so that anyone who caught a horse might keep it. Not to be outdone, a number of English earls, including the king's brother Edmund and the formerly fractious Gilbert de Clare, repeated the exercise, releasing several hundred more.[64]

Whatever the truth of the story, the coronation of Edward I had clearly been an occasion of great joy. And, as the presence of the king of Scots reminds us, simply everyone had been there to share in it.

Everyone, that is, except the prince of Wales.

5

The Disobedient Prince

It might seem strange – it is certainly ironic – that the earliest surviving evidence of preparation for Edward's coronation is a polite letter from Llywelyn ap Gruffudd acknowledging receipt of his invitation. Given the differences between the two men in the not-too-distant past, one might well wonder why the Welshman was even included on the guest list. The full story of their relationship, however, has yet to be told.[1]

We parted company with Llywelyn in 1263 at a moment of great triumph. In September that year the self-proclaimed prince had finally captured the royal castles at Dyserth and Deganwy, thereby achieving an objective that had occupied him since the start of his war against the English some seven years earlier. Henry III had spent thousands of pounds on these new fortresses, intending that they should secure his grip on the Four Cantrefs, his 'new conquest in Wales'. But, thanks to the comprehensive destruction wrought by Llywelyn that autumn, all that remains today of these once mighty buildings is a few scattered rocks. After their fall, the prince's power in Wales was entirely uncontested.[2]

Edward might have avenged these assaults had it not been for Simon de Montfort. As it was, that same summer saw Montfort supersede Llywelyn as Edward's principal *bête noire*. Not that Llywelyn was forgotten or forgiven in the course of the struggle that followed. During the next two years the prince compounded his crimes by lending material support to Montfort, though he had the good sense not to turn up for the fatal encounter at Evesham.[3]

It was in the months immediately after the civil war that the long-standing quarrel was officially patched up. Edward, as part of his preparations for crusade, became a signatory to the peace his father agreed with Llywelyn in 1267. This provided the occasion for what was apparently their first meeting, and it evidently marked the beginning of some sort of personal understanding. Two years later, after they had met for a second time, Llywelyn wrote to Henry III that he had been 'delighted' by Edward's visit. Similarly, once Edward had departed for the East, the king could write to Llywelyn and describe his son as 'the friend of the prince'. Relations, therefore, were cordial. There was nothing insincere or implausible about Edward's wish to have Llywelyn attend his coronation.[4]

And yet, in the event, the Welsh leader chose not to come. To understand why – and why his absence was significant – we need to travel back to 1267, and the peace that was made between England and Wales.

By the summer of 1267 it had become clear to even the most insensible Englishmen that peace with Wales was no longer an option but a necessity. Henry III, for example, had once hoped to reverse Llywelyn's conquests, and for this reason had long refused to grant the prince anything more than a series of temporary truces. Four years of civil discord in England, however, had forced him to reconsider his position. With his subjects bitterly divided and his treasury completely drained, the king realised that he had no option but to recognise the reality of Llywelyn's power. In August 1267 he took his court, including both his sons, to the Welsh border, and began for the first time to negotiate in earnest.

The outcome, the so-called Treaty of Montgomery, handed to Llywelyn almost all the prizes he had sought since the start of his career. The Four Cantrefs of Perfeddwlad, his first and most significant conquest, were officially surrendered; so too was Edward's castle and lordship of Builth, snatched in the summer of 1260. These and other territorial gains, however, constituted only one part of the package: equally momentous was the English king's acceptance of Llywelyn's supremacy throughout Wales as a whole. The homages of other Welsh lords, which Henry had once claimed as his own, were now ceded to Llywelyn, making him truly the master of his country.

Lastly, in accordance with his pre-eminent status, Llywelyn was afforded recognition of the title he had selected for himself back in 1258. In the words of the Treaty of Montgomery itself, drawn up by delegates on 25 September, 'the king, wishing to magnify the person of Llywelyn,' granted that 'Llywelyn and his heirs shall be, and shall be called, princes of Wales'. This was indeed the glittering jewel in the Welsh leader's new crown, for such recognition had never been afforded to any of his predecessors, not even his namesake grandfather, Llywelyn the Great.

When, therefore, the peace process at Montgomery was concluded four days later, it represented a climax not merely for Llywelyn but for his dynasty as a whole. He and Henry came face to face, probably at the ancient ford across the River Severn where their ancestors had been accustomed to meet in times past, in order that the newly minted prince could perform his homage. Llywelyn knelt before the king of England with pleasure. This act of subservience promised to cement his achievement, and thus marked the greatest moment to date in his astonishingly successful career.[5]

The problem was that a lasting peace between England and Wales required more than the restoration of cordial relations between Henry and Llywelyn, or, for that matter, between the prince and the king's eldest son. It also depended on a similar degree of civility being maintained between Llywelyn and his immediate neighbours, and this was an altogether more ambitious aspiration. The Marcher lordships that fringed the heartlands of native Wales were, almost by their very nature, opposed to the preservation of such stability; in general, their owners were inclined by temperament and tradition to expand their power at Welsh expense. In 1267 the chances of peace in this turbulent arena looked even more remote than usual, for all the recent expansion had been achieved by Llywelyn. During the course of his struggle with the English Crown, the prince had carried war into the March and occupied large swathes of territory. The drafters of the Treaty of Montgomery had done their best to address the disputes that had arisen as a result; it was agreed in general terms that Llywelyn would restore all the Marcher lands he had taken. There were, however, certain named exceptions that the prince was permitted to retain, much to the chagrin of their former owners. Worse still, there were ominous silences in the treaty, which suggest that some disputes had been too contentious even to consider for inclusion. The lords of these areas were not about to take their losses to Llywelyn lying down.[6]

The most glaring omission from the new peace was any mention of the argument already brewing between the prince and Gilbert de Clare, earl of Gloucester. Gilbert, as we have seen, was an irascible young man, enormously powerful and determined in defence of his rights. After the recent civil war in England, his sense of self-importance must have been running more than usually high – he was, after all, the only figure of consequence to have fought on the winning side at both Lewes *and* Evesham. He was, therefore, unlikely to disregard what he saw as an unwarranted intrusion into his lands in south Wales by Llywelyn: at the beginning of 1267, the prince had pushed into Gilbert's lordship of Glamorgan. In April the following year, therefore, the earl responded in kind, moving his men into the disputed region and commencing the construction of a new castle.[7]

The fear that this escalating row would upset the fragile peace was what brought Edward back to Montgomery in the summer of 1269 for his second meeting with Llywelyn. It is further proof of the amicable turn their relationship had taken in the wake of the treaty that Edward actually favoured the prince in his arbitration, accepting his right to hold some of Gilbert's territory. The earl, when he learned of this, was furious – it became one of his chief grievances in the subsequent row with Edward that threatened to derail their planned crusade, and dictated one of the key provisions in their subsequent peace agreement. Gilbert agreed that he would follow Edward east, but only on condition that Henry III intervened in Wales and sorted out the earl's quarrel with Llywelyn.[8]

Gilbert never set sail. On 13 October 1270, just a few weeks after Edward's departure, Llywelyn invaded Glamorgan and destroyed the earl's new castle. From that point on, their dispute became a matter of pure force, and the earl proved that he could deliver an enormous punch. In 1271 he was back in possession of his lordship, and work on his castle was resumed. The scale of his effort can still be appreciated today, for the fortress he fashioned – Caerphilly – remains one of the mightiest examples of medieval architecture, and was at that time the single greatest castle in the British Isles (its concentric design predated Edward's similar work at the Tower of London by several years). Llywelyn swore he would destroy it, but in the end his resources proved unequal to the task. By 1273, Caerphilly was almost completed, and it was clear that Gilbert had won their struggle.[9]

From that point on Llywelyn's problems began to multiply. The failure of his speculative expansion into Glamorgan and the earl of Gloucester's success in resisting it, encouraged other Marcher lords to start trying their luck in the hope of reversing the prince's earlier gains, even those ones supposedly guaranteed to him by the Treaty of Montgomery. Humphrey de Bohun, for example, heir to the earldom of Hereford, began in 1273 to reassert with force his ancestral claim to Brecon, operating in conjunction with several of his Marcher neighbours. This was a clear violation of the treaty's terms but, following the death of Henry III, Llywelyn found it almost impossible to ensure that those terms were properly enforced. It was not so much that royal government was weaker after the old king's departure – Henry had hardly been much more effective while he was alive; rather the problem lay in the inherent bias of the regency regime. There were good reasons behind Edward's decision to include his old friend Roger Mortimer on his team of caretaker-governors; Montfort's killer was a strong man to have holding the reins of power. Yet Mortimer, as the most pugnacious Marcher lord of all, was unlikely to lend a sympathetic ear to any complaints from Llywelyn, his long-time enemy. Nor, more surprisingly, were his fellow regents, not even the normally judicious Robert Burnell. Their conniving collective mindset in the case of Humphrey de Bohun's illegal intervention in Brecon is strikingly revealed in a surviving letter. Having inspected the Treaty of Montgomery, Burnell discovered that, alas, 'the land of Brecon' had indeed been ceded to the prince of Wales; but, as he went on to explain to Mortimer, nothing was written about who should hold the *castles* in the region. It was, therefore, 'very expedient to defend them, and to give effective assistance for their defence'. Unsurprisingly, Llywelyn took the view that his right to Brecon comprehended the possession of the fortifications within it, and continued with his efforts to expel Bohun and his allies. The regents responded by adopting a morally superior tone, declaring themselves shocked that the prince 'had presumed to besiege and occupy the castles', and tut-tutting that his behaviour led to 'the very great disturbance of the peace'.[10]

Thus the antagonisms between Llywelyn and the Marchers, exacerbated by the attitude of the regents, continued to mount. The summer of 1273 saw what amounted to an arms race between the prince and Roger Mortimer, with both men rushing to build or repair castles in the vicinity of Montgomery. When the regents, writing in the king's name, ordered the prince to cease construction of his new castle at Dolforwyn, his response was brilliantly contemptuous. 'We received letters in your majesty's name,' he began, 'but we are sure that they did not have your consent.' Nevertheless, for all his mocking, his letter to the absent Edward contains one sentiment that was undoubtedly sincere. 'If you were present in your kingdom, *as we hope*, such an order would not have been sent.' Llywelyn knew that the best chance for détente between England and Wales was Edward's swift return.[11]

Why, then, did he pointedly snub the king by failing to attend his coronation? The answer must be in part that Anglo-Welsh relations had deteriorated to such an extent by August 1274 that the prince would not have felt safe travelling to the ceremony. There was, however, another reason for his decision to stay away that day. Llywelyn had an additional difficulty, bigger even than his dispute with the Marchers, a problem so fundamental that it can be summed up in a single word: Wales.

Today Wales is celebrated for its untamed natural beauty. Forests, fast-flowing rivers and mountains: all are marketed to tourists in search of splendid scenery and adventure. In the Middle Ages the landscape excited much the same kind of response. Llywelyn's great-great-grandfather, Hywel ab Owain Gwynedd, was given to writing poetry in praise of his homeland. 'I love its beaches and its mountains,' he declared, 'its water meadows and its valleys,' before going on to enumerate a few more of his favourite things: its soldiers, its horses, and, of course, 'its lovely women'.[12]

No doubt his great-great-grandson enjoyed listening to such songs at his court and shared the sentiments they expressed. However, for a man who wanted to build a strong, united state, the Welsh landscape was an enormous hindrance. A more prosaic and analytical twelfth-century writer summed up the problem precisely. 'Because of its high mountains, deep valleys and extensive forests,' wrote Gerald of Wales, 'not to mention its rivers and marches, Wales is not of easy access.' Such natural obstacles frustrated travel and communication, rendering government slow and laborious. The Welsh landscape, in short, promoted division rather than unity.[13]

A more serious problem for the rulers of Wales, which flowed from the landscape, was the state of the Welsh economy. Mountains and forests might move men to poetry, but they are not terribly productive in financial terms. Llywelyn, in a letter written at the very end of his career, candidly admitted as much, contrasting the 'fertile and abundant land in England' with 'the barren and uncultivated land due to him by hereditary right'. Of course, upland to a certain height could be used for pasturage, and this was an important mainstay of the Welsh economy, but in many other respects Wales was severely underdeveloped. There were, for instance, almost no towns worthy of note. The amount of coin in circulation was extremely limited, and what little currency there was came from England. Matters were starting to improve somewhat in Llywelyn's day, thanks in part to the attempts that he and his immediate ancestors had made to foster and encourage trade. Change, however, was exceedingly slow in coming, and the returns were meagre in the extreme. To take one particularly telling example, it has been calculated that Llywelyn's total customs revenue was around £17 a year – hardly a lordly sum, never mind a princely one, but above all a figure that pales into utter insignificance when compared with the annual £10,000 that Edward collected in England.[14]

The comparative poverty of Wales would not have been such a problem for Llywelyn had he not set such a high value on being a prince. Unfortunately, the Treaty of Montgomery had come at a hefty premium. Since the 1250s Llywelyn's desire to have his title recognised by Henry III had led him to offer the king larger and larger sums of money.

When his status was finally admitted in 1267, the price of acknowledgement was fixed at 25,000 marks (£16,667). Llywelyn agreed that, after an initial down payment of 5,000 marks, he would pay off the remainder at a rate of 3,000 marks (£2,000) a year. This was, to say the least, a plan predicated on an extremely optimistic assessment of his spending power. A generous modern estimate of his income suggests that it might have peaked in the 1260s at around £6,000 a year. At the very least, therefore, the prince had agreed to forego a third of his annual revenue, possible more, and this at a time when he was having to find extra money to defend a much-enlarged border, building and garrisoning castles like Dolforwyn.[15]

Llywelyn, in short, had mortgaged his principality at a rate that was impossibly high. As early as 1270 he was having difficulty keeping up with repayments, and the following year he stopped paying altogether. By the time Edward returned he was three years in arrears. Of course, the prince himself would never admit that this descent into debt was caused by his insurmountable financial difficulties. Instead, he chose to maintain that non-payment was a political decision – retaliation for the English government's failure to address his grievances. 'The money is ready to be paid to your attorneys,' he wrote to the regents in February 1274, 'provided that . . . you compel the earl of Gloucester, Humphrey de Bohun and the other Marchers to restore to us the lands they have unjustly occupied.' But this was bluff and bluster. Later complaints about his oppressive rule show that Llywelyn was relying on increasingly extortionate methods to raise money; the notion that he was sitting on a big pile of treasure in 1274 is ludicrous. The reality was that by this date he had bled his principality dry and could not afford to have his grievances settled. What he needed was renegotiation with England, and this explains the provocative stance he took against its new king.[16]

For the same financial reasons, Edward, when he finally returned to England, was prepared to be extremely patient with Llywelyn. His crusading debts were so great that he was willing to overlook the prince's snub if it meant getting his hands on the outstanding cash. As early as December 1272 the regents had stressed in their letters to Llywelyn that their master was in urgent need of the annual payment because he was 'bound to diverse creditors in a great sum of money'. Edward's own attitude is revealed in a letter he sent in the spring after his return to the sheriff of Shropshire, who was charged with bringing an end to the ongoing hostilities in the March. When the king stressed that 'he did not want Llywelyn to have any reason for complaining about the settlement made', and urged the sheriff to 'act with circumspection' to ensure that the prince was satisfied, the logic was clear enough: if Llywelyn had no reason to complain, he would have no excuse not to pay up.[17]

Despite the fact that the two men evidently viewed the annual render for Montgomery in very different terms, it was not impossible that a compromise solution might have been found. Edward was not averse in principle to negotiation over repayments (certain English magnates, for example, were pushed at the start of the reign to acknowledge their debts to the Crown, but also granted reasonable terms to pay them off). In the autumn of 1274, just a few months after the coronation, Edward and Llywelyn were scheduled to meet at Shrewsbury. Had they done so, perhaps a similar amicable arrangement might have been devised, and the good relations that had obtained a few years earlier might have been rekindled. In the event, however, this meeting never took place; a few days before they were due to meet Edward fell ill and was unable to attend. Then, just a few days later, Llywelyn discovered that his difficulties ran far deeper than he had ever dared to imagine.[18]

The prince was, in general, under no illusion about his diminishing popularity within Wales, especially in certain quarters. Earlier in 1274 he had uncovered a plot against him led by Gruffudd ap Gwenwynwyn, lord of Powys, a man who had long resisted the expansion of Gwynedd and resented having to kowtow to Llywelyn. Gruffudd had paid for this disloyalty – the prince had obliged him to surrender some of his lands, as well as his son, as guarantees of future good behaviour – but, all told, Llywelyn's retribution had been mild, suggesting that he had not at the time realised the full extent of the conspiracy against him. Only in November, following a full confession from Gruffudd's son, did he understand the true enormity of the plotters' intentions. Their plan, it emerged, was not just independence for Powys, but death for the prince himself. And their leader was not Gruffudd ap Gwenwynwyn. It was Llywelyn's own brother, Dafydd.[19]

Dafydd ap Gruffudd, the youngest of Llywelyn's four brothers, has a poor reputation among modern historians of Wales, and not without reason: when it came to treachery, Dafydd had all the makings of a serial offender. Over a decade beforehand, he had abandoned Llywelyn's war with England and defected to support Edward; earlier still, in the course of the original struggle for supremacy in Gwynedd, he had opposed Llywelyn by siding with their eldest brother, Owain. And yet, in the wake of both these unsuccessful adventures, Dafydd had not merely been forgiven, but rewarded into the bargain. In 1256 Llywelyn granted him lands in the newly conquered Four Cantrefs, and in 1267, following their second reconciliation, these lands were restored.[20] Given Dafydd's unreliable record, such lenient treatment might seem like evidence of indulgence or even naivety on the prince's part, and there may have been an element of both in his attempts to deal with Dafydd. The basic fact was, however, that Llywelyn was struggling against the Welsh custom of partibility – that ancient obstacle to unity as impassable as the mountains and forests. Dafydd was Llywelyn's younger brother, and in Wales even younger brothers expected a share of the ancestral estate. By granting him lands elsewhere in Wales, the prince seems to have hoped that he might persuade Dafydd to drop his demand for a portion of Gwynedd. Now, in 1274, he realised that this strategy had failed. Dafydd still regarded himself as hard done by, and could clearly count on the support of other disaffected Welshmen, like Gruffudd ap Gwenwynwyn, to help him prosecute his claim.

The immediate problem for Llywelyn in 1274 was not the discovery of his younger brother's latest treachery but its wider effects. As soon as their plot had been exposed, Dafydd and Gruffudd fled across the border into England, and this led to an immediate deterioration in Anglo-Welsh relations.[21] The prince demanded that the conspirators be handed over at once, claiming that their reception was contrary to the terms of the Treaty of Montgomery. In actual fact it was not: Llywelyn had promised not to receive English fugitives, but all that the English had promised in return was not to furnish his enemies with material support. In any case, the legal merits of the prince's complaint hardly mattered. Edward must have reasoned that in Dafydd and Gruffudd he had acquired a useful bargaining chip, which might be used to counter Llywelyn's assertion that he was deliberately withholding his treaty payments. More to the point was the fact that, as it stood in the winter of 1274–75, the king had no formal obligation to the prince whatsoever, for Llywelyn had yet to appear before Edward and perform his homage.[22]

It was on this issue that Llywelyn made his biggest blunder. As we have seen, he had no objection in principal to acknowledging the English Crown's superior lordship. At the ford of Montgomery in 1267 he had been only too happy to kneel before Henry III and become his man. Homage in this context was hardly a recent innovation; Llywelyn's predecessors, and other Welsh lords, had been doing the same for generations. As Matthew Paris had once rhetorically demanded, 'who does not know that the prince of Wales is a petty vassal of the king of England?'[23]

Since Henry's death, however, Llywelyn had begun to link the question of his vassal status, like the question of his financial contributions, to the resolution of his grievances. For this reason he had not even performed the basic first step of swearing fealty, or fidelity, to Edward in his absence. When, early in 1273, the regents had sent ambassadors to the border expressly for this purpose, the prince had failed to appear before them.

Edward, to his credit, did not attach too much importance to this initial dereliction of duty on Llywelyn's part, just as he chose to ignore the prince's failure to attend his coronation. His desire to see good relations restored – and payment made – meant that he was prepared to go to considerable lengths to sort the matter out. In 1274, until prevented by illness, he had been ready to travel to the border to meet Llywelyn; the following year he was ready to do so again. In the summer of 1275 the king and his court made their way north to Chester, where Llywelyn had been told to come and render his due obedience.[24]

The prince did not appear. As he explained in a letter, he considered that it was unsafe for him to travel into England, where his enemies were being sheltered. There was evidently some sincerity in this: Llywelyn was hovering close to the border as he wrote, seemingly in the hope that Edward would go the extra mile and come to meet him there.[25]

As far as the king was concerned, however, he had gone quite far enough. The suggestion that his court was an unsafe place was insulting, for it implied that his word was not to be trusted. Much more offensive was the challenge to his authority. Llywelyn's homage was not a conditional thing about which they might debate indefinitely; it was a non-negotiable necessity, already long overdue. Yet it looks very much as if the prince now began to suggest precisely the opposite, giving out that his homage would be forthcoming only once Edward had remedied all his grievances in the March.[26]

Such insubordination was not to be tolerated. Edward was not about to make his father's mistake of allowing the authority of the Crown to be disrespected in this way. After waiting in vain at Chester for more than a week, the king finally gave up and began his journey south – 'in a rage', as one Welsh chronicler noted. He felt he had gone out of his way to oblige Llywelyn, and that for his efforts he had been gratuitously insulted, even to the point of humiliation. 'In order to receive his homage and fealty,' he later wrote to the pope, 'we so demeaned our royal dignity as to travel to the confines of his land.'[27]

Chester clearly marks a turning point in relations between Edward and Llywelyn. From that point on it is difficult to see how their personal relationship could have been repaired. Before he left the city in September, the king bluntly instructed the prince to present himself at Westminster the following month. Llywelyn, of course, did not appear – his dignity too was now at stake.[28]

And yet, despite his well-attested rage, Edward took no retributive action. The Treaty of Montgomery had taken a long time to negotiate, and Llywelyn still owed a great deal of money for it. Pride prevented the king from making any more friendly overtures to the prince, but in late November he was still writing to his officials in the March, urging them to see that there was no fighting in the region, and stating categorically that he wanted the peace 'to be well maintained'. It took a final, astoundingly provocative act on Llywelyn's part to make him change his mind.[29]

At some stage in 1275 – the precise date is sadly unknown – the prince of Wales decided to get married. From an abstract, dynastic point of view, this might have been regarded as a sensible decision. Llywelyn, although now in his early fifties, was still a bachelor, and had no sons, legitimate or otherwise, to succeed him. His heir was the treacherous Dafydd, and it may have been his younger brother's defection that belatedly spurred the prince in the direction of matrimony.

From the point of view of Anglo-Welsh relations, however, Llywelyn's marriage was the last nail in his coffin, for his intended bride was Eleanor de Montfort, daughter of the late Earl Simon. This match may have been contemplated a decade earlier, when Montfort was in power and in alliance with the prince; its resurrection in 1275 was certainly guaranteed to stir up trouble. At best a tit-for-tat response to Edward's sheltering of the Welsh fugitives, it may have been much more – an attempt to stoke the ashes of the recent English civil war, in the hope of sparking the conflict back into life. When, at the very end of 1275, Eleanor set out in secret from her home in France, the ship that carried her across the Channel had the arms and banner of the Montforts hidden beneath its boards. They were found there by the king's agents, who captured the vessel and its passenger on the high seas.[30]

The scale of Edward's anger on discovering Llywelyn's intentions is not hard to imagine. The Montforts may seem like a spent force in retrospect, but in the 1270s this was not nearly so apparent; at that time memories of the divisive war were still vivid, and its re-ignition was precisely what the authorities in England feared. More importantly, the mere mention of the name of Montfort must have touched the rawest of nerves as far as the king himself was concerned. Apart from his own humiliating experiences at the hands of Earl Simon, Edward also had to consider the unforgivable murder of his cousin, Henry of Almain, by Montfort's sons. His reaction to the foiled marriage speaks for itself. Eleanor de Montfort was kept in close captivity at Windsor for the next three years; her clerical brother and escort, Amaury, was cast into prison at Corfe, where he waited twice as long for the royal wrath to cool. Most significant, however, was the king's retaliation against the disappointed bridegroom. All efforts to preserve the peace with Llywelyn were now abandoned. From the start of 1276 the Marchers were encouraged to renew their attacks, and Welsh fugitives were finally granted material aid. A cold war between England and Wales was begun.[31]

A full-blown war was on the agenda. Edward also marked the new year by sending a final summons to Llywelyn to come to Westminster in April and perform his homage. If the prince did not appear, he was warned, the king would consider the matter in parliament – the clear implication being that parliament would provide a verdict that would legitimise military action. Llywelyn, of course, did not come. He had made his decision to defy Edward at Chester the previous summer based on the erroneous assumption that the king was already bent on war. When Edward's ultimatum arrived it merely confirmed in the prince's mind what he had suspected all along.[32]

Llywelyn, for his part, professed not to want war. On the very day that Edward had left Chester in anger, the prince had written to the pope, asking him to intervene lest new discord should arise between England and Wales, 'which God forbid'. In a similar spirit, he approached the archbishop of Canterbury, Robert Kilwardby, in the weeks between receiving the king's final summons and its April deadline. Their correspondence during the summer shows Llywelyn struggling to maintain the peace in spite of the attacks being launched into Wales by the Marcher lords. 'We have strictly ordered all our vassals and other men to commit no trespasses in the lands of the king or in any part of the March,' he told the archbishop in June, and other evidence proves that this was indeed the case. Such efforts indicate that the prince's wish for peace was far from insincere.[33]

And yet, at the same time, Llywelyn was determined to take a stand. While his letters to the archbishop stressed his restraint, those he sent to the king simply complained of his sufferings at the hands of the Marchers and demanded justice.[34] For all the prince's earnest declarations in favour of peace, one cannot dispel the feeling that a strong part of him relished the prospect of a straight fight. In contrast to his fruitless diplomatic efforts in recent years, Llywelyn's earlier military career had been one of unbroken success. His brothers, his rivals, the English – all had been roundly defeated as a result of his celebrated prowess. The royal host that had marched into Wales some two decades earlier had failed to dislodge him. The man who now threatened him had done so many times in the past, and on each occasion he had failed. His earlier victories gave the prince his confidence. If he did not want a war, it is equally plain that he did not fear it either.

And so war was declared. In spite of the prince's non-appearance at Easter, Edward stayed his hand in the course of the summer of 1276, perhaps at the bidding of the archbishop, who clearly still believed at that stage that a peaceful outcome was possible. By the autumn, however, the king could wait no more. On 12 November, as that autumn's parliament drew to a close, Edward consulted with the great men of his realm, and the decision was taken. The prince of Wales was pronounced 'a rebel and a disturber of the peace'. The king and his men would go against him.[35]

Even then war was not utterly inevitable. There could be no invasion of Wales during the winter: Edward's verdict indicated that his army would not assemble until midsummer the following year. It is not impossible that this long delay was deliberately contrived, a final concession to an archbishop still endeavouring to find a peaceful solution. Either way, by passing sentence so late in the season, the king effectively gave the condemned man one last chance to escape his punishment.

The prince, certainly, was not slow in coming forward with last-minute proposals for peace. In some respects these were outrageously generous. At the start of 1277 he offered to pay 11,000 marks (£7,333) for Edward's grace – this to be in addition to the money he still owed for the Treaty of Montgomery. But Llywelyn's letters of supplication still came laced with demands: he wanted the treaty confirmed; he wanted its terms upheld; he wanted his wife released. It all amounted to the same thing: the prince wanted to submit on his own terms, and this the king would never accept. As the hour of reckoning approached, the unmistakable spirit of defiance remained. Early in the new year the archbishop of Canterbury finally abandoned his efforts after his envoys were turned away from Llywelyn's court; on 10 February, as a result, the prince was excommunicated. Only in his last letter to Edward, dated 21 February, did Llywelyn come close to adopting the unconditional tone that the king required.

'We swear before God,' he wrote, 'that we love and esteem your illustrious person more truly, more faithfully and more intimately than those who incite your spirit to indignation against us.'

'We will be of greater value to you,' he concluded, 'than those who, by your war, now attempt to gain their own profit and advantage rather than your honour.'[36]

But by then it was too late. War was already upon him.

Even as Llywelyn was drafting his last proposals for peace, his adversary was advancing towards him with hostile intent. Edward may not have intended to lead an army in person until the summer, but he had plenty of other resources that he could marshal in the meantime. In January he moved west to Worcester in order to supervise their deployment.[37]

Chief among these resources was his own household. Since he had become king, Edward's domestic establishment had grown to somewhere in the region of 600 people. The increase in size was a precondition of his new role. Medieval monarchs were no different from modern heads of state in needing extensive entourages to magnify their importance. As a consequence, the household was dressed to impress: one of the ways we are able to gauge its size is through surviving records that reveal the twice-annual distribution of robes to its (mostly male) members. Wherever Edward went, this splendid retinue went too, trotting after him on horseback and trundling along in carts. And in their wake followed others – merchants, players, beggars, prostitutes – all drawn by the household's unrivalled ability to disgorge money. As it made its ceaseless way around the country, it resembled nothing so much as a small army on the move.[38]

The resemblance was far from coincidental. While many household men – cooks, carters, clerks, grooms, doctors, tailors, huntsmen – had non-military roles, those individuals who really stood out, arrayed in the finest clothes and seated on the noblest horses, were the household knights, and their primary purpose was violence. A personal bodyguard for the king in times of peace, they were also effectively a standing army, an elite unit that formed the core of any force when the king went to war. The same was true of their lesser counterparts, the esquires and sergeants of the household, whose day-to-day tasks might be more menial, but whose fundamental function was also to fight. Together, both groups proved that the household, for all its elaborate routines and courtly veneer, was a direct descendant of the warrior band of an earlier era. Numbers tended to fluctuate, but on average the king employed around fifty knights and around two to three times as many esquires and sergeants. This meant that in general a quarter to a third of the royal household were experienced military men who could be deployed at short notice. In the immediate circumstances of January 1277, it meant that Edward was able to detach from his side some forty knights and seventy esquires to begin operations on the ground for the coming war in Wales.[39]

The size of Edward's household, and the proportion of warriors within it, were neither new nor unusual: Henry III had at times maintained an entourage of similar size and composition. Fighting may have been the ultimate *raison d'être* of a household knight, but they were

versatile creatures, well suited to other functions – a special intervention in some distant part of the realm, a delicate diplomatic mission
overseas. All kings had use of such men. If, however, there was a difference between the households of Henry III and his son, it surely lay in
their sense of purpose and in the reputation they had already earned.
Edward's knights shared a strong *esprit de corps*, forged from their common
experience in arms. Many of them had served Edward since his youth.
They had fought together in tournaments, campaigned together in war,
travelled together to the Holy Land and back. Strong bonds of love
and loyalty bound them to each other and to the man they now served
as their king.

What was true of the household was equally true of Edward's newly
appointed captains of war. A cursory glance at their names reveals that
the king's other great resource was his long-established friendship with
a wide circle of formidable warriors. Roger Mortimer, assigned to
command the royal forces in the middle March, was a choice so obvious
as to require no further explanation. Based at Montgomery, his role
was essentially to continue his existing private war with Llywelyn, albeit
in Edward's name and with the Crown's financial backing. Supporting
him in the same region were other men with equally distinguished
records of service. Roger Clifford, for example, was both Mortimer's
neighbour and one of the king's oldest associates – his entrée had been
occasioned by Llywelyn's first war over two decades before, and he had
celebrated his fiftieth birthday with Edward on crusade. Otto de
Grandson and John de Vescy, also appointed to the middle March, were
likewise veteran crusaders, as was Payn de Chaworth, the young man
whom Edward had assigned to command his forces in the south, and
who had been harassing Llywelyn from his castle at Kidwelly since the
spring of the previous year. William de Beauchamp, earl of Warwick,
was only marginally less qualified for his role as commander of the
northern forces. A man much the same age as Edward, Beauchamp had
evidently commended himself through his support for the royalists
during the civil war, and by his recent services in negotiating with
Llywelyn on the king's behalf. In fact, of all the men placed in positions of trust in Wales, only Henry de Lacy, the twenty-seven-year-old
earl of Lincoln, appears to have lacked any prior experience. The fact
that he had grown up in the household of Edward's mother no doubt
explains the earl's closeness to the king, and hence his appointment as
one of Mortimer's lieutenants.[40]

Lacy apart, Edward's commanders were thus well rehearsed for the
roles the king wanted them to play. To a large extent his declaration
of war on Llywelyn simply meant that the old firm established in the

1260s was back in business. These were men whom Edward could trust to start the conflict on his behalf. At the end of January 1277, after taking counsel with his friends for a final time, the king left the border and left them to it.[41]

Assaults began at once on all fronts. In the south Payn de Chaworth advanced from the royal castle at Carmarthen into the same region where, twenty years earlier, Edward's forces had been completely obliterated by Welsh attack. In the north, meanwhile, the earl of Warwick, operating in tandem with Dafydd ap Gruffudd, pushed out from his base at Chester and into Powys, where he encountered stiff resistance at Castell Dinas Brân. The fiercest fighting, however, seems to have occurred in the middle March, where Llywelyn concentrated his resources in the hope of opposing the onset of Roger Mortimer from Montgomery. Mortimer's objective was the prince's newly completed castle at Dolforwyn, and Llywelyn was determined that he should not achieve it.[42]

While his friends and the troops of his household began to drive into the principality of Wales, Edward was attending to the preparations for his own advent in the summer. These were, in the first instance, spiritual. Even as Mortimer and company were hacking their way into hostile territory and raining down arrows on Dolforwyn, the king was touring the quiet countryside of East Anglia in order to pray before the shrines and relics at Walsingham, Bromholm and St Faiths. His thoughts, though, were rarely far from matters military. During the same month of pilgrimage, for example, Edward ordered no fewer than 200,000 crossbow bolts from the chief centre of their manufacture, St Briavel's Castle in the Forest of Dean. At the same time, royal agents were active in France, buying up warhorses for the king's use, and carts were being requisitioned from abbeys and priories in order to transport his tents from London to Wales. Henry III had failed in his fight against Llywelyn by rushing into north Wales unprepared. Here, as elsewhere, Edward was determined not to make his father's mistakes.[43]

By May the king had returned to Westminster and a parliament buzzing with the news of his lieutenants' success. Payn de Chaworth had won over south Wales using a combination of force and negotiation: in a letter to Edward he indicated that the Welsh lords of his region would soon be heading towards England, ready to acknowledge the king as their new master. In like manner the earl of Warwick and his Welsh allies had recovered all of Powys – Dinas Brân had been abandoned by 10 May – and its former lord, the conspirator Gruffudd ap Gwenwynwyn, was back in possession. Perhaps the most symbolic victory had been won in the middle March, where Roger Mortimer and his companions had taken Dolforwyn at the start of April after a siege that had lasted only a week (signs of the castle's bombardment are still apparent from its surviving masonry). By the middle of May, when Mortimer wrote to Edward, it was essentially to report the total collapse of Llywelyn's power in the March. It was a sure sign of how much had been achieved that several of the king's commanders – Chaworth, Clifford and Vescy – were able to leave their posts in order to attend parliament in person. In the space of a few short months almost all of Llywelyn's earlier conquests had been reversed. In southern and central Wales the prince's vassals, tired of his extortionate rule, had deserted in droves and were preparing to fight against him. For the English it remained only to tackle Gwynedd, and the prince himself. Now that the summer was approaching, the time for that task was at hand. And, thanks to his careful preparations, Edward was now ready.[44]

On 3 July the king arrived in Worcester to meet the force with which he intended to reduce Llywelyn to submission. Six months earlier, the same city had seen him deploy the crack troops of his household. Now it was host to all the remaining cavalry he had the ability to command. Which is to say, in response to Edward's earlier orders, the great men of his kingdom had turned out in all their power and splendour.

Ever since the Norman Conquest (and very likely well before) all those in England who held their lands directly from the king had been obliged to provide him with military service when he demanded it. The men assembled in Worcester in the summer of 1277 were there because Edward, on the same day that he had declared Llywelyn 'a rebel and disturber of the peace', had simultaneously summoned 'all who held of the king "in chief", and owed him service . . . to be at Worcester . . . with horses and arms'.[45]

Had Edward relied solely on obligation, his cavalry host would have been a small one. Naturally, the number of warriors each landowner was expected to provide varied according to the number of estates he or she held, but, thanks to a fairly recent adjustment, the numbers themselves were very low. In earlier centuries the burden of military service had been heavy indeed: at the time of the Conquest, two hundred years before, the king's greatest tenants had been expected to furnish him with dozens of knights when required. It was during the reign of Henry III that these long-established obligations had been drastically reduced, probably in deference to the rising costs of knightly arms and armour. As a consequence, many men were obliged to serve only in their own person, or perhaps with one other companion. Even the very greatest individuals – the earls – had knightly quotas that for the most part could be expressed in single figures.[46]

Luckily for Edward, however, his great men shared his own attitude in their need to have magnificent entourages. An earl might be required to provide only half a dozen horsemen when the king called him to war, but his stature and sense of self-worth demanded that he be surrounded by many times that number. Most of Edward's earls typically rode to war with at least thirty knights and esquires in tow, and in some instances twice that number. Other great landowners also brought contingents well in excess of their nominal quotas. The king's total cavalry forces, therefore, tended to be far more impressive than the minimal force to which he was theoretically entitled. In the summer of 1277 they totalled somewhere in the region of 1,000 mounted men.[47]

Not all of these men turned up at Worcester. Edward's plan for invading Gwynedd was a two-pronged assault: one force would drive northwards from Carmarthen, while another would push west from Chester. In other words, the operation would be launched from the bases established during the preliminary campaign, and it therefore made sense for those cavalrymen already under the commands of the earl of Warwick (at Chester) and Payn de Chaworth (at Carmarthen) to remain at their posts. Both men, however, were about to be superseded. When the troops mustered at Worcester divided, those who rode south joined an army that was now captained by Edmund, earl of Lancaster, Edward's younger brother. Thanks to the king's earlier generosity, Edmund was the biggest landowner in south Wales, and Carmarthen was his lordship: it was only fitting that the responsibility, and the honour, of leading the southern army should be given to him.[48]

Important though it was, Edmund's role was essentially a supporting one. His army was allocated only a fraction of the forces that came to Worcester, bringing his total cavalry to somewhere in the region of 200 men. The great majority of the assembled host – including all the other earls and their militarised households, rode north to Chester, where (together with Warwick's contingent) they formed a company of horse in excess of 800 strong. They were to be the main strike force that would bring down Llywelyn. And their captain was, of course, the king himself.[49]

Edward arrived in Chester on 15 July. The old Roman city was already humming with activity, and swollen to many times its normal size by thousands of other outsiders. The coming of the king and his cavalry appears to have coincided neatly with the arrival of a fleet of eighteen ships from the Cinque Ports. They, their crews and their captains, like the army they were there to support, had also turned up as a matter of ancient obligation. Other ships, some local, some from as far afield as Gascony, were soon hired by royal agents, bringing the total number of vessels squeezed along the quayside to thirty-five. In the city itself, some 700 or so sailors jostled for space with the 800 or more cavalrymen and an even greater number of horses.[50]

Both the seamen and the horsemen together, however, were outnumbered by the foot soldiers, who at the time of Edward's arrival accounted for almost 3,000 additional souls. Theirs was an altogether more mixed company. Some of them, like the sailors, were evidently men of prior experience. The 270 individuals who came carrying crossbows, for example, clearly constituted an elite group by virtue of owning one of the deadliest weapons of their age (and, presumably, the knowledge of how to use it). For the most part, though, the infantry were a ragbag, whose skill and equipment varied from the merely adequate to the virtually non-existent. Unlike the other elements in Edward's army, there was no formal obligation for foot soldiers to turn up and fight in his wars. The humblest freeman was required by law to furnish himself with a helmet, spear and gambeson (a padded tunic), but seemingly only for reasons of local defence. Obligation, if anything, operated in the opposite direction in the infantry's case, for those who turned out expected the king to pay them the respectable wage of two pence a day (or four pence in the case of the crossbowmen).[51]

The unknown factor is how much coercion and compulsion were involved when the sheriff or other royal officers rode into a village looking for raw recruits. Sometimes the compulsion may have been economic; for the poor and unskilled, the king's money must have been hard to refuse. Others, by contrast, may have been conscripted by their communities in order to meet the king's demand. What seems more certain is that the quality of foot soldiers raised by such methods was generally pretty lamentable. The best may have been practised bowmen, but many – probably the majority – may have turned out armed only with swords and knives. Whatever the case, exceedingly few of the 3,000 men who trudged to Chester in the summer of 1277 can have mustered the same level of enthusiasm as the knights who had ridden there alongside the king.[52]

Chester was therefore busy – yet apparently not busy enough. We lack good eyewitness reporting, and are reliant on the detailed but dry financial records kept by the king's ministers. But, from these, it seems that the initial groundwork carried out by the earl of Warwick and his deputies was deemed insufficient by the king and his advisers on their arrival. Take, for example, the fundamental question of food. Some preparations, it is plain, must have been made in order to feed the thousands of men and animals already in Chester by the middle of July. Edward's local officials in Cheshire had been seizing corn in his name as early as January, and in February the king himself had ordered his ministers in Ireland to ship 1,600 quarters of cereal to Chester by midsummer at the latest. It is striking, however, that on 17 July, just two days after Edward's arrival, fresh stocks of grain were ordered from nine English counties. 'Other misfortunes can in time be alleviated: fodder and grain supply have no remedy in a crisis except storage in advance.' So wrote the Roman general Vegetius in his manual *De re militari*, which Edward owned and had therefore almost certainly read. Of course, the book offered no advice as to how much food should be stockpiled. That was a lesson that could be learned only from experience, and experience told Edward that, at the start of his campaign in the summer of 1277, he did not have nearly enough.[53]

The same may well have been true of the men he was hoping to feed. Three thousand foot soldiers was not the making of a great army of invasion. Again, we have to guard against the limitations of our sources. It may be that the king intended from the outset that his infantry should accumulate gradually, increasing in number as his advance gathered momentum. If, however, this was indeed the case, it is difficult to see why he should have mustered all his cavalry at the beginning of July or have had all his ships assembled in the middle of the same month. The aristocracy and the Cinque Ports were both bound to assist Edward, but their obligations were not indefinite. Cavalry service was compulsory for only forty days, while the Portsmen were required to turn out for only two weeks. The king might appeal to both to serve for longer, either in return for payment, or simply as a favour, but his appeal might well fall on deaf ears.[54]

The clock, in short, was ticking. Within a matter of a few more weeks, the men Edward had with him would be obliged to offer him nothing, and might well decide to return home. Despite the fact, therefore, that his resources might have been considerably less than he had hoped, the king had to make a swift start. A week after their arrival in Chester, he and his army left the city and crossed the border into Wales.[55]

There was no Welsh army with Llywelyn at its head advancing to meet them. The events of the spring, and the fall of Dolforwyn in particular, had shown beyond any doubt that the prince's resources were no match for those of the king of England. Even at the height of his power, Llywelyn was able to deploy only 300 mounted men, and they were unlikely to have been equipped to the same high standard as Edward's knights, with their great warhorses, heavy armour, mail shirts, swords and lances. When it came to warfare, the economic and industrial gulf between England and Wales was all too apparent. Llywelyn had no fleet to speak of and no money to hire one. He could not afford to bring crossbowmen from Gascony, nor to furnish them with an almost unlimited supply of ammunition. His resources were those of a primitive and underdeveloped society, set against those of a thirteenth-century superpower. Direct confrontation was out of the question.[56]

But the prince did not need to meet the English army head on to see it defeated. Geography could do that for him. Wales, it bears repeating, was 'not of easy access'. The same physical obstacles that limited Llywelyn's dreams of expansion – marsh, forest and mountain – also served, in the final analysis, to protect the core of his power. What nature had made difficult, moreover, man might make doubly so. During the previous English invasion of 1257 Llywelyn had gone to great lengths to obstruct his enemy's advance. Holes had been dug in the middle of fords to render them impassable; meadows had been ploughed up; bridges had been broken. The prince, so it was said, had even destroyed the mills of his homeland rather than see them used to grind corn to feed an English army.[57]

No doubt similar preparations were made in 1277. But, whatever else he might have done, the fact was that Llywelyn had already ensured that this new invasion would face far greater difficulties than its precursor. The destruction of the castles at Dyserth and Deganwy meant that Edward had no secure bases at which to aim his army. Everything west of Chester was hostile terrain that afforded neither shelter nor safe haven. In this environment, unforgiving and inhospitable, even the greatest armies might become entangled or bogged down, and once that had happened the eerie silence might suddenly be broken by the noise of a surprise attack. The Welsh might have lacked the latest military hardware, but they themselves were famously fierce and fearsome. Dressed in leather, armed with bows, arrows and spears, they would sweep down on their enemies, catching them unawares and wreaking havoc, before retreating with equal swiftness into the woods and hills. Such guerrilla tactics had served them well against would-be invaders for centuries. They were precisely the tactics by which a small nation might defeat a superpower.[58]

Edward was determined to avoid such a fate. Well aware of the challenges presented by the terrain he wished to traverse, he had already devised a strategy by which it would be tamed. The essential feature of his plan was new and better castles. Since early June royal agents had been busy recruiting hundreds of masons, carpenters, diggers and woodsmen, and this separate army of workers now marched with the main host as it advanced from Chester to the edge of hostile territory. Their first stop was a spur of rock on the estuary of the River Dee, which they christened 'the Flint'. Work began immediately on the castle that has borne that name ever since.[59]

Protection was the first priority. More than half the 1,850 or so men engaged in the initial stages of construction were diggers, who laboured to create huge ditches around the site, 'for the security of the king and his company'. Speed was also of the essence. Almost all of the initial building work was carried out in timber; carpenters outnumbered masons by more than two to one.[60]

Once again, however, speed was not all it might have been. Despite the impressively large workforce, it is clear that not enough building materials had been gathered in advance. At the end of July, by which point Edward had already been at Flint for over a week, trees were still being felled in the forests of Cheshire for use at the castle. The king was therefore obliged to retrace his steps in the direction of Chester in order to hasten the shipment of further supplies. The fact that his journey was a short one only served to emphasise how little had been achieved thus far. One month on from the muster, one week since beginning his assault, and Edward had advanced all of twelve miles.[61]

In the south things were moving faster. Edmund of Lancaster and his army had set out from their base at Carmarthen at some point after 10 July, and in the space of the fortnight that followed had driven more than fifty miles through the valleys of the Welsh interior. By 25 July they had reached Aberystwyth, their intended goal on the western coast. Their progress was, of course, considerably easier than that of their allies at Chester. The landscape of south Wales was no more forgiving in physical terms, but politically it had already been surrendered. Those Welsh lords who had not sought the king's peace earlier in the year now fled north at the advent of his younger brother, leaving their lands to be conquered, and seeking sanctuary in Snowdonia with Llywelyn. Consequently there was little for Edmund to do by the end of July except consolidate his gains. At the start of August, another new royal castle was founded at Aberystwyth. Men and materials were shipped around the coast from Bristol to facilitate its speedy construction.[62]

Meanwhile, back in the north, a similar naval exercise was under way. Great quantities of timber were being sent from Chester to Flint, some of it on large rafts constructed specially for the purpose. At the castle site itself, diggers were encouraged to work harder by the payment of bonuses 'by the king's gift'. For those in charge the sense of urgency was doubtless compounded by the fact that the sailors of the Cinque Ports now had to be paid as well, their period of obligatory service having already expired.[63]

Yet if the man who was ultimately in charge was concerned about the rising costs and the lapse of time, he did an excellent job of disguising it. Edward was naturally anxious that the business in Wales be expedited as quickly as possible – that much is proved by his itinerary during the first half of August, which shows him touring those areas (the Wirral and the Mersey estuary) where requisitioning was most intense. His movements at this time, however, also reveal a characteristic assuredness; a calm confidence that enabled him, at a moment when his resources already seemed stretched, to extend them further still, and in a rather different direction.[64]

Until this point, the king had still done little to further his youthful vow to build a great Cistercian abbey. The site he had sponsored before departing on crusade, Darnhall, had proved unsuitable, and the project had been left to languish. Now, on the eve of another great military adventure, Edward clearly felt that it ought to be revived. In the middle of the first fortnight of August, therefore, he abandoned his logistical concerns and travelled to the eastern edge of the lordship of Cheshire. On 8 August the court was stopped near Northwich, and it was probably on the following day, a Sunday, that they came to the empty place on the banks of the River Weaver where the king's new abbey was to be founded.

The occasion was deliberately grand and participatory as well as solemn. Surrounded by an assembly of his greatest subjects, Edward himself laid the first stone on the spot where the high altar was to be built. Eleanor laid the second and third – for herself, and for their son, Alfonso. Other stones were then placed by a long line of nobles, including the earls of Gloucester, Cornwall, Surrey and Warwick. The king's friend and chancellor, Robert Burnell, celebrated mass, emphasising that the event was above all a pious act, intended to bring God's blessing on their enterprise in Wales. At the same time it was a bold statement of Edward's own power. His new abbey was laid out to be the largest of its kind in Britain, bigger than its sister house at Fountains in Yorkshire, an equal for his father's house at Westminster. He named it Vale Royal, intending (so its historian later asserted) 'that no monastery should be more royal in liberties, wealth, and honour'.[65]

Back at Flint, work progressed apace in anticipation of the king's imminent return. The timber shipped from Chester was being raised, and the workforce was still increasing in number. The same day, 9 August, that Edward was at Vale Royal, a further 300 diggers arrived from Lincolnshire at the castle site. They were brought under armed escort, 'lest they should flee on the road', as well they might, given the hazardous nature of their assignment. For the next stage of his advance the king had to pass through the interior of the Four Cantrefs, and what one English chronicler called 'a forest of such denseness that the royal army could by no means penetrate without danger'. Edward, of course, had no intention of taking any such risks. In advance of his arrival, the workmen, guarded by the men with crossbows and supervised by certain household knights, were charged with the task of cutting back the enveloping trees. In this way, as the same chronicler explained, 'the king opened out for himself a very broad road', and he may have had little scope for exaggeration. When, some years later, Edward introduced similar road-widening measures in England, for similar reasons ('so that there may be no ditch, underwood or bushes where one could hide with evil intent'), he required clearance and levelling 'within two hundred feet of the road on either side'. This conjures the arresting image of the king's workforce in Wales (assuming similar standards were applied) cutting and burning a path some 400 feet wide – around four times the width of a three-lane motorway.[66]

By the time, therefore, that Edward returned to Flint on 18 August, almost everything was ready. Infantry were at last starting to rise to respectable levels. The new road must have been well advanced. The king and his army were finally ready to embark on their major offensive. Only one question remained.

To what end were they about to march? Did they go to conquer Gwynedd or merely to punish its disobedient prince? One man, above all, who wanted clarification on this issue was Dafydd ap Gruffudd. Llywelyn's treacherous younger brother had at first been pleased to have Edward's support in his lifelong struggle for a share of his patrimony, but latterly he had begun to appreciate its inherent disadvantages. The English military and political establishment, once up in arms, acquired a momentum and an agenda of its own. If there was land to be conquered, the king and his greatest subjects would inevitably want their share. According to the earl of Warwick, who wrote to Edward on the matter, Dafydd was becoming dangerously disaffected, already irked by what he perceived as the diminution of his rights to payment and booty.

The king took heed, and sought to reassure Dafydd by issuing a formal statement of his intentions. According to this document, their aim was indeed the outright conquest of Gwynedd and, by implication, the deposition of Llywelyn. In future, north-west Wales would be shared. Dafydd would, at last, receive his portion, as would his other brother, Owain. But, as the document also made plain, the matter would not end there. Edward, not unnaturally, intended to keep a large slice of whatever was conquered for himself, and he further expected that both Dafydd and Owain would attend his parliaments at Westminster, 'just like our other earls and barons'. Whether Dafydd was satisfied with this proposal is a moot point. Another is whether Edward was entirely in earnest. His promise to Dafydd was only a piece of parchment that sketched out a future yet to be realised. Its date of issue – 23 August – suggests a temporary expedient for appeasing an unstable ally at a crucial moment in the campaign. That same day, Edward and his army set out.[67]

If there was hard fighting it took place in the course of the week that followed. English chronicle accounts are sparse, and tend to give the impression of an easy progress. One speaks of the king advancing along his newly cut road 'in triumph', but concedes that it had to be occupied 'by strong attacks'. On the first day out from Flint, the army moved some fifteen miles to Rhuddlan, a settlement on the River Clwyd, two miles downstream from the cathedral town of St Asaph. The bishop there, no friend of Llywelyn, was nevertheless appalled by the onslaught of Edward's war machine, and complained to the archbishop of Canterbury about the destruction of church property, sacrilege and rape carried out by English soldiers. Royal records, though more voluminous, are more difficult to interpret with certainty. From them we can see the king's stay at Rhuddlan was short, lasting no more than a few days. While there he began to raise another new castle, preferring a site by the side of the Clwyd to the hilltop position his father had favoured at nearby Dyserth. Edward's overriding objective, however, was sustaining the forward momentum of his forces. For all those who stopped to secure this second camp, many more must have poured across the river to continue the advance and the clearance of a path to the west. By this stage, Edward had soldiers to spare. At Rhuddlan the infantry swelled to more than 15,000 men.[68]

When Edward and his army reappear, it is the end of August, by which time they have reached Deganwy, the lofty hill on the eastern side of the River Conwy, where Henry III's castle stood in ruins. Suddenly, everything does not seem so sanguine. No new building works are begun, though perhaps none were ever intended. More striking is the sharp drop in the number of infantry: numbers have fallen by half, from 15,000 to just under 7,500. This might be interpreted in several ways. The first, and by far the most favourable, is the traditional explanation that the missing men were dismissed, and that the reduction was therefore a conscious decision on the king's part, by which he hoped to render his army more manageable. Another, arguably more plausible scenario is that these troops left of their own accord. From what we know of Edward's later campaigns, desertion among the rank and file was rife, and easily the most common cause of attrition. The third possibility is perhaps less significant but nevertheless impossible wholly to discount: some of these soldiers must have been killed in the course of the advance.[69]

Dismissal, desertion, death: whatever the cause, the fighting strength of the king's army was substantially diminished, and at the critical moment of his campaign. It had been here at Deganwy, twenty years before even to the very day, that Edward had stood with his father and contemplated the conquest of Gwynedd, only to have Henry decide that the task was beyond them, and order a retreat. Would Edward now be forced to do the same? Even the most charitable estimation of his predicament – dismissal – would suggest that he was running out of the wherewithal to pay or feed his infantry forces. His cavalry, meanwhile, had already served well beyond their obligatory forty days. According to one chronicler, the king had to dismiss some of their number, presumably because he could not afford to retain them. Faced with such circumstances, the king may well have stared at the mountains of Snowdonia and concluded that they were slipping beyond his reach.[70]

There was a possible solution to Edward's problem, however, provided that he acted fast. To the north-west of Gwynedd lay the island of Anglesey, a large area of lowland that might be occupied with comparative ease. The challenge of access remained, but the obstacle now became an expanse of water. Could sufficient numbers of troops be sent across the strip of sea that separated the island from the mainland? Henry III had considered this question in 1257 and decided that the answer was no, for he lacked the ships and the necessary will. His son, by contrast, was in possession of both. In the early days of September, courtesy of the sailors of the Cinque Ports, Edward was able to dispatch some 2,000 soldiers across Conwy Bay and the Menai Strait, captained by his friends Otto de Grandson and John de Vescy. Within a matter of days, Anglesey was occupied.

For Llywelyn this was a devastating blow. Of all the territories he had lost to date, his offshore island was by far the most important. To the prince and his fellow countrymen, Anglesey was *Môn mam Cymru* (Mona, mother of Wales) because it contained the best arable land in the country. 'This island produces far more grain than any other part of Wales,' said the knowledgeable Gerald of Wales; indeed, it was 'so productive that it could supply the whole of Wales with corn over a long period'. Anglesey, in other words, was Llywelyn's granary, and Edward had snatched it from him. Along with his soldiers, the king had shipped to the island 360 other men, armed only with scythes, whose job it was to get in the harvest. It was a brilliantly executed, perfectly timed move: at a stroke Edward had resupplied his own army, while simultaneously depriving his opponent of the means to survive the coming winter. Perhaps for this reason, more than any other, a later English chronicler would describe this campaign as 'the siege of Snowdon'. As in the bitterest sieges, the attacker hoped to starve the defender into submission.[71]

Llywelyn submitted. He had no other option. We do not know precisely how or when, but all indications are that he must have communicated a readiness to surrender soon after the fall of Anglesey, and possibly as early as 11 September, for by that date the English army was clearly standing down. Edward had left Deganwy and retired to Rhuddlan, where he busied himself building his new castle. Within a few days most of his infantry had been dismissed: in the middle of the month only 1,600 foot soldiers remained in the royal camp. The cavalry must have been released around the same time. Among the magnates, the earls of Warwick and Lincoln, Edward's close friends, stayed by his side, but the other earls disappear from the records. The permission granted to the earl of Norfolk on 15 September to hunt in the king's forest in Cheshire looks very much like a farewell gift. Edward had evidently sent immediate word to his brother advising him that the war was over: on 20 September Edmund disbanded his southern army and returned to England, leaving a small contingent to continue the castle-building at Aberystwyth. Finally, at the end of the month, the ships of the Cinque Ports were sent home, presumably with thanks for the sterling service they had rendered.[72]

It remained to negotiate the terms of the surrender, and this took several weeks. There had evidently been some progress by 10 October, at which point Edward granted two of the Four Cantrefs to Dafydd ap Gruffudd – compensation for a prickly ally who now had to accept that, since the invasion had been called off, he would not be getting his hands on any part of Gwynedd in the immediate future. Gwynedd, it was allowed, would remain to Llywelyn. It was, however, just about the only territory he was permitted to retain: more or less everything else was to be kept by the conquerors. The prince was given to understand, for example, that the other two of the Four Cantrefs would once again become the property of the English Crown, controlled from the new castles at Rhuddlan and Flint. Anglesey, by contrast, would be returned to him, but only on the understanding that he should pay

1,000 marks (£666) a year for this privilege. On the same subject of money, it was felt appropriate that Llywelyn should make reparations for the injuries and damages he had inflicted: a sum of £50,000 was suggested. As for the rest of his once extensive empire, that was treated from the outset as a thing of the past. Authority in south and central Wales had slipped from the prince many months before; the lords of these areas had already accepted that their rightful overlord was the king of England. As a small sop to his dignity, it was allowed that Llywelyn should retain the homages of five minor Welsh lords, and also his title 'prince of Wales'. But this was tantamount to a mockery, for he was patently nothing of the sort. The reality was that Edward had turned back the clock by thirty years, and Llywelyn's life's work had been undone.[73]

The prince agreed to these terms with English negotiators at Conwy on 9 November 1277, but his humiliation did not end there. There was still the matter of his personal subjection to Edward, so long resisted and at such great cost. The following day, therefore, Llywelyn was escorted from Snowdonia into the part of north Wales now under English occupation. Three miles west of Rhuddlan he was met by Robert Burnell and the earl of Lincoln. Finally, he was brought within the confines of the new royal castle, and before the king himself.

Edward was magnanimous in victory. Llywelyn had done all that had been required of him and placed himself entirely at his overlord's mercy. The king acknowledged this with a gesture of his own, pardoning the prince his £50,000 fine and waiving the annual rent for Anglesey. He was not, however, minded to revisit the issue of homage – not yet. Rhuddlan was too remote an arena for a submission so significant and symbolic. On 20 November the king left the castle and returned to England.[74]

With him went Llywelyn. Westminster, not Wales, was to be the venue for the final act of this piece of political theatre. The king and his guest arrived there shortly before Christmas. It was on Christmas Day, surrounded by an assembly of English magnates, that Llywelyn finally knelt before Edward, placed his hands within the hands of the king, and promised to be an obedient prince.[75]

6

Arthur's Crown

From the declaration of war on 12 November 1276 to the proclamation of peace on 9 November 1277, it had taken Edward just
short of a year to reduce Llywelyn ap Gruffudd to obedience.
After such a sustained military effort the king was anxious to ensure
that the gains he had made and the terms he had imposed would not
be undone or reversed. Consequently, for much of the year that followed,
he remained highly engaged with Welsh affairs, directing his energy
and resources to the task of creating a settlement that he intended
would be permanent.[1]

The most visible manifestation of Edward's will in this regard were
his new castles. At Rhuddlan, Flint and Aberystwyth, as the king's armies
withdrew, his workmen stayed on, labouring in their thousands to transform the temporary timber stockades thrown up during the campaign
into the stone fortresses that have survived to this day. Rhuddlan, in
particular, required a tremendous deployment of manpower, for besides
the castle (itself the largest of the three), Edward had foreseen the necessity of straightening the adjacent River Clwyd. Teams of diggers – at
one point they numbered almost a thousand men – would work on
this project for the next three years to ensure that in future the inland
garrison could be kept supplied by sea.[2]

Nor was it just new foundations that received such attention. In
mid-Wales Roger Mortimer had recovered for the king the castle at
Builth that he had lost to Llywelyn some seventeen years before. Building
work there was under way even before the main assault on Wales had
begun. Meanwhile, elsewhere in the same region, and also further south,
the Crown had obtained many other new lands and castles by virtue
of depriving their former Welsh owners. Consider, for example, the fate
of Rhys Wyndod, one of the most powerful lords of south Wales. He
had offered minimal resistance in 1277 and come to terms swiftly, yet

he was still obliged to surrender all his fortresses along the River Tywi – Dinefwr, Llandovery, and the lofty eyrie that is Carreg Cennen. All three now passed to Edward, expanding his stock of strongholds, but also increasing his already massive construction programme.[3]

To oversee such a major exercise in castle-building required a project manager of considerable genius, and so it was fortunate that Edward had just such a man at his disposal. Five years earlier, in the course of his return journey from the Holy Land, the king passed through the lands of his mother's relatives, the counts of Savoy; for a week or so in the summer of 1273 he and his fellow crusaders had paused at Count Philip's new castle of St Georges de Espéranche, not far from the French city of Lyon. And there, it seems, Edward was probably introduced to the castle's designer and builder, a young master mason who came to be known as Master James of St George. For some years James and his father had been selling their building services to the counts of Savoy and their nobles; a string of towns and castles in the Swiss and Italian Alps still stand as witness to the duo's industry and skill, and also their flair for organisation. In the autumn of 1275, however, Master James himself vanishes from the administrative records of Savoy. When he reappears, some two and a half years later, it is in the pay of a new employer. On 8 April 1278 Edward I sent him from England into Wales 'to ordain the works of the castles there'.[4]

The new castles were not intended to be isolated outposts where lonely English garrisons would guard against future Welsh insurgency. On the contrary, they would be the focal points of the new and better Wales that Edward saw it as his job to build. Rhuddlan and Flint were administrative centres, attached to the justiciar of Chester, from which royal bailiffs could superintend the Welsh interior, and to which the Welsh were regularly summoned to attend the king's courts. Aberystwyth played a similar role in the west, ultimately answering to a new 'justiciar of west Wales', based at Carmarthen. Edward, it is fair to say, did not try as part of this exercise to introduce English law into Wales. When, in January 1278, he appointed a seven-man legal team (the so-called Hopton Commission) 'to hear and determine all suits and pleas . . . in the Marches and in Wales', three of its members were Welsh, and they were instructed to do justice 'according to the customs of those parts'. Nevertheless, he intended that both Welsh law and Marcher law should be brought firmly within the framework of his own overarching jurisdiction. The king's high estimation of his authority in Wales is well demonstrated by his ongoing efforts to thin out its forests and widen its roads. Marcher and Welsh lords alike were ordered to see to it that this work was done in their districts, or else the king's agents would do it for them and charge them for the privilege.[5]

And if, moreover, it was impracticable to introduce English law into Wales, anglicisation could still be advanced by other means. At Flint, Rhuddlan and Aberystwyth, the king's new castles were paired with new royal towns, not for the benefit of the natives, but in order to host immigrant communities of English settlers. England's population was rising in the thirteenth century, and the country was already approaching a stage where it had more people than the land could support. Consequently there was no shortage of Englishmen and Englishwomen ready to accept the offer of a new life in Wales, even if it meant living in the midst of a hostile people. Edward's new boroughs were surrounded by palisades and ditches, and ultimately protected by their adjacent castles. The settlers would supply the soldiery by providing local services and – here was the ultimate hope – soften the natives by their peaceful, law-abiding and industrious example.[6]

And what of the man who, despite his reduced circumstances, remained the greatest and potentially the most hostile native of them all? It is clear that, despite his symbolic submission at Christmas 1277, Llywelyn ap Gruffudd was still regarded with considerable suspicion in England, especially by the king. Although in the new year Edward allowed his erstwhile adversary to return to his diminished principality, he had already taken steps that effectively placed the prince on probation. One of the conditions of the surrender, for example, had been Llywelyn's agreement to an annual oath-taking ceremony, by which twenty men from every district in his possession would swear that their belittled leader was behaving himself. In the more immediate term, the prince had also been required to hand over ten hostages, and at the start of 1278 these men remained in the Crown's custody. And to their number, of course, could be added Edward's long-term guest, Eleanor de Montfort. Her release was probably discussed during Llywelyn's visit to England, but was not carried out. For a while longer, she too would remain in the king's keeping as a guarantee of her fiancé's good conduct.[7]

Within a few months, however, Edward started to soften in the face of Llywelyn's ready compliance. As early as March he was pleased to note that the prince was submitting his territorial disputes to the Hopton Commission. 'With goodwill,' the king told his chancellor, Robert Burnell, 'he seeks and receives justice and judgement.' By the end of the summer Edward was ready to release the hostages; in September he returned to Rhuddlan for this purpose, and to rule on the territorial disputes between Llywelyn and his brothers. Finally, in the early autumn, the king travelled to Worcester in order to attend the prince's wedding.

This could go ahead, of course, only because Edward had agreed to release the bride, and the ceremony showed other signs of being arranged to suit the king's own agenda. Not only did it take place in an English cathedral; it was celebrated – with what Edward no doubt considered to be mischievous humour – on 13 October, the feast of the translation of Edward the Confessor, patron saint of the English monarchy. Nevertheless, it remained an act of royal generosity, and the best dynastic match ever made by a Welsh ruler. Eleanor de Montfort, for all her father's crimes, was still the king's cousin. It was Edmund of Lancaster who gave her away at the church door, and Edward himself who paid for the wedding feast.[8]

Edward, then, was much engaged in the business of settling Wales during 1278. Given this evident preoccupation, it is astonishing that his most interesting act of the year, which fits squarely into this context, has received so little attention from historians, or been noted only briefly and in passing in order to deny that it was in any way relevant. At Easter 1278 Edward took his court to Somerset, and to the abbey at Glastonbury, to visit the tomb of King Arthur.[9]

The tomb of King Arthur at Glastonbury, regrettably destroyed in the seventeenth century, was obviously a fake. 'Obviously' because, as all sane historians will nowadays readily attest (whatever the assertions of lamentable Hollywood films to the contrary), Arthur himself never existed. Beyond any reasonable doubt, the legendary 'king' began life as an elemental figure or demi-god – a sort of low-grade Thor or Wodin. What is also unquestionably clear, however, is that his otherworldly origins were in no way apparent to Edward I and his contemporaries. To them, Arthur was a historical personage as real as Richard the Lionheart, William the Conqueror or Edward the Confessor.[10]

Diligent and painstaking modern scholarship reveals to us what thirteenth-century folk could not possibly know: that Arthur was not historic, but had been 'historicised'. That is to say, a number of earlier medieval writers, at different times and for different reasons, had taken the legendary or god-like figure and written about him as if he had been a real person. In the early ninth century, for example, an author known to posterity as Nennius wrote Arthur into his account of the struggle between Britain's original inhabitants, the Ancient Britons, and the Anglo-Saxon invaders who eventually displaced them. The deity was thereby demoted into a warrior who successfully battled for the Britons around the year AD 500.

This Arthur was shadowy and obscure, brief and boring; had his development ended there and then he would have undoubtedly remained a little-known and seldom-mentioned curiosity. But Arthur underwent a subsequent re-imagining that transformed him out of all proportion. In the 1130s a mischievous Oxford scholar called Geoffrey of Monmouth sat down and perpetrated what stands to be regarded as the most brilliant and audacious literary hoax of the Middle Ages, if not of all time. *The History of the Kings of Britain*, as his book has come to be known, was in reality nothing of the sort. It was a work of fiction, laced with just enough snippets from more sober and bona fide chronicles to convince the credulous. And into his long, tall tale of imaginary kings in a distant imaginary past, Geoffrey inserted Arthur – King Arthur, as he now became – the greatest of all Britons, one-time ruler of the whole world.[11]

Not everyone was taken in by such nonsense. 'It is quite clear,' wrote the infinitely more responsible William of Newburgh some fifty years later and with palpable irritation, 'that everything this man wrote about Arthur and his successors, and indeed his predecessors . . . was made up!' By this stage, however, it was far too late: Geoffrey's book had become a runaway success, a medieval bestseller. Even today, some 215 manuscript copies of the *History* still survive, putting it way ahead of its nearest rivals, and second only to the Bible. And as for Arthur – the part of the book that everyone liked best – he rapidly spawned an entire industry. Tales of his exploits were taken up by other writers and poets, especially Continental ones, and made taller still. Soon Arthur acquired a castle called Camelot, a host of knightly companions, and a Round Table.[12]

It was only a matter of time before he acquired a tomb. When the church at Glastonbury Abbey burned down in 1184, it quickly dawned on the monks there that a sure-fire way to increase the number of paying visitors was a spot of creative marketing involving everyone's favourite king. Accordingly, they dug around in the churchyard and unearthed a pair of skeletons that, they claimed, were those of Arthur and his queen, Guinevere. To the monks' credit, their forgery was first-rate: the excavations were carried out in secret, and the bones were discovered under an inscribed lead cross that confirmed, with convenient explicitness, the identities of their former owners. As with other famous hoaxes (Piltdown Man, the Hitler Diaries, Geoffrey of Monmouth's *History*), even the very clever and sceptical were taken in. Gerald of Wales, a man who considered himself nothing less than a genius, saw both the bones and the cross and was convinced of their authenticity. Other writers followed suit, and Glastonbury's claim to be Arthur's final resting place was rapidly accepted as a matter of fact. By the early thirteenth century it was proof positive that the fabulous king about whom Geoffrey of Monmouth had written had once really existed.[13]

Thus, by Edward's day, Arthur-mania knew no bounds, and evidence of enthusiasm for the king was abundantly apparent. Richard of Cornwall, for instance, soon after gaining his earldom, spent considerable sums building the remote castle at Tintagel, a place that offered neither strategic nor domestic benefits but that was, according to Geoffrey of Monmouth, the location where Arthur had been conceived. Eleanor of Provence, it is touching to note, was taken to Glastonbury soon after her arrival in England, by a new husband evidently anxious to please a twelve-year-old queen who (as other evidence shows) loved all things Arthurian. By this time, moreover, one did not even have to be a great reader like Eleanor to join in the fun. Even those knights who were insufficiently in touch with their feminine sides to endure interminably long tales of courtly love were still able to fill their leisure time with Arthur-themed entertainment. It is in the middle decades of the thirteenth century that we first begin to hear of special tournaments called 'Round Tables', where the emphasis was on jousting, pageantry and prizes. Edward's good friend Roger Mortimer would organise just such a tournament at Kenilworth Castle in 1279 in order to celebrate the end of his military career.[14]

In Gascony and Germany, Italy and Sicily, France, Scotland and even in the Holy Land – everyone everywhere loved Arthur and told tales about him. In England, however, the famous king, fantastic though he was, did present something of a problem. Geoffrey of Monmouth, sticking to his earlier sources (like Nennius), had located his superhero at the turn of the fifth and sixth centuries. Arthur was not merely a British king, but a British king who had fought against the Anglo-Saxons – that is, the founding fathers of the kingdom of England. The English, in other words, were the bad guys in the Arthur story; the invaders who had ultimately defeated the Britons and driven them into the northern and western extremities of their island. Arthur, the most excellent king that had ever been, might be admired by the English, but he did not belong to them in any meaningful sense. On the contrary, he belonged to the descendants of the Britons – the Welsh.

The fact that Arthur was Welsh, though galling, was not his biggest problem as far as English audiences were concerned. A more disturbing difficulty was that he was apparently due for a come-back. According to Geoffrey of Monmouth, the king was merely wounded in his last battle with the Saxons; nothing was said about his death. Arthur, Geoffrey maintained, had been taken to the mysterious island of Avalon, in order that he might recover from his injuries. And when he did, so the story went, he would return and lead the Britons to victory once more. For fairly obvious reasons, the Welsh were very fond of this idea.

The English, for reasons that are equally obvious, preferred the version of the story that ended in Glastonbury. Not only did the tomb there prove that Arthur had really lived, and was therefore apt to be emulated; it also proved that he was really dead, and would not be coming back to cause any trouble. One of the few people who seems to have been in on the original fraud at Glastonbury was Edward's great-grandfather, Henry II, who had problems of his own with the Welsh. It was reportedly his suggestion – and one imagines him tapping his nose and winking as he made it – that had set the monks digging in the first place. If, however, it was indeed Henry's aim to discomfort his Celtic neighbours by this discovery, his propaganda missed its mark. The English might have been predisposed to accept that Arthur was dead and buried, but the Welsh simple refused to believe it. 'In their stupidity,' scoffed Gerald of Wales, '[they] maintain that he is still alive.'[15]

It was, therefore, more than just idle curiosity or exaggerated devotion that brought Edward I to Glastonbury in the spring of 1278. The king, like his mother and his wife, owned Arthurian romances and appears to have been well versed in their contents; but, as has been rightly observed, there is nothing to show that his enthusiasm in this regard was anything other than ordinary.[16] So far as we can tell, Edward's trip to Glastonbury in 1278 was his first and only visit, and it was not a secular pilgrimage of the kind that had drawn his parents there forty years earlier. Edward came not to praise Arthur, but to bury him. Again.

Two days after Easter, which the court celebrated at the abbey, the king ordered Arthur's tomb to be opened. 'There, in two caskets,' said a local chronicler, 'were found the bones of the said king, of wondrous size, and those of Guinevere, of marvellous beauty.' The next day, Edward had these remains removed to the abbey's treasury, there to be kept while a new and better tomb was constructed. From a description in the sixteenth century it seems that the eventual outcome was a box of black marble with a lion at each end, and an effigy of Arthur at its foot.

What took place at Glastonbury was a piece of political theatre every bit as pointed and significant as Llywelyn's homage the previous Christmas, or the prince's marriage the following October. As on these occasions, every effort was taken to ensure that the event was momentous and memorable. The disinterment of the bodies, we are told, took place at twilight, no doubt deliberately to heighten its dramatic effect. The following morning the court was treated to an equally arresting spectacle when Edward personally wrapped Arthur's bones in silk, while Eleanor of Castile similarly prepared the remains of Guinevere for reburial. There may even have been, in addition to these macabre solemnities, some kind of celebratory jamboree. Immediately prior to its arrival at Glastonbury, the court had gone out of its way to stop at Eleanor's manor of Queen Camel, which stands close by the giant Iron Age hill-fort at South Cadbury. Since Cadbury had already been identified by this date as Camelot (presumably because of its proximity to Camel, as well as to Glastonbury), it seems likely that the two visits were connected, and that there might have been a chivalric prelude to the exhumation.

Such efforts, coming as they did within a few months of Edward's humbling of Llywelyn, and at a time when the king was engaged in a general drive to redefine the relationship between England and Wales, can hardly be interpreted as anything other than an exercise in propaganda directed squarely at the Welsh. The attempt to deal decisively with Arthur shows in the attention to detail: having wrapped the skeletons and returned them to their caskets, Edward and Eleanor affixed their seals, so as to certify that the contents were indeed authentic. More telling still is the intention to ensure that the evidence was left on permanent display: the skulls of 'Arthur' and 'Guinevere' were not reinterred, but placed outside the tomb, 'on account of popular devotion'.[17] Edward, it would seem, was determined to prove to his turbulent neighbours, once and for all, that Arthur would not be coming back to save them.

Before we leave Arthur and Glastonbury, it is appropriate to ask one final question. Why did Geoffrey of Monmouth write *The History of the Kings of Britain*, the startlingly inventive book that set the whole Arthurian avalanche in motion?

For his chief critic, William of Newburgh, there were two possible answers. It was 'either from an inordinate love of lying, or for the sake of pleasing the Britons'.[18]

There can be little doubt that Geoffrey took pleasure in spinning his stories, but Newburgh probably came closer to striking the nail on the head with his second suggestion. Geoffrey of Monmouth was only latterly an Oxford scholar. Originally, as his surname implies, he hailed from Wales. And, as a Welshman living in England during the 1130s, he found himself having to listen to a lot of racism from his clever contemporaries.[19]

The English and the Welsh, it must be admitted, had never really seen eye to eye. From the moment that the first Anglo-Saxon settlers had arrived in Britain, their relationship with the Britons was characterised by mutual distrust and suspicion. *Welisc* was the Anglo-Saxon name for the Britons: it meant 'strangers'. And all too often this estrangement resulted in bursts of war and violence. Offa's Dyke, the great earthwork erected between England and Wales in the eighth century, stands as an eloquent reminder of the extent to which the two peoples were divided.

In Geoffrey of Monmouth's day, however, this age-old antipathy was given a new twist. Latterly, the English had decided that the Welsh were not only different and dislikeable; in addition, they had now concluded that Welsh society was, by almost every conceivable measure, inferior to that of England.

The instigator of this new attitude, or at least the individual responsible for its earliest and most trenchant expression, was an English monk called William of Malmesbury. Writing in the 1120s, Malmesbury looked at his own society and saw that it was good. England, he noted, had abundant, well-tended fields, thriving nucleated villages and bustling market towns; its people used a plentiful silver coinage, built impressive castles and cathedrals, ate good food and drank good wine. The Welsh, on the other hand, had none of these things. Theirs was a pastoral economy of scattered settlements, lacking money, towns and trade. We have already noted this, and accounted for it chiefly in terms of an unforgiving upland landscape. William of Malmesbury, however, made no such allowances. To him, the differences between England and Wales were to be explained by the different characters of their inhabitants. If Wales was unproductive, it was because the Welsh were indolent and ignorant, preferring to stand around all day idly tending sheep, rather than setting their hands to the plough like industrious Englishmen.

Nor was that their only moral failing. Malmesbury and his contemporaries also noticed that, whereas the English chivalrously spared their enemies in battle, the Welsh gave no such quarter, nor did they spare the lives of non-combatants. Similarly, when it came to sex, the Welsh were way out of step with what was normal or acceptable. Marriages in Wales were celebrated within degrees of consanguinity that were prohibited in England, and furthermore could be dissolved or disregarded with unreasonable ease.

Lazy in their work, savage in warfare, lax in their love lives: there was only one word fit for such a people, the English intelligentsia decided. They were barbarians.

It was almost certainly with the intention of challenging such hostile attitudes that Geoffrey of Monmouth put pen to parchment in the 1130s. *The History of the Kings of Britain* sets out to show that, whatever the current state of the Britons (which, Geoffrey conceded, was pretty bad), they had once been a great and noble people. Their pedigree, he said, stretched all the way back to the fall of Troy, 1,200 years before the birth of Christ. Britain had been founded by and named after

Brutus, the leader of a doughty band of Trojan exiles and forefather of the British people. In all their deeds, Brutus and his successors (who included Camber, ruler of Cambria; Corineus, founder of Cornwall; and, of course, Arthur) showed themselves to be truly heroic individuals, leaders of the greatest people on Earth. What is most striking, however, is the frequency with which they indulged in the kind of activities that contemporary Englishmen alleged were alien to Welsh nature. From the minute of their arrival, Geoffrey's Britons 'began to cultivate the fields'. Not long afterwards they started founding towns and cities. Thus Carlisle was the creation of King Leil, and Colchester the work of Old King Cole. London, we are assured, was so called after being rebuilt by an enterprising Briton called Lud. The subtext of such assertions seems undeniable. Geoffrey of Monmouth was not merely praising the Britons for the sake of it; he was attempting to prove that, contrary to the claims of their English critics, the Welsh were indeed a civilised race.[20]

In this respect, *The History of the Kings of Britain* was a grand failure. The English bought copies of the book in their thousands, but it did not alter their attitude to the Welsh one little bit. They loved Geoffrey's stories, but proved remarkably able to separate in their minds the old British heroes they admired from the contemporary Britons they despised. (This disconnect is well illustrated in the Arthurian Romance *Perceval*, when one knight of the Round Table turns to another and informs him that 'all Welshmen are by nature more stupid than beasts in the field'.) In spite of Geoffrey's valiant literary efforts on behalf of his countrymen, English hostility towards Wales and its inhabitants continued to grow inexorably during the twelfth century, with the result that, by the thirteenth century, the barbarity of the Welsh was treated as a matter of fact. Old socio-economic proofs, for example, could still be trotted out as late as 1265. When Simon de Montfort led his followers into Wales that year, one English chronicler noted casually that they had to subsist on milk and meat because the Welsh, 'that wild people', did not know how to make bread. Welsh warfare was likewise still regarded as unreasonably savage by Matthew Paris, who noted that it spared 'neither churches nor churchmen, women or girls'. And as for their other moral failings, these continued to excite comment in England, especially among churchmen. When, in 1280, the archbishop of Canterbury examined Welsh law, he concluded that much of it was contrary to the teachings of the Bible and should be abolished.[21]

In October 1278, having presided munificently at the wedding of his cousin Eleanor and Llywelyn ap Gruffudd, Edward left Worcester and turned his mind to other business.

The highest matter on the agenda, it seems, was how he was going to pay for the settlement of Wales. Before the outbreak of hostilities, thanks to the generosity of his first parliament, the king had been comfortably in credit. Now, three years on, his finances were once again in the red. The war itself had cost around £23,000, and during the campaign Edward had borrowed a sum equivalent to this amount from his Italian bankers, the Riccardi of Lucca. Of course, thanks to their special relationship with the king, the Riccardi could look forward to recovering this money from their control of the customs. That process, however, might take a very long time, for Edward's expenses in Wales were ongoing. Road clearance, canal construction and, especially, the building of the new royal castles – by October 1278 the settlement was running up a substantial additional tab that would eventually exceed the cost of the conflict itself. After the war Edward was still taking out new loans from the Riccardi, his borrowing on average three times what it had been at the start of the reign. If, therefore, the system was not going to collapse in bankruptcy and mutual recrimination, more money would have to be found from somewhere.[22]

The king was evidently anxious that it should not come from parliament. To get another grant of taxation so soon after the last one would probably have proved impossible in any case; it would certainly have required political concessions on a scale that Edward would have regarded as unconscionable. The king, therefore, cast around for other ways of raising cash that did not require parliament's consent. In the summer of 1278, for example, he resorted to an old fashioned money-raising expedient by ordering a so-called 'distraint of knighthood', a measure that compelled all landowners with property above a certain value (on this occasion it was £20 a year) to become knights before a certain date (in this case, Christmas). Since knighthood was an expensive business and generally beyond the means of such men, most of them chose to avoid the obligation by paying an exemption fine, which was the point of the exercise. But this, and the other traditional devices he tried, could not raise the large sums that Edward required. And so, in the autumn of 1278, he embarked on a far more drastic course of action.[23]

For some time, it seems, the king had been concerned about the state of his coinage. Some new coins had been struck since the start of his reign, but there had been no general reminting for over thirty years. Consequently, many of the silver pennies in circulation were old and worn, and still bore the name and image of Henry III. To Edward's tidy mind, this must have seemed a fairly shameful state of affairs, and would probably by itself have constituted sufficient reason for reform. But there were other incentives for improvement besides appearances. Poor currency pushed up prices, deterred foreign merchants and made tax collection unduly taxing for the collectors. Perhaps most importantly, however, a king who issued new coins stood to make a handsome profit. In exchange for reminting their old currency, Edward could charge his subjects a small fee, and, by making subtle alterations to the weight and silver content of new specie, he could increase his profits further still. There was nothing especially extortionate or exploitative in this process: the king stood to make money, but his subjects also benefited from having a superior quality coin. It was a mutually beneficial proposition.[24]

Nevertheless, a desire to derive maximum advantage from this proposition led Edward to commit one of the most exploitative and shameful acts of his career. He appears to have decided that a good way to increase the efficiency of a recoinage would be to round up in advance all those guilty of coinage offences. Coins, it was widely appreciated, diminished in size and weight not only through long use; they also shrank as a result of a practice known as 'clipping', whereby small amounts of silver were shaved off each penny and melted down into new ingots or plate. Needless to say, altering the currency in this way constituted a serious crime: convicted coin-clippers stood to lose either their lives or the readily detachable bits of their bodies. Where the criminal suffered, however, the Crown prospered. Fines imposed on the guilty, property confiscated from the condemned: it all amounted to an appreciable increase for the treasury if enough convictions could be secured. And it was apparently for this reason that Edward, in February 1278, sent two of his clerks to tour the country with the instruction to buy up melted silver. At best it was a sting operation to catch known criminals; at worst, it was a mission to entrap the unwary. By the autumn these undercover agents had obviously accumulated enough evidence for the government to act. In late October Edward and his council authorised the arrest of the suspects, and in November the king's officers swooped.[25]

Every single Jewish adult male in England was seized and imprisoned – at least 600 individuals out of a total community of only 2,000 to 4,000 people. They, it seems, were the special target of the sting operation. Of course, the Jews had a long-standing dominance of the money and metalworking trades, so to some extent an investigation into coin-clipping was bound to focus on their activities. There can be little doubt, too, that some Jews were guilty of coinage offences: the king's recent prohibition of moneylending must have driven many of them to desperate measures in order to survive. But Edward's readiness to believe that *all* Jews were involved in devaluing his currency, and the disproportionate conviction rate of Jews and Christians, tell us that there was a darker dimension to the story. Early in the new year of 1279, when the trials of the accused began, some twenty-nine Christians were hanged for their crimes, but around ten times as many Jews suffered the same fate. In his drive to improve his finances – and the recoinage, by the way, was a glowing success, generating a profit of around £36,000 – Edward executed half of the adult males in a minority population. Almost incidentally, he had committed the single biggest massacre of Jews in British history.[26]

The next item on Edward's agenda was France. A year earlier, in February 1278, he had dispatched two of his closest companions, Robert Burnell and Otto de Grandson, to deal with the ongoing problems in his Continental dominions. 'We have no one about us,' he told them in a revealing letter, 'whom we believe could know [these affairs] and do our will better or more advantageously than you', adding that he would stand by whatever they decided to do, for he would regard their deeds as his own.[27]

One year on, and it was evident that the king's trust had not been misplaced. There had been substantial progress on all fronts. Gascony itself, extremely fractious at the start of 1278, was now pacified. Burnell and Grandson had taken it upon themselves to dismiss the abrasive and unpopular English seneschal, Luke de Tany, and replace him with John de Grilly, a Savoyard with a softer touch. More impressive still was the deft way in which the two ambassadors had handled the king's biggest headache in the duchy, the turbulent vicomte Gaston de Béarn. In the wake of his earlier rebellion, Gaston had continued to cause trouble. It had not helped matters, for instance, that he had subsequently defamed Edward, publicly calling the king 'a faithless traitor' and challenging him to a duel. By the start of 1279, however, this row too had been mended. Gaston obtained Edward's forgiveness, and also a generous pension from the customs of Bordeaux to keep him sweet in the future. In this respect, his fate forms an interesting contrast with that of the king's other defiant vassal, Llywelyn ap Gruffudd. The difference, of course, was that Gaston, unlike Llywelyn, had the advantage of being able to appeal over Edward's head to the king of France, underlining the fact that the relationship between Gascony and France remained the fundamental question on which all others turned. And here, too, Burnell and Grandson had made substantial progress. By February 1279 it had been agreed that the two kings should talk together in person in order to take matters forward.[28]

So it was that, three months later, Edward and Eleanor crossed the

Channel and travelled to the northern French city of Amiens in order to meet with King Philip. It was a timely rendezvous in more ways than one. A few weeks earlier, news had arrived in England of the death of Eleanor's mother, Joan of Dammartin. Joan, although a former queen of Castile, was not herself Castilian. She originally hailed from France, and it was to France that she had returned in 1254, to rule the small county of Ponthieu, which belonged to her by hereditary right. Now, by the same right, the county passed to Eleanor, who was able to do homage to Philip III at Amiens, and visit the newly acquired lordship, which lay nearby. As for the main purpose of the visit – the very necessary clarification of Franco-Gascon relations – this was a resounding success. Philip made significant concessions on several scores, but none more so than by his agreement to cede the Agenais. This large and prosperous swathe of territory, lying on Gascony's eastern border and centred on the city of Agen, was due to Edward under the terms of the Treaty of Paris, and had been his chief demand during the past five years. The French king's readiness to let it go was testimony to the hard work of Burnell and Grandson, but it also proved that the warm personal relations achieved between Henry III and Louis IX were being carefully maintained by their sons. The meeting at Amiens was a diplomatic triumph. The two courts came together in feasts and banquets, tournaments and jousts, as well as high religious ceremonies in the city's cathedral.[29]

Edward returned to England just in time for his fortieth birthday; such celebrations as there were must have taken place at Dover Castle. One wonders if the anniversary and the location gave him pause to take stock. It was almost five years since his last landing at Dover, when he had returned as a new king to take up his father's crown and to confront a host of problems, the roots of which in some cases stretched back a generation or more. Five years on, and most of those problems had been solved. In England, royal authority had been restored, political and provincial unrest quietened, and the Crown's finances placed on a new and secure footing. In Wales, Llywelyn ap Gruffudd had been reduced to obedience, his inflated principality torn down to its proper size. Gascony, thanks to the king's friends, was now at peace, and relations with France were in an excellent state.[30]

For the first time since his boyhood, Edward discovered he had little to do. In the months after his return from Amiens there was no urgent business to be getting on with. Indeed, if we consider the four-year period after the war with Wales, 1278–81, as a whole, we see a remarkably regular pattern. Parliaments meet every Easter and autumn, without fail and without controversy. By providing an outlet for his subjects' grievances, Edward had ensured that they did not mount up. There were, of course, some disagreements. The new archbishop of Canterbury, John Pecham, who replaced Robert Kilwardby in 1279, brought an earnest desire for reform to his role that to some extent set him against royal interests and antagonised the king. But the dispute, such as it was, did not impair relations between the two men, let alone more general relations between Church and State. It was a measure of the clergy's goodwill that in 1280, having resisted the request since the start of his reign, they finally obliged Edward with a grant of taxation.[31] Similarly, the king's resumption in 1278–79 of his investigation into the rights and liberties that went with landholding gave some concern to his lay magnates. Yet an examination of the witness lists to Edward's charters shows that all his earls, and other great men besides, continued to attend his court, and not just when parliament was in session. The king was firm with his magnates, as he was with his prelates, but he remained friendly with both, and did not make his father's mistake of alienating either group.[32]

And as for Edward himself: never was he more leisured. An examination of his itinerary in this period shows him devoid of any major political agenda. It was seemingly for want of anything better to do in the summer and autumn of 1280 that he embarked on a tour of northern England, taking in Carlisle, Newcastle, Durham, Lincoln and York. In January 1281 he travelled to East Anglia to visit his preferred places of pilgrimage. Edward remained, at forty, as vigorous as ever. On several occasions during these years we catch him on what are evidently hunting trips, in Essex, Northamptonshire and the New Forest. And even when he was in Westminster, it cannot have been all business. At least some of his time there must have been spent enjoying the new Royal Mews that he had established at Charing (the site on which Trafalgar Square now stands). Arranged around a garden courtyard, complete with an elaborate ornamental bird bath at its centre, this home for his hawks and their keepers must have afforded the king many hours of pleasure. Of all his various pastimes, falconry was clearly the favourite.[33]

The leisured lifestyle of the queen in these years is also evident. For the most part Eleanor's interests, like her itinerary, overlapped with those of her husband. She too, for example, liked to hunt, though she used dogs rather more than he did, and she probably preferred the bow whereas he reportedly favoured the sword. Something more of Eleanor's individual tastes can be gleaned from the accounts of her estate management. The occasional purchase of citrus fruits and olive oil from overseas merchants suggest the appetites acquired in childhood were not wholly forgotten. Similarly, her employment of two Spanish gardeners at her manor of King's Langley in Hertfordshire (visited several times in 1280–81) and the creation there of ditches and wells may imply an attempt to reproduce in England the kind of water gardens favoured in southern Castile. Perhaps most evocative of royal tastes, however, is the way in which the king and the queen together transformed Leeds Castle in Kent. Acquired by Eleanor in 1278 and rebuilt with her husband's help in the years that followed, Leeds became a veritable pleasure palace (an aspect it retains today, despite considerable modern alterations). The inclusion of a bath for the king may hint at another attempt to re-create something of that same Spanish style in balmy Kent, but the castle's most notable features – its wide moat and its isolated 'gloriette' of privy apartments – indicate that Edward and Eleanor's tastes were chiefly informed by their shared love of romance and fantasy.[34]

These easy days would have allowed both the king and the queen to spend more time with their children. Since her return to England, Eleanor's relentless round of pregnancies had continued: new and lasting additions to the royal nursery in the late 1270s came in the shape of Margaret (b. 1275) and Mary (b. 1279). Edward's visits to Windsor and Woodstock, while by no means rare, remained occasional, so neither baby daughter would have seen much of their father, nor perhaps their mother. But the same was not necessarily true of their older siblings. By the end of the decade, Eleanor (b. 1269), Joan (b. 1271) and Alfonso (b. 1273) would have been old enough to accompany the court as it travelled, at least for short periods, and certainly able to join their parents for Christmas, Easter and other festivities.[35]

Perhaps, therefore, it was with his family that Edward paid his mysterious springtime visits to Gloucestershire. From 1278 until 1282, and always in the month of March, the king spent an average of two to three weeks each year at Quenington and Down Ampney, two manors in the neighbourhood of Cirencester. Since these visits had no discernible purpose, political, religious or otherwise, the assumption is that they too were a luxury afforded by the relative calm of these years, a regular period of relaxation in a rural locale for a king and queen whose tastes, when given free rein, tended towards escapism.[36]

Such freedom could not last forever. It was just after leaving Down Ampney in March 1282 that Edward began to receive urgent messages from every corner of Wales.

While Edward's existence had become increasingly easy, Llywelyn's life had become correspondingly hard. Publicly, the post-war relationship between the two men had been all smiles and handshakes; privately, the prince felt unduly put upon. On the day of his wedding, for example (a spectacle already contrived in part for English amusement), Llywelyn, so he later alleged, was 'compelled by fear' into making additional written concessions to the king, in contravention of their earlier peace agreement.

Further indignities and irritations had followed. Llywelyn's messengers were arrested without reason at Chester; his huntsmen were maltreated by the king's men near Aberystwyth. Most trying of the prince's patience was his legal effort to recover a strip of territory on his south-eastern border (Arwystli) from his old adversary, Gruffudd ap Gwenwynwyn. The case, Llywelyn contended, should be decided by Welsh law. Not so, said Gruffudd: English law should apply. Edward, in his capacity as supreme judge, responded by ordering one inquiry after another, repeatedly adjourning his decision, but always obliging the prince to jump through the tangled loops of English judicial procedure. After four years of pleading, Llywelyn had achieved nothing, and it was beginning to tell on his patience. Once a great man, he knew the war had made him small, but latterly he had been made to feel it.[37]

And yet, irritating though the prince's experiences undoubtedly were, they were nothing compared to the oppressions being endured elsewhere in Wales. New English castles thrusting their way skywards; intolerant English administrators trying to govern their districts in line with their own notions of normality: outside of Snowdonia, the Welsh were suffering on an altogether different scale. Indeed, that they 'were treated more cruelly than the Saracens by the king's bailiffs and other royal officers', was one later complaint. To the men of the north-east it was a throwback to the worst days of the 1250s, when Henry III had imposed a similar regime on the Four Cantrefs. To their countrymen in south and west Wales, it was domination of a kind they had neither experienced nor anticipated. Life under Llywelyn had seemed taxing at the time, but now, with the advent of English officialdom, the prince's rule was assuming the retrospective aspect of a golden age.[38]

We scarcely need to look for specific reasons for such oppression. Edward was in general terms anxious to avoid his father's mistakes; he did not set out deliberately to provoke Wales, its inhabitants or its prince. Nor, in all probability, did the men whom he appointed to administer his conquests. But both the king and his lieutenants were conditioned from birth to regard the Welsh as an inferior race. If they preferred to conduct business along English lines, it was because those lines were to them self-evidently more sensible than the backward and barbarous ways of a people whose language, habits and culture they could not comprehend.

Nevertheless, specific reasons did exist. Just as Llywelyn felt belittled by Edward, so Edward felt antagonised by Llywelyn. From the king's perspective, it seemed that the prince was engaged in a deliberate attempt to test the limits of their peace agreement, and was trying to force him into a judgement that would damage the rights of his Crown. When Llywelyn reactivated his plea for Arwystli in the autumn of 1281, Edward's patience – febrile at the best of times – seems to have snapped. He responded by removing the justiciar of Chester and replacing him with the hard-liner Reginald de Grey. The result was an immediate intensification of the English grip on north-east Wales.[39]

This change had little direct impact on Llywelyn, ensconced as he was in Snowdonia. It did, however, affect his younger brother. Dafydd ap Gruffudd, prickly by nature, already considered himself a man hard done by. The English failure to cross the Conwy in 1277 had denied him the prize he most desired, his rightful share of Gwynedd. In acknowledgement of this disappointment, Edward had granted him lands in lieu; but since this compensation amounted to two of the Four Cantrefs, it meant that Dafydd's lordship bordered that of the king himself. Consequently it was Dafydd rather than his brother who bore the full brunt of the new and high-handed English regime at Chester. In later letters to the archbishop of Canterbury Dafydd complained of how, on one occasion, the justiciar had wrongly accused him of harbouring fugitives; of how, at another time, his woods had been chopped down and sold off by the justiciar's men; and of how, most contentiously, he had been summoned to be judged at the king's court at Chester for lands that he held in Wales.[40]

Dafydd was not alone in feeling mightily oppressed. Elsewhere in Wales, wherever newly extended English power marched with that of the natives, other Welsh lords, some of whom had helped to bring down Llywelyn, also wondered at their newly straitened circumstances. Rhys Wyndod, the southern lord who lost no fewer than three castles in 1277, complained that six of his men had been killed by the English and yet no amends had been made. Faced with such injustices, such men, like Dafydd himself, began to borrow from the script written by Llywelyn. They were unable to obtain redress; they were compelled to attend English courts; their own law was being denied. And, if their law was being denied, it followed that their identity as a people was being denied. 'Let the law of Wales be unchanged,' Dafydd told Edward I, 'like the laws of other nations.' It was a powerful and popular idea for a downtrodden people. In the spring of 1282, it became their cry to arms.[41]

★　★　★

It was the night of 21 March 1282, and Roger Clifford, one of Edward's oldest friends, was asleep in Hawarden Castle. Some five miles to the west of Chester, Hawarden had come to the Crown as a result of the recent war, and its castle was seemingly new. Most likely the building works there had begun soon after Clifford's appointment as keeper of the lordship just over a year earlier. That being the case, they can scarcely have been finished on the night in question – it happened to be the eve of Palm Sunday – when Dafydd ap Gruffudd and a band of armed Welshmen descended, burned the castle, killed several members of Clifford's household, and carted the constable himself off into captivity.[42]

A widespread revolt against English rule was under way. The following day Flint and Rhuddlan were subjected to identical assaults; two days later Aberystwyth was taken by trickery. In each case the castles were attacked: Aberystwyth was destroyed, and Rhuddlan too may well have fallen. But, in each case, the castles formed only part of the target. The rebels' fury was directed equally at the attendant towns, those enclaves of English privilege, where the Welsh were obliged to trade but could not live, and where the legal discrimination between the two peoples was a fact of everyday existence. Property was looted, houses were burned, and those settlers who could not flee were killed.[43]

The scope and success of the revolt shows that it was popular; its timing reveals that it was planned. As Dafydd and his followers launched his attacks in the north, Rhys Wyndod and his allies mounted copycat assaults in the south, recovering the castles at Llandovery and Carreg Cennen. Meanwhile, other Welsh lords led the attacks on Oswestry, an English town on the eastern border, subjecting it to the same fate as the other new boroughs. Clearly these leaders had leagued together in the weeks and months beforehand and agreed on the date that their pent-up anger would be released.[44]

It seems equally clear that Llywelyn was not among their number. The prince, when later given the chance to account for his actions, claimed to have had no prior knowledge of the rebellion, and indeed there is no good evidence of his involvement. The sudden outbreak therefore placed him in a terrible dilemma: whether to support Dafydd's intemperate action or to assist Edward I in suppressing it. If patriotic sensibility urged him to back his brother, his sense as a politician restrained him, for the timing was wrong, and the chances of success impossibly slim. For a while, at least, Llywelyn must have debated, with his councillors, and with himself. It has been suggested, temptingly, that he may have waited until as late as June before making his decision.

In 1282 Llywelyn's own time was running out. He was approaching, if he had not already attained, his sixtieth year. But in the spring of that year, his young wife, Eleanor, was pregnant. If their child was male, then it might be worth playing the long game: putting down his perfidious brother to protect the patrimony for his son, and thereby preserving an independent Gwynedd, and a principality that might one day recover its greatness.

On 19 June this hope for the future evaporated. Eleanor died in childbirth. The child, which survived, was a girl, christened Gwenllian. It was, perhaps, a broken and desperate prince who finally joined his brother and his people that summer, to face the king of England's immeasurable wrath.[45]

It was 25 March, three days after the first attacks, that Edward heard the news. More than anything else, it was the treachery that seems to have astonished him. Dafydd, the king was later minded to recall, 'had been received as an exile, nourished as an orphan, endowed with lands and placed among the great ones of the palace'. That such generosity should be repaid by rebellion almost beggared belief. When, later that same day, writs began to emanate from the royal chancery, they naturally dwelt on the killing, burning and kidnapping. But when Edward said the Welsh were 'unmindful of their own salvation', he meant they had sworn sacred oaths to obey him, and these oaths had now been broken.[46]

And how the writs flew. Edward, as we have noted, was effectively on holiday at the time of the revolt, caught off-guard and with few of his great men about him. But as soon as the news broke messengers sped out in all directions. Within ten days the council was in session. On 6 April the other magnates were called to muster in mid-May, at Worcester, as before. On 7 April the knights of the household began to draw pay, and a contingent galloped north to see to the relief of Rhuddlan. Orders started to pour out for supplies. Food was demanded from Essex, Surrey, Kent and Hampshire. Workmen – 345 carpenters and more than 1,000 diggers – were summoned from no fewer than twenty-eight counties. The men of the Cinque Ports were warned to prepare their ships, the Riccardi to be ready with their money. Naturally this activity was not confined to England. Crossbowmen were ordered from Gascony, horses were purchased from France, and other supplies were requested from Ponthieu, Ireland and even from Scotland.[47]

It was only in May, when the king arrived at Worcester, that his tremendous momentum suffered a setback. Edward's call to arms had been highly unusual. He had not, as was conventional, asked men to serve him out of obligation, nor had his summons been universal. Instead, some half a dozen earls and 150 other named individuals had been 'affectionately requested' to serve in return for pay. It was, it seems, the king's intention to avoid the limitations of the customary forty days' service, and instead to put the relationship between him and his cavalry forces on a more businesslike basis.

Some of the earls, at least, must have agreed to this idea, for they were with the king in early April when the orders had gone out. It was probably the unconsulted majority, beyond the council, who objected to a scheme that would have effectively made them the king's mercenaries. Moreover, the suggestion that they should forget their ancient obligations and embark on a novel arrangement must have seemed more than a little rich, coming as it did from a king who, from the moment of his accession, had insisted on the most traditional interpretation of his own rights. No official protest is recorded, but the idea of paid service was quietly dropped. Three days into the muster, new writs were issued of the conventional kind: the magnates were summoned to reassemble at Rhuddlan at the start of August. None of the earls, in the event, accepted pay. It is not impossible that two of them, the earl of Hereford and the earl of Gloucester, had some hand in leading the opposition to the king. Hereford held the hereditary honour of 'constable of England', with responsibility for compiling the lists of men who served in a campaign, as well as for their discipline. As early as 6 April he had insisted on receiving the traditional perquisites that went with his office. Meanwhile, Gloucester (that is, our old friend Gilbert de Clare) was clearly put out at the suggestion that he should serve in an army under the command of the new justiciar of south Wales, Robert Tiptoft. On 10 April, the earl had evidently insisted that the honour of leading the southern forces should be his.[48]

As this mention of a southern army suggests, Edward's strategy in 1282 was much the same as it had been five years earlier. Having left Gloucester in charge of the south (albeit with Tiptoft as his deputy), the king proceeded north towards Chester, from where, as before, he would lead the main force into north Wales. En route he stopped in Shrewsbury, and parted company with Roger Mortimer. The old warrior who had said farewell to arms three years earlier was once again called upon to do what he did best, and hold the line in the middle March.[49]

Nevertheless, although the strategy was the same in broad terms, there were important differences this time around. In 1277 Llywelyn had been quite isolated; Edward's main opponent that year had been the Welsh terrain. On this occasion, by contrast, the opposition was far more general, the fighting fiercer and more widespread. Before he could advance along the coast road to Rhuddlan, the king had first to tackle the resistance in the interior of the Four Cantrefs, led by Dafydd ap

Gruffudd. The rebel leader and his Welsh allies had made their chief stronghold at Denbigh, and also held a number of other castles in the same region.[50]

The initial stage of this operation was carried out in early June, soon after Edward had arrived at Chester. While the king remained in the city supervising the assembly of men and materials for his push along coast, it fell to Reginald de Grey – justiciar of Chester, antagoniser of Dafydd and, since March, captain of the king's northern forces – to lead the first inland assault. With some 7,000 foot soldiers already at his disposal, many of them archers, Grey made swift progress. In the middle of June he recovered the castle at Hope (Caergwrle), which Dafydd destroyed in his retreat, and where over 1,000 English workmen immediately began the business of reconstruction. By the end of the month the king's forces had retaken another castle at Ewloe, and also Hawarden, the point from which the whole conflagration had been started.[51]

But by this time they had heard the bad news: Gloucester and his army had already been defeated. The haughty earl, having insisted on leading the king's southern forces, had succeeded in advancing all of four miles before being overtaken by disaster. On 11 June some 1,600 English foot and at least a hundred horse had set out under his command from their base at Dinefwr to retake nearby Carreg Cennen. Five days later, their objective achieved, they were retracing their steps when the Welsh attacked. Gloucester himself escaped, but others were not so lucky. Among the knightly casualties was William, son of William de Valence, a cousin of the king. Many of the foot soldiers must also have perished; English military activity in south Wales came to an abrupt and inglorious halt.[52]

Gloucester's incompetence obliged Edward to alter his plans. The king had hoped to bring the full weight of his cavalry forces to bear against Snowdonia; now he had to divert some of these troops into the southern theatre. On 2 July the knights of the south-western counties of England were advised that their new muster point was Carmarthen; those of the west Midlands were told to go to Montgomery. Four days later, Gloucester, who by this time had appeared before the king to explain himself, was deprived of his command. In his place was appointed William de Valence, who may have been grateful for the opportunity to avenge the death of his son.[53]

That same day Edward moved out of Chester and advanced towards Rhuddlan. His new castle there, far from complete at the time of his last visit, had been swiftly recovered by the knights of the household in April. Nevertheless, the Welsh had apparently done substantial damage with their siege engines before they departed: repairs were put in place immediately after the king's arrival. Now was the time for Rhuddlan, as the foremost base of English operations, to prove it was worth its expensive price tag. At once the newly canalised River Clwyd was seen to have been a sound investment, when the forty-strong fleet of the Cinque Ports sailed up to the walls of the castle.[54]

From Rhuddlan, Edward intended to achieve two separate but simultaneous objectives: the capture of Denbigh and the occupation of Anglesey. Both waited on the build-up of troops and supplies, but early August saw the arrival of the cavalry for their postponed muster, and by the middle of the month there were 6,000 infantry in pay.[55]

The Anglesey divisions were the first to leave. Under the captaincy of Luke de Tany, erstwhile seneschal of Gascony, at least 200 horse and 2,000 foot occupied the island and, as before, secured its harvest. This was not, however, simply to be a repeat performance of the exercise of five years earlier. That August, while Tany and his troops fought to secure a beachhead, the men of the Cinque Ports began to ship great quantities of timber, nails, rope and iron from Chester to Rhuddlan, and from Rhuddlan to Anglesey. This was the makings of the most ambitious part of the campaign plan: a bridge of boats that would link the island to the mainland, allowing Tany's army to penetrate Snowdonia from the rear. In early September hundreds of carpenters were engaged in its construction.[56]

By that time the king's army had also moved out. To them fell the more tedious task of securing every strongpoint and valley in the Four Cantrefs. Edward marched first to Ruthin, a castle further up the Clwyd that had fallen to Reginald de Grey before the end of August. Later he pushed west to Llangernyw, just a few miles from the upper reaches of the Conwy. Progress was painfully slow, no doubt out of caution. This was a war being fought on ground where mounted cavalry were of limited, not to say negligible use, but where guerrilla tactics could easily hand victory to the Welsh. Throughout September the king's forces were divided into three smaller armies, each one inching their way forward, anxious not to repeat the earl of Gloucester's error.[57]

As the autumn began to set in, their task approached completion. In early October Edward was back at Rhuddlan, where he began to hand out portions of conquered territory to his friends as reward for their services. By this time, too, the south was secure. William de Valence had led a successful month-long mission from Carmarthen to Cardigan by way of Aberystwyth. It remained only to take out Dafydd's main base at Denbigh, and this was done three weeks into the month. On 22 October the king arrived there in person, but Dafydd was nowhere to be seen. The rebels had retreated into Snowdonia, and the mountains that had always been their surest refuge. This time, however, Edward was quite determined: there would be no escape. His armies remained intact and, moreover, his bridge of boats was ready.[58]

It was at this critical juncture that the archbishop of Canterbury arrived with the notion of ending the war by peaceful negotiation. Given the royal rebuffs he had already received since taking office three years earlier, John Pecham can hardly have expected that his latest idea would elicit the king's unqualified enthusiasm. Apart from anything else, winter was now setting in; even a short delay at this stage could prove costly, if not calamitous, to English military plans. And yet, at the same time, Edward could not reasonably refuse a request by his most senior churchman to send an emissary into Gwynedd with the hope of inducing a Welsh surrender. Pecham, after all, was not proposing to act as an impartial arbiter: the letters he sent to Llywelyn were on a par with his earlier condemnation of Welsh law. The prince and his countrymen were reproached for their crime of rebellion, and exhorted to make an immediate and unconditional submission.[59]

Within a few days, however, the archbishop had received a response that gave him pause. In a lengthy written statement Llywelyn and his councillors set out a justification for their actions (this is the principal record of Welsh grievances discussed earlier in this chapter). They also enumerated what they claimed were the crimes of the English in recent weeks: the burning of churches, the killing of monks and nuns, the indiscriminate slaughter 'of women and infants at the breast and in the womb'. It was enough to persuade Pecham, when he came before the king in the closing days of October, to suggest that such complaints merited investigation and correction.[60]

Edward would not stand for this. As far as he was concerned, the Welsh had always had the opportunity to present him with any complaints they might have had; he was not about to start a dialogue at this late stage with men who had attacked his castles and killed his other subjects. From what we can tell – for we have only the archbishop's account – these exchanges with the king must have been very difficult indeed. Edward told Pecham that he would not issue safe-conducts for the Welsh to come and go from his court. In that case, Pecham informed Edward, he would go to see Llywelyn himself. The king made it clear that he did not approve. The archbishop went anyway.[61]

More days were therefore lost as Pecham, in defiance of Edward's wishes, travelled into Snowdonia to hold talks with the Welsh leader. When he returned, in early November, it was with the unhappy knowledge that both parties were wedded to irreconcilable positions: Edward's insistence on unconditional submission was matched by Llywelyn's refusal to surrender except on guaranteed terms. In desperation, the archbishop, this time with Edward's consent, tried to devise a formula that could satisfy both sides. Certain English magnates promised that, if the prince submitted, they would lobby the king on his behalf. In secret, a document was sent to Llywelyn, offering him an earldom in England if he would give up the fight for Wales.[62]

Before the prince could respond to this offer, however, its credibility was hopelessly compromised by events elsewhere. During his negotiations with Pecham, it appears that Llywelyn had based himself at his hall of Garth Celyn, which lay on the coast, not far from Bangor. This meant that, thanks to the recently completed bridge of boats, he was also not far from the English base on Anglesey, and the temptation was evidently too great for the army there to resist. On 6 November Luke de Tany and his forces poured across the bridge, almost certainly with the intention of catching the prince and his council unawares and bringing the war to a swift conclusion. They rode out, in the words of one chronicler, 'to acquire glory and reputation'.

What they found was death. That day saw the greatest English disaster in Wales, not just of this campaign, but in the course of Edward's life to date. Reports of precisely what happened, as ever, differ in their detail. From the best of them it would seem that the cavalry had crossed the bridge and moved some distance along the coast when, suddenly, the Welsh swept down from the mountains and attacked. Outnumbered and outflanked, the horsemen turned to flee but, the tide having changed in the meantime, they found that they could not get back to the bridge. 'Panic-stricken at the sight of their numbers,' wrote one English chronicler, 'our men preferred to face the water than the enemy. They plunged into the sea, burdened as they were with their armour, and were drowned all in a moment.'

At least sixteen English knights were lost, including Luke de Tany himself, and Roger Clifford, namesake son of the king's captive friend. Also among the dead were two young relatives of the chancellor Robert Burnell, possibly his nephews, perhaps his bastard sons. Notable survivors included the redoubtable Otto de Grandson, and the household knight William Latimer, whose horse swam him through the waves to safety.[63]

We do not know on whose authority the decision to launch the attack was taken. Some chroniclers are adamant that the initiative lay with the commanders on Anglesey, and others imply that Edward himself had not approved the action. We might reflect, however, that it would have taken a bold commander to have acted in this way without seeking the highest approval, and also note further that it would have been entirely in keeping with the king's earlier daring stratagems – his raid on Kenilworth, his escape from Hereford – to have given such a scheme the go-ahead.

What is certain is that, in the wake of the thwarted assault, all talk of submission and secret deals was ended. Five days after their victory on the shores of Snowdonia, Llywelyn and his councillors sent their final reply. Nominally addressed to Archbishop Pecham, but surely written above all for the ears of Edward I, it rang with defiance. The king, they declared, had no legitimate claim to the Four Cantrefs or to Anglesey, for he had only ever held them by force, and using officers who had exercised 'the cruellest tyranny'. These lands, they averred, belonged 'purely to the prince, and the princes and their predecessors from the time of Camber, son of Brutus' – the founding father of the British people was invoked in the document no fewer than three times. As for the secret offer of an earldom in England, Llywelyn publicly rejected it as a worthless promise made by men out to disinherit him. And even if the prince had been minded to accept, his council would have prevented him. 'The people of Snowdonia,' the letter concluded, 'do not wish to do homage to a stranger, of whose language, manners and laws they are entirely ignorant.'[64]

So this was it: not a struggle between an offended overlord and his rebellious vassals, as had earlier been pretended. This was a war between peoples; a veritable clash of civilisations. As soon as he heard the news from Anglesey, Edward returned from Denbigh to Rhuddlan to consult with his magnates and plan his next move. By any assessment their situation was no longer strong. The recent disaster apart, numbers of horse and infantry were falling, the obligation to serve having long since expired. But when Llywelyn's letter arrived, there was no question about what would have to be done. On 24 November writs were dispatched to every county in England.

The king, they announced, proposed 'to put an end finally to the matter that he had now begun of suppressing the malice of the Welsh'. This, it was explained, was an historic struggle that it fell to their generation to end. It would entail labours and expenses beyond what was customary; the burden might therefore seem hard. But it was better that they bear it now than be tormented by the Welsh in the future. In separate letters to the clergy of England, Edward added that he wished to finish the business in Wales for 'the praise and honour of God, the increase and renown of him and his realm, and the perpetual peace of his realm and people'.[65]

No doubt these writs reflected a genuine resolve on the part of the king and his magnates, ensconced at Rhuddlan in the deepening winter of 1282. Scores of other orders were sent out simultaneously, requiring new levies of infantry to be raised and new contingents of crossbowmen to be recruited. Nevertheless, the rallying cry to England was propaganda with a specific purpose. What Edward needed above all else was cash. Already this second Welsh war had gone on far too long; it would not be possible to pay for it using the kind of expedients that had eventually paid for its predecessor, nor, for that matter, with the emergency loans that the king's ministers had managed to extract from various English towns and cities during the course of the summer. For the fight to be continued on the scale that was necessary, there was only one possible solution, and that was a grant of general taxation. This was the burden Edward needed his people to bear, and the reason behind his extraordinary writs. In January, he intended, two great assemblies would gather, one in Northampton, the other in York. Each would be larger than any parliament ever summoned: not only four knights from every county and two men from every town, but also every landowner with an income of more than £20 a year. All would come at the king's command to help him in this hour of great national need.[66]

Llywelyn and his allies could not afford to wait for this to happen. At present they were encircled, but, with the respite granted by their recent victory, they might open up new fronts. Already in the second half of November there were fresh risings in south and west Wales, perhaps fomented by the presence of the prince himself in those areas. It was in the middle March, however, that Llywelyn was hoping for the greatest gains. There, on 26 November, Roger Mortimer, not only the king's commander in the region but also the most powerful lord in his own right, had died of natural causes. ('His long and praiseworthy services,' wrote Edward to Mortimer's namesake son, 'recur frequently and spontaneously to our memory.') The old warrior's passing had led to immediate fears of an English collapse in central Wales: within weeks the sheriff of Shropshire was reporting that Mortimer's 'fickle and haughty' tenants were 'on the point of leaving the king's peace'. In Edward's second set-back that autumn, Llywelyn saw his best opportunity. Leaving Dafydd in charge of Snowdonia, the prince took his army and struck out in the direction of Builth.[67]

He arrived there on 11 December to find the might of the entire middle March ranged ready to meet him. Coincidence or conspiracy? There is circumstantial evidence to suggest that the Welsh leader had been lured into a trap devised by Mortimer's sons and perhaps by some of his own men too. Whatever the truth, it is clear enough what happened next. On the high ground to the west of Builth, at a place called Cilmeri, a substantial battle took place between the English and Welsh forces, and in the course of the fighting the prince of Wales fell. Most accounts agree that he somehow became separated from his men, and was killed unrecognised by his English assailant. It was only when the battle was over, and the bodies were examined, that his corpse was identified.

'Know, Sire,' wrote Roger Lestrange, captain of the English forces, to his royal master, 'that Llywelyn ap Gruffudd is dead, his army broken, and the flower of his men killed.' Accompanying the letter as proof was the prince's severed head. Edward had it sent on to Anglesey to cheer his other troops, and from there dispatched to London, where its arrival was greeted with a fanfare of trumpets and horns. Carried through the city's streets on the end of a lance, it was finally placed on an iron spike above the Tower of London and crowned with a mockery of ivy. The prophecy that a Welshmen would one day wear a crown in London was in this grisly way seen to have been fulfilled.[68]

While the English rejoiced, Wales despaired. 'See you not that the world is ending?' asked one Welsh poet. 'Ah, God, that the sea would cover the land!' For his countrymen, Llywelyn's death was an unmitigated disaster. Their leader for more than thirty years, he had once given them a greater unity than they had ever known before. It is doubtful whether, had he lived longer, they would have recovered it. Without him, however, the hope of doing so evaporated entirely. Dafydd ap Gruffudd now took up the princely title and entered into the inheritance that he had coveted for a lifetime. But Dafydd was not a man to fill his brother's shoes. Just a few weeks earlier he had been pleased to send his own letter of defiance to Archbishop Pecham, proudly proclaiming that the Welsh were fighting a just war, and hopeful of God's help. Now he was ready to plead for peace, and (according to one English chronicler) sent the captive Roger Clifford to beg Edward for terms.[69]

It was a request that, unsurprisingly, the king was not minded to consider. Already by the time of Llywelyn's death, ships were arriving at Rhuddlan from Gascony, bringing 200 new horse, 1,300 foot soldiers and 70,000 crossbow bolts. Other ships from Ireland brought the food to feed the troops — cows, pigs, sheep, oats, wine, cheese and beer. Meanwhile, the knights of south-western England were dutifully reassembling at Carmarthen. By January new drafts of infantry were massing in both north and south.[70]

Nor was it just a case of material preparation. The death of the Welsh leader had infused the English with an even greater sense of destiny and the righteousness of their cause. 'Glory be to God in the highest, peace on earth to men of good will, a triumph to the English, victory to King Edward, honour to the Church, rejoicing to the Christian faith, confusion to jealous men, dismay to envious ones, and to the Welsh everlasting extermination.' So wrote an English clerk in Rome in January when he heard the news of Llywelyn's death. Edward, the same writer added, was the king 'whose footsteps the heavenly king directs . . . long may he live and reign and conquer and rule'; in tackling the Welsh, he and his soldiers were 'powerfully removing the reproach of their people, that domestic enemy . . . the disturber of English peace'. There can be little doubt that Edward himself shared this sense of missionary purpose. His war with Wales had taken on the aspect of a secular crusade. His infantry were issued with armbands bearing the cross of St George. His armies, when they advanced, marched behind St George's banner.[71]

They advanced in January 1283. In a co-ordinated offensive, William de Valence led 1,500 foot-soldiers north from Carmarthen and retook Aberystwyth. In the north Edward's army, some 5,000 strong, marched south-west out of Rhuddlan and struck into the heart of Snowdonia. Their target was the Welsh castle at Dolwyddelan, birthplace of Llywelyn the Great. It fell after the shortest of sieges and was occupied by a new English garrison. By the end of the month the brief campaign was over. Edward was back at Rhuddlan, Valence was ensconced at Aberystwyth, and the back of Welsh resistance had been broken.[72]

For a short while Edward stayed his hand. The Welsh were now weak, crippled even, but the occupation of Snowdonia remained a daunting proposition, especially in the dead of winter. Royal resources, moreover, were not infinite: having achieved his targeted objectives, the king let go most of his infantry and mercenaries. Nevertheless, the means for achieving a decisive victory would soon be at Edward's disposal. In January his two great assemblies had gathered in England and, in an atmosphere no doubt exhilarated by Llywelyn's demise, agreed to a grant of taxation. On the last day of February the king sent out writs ordering its collection.[73]

Two weeks later the invasion of Gwynedd began. On 13 March 1283 Edward sailed across the mouth of the Conwy and established a new base camp on the river's western shore. With Eleanor by his side, the king took up residence in the hall that had been built there by Llywelyn, while his troops occupied the grounds of the nearby Cistercian abbey where the bones of the prince's ancestors lay buried. The following day new writs went out. The earls and barons of England were summoned once again to muster at Montgomery and Carmarthen. One week later, a further 5,000 English infantry were ordered. The occupation of Wales was finally under way.[74]

There was one man, above all, whom Edward wanted to catch, and Dafydd ap Gruffudd responded by running. At first he fled south, into the mountains of Meirionnydd, holing up in the isolated Castell-y-Bere at the foot of Cadair Idris. That fortress soon came under siege by English forces, and fell in the last week of April, but by then the fugitive prince had fled again. As a consequence, the English invasion of Snowdonia began to assume the character of a massive manhunt. Roger Lestrange led his men into Wales from the middle March; Valence pushed up from the south; the army of Anglesey, now under the more competent command of Otto de Grandson, crossed the pontoon bridge and penetrated the interior. Finally, in the second week of May, the king himself marched up the Conwy with 7,000 men and set up a temporary headquarters at Dolwyddelan. Bands of Englishmen swarmed through the valleys and over the mountains, finding many Welshman who were ready to make their submission. Dafydd, however, still could not be found.[75]

No doubt somewhat frustrated, Edward returned to his camp at Conwy in early June, and a fortnight later retired to Rhuddlan in order to celebrate his birthday. He was still there a week or so later when, like a belated birthday present, the longed-for news arrived. Dafydd had been taken, captured near Llanberis at the foot of Mount Snowdon. On 28 June the king sent out jubilant letters to his people in England, announcing that the prince, 'last of a treacherous line', was now in his custody, having been caught by 'men of his own tongue'. Edward immediately returned to Snowdonia for a two-month tour, during which hostages were taken and the submissions of communities were received. It was only at the end of August, after an absence that had lasted more than a year, that the king finally returned to England.[76]

The conquest of Wales, so often contemplated by previous English kings but never carried through, was at last complete. It had taken a monumental effort on the part of Edward, his magnates and his people. The financial cost alone was colossal. As far as can be determined, the total budget stood somewhere in the region of £120,000 – that is, around five times the amount spent on the previous Welsh war. The king's subjects in England had dug deep into their pockets to find him a tax of nearly £50,000; the Riccardi of Lucca, his bankers, had strained to keep the river of silver pennies flowing into the war zone in order that the troops could be paid. In terms of those troops, the cost had been higher still. Among the English nobility, the sons of William de Valence, Robert Burnell and Roger Clifford were just a few of the numerous high-status casualties; among the common foot soldiery, the numbers must have run to countless hundreds, probably thousands. As early as October 1282, before the invasion of Snowdonia had even started, the military cemetery at Rhuddlan had already run out of room for bodies. The bitter cold of a winter campaign – itself an unprecedented under-taking – must have accounted for the fact that many of those who had been marched to Wales from distant villages in England would not be returning home. Nor, of course, had the burden been borne by England alone: men and supplies had poured into Wales from Ireland, Gascony and Ponthieu at Edward's behest.[77]

But nowhere, naturally, was the impact of conquest felt more force-fully than in Wales itself. 'What is left us that we should linger?' wondered the author of Llywelyn's lament. 'No place of escape from Terror's prison/No place to live – wretched is living!' The trauma of 1282–83 was not to be measured merely by the loss of a prince, however mighty. It was also to be reckoned in the appropriation of the halls, houses and castles that had belonged to Llywelyn's dynasty since time out of mind; the confiscation of Welsh secular treasures and holy relics; the destruc-tion of churches and abbeys, most notably in the case of the abbey at Conwy. It must have been felt, above all, in terms of human suffering and loss, to an extent that is now unknown but that must have exceeded the English death toll many times over.[78]

And yet, with the conquest now complete, the killing came to an end. Choleric English clerics at the Roman Curia, of course, full of Christian charity, might well wish the Welsh 'extermination', and no doubt other Englishmen, their deep-seated antipathy stoked by Edward's propaganda, must have felt the same way. The king himself, however, subscribed to higher ideals of justice and chivalry. In victory, it behoved him to be fair, magnanimous and merciful. Thousands of Welshmen might have died, but they had died fighting. Those who had submitted or were captured might suffer imprisonment, but their lives would be spared.

Except Dafydd ap Gruffudd. His crimes, in Edward's eyes, were too great, and his treachery too profound, to be punished or pardoned in the normal way. As the instigator and inciter of rebellion, Dafydd was deemed to deserve death, just as surely as that earlier troublemaker, Simon de Montfort, had done. But Montfort, and for that matter Llywelyn, had obliged the king by dying in battle; Dafydd had merely been wounded in the course of his capture. This may have been a cause of regret for Edward, for it meant that he had to take unprecedented action in the autumn of 1283. No one, however, would have more cause to regret his failure to die on the slopes of Snowdon than Dafydd himself.

In September the captive prince was brought under armed escort from Rhuddlan to Shrewsbury, and there, on the last day of the month, a parliament assembled to decide his fate. Edward proposed, and his magnates agreed, that the prince was guilty of treason: the crime of plotting the king's death. Notionally, treason had existed for a long time, but never before had it been twisted to apply to rebellion, or attributed to someone of such exalted rank. The chroniclers who described what followed were aware that they had witnessed something 'in previous times unknown'. On 2 October Dafydd was subjected to a four-fold punishment. For his treason, he was dragged through Shrewsbury 'at the horse's tail' to a scaffold; there, for his homicides, he was hanged alive. Next, for having committed his crimes in Holy Week, he was disembowelled, and his entrails were burned. Lastly, for having plotted the king's death, his body was quartered, and the parts were dispatched to the four corners of Edward's kingdom. His head was carried off by the citizens of London, to be displayed next to that of his brother.[79]

After the blood-letting came the thanksgiving. From Shropshire, Edward moved south, touring the cathedrals, abbeys and priories of Herefordshire, Gloucestershire and Worcestershire. Having returned to Rhuddlan for Christmas, in the New Year he crossed the Pennines to repeat the exercise in Yorkshire and Lincolnshire. There can be no doubt that the king considered that the offerings he made during these months and the ceremonies he attended were entirely fitting and important in the wake of his victory. Yet the suspicion remains that he was also deliberately killing time, awaiting the onset of spring for the momentous finale he had planned.[80]

When the spring arrived, Edward returned to Wales for a second time, and he came fully conscious of his rights and responsibilities as a conqueror. On 19 March, at Rhuddlan, a great statute was promulgated, setting out how Snowdonia and the other royal lands in Wales would be governed in the future. It was, on the whole, a wisely worded and well-balanced document, insisting, for example, that English law should apply in criminal cases, but also allowing that, for civil pleas (inheritance, debts and contracts) Welsh procedures might be maintained. Nevertheless, this synthesised system was to be administered on purely English lines. From now on, Snowdonia would be run by the full panoply of royal officials familiar in England – sheriffs, coroners, bailiffs and their deputies – all answering to a new justiciar of north-west Wales. As the king explained in the statute's preamble, 'Divine providence, which is unerring in its dispositions ... has now, of its grace, wholly and entirely converted the land of Wales ... into a dominion of our ownership.'[81]

From Rhuddlan Edward moved west, back into Snowdonia itself. There he was able to assess how the physical process of transformation was progressing. Just as with his earlier campaign, the king's new conquest was being cemented with a trio of new castles. Each of them, like their precursors, was located on the coast so as to be suppliable by sea, and each of them, more so than before, was state of the art in terms of its defensive capabilities. These latest castles, too, were set to possess a glamour that their counterparts at Flint, Rhuddlan and Aberystwyth would lack by comparison. At Conwy, for instance, where Edward and Eleanor arrived on 26 March, a castle was rising every bit as fantastical as the one they were still fashioning at Leeds. Meanwhile, across the other side of the mountains, on a rock called Harlech, a similar fortress, replete with multiple towers and turrets, was also being founded.[82]

It was for his third new castle, however, that the king had instructed Master James of St George and his colleagues to create something truly exceptional: Caernarfon, he intended, would be the greatest of all their many projects. The prominence it was afforded was, in part, a reflection of its future role. Situated at the southern end of the Menai Strait, the settlement was conveniently located in the heart of what used to be Gwynedd; from here the other parts of the king's new conquest could be most easily reached. It was, therefore, an appropriate place for the new justiciar of north-west Wales to have as his base.

But Caernarfon had a stronger appeal still, and that was the pull of its past. A thousand years and more beforehand, the Romans had come to this part of Wales, and the remains of their legionary fort, Segontium, still stood close by (where, less extensive, they can still be seen today). Since that time, however, its origins had become the stuff of legend. According to Welsh tradition, the fort had stood since the time of Magnus Maximus, a Roman emperor who had seen it a dream, and who had come to Wales to discover it was a reality: 'a great castle, the fairest that mortal had ever seen.' And this was what Edward and his architects aspired to recreate, albeit on a new site at the mouth of the River Seiont: a truly tremendous castle, bristling with towers and turrets, amply supplied with arrow-loops, and apartments appropriate for future royal visits. To their design, moreover, they also decided to add a telling detail. The Emperor Maximus, so it was said, was the father of the Emperor Constantine. Caernarfon was therefore going to be built with polygonal towers, and different coloured bands of masonry, so as to resemble the walls of Constantinople.[83]

When Edward arrived at Caernarfon at the start of April 1284, he was no doubt pleased to inspect the progress of the building works, but he had other, more important motives in mind. With the king, as ever, travelled the queen, who at that time was entering the ninth month of what was probably her sixteenth pregnancy. As a consequence, every effort was made to ensure that the royal couple felt as comfortable as possible in the midst of a busy construction site. Temporary timber apartments, constructed the previous year, were improved in advance of their coming by the addition of new glass windows; nearby, as at Conwy and Rhuddlan, a garden was laid out for Eleanor's enjoyment. After keeping the court waiting for three more weeks, and missing St George's day by just forty-eight hours, the queen gave birth on 25 April. To general rejoicing, the child was a boy, and a few days later he was baptised Edward after his father. The tradition that the king presented this new arrival to the Welsh as their future prince is a later improvement of the story, not recorded until the sixteenth century; precisely what future Edward senior foresaw for his second son at this stage we will never know. What can hardly be doubted, however, is that the child's birth at Caernarfon was intentional. In the person of this new Edward, Wales's distant imperial past and its future as an English dominion were deliberately linked.[84]

Other symbolic events had already been contrived at Caernarfon to reinforce the connection. The previous year, during his hostage-taking tour, Edward had 'discovered' the body of the Emperor Maximus there; on the king's orders, it was exhumed and then reburied in the local church. Here, in other words, was a repeat performance of the disinterment of Arthur some five years earlier, and to much the same purpose. Maximus was said to be the father of Constantine; Constantine was known to be the grandfather of Arthur – Geoffrey of Monmouth had said so. It was no coincidence that, around the same time, Edward had been presented with a coronet that had once belonged to Llywelyn, which was said to be 'Arthur's crown'. In the spring of 1284, once the royal goldsmith had rendered it more impressive, this trophy was sent to England. At some point soon after, Edward's oldest son and heir, Alfonso, presented it at the shrine of Edward the Confessor in Westminster Abbey.[85]

Back in Wales, the search for symbols of conquest and the celebration of victory continued in a similarly Arthurian vein. For most of June, including his forty-fifth birthday, the king chose to keep his court at Llyn Cwm Dulyn, a deep, dark lake in the mountains to the south of Caernarfon, reputed to have mystical properties. At the end of July he held a magnificent 'Round Table' tournament at Nefyn, a remote little town where the prophecies of Merlin were said to have been found. In early August he toured the far reaches of the Llŷn peninsula, even the tiny islands off the coast. Edward was evidently revelling in his discoveries, and the knowledge that he had been further and seen more than any of his predecessors. Excepting Arthur, of course.[86]

It was not until the middle of August that the festivities began to wind down. By 13 August the king was back at Caernarfon, and on 22 August he set out east along the coast, back in the direction of England. It was probably on that day that messengers from England arrived to meet him, with the news that Alfonso was dead.

7

Peaceful Endeavours

Contemporary chroniclers, if they noticed it, maintained a discreet silence; posterity, as a result, has also failed to register its alarming significance. But it can hardly have escaped the attention of Edward I, engaged as he was in the summer of 1284 with the manipulation of myth and search for historical validation: Alfonso, the son and heir to whom he had recently dispatched 'Arthur's crown' for presentation at the high altar of Westminster Abbey, had died on 19 August – the very date on which, ten years earlier, the king himself had stood in the same sacred space on the day of his coronation.[1]

To a man who had proclaimed that his recent conquest was proof of the unerring dispositions of divine providence, such a coincidence must surely have been more than a little jarring. Alfonso, ten years old at the time of his death, had passed beyond the more perilous years of infancy that had claimed the lives of his predeceased brothers. The toys that Edward had bought him – which included a wooden castle and a miniature siege-engine – had already been exchanged for hawks, hounds and horses. It was premature to call the boy, as one chronicler did, 'the hope of knighthood', but surely no exaggeration for the same writer to suggest that Alfonso had been 'a comfort to his father'. As Archbishop Pecham put it his letter of condolence to the king, 'the child . . . was the hope of us all'. Once again, death had robbed the realm of its future security, and left the succession dangling on the fate of a four-month-old baby.[2]

Nevertheless, Edward, as usual, succeeded in disguising his discomfort. Alfonso was swiftly buried in Westminster Abbey, a week after his death, and with neither of his parents present. Such apparent indifference might seem callous, or perhaps be thought typically medieval, but neither was necessarily the case. Henry III and his queen, for example, had shown great and public concern during the sicknesses of their children and exhibited extreme grief when one of them (a girl called Katherine) had died at a young age. But Katherine was seemingly their sole casualty; their eldest son and his wife, by contrast, had not been nearly so lucky. Edward and Eleanor's first three children – all daughters – had died before the couple departed on crusade and, within four more years, their eldest sons had likewise been lowered into early graves. Given such a record, it would be understandable if the king and queen came to regard their children with greater detachment than most parents. Other evidence, however, suggests that, in spite of their frequent absences, the king and queen were neither emotionally distant nor uninvolved. Edward's presents for his son, like the similar gifts he showered on his daughters, are reasonable indicators of genuine affection. Eleanor regularly wrote letters asking after her children's health. And, while she was unable to attend his funeral, the queen had Alfonso's heart preserved, in order that it could one day be buried with her own.[3]

What prevented Edward and Eleanor from rushing back to Westminster that August was an overriding commitment to completing their business in Wales. With the conquest and the celebrations over, the king had elected to embark on a victory tour that would take in the whole country. In September, as a prelude, he travelled to his new abbey at Vale Royal in Cheshire and presented the monks with yet another significant trophy – a silver chalice, made from the melted seal matrices of Llywelyn, Dafydd and Eleanor de Montfort. This was followed a few days later by another festive assembly, which took place on the border at Overton. According to royal financial accounts, a thousand Welsh minstrels gathered there, presumably to perform for the court's entertainment during the fortnight that followed. It was not until early October that Edward crossed the River Dee and the tour began in earnest. The rest of that month was spent visiting each of the new castles in north Wales – Conwy, Caernarfon and Harlech. Then, in November, it was the turn of west Wales, and for the first time the king got to see his castles at Aberystwyth and Cardigan, as well as the cathedral at St David's. Finally, in December, Edward and Eleanor moved into the south of the country. Until this point they had been accompanied only by their friends and servants (Robert Burnell, Otto de Grandson and John de Vescy are the foremost witnesses to royal charters), but now they were joined, and welcomed, by several of their great magnates in turn. At the castles of Cardiff, Caldicot and Chepstow, the earls of Gloucester, Hereford and Norfolk were all pleased to play host to the court, which consequently swelled in size as the tour, and the year, drew to a close. Around 21 December the king and his companions took ship across the Severn estuary to Bristol, where they stopped to celebrate Christmas.[4]

The overriding question now became: what next? Wales was completely subjugated, its native dynasties tamed or extinguished, its history and symbols of independence erased or appropriated. England was at peace, its people inspired by their king's triumph, its nobles united as never before in their sense of shared achievement. Gascony was beset by its normal array of problems, but faced no immediate crisis and required no urgent intervention; Ireland was no more troublesome, nor alluring, than usual. Edward, and the tireless Eleanor, given their recent exertions, might well have been forgiven had they decided to take a well-earned rest, and allowed themselves to lapse into the kind of easy routine they had been enjoying before the fateful rebellion had been raised.

Instead they decided to go on crusade again. Edward had always intended to return to the Holy Land. But, as he had made clear in his correspondence with one pope after the next (the turnover since 1274 had been tremendous – no fewer than six in ten years, including one who had lasted only a month), affairs in England must for the time being take first priority. During this decade, Edward had repeatedly emphasised that his brother Edmund was an experienced crusader who would be more than happy to lead an English army in his place. The popes, however, had ultimately rejected this suggestion. What was needed, they averred, was a leader of international renown who would rally all of Christendom behind his banner. And only Edward, whose earlier exploits in the East were already the stuff of legend, could truly take on such a role.[5]

And so, in the end, Edward agreed to go. His decision was announced early in 1284, in the wake of his Welsh conquest, and the two events are probably not unconnected. At the height of his power, filled with a sense of divine purpose, grateful to God for granting him victory: here was a king newly inspired, ready again to confront the greatest challenge his age could offer.[6]

To follow one colossal and costly conflict with another in this way might seem to be imprudent, even wholly impracticable; but in fact this was not the case. This time, Edward would not be a junior partner, scrabbling around for funds. On the contrary, as the papacy's chosen leader, he expected the papacy's full financial support, and by 1284 this looked set to be very substantial. For much of the past decade, and in the face of strong opposition in England, Rome had been taxing the churches of Europe in anticipation of a new expedition. For six continuous years from 1274, 10 per cent of all ecclesiastical income had been relentlessly harvested, with the result that, in every major church and abbey, sacks of silver pennies were sitting, waiting to be spent. (Edward, indeed, was well aware of their existence: in the spring of 1283, incensed by the clergy's refusal to subsidise the Welsh war, he had angrily ordered this money seized. It was a move that had made even his bankers blanch, and the sacks were soon returned, for the most part unopened.) Impressive as these funds were, however (they totalled about £130,000), Edward knew from experience that they would not be enough; his first, unsuccessful crusade had cost at least £100,000. Negotiations with Rome were therefore ongoing in 1284. Pope Martin IV – three years into his pontificate, and still going strong – had offered to tax the Church for another three years; Edward, in response, had suggested that ten years might be nearer the mark.[7]

Such long-distance haggling was time consuming and tedious, but there was no question that a compromise could be reached in due course. The obstacle to a new crusade in 1284 was not financial, nor volitional, but political. Edward could hardly lead a great Christian coalition to fight the infidel when the kings of western Europe were poised on the brink of war with each other.

The cause of contention, once again, was Sicily. In the thirty years since it had ensnared Henry III, the island had continued to act as a focus for the rivalries of Europe's rulers. For a while, it is true, matters there had seemed settled. In the late 1260s Charles of Anjou had taken up the pope's offer of the Sicilian crown and forcefully established his authority. Within a few years – even by the time of Edward's visits during his first crusade – his power appeared to be unshakeable. But Charles had gone on to overplay his hand in pursuit of a dream of Mediterranean empire. In 1271 he had acquired the kingdom of Albania; in 1277 he bought the title 'king of Jerusalem'; by the start of the 1280s he was planning to capture the city of Constantinople. And yet, all the time he was expanding east-wards, the ambitious Angevin was neglecting, and abusing, the core of his power. To raise the armies for his campaigns, Charles subjected Sicily to the harshest measures: taxes were raised in ever greater sums, deserters were punished with death, and the threat of reprisals against their wives and children. By the spring of 1282 the islanders had decided that they would stand for no more. On Easter Monday that year, with the cry 'Death to the French!', they rose up, killing their oppressors, or sending them fleeing to the Italian mainland.[8]

This revolt, known because of its timing as the Sicilian Vespers, came just a week after the similar anti-colonial uprising in distant Wales, and provoked a similar reaction from the ousted overlord. 'We intend,' said Charles of Anjou, 'to confront the rebel island of Sicily with an army

by land, and a fleet by sea, to bring about the total collapse and confusion of our enemies and rebels.' And had the Sicilians, like the Welsh,
stood alone, he might well have succeeded.[9]

But the Sicilians were not alone. On the contrary, they were backed
by an international coalition of malcontents, all of whom had been itching
to curb the rise of Angevin power. The emperor of Constantinople,
fearful for his own security, was one. Peter of Aragon, king of Spain's
second most sizeable kingdom, was another. His queen was a daughter
of the Hohenstaufen – the once great dynasty whose power Charles
of Anjou had terminated – and, as such, regarded herself as Sicily's
rightful heir. Within a few weeks of the rebellion, Peter set sail from
Spain to aid the islanders in their struggle and to uphold his wife's
claim. On 1 September he reached Palermo, where he was greeted by
rapturous crowds, and had himself crowned as Sicily's new king.[10]

This intervention by the king of Aragon dragged in the king of
France. Philip III was Charles of Anjou's overlord (for Anjou itself) and,
more to the point, his nephew. He had warned Aragon in advance that
any action taken against Sicily would be regarded as an attack on France.
Since King Peter had chosen to ignore this admonition, a new war
across the Pyrenees threatened.

Such a war was actively encouraged by the papacy, the last player in
this international crisis. Rome had long regarded Sicily as its own special
preserve; it was the pope, and no one else (certainly not the Sicilians)
who should decide who ruled there, and Charles of Anjou had long
been the approved papal candidate. The fact that Pope Martin was a
Frenchman merely reinforced his determination to see Angevin power
on the island restored. In short order, he excommunicated Peter of
Aragon, then deprived him – which is to say, he declared that the king
should rule no more – and empowered the French to put the sentence
into effect. In 1284, therefore, Philip III began dutifully to raise an army
and fleet to attack his southern neighbour. By the start of 1285 his
stores were assembled on the Mediterranean coast, his ships were set
to sail, and an army of 8,000 men was mustering, ready to march.[11]

Edward had done his utmost to discourage an escalating conflict in
which both sides had looked to him for help. Peter of Aragon regarded
the English king as a friend (for years they had been planning the
wedding of their eldest children); Philip III claimed Edward's allegiance
as a cousin and, more contentiously, as his overlord (for Gascony). Most
troubling of all, Pope Martin had designated the war against Aragon as
a crusade. Edward had previously been able to offer his apologies to
all three, explaining that he was preoccupied with the rebellion of his
own subjects in Wales. But now, at the start of 1285, he was faced with

two equally unappealing alternatives. Either he could offend one side by backing the other, or he could do nothing, and watch as the papacy squandered its carefully husbanded crusading funds on a war between Europe's Christian kings.[12]

Edward was certainly not inclined to fight, but nor was it in his nature to stand aside and do nothing. His stay at Bristol during Christmas 1284, surrounded by his great magnates, was more than just a culmination of that autumn's royal progress around Wales. Locals (if not later historians) were proud to regard it as a parliament, indicating that the festivities must have been mixed with much serious debate. The question under discussion was what should be done about the imminent conflict on the Continent. And, by the start of the new year, the king had decided on a course of action.[13]

He had decided, it seems, to intervene in person to stop the war. In early January Edward departed from Bristol, leaving the chancery behind him in his haste, and sped eastwards across southern England. After a fleeting visit to London, he rode on to Dover, from where he intended to cross to France. This was clearly not a military mission: no troops were raised, and the letters of protection issued to the king's small entourage were set to expire at Easter. What Edward appeared to have had in mind was an eleventh-hour meeting with Philip III, by which he hoped to talk his cousin out of launching his invasion.[14]

This being the case, he must have been disappointed. By the middle of February the king had left Kent for East Anglia, where he remained for the next two months. Contemporary chroniclers and modern historians have speculated as to why he suddenly changed course in this way. What seems most likely is that, after several weeks of waiting, he received word from Philip, telling him not to come. Denied the opportunity to petition the French king in person, Edward embarked on the only other route that remained open to him. The shrines and altars of Norfolk and Suffolk were a favourite recourse when divine assistance was required.[15]

No doubt frustrated by his inability to intercede, but still hopeful perhaps that war was not yet inevitable, Edward summoned a parliament to meet in May 1285 – one of the most important of his entire reign. Apart from his brief visit in January, the king had not been seen in London for over three years; at the same time, because of the prolonged emergency in Wales, much of the normal business of government had necessarily been retarded. The long delay, the need for a fresh start and, once again, a desire to celebrate his great victory: Edward acknowledged all of these by the spectacle he staged to mark parliament's opening.

On Friday, 4 May, the king, together with the queen, set off on foot from the Tower of London – still decorated with the mouldering heads of Llywelyn and Dafydd ap Gruffudd – towards Westminster Abbey. With them walked all the magnates of the land and no fewer than fourteen bishops, while at the front of the procession went Archbishop Pecham, carrying before him the most precious of the many relics that had once belonged to the vanquished princes. The Croes Naid, as it was known, was believed to be a piece of the cross on which Christ himself had been crucified. Placed at first on the abbey's high altar, at some point thereafter it was committed to the keeping of the nuns of St Helena at Bishopsgate. Here, again, Edward was advertising his awareness, and his command, of history: it was Helena's special claim to have been the discoverer of the True Cross. That she was also known to have been the mother of the Emperor Constantine was merely a fitting coincidence.[16]

Having staged what amounted to a virtual re-enactment of his coronation procession, the king and his parliament settled down to business. First on the agenda was the situation in Europe, and the question of whether Edward, as duke of Gascony, was really obliged to respond to the military summons of the king of France. As with most aspects of their complex relationship, there was no certain answer, but the Gascons themselves were clearly very concerned: already they had sent word to Edward, emphasising the dangers and subjugation that would undoubtedly ensue should he accede to the French demand. No doubt many English magnates, like the king himself, also viewed such a prospect with considerable unease. It was decided, therefore, to reply in uncertain terms. Before the end of May, English ambassadors were dispatched to Paris with an offer of debate. It is also likely that they took with them the message that Edward's offer to act as an arbitrator between France and Aragon still stood.[17]

While they waited for a response, there was much domestic business to transact. The king, it was noted, confirmed many of the charters of his ancestors in this parliament and knighted many of the sons of his magnates. New laws were also promulgated. The second Statute of Westminster sought to provide a comprehensive statement on questions relating to land law, while a new Statute of Merchants laid down procedures for those trying to recover their debts.[18]

The most dramatic legal and mercantile developments, however, were those that affected the city of London. The capital and its citizens, as we have already seen, had a love–hate relationship with England's kings – a standing disagreement about the proper limits of royal power and civic liberty. London had long claimed special rights of self-government

– the right to elect its own mayor, and its own sheriffs – and when the Crown needed popular support, it tended to agree with the city's estimation of its own independence. When, on the other hand, the Crown felt strong or vengeful, it acted as if these rights did not exist. Henry III, for example, had suspended London's liberties at least ten times during the course of his reign. As this high number suggests, however, such suspensions were only ever temporary. Even Henry's most wrathful intervention – his punishment of the capital in the wake of its support for Simon de Montfort – was soon moderated, and within five years the mayor and sheriffs were restored to their full independence.[19]

London had more reason to fear the coming of Henry's son – the dislike between Edward and the citizens ran much deeper, a result of their attack on his mother and his bloody retribution at Lewes. And yet, once the new reign had started, the capital's worst fears were not realised. The king's massive redevelopment of the Tower – begun not long after his accession, and largely finished by the summer of 1285 – radiated the threat of royal power, but thus far there had been no direct assault on the city's franchise.[20]

During his first decade, Edward had been content to meddle in London's politics indirectly. Soon after the coronation, for example, Mayor Henry le Waleys ('the Welshman') – an instinctive authoritarian of whom the king thought highly – was voted out and replaced by the more moderate and conservative Gregory of Ruxley. Edward had responded by gradually packing the city's narrow electing council with royalists, with the result that, in 1281, Waleys was returned to office.[21]

Edward had two quite specific objectives in getting his own mayor elected. The first was to make the capital more competitive. Full civic privileges extended to only a narrow and self-sustaining oligarchy, which protected the vested interests of a few long-established families, while denying a fair and free market to both lesser citizens (such as fishmongers and cordwainers) and foreign merchants (such as the Riccardi). The king's second objective was to reduce crime. London was growing rapidly in the thirteenth century – its population had probably doubled from 40,000 to 80,000 in the time since Edward's birth – and rapidly growing more lawless. At best this manifested itself in noisy and violent games being played in the streets; at worst, it meant armed gangs roaming around after dark, and hiring themselves out to settle – and hence to perpetuate – civic feuds. Waleys, as Edward's placeman, responded with a series of hard-line measures: tougher sentences for curfew-breakers, plus the building of a brand-new prison. The Londoners responded, once again, by voting him out, and returning to power his more lenient predecessor. Given the choice, it seems, the citizens prized liberty more highly than public order.[22]

Such a line would have been difficult to defend before Edward I at the best of times; in the charged atmosphere that existed in 1285 it proved impossible. Not only did the king return that spring at the height of his power; he also came back, after his long absence, to a capital recently rocked by scandal. The previous twelve months had witnessed rioting in the streets, a break-out from Newgate Prison, and a notorious murder in which several leading councillors were implicated. It was a sufficiently damning litany of failure to merit some form of intervention on the part of the Crown, but Edward used it as his pretext for going much further than anybody expected. At the start of the summer the king announced that he was appointing a special commission to look into matters of law and order, but before it sat he ordered the enclosure of St Paul's Churchyard – the area where, since time immemorial, London's public assemblies had been held. On the last day of June, Mayor Ruxley resigned his office in protest and remonstrated with the royal commissioners at the Tower. They, in response, ordered the detention of some eighty Londoners and announced that the city was being taken into the king's hands. The following day royal officers, headed by a new royal warden, moved in. London was now Edward's city, to be governed as he alone saw fit.[23]

The same day, with parliament finished and the capital constrained, Edward left Westminster and embarked on a more leisurely round of summertime activities. Along with his family – all his daughters, and even the little Lord Edward – the king went on pilgrimage to Canterbury, where he marked the feast of Thomas Becket by presenting four gold figures at the saint's shrine (Edward the Confessor and St John for the sake of Henry III; St George and his horse for their help in conquering Wales). A week at Leeds Castle and some hunting in Hampshire were followed by another family occasion at Amesbury in Wiltshire, where Edward's six-year-old daughter Mary was veiled as a nun (a move that pleased his mother, who had a strong attachment to Amesbury, far more than it pleased his wife).[24] Finally, as the summer drew to a close, the king was reunited with his magnates at Winchester Castle. Because their gathering saw more law-and-order legislation (the Statute of Winchester), it has sometimes been mistaken for a parliament. In fact, this was a more select assembly, almost exclusively secular and military in character. It was, in all probability, the occasion for another chivalric celebration of the conquest of Wales: a much grander restaging of the smaller scale tournament held at Nefyn the previous year. And, although we cannot be entirely certain, it was most likely the event for which Edward had fashioned a real

Round Table, eighteen feet across and weighing three-quarters of a ton. Repainted in the sixteenth century and restored in the twentieth, it now hangs on the wall of Winchester's Great Hall. Around this table, for several glorious days that September, the king and his knights must have feasted.[25]

Throughout these leisured weeks of summer, Edward had, of course, been waiting for news from across the Channel. By the time the court reached Winchester he had heard the worst: France had begun its invasion of Aragon. Neither the death of Charles of Anjou (which had occurred in January) nor the death of Pope Martin IV (in March) had been enough to dent Philip III's resolve, and Edward's ambassadors had come too late: by the time they had reached Paris, the French king and his army were already crossing the Pyrenees. The knowledge that a fratricidal war among Christians was under way must have soured the celebrations at Winchester. By this French action, English plans for a new crusade seemed irreparably compromised.[26]

But, just a month or so later, Edward – by this point on the Isle of Wight – received fresh intelligence, at once terrible and hopeful. Philip III was dead. The French king and his troops had barely entered Aragon before being struck by plague, and forced into an ignominious retreat. Like his father Louis, Philip had died in the midst of a diseased and defeated army, his crusade a similarly misdirected disaster. It was a lucky escape for Peter of Aragon, who must have breathed a sigh of relief – but little else. On 10 November, just six weeks after the death of his rival, the Spanish king also gave up the ghost.[27]

Thus, by Christmas, which the English court spent in Exeter, Edward would have known that all four protagonists in the great European feud were dead. The issues that had divided them, of course, still remained, but the war, for the moment, had ground to a halt. Moreover, Philip III and Peter of Aragon had both been succeeded by young sons – a teenager and a twenty-year-old – who might hesitate before continuing their fathers' fight. What a difference, then, a year had made. Peace, which had seemed such a forlorn hope the previous Christmas, was suddenly a much stronger prospect.[28] According to one chronicler, the solemn French embassy that arrived in Westminster in February urged Edward to cross the Channel as soon as possible in order to act as peacemaker; if so, then the contrast with the previous year, when the king's overtures had been rebuffed, was even more pleasing. In any case, Edward now had to go to France: as duke of Gascony, he was obliged to do homage to the new French king. Accordingly, a short parliament was called for April, in which the king's cousin, Edmund of Cornwall

(Richard of Cornwall's younger son) was entrusted with the custody of the kingdom. Edward then went immediately to Dover and, on 13 May, set sail for France.[29]

We are well informed about Edward's Continental visit, thanks to the voluminous surviving records of his household. These tell us, among many other things, that the king travelled to France in great state, taking with him not only the queen and close advisers like Burnell, Vescy and Grandson; his entourage also included several earls, including his brother the earl of Lancaster, his friend the earl of Lincoln, and his uncle, William de Valence – an earl in all but name. Even Gilbert de Clare, the prickly earl of Gloucester, had agreed to accompany the royal party, at least as far as Paris. These men and their attendants, combined with the already large staff of the royal household, made for a total contingent that numbered well into four figures. It took several days to ferry them all, and at least 1,000 horses, across the Channel. Eight ships were needed for the kitchen equipment.[30]

Once in France, this great company rode first to Amiens, where they were greeted by the new French king. Philip IV, son of Philip III, although already knighted and married before his father's death, was still only seventeen years old at the time of his recent coronation. Dazzlingly beautiful – Philip le Bel (the Fair), his countrymen called him – he was also apparently painfully shy. This reserve may explain why some people found him aloof; later in his reign the king was famously described by a hostile French bishop, who caustically compared him to an owl. 'The handsomest man in the world, [he] can do nothing except stare at men.'[31]

Nevertheless, the new French king seemed to hit it off reasonably well with his second cousin. From Amiens, Edward and Philip moved quickly to Paris, where the English court remained for several weeks, lodged on the Left Bank, in the monastery of St Germain-des-Prés. The length of their stay, the feasts thrown by both kings, and Edward's repeated boat trips across the Seine to visit Philip at his palace of the Louvre – all of this has been taken as good evidence that genial relations were being maintained and developed.[32]

No doubt they were, at least in some quarters. But the duration of the visit and the frequency of contact is also as likely to have been the result of the arduous negotiations that were taking place on two fronts. In the first place, there was the delicate matter of the relationship between France and Gascony, which required renewal, but which had also been tested by the recent French demands for military service. When Edward did homage to Philip on 5 June, he had been careful, once again, to use words that were imprecise and conditional. 'I become your man for the lands which I hold overseas,' the English king had said, 'according to the terms of the peace made between our ancestors.' Before he did so, Robert Burnell had made the English position more explicit, explaining that they considered that France had not fulfilled its obligations under the Treaty of Paris; that, indeed, Edward's rights had been threatened by French behaviour and that, for this reason, some Englishmen had advised their king to challenge Philip's claim to homage. It was a bold opening statement that must have occasioned much debate.[33]

More intractable still was the question of peace between France and Aragon. Philip IV himself appears to have been opposed to his father's war (his mother, who had died when Philip was a small child, had been Aragonese), and the Aragonese, for their part, were willing to talk (their ambassadors were in Paris). As far as the papacy was concerned, however, the struggle should continue as long as Aragon remained defiant over Sicily – the root cause of all the contention – and the Aragonese were equally adamant that the island would not be relinquished.[34]

On this issue the Aragonese could afford to be dogmatic. At an earlier stage in the fight for Sicily, the fortunes of war had dealt them a card that trumped all others. In June 1284 a naval battle had been fought off the coast of Naples between the Aragonese fleet and the forces of Sicily's ousted overlord, Charles of Anjou. Charles himself was not present at this engagement, but his namesake son and heir was. Victory had gone to Aragon, and Charles, prince of Salerno, had been captured in the course of the fighting.[35]

Two years on and Charles of Salerno was still being held in an Aragonese prison. His continued detention was a source of great concern to his immediate family, and to his cousin, Edward I. The two men had met on at least one occasion (a tournament in 1279) and had evidently got on well. When, in 1281, it had looked as if another French feud would pull them into rival camps, the king had written to the prince, expressing his reluctance to get involved. 'My heart is not in it,' he told his cousin, 'on account of the love between you and me.' At a more practical level, Edward knew that there could be no crusade to the Holy Land while Charles – now nominally a king after the death of his father in 1284 – continued in his confinement. The prospect of his liberation, however, looked bleak. Unless Aragon agreed to withdraw from Sicily, the papacy would not drop its anathema; unless the papacy dropped its anathema, Aragon would not agree to Charles's release.[36]

There was no way, therefore, that Edward could have brokered a

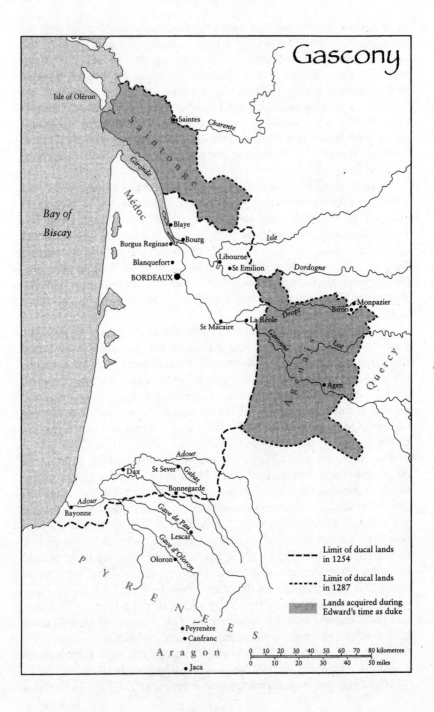

Gascony

Isle of Oléron

Saintes

Charente

Saintonge

Gironde

Médoc

Bay of Biscay

Blaye

Bourg

Burgus Reginae

Isle

Blanquefort

Libourne

St Emilion

Dordogne

BORDEAUX

Dropt

Biron

Monpazier

La Réole

Lot

St Macaire

Garonne

Agenais

Quercy

Agen

Adour

St Sever

Gabas

Dax

Bonnegarde

Adour

Bayonne

Gave de Pau

Lescar

Gave d'Oloron

Oloron

P
Y
R
E
N
E
E
S

N

E

S

Peyrenère

Canfranc

A r a g o n

Jaca

Limit of ducal lands
in 1254

Limit of ducal lands
in 1287

Lands acquired during
Edward's time as duke

0 10 20 30 40 50 60 70 80 kilometres

0   10   20   30   40   50 miles

conclusive peace agreement during his stay in Paris that summer. Nevertheless, after several weeks of negotiation, he did succeed in arranging
a ceasefire. In the last fortnight of July, having been empowered by
both Philip IV and the Aragonese ambassadors, the English king ordained
a truce that would begin in August and last until September the
following year. This was at least a start: one which gave him just over
twelve months to broker something more decisive.[37]

A few days later similarly patient bargaining on Anglo-French relations also bore fruit. Philip IV made concessions to Edward involving
his jurisdiction as overlord, and also regarding the lands promised to
the English king under the long-standing peace treaty. Edward's rights
in Saintonge (that is, the area around Saintes, a town on Gascony's
northern frontier) were finally acknowledged, while Edward, for his
part, agreed to drop his claim to Quercy, a region to the east of the
duchy, in return for an annual payment of several hundred pounds.[38]

This breakthrough on both fronts in Paris was accompanied by
equally encouraging news from a third direction. Around this time, the
English must have learned that the new pope, Honorius IV, had improved
on the financial package offered by his predecessor. The papacy was
now prepared to grant Edward a new six-year crusading tax, provided
that he took up the cross by May the following year. If this was not
quite everything the king wanted – he wrote back asking for payment
in advance – it was nevertheless excellent news. When the English court
finally quit the French capital at the end of July, there must have been
a general consensus that they had already achieved a great deal.[39]

Their next destination was Gascony, but they set off in no great
hurry. Having bought himself some time, Edward chose to spend it
partly on pilgrimage. From Paris he led his retinue south-east, to the
city of Auxerre and the abbey of Pontigny (where Edmund of Abingdon,
the archbishop of Canterbury who had officiated at Edward's baptism,
lay buried). From there they went west, and along the River Loire to
Fontevrault, burial place of Edward's Angevin ancestors (Henry II and
Richard the Lionheart). Consequently, it was September before the
king started south in the direction of his own lands. These, of course,
had expanded greatly since his last visit twelve years earlier, and Edward,
as was his wont, made a special effort to appear in each new area under
his lordship, inspecting its management and impressing himself on the
inhabitants. From mid-September to mid-October he toured newly
acquired Saintonge; then, in the later part of the autumn, he moved
east along the Dordogne, until he reached the Agenais, ceded to him
in 1279. By 15 November he had reached Agen itself, and he stayed
in the city, or its environs, for a month. Not until mid-December did

he head up the River Garonne towards Bordeaux, and in the event the English court spent Christmas and the New Year in the small town of St Macaire.⁴⁰

If his itinerary sounds laid back and listless, this is probably because it was partly so. No one was more anxious than Edward to settle the great problems of Europe, but the wheels of international diplomacy turned slowly, not least because of the distances involved. It took weeks, running into months, for letters and ambassadors to pass through the Pyrenees to Aragon or across the Alps to Rome. When, in early January, the king finally reached Bordeaux, there were some preliminary talks with an Aragonese delegation. But, once they had departed, Edward necessarily focused his attentions on Gascony which, as usual, had problems of its own. John de Grilly, the seneschal appointed in 1278, had proved capable but corrupt; removed before the king's arrival, he was put on trial the following year. For royal and ducal officials, at least, there was much work to be getting on with. Edward himself spent most of February exploring the far reaches of the Médoc. At one point in March we catch him hunting wolves.⁴¹

At Easter, however, events suddenly and dramatically sped up. Once again, we are able to reconstruct what happened in forensic detail thanks to the records of the royal household. On Wednesday, 2 April, the king came back to Bordeaux in time to celebrate Easter on the Sunday. Two days after his arrival the Aragonese ambassadors also returned, in what even the dry financial accounts acknowledge was 'a solemn embassy': some eighty-three men and forty-six horses were accommodated in the city at Edward's expense. Perhaps, like the king himself, they were entertained by the little boy who was paid two shillings for playing the bagpipes, or the damsel who received seven pence for her dancing.⁴²

Then came Easter Sunday itself – a day of such drama that it made the news back home in England. As the best-informed chronicler explains, 'a great misfortune befell the king'. Edward, we are told, was standing with his nobles in a certain solar (the topmost room in a tower) when the floor beneath their feet suddenly fell away. The assembled company tumbled from an estimated height of eighty feet. Some of them were crushed, some suffered broken bones. Three knights were said to have been killed, while others apparently walked away unscathed. As for Edward himself, he was not nearly so unlucky, nor quite so fortunate. Found under a Gascon knight who had broken his leg, the king emerged from the wreckage with a broken collarbone.⁴³

A tragedy for some, the incident was generally held to have been a miraculous escape: proof that Edward and those around him had been spared for a reason. If, as one later chronicler seems to suggest, the collapse was caused by a bolt of lightning that passed through a window, it can only have reinforced the impression that the event was heaven sent. As it was, the fact that it had happened on Easter Sunday – the day of Christ's passion – must by itself have been seen as significant. Edward had been expressing his willingness to go on crusade – that is, to recover Jerusalem, the site of Christ's passion – for more than three years by this point. In spite of this, however, he had still not yet taken the cross.[44]

That was now set to change. The king, for the time being, could go nowhere. It may have taken him as long as five weeks to recover from his injuries. But within days of the near-disaster, three of his servants were given money for their journey to the Holy Land. Soon afterwards, letters arrived from the pope, dated three weeks before the accident, offering final terms for the payment of crusade funds, provided that Edward accepted the offer before 24 June.[45] The king, once he was able to move, needed no further encouragement. By 12 May he had left Bordeaux for nearby Blanquefort, a recently acquired castle that served as a retreat from the city, and there made his vow. Many others joined him in doing so. The ceremony was conducted by the archbishop of Ravenna, a papal legate empowered for the purpose. Edward was recognised as 'captain of the Christian army'.[46]

It must have been just a few days later that they had further news from Rome. Pope Honorius was dead – he had passed away nineteen days after sending his last letter. This meant that the legate's authority had expired before he had signed the king with the cross. Worse still, it meant that the tortuous and protracted business of negotiating the financial terms of the crusade would have to begin all over again with Honorius's successor.[47]

At least negotiations with Aragon were moving forward, perhaps impelled by the same sense of divinely ordained purpose. In the first week of May, after a stay that may have lasted longer than they intended, the Aragonese ambassadors left to return home. At the same juncture, and probably in their company, Edward's close associate John de Vescy rode south to finalise plans for the two kings to meet in person. By 10 June he was back with a date and a place. At once Edward dispatched certain members of his household to make the necessary arrangements for his coming. Then, twelve days later, the king and his company set out.[48]

Their destination was Oloron, a substantial town on the southernmost fringes of Edward's power, just twenty miles distant from the peaks of the Pyrenees. The English court had arrived there by 11 July; the Aragonese court must have arrived a few days later, and Edward would have welcomed Alfonso III, the twenty-two-year-old successor to the late King Peter. Of Alfonso himself little is known. Like Edward, though, he seems to have travelled in great state. Just as the English king had brought with him some Welshmen in order to advertise the extent of his power, so the Spaniard had come attended by several Saracens, reluctant recruits from his own wild frontier. Their meeting was characterised by the kind of celebratory festivities that generally accompanied such royal rendezvous. Jousts and other games took place outside the town, destroying cornfields and vineyards, whose owners Edward later felt obliged to compensate. Exotic gifts were exchanged: Alfonso presented Edward with a lion and a wildcat. The lion later killed a horse belonging to a local, further increasing the English bill for compensation. And two of Alfonso's Saracens absconded, taking with them a mule. But otherwise the chivalric ice-breaker appears to have passed without incident.[49]

Amid the gaiety and the gift-giving, of course, there was serious business to be getting on with. Edward's primary reason for coming to Oloron was to secure the release of his cousin, Charles of Salerno. Until Charles was a free agent there could be no lasting European peace; anything he promised in captivity was likely to be obviated by a later claim that it had been exacted under duress. Alfonso, for his part, was happy to consider Edward's request, but made it clear that he would require a lot in return. It was not a question of greed: the captive king was Aragon's best guarantee against future French and papal aggression. Charles was not going to be liberated unless he agreed to hand over very substantial new securities by way of exchange. In a nutshell, Alfonso wanted hostages and money: three of Charles's sons, including his heir, were to be handed over, along with sixty nobles from his French county of Provence. In addition, Charles was bound to pay 50,000 marks. All of these were in return for a three-year truce and would be restored if a lasting peace was sealed by the end of that term. If not, they would be returned only if Charles returned to captivity, and Provence would be forfeited to Alfonso.

These, at least, were the conditions that Edward accepted on 25 July, when an agreement at Oloron was reached. In order to move matters forward more quickly, the English king made himself personally involved, taking on the responsibility for finding 20,000 of the 50,000 mark security. He also promised to seek papal permission for his daughter, Eleanor, to marry Alfonso. Their long-planned wedding had latterly been forbidden by the papacy in view of Aragon's pariah status.[50]

Papal approval was the point on which the whole deal pivoted. As his eagerness to ally himself with Edward shows, what Alfonso wanted most was to be welcomed back into the fold of European princes. But he was also determined to retain Sicily, and it was a central require-ment of the Oloron agreement that both France and the papacy should acknowledge his right to the island. In any circumstances, therefore, Edward's ambassadors were going to have a hard time persuading both powers to accept the results of his honest brokerage. But in the summer of 1287, when they set out for the attempt, there was a more funda-mental problem. Despite the fact that Honorius IV had died in April, the college of cardinals had still not agreed on who should be his successor. This was the great short-term stumbling block to peace. There could be no papal approval (or, for that matter, disapproval) while there was no pope.[51]

For a while Edward was evidently optimistic that matters might be wrapped up quickly. Once the summit at Oloron was over and the two courts had gone their separate ways, the English king remained in the south of his duchy. As the summer turned to autumn, he spent one listless week after another, first at Dax, then at St Sever, waiting hope-fully for news that would allow the early release of his cousin. During this time, he was pleased to receive an unexpected visitor in the form of Rabban Bar Sauma, a Chinese monk who had come to Europe as an ambassador for the Mongols. His master, il-khan Arghun, son and successor of Edward's erstwhile ally il-khan Abagha, was contemplating renewed military action in the Middle East against the forces of Islam, and hoped for European support. Encouraged by this news, the king made a statement that the ambassador recorded in his journal and that reveals the strength of conviction that underlay his actions at this time. 'We . . . have taken the sign of the cross upon our body,' Edward said, 'and have no other thought than this affair. My heart swells when I learn that what I am thinking is also being thought by King Arghun.'[52]

As autumn turned to winter, however, the hope in the king's heart of an early settlement of Europe's affairs began to fade. Part of the problem was Philip IV. Having given Edward a free hand to negotiate, the French king now balked at the provision that Aragon should occupy Provence if peace did not ensue. The main obstacle, though, was the continuing vacancy of St Peter's throne. In November the cardinals wrote to Edward commending him for his efforts but, before these letters reached him, the king had already concluded that Charles of Salerno would not be freed that year. On 21 November he turned and headed north, back to Bordeaux, where the English court stayed for Christmas. Until a new pope was in place, everything – the truce, the peace, the projected crusade – hung in the balance.[53]

Perhaps to occupy his time more than for any other reason, Edward elected to spend the early months of the new year founding a new town. For most of February, March and April 1288 the king and his court were camped on the banks of the River Garonne, some twelve miles north of Bordeaux. At this point the Garonne joins the region's other main river, the Dordogne, and together they form the wide estuary of the Gironde, which flows out into the Bay of Biscay and beyond into the Atlantic. It was here, at the confluence of the two main commercial arteries of his duchy, that Edward chose to plant his new settlement. From the first it was given the Latin name *Burgus Reginae*, in tribute to Eleanor of Castile. In England it would have been known as Queensborough.[54]

Although Edward's decision to involve himself (and Eleanor) so directly in the creation of Burgus Reginae looks slightly self-indulgent, in general there was nothing whimsical about such urban initiatives. The creation of new towns had been official policy in Gascony from the moment of Edward's accession as duke. Following the example of the counts of neighbouring Toulouse, who had begun a similar programme some two decades earlier, in 1274 Edward had ordered his seneschal in Gascony to plant new settlements wherever in the duchy he saw fit. As a consequence, dozens had sprung up in the twelve years that had elapsed since the king's previous visit, and many more were still being laid out at the time of his return in 1286.[55]

The local word for such new towns was 'bastides' – it derived from a southern French word meaning 'to build'. For those who equate medieval with muddle, the most striking thing about the majority of these places is the regularity of their design. Planned with precision, and with each plot laid out to the same size as its neighbour, the streets of a bastide form a perfect gridiron: the kind of effect more commonly associated with the towns and cities of modern America than those of thirteenth-century Europe. Of the scores that were created, some have swollen to become substantial modern towns, while others have shrunk to the smallest of villages. Perhaps the best preserved, in terms of overall ambience as well as original size, is the bastide in the Agenais known as Monpazier. Founded in 1285, and visited by Edward himself during his tour of the region the following year, Monpazier still exhibits many of the original details that made bastides so distinctive. Its regular grid of streets give out onto a central square, with an open market hall at one end, where even the original metal bins for measuring grain still survive. Around the square, the buildings with vaulted archways known as *cornières* are another characteristic medieval feature. Monpazier is also the only place, to the best of this author's knowledge, that can boast a Hotel Edward Premier.[56]

The creation of bastides served Edward in two ways. First, and most obviously, as commercial centres they were a source of profit, both direct (in the form of local tolls and taxes) and indirect (they increased trade that was taxed at other points, such as Bordeaux). Secondly, and perhaps less obviously, they were a means by which he could increase his authority as duke. As we have already noted, Edward's power as duke of Gascony was nothing like his power as king of England. In Gascony he had comparatively little land of his own, and far less money. Towns founded in his name not only swelled his coffers; they also looked to him as their lord and protector. As the bastides spread, therefore, so too did Edward's seigneurial influence.[57]

As such, it was wont to run up against existing vested interests. Other landlords were often quick to object when a new town was being planned or planted on their doorstep, recognising that their own profits were bound to suffer, not least because their tenants tended to slope off to become townsmen. The lowest sections of society were lured to bastides not only by the prospect of becoming richer, but by the promise of freedom that urban life would bring.[58] For this reason, around half of all bastides were founded on the principle of *paréage*, a public-private partnership, whereby the local lord or lords would put up the land, the duke provided the authority and the permission, and the profits were split between all parties. Monpazier again supplies a good example: the town was created by an act of *paréage* between Edward and the lord of Biron, whose castle still stands some four miles to the south of the town. By such a method, it was possible for all parties – duke, lords and peasants – to profit from a new foundation.[59]

The whole initiative of creating new urban communities on virgin sites was possible only because Gascony, at the time of Edward's accession, was an economically underdeveloped region. Although it still preserved the visible traces of its civilised, Roman past, the duchy had latterly fallen on hard times (in the early thirteenth century, for example, it had been ravaged by decades of war). Consequently, it lagged behind other regions in western Europe and was ripe for economic exploitation. With the advent of stability from the middle of the thirteenth century and a growing reliance on the wine trade with England, there was a great incentive to clear the surrounding forests and plant vineyards in their place (some bastides even provided for this in their foundation charters). It was all for the greater good. New towns meant new roads; new roads and fewer forests meant fewer places for rebels and robbers to haunt. A region that had grown wild was once again being tamed and civilised.[60]

In this respect alone – its economic underdevelopment – Gascony resembled Wales, and for this reason Edward saw fit to plant new towns there as well. After the first Welsh war he had laid out new settlements at Flint, Rhuddlan and Aberystwyth; the conquest of Wales had led to the creation of several more, at Conwy, Caernarfon, Harlech, Bere and Criccieth. Of course, in Wales Edward was supreme lord and conqueror: there was no need for him to purchase land or split profits in these cases. But, from a physical point of view, his Welsh towns closely resembled the bastides that were simultaneously being laid out in Gascony. The streets of Flint still preserve a near-perfect medieval grid. Conwy and Caernarfon, slightly less regular, are nonetheless the most impressive, surrounded as they are by splendid circuits of stone walls, among the best preserved in Europe.[61]

In the immediate aftermath of the conquest of Wales, in fact, Edward seems to have been infected with such an enthusiasm for town foundation that he attempted one or two similar projects in England. His trip to the Isle of Wight in the autumn of 1285, for example, was to inspect the town of Francheville (Newtown), bought from the bishop of Winchester the previous year with a view to further development. A few weeks later in 1285, in the wake of a visit to Corfe Castle, he ordered a new town to be laid out on the nearby Dorset coast. Neither of these initiatives, however, was successful – indeed, the Dorset project never seems to have got past the planning stage. The fact was that, by Edward's reign, if not before, England already had enough new towns – they had been increasing steadily in number, thanks largely to the lead of enterprising local lords, since the eleventh century.[62] Edward's only truly successful foundation in England was the new settlement he created at Winchelsea, and in this case the circumstances were special. Winchelsea was an existing port on the Sussex coast that became imperilled in the middle of the thirteenth century due to the shifting shingle beds of the sea floor. By the time Edward came to the throne the old marketplace was disappearing under water and the waves were lapping at the church door. From 1281, therefore, and by royal command, a new town was laid out for the citizens on the crest of a nearby ridge. One of the men in charge of the project was Henry le Waleys, the king's favourite townsman and erstwhile mayor of London. The result was the closest thing in Britain to a French bastide (Waleys was also later responsible for several new sites in Gascony). This was highly appropriate, since Winchelsea, lying on England's south coast, was one of the principal places of import for Gascon wine. Beneath the empty grass plots in the town today are several well-preserved, expensively fashioned stone cellars, where once the barrels of wine and cheese were rolled and stacked, and that once echoed to the sound of Gascon as well as English voices.[63]

Even in Gascony itself, by the time of Edward's visit in the late 1280s, there were signs that the countryside was approaching a point where it had sufficient new urban settlements. The earliest bastides, provided they were well located and well managed, flourished and prospered. Libourne, a pioneering early effort of 1270, founded by and named after Edward's friend and sometime seneschal Roger Leybourne, is now a modern French town of some consequence. By contrast, the bastide known as Baa, founded by the king himself in 1287, and so called as a compliment to Robert Burnell (bishop of Bath), has long since disappeared. In fact, of all the king's personal foundations in Gascony, not one has survived as a modern settlement. Even Burgus Reginae, on which the king lavished the greatest personal attention, and no doubt considerable sums of money, has now vanished. The only clues to its existence, beyond the written record, are the suggestive shapes of the surrounding vineyards, the plausible path of some banks and ditches, and the name of the nearby village – La Bastide.[64]

At some point towards the end of his protracted stay at Burgus Reginae in the spring of 1288, Edward received news from Rome. At last, the cardinals had elected a new pope. Nicholas IV had ascended to the papal throne on 22 February 1288 – and immediately decreed that the Treaty of Oloron should not stand. Negotiations with Aragon would have to begin all over again.[65]

At the start of June, therefore, the English king and his entourage set out for a second time on the long journey south, determined to find a new way out of the diplomatic impasse. By the end of the month they were back at Oloron. On this occasion, we are not nearly so well informed about their activities, but it seems fairly certain that exchanges with Aragon were more difficult. Whatever discussions took place at Oloron, for example, proved abortive: by the end of July Edward had retreated to the small cathedral city of Lescar, some fifteen miles to the north-east. It was probably not until September that the two kings came face-to-face for their second meeting, and when they did so it was in Aragon. Presumably at Alfonso's insistence, the English court trekked through the high passes of the Pyrenees in the late summer and were received by the Spanish king in his mountain city of Jaca. It must have been there, in early September, that a new deal was brokered.[66]

The only way forward was for Edward to take on more responsibility for the security of the deal. His previous offer to provide some of the money was repeated, and indeed fulfilled – 23,000 marks were handed over at once, and 7,000 more were promised. Moreover, the

English king now agreed to supply some of his own men as temporary hostages, until they could be replaced by hostages gathered from the domains of Charles of Salerno. Accordingly, in the early autumn Edward was obliged to make another long journey back and forth across the Pyrenees in order to round up the necessary recruits. Eventually, on 28 October, at the small town of Canfranc, the northernmost settlement in Alfonso's realm, the two courts came together once more. No fewer than seventy-six hostages were handed over to begin a captivity that they earnestly hoped would be impermanent. Most of them were Gascons, but included among their number were several leading members of the English court, including Otto de Grandson. Also, as per the earlier agreement, three of Charles of Salerno's sons at this moment became involuntary guests of the Aragonese king. But Alfonso was at last satisfied. In exchange for this extensive supply of human collateral, Charles of Salerno himself was finally set free.[67]

For Edward and his diminished entourage, it was now an anxious waiting game. While the grateful Charles sped off to raise the rest of the money and the replacement hostages, his English cousin had little choice but to sit out the winter months in the south of his duchy. Edward, however, was incapable of remaining idle, even when motionless, and so selected a site for this enforced sojourn where he could profitably expend his energies. The English camped themselves at a place called Bonnegarde, an ancient fortified site high above the River Luy, which marks the boundary between Edward's own domains and those of his once turbulent vassal, Gaston de Béarn. A few years earlier Bonnegarde had been reinvented as a small, irregularly shaped bastide, but now, during the winter of 1288–89, it was apparently extended on a massive scale, with a great expanse of adjoining land to the south and east being enclosed within new banks and ditches. Today in private ownership, Bonnegarde has proved the most enduring of Edward I's personal initiatives during his time in Gascony.[68]

Charles of Salerno had been given three months to find his own hostages, and in February, as this deadline looked set to expire, the English court became visibly more restless. But, at last, as the end of the month approached, Charles reappeared, and together he and Edward set out for the border. Queen Eleanor, for once, did not accompany her husband. At this time of year the Pyrenees were almost impassable. The king, his cousin and the replacement hostages had to ride through snowy peaks, guided by hundreds of specially recruited foot soldiers. Their destination was Peyrenère, the highest point of the mountain pass, more than 5,000 feet above sea level. When they arrived there in early March, Edward had a great wooden cross erected, to mark the boundary between his power and that of the king of Aragon. Around 6 March Alfonso arrived, and the exchange of hostages took place. The reunited English court rode back to Oloron, where they were received with relief by the anxiously waiting queen.[69]

The task that Edward had set himself in Gascony was at last complete. Charles of Salerno was free, and would remain forever grateful to the cousin who had secured his deliverance. 'You proved your sincerity,' he later told the English king, 'unloosed my bonds, and broke the walls of my prison.' There was also great joy in Oloron that the English hostages had returned safely.

But there was no disguising the fact that Edward's time in Gascony had been tedious and frustrating. A week after the king's return to Oloron, a clerk in his company sent a letter to a friend in Canterbury.

'I would have written more often,' he explained, 'if things had gone smoothly with our lord the king during his stay in Aquitaine; but things were rather bad than good.'

'Soon, I hope,' the same clerk concluded, 'the king will be on his way home again. The stay in these parts has seemed too long, both to him and his.'

In this hope our correspondent was not disappointed. Edward spent just three more months in Gascony, finalising the arrangements for the duchy's future government and its relationship with France. As soon as this business was concluded, on 13 June 1289, the king and his court set out north in the direction of home.[70]

Back in England, Edward's regency government had by no means had an easy time during their master's absence. Several major problems had arisen to test the capabilities and the resolve of Edmund of Cornwall and the other home councillors. In 1287, to take the most major example, a sizeable rebellion had erupted in south Wales. Rhys ap Maredudd, one of the few Welsh lords to have consistently supported the Crown, seems to have belatedly decided that he had been backing the wrong horse all along. In June that year he seized a number of castles and burned several towns. His rising, however, was short lived. The regents, perhaps fearing that a revolt on the scale of 1282–83 was in the offing, responded with a magnificent overreaction. Twenty-four thousand men were mobilised in order to bring Rhys to heel, a sledgehammer to crack a walnut. By the start of the new year it was all over, and English power in south Wales was undisputed. Rhys's chief castle at Dryslwyn fell to English siege-engines and was added to the list of the king's Welsh fortresses. In its shadow yet another new town was laid out, and English burgesses were soon moving in to take up residence.[71]

Rhys ap Maredudd himself evaded capture in 1288, and the following year it was rumoured that he was likely to escape to Ireland. How well he might have fared had he done so is an open question, for there too royal power was waxing irresistibly strong. Edward, as will now have become quite clear, had very little interest in Ireland. It was over thirty years ago, at the time of his first visit to Gascony, that he had received letters from his father telling him that Dublin should be his next port of call. Since then he had crossed the Channel to visit his French lands on four further occasions; but he had still yet to sail across the Irish Sea.[72]

There were obvious reasons for this preference. Gascony was cultured, civilised, warm and alluring. Its castles and cathedrals were the work of Edward's ancestors, its cities and roads had been laid out by the Romans. Its people might be fickle and devious (such was the king's opinion of them as expressed in a letter), but they were recognisably men of his own kind: wily, indeed, but also French-speaking, sophisticated and chivalrous.[73]

Ireland, by contrast, was a wild place – inhospitable, inclement and in many respects abhorrent to civilised sensibilities. The English clerk who wrote that he would rather go to prison than have to go back there probably spoke for many of his fellow countrymen.[74] Culturally, the country was thought to contain little worthy of curiosity. Edward, for example, displayed no interest in Irish history to compare with his marked fascination with the legendary past of Wales. The biggest problem with Ireland, however, was the people – or rather peoples. Ireland's problem was that it had not one people, but two.

A century before Edward's accession, the first English settlers had crossed the Irish Sea. Adventurous lords, enterprising townsmen and land-hungry peasants – all had set out into the west, tempted by the prospect of a fertile landscape they might profitably tame. The kings of England – Henry II and John – had soon followed, and Ireland was integrated into a royal empire that stretched from Dublin to Westminster and beyond to the Pyrenees.

But not wholly integrated. When those first English settlers had arrived in Ireland, they discovered a people whom they quickly concluded were the worst kind of savages. This was the late twelfth century: the English had been honing and developing their hostile attitudes towards the Welsh for more than fifty years, and found that such attitudes could be easily exported and applied to the Irish. Socially and culturally, there could be no question of mixing with such people. Moreover, by this stage, English governmental institutions and practices were also well developed and inflexibly hidebound, so political integration proved similarly impossible. English lords therefore took what they could by force of arms, and English settlers shut themselves away in self-contained and self-sustaining new towns. The Irish found themselves denied the most fertile parts of their island and driven to subsist on its less productive margins – the hills, the forests and the bogs. The result was a deeply divided society: English colonists and restless natives.[75]

For three generations, this English colony prospered. New castles, towns, abbeys and churches were built, the area under cultivation was expanded, flocks were increased, trade boomed, and some men made a fortune. But, around the middle of the thirteenth century – that is, around the time that Edward took over the island's lordship – the colony began to stall and stagnate. Several of the great English lordly dynasties died out, and the flow of settlers from England dried up. From this point on, more often than not, the lords of Ireland were absentees, rarely if ever crossing the sea to visit their Irish estates.[76]

This, of course, was true above all of Edward himself. Distracted by events in Wales from 1256 and then by political upheaval in England from 1258, the future king had little time or thought to spare for Ireland. As a result, the decline there steepened: English colonists began to fight among themselves, and the native Irish began to reassert their power. In 1258 one Irish chieftain even went so far as to declare himself 'king of Ireland', much as Llywelyn ap Gruffudd had proclaimed himself 'prince of Wales'. This would-be king, and hence his revolt, proved short lived. But other revolts followed in its wake. Provinces formerly under English power began to be lost. A Gaelic revival was under way.[77]

Hence, at the time of his accession, Edward knew that something had to be done about Ireland. The country might have held no personal attractions for the king, but he appreciated its value as a source of soldiers, food and money, and by 1274 these useful returns were suffering badly. After twenty years of his lax lordship, for instance, profits from the Irish exchequer had halved, from £5,000 to just £2,500 a year.[78]

Edward's solution was delegation. As with Gascony, so too with Ireland: the king dispatched a number of capable, trustworthy men, armed with wide powers of discretion to turn the lordship around. But whereas the individuals he sent south were smooth conciliators, those who went west were tough enforcers, licensed to use almost any means to restore order. Consider the example of Thomas de Clare. The younger brother of Earl Gilbert of Gloucester and one of the key players in Edward's escape from Montfort's clutches, Thomas had subsequently cemented his friendship with the future king by following him on crusade. Within weeks of his return and coronation, Edward had dispatched this daring and militaristic young man to Ireland to exercise his talents. As a younger son, with no inheritance to look forward to, Clare had a strong personal incentive to make a name and fortune for himself. The lordship he carved out in south-west Ireland was based on the former Irish kingdom of Thomond, centred on the estuary of the River Shannon. For a decade from 1276, Clare behaved like an old-school English conquistador of the previous century. Settlers were drafted in from England and planted on the Shannon's north shore. New stone castles were constructed. At Bunratty, the giant fortress that Clare erected has now vanished, but an impressed contemporary described it as 'girt with a thick outer wall, containing an impregnable roofed tower, and other buildings, large and limewashed'. By such irresistible methods, and with the Crown's backing, the ambitious Englishman was able to impose his domination on a wild frontier.[79]

Part of Edward must have realised that such a policy of repression could not provide a lasting solution. At some stage, and to some degree, the Irish would have to be included. That, after all, was very much the wish of the Irish themselves. In 1277 they collectively petitioned the king to allow them to use English law, and offered to pay handsomely for the privilege. But, while Edward may have been minded to accept such a move, the English settler community made it clear that they were not. To allow the Irish to use English law would be tantamount to treating them as English, and that would never do. The colonists jealously guarded their law as a marker of their identity, and so the proposal was ultimately rejected. The alternative path to integration, of course, would have been for the king to recognise Irish law and bring it under the umbrella of the Crown's jurisdiction. Edward, after all, had been prepared to do this with Welsh law before 1282, and parts of Welsh law had been allowed to stand after the Conquest. In Ireland's case, however, incorporation was regarded as a bridge too far; Irish law was so perverse and barbarous that its absorption was completely unconscionable. As the king himself declared in 1277, 'the laws the Irish use are detestable to God, and so contrary to all law that they ought not to be deemed law'.[80]

Denied the right to use English law and condemned for using their own, Ireland's original inhabitants were thereby destined to remain a race apart, and the only way left for the newcomers to deal with them was further marginalisation and military repression. Thus in 1277 Thomas de Clare dealt with one of his Irish rivals, Brian O Brian, by personally executing him at Bunratty, while in 1282 the English justiciar of Ireland – a bishop, no less – dealt with the troublesome MacMurrough brothers, native leaders of the south-east, by having them assassinated. It was hardly chivalrous, never mind Christian, but chivalry did not extend to the Irish. They were literally outlaws, living beyond the rules of civilised society.[81]

In any case, the proof of the pudding was in the eating. By 1289, as Edward prepared to leave Gascony, English royal policy in Ireland was seen as having succeeded. Profits at the exchequer in Dublin were back at the former high levels, boosted in part by the need to supply food to the troops and construction workers in north-west Wales. Thomas de Clare himself died in 1287, apparently of natural causes. But at the end of that same year, an anonymous Englishman in Ireland could write that the country 'was so pacified these days that in no part of the land is there anyone at war, or wishing to go to war, as is known for sure'.[82]

In many respects, therefore, royal power was at its height when Edward and Eleanor returned to England in the summer of 1289. (They were met off the boat at Dover on 13 August by five girls and one five-year-old boy, all pleased to see their parents after a separation of three years.) The king's patient diplomacy had given him a standing in Europe that was beyond compare, his rule in Gascony had been consolidated peacefully in person, and his power in Wales and Ireland had been consolidated forcefully by his deputies.[83]

In England itself, however, there was considerable disquiet. General lawlessness, for example, appears to have increased, in spite of the king's earlier legislation. There had been violent feuding between both magnates and merchants; men had ridden about the country in armed gangs. At Boston in Lincolnshire there had been a particularly notorious incident in 1288 when certain individuals had conspired to rob the town's famous annual fair, with the result that much of it went up in smoke.[84]

Some of these disturbances were a natural consequence of Edward's absence; robbers as well as rebels would seize the opportunity if they thought the government seemed weak. But England's restlessness during these years was also fuelled by a deepening sense of political discontent. The citizens of London, for instance, still bridled at their loss of liberty in 1285; the clergy, too, had become increasingly resentful of royal interference in their affairs and challenges to their jurisdiction. Above all, though, the trouble lay with the magnates, who were furious at the treatment they had been receiving from the Crown. When the regent had warned certain men against riding around causing trouble in 1288, four of them were earls. Before the king's departure these men had been reasonably quiescent, but soon after he left they were literally up in arms.[85]

The principal reason for disgruntlement among England's great men was the ongoing royal investigation into their rights and liberties as landowners. Launched by Edward soon after his coronation, but then postponed on account of the first Welsh war, the long-running inquiry had resumed in earnest in 1278–79. At that point the king's justices had begun to summon men to court to defend their claims, and their insistent question 'quo warranto?' had given the whole process its popular name. In every case, the justices demanded to know 'by what warrant' an individual claimed his or her special privileges.[86]

From the first the magnates had found this all very tedious, frustrating and expensive. It meant having to hire lawyers to defend perfectly legitimate ancient rights, and having to bribe jurors where those rights were not quite so old and unimpeachable. As one piece of contemporary doggerel put it, 'And the Quo Warranto/Will give us all enough to do!' The main problem was one of evidence. Naturally, the best rejoinder to the question 'by what warrant' was to say 'by this one', and wave under the inquisitor's nose a royal charter that set out in precise detail all the rights that one was defending. But in most cases such a charter simply did not exist; only latterly had society come to place such a heavy reliance on documentary proof. Often the only defence a landlord could offer was that he and his ancestors had enjoyed such rights since time immemorial, and hope that local jurors would back him up in his assertion.[87]

This is why, latterly, the magnates had become so agitated. In 1285 royal justices had announced that, in future, claims of long usage would not be admissible as evidence – only a charter would do. (Hence, probably, the rush to get old charters confirmed by the king during that year's summer parliament.) When, therefore, the hearings had resumed in Edward's absence, the landowning classes had found themselves losing out badly to the king's lawyers. As one chronicler succinctly explained, 'a great many men who did not have charters lost, without recovery, liberties and free customs of which they had been seized for a long time before'.[88]

One can well understand the magnates' frustration. They had helped Edward reduce and conquer Wales in two separate campaigns, in many cases at considerable personal expense and in return for little, if anything, by way of compensatory reward. More recently they had given the same support to the regency government in suppressing the rebellion of Rhys ap Maredudd. Their reward for this service, it seemed, was to be dragged through the courts by arrogant royal justices and forced to defend the hard-won liberties of their ancestors. So much for the king's pretence that they were like Arthur and his knights, a brotherhood of equals sat at a Round Table. Of late, it felt more like a conventional domestic setting, with Edward and his lawyers sat together at the high table, while the magnates sulked on the benches below.

It is no coincidence that this period saw the production of anonymous tracts, not only attacking royal justices but also simultaneously asserting the rights of the magnates. *The Mirror of Justices*, for instance, as well as demonstrating a pronounced hostility for the king's lawmen, begins with a fabulous justification for restricting royal power. Its author explained how, when the Anglo-Saxons had first arrived in Britain, it was the earls who had been the sovereigns; only after many years of infighting had they agreed to elect one of their number as king. Edward's great men, in other words, had begun to follow his own example, and were appealing to (and, in this case, inventing) history to justify present politics. According to a well-known chronicle tradition, either the earl of Gloucester or the earl of Surrey made a similar, impassioned appeal to the past when he came before the Quo Warranto judges. When asked by what warrant he claimed his rights, the earl brandished an ancient, rusty sword. 'Behold, my lords!' he said. 'This is my warrant. For my ancestors came with William the Bastard and conquered their lands with the sword – and by the sword I shall defend them from anyone wishing to seize them. The king did not conquer and subject the land by himself, but our forebears were sharers and partners with him.'[89]

Edward therefore returned to England realising that he faced opposition on several fronts – a situation similar to the one that had greeted him at the start of his reign. If the discontent and disorder did not run as deep as they had done fifteen years earlier, the disillusionment was greater, and the grounds for optimism were fewer. There was, moreover, a strong similarity between the Crown's financial position in 1274 and 1289: once again, the king was coming home in serious debt. His time in Gascony had been massively expensive, and not just because of obvious costs, such as his payment to free Charles of Salerno or the lavish hospitality laid on for the Aragonese court. The main cause of insolvency was that Gascony's resources were totally inadequate for maintaining an entourage on the scale that royal dignity had demanded. For three years, Edward had been keeping up a kingly appearance on a ducal income, and as a result he had run up a debt to compare with the cost of his crusade or the conquest of Wales. On the day he had sailed for England, the king acknowledged that he owed the Riccardi a sum of almost £110,000. Attempts to alleviate this burden in his absence had already run aground. Asked for an aid at the start of 1289, the discontented magnates, led by the earl of Gloucester, had assured the regency government that no tax would be granted as long as the king was outside his kingdom. Whether or not they would change their tune now he was back remained to be seen. As at the start of his reign, Edward needed to do some serious conciliating.[70]

He began in the autumn of 1289 with the same kind of move that had won him popularity on that earlier occasion. In October it was announced that all those who had grievances against the king's local officials could come forward and complain. This time around, however, the strategy fell flat, probably because it was perceived as overtly cynical. Edward obtained more popularity – and a convenient windfall of cash – from a simultaneous crackdown on corruption among his judges. Most of the leading lights of the judiciary were found guilty of one charge or another, lost their jobs and were made to pay large fines. The chief justice, Thomas Weyland, was sent into exile. But, unpopular as the judges were, this purge produced no corresponding boost for the king. When a parliament met at the start of 1290 – the first since 1286 – there was naturally much business to be discussed, but nothing was done to improve the king's finances.[91]

For Edward to get the support and the money he needed, he was going to have to do more than conciliate. Concessions were required, and, as far as the magnates were concerned, the key was Quo Warranto. When parliament met again after Easter, the protests and petitions on this issue reached their highest pitch. For several weeks, in spite of his need, the king remained obstinate: as far as he was concerned, any rights without proof of entitlement were usurpations, and he had sworn at his coronation to recover them for the Crown. Eventually, however, around 21 May, a compromise was reached. Edward allowed that liberties could stand where landowners could prove continuous and responsible usage since 1189 (the start of the reign of Richard I). The face-saving formula was that all claims accepted in this way had to be confirmed by the king, thereby preserving the fiction that the Crown had conceded them in the first place.[92]

By this partial royal climbdown, the magnates were partially appeased. It helped Edward's cause that he had successfully neutralised his chief opponent, the earl of Gloucester, by making him an offer he couldn't refuse. At the start of the parliamentary session, in a private ceremony in the royal chapel, Earl Gilbert was married to the king's daughter, Joan. The spirited eighteen-year-old princess may have presented obvious attractions to the forty-six-year-old divorcee, but the match's principal enticement was the proximity it promised the earl to the centre of royal politics, allowing him a prominence he had not enjoyed since the 1260s.[93]

By themselves, however, the magnates – as Edward must surely have appreciated – were in no position to grant him the huge amount of money that he needed to achieve solvency. In their capacity as his principal tenants, they offered him the kind of levy that any lord might demand on the occasion of his daughter's wedding, but this promised to yield such a nugatory sum that the king did not even bother to collect it. What he needed to clear his debts was a grant of general taxation, and, while mending fences with the magnates was an essential first step, consent for such a measure could come only from the knights of the shires. In the middle of June writs of summons were sent out to the counties, and parliament went into recess until their arrival.[94]

The lesser landowners of England, like the magnates, had one outstanding grievance: in spite of successive rounds of legislation, for which they had paid through the nose on two earlier occasions, the problems associated with Jewish credit had persisted. The ban on moneylending that Edward had imposed at the start of his reign had not worked – all it had succeeded in doing was to drive the practice underground. The Jews had continued to lend money as before, albeit covertly, with some concealing their deals with false contracts for commodities. Moreover, the king's ban had not eradicated debts taken out before 1275, and so the dubious trade whereby Christian speculators could snap up encumbered estates had also continued unabated.[95]

  As of old, the most notorious speculators were the richest members of society who congregated at the king's court, and none was more notorious than the queen. Eleanor of Castile, a smart and shrewd woman, had never assumed a political role in England – there were no rival factions at her husband's court to compare with those of the previous reign. Instead, and with Edward's encouragement, Eleanor had directed her energies into playing the property market, pouncing on estates whenever their owners looked vulnerable. 'The king would like to get our gold/The queen, our manors fair, to hold,' ran one scurrilous rhyme. The fair Leeds Castle was one of many properties acquired in this way. It had been obtained from William Leybourne (son of the king's friend, Roger) in exchange for clearing his debts to the Jews.[96]

  Such sharp practice had a corrosive effect on Eleanor's reputation – so much so that, while the queen had been away in Gascony, Archbishop Pecham had felt compelled to write to one of her leading clerks. 'A rumour is waxing strong throughout the kingdom,' Pecham began, 'and has generated much scandal. It is said that the illustrious lady queen, whom you serve, is occupying many manors, lands, and other possessions of nobles, and has made them her own property – lands which the Jews have extorted with usury from Christians under the protection of the royal court.'

  'There is public outcry and gossip about this in every part of England,' the archbishop continued, before urging the recipient of his letter to intercede. For her own good, he averred, the queen must desist: her dealings were damnable.[97]

In 1290, therefore, Edward was almost as fed up with the Jewish problem as the knights of the shires themselves. In several different ways, on several different occasions, he had tried to solve it by means that, to his mind, seemed very conscientious. In 1275 he had banned moneylending and exhorted the Jews to live by lawful trade; in 1280 he had ordered all Jews to attend special sermons, preached by Dominican friars, with the hope of persuading them to convert. But his ban had not been obeyed, and his exhortations were ignored. The problem was as bad as ever, and its taint now reached so high, touching even the queen, that it threatened to discredit the king himself. Something would have to be done.[98]

One option was simply to get rid of the Jews altogether. Wholesale expulsions were nothing new in thirteenth-century Europe. The king of France had expelled all Jews from his own lands in 1182; the duke of Brittany had driven them out of his duchy in 1239. In England, as we have already seen, both Simon de Montfort and Eleanor of Provence had ordered local expulsions from their own estates. According to one chronicler, it was his mother who suggested to Edward that he expel the Jews from England in 1290. For those who ordered them, such expulsions were a matter of Christian conscience and, for this reason, they were sometimes ordained as a preparatory step towards going on crusade. In the late 1240s Louis IX had expelled the Jews from the French royal demesne in advance of his first passage to the East. And Edward, having taken the cross for the second time in 1287, had ordered the Jews out of Gascony. After God had spared him from falling to his death, it seemed the least he could do.[99]

The downside for any prince or potentate who acted in this way was that, while spiritually beneficial, it was commercially disadvantageous. Of course, the property of expelled Jews could be sold off, but the profits involved were not huge and, besides, profiteering was hardly in keeping with the piety of the exercise. When Edward had expelled Gascony's Jews, he had given the proceeds to the local friars.[100]

An expulsion, therefore, might cut the Gordian knot of England's Jewish problem, but financially it would be a backward step. The Jews were no longer the great cash cow they had once been – successive royal depredations, culminating in the king's own coin-clipping pogrom of 1279, had seen to that – but 1290 was not a year for doing away with any form of revenue, no matter how small. Indeed, it looks very much as if, in June that year, Edward was preparing to tallage the Jews, hoping to squeeze out of them what little money remained.[101]

But then, it seems, someone – we don't know precisely when, where or with whom the idea originated – had the happy notion that the king might be able to copy his cousin. Following his release from captivity, Charles of Salerno had expelled the Jews from his counties of Maine and Anjou. Naturally, his expulsion edict made much of the Jews manifold crimes (usury, in Charles's mind, was apparently trumped by the Jews tendency to 'cohabit evilly with Christian maidens'). But – and this was the notably pioneering part – Charles also made no bones about the fact that, by expelling the Jews, he was hurting his own pocket. As the edict went on to explain, it was for this reason – 'as some recompense for the profit which we lose through the said expulsion' – that Charles's subjects had agreed to vote him a tax.[102]

In the second week of July 1290, parliament resumed in Westminster. The session re-opened with another royal wedding, as Edward's fifteen-year-old daughter Margaret married John, heir to the duchy of Brabant. In contrast to the private ceremony of the spring, this match was deliberately presented as a great affair of state, and celebrated on a maximum scale. The marriage itself took place in Westminster Abbey, and hundreds of lords and ladies attended, along with almost a thousand Londoners. At the wedding feast no fewer than 426 minstrels entertained the throng. Immediately afterwards – again, no doubt by deliberate design – Archbishop Pecham preached the cross. Gilbert de Clare and his new wife swore to go east, as did many other nobles and bishops.[103]

In this atmosphere of celebration and heightened religious fervour, the knights of the shire assembled. The magnates, mindful of the king's concession on Quo Warranto and appeased by a raft of other recent measures, approved the grant of a tax. Would the knights oblige the king by doing the same? We do not know if the idea was put to them first (as seems most likely) or whether they demanded it as the price of their consent. Whatever the case, the deal was quickly done. Edward was granted his tax. And, in return, on 18 July the royal orders went out. All Jews were to leave the realm before the 1 November.[104]

For what was very definitely the final time, the Jews were made to pay the price for the king of England's insolvency. That summer, the small, impoverished and broken community – perhaps numbering only 2,000 souls by this time – gathered together their belongings, and the enforced exodus began. In general, their departure was peaceful, and they made their way to the coast without incident. Once on board ship, some groups fell victim to murderous Christian captains, who were later punished, though more for their failure to respect royal authority than on account of any belated sympathy for the Jews. In his anti-Semitism, as in other aspects of his bigotry, Edward marched in step with his subjects. The knights of the shire were so pleased at the prospect of being rid of the Jews that they had agreed to a generous grant of one-fifteenth of their goods. Its yield, a massive £116,000, was not only the biggest of the whole reign, but the single biggest tax collected in Britain during the entire Middle Ages. The Church was so delighted with the king's pious performance that they voted a thank-you tax of their own in the autumn. Without doubt, the expulsion of the Jews was the most popular act Edward ever committed.[105]

By this expedient, the king had once again squared the circle. His critics were appeased, his finances restored. He could now devote his attention fully to the great project of his crusade. Already in 1290 he had received a further embassy from the Mongols and sent Otto de Grandson to the Holy Land on an advanced reconnaissance mission. There was also excellent news from Europe: in spite of further difficulties since his departure, a universal peace between France, Aragon, Anjou and Rome now seemed to be in train. Meanwhile, during negotiations with his subjects in England, parallel negotiations with Rome had come to final fruition. By the start of the year the new pope had endorsed the financial package agreed by his predecessor, and by the end of the summer, after further fine-tuning, Edward held in his hands a document to which he was ready to commit. A special, select parliament of magnates was summoned. They met in October, at Clipstone, a royal hunting lodge in Sherwood Forest. There, surrounded by his great men, with whom he was once again united, Edward set his seal to the pope's offer. He would be paid the £130,000 of crusading funds already collected, and would receive the proceeds of a new, six-year tax as quickly as they came in. The date for departure was set. The king and his fellow crusaders would leave at midsummer 1293.[106]

Then the queen fell ill, and Edward's world fell apart.

8

The Great Cause

Within a month of the close of the autumn parliament of 1290 Queen Eleanor was dead. During her stay in Gascony she had contracted a malarial fever that, although it obviously did not prevent her from travelling, probably lingered and left her susceptible to the sickness that took hold at Clipstone in the last days of October. At that point a household sergeant was dispatched to Lincoln, twenty-five miles to the east, to procure better medicines. But a further fortnight brought no improvement, and it was evidently decided that the only hope was to get the queen to Lincoln in person, almost certainly so that she could be near the shrine of St Hugh in the city's cathedral. The royal party proceeded by short journeys and managed to cross the River Trent, but by that stage it must have been clear that Eleanor could cope with no more. On 20 November the court was forced to stop in Harby, a small village six miles short of their destination, and for another week the queen rested in the modest home of Richard Weston, a local knight. These, though, were to be her last lodgings. During the evening of 28 November Eleanor died. She had recently passed her forty-ninth birthday.[1]

Contemporary Englishmen who recorded the queen's passing composed only the shortest of obituary notices, and what little they wrote was hardly positive. 'A Spaniard by birth,' said the annalist at Dunstable Priory, 'she acquired many fine manors.' As far as most people were concerned, there was not much more that could be said. Since her arrival in England thirty-five years earlier, Eleanor had made scant effort to cultivate popular affection. Medieval queens could endear themselves by the personal distribution of alms to the poor, and by interceding with their husbands on behalf of the needy, the oppressed or the condemned. But Eleanor had preferred to let others make donations on her behalf and − to judge from comments once made by

Archbishop Pecham – was reckoned to have encouraged Edward to be more severe in his judgements, not less so. As the Dunstable annalist implies, foreignness was one part of her problem. Unlike the king, Eleanor had never learned to speak English. Acquisitiveness – the accumulation of 'fine manors' – was another. In the course of her career Eleanor had amassed lands worth a total of about £50,000 (or £2,500 a year). This was not simply a question of greed: at the time of her arrival in England the queen's resources had been quite inadequate and required development. Yet the means employed by Eleanor and her officials to effect this expansion, especially the snapping up of estates encumbered by Jewish debts, had become notorious. So too had her methods of estate management, which inquests carried out after her death revealed to have been high-handed and ruthless. Not until her last moments did Eleanor seek to make amends. 'After she had devotedly received the sacrament of the dying,' wrote one chronicler, 'she earnestly prayed her lord the king, who was listening to her requests, that everything unjustly taken from anyone by her or her ministers should be restored.'

Edward saw to this and much more besides. Indeed, his reaction to his wife's death was such that it all but eclipsed the muted response of his subjects, and ultimately served to disguise the damage that the queen's reputation had sustained during her own lifetime. It began with an elaborate funeral procession. From Harby Eleanor's body was taken to Lincoln, where her viscera were removed and interred in the cathedral, while her heart, in accordance with her wishes, was reserved for later burial at the Blackfriars in London with that of her son Alfonso. Then, on 3 December, the king and his court set out to conduct the queen's embalmed corpse south to Westminster – a slow, mournful progress that lasted the best part of a fortnight, and that ended on 17 December, when Eleanor was entombed near the high altar in Westminster Abbey.[2]

The king's effort to honour his wife, however, was only just beginning. In the months and years that followed, a team of royal artists and artisans was commissioned to create what has been called 'the most magnificent funerary display ever accorded an English monarch'. At Lincoln, Blackfriars and Westminster, three separate tombs were fashioned. Only the last survives, but it is a work of striking sophistication: the representation of Eleanor shows her with her hair unfastened and her eyes wide open. Cast in bronze and finished in gold, it took two years to produce and is rivalled only by the similar effigy created simultaneously for the tomb of Henry III.

In overall terms, though, Eleanor's commemoration has no equal. In addition to the tombs, Edward ordered the creation of no fewer than twelve additional memorials – a dozen monuments of stone and marble, one to mark each place that the queen's body had rested on its journey from Lincoln to London. These were the celebrated Eleanor Crosses, so called because each was originally surmounted with a devotional cross. Memorial crosses, the primary purpose of which was to encourage prayers for the departed, were not unknown in thirteenth-century England, but nothing on this scale had even been seen before, nor would it be attempted again. The only precedent, and the probable inspiration, were the series of monuments, known as *montjoies*, built in France to mark the last journey of Louis IX. None of these survives, however, whereas – miraculously – three of the twelve crosses erected for Eleanor are still standing (at Hardingstone and Geddington in Northamptonshire, and at Waltham in Hertfordshire). The building accounts indicate that these are lesser examples – their vanished counterparts that once stood in Cheapside and Charing (hence Charing Cross) cost up to seven times as much. Nevertheless, the three survivors, weathered and damaged as they are, stripped of their paint and their gilding, are generally acknowledged to constitute a watershed moment in English art – a novel fusion of sculptural and architectural forms that heralds the beginning of the English Decorated style.[3]

An appreciation of their aesthetic qualities, though, and of the contribution they made to the prestige of the Crown, had led some commentators to downplay what was surely the primary motivation for the crosses' construction, namely, the profound grief of the king. Edward and Eleanor had been married for thirty-six years, and during that time they had hardly ever been apart. Their tastes and interests – hunting, chess, chivalry and romance – appear to have coincided almost exactly. Above all, they had shared a sense of adventure. On all the king's travels, on crusade or on campaign, the queen had been his most constant companion. Her fifteen or sixteen pregnancies are another testament to their closeness, and there is no credible evidence to suggest that either was anything other than faithful. The English may never have taken Eleanor to their hearts, but Edward had always adored her. After her funeral in December 1290 he retreated to Ashridge, a religious house in Hertfordshire, to spend Christmas in what must have been the deepest sorrow. He was still there in January when he wrote a letter to the abbot of Cluny in France, in which he referred to the wife 'whom in life we dearly cherished, and whom in death we cannot cease to love'.[4]

Deep as the king's desolation assuredly was, there is no reason to suppose that it diminished in any way his enthusiasm for the planned crusade.

If anything, Eleanor's death may have intensified Edward's desire to return to the Holy Land: a picture on the side of the queen's tomb shows a knight, believed to be Otto de Grandson, offering prayers for her soul there.[5] The king *was* distracted from his declared purpose in the autumn of 1290, but not by the loss of his wife. Rather his plans were disrupted by the death of a seven-year-old Norwegian girl in the distant islands of Orkney.

To explain this cryptic comment, it is necessary to travel back in time, and north in space, and consider the career of Edward's brother-in-law, King Alexander III of Scotland. Like Edward, Alexander was a strong and successful king. In the 1250s, still in his teens, he had asserted his independence in the face of aristocratic efforts to control him. In the 1260s – much as Edward would do in Wales a decade later – he turned his attention westwards and imposed his authority on a debatable frontier. The islands on Scotland's western seaboard, nominally under the control of the king of Norway, were effectively independent; but by 1266 the Norwegians had been forcibly persuaded to bow out, and the locals were obliged to acknowledge the superior lordship of the Scottish royal house. So successful, in fact, was Alexander's rule, that the latter part of his reign suffers from documentary silence. Contrary to the belief of Walter Scott, who once opined that everybody in medieval Scotland was too busy fighting to write anything down, the hush that descends on Scottish affairs in the 1270s is testimony to the peace that their king had succeeded in establishing.[6]

But, forceful and fortunate in politics, Alexander was far less lucky in his family. First, in 1275, came the death of his queen (and Edward's sister), Margaret. Then, in the decade that followed, came the successive loss of all their children: their younger son David died in 1281, their only daughter, also Margaret, in 1283, and lastly their elder son, Alexander, in 1284. It was an incredible run of dynastic bad luck, and inevitably raised the question of who would succeed to the Scottish throne when Alexander himself died, for the king had neither brothers nor uncles who might step in and replace him. Prudently, therefore, Alexander – still only in his early forties – elected to remarry. In 1285 he took as his second queen a young Frenchwoman by the name of Yolande of Dreux. Imprudently, however, just a few months into their marriage, the king set out to meet his new wife in a terrible storm. On the evening of 18 March 1286 he rode from Edinburgh to Queensferry, crossed the Firth of Forth by boat, and continued along the coast towards Kinghorn, where Yolande was waiting. But she waited in vain. At some point during the last stage of his ill-advised journey, her husband lost his escort, tumbled over a cliff and broke his neck. Not until the next day dawned was his lifeless body found lying on the shoreline.[7]

At this point the king of England was readying himself to leave for France, a trip on which the peace of Europe and the fate of the Holy Land were seen to hinge. Discomforting as was the news from Scotland, therefore, it could not be permitted to disrupt or even to delay the urgent business on the Continent. In May Edward set sail from Dover, having heard of Alexander's sudden death, but not of its drawn-out sequel.

That news reached him sporadically during his stay in Gascony. In the summer of 1286 it was hopeful: Yolande of Dreux, the new and newly widowed Scottish queen, was pregnant. King Alexander, it seemed, had not failed after all. His subjects were now preparing themselves for a long minority, at the end of which the late king's as-yet unborn child would succeed him. Until that time, Edward learned, Scotland was to be governed by a regency council. By common consent, power had passed to six 'Guardians' – two earls, two bishops and two barons – who had sworn to protect the kingdom for Alexander's heir.[8]

The following year, however, the intelligence was altogether more desperate. The queen's pregnancy had ended unsuccessfully with the delivery of a stillborn child. As a result, Scotland had been thrown into confusion. Rebellion had been raised in the south-west of the country, and although the Guardians had suppressed the rising, their authority was now weak and the peace they maintained fragile. What they needed, and what they sought above all, was Edward's assistance. The Scots would remain on anxious alert until the English king could come there and help them solve their succession crisis.[9]

The terrible and tragic turn that events had taken in Scotland concerned Edward in more ways than one. Obviously, as king of England, he was bound to take an interest, if only from the point of view of security, in any disarray north of the Border. But far more disturbing were the general ramifications of the Scottish crisis, for it held up a mirror to Edward's own domestic situation, and presented an alarming future vision of England overtaken by a similar dynastic disaster. Alexander's untimely end emphasised that death was no respecter of high office and that even vigorous and active kings might be struck down in their prime. Edward's luck was already legendary. He had emerged unscathed from two bloody battles, survived storms at sea, and had miraculously recovered from the seemingly deadly wound inflicted by an assassin's blade. But such luck could not last forever. The broken collarbone that the king sustained in Gascony could easily have been a broken neck.

Had that been the case, the English crown would have passed to Edward of Caernarfon, a child barely two years old at the time of his parents' departure for France. Needless to say, it would have been quite unwise, given the fate of all his other sons, for Edward to have pinned too much hope on the boy's survival. By the same token, it must have been equally clear by 1287 that he and Eleanor could expect no more children. Little Edward, their only surviving son, would also be their last.

It was almost certainly with the example of Scotland uppermost in his mind that Edward set about formalising the arrangements for the English succession soon after his return from Gascony. In the spring of 1290 the king summoned a special meeting of counsellors, including the archbishop of Canterbury and five other bishops, to assemble at Amesbury in Wiltshire. The choice of location is revealing. In 1285, as we have seen, the priory at Amesbury had received Edward's daughter, Mary, as a nun. But, more significantly, the priory had in the meantime also become home to the king's mother. Eleanor of Provence was also making preparations for the end of her life, and had quietly followed her granddaughter in taking the veil during her son's absence. Now in her late sixties, the dowager queen had lived a far less conspicuous and controversial life in the West Country since the death of Henry III some eighteen years earlier. Gone were the days of plotting revenge on her enemies and raising armies to rescue her husband's realm. Mindful of the divisive and unpopular figure his mother had once been, Edward, while according her great personal respect, had allowed Eleanor no role in politics, just as he had marginalised the political position of his own queen.[10]

When it came to family matters, however, the king was wont to consult both women, and the question of the succession, although a political concern of the highest order, was ultimately a family affair. For this reason, Edward, his wife and his mother were joined at Amesbury not only by a crowd of senior churchmen, but also by Edmund of Lancaster, the king's brother, and William de Valence, his half-uncle. Also in attendance was Gilbert de Clare, earl of Gloucester, who was about to enter this family circle by virtue of his impending marriage to Edward's daughter, Joan. Indeed, Earl Gilbert's presence, as the promissory documents he was induced to issue make plain, was most important, for the king's daughters were revealed to be his back-up plan. All those gathered at Amesbury agreed that, in the event of Edward's death, and the premature death of his only son, the kingdom would pass to the eldest of his five surviving daughters.

This was a remarkable provision. From a legal point of view, it was anomalous, in that primogeniture did not normally apply to female heirs. Ordinarily in such circumstances, estates were divided between daughters regardless of precedence of birth. By this decision, therefore, the kingdom of England was understood to be exceptional in its impartibility. But more remarkable still was the daring of the ordinance in the light of historical precedent. Only one earlier king of England, the imperious Henry I (d. 1135), had insisted that his daughter should succeed him, with the result that England had been torn apart by civil war for a generation. For Edward similarly to rule in favour of female succession, even in concert with the episcopate and his extended family, was thus a mark of his supreme self-confidence. At the same time, it exposed his shrinking range of options. The best that all of them could hope for was that Edward himself would continue to reign for many years to come, and that his only remaining son would beat the odds and survive to adulthood.[11]

There was, however, a better hope still, and it lay with Scotland. Alexander III had died before he could father any more children of his own, but he was not without a direct heir. Between 1281 and 1283 his late daughter, Margaret, had been briefly married to the king of Norway, and at some point towards the end of that period she had given birth to a daughter of her own. This child, also called Margaret, had grown up in Norway, unaware that she would one day become the last hope for her grandfather's dynasty. In 1284, when his last son died, Alexander had obtained general recognition of her right to succeed him in default of any new children he might have. And when, two years later, the king himself perished, the broad political consensus remained: Margaret, 'the Maid of Norway', had the best right to the Scottish throne.[12]

What if this little girl, aged only three at the time of Alexander's death, were to be married to Edward's only son, then approaching his second birthday? The boy would not only succeed his father as king of England, but also become king of Scotland in right of his wife. Their children would become rulers of a double kingdom – perhaps a united kingdom – which would stretch from the English Channel to the Western Isles. The idea appears to have been floated as early as 1284, by Alexander himself, following the death of his last son. In response to a letter of condolence from Edward I, the Scottish king had mused that, through his tiny granddaughter, 'much good may yet come to pass'. It was an intriguing idea, though at that time only one of many possible futures; if Alexander had more children of his own, the vision would dissolve, and the future king of England would be committed to a disadvantageous match with a Norwegian princess, nothing more. But when Alexander died, the Maid's succession seemed certain. Messengers began to travel between the English and Norwegian courts. In the spring of 1289, in anticipation of Edward's imminent return to England, negotiations began in earnest. Finally, on 6 November that year, an international summit was held at Salisbury. Edward and his advisers met with the Norwegian ambassadors and the Scottish Guardians, and it was agreed: within the next twelve months, Margaret of Norway would marry Edward of Caernarfon.[13]

The Scots were far from unhappy with this prospect. It promised an end to the years of uncertainty since 1286 and to the latent threat of further disorder. A marriage alliance with England would give the Maid a powerful protector, and would mean that her claim was most unlikely to be contested in the future. Accordingly, when the political community of Scotland assembled on the Border at Birgham in March 1290, the Salisbury agreement was unanimously ratified. More than a hundred Scotsmen of substance wrote to Edward I expressing their will to proceed with the wedding.[14]

Nevertheless, the Scots proceeded with caution. This was not just the union of two royal children but the union of two kingdoms. The fact that Edward was a force to be reckoned with also carried certain negative implications. Would he be too powerful, or too demanding? Realistically, the Guardians recognised that their options were limited, and accepted that England would be the dominant partner in the marriage. But, at the same time, they had sworn an oath to preserve Alexander III's kingdom intact and undiminished for his eventual heirs. As such, their overriding concern was to safeguard Scotland's future independence.[15]

What the Scots needed, in short, was a prenuptial agreement, and to this end negotiations with England dragged on into the summer of 1290. On many issues it was possible to reach consensus. Everyone, for example, accepted that, although the two children were not yet of marriageable age, they should nonetheless be regarded as if married from the moment of the Maid's arrival, and that Edward of Caernarfon should therefore be regarded as king of Scotland from that point. There was agreement, too, on the question of the routine business of Scottish government. The Scots were concerned to ensure that they would not have to travel to England to do homage to their new king, or to answer or initiate lawsuits. What they demanded – and what Edward conceded – was that such matters should be dealt with in Scotland by a resident viceroy or lieutenant.

When they came to consider the matter of Scotland's castles, however, the two sides could find no common ground. Edward was determined that all royal fortresses must come under his control, and insisted on his right to appoint their custodians in every case. His attitude was probably borne of bitter memories of 1258, at which point control of England's royal castles had been handed to a council. Also, no doubt, the king recollected the unpleasant experiences of his sister Margaret after her marriage to Alexander III, whose minority had been blighted by one aristocratic coup after another.

But what seemed to Edward to be a commonsensical means of ensuring Scotland's future security sounded to the Scots like an unconscionable demand for the surrender of sovereignty. Castles were the instruments of raw power, and for this reason neither side was prepared to compromise. When, in July 1290, the Scots reassembled at Birgham to meet the English king's ambassadors, articles were drafted with a view to producing a final treaty, but, because of the disagreement on this crucial issue, no treaty was sealed.[16]

The deadlock was broken, it seems, by the news that the Maid had already set sail from Norway and was en route for Scotland. This intelligence, which apparently reached Edward's ears in the last days of August, forced him to settle, for fear that the Scots' bargaining position would be strengthened if they took possession of the girl. On 28 August, therefore, while the English court was at Northampton, the articles drafted earlier in the summer were approved. The contentious matter of castles was fudged: those Scottish envoys present accepted that keepers would be appointed 'on the common advice of the Scots and the English king'. But the Scots did get a clear statement to safeguard their independence, of the kind they had been seeking since the start. In the most resonant phrase of their agreement, Edward promised that Scotland should remain 'free in itself, and without subjection, from the kingdom of England'.[17]

All thoughts now turned to the Maid's impending arrival. Edward immediately sent his friend, the bishop of Durham, to see to her reception, and a few days later dispatched a welcoming gift of jewels for the little girl who was about to become his daughter-in-law. Meanwhile, the magnates of Scotland, as was traditional, began to assemble at Scone Abbey near Perth in readiness for the enthronement of their new queen. In late September representatives of both nations rode into Scotland's extreme north, to greet the Norwegian ship which, unexpectedly, had put into the islands of Orkney. Only in the course of their journey did they learn that, during her voyage, the Maid had fallen sick, perhaps from having eaten decayed food. And when, in early October, they returned south, it was with the news that the girl was dead.[18]

The death of the Maid of Norway finally extinguished the flickering flame that was the bloodline of King Alexander and threw the

Scotland

question of the Scottish succession wide open. It was necessary to forage far back into the royal family tree – over a hundred years – to find other branches that had flourished into the present. But these collateral descents were many, and consequently there was no consensus on who was next in line to the throne. The respective merits of the most important candidates will be considered later in this chapter; for now, it will suffice to note that, in the eyes of many Scots, the man with the best claim to succeed was John Balliol.

Twenty years earlier only a madman or a mystic would have put money on this candidate, and not just because the Scottish royal house had yet to be overtaken by disaster. Born around the middle of the thirteenth century, Balliol was the youngest of four brothers, and as such was apparently destined for a career in the Church. But in the course of the 1270s his family were also visited by an exceptional mortality: during that decade, all three of his elder brothers died without issue, leaving John as the heir to their father's estates in England and France.[19]

As this paternal inheritance implies, Balliol was to all intents and purposes an Englishman. His father had been lord of Barnard Castle in County Durham, had fought for Henry III in the Battle of Lewes and, around the same time, had achieved lasting fame as the founder of Balliol College, Oxford. John, it is true, was Scottish on his mother's side, and it was from his mother that he inherited his claim to Scotland's empty throne. But Dervorguilla Balliol lived to be a very old lady, surviving until January 1290. Only at that point did her son, around the time of his fortieth birthday, enter into her extensive estates in Galloway and become a major Scottish landowner in his own right.[20]

Nevertheless, Balliol had another connection with Scotland in the form of his brother-in-law, John Comyn. Having married Balliol's sister, Eleanor, in the early 1270s, Comyn had gone on to become the lord of Badenoch, and as such wielded especially great power in the northern part of the kingdom. Together with his other relatives, moreover, he held lands and castles in almost every corner of Scotland. It was an indication of the Comyns' importance that two of their number – John and his great-uncle Alexander – had been among the six Guardians elected in 1286. All of which is to say that John Balliol, although he was a newcomer to the ranks of the Scottish nobility, had major and influential backing for his claim to the throne from a family that was arguably the most formidable force in Scottish politics.[21]

That claim, however, did not go unchallenged. Balliol and the Comyns had a powerful opponent in the shape of Robert Bruce. Despite the fact that he too held lands in England, Bruce was the more obviously

Scottish candidate: Annandale, a lordship in south-western Scotland, was his paternal inheritance (although, like Balliol, his claim was on his mother's side). An elderly man – in 1290 he was about seventy years old – Bruce was nothing less than ferocious in prosecuting what he regarded as his superior right. Indeed, he evidently considered his right to be superior not only to that of Balliol, but also to that of the Maid of Norway. It was Bruce who had raised rebellion in the winter of 1286-87, on learning that Yolande of Dreux's pregnancy had failed.[22]

At that point the majority of Scots, represented by the Guardians, had given their backing to the Maid, and Bruce's pretensions had been forcibly held in check. But in the autumn of 1290, once the Maid was revealed to be dead, the renewal of armed conflict seemed all but inevitable. Support was split between the two camps: neither Bruce nor Balliol could command sufficient backing among Scotland's political community to impose a decisive settlement.

What the Scots needed was a powerful outside agency to help them choose between these two contenders: an honest broker to come and arbitrate. Once again, there was only one realistic option, and that was the king of England. He, after all, had been playing the role of international peacemaker in Europe for the past five years. On 7 October 1290 one of the Guardians, the bishop of St Andrews, wrote to Edward, stressing the turmoil in Scotland, and urging him to hasten north and prevent the outbreak of civil war.[23]

The king's response to this request has, unfortunately, not survived. The Scots would later allege that, after the death of the Maid of Norway, Edward sent them a letter of condolence, in which he promised that he would indeed come to Scotland in order to give his advice as 'a friend and neighbour'.

The king's intentions, however, were far from friendly or neighbourly. Death, in taking the Maid, had robbed him of a rich prize and within just a few weeks had also deprived him of his own beloved queen. Edward retreated to Ashridge, and there, in his mourning, he began to formulate a new plan. According to one English chronicler, this was revealed to his magnates when they assembled early in the new year. The king, we are told, 'said that it was in his mind to reduce the king and kingdom of Scotland to his rule, as he had recently subjected Wales to his authority'.[24]

If these words attributed to Edward are genuine, they show either supreme self-confidence or immense naivety – or perhaps both, the one born of the other. Scotland and Wales, of course, do share certain physical characteristics: most obviously, a large proportion of their landscape consists of hills and valleys. This meant, in the thirteenth century, that they also possessed some economic similarities. The predominance of upland meant that Welsh and Scottish societies were for the most part pastoral and hence poor in comparison with England. Viewed from Westminster, therefore, the two Celtic countries might have appeared to have much in common. In fact they were very different places.

In one respect, Wales was a more united country than Scotland. The Welsh, as we have seen, were a single ethnic group – the last survivors of an ancient civilisation that had once occupied all of Britain, but that had been gradually driven into the western margins of the island by the English. Hence, in terms of culture and language, Wales was homogenous. Scotland, on the other hand, was a complicated ethnic mix. Here too, in the south-western corner of the country, there were Brittonic elements that had been pushed out of England. Yet in south-eastern Scotland the population was mostly of English stock, a remnant of the once extensive Anglo-Saxon kingdom of Northumbria. In the west, meanwhile, the natives were mainly of Gaelic origin, having immigrated from Ireland in ancient times, or of Norwegian (Viking) descent. Ethnically and culturally, medieval Scotland was a melting pot.[25]

But politically – and this was its other major difference from Wales – Scotland was united. The kings of Scots, whose rule had once been restricted to the area around the River Tay, had over the centuries expanded their power first southwards, then westwards. By the thirteenth century their authority was acknowledged, albeit loosely in some quarters, by all of Scotland's multi-ethnic, multi-cultural inhabitants. An important factor in promoting this political unity had been the Scottish monarchy's adoption during the eleventh century of the practice of primogeniture. As a consequence, while the petty kings and princes of Wales continued to squabble for power with each successive generation, in Scotland the throne passed smoothly – or at least smoothly in relative terms – from one occupant to the next.[26]

These fundamental differences between Wales and Scotland had huge ramifications after 1066 when England was brought under new, Norman management. It meant that when those Frenchmen who acquired lands along England's northern and western borders went looking for further opportunities to expand their power, they were confronted with two very different prospects. In Wales they saw a fragmented society, with no existing political structures within which they could realise their objectives. They therefore simply took whatever they could and set themselves up in competition with the natives – which is to say, they created the March of Wales and became Marcher lords. Those Normans who harboured ambitions to expand into Scotland, however, saw a society that, in its barest essentials, conformed to their expectations. The kings of Scots were not only too strong to challenge for supremacy; they also possessed sufficient stature that it was possible to offer them military service in return for landed reward. In Scotland, therefore, the Norman newcomers were absorbed into the existing society, thereby adding yet another new ethnic layer to the country's already complex combination.[27]

Thus, as Wales was left drained and diminished by the advent of parasitical Norman neighbours, Scotland was strengthened by what was in effect a transfusion of new Norman blood. Thanks to the arrival of these Continental adventurers, Scottish kings and their subjects were soon drawn inexorably into the mainstream of European culture. A good indication that this process of assimilation was well under way by the end of the eleventh century is provided by the names of Scotland's kings. Prior to this point they were exclusively traditional and Celtic – Donald, Malcolm and Duncan – but thereafter the names that predominated were classical, biblical or French – Alexander, David and William.[28]

The key moment, indeed, in this transformation of Scottish society took place in the middle of the twelfth century during the reign of King David I. Although descended from the Celtic dynasty that had ruled in central Scotland since the late eighth century, David had grown up at the court of Henry I of England, where he received what contemporaries regarded as the benefits of a civilised education. Exposed in his youth to European cultural norms – modes and morals of warfare, methods of government and manners in general – David returned home to Scotland as king and began the business of acquainting his subjects with these new standards. In this he was helped by a number of friends he had made during his time in England, who accompanied him on his return, and whom he rewarded with lands and honours north of the Border. To take just one obvious example, David brought with him a certain Robert de Brus, a man who originally hailed from Brix in Normandy, and who was the forefather of the Robert Bruce who claimed the Scottish throne in 1290.[29]

Nor were Anglo-Norman aristocrats like the Bruces the only newcomers. In the same period Scotland was engulfed by a veritable wave of more humble settlers – merchants and labourers in search of new markets. Some came from as far afield as France or Flanders, but, in the overwhelming majority of cases, they were drawn from England. The Scottish kings endorsed and encouraged this immigration, founding new towns or 'burghs' in the more prosperous eastern parts of their realm. In fact, at almost every level, twelfth-century Scotland threw its doors wide open to outside influences. As well as the new burghs, and also in response to royal initiative, new abbeys and priories began to be founded on the Continental model; the king's household, with its new officers, such as the constable and the steward, increasingly resembled those of other European rulers; royal government adopted the coins and charters common to the other civilised countries of western Europe. Above all, though, Scotland was approximating itself to England. Existing Scottish regions were recast as 'shires' – the characteristically English division of local government – and new shires were created along English lines. The English language, already the established vernacular in south-eastern Scotland, began to gain ground in other areas as the new burghs and burgesses spread. As one modern English historian has memorably (and rather provocatively) put it, 'it is almost as if we are looking at two Englands, and one of them is called Scotland'.[30]

The anglicisation of David I, and the subsequent anglicisation of Scotland, occurred at a critical moment. As we have already seen, it was in the middle decades of the twelfth century that attitudes in England towards the people beyond its borders underwent a fundamental shift. At first, the Scots were deemed to lack the essential hallmarks of civilisation, and, like the Irish and the Welsh, were stigmatised as barbarians. But, by the end of the twelfth century, the English were obliged to admit that their northern neighbours had effected a remarkable transformation. They waged warfare according to the proper rules; they held respectable attitudes towards sex and religion; and, as their new towns, castles and abbeys attested, they had achieved a commendable level of economic advancement. Whichever way one looked at it, the Scots were manifestly eligible for membership of the civilised club.[31]

That they had been admitted by the thirteenth century is confirmed by the rising number of important Anglo-Scottish marriages. In 1221 Henry III's sister, Joan, was married to Alexander II of Scotland, and thirty years later Alexander III married Henry's daughter, Margaret. In the meantime the earls of Norfolk, Kent and Pembroke were all partnered with Scottish princesses; John Balliol's father, a northern English magnate, married Dervorguilla of Galloway, and Robert Bruce was married to a daughter of the earl of Gloucester. The multiplication of such matches, along with other social, cultural and economic links, suggests that the border between the two nations was beginning to blur.[32]

Over and above this general bonhomie, however, an important question still loomed. What was the proper political relationship between the two kingdoms? Was Scotland, the weaker of the two by a very long chalk, in any way subservient to England? This was clearly the case with Wales, whose rulers had for centuries accepted that the king of England was their rightful overlord. In the 1250s and 1260s Llywelyn ap Gruffudd had been desperate to do homage and swear fealty to Henry III, seeing this as the only way in which his territorial gains and title 'prince of Wales' could be legitimised. Even when the same prince fell out with Henry's son, the argument was over exactly what dependency entailed. That such dependency existed was not denied – not until native Wales was in its death throes.

The Scots, however, squarely refused to accept any suggestion that a similar subservient relationship applied in their case. While relations with England during the twelfth and thirteenth centuries were for the most part amicable, the issue would surface during times of tension. The most consistent cause of stress in this period was the question of where the border between the two kingdoms should be. The kings of Scots would have liked to have redrawn it considerably further south than its present position, which is defined by the Cheviot Hills and the River Tweed. Their ambition was to gain control of Cumbria and Northumbria, and on occasion – when England was distracted by civil or Continental wars – they succeeded in doing so. It was for this reason that the castle keep at Carlisle, begun by Henry I, was finished by his former protégé, David I of Scots. When they regained their composure, however, the kings of England were always able to reverse such Scottish gains, and typically took the trouble to spell out, from a position of dominance, how they felt Anglo-Scottish relations ought to operate in the future. The most significant of these occasions came in 1174, when King William the Lion of Scotland, grandson of King David, was taken prisoner by Henry II of England and compelled to perform a humiliating act of homage. After his release the Scottish king renounced his oath, complaining that it had been exacted under duress, and in 1189 the English accepted the original state of affairs. King Richard I of England, desperate for funds to finance his crusade, agreed to drop the English claim to overlordship in exchange for a large cash payment.

For the next hundred years the question was never revisited with the same directness or intensity. It helped that in 1237 the line of the Border was fixed in its present position by mutual agreement, thereby removing the likeliest cause of future contention.[33] Nevertheless, the issue of overlordship remained a live one. A good example of the kind of diplomatic tightrope that the kings of Scotland were sometimes forced to walk can be seen on the occasion of the marriage of Alexander III and Margaret, daughter of Henry III, which took place in York at

Christmas 1251. The English king evidently assumed that, in the course of this sustained display of his superior power, he could easily extract from his new ten-year-old son-in-law an admission of political dependence. Young Alexander, however, had clearly been well coached by his advisers: he answered the request with a polite refusal, and Henry had sufficient wisdom to let the matter rest.[34]

What might Edward I, then aged twelve and present as a witness, have made of this exchange? In the minds of thirteenth-century Englishmen the superiority of their country to Scotland was not merely based on the self-evident balance of power in the present; it was a matter of unimpeachable historical fact. Anybody who had read or heard Geoffrey of Monmouth's *History of the Kings of Britain* – and that must have included just about everybody, to judge from the number of surviving copies – would have understood that Scotland had always been subordinate to its southern neighbour. Geoffrey, for example, told the story of Belinus and Brennius, two brothers who, in the days before the Romans, had battled for control of Britain. When they finally agreed to divide the island between them, Belinus took all the lands south of the Humber (that is, England and Wales), while Brennius was to hold those to the north (including Scotland). Only Belinus, however, the elder brother, was crowned as a king. Brennius, it was agreed, 'who was the younger, should be subject to his brother'. More famous still was Geoffrey's account of the northern adventures of King Arthur. Having first waged war on the Scots for rebelling against him, Arthur went on to grant Scotland to a certain distant royal relative called Auguselus. This client ruler later honoured Arthur by attending his coronation, during which he carried one of the processional swords as a mark of his subservience.[35]

This, then, was how Edward I understood the relationship between England and Scotland. In Scotland, however, little boys were told a very different story. When Alexander III was installed as king of Scots in 1249, a Highland historian appeared before him and read out, in Gaelic, a list of Scottish kings. Like the royal pedigrees recited in England, immeasurably elongated and enhanced by the fantasies of Geoffrey of Monmouth, the Highlander's list was a genuine genealogy of recent rulers, extended into the remotest past by invention. The eight-year-old Alexander was reminded that his dynasty began with Scota, a warrior princess, daughter of Pharaoh of Egypt, who had wrested northern Britain from the heirs of Brutus and renamed it in her own honour.[36]

As well as highlighting the different histories that the English and Scots told themselves in the thirteenth century, Alexander's inauguration also reveals another source of contention on the issue of overlordship.

The king-making ceremony of 1249 took place, as it had always done, at Scone Abbey. A hefty stone of ancient provenance, used for such occasions since time immemorial, was carried out of the abbey church and into the churchyard, where it was probably placed in the base of an oaken chair. On this the young Alexander would have been seated for his transformation into a king. He was acclaimed, mantled and invested with the Scottish regalia, which included a sword, sceptre and a crown. Despite the use of this last item, however, and in spite of the best efforts of the Scots, this was not quite a coronation. Alexander was not anointed by anyone, nor was his crown blessed by any of those churchmen present. Since the start of the thirteenth century, Scottish kings had been applying to the pope for permission to sacralise their ceremony at Scone. Every time, though, they were rebuffed, thanks to English intervention. Their friends south of the Border might acknowledge that the rulers of Scotland were kings, but they firmly maintained that there was only one true Crown in Britain – the one worn by the king of England.[37]

All of this makes it sound as if the English and the Scots, with their differing histories, asserting superiority on the one hand and independence on the other, were bound to fall out. In fact, Edward I remained on quite cordial terms with Alexander III for the rest of the latter's life. Henry III may not have succeeded in exacting homage from the Scottish king in 1251, but that hardly mattered. Alexander had witnessed the awesome power and majesty of the English court at first hand, and realised from a young age that he was in no position to challenge it. The result of the royal wedding in 1251 was not hostility but increasingly warm and friendly relations. Five years later, following his own marriage to Eleanor and his return from Gascony, Edward took the trouble to visit Scotland to see his sister and brother-in-law; a little later still, at the end of that same summer, Alexander and Margaret journeyed south to be entertained at the English court. In 1260 they came south again, this time for the birth of Margaret's first child. And when, in the summer of 1268, Edward paid another brief visit to Scotland, he was reportedly delighted with his sister's children. The evident affection between the English and Scots now that they were part of one extended royal family meant greater political co-operation, not increased friction. Alexander sent a force of Scots to fight for Edward at Evesham (too late to be of any use, but surely appreciated as a gesture) and also permitted Scottish nobles – Robert Bruce, for example, and the older brothers of John Balliol – to join Edward's crusade.[38]

Such amicable relations meant that for a long time the issue of overlordship could be avoided. Those occasions that might in other circumstances be interpreted legalistically, as one king rendering service to another, could be cast simply in terms of friendship. When Edward returned from his crusade and was crowned at Westminster, nothing could have been more natural than for his sister and brother-in-law to take precedence among the distinguished guests. Edward himself may have attempted to exploit the situation: in a letter written a few weeks beforehand he alluded to 'the service' owed by the Scottish king, perhaps anticipating that Alexander would agree to carry a sword during the coronation procession, just as Auguselus had done for Arthur. Sadly, we have no way of knowing whether or not Alexander obliged, though it seems most unlikely: at this point the Scottish king also seems to have been able to avoid doing homage to Edward.[39]

What undoubtedly refocused everyone's attention on the overlord-ship question was the behaviour and subsequent punishment of Llywelyn ap Gruffudd. The Welsh prince, having pointedly failed to attend Edward's coronation and then withheld his homage, was torn down to size in 1277 by an angry Edward at the head of devastating armies. When, the following year, a much diminished and chastened Llywelyn was permitted to marry his fiancée (in England, before the English king, on the feast-day of England's premier royal saint), Alexander, now a widower, was again among the guests. Before crossing the Border he had insisted on an escort of English earls and bishops to emphasise his importance and his independence. But the knowledge of what had happened to the prince of Wales must have impinged heavily on the king of Scotland's consciousness, for Alexander had come south at Edward's bidding in order to perform his homage.[40]

This was not necessarily the major concession it might sound. From the mid-twelfth century the kings of Scotland had held certain lands in England (Tynedale and Penrith). Since Alexander held these estates from Edward, it was entirely right and proper that he should formally acknowledge the fact. The homage he owed, in other words, was personal and private, and should not have affected his status as king of Scots. After all, Edward I, as duke of Gascony, had himself done homage on two occasions to consecutive kings of France, with no prejudice to his position as king of England.

Edward, however, was determined on this occasion to make more of it. When Alexander offered to do his homage soon after the wedding at Worcester, his brother-in-law demurred. It would be better, Edward explained, if the act took place before his full council in Westminster in a fortnight's time. The English king was clearly angling for a major concession and wanted to be sure that everyone saw him land his catch. Anxious not to offend, Alexander and his advisers agreed, but once again stressed that they were only condescending as a favour. The ceremony finally took place on 28 October in the king's chamber at Westminster, as Edward had planned, but accounts of what happened differ depending on whether they are Scottish or English. What is clear is that, as in a game of poker, everyone kept their cards concealed until the last possible moment. When Alexander came to speak his lines, he did the limited, personal homage that was appropriate for his English estates. Only then did the English show their hand, when the bishop of Norwich interjected that the Scottish king should also do homage to Edward for Scotland. According to the Scottish source, this provoked Alexander to respond with a robust rejoinder. 'Nobody but God has the right to homage for my kingdom of Scotland,' he declared, 'and I hold it of nobody but God himself!'[41]

At the time of Alexander's death, therefore, overlordship was an old controversy, but still a live one. It would remain so until the English agreed to drop their pretensions or until the Scots agreed to accept them. Consecutive kings of Scotland had proved staunch in defence of their independence. But now the Scots had no king, only a succession crisis that they needed English help to resolve. Edward I saw a great opportunity.

In the spring of 1291 the Scots were given to understand that the king of England was ready to offer them the friendly and neighbourly advice that he had allegedly promised the previous autumn. We do not know precisely what messages had been exchanged in the interim. But by May that year, probably at Edward's suggestion, the Guardians and many other leading Scots had assembled in Berwick. This was an obvious location for the transaction of Anglo-Scottish business. Not only was it the largest and richest of Scotland's royal burghs; it was also the closest to England, for it sits by the coast on the north shore of the River Tweed, fixed since 1237 as the eastern part of the Border. As for Edward himself, the Scots knew that he was headed for Norham, where an English parliament had evidently been summoned for 6 May. Situated some five miles upstream from Berwick on the Tweed's opposite bank, Norham was a much smaller settlement, but had the outstanding attraction of a magnificent stone castle, established in the twelfth century by the bishops of Durham. It was the northernmost point at which the king and his court could be accommodated in any comfort prior to leaving England.[42]

Leaving England, however, was not part of Edward's plan. By 9 May the Scots gathered in Berwick had received the news that the king expected them to come to him. This was an unsettling invitation:

they had assumed that the business of choosing between John Balliol and Robert Bruce, being a Scottish matter, would be transacted in Scotland. If it were done in England, there was the risk that, now or later, this might be interpreted as a sign of Scottish submission. Against such anxieties, though, the Scots did have Edward's promise from the previous year that Scotland would remain 'free in itself, and without subjection, from the kingdom of England', and their confidence was further bolstered by the letters they secured from Edward on 10 May, promising that no prejudice should arise from their actions. Thus reassured, a delegation of Scotsmen crossed the Tweed to Norham later that same day.[43]

It was, in fact, far worse than they had feared. Once inside the castle at Norham, the Scottish delegates were treated to an introductory speech by Roger Brabazon, an English royal justice. After a lot of flowery rhetoric about the beauty of peace and so on, they were told that Edward had come north to do right to *anybody* who had a claim to the Scottish throne. This implied that the king envisaged other candidates besides Bruce and Balliol, which would, in turn, alter the nature of his intervention. With more than two claimants, a straightforward arbitration of the kind anticipated by the Scots would become impossible. Edward was therefore proposing an alternative arrangement, namely that he should act, not as arbiter, but as judge. This was a role that he naturally felt entitled to assume, given the fact that he was Scotland's rightful overlord.

The Scots were stupefied. It was surprising enough to discover that there were apparently other claimants besides Bruce and Balliol, but the corollary was outrageous. The king of England their overlord? They protested, with pardonable exaggeration, that they had never heard of such a novelty.[44]

Edward had expected such a reaction – he had, after all, received a similar response from his late brother-in-law in 1278. Accordingly, he had taken the trouble on this occasion to prepare his ground thoroughly in advance. Two months earlier, a search of the archives had been ordered – and not just the royal ones. In abbeys and priories all over England, monks had been made to ferret through their chronicles and muniments in an effort to build the king's case. Given that the trawl was so extensive, the haul was disappointing (inevitably, of course, given that the superiority that Edward took for granted was built on exceedingly weak, and for the most part fantastical, foundations). Nevertheless, in the days before the Scots had crossed to Norham, a crowd of clerics had told the king what he wanted to hear: his was indeed the superior right. This enabled Edward to present the Scots with a two-fold challenge. If they would not concede his overlordship as a matter of course, he said, they should disprove the facts set out in his new dossier. Or, as an alternative to both these options, they could decide the matter by force.

It was Robert Wishart, bishop of Glasgow and Guardian, who recovered himself sufficiently to respond on behalf of the startled Scots. In the first place, he said, it did not matter what they, as temporary custodians, might or might not concede: only a king of Scotland could answer such a momentous demand. Secondly, the bishop took Edward to task over his reasoning: *they* were not obliged to prove him *wrong*; rather *he* should prove himself *right*. Thirdly, and more caustically, Wishart reminded the English king that he was supposed to be a crusader, and observed that a threat to unleash war against a defenceless people did him no credit. At this last Edward was predictably enraged, and prompted to issue a new threat. He would indeed lead a crusading army, he declared – against the Scots![45]

Amid these acrimonious scenes, the meeting at Norham broke up, with nothing agreed between the two sides beyond the need for a three-week adjournment. For the Scots, obviously, it had been a total disaster: they had come to the Border expecting the happy resolution of their problems by a friend, only to be confronted with ultimatums and undisguised belligerence.

Yet for Edward, too, the encounter had been highly unsatisfactory, and had turned out quite contrary to expectation. The king, to be sure, had anticipated some opposition to his demands – hence the massive effort to prove himself right by documentary means. But the scale and fervour of Scottish resistance had left him reeling, with no response other than angry threats of force. And force, as the bishop of Glasgow had discerned, was an inappropriate answer in present circumstances.

The fact of the matter was that Edward, like the Scots, had been misled. In February the king had received a letter from Robert Bruce, in which the latter had made it abundantly clear that he and his supporters were willing to endorse the English interpretation of Anglo-Scottish relations. At one point in this letter, for example, Bruce had referred explicitly to the submission made by William the Lion in 1174 and the subsequent decision by Richard I in 1189 to nullify it. This reversal, Bruce suggested, could hardly have been right, for Scotland was a limb of the English Crown, and surely 'one must keep the Crown whole'. Edward, of course, did not need to be convinced that this was the case, but to hear it coming from a Scotsman must have been music to his ears. Bruce had gone on to say that, whenever the English king was ready to come north and demand his right, the Bruce family and their friends would be ready to obey him.

Edward, therefore, had come north expecting a far easier ride than the one he had in the event experienced. Bruce, it was now clear, had not spoken for the majority of his countrymen, with the result that they and the English king now found themselves in a bitter impasse. The three-week adjournment ended, predictably, with a flat refusal from the Scots to return to Norham.[46]

By this stage, however, Edward had come up with a new way to exploit the situation. The Scots maintained that only a king of Scotland could answer the demand for an admission of English overlordship. Edward's rejoinder was to seek individual admissions of his superior right from all those contending for the royal title. If all the men who might one day be king were willing to acknowledge England's superiority, so this logic ran, then Scotland's current custodians – the Guardians – could have no grounds for further objection. The English king could take possession of the vacant kingdom, and award it to whichever candidate he adjudged to have the strongest claim

In deciding on this strategy, it is likely that Edward acted in collusion with Robert Bruce. Certainly, when the suggestion of individual submissions was made public around 5 June, Bruce was among the first to throw his hat into the ring and recognise the English king's right. John Balliol, who was probably still in Berwick at this point, evidently held out a little longer, and may have made a last-ditch appeal for arbitration rather than judgement. But the following day, no doubt fearing that he would be ruled out of the race, Balliol too returned to Norham and agreed to Edward's terms.

The swift submission of the two principal competitors (now joined by a host of other less likely candidates) had the inevitable effect of weakening Scottish resistance. Balliol's capitulation was all the more significant in that he was accompanied across the Tweed by John Comyn, not only his brother-in-law but also one of the Guardians. The six men entrusted in 1286 with safeguarding Scotland's future had since been reduced to four, but only by death's intervention; Comyn's surrender on 6 June represented the first desertion from their company for political reasons.[47]

The three remaining Guardians, however, and those Scots still with them at Berwick, continued to hold out. (No doubt the presence among their ranks of the indomitable bishop of Glasgow served to stiffen their resolve.) Unlike the claimants, they had nothing to gain by falling in with the king of England's wishes. On the contrary, they could easily end up violating the solemn oath they had sworn to preserve Scotland for Alexander III's heirs. The same was true for the twenty or so constables who had been entrusted with the keeping of the kingdom's royal castles. These men were not going to give up their custodies to Edward I until they were satisfied that he would abide by his promise of the previous year to leave Scotland free and independent, and they were certainly not about to surrender anything to the king while he was claiming to be their overlord. When Edward tried to claim the castles in that capacity after the submission of Bruce and Balliol, he met with a firm refusal.[48]

Nevertheless, the stalwart Scots at Berwick could not hold out for ever. Nor could the threat of force, no matter how improbable or unconscionable it might appear in retrospect, have been entirely absent from their minds. It was not just an impatient English king waiting on their doorstep, but the English royal household, swelled by the presence of half a dozen English earls. Moreover, from the start of June this implied might had been reinforced with 650 crossbowmen, and all the while the Scots negotiated they were conscious of an English fleet lurking off the coast near Lindisfarne. This might not have been gunboat diplomacy, but it came pretty close.[49]

Eventually, after six more days of argument, a compromise solution was found. Despite the intense English pressure, the Scots remained staunch in their refusal to admit Edward's overlordship, so the way forward became a complicated legal fiction. The king himself now put in a claim to the Scottish throne, and proposed that he should take custody of the kingdom and its castles, not as an overlord, but simply as one claimant acting on behalf of all the others.

This was a formula that the Guardians felt able to accept: it meant that Edward would gain control of Scotland, not by dint of any existing superiority, but because the Scots themselves had agreed to grant him its keeping for a limited period. Put more concisely still, he was not taking the kingdom from them: they were giving it to him. The significance of this crucial distinction was reinforced by the fact that the transfer took place not in England but in Scotland. To the last, the Guardians had refused to cross the Tweed, and in the end it was Edward who was obliged to make the short boat trip from Norham Castle. It was in the meadow of Upsettlington, on the river's north shore, that the deal was finally struck. On 12 June the Guardians surrendered their seal, along with the custody of the royal castles, and the English king promised to maintain the laws and customs of Scotland. The following day all those Scots present swore fealty to Edward in his capacity as Scotland's temporary caretaker – 'chief lord and guardian of the kingdom, until a king is provided'.[50]

★ ★ ★

Now that Edward had obtained seisin of Scotland, the momentous business of providing a king could begin. The preliminaries for hearing this great case – 'the Great Cause', as it was dubbed in the eighteenth century – began at Norham immediately after the agreement of 12 June. But the proceedings proper were adjourned to the start of August, at which point the case was set to resume on the Scottish side of the Border. The delay gave the various claimants – now thirteen in number, excluding Edward himself – a few weeks to consult their legal teams and prepare their arguments. At the same time, it also offered Scotland's new custodian the opportunity to obtain a wider recognition of his role. In July Edward embarked on a tour of the heartlands of the Scottish kingdom – the prosperous royal burghs clustered around the Firth of Forth. At Haddington, Edinburgh, and Linlithgow, Stirling, Dunfermline and St Andrews he stopped to receive oaths of fealty of the inhabitants. Given that his lordship was expected to last only a little while longer, the English king was going to considerable lengths to have it acknowledged by as many Scots as possible.[51]

By 2 August Edward was back at the Border, only this time in Berwick, and the following day the proceedings to decide the Scottish succession began. The case, it had been agreed in June, would be determined by a special tribunal of 105 men – the number apparently suggested by the courts of similar size that had sat to consider inheritance disputes in Ancient Rome. Twenty-four of these auditors had been chosen by Edward (whose own inclusion brought the royal contingent to twenty-five); the remaining eighty men had been selected by Bruce and Balliol, who were thereby evenly represented with forty auditors apiece. The shape of the tribunal, in other words, reflected the reality of the contest, and was probably a concession to the Scots. In spite of the multiplicity of candidates that Edward had encouraged in his attempt to wrangle an admission of overlordship, this was now implicitly acknowledged to be a two-horse race.[52]

Nonetheless, the other candidates had to be heard, even if only to have their claims dismissed. Accordingly, much of the opening business at Berwick was devoted to a consideration of the case of Florence, count of Holland. By any reasonable reckoning, Count Florence was a no-hoper, but his arguments do take us to the heart of the debate about who should be Scotland's next king.[53]

In the decade 1280–90, as we have seen, three generations of the Scottish royal family – Alexander III, his children, and his only grandchild – had died out entirely. The same was also true of the previous generation, at least in the legitimate lines. The search for a new king of Scots therefore had to begin one generation further back, in the time of Alexander's grandfather, William the Lion (who reigned from 1165 to 1214). Now that William's own bloodline had failed, the succession was generally reckoned to have passed to his younger brother, David, whose descendants were several, and included both Balliol and Bruce.[54]

Count Florence, however, claimed to have an additional piece of information that crucially altered the story. It was his contention that David, in return for a grant of land from his older brother, had resigned his right to the Scottish throne. That right had consequently been fixed on their sister, Ada, who – it just so happened – was the great-great-grandmother of Florence. The count contended that he could prove all of this from documents, given time to find them. It was, to say the least, an optimistic claim, and unlikely to have commanded much credence with the majority of the 105 auditors, not least because both the Bruce and Balliol camps had a vested interest in throwing it out. It must, therefore, have come as a considerable surprise to most of the court when, just nine days into their deliberations, Edward announced that there would be a second adjournment to allow Florence to unearth his alleged evidence. Surprise, moreover, must have quickly turned to anger when the king went to declare that this new adjournment would last ten months.

What was Edward up to? One possibility, which cannot be entirely discounted, is that both he and Florence were sincere in their belief that the necessary proof existed, and that Edward was actually entertaining the thought of passing judgement in the count's favour. Florence's son John was engaged to be married to Edward's daughter Elizabeth (b. 1282), so the count's candidacy represented a second chance to construct a marriage alliance between England and Scotland. Florence was also financially beholden to Edward, and would doubtless have made a pliable client king.

It is more likely, however, that the lengthy delay was a deliberate ploy on Edward's part to extend his temporary tenure of Scotland. In ten months' time the king would have had custody for more than a year and a day – a period that, from a legal point of view, might be deemed at a later date to strengthen the English claim to overlordship. As such, the long adjournment was another piece of chicanery by Edward in keeping with his earlier efforts to exploit Scotland's difficulties to England's advantage, and no doubt explains the care he had taken to extract oaths of fealty from the Scots during the previous month. The Scots themselves must have been infuriated, especially in view of the fact that the king had promised at the outset to provide a speedy resolution to the succession crisis. But the transfer of lordship and of castles that had taken place in June meant that this was now Edward's show. It would stop and start at his discretion, and it would run for as long as he deemed necessary.[55]

The court at Berwick therefore broke up. Florence hurried off, ostensibly to hunt for his documents, the other competitors went to their own parts, and Edward returned to England. The king's affairs in the south had remained for the most part quiet and orderly during his absence, but there were nonetheless one or two items that required his immediate attention.

The first was the funeral of his mother. Eleanor of Provence had died, aged sixty-eight or very nearly so, on Midsummer's Day, but her burial had been purposely delayed until her eldest son could be present. To the evident surprise of some people – including, it seems, Eleanor's younger son, Edmund – the queen was not laid to rest in Westminster Abbey, but in the more remote surroundings of her latter-day home at Amesbury. Possibly this was Eleanor's own, quietly kept intention; it is hard to imagine that Edward would have deliberately disregarded his mother's last wishes had she wanted to be buried at Westminster. At the same time, it is also fair to remark that, following the recent decision to create new golden effigies of Henry III and Eleanor of Castile, the abbey already had its idealised images of kingship and queenship. Edward was therefore quite content to see his mother – beloved by the king himself but still remembered throughout the kingdom as a virago – interred in the quiet Wiltshire countryside. On 9 September a great crowd of magnates and prelates attended Eleanor's funeral at Amesbury; but thereafter, except in Amesbury itself, her memory was allowed to fade away.[56]

The other major item on Edward's agenda in the autumn of 1291 was the March of Wales, which for the past two years had been disturbed by a violent dispute. The earls of Hereford and Gloucester, respectively the lords of Brecon and Glamorgan, had locked horns over a debatable strip of land that lay between their two territories. In 1289 Gloucester had begun to build a castle, Morlais, to assert his claim, Hereford had in due course retaliated, and the result had been a private war. This in itself was uncontroversial: one of the benefits (or burdens, depending on one's viewpoint) of being a Marcher lord was the right to settle disagreements at sword-point, and without reference to the Crown. The issue had become contentious on this occasion because, at an early stage, the king had called on both earls to desist, yet Gloucester had continued to make raids into Hereford's territory. A subsequent royal commission sent to the March in 1291 had been similarly disregarded.

Gloucester had not even bothered to attend its hearings, and those other Marchers called to bear witness against him had closed ranks in refusing to do so. The old maxim that 'in the March of Wales, the king's writ does not run' was clearly felt to be under threat.[57]

The scale of the threat was made manifest in October when Edward arrived in the March to assert his authority in person. In a specially convened session of the council at Abergavenny the king imperiously insisted that the rights and dignity of his Crown were superior to any Marcher liberties. Gloucester was called before the court and found guilty, not of having waged war, but of having done so in spite of Edward's express prohibition. Hereford too, much to his surprise and chagrin, was found guilty on similar charges of contempt (for having retained some cattle his men had seized during the course of the dispute). Both earls were bailed to appear before a parliament at Westminster in January, at which point they were sentenced to imprisonment and the loss of their Welsh estates.[58]

Naturally, neither of these great men was deprived of his lands or liberty for very long (Gloucester, after all, had lately become the king's son-in-law). Within a few days both had been released from captivity, and a few months later their lordships were ordered restored. What Edward had wanted from each of them, and from the Marchers in general, was an acknowledgement of the Crown's supremacy. That point had now been clearly conceded. The Marchers, it was allowed, could keep their liberties, but on the understanding that in the final analysis there were no areas into which the king of England's authority did not reach. This fact was nicely reinforced in the spring of 1292 when fate finally caught up with Rhys ap Maredudd, the fugitive leader of the last Welsh rising. Taken in the Tywi Valley, Rhys was sent in chains to Edward and sentenced to be drawn and hanged. Whether in the March, or in the valleys of the interior, the English king's mastery in Wales was now seen to be complete.[59]

It remained to demonstrate that the same was true in Scotland. By 1 June 1292 Edward was back in Berwick, and on the following day – even as Rhys ap Maredudd was being dragged to his death through the streets of York – the proceedings to select the new king of Scots were resumed.[60]

Unfortunately, the first two weeks of this second session are shrouded in mystery. One would assume, since he was officially the cause of their long adjournment, that the auditors began their deliberations by considering the business of Florence of Holland. If this was the case, however, then no verdict was reached: during this fortnight the count's claim was neither upheld nor thrown out. The tribunal, it seems, was experiencing procedural problems – hardly surprising, given its unwieldy size and experimental nature. By the middle of June the auditors had admitted as much to Edward, who responded on 16 June by announcing that he wished to 'hasten' the proceedings. Accordingly, Florence was persuaded, not to abandon his claim, but to stand aside while others advanced theirs (possibly in return for a payment of £1,250, which he received from the king around this time). As far as Edward was concerned, the count had already served his purpose by prolonging English overlordship of Scotland. It was now imperative that they got to the heart of the matter and heard the arguments between John Balliol and Robert Bruce.[61]

These arguments hinged, as we have already noted, on the descent of both men from David, the younger brother of William the Lion, sometime king of Scots. David had continued his family's line by fathering three daughters. Bruce was the son of the middle daughter; Balliol was the grandson of the eldest. In the view of Balliol and his supporters, the argument was therefore simple. Their candidate was descended from the senior line, and thus his was clearly the superior right.[62]

Not so, said Bruce, whose argument was much more complex, and yet had a certain compelling logic. In the first place, Bruce observed, primogeniture did not apply to women. If matters really were as simple as Balliol made out, and Scotland were an estate like any other, then by rights it should be split up and shared equally between all the descendants of David's three daughters. From the outset, however, all the parties involved in the Great Cause had agreed that the kingdom should remain intact. In other words, said Bruce, kingdoms were clearly exceptional. Their descent was not governed by the customary law that applied to other estates, but by a higher law, which was written, ancient and imperial (and, he might well have added, were they not sitting in a court configured along ancient, Roman lines?). According to this law, Bruce asserted, primogeniture was irrelevant; what mattered most was nearness of degree in blood. He was the son of one of David's daughters; Balliol was merely the grandson of another. Therefore he, Bruce, had the stronger claim.[63]

Thus, for the auditors, it was not simply a matter of deciding between two rival candidates; it was also a matter of deciding which species of law ought to apply, and this proved altogether too taxing. After ten days of debate the court was still deadlocked, and Edward called proceedings to halt. It was clear that, unless they took wider consultation, their deliberations could go on for ever. The question of which law ought to be used, the king determined, should be put to the lawyers at the university of Paris, whose authority on such matters was second to none. This meant, frustratingly, that there had to be a third adjournment, albeit not as long as the second, spurious interruption. On 25 June the court was disbanded and told to reconvene in three months' time.[64]

It was not, therefore, until mid-October that the English and Scots reassembled in Berwick for what all hoped would be their final session. Edward (who had occupied himself in the interim by touring northern England) was by this time as anxious as anyone to wrap things up. Although his decision to suspend proceedings in the summer had apparently been conscientious, his actions in the autumn were rather more impatient and less even-handed. In terms of personalities, the king probably had no strong preference for Bruce or Balliol (even though he might have been expected to favour Bruce, as the more obviously obsequious candidate). When it came to the law, however, Edward leaned instinctively towards Balliol's customary case. In this he was almost certainly in step with the majority on both sides of the Border. Bruce's arguments were certainly cogent, and they did flag up the inherent contradictions in the customary claim. But were the traditions common to England and Scotland really to be set aside in favour of the ancient but alien concepts advanced by Bruce? And was the contradiction of accepting female primogeniture but rejecting partition really so insuperable? After all, just two years earlier, the English succession had been fixed, in default of male heirs, on whichever of Edward's five daughters was eldest. There had been no question of dividing England among them.[65]

The English precedent was probably a crucial factor in finding a verdict for Scotland. It was awkward that, when the time came to consider the opinions of the learned clerks of Paris, they weighed in favour of Bruce's imperial law. But only slightly awkward because, while the court had been in recess, Edward had decided to adjust its workings. In October it was not the eighty Scottish auditors who were asked to rule on which law should be used, but the English king's council. By 5 November the latter had reached their decision, and the following day the auditors concurred: customary law should apply. Bruce's appeal for imperial law was thrown out.[66]

This did not make Balliol the winner by default, for there was still the matter of hearing the claims of the other, lesser candidates. But it did make Bruce the loser, and prompted the old man to try a series of drastic last-minute expedients. On 10 November, for example, Count Florence of Holland put forward his claim for a second time, only now with Bruce as his backer. During the summer, at the moment when Florence had been induced to stand aside, the two men had struck an extraordinary agreement, whereby whichever of them became king would compensate the other with a third of the kingdom. The count's candidacy therefore held for Bruce the prospect of a considerable compensation prize (or perhaps even the throne, if he could buy his partner out). When Florence went on to present his case, however, it was an embarrassing mess. Despite his ten-month adjournment, the count was still unable to produce the alleged documents on which his claim depended. They had, he now claimed, been stolen. But if the court would permit him an inquest . . .[67]

Seeing Florence flounder, Bruce tried one last, desperate roll of the dice. From the outset he had reasoned that, if the kingdom was indivisible, customary law should not apply. Now, since that reasoning had got him nowhere, he stood the argument on its head. If customary law *did* apply, it surely followed that the kingdom should be divided. On 14 November both Bruce and John de Hastings (a claimant descended from the youngest of David's three daughters) applied in this way for a third share of the kingdom. The following day they received their final answer. The kingdom was not partible. There would be no three-way split. And there would be no further argument.[68]

Edward desired to draw matters to a close. He had expected that the business of selecting Scotland's new king would be concluded during the summer, yet here he was, still north of the Border, watching as the winter set in. In the final days of the proceedings, his council not only summarily rejected the plea for divisibility; they also dealt swiftly with the lesser claimants, including Florence of Holland. Edward had no further use for the count's far-fetched story that had earlier enabled him to prolong his overlordship. Now the king wanted resolution, not a pantomime that would run and run. Bruce had had his day in court and lost. Balliol was the popular favourite, whose claim was supported by the law that Edward, the English and the great majority of Scots felt was the most natural. On 17 November judgement was pronounced in Balliol's favour. Two days later, Edward gave orders that the kingdom and its castles should be handed over.[69]

For the Scots, the most important matter now became the enthronement of their new king. As luck would have it, the Great Cause had concluded with just enough time for everyone to get to Scone Abbey before the end of the month. There, in the abbey churchyard, Balliol was seated on the sacred stone and crowned as King John I. The ceremony took place on 30 November, the feast of St Andrew, Scotland's patron saint and protector.

Edward was not present to witness it. To his mind, kings of Scotland should attend the creation of kings of England, but not vice versa. It was sufficient for English interests that two royal henchmen oversaw Balliol's inauguration. For Edward, the installation of a new king of Scots was only a secondary concern, just as the selection process had been. His declared priority over the past two years had been 'to reduce the king and kingdom of Scotland to his authority': an attributed declaration, admittedly, but one entirely borne out by his bullying behaviour at Norham and the preposterously long adjournment he had ordered at Berwick. English domination was the major project, and it had yet to be completed. As far as Edward was concerned, the crucial ceremony was still to come.

Before leaving for Scone, Balliol had sworn fealty to the English king, and done so in the most explicit terms. Not only were his words spoken in England (Edward had returned to Norham especially in order to hear them); they also applied unambiguously to the kingdom of Scotland. To complete the process, therefore, it remained to receive Balliol's homage, and this was duly obtained at Christmas. It was at Newcastle, on 26 December, that the newly made king of Scots knelt before Edward and became his man.

For those Scots who had taken a stand against English assertions of overlordship, this was a grave disappointment, but not unexpected. Balliol, like all the other candidates, had entered the race admitting that the king of England was his overlord. Now he had emerged as the winner, the new Scottish king was simply being made to reiterate his previously stated position.

Far more startling to the Scots, though, was the subsequent behaviour of Edward. In the short interval between Balliol's fealty at Norham and his homage at Newcastle there had been a small but alarming development. On 7 December a burgess of Berwick, dissatisfied with several judgements given against him during the time of the Guardians, had appealed to the English king as his superior lord; Edward, in response, had proceeded to review the case at Newcastle and, on 22 December, had overturned one of the original verdicts.

To the Scots at Newcastle this constituted a clear breach by the English king of his earlier promises. Had he not assured them, in June the previous year, that their laws and customs would be maintained? And had he not, more to the point, accepted in 1290 that Scotland should remain 'free in itself, and without subjection, from the kingdom of England'?

Edward's answer was given in two parts, first by proxy, then in person. On 30 December an English royal justice informed the Scots that any promises that had been made before Balliol's enthronement had been only 'for the time being': they were no longer applicable in the present. This was affirmed the following day, when Edward addressed his critics directly. In no uncertain terms, the king declared that he would not be bound by his earlier words. As superior lord of Scotland, he would hear appeals wherever and whenever he wanted; if necessary, he would summon even the king of Scotland himself to appear before him in England. Lest there should be any doubt on these matters, Balliol was obliged in the days that followed to seal a series of written instruments, acquitting his overlord of any earlier promises he might have made, and specifically those resonant assurances of independence made in 1290.[70]

Edward's mastery had been acknowledged and demonstrated beyond doubt; his two-year scheme to establish Scotland's subservience was finally complete. The time had now come to consider his last and greatest project, especially in light of Christendom's recent and appalling loss.

9

The Struggle for Mastery

While Edward had been duping and bullying the Scots into submission, the Christian communities of the Holy Land had been driven into the sea. On 5 April 1291 the new Egyptian sultan, al-Ashraf Khalil, had drawn up a massive army before the walls of Acre, much as his predecessor Baybars had done twenty years before. On this occasion, however, it was to be no mere display of Muslim might. In the six weeks that followed, the great city was subjected to a sustained siege that heralded nothing less than the total destruction of crusader power. On 18 May the sultan ordered a general assault, and within hours it was all but over. Caught up amid the chaos and the carnage were Otto de Grandson and the small force of English knights that Edward I had sent east the previous summer. Dispatched for diplomatic purposes, these men unexpectedly found themselves fighting for dear life. Otto himself was among the fortunate few who managed to buy their way onto a boat, saving his skin but losing everything else, and sustaining no small damage to his reputation into the bargain. Thousands of others were far less lucky, among them the English esquire seen burning to death inside his armour like tar in a barrel. By the end of May Acre's last outpost, the Templar stronghold by the sea, had fallen, and by the end of the summer every other city, castle and province had also been taken. So ended the kingdom of Jerusalem and the other colonies of Outremer. In a few short months, two centuries of Christian rule in the East had been brought to an abrupt and inglorious close.

The reaction in the West was one of profound shock. It had been widely appreciated that the situation in the Holy Land was deteriorating, but no one had expected a disaster on a scale such as this. News of Acre's fall engendered both horror and an acute sense of guilt, and provoked a fresh round of crusade planning and propaganda. The Church, in response to a call from the pope, drew up ambitious schemes for remodelling society in order to recover the lost territories. The threat to Christendom, meanwhile, was emphasised by a sensational and widely circulated letter, purporting to be from the sultan himself, gloating over the slaughter and slavery of Acre's citizens, and promising that worse was to come.[1]

No one could have been more startled than Edward I. Just weeks before the disastrous news broke in England, he had dispatched (at what eventually proved to be colossal expense) an embassy to the il-khan Arghun, his putative Mongol ally. (The timing turned out to be doubly unfortunate, for Arghun was already dead.) Nevertheless, once Acre's fate was known, the king clearly showed himself determined to press ahead with his long-planned expedition. That much is suggested by the letters he exchanged with other sworn crusaders, and especially by the new architectural and artistic works that he decided to commission.[2]

Not long before, Edward had suddenly cut all funding to Vale Royal Abbey, the foundation closely associated with his original crusading adventure. 'The king has ceased to concern himself with the works of that church,' noted one financial official, 'and henceforth will have nothing to do with them.' His mysterious decision may have had some-thing to do with the monks' misuse of money; it certainly freed up funds for the two projects ordained in the spring of 1292. The first was the complete reconstruction of the royal chapel of St Stephen in the Palace of Westminster. The design of the new building was closely modelled on that of the Sainte Chapelle in Paris, created half a century earlier by Louis IX in preparation for his first crusade. That Edward was responding to a similar stimulus in 1292 is strongly suggested by the other project he began at precisely the same time. Royal artists at Westminster were also ordered to redecorate the king's chamber: the room where Henry III had died and where Edward had spent his coronation vigil. To the existing, peaceable wall-paintings that showed the Confessor being crowned and virtues triumphing over vices, exten-sive new murals were added depicting biblical scenes of war and suffering. Mostly based on stories from the Book of Maccabees, these images were seemingly an allusion to the recent fate of the Christian commu-nities in the Holy Land, and intended to inspire thoughts of vengeance in those who saw them.

They evidently inspired wonder. Two Irish friars who regarded the 'Painted Chamber' in the early fourteenth century wrote of their 'great admiration' at 'the greatest royal magnificence'. Similarly awe-struck were the antiquaries who rediscovered the friezes in the early nine-teenth century, concealed beneath thick layers of whitewash. And yet, tragically, the inferior copies made by these men are the only visual record we have today of Edward I's most extensive artistic endeavour: in 1834 the Painted Chamber was consumed by fire, along with St Stephen's Chapel and the rest of the medieval Palace of Westminster.[3]

When, therefore, the English king returned from Scotland at the start of 1293, he was still clearly committed to effecting Jerusalem's recovery. At the same time, it was equally plain that he would not be setting out that summer, as had previously been planned. Scotland was partly to blame: for the past two years Edward's attention had admittedly been somewhat distracted. Yet a preoccupation with affairs in the north can only go so far in explaining why no material preparations had been made for the East. More significant, probably, was the failure on the part of the papacy to hand over all of the money promised in 1290. The king had, as agreed, received half of the accumulated crusade funds (100,000 marks) in the summer of 1291; but the following year the second instalment had failed to materialise. Presumably this was due to the death, in April 1292, of Pope Nicholas, which itself served to scupper any chance of a new crusade leaving in the immediate future: once again, the college of cardinals had been unable to decide on a successor, and at the start of 1293 they were still debating. Until Christendom had a new leader, and until Edward had received the balance of papal payment, no new departure date was likely to be set. Accordingly, the king's journey south from Scotland was slow and unhurried. It was not until the middle of April that he arrived back in Westminster, in time for the first proper parliament for over a year.[4]

The king's absence meant that there was much routine business to discuss. Top of the agenda, however, was a sudden and mysterious quarrel that had arisen in the past year between English and French sailors. According to one north-country chronicler, trouble had started when a brawl in a Norman port had gone too far: swords had been drawn and one man had ended up dead. Since then, in spite of efforts on Edward's part to intervene, the dispute had intensified, to the extent that the two maritime communities were now virtually at war with each other. So serious was the problem by the spring of 1293 that the king appointed a high-ranking embassy, including two earls, to cross to France in order to devise a solution. But before it had set out, news arrived of a great battle at sea.[5] On 15 May English and Gascon ships had been assailed off the coast of Brittany by a large and overtly hostile Norman fleet. As the men of the Cinque Ports later testified, their attackers had flown red streamers, 'which everywhere among mariners means killing without quarter and war to the knife'. In the bloody engagement that followed, though, it was the English and Gascons who had evidently had the best of the fighting: several French ships were captured, along with their crews and their cargoes. And the Gascons, for an encore, had gone on to sack the French port of La Rochelle on their way home.[6]

What had started as a scrap between sailors had escalated into a major diplomatic incident. Soon letters arrived in England from the king of France, requiring the release of those taken prisoner and the restitution of goods. Edward, in response, now proposed three different ways by which the matter might be resolved. First, he offered to do justice in England to any complainants. For obvious reasons, the French were unlikely to accept this, which probably explains Edward's second suggestion, that the dispute be settled by a joint Anglo-French commission, which would rule according to 'the Law of the Sea' (evidently a kind of maritime Marcher law). Lastly, in case neither of these options found favour in France, the king proposed that the quarrel be put to the arbitration of the pope. Edward clearly continued to regard the business as very serious. His threefold offer was carried to France by a new embassy, more legally qualified than the aborted original, which set sail from Dover at the end of July. The king then turned and headed west, to spend what remained of the summer in the comfortable environs of Windsor, Winchester and Corfe, before moving to Bristol in September, where he celebrated the wedding of his eldest daughter, Eleanor, to Henry, count of Bar (in eastern France).[7]

By the time the court returned to Westminster for the customary autumn parliament, however, it was clear that the English embassy had (metaphorically speaking) run aground. All three of Edward's proposed solutions had been rejected. Joint commissions, arbitration – these rested on the assumption that this was a matter between two sovereign powers. The French had chosen to see it very differently. In their view it was not a disagreement between two kings, both alike in dignity, but a dispute between the king of France, a superior lord, and the duke of Gascony, his vassal. For this reason, the French had made much of the involvement in the maritime clashes of the men of Bayonne, and had demanded the surrender of the mayor and jurats of the town, as well as one hundred of its citizens. When the Bayonnais had inevitably refused to comply, the French had further upped the ante, demanding the surrender of Bordeaux and the Agenais. This process culminated on 27 October, when Philip IV peremptorily summoned Edward, his disobedient liege-man, to appear before him in Paris.[8]

The timing of this summons, which must have arrived in Westminster around mid-November, could not have been more ironic. At that very moment, John Balliol, the newly installed king of Scots, was up before the king of England and his parliament in response to a similar summons – obliged to explain why he, Balliol, had acted against one of his own Scottish earls, who had appealed to Edward as his superior lord. Balliol, having meekly accepted English overlordship at the start of the year, but no doubt having had the gravity of his mistake explained to him in the meantime, now put up more of a fight. 'I am king of the kingdom of Scotland,' he told the assembled magnates, 'and I dare not answer . . . anything concerning my kingdom without the advice of the responsible men of my realm.' Confronted by King Edward, however, Balliol swiftly buckled, and reaffirmed his vassal status. Indeed, he did not even use his royal title, accepting his position as 'your man of the realm of Scotland'. Judged in contempt of court, he was sentenced to lose three of his castles and towns. 'Like a lamb amongst wolves,' said a contemporary English chronicler, Balliol did not dare to open his mouth.[9]

The irony was probably not altogether lost on Edward, but he would not have seen the two situations as analogous. In Edward's view, Balliol was his vassal in every respect: the king of Scotland exercised no authority beyond what was delegated to him by the king of England. The situation on the Continent was seen as very different. Edward, as duke of Gascony, was a vassal of the French king and had always admitted as much. But he was also king of England, in which capacity he answered to no one (except God). He was certainly not about to trot to Paris at the king of France's command.

What, Edward must have wondered, was Philip playing at? The French king's summons had not only been unwarranted but gratuitously offensive, failing even to address Edward with his title as duke of Gascony. By November it was creating unnecessary tension in the duchy, where French officials were riding from town to town to read it out and being treated with predictable contempt in return. This was simply not the way the English and French did business. For forty years the two royal families had avoided confrontation by cultivating warm personal relations. Their friendship had blossomed in 1254, when Henry III, passing through Paris, had first met Louis IX. The two men had hit it off immediately, but the real credit for the concord belonged to their queens. Margaret and Eleanor of Provence had also been present in Paris that December, along with their younger sisters Beatrice and Sanchia – respectively the wives of Charles of Anjou and Richard of Cornwall. Louis had looked at their gathering and seen the seeds of a lasting European accord. 'Have we not married two sisters,' he said to Henry, 'and our brothers the other two? All that shall be born of them, sons and daughters, shall be like brothers and sisters.'[10]

And how wonderfully prophetic these words had proved. Edward I, Philip III and Charles of Salerno had all endeavoured to maintain this spirit of affection and unity, in spite of the powerful contrary forces that had sometimes threatened to pull them apart. When the three of them had met at Amiens in 1279, Philip and Edward had worked diligently to resolve their outstanding differences as lord and vassal. And, of course, when Charles was later captured and imprisoned, it had been his English cousin who had come riding to his rescue.

With this long history of family friendship in mind, it was perfectly natural that Edward should entrust the task of calming Anglo-French relations in 1293 to his brother: Edmund of Lancaster was, of course, part of the same circle of cousins. He was, moreover, in some respects better qualified in this respect than Edward himself. In 1275, following the death of his first wife, Edmund had married into the French aristocracy, taking as his second wife Blanche of Artois, countess of Champagne. Blanche, a widow herself, had a daughter called Jeanne of Navarre, who had subsequently become the wife of Philip IV. Thus Edmund was not only second-cousin to the king of France, but also stepfather to the French queen.[11]

And he was in Paris in the autumn of 1293. No doubt thinking that his brother's entrée into the highest circles of French royal power might prove useful, Edward had dispatched Edmund in the summer, an informal attaché to the official English embassy. Now that the formal, legalistic pleading had apparently failed, the king looked to his brother to play the family card.[12]

And so, early in the new year 1294, Edmund sat down to negotiate with his wife, his stepdaughter and Mary of Brabant (Philip III's widow and stepmother of Philip IV). In friendly fashion, the earl and the three royal ladies devised a secret scheme that would simultaneously salve wounded French pride, simplify the relationship of England and France over Gascony, and strengthen the existing bonds of amity between the two Crowns. Together they agreed that several important Gascon towns, including Bordeaux, would be surrendered to Philip, along with a score of Gascon hostages. Edward would submit to this public dressing-down on the private understanding that it would be quickly reversed. A summit meeting between the two kings would follow at Amiens, as of old, and Philip would regrant Gascony to Edward on new, favourable terms that would reduce the likelihood of future contention. Lastly, to seal the deal, Edward would marry Philip's sister, Margaret. Honour would be satisfied, stability would be secured, and the family settlement created by Henry III and Louis IX would be renewed for generations to come.[13]

In all of this, the English king, his brother and the royal ladies of France were deceived. Their secret negotiations at the start of 1294 were not the beginning of a new period of friendship, but the last part of a carefully contrived plot to deprive Edward of his Continental dominions. A crucial player in this plot was Philip IV himself. Throughout the secret negotiations the French king looked in several times on Edmund and the ladies, to reassure them that the harsh words and aggressive noises being made by his council were all a front, necessary for appearances' sake. The reality, he averred, was the confidential business they had in hand, and all would soon be well. A question mark hangs over Philip's sincerity. Either he was a brilliant actor and an accomplished liar who intended to deprive Edward all along; or he may genuinely have intended to honour the secret deal but been overruled by his own council. One thing is certain: whether he was part of it or not, there was powerful faction at Philip's court that had gained the upper hand in the 1290s, and its aim was the destruction of Edward I's rule in Gascony.[14]

At its head was Philip's younger brother, Charles of Valois. He most of all had special reason to hate the English. When, a decade earlier, France had been preparing to invade Aragon in order to remove its excommunicated king, Charles, then thirteen years old, had been crowned as his anticipated replacement. Subsequently, however, his crown had been bartered away by Edward I during the negotiations for a European peace. The rest of the Continent, including his older brother Philip, may have been pleased, but Charles was evidently not. As one modern historian has memorably put it, 'he had been addressed as a king when he was still in his teens and had never quite recovered from the experience'. Even in 1294, by which time he was in his mid-twenties, Charles was still refusing to relinquish his royal title. And, though the prospect of realising his claim was long gone, he was determined to revenge himself on the man he regarded as responsible for his loss. English chroniclers recognised Charles as the author of the war at sea. The Normans who had plundered English ships and killed their crews had been acting on his orders, said one writer. 'He persecuted the English with an inveterate hatred,' wrote another.[15]

None of this would have mattered so very much had Charles been a lone loose cannon. But the fact was that, by the 1290s, his 'inveterate hatred' was shared by many others at the French court. Edward's last trip to the Continent, a triumph in English eyes, had been viewed as so much grandstanding by envious Frenchmen. Philip IV, like Edward, might have intended to preserve amicable relations, but he too was surrounded by aggressive royal lawyers, whose *raison d'être* was to push the rights of the French Crown to their utmost logical limits. Such men must have been particularly annoyed by the swagger of the English king's entourage during their visit to Paris in 1286. Robert Burnell's speech, querying the extent of Edward's vassalic obligations on the eve of his homage for Gascony, was seen as a gauntlet thrown down. Charles of Valois and his co-conspirators were now ready to pick it up.[16]

Had Burnell been involved in the negotiations with France in the winter of 1293–94, it is impossible to imagine that they would have been so badly handled. But the great chancellor, after eighteen years in office and a lifetime in Edward's service, had died at Berwick the previous year, towards the end of the Great Cause proceedings. His replacement, John Langton, was no fool but, as a mere chancery clerk, did not command the king's respect as Burnell had done. When the new chancellor advised against the secret deal, Edward simply ignored him.[17] In February 1294 the order to surrender Gascony was given: in March English officials packed their bags and started to ship out, dismayed to be handing over towns, cities and hostages to the French on the express orders of their king.[18]

In fact, throughout the negotiations that winter, Edward seems to have ignored almost everyone, and kept no counsel other than his own. The men who were normally consulted in such matters – the magnates – appear to have sensed that important business had been concluded without their involvement. During Lent the king moved into East Anglia, touring his favourite shrines and churches, praying for a successful outcome to his daring and highly personal diplomatic initiative. At this time, noted one local chronicler, the magnates did not attend his court.[19]

The denouement came at Easter. Edward had moved into Kent, partly to bid farewell to his eldest daughter and her new husband, but mainly in anxious expectation of good news from France: a safe-conduct from Philip to come to Amiens, to marry his sister, and to receive Gascony back on new, improved terms. The newly-weds sailed, and Easter came and went, but still no messengers arrived from France. Then, on 20 April, a sorry band of Englishmen arrived, led by John of St John, the man who until just a few weeks earlier had been seneschal of Gascony. From the horse's mouth, Edward learned what the king of France's men had said and done as they had occupied the duchy, and the awful truth finally dawned. 'The king went red,' said the best informed chronicler, 'and became very afraid, because he had acted less than wisely.'[20] In France, more or less simultaneously, Edmund of Lancaster was also discovering the enormity of his error, and being told by Philip's counsellors that Gascony would remain in French hands. A few weeks later Edward was condemned in Paris for failing to attend the French king's summons, and the duchy was declared forfeit.[21]

As the news of the confiscation spread, the English people weighed the evidence available and concluded that their king must have gone mad. 'Up till now,' said one writer, 'Edward . . . had in all his acts shown himself energetic, generous and triumphant, like another Solomon.' His departure from reason, it was popularly decided, was down to that old demon, Lust. The prospect of marrying a beautiful young woman had clearly turned the head of the fifty-four-year-old king.[22]

Accordingly, when parliament assembled on the last day of May there were extraordinary scenes: Edward, usually so masterful, appeared almost meek, while his magnates, normally so agreeable, were furious. Having not been consulted, they felt no obligation to meet his request for help. According to one well-informed chronicler, it took a public act of contrition from the king to turn the situation around. Before all who were present, Edward swore an oath that he had not acted out of lust for the girl, but in order to have peace with France, without which he could not fulfil his vow to go on crusade. The magnates, moved by this declaration, now promised to help the king win back the lost duchy, saying they would follow him 'in life and death'. 'Mount the warhorses!' urged Anthony Bek, the bellicose bishop of Durham. 'Take your lance in your hand!'[23]

The challenge that lay before them was enormous. France was not Wales. A war there was a fight against a formidable opponent, whose resources, by even the most charitable estimate, were the equal of Edward's own, and in many respects much greater. Moreover, Philip IV was already prepared for war: since 1292 the French king had been building a fleet of galleys. The professed reason for this project had been a desire to assist in the ongoing 'crusade' against Sicily. Now, in retrospect, it was obvious that these ships had been intended all along for a conflict with the king of England.[24]

Of course, Edward's fury at the French action was fuelled by the knowledge that his own crusade, the true crusade, was now dead in the water. The quest for peace, the years of planning, the endless diplomacy: at a stroke it was all rendered obsolete. In June, the king wrote to the prince of Achaea in Greece, who was to have been an ally in the East, angrily lamenting the sudden change in circumstances.[25] The only consolation was that he was comfortably in credit. Conscious of the gargantuan task ahead of him, and resigned to the eclipse of his crusade, Edward determined to do as his enemy had done, and use his crusading resources to fund what was now an inevitable secular conflict. Accordingly, he turned to his bankers, the dependable Riccardi of Lucca, and asked them for the 100,000 marks that they had received from the papacy some three years earlier.

But the Riccardi, like Edward, had been caught completely off guard. They, like he, had conducted their business on the not unreasonable assumption that Anglo-French relations would remain amicable. The money they had been holding on his behalf was, it seems, tied up in overseas investments, and could no longer be recovered. And so, presumably with a good deal of trepidation, the Italians regretfully informed the king that, in present circumstances, they were unable to meet his request.

Edward's reaction, sadly, is not recorded, nor is it known for certain when he received this devastating news. The evidence, however, suggests it must have been early, and probably before mid-June, for at that point parliament instituted a series of drastic emergency measures. First, on 12 June, it was ordered that all the wool in the country should be seized; then, four days later, notice was given that all churches were to be searched for monetary deposits – in particular the proceeds of the crusading tax that was still being collected. The king was clearly engaged in a desperate hunt for funds, rendered more frantic by the realisation that his bankers had failed him. The Riccardi themselves may have been granted a period of grace to see if they could recover any of the lost money, but by the autumn Edward had ordered their arrest. They were, he later opined, 'men who had deceived him'. In this way the profitable relationship that had served them both so well for more than two decades, and that had underpinned all of the king's earlier military enterprises, came to an end. The clever system of customs-for-credit was left in tatters.[26]

More than ever before, Edward needed the voluntary support of his subjects. Thankfully, the English magnates in parliament were as good as their word. One of the first off the mark was Roger Bigod, the earl of Norfolk. A decade earlier he had rendered the king inestimable good service, not only fighting in Wales but also shipping large quantities of produce from his Irish estates to feed the conquering armies. Now the earl showed himself ready to perform the same task again, ordering his servants in Ireland to buy up all the food they could and ship it to Gascony in advance of his arrival. Edward would need exactly this kind of altruism to be widely replicated if he was to succeed. Throughout June the writs flew, first to England, then to Ireland and Scotland. All the king's lieges were enjoined to be at Portsmouth, ready to sail, on 1 September.[27]

By the end of June, when the last of these orders were issued, Edward himself had already arrived in Portsmouth – the great royal naval complex developed a century earlier by his illustrious ancestor, Richard I, for prosecuting a war against France – and was overseeing the build-up of his invasion force. As ever, the troops and clerks of the royal household had sprung into action like a well-oiled machine. They had already been in Portsmouth for over a fortnight, requisitioning warehouses, commandeering horses and carts, and impressing ships. Around the town, fields had been hired to accommodate hundreds of head of cattle, driven on the hoof from as far afield as Salisbury. Other produce – pigs, fish, cheese, chickens and some 24,000 eggs was pouring in from local suppliers and from London.[28]

Already, as well, troops were starting to arrive. 1 September was the date for a general muster: before that, Edward intended to dispatch a smaller, rapid-reaction force to lead the first assault. As early as 8 June he had summoned a select number of barons to come to him as quickly as possible to this end. Some of these were young men, or must have brought young men with them, for the king knighted certain of them after their arrival in Portsmouth. As Edward explained in letters to his Gascon subjects (dated 1 July), this first force would be led by one such young man, his nephew, John of Brittany, aided by the more experienced John of St John, Gascony's ousted seneschal. The second, larger fleet would then follow, captained by Edmund of Lancaster and the earl of Lincoln. Finally, in the fullness of time, Edward would come to the duchy in person.[29]

This scheme, however, was disrupted by the appalling weather noted by many chroniclers that summer. In Ireland, monks wrote of a great storm in mid-July that destroyed the crops and caused widespread famine. A writer at Bury St Edmunds confirmed that there was similar dearth and want throughout England. 'Worse still,' he added, 'during August and September there was a continuous drenching downpour of rain.'[30]

This deluge, and the contrary winds that accompanied it, delayed the departure of the first fleet, probably for several weeks. It was not until the third week of August that the ships were able to put to sea. This meant that they would not be back in time to transport the main muster, which was accordingly postponed from the start of September to the last day of the month. No doubt frustrated by the delay, but glad to have finally blessed his troops and bidden them farewell, the king left Portsmouth on 21 August and went on pilgrimage to Worcester. God's blessing, and the intercession of St Wulfstan, were also deemed necessary for the great English enterprise that was finally under way.[31]

The Church was much on Edward's mind. The scrutiny of funds that had taken place on 5 July had succeeded in locating such crusade funds as still existed – a useful £32,000. But it had also revealed that the English Church itself was rich, and therefore able to help finance the French war. Finance was still the king's major concern. By this stage he had thought better of his plan to seize all the country's wool, having been persuaded by the mercantile community that an increase in customs duties would be more workable and render better results. But the scale of the increase – a punitive six-fold hike – shows that the need for money remained desperately acute. As the king prepared to leave Portsmouth, therefore, he instructed his clergy – his apparently comfortably off clergy – that he wanted to talk with them in Westminster in one month's time.[32]

The trip to Worcester was accordingly of short duration: a flying visit to secure the necessary spiritual aid. Meanwhile, the material build-up continued. On his way to and from the cathedral city, Edward ordered the infantry levies that would accompany the second fleet – these were to come from Wales. The king's lieutenants there were enjoined to raise as many of the strongest and most powerful men as possible and have them ready at Shrewsbury by the end of September.[33]

When Edward returned to Hampshire in the middle of the month, however, it was to news of fresh disaster. The first fleet, once out in the English Channel, had been dashed by the same contrary winds that had earlier delayed its departure. Some ships had been blown back to Portsmouth, but others had been swept as far afield as Plymouth, 150 miles to the west. Weeks after it should have arrived, his rapid-reaction force for Gascony was now scattered along the coast of southern England.[34]

By itself, this latest setback was probably enough for the king and his advisers to decide that the main muster would have to be postponed indefinitely. There would be no point in having an army assembled at Portsmouth at the end of September without the means to transport it into the war zone. At the same time, it is possible that Edward was aware by this point of a more insidious problem. Some men, it seems, were refusing to obey his summons. The ancient obligation to provide the king with military service, as we have already seen, was limited by time – forty days being the longest period upon which the king could insist. But service was also subject to geographical limits – or so the landowning classes claimed. The question of whether Englishmen were duty bound to fight overseas had arisen on several occasions in the thirteenth century, and in the summer of 1294, prompted by Edward's demand, the argument appears to have flared back into life. In Cambridgeshire, for example, the abbot of Ramsey was distraining his tenants – that is, seizing their horses and cattle – in order to compel them to turn out for the king. When this failed, he confronted the same men with the abbey's own records, which showed that their grandfathers had fought on the Continent over fifty years earlier. But this too produced no compliance and, in desperation, the abbot paid out of his own pocket to send substitute knights to the king in order to fulfil his obligation. In the event, the fact that the muster had been abandoned meant that they were sent home again and told to await further orders, as were presumably the other knights who came to Portsmouth, and the 5,000 Welsh infantry who marched as far as Winchester before being turned back. There was no recorded reaction on Edward's part to the opposition, but he would surely have been aware of it. As he set out for Westminster, therefore, it was probably with the knowledge that he would have to talk with his lay subjects, as well as his clergy, about the extent of their obligation to the Crown.[35]

But the clergy came first. Edward met the assembled bishops, abbots and lesser churchmen on 21 September, as agreed, and found them champing at the bit. The cause of their ire was the scrutiny of church funds that had taken place in July. The fact that the king had chosen to lay hands on the crusading tax was one thing: a matter for his own conscience and the pope. In their quest for cash, however, royal agents had been quite indiscriminate, and had made off with an additional £11,000 of private deposits. This seizure, moreover, had been handled with gross insensitivity, with the king's men forcing their way into ecclesiastical buildings and breaking open chests with axes. It was an act in many ways reminiscent of Edward's personal smash-and-grab at the Temple Church in London some thirty years earlier, but carried out on a nationwide scale. And, to add insult to injury, it had taken place on a Sunday.

The king, in response, came close to apologising, and promised redress where offence had been caused. But, as he went on to explain, this was a national emergency – a war forced upon him, a peacemaker and a sworn crusader, by the deceitful king of France. He needed their help, which meant he needed their money. The clergy considered the matter for three days and offered him a tax of 20 per cent.

Now it was Edward's turn to be angry – so much so that the elderly dean of St Paul's who came to deliver the clergy's response collapsed and died in the royal presence. A troop of knights was dispatched to the assembled churchmen, with the message that Edward wanted half their money, or else they would be outlawed – that is, literally placed outside the king's protection, and exposed to all the dangers of robbery and physical violence that that implied. Anyone wishing to oppose Edward was invited to stand up and identify himself as a breaker of the king's peace. Unsurprisingly, there were no takers. At this critical moment, the English Church lacked a leader: Archbishop Pecham had died almost two years earlier, and his replacement was still in Rome awaiting papal confirmation. Fearing for their safety, the clergymen crumpled and agreed that the tax, unprecedented in its severity, could be levied.[36]

Shocking as Edward's bullying tactics appear, his anger is readily understandable. Not so long ago, he could have imagined himself in the Holy Land in the autumn of 1294, perhaps even in the Holy City itself. But it had been a year of accumulating disasters: the treacherous occupation of Gascony by the French; the loss of the crusade funds and the consequent collapse of his financial system; the failure, in spite of his preparation and his prayers, of the first fleet to reach the troubled duchy; the rumour, and perhaps more than the rumour, that at least some of his subjects might refuse to fight for its recovery.

Edward felt every right to be angry. It was now early October, and still no help had reached Gascony. The first fleet was still regrouping in Plymouth; the magnates were talking in Westminster when they should have been fighting in France. There were also reports of trouble in Wales – apparently some of the infantry ordered to Shrewsbury had revolted. Moreover, whatever money Edward had been able to grab or extort, it was still clearly not enough: on 8 October, the king summoned the knights of the shire to meet in Westminster with the intention of negotiating a new tax.[37]

One week later, the next hammer blow fell. The trouble in Wales, it transpired, was not local at all, nor was it spontaneous. It was planned, it was national, and it was deadly serious. Three baronial castles had already been taken. The royal castles at Harlech, Conwy and Criccieth were surrounded and under siege. And Caernarfon, the great, unfinished fortress, centre of royal power and symbol of Edward's imperial rule, had fallen. The castle walls were being thrown down. The new English borough burned.[38]

'The stirrers of this sedition were a duo called Madog and Morgan.' So wrote Walter of Guisborough, one of the most important chroniclers of the last part of Edward's reign, and to some extent he was right. Revolt in north-western Wales had been raised by Madog ap Llywelyn, a distant relative of the late prince of Wales who, rather ambitiously, sought to revive the title for himself. Meanwhile, in the south, the rebels were being led by Morgan ap Maredudd, a disinherited local lord whose particular grudge was against the earl of Gloucester. It would be a mistake, however, to imagine that the major spur to action in 1294 was the frustrated ambition of fading Welsh dynasties. More than ever before, the rising was popular. Madog, Morgan and other leaders like them were not exciting a docile people to rebellion: they were riding a tidal wave of popular indignation. Welsh resentment against English rule had been building for over a decade, encouraged by the familiar pattern of oppression and apartheid that had fuelled earlier outbreaks. What had caused it to swell so spectacularly in the early 1290s had been Edward's effort to raise taxes – specifically, the fifteenth granted to him in 1290 for the expulsion of the Jews. There was no tradition of taxation in Wales, and unreasonable assessment had meant that, in some areas at least, the Welsh – a much poorer people to start with – had been expected to pay more than double what had been asked of the English. Collection was culminating in 1294, just as Edward's Continental crisis broke. With what must have been considerable curiosity, the Welsh watched as their oppressors departed from the new towns and castles, leaving behind only the most minimal of garrisons. Then, with what must have been utter amazement, they learned that they would be required to fight – to band together in their thousands and be issued with arms. Unsurprisingly, when the day of the muster arrived, they needed no further encouragement.[39]

'May Wales be accursed of God and St Simon / For it has always been full of treason!' So rhymed another important north-country chronicler, Peter Langtoft, on hearing of the Welsh rebellion, and one can well imagine similar (albeit less poetic) oaths forming on the lips of his king. By the middle of October Edward realised that the rising in Wales was so serious that the troops and supplies originally intended for Gascony would have to be redeployed. It was a minor blessing, perhaps, that by this date the long-delayed first fleet had finally put out of Plymouth and sailed beyond recall. But writs reached Portsmouth instructing the earls of Lancaster and Lincoln to send their men and *matériel* westwards; they and the king's other lieges were requested to rendezvous at Worcester, as on previous occasions. Requested, not required: as the scale of the crisis continued to increase, so Edward recognised the need to moderate his natural imperiousness. Fighting the French and the Welsh simultaneously, and having already browbeaten the Church into submission, he could not afford any additional confrontation with his lay magnates.[40] When, after what must have been an intensely frustrating four-week wait, the laity assembled in Westminster to consider the royal request for cash, it was the cue for more concessions. The controversial Quo Warranto inquiry, moderated in return for the last tax, was now dropped altogether – and at a knock-down price. The laity, unlike the clergy, did not lack a leader. When the king asked for a tax of a third, his old sparring partner the earl of

Gloucester stepped forward to object. A tenth was all Edward was able to obtain in exchange for abandoning one of his most cherished projects. It must have been with a new, bitter taste in his mouth that, immediately after the tax was agreed, the king set out for Wales.[41]

The military strategy was by now familiar: three armies, from three bases, would drive into north, south and central Wales. The scale, by contrast, was extraordinarily novel: no fewer than 35,000 foot soldiers were mobilised, a figure that dwarfed the total deployed during the conquest by a factor of four. Leaving his earls to tackle the other theatres, Edward, as ever, commanded the northern assault. With some 5,000 men by his side, the king pushed through the valleys of the interior, while another 16,000 marched along the coastal road. Progress was swift, resistance seemingly slight: within a week or so, his forces were reunited and, as the end of the year approached, Edward drew up his whole army on the eastern edge of the River Conwy.[42]

There, on the opposite shore, was a sight to lift all their spirits. Conwy Castle, which can only have stood a few feet high at the time of the king's last visit, was now completed. Master James of St George and his fellow masons had worked at lightning speed to finish the fortress, and its close counterpart at Harlech, in just six building seasons. Grafted onto its platform of rock, surrounded on three sides by the sea, Conwy stood like a ship in harbour, its whitewashed walls rising sheer and tall, the royal flags flying from its turrets. When Edward and some of his soldiers crossed the river to celebrate Christmas in the castle's great hall, he may well have reflected that it represented the best £15,000 he had ever spent.[43]

At the start of the new year (1295) Conwy certainly proved it was worth every penny. In early January, for reasons unknown, the king decided on an immediate advance. Possibly he hoped to relieve Caernarfon, or even the castles further round the coast; perhaps he had intelligence concerning the whereabouts of his enemies on which he aimed to capitalise. Impatience almost certainly played a part – Edward was anxious to deal with Wales so he could return to the business of Gascony. Whatever the case, without waiting for the rest of his army to cross the Conwy, on 7 January the king took such soldiers as he had with him and struck out into the west.

At some point during this sortie they were attacked. We do not know precisely when, because even the routine royal record-keeping was disrupted as a consequence. Immediate losses were apparently small – it was not the king and his soldiery that were targeted, but their baggage train. This, however, had the effect of creating a more pernicious problem. They were deep inside enemy territory and had been deprived of supplies. Having penetrated as far as Nefyn – ironically, the scene of his earlier victory celebrations – Edward ordered a retreat. By 20 January he and his army were back at Conwy Castle.[44]

But they were still cut off. Outside the castle walls, the worst storm in living memory raged. 'It was so terrible,' wrote one English chronicler, 'that even men who were a hundred years old could recall nothing similar.' The harsh conditions meant that no contact could be had with the reinforcements stationed on the opposite side of the estuary. Edward and his troops found themselves in the uncomfortable position of being under siege and running out of rations. Walter of Guisborough has a nice story, not too tall to be entirely incredible, of how the soldiery had set aside the last barrel of wine for the king's personal consumption, but that Edward insisted on sharing with everyone.[45]

Their isolation was comparatively short lived. By the start of February, if not before, contact with the main army had been re-established and supplies were able to get through.[46] During that month ships arrived from Bristol and Chester, Lancashire and Dorset, Ireland and even Gascony. The seaborne operation served to emphasise the wisdom of Edward's choice of coastal sites for his castles; yet it also highlighted the folly of his recent, impetuous foray. After his brush with disaster, the king showed himself in no hurry to move anywhere until victory seemed more certain. By the second week of March his well-fed soldiers were so bored from inactivity that they begged to be allowed out for a bit of adventure. A brief sortie led to the killing of some Welshmen and the recovery of items from the lost baggage train.[47]

The eagerness of the troops at Conwy was probably encouraged by the knowledge that elsewhere in Wales a renewed English assault was well under way. As early as the middle of February the earl of Hereford had struck out from his base in the south and successfully recovered the town and castle at Abergavenny. A few weeks later, on 6 March, the royal forces in the north-west had marched out of Rhuddlan and into the interior. The best news, however, had emerged from mid-Wales. On 5 March, some eight miles north-west of Montgomery at a place called Maes Moydog, the earl of Warwick had fought a pitched battle with the army of Madog ap Llywelyn. 'They were the best and bravest Welshmen that anyone had seen,' an English eyewitness admitted, but explained that 700 Welsh soldiers fell compared with just seven Englishmen. Madog himself evaded death and capture, but his power had been decisively broken.[48]

At last, in early April, the king moved out of Conwy. His target was Anglesey, which had been the centre of the revolt in the north. Thanks to the ingenuity of James of St George in the preceding weeks, the island was quickly retaken by amphibious assault, using an armada of ships, pontoons and siege-engines. By 10 April Edward had arrived at Llanfaes, Anglesey's most populous and prosperous settlement, where seven months earlier the rebels had executed the English sheriff. As punishment, the king had the town levelled and its inhabitants moved to a virgin site on the other side of the island that still bears the name Newborough. Llanfaes, for the sake of future security, was to be super-seded by another new English plantation, protected by yet another new castle. Within a week of the king's arrival, Master James had begun work on a marshy site christened Beaumaris.[49]

What followed was also largely an exercise for ensuring future security. In early May Edward set out southwards, probably passing via Criccieth and Harlech to inspect his new and reconditioned castles, both of which had held out for the duration of the revolt, supplied by ships from Ireland. By the middle of the month, some ten miles north of Aberystwyth, the king was reunited with his other commanders – the earl of Warwick and the Rhuddlan garrison under Reginald de Grey – who had pushed right through the Welsh interior to reach the western coast. As he moved through each district, Edward was all the while receiving submissions and taking hostages in large numbers. The pacification process drew to a close in June as the king moved into the south, where he received into his peace the rebel leader Morgan ap Maredudd – much to the chagrin of the earl of Gloucester, who had once again bungled his allotted task, and now suffered the additional ignominy of having Edward confiscate his lordship of Glamorgan. By midsummer, the business of restoring order was complete. On 30 June the king was back at Conwy, with only a token military force.[50]

One last place remained to be visited. Until this point, it seems, Edward had not stopped at, and perhaps had not seen, his castle at Caernarfon.[51] Now, at last, he was ready to behold the stricken giant. Incomplete at the time of the revolt, Caernarfon had latterly suffered substantial damage at the hands of the rebels. Any wooden buildings are likely to have been destroyed by fire, and the town walls, in par-ticular, must have suffered considerable damage – repairs later came to more than £1,000. But enough masonry remained standing in 1295 for Edward to appreciate that the majestic building he and his masons had envisaged twelve years earlier was well on the way to being realised. The king's last concern that summer was to ensure that enormous resources were earmarked for Master James and his team, so that Caernarfon and the new fortress at Beaumaris could be speedily finished. That done, his tour of inspection complete, and with some 250 Welsh hostages in his custody, Edward returned to England.[52]

Gascony, of course, was uppermost in his thoughts. During the winter, while he and his magnates had been effectively reconquering Wales, the first fleet had finally arrived in the duchy and had met with moderate success. John of Brittany and John of St John, although they had failed to retake Bordeaux, had managed to recapture several towns along the Gironde estuary and the River Garonne. The onset of spring, however, had brought with it the inevitable French counter-attack: a large army led by the war's principal architect, Charles of Valois, had quickly reversed these gains, and captured some dozen English knights as they were retreating. Within a few days, all that remained in English hands were Bourg and Blaye, two embattled outposts on the Gironde, and Bayonne, the maritime town in the south-western corner of the duchy.[53]

These places would not be able to hold out for ever, as Edward keenly appreciated. In March, even before the French counter-offensive had begun, the king had been trying to ship excess supplies from Wales to Gascony, where he knew the need was greater. According to one well-informed chronicler, he also succeeded in sending several thousand infantry to the duchy under the command of John de Botetourt, a knight of the royal household. Such measures, however, were only sticking plasters, insufficient to provide anything more than temporary succour to what was, after all, only ever intended to have been an advance expeditionary force. What Gascony needed more than ever was the deployment of the large English army that Edward had ordered, then cancelled, then finally redirected into Wales the previous year. It was probably to discuss this matter more that any other that the king summoned a small, select parliament to meet in Westminster at the start of August.[54]

This assembly had barely had time to gather when the news arrived that the French were attacking England's south coast. On 2 August Dover was raided and burned. It was a short-lived assault and not too serious. Although some locals lost their lives (including a monk who achieved sainthood as a result), the raiders were successfully repulsed. More than anything else, the attack was ironic in its timing, coinciding as it did with Edward's return to Westminster after an absence of eight months. Prior to his departure for Wales, the king had been visibly anxious at the prospect of leaving England undefended. Before leaving London he had spent a week at the Tower (his longest stay for seventeen years) and en route to Worcester he had ordered the construction of a fleet of galleys. The raid on Dover probably explains why the parliament summoned for the start of August did not get under way until the middle of the month. It certainly explains why the cardinals who had arrived in England a few weeks earlier made little headway in their effort to secure an Anglo-French peace.[55]

War with France was still the order of the day, and Edward had given some thought as to how it could be successfully prosecuted. Back in February, during his self-enforced sojourn as Conwy Castle, the king had ordered his sheriffs to identify all those men in their districts with lands worth more than £40 a year and warn them to be ready to fight at three weeks' notice. Here, in other words, was a radical attempt on Edward's part to redefine his subjects' obligation to provide him with military service – a move no doubt inspired by the difficulties that had started to emerge the previous year. By such a measure the vagaries of the existing, ancient system, wherein duty was determined by an individual's tenurial relationship with the Crown, would be swept away, replaced by a more straightforward arrangement based on an assessment of landed wealth. The idea was not entirely new: on the eve of the conquest of Wales, and apparently after an argument with his magnates about the terms of their service, the king had contemplated a similar scheme, only to abandon it at an early stage. Now, with the need in Gascony so great, it seemed imperative that the plan be revived in earnest.[56]

But when the parliament of August 1295 finally settled down to business in the middle of the month, the magnates were already restless. At that very moment, royal tax collectors were moving into their estates in order to collect the tenth that had been granted the previous year. Having responded to the king's 'affectionate request' to fight in Wales at their own expense, the military men evidently expected that they might be excused payment. Yet all that Edward had been prepared to grant them since the campaign's outset were individual, temporary respites that (in the longest cases) had expired on 1 August.[57] It may have been to appease his magnates on this issue that Edward publicly sacked his treasurer (a man already unpopular with the Church and the citizens of London) at the start of the parliament. As a next step, the king may have floated the idea that the demand for tax would indeed be dropped – for those who agreed to serve him in Gascony. On 20 August some men who were already fighting in the duchy received just such an acquittance, as a mark of the king's 'special favour'.[58] Within three days, however, Edward's attempts at persuasion were seen to have failed. When the king ordered some of the assembled magnates to fight in Gascony, fourteen of them – about a quarter of those present – flatly refused to go.

None of these men were especially powerful, nor did they constitute an organised political clique. The most important among them was the earl of Arundel, Richard fitz Alan, but even he was a relatively unimportant figure, a newcomer to the ranks of England's earls and apparently quite hard-up as a result. Poverty – or what passed for poverty among the ruling classes – was likely to have been the chief complaint of all of these men, most of whom can be proved to have fought in Wales earlier in the year. Their stand, though, was probably taken on a matter of principle: namely that, no matter what innovations their king might care to devise, Englishmen were not obliged to provide military service overseas.[59]

Edward was massively angry at their refusal. On that day – 23 August – he instructed his officials to distrain these men, just as the abbot of Ramsey had done when he had come up against similar refusals the previous year. Distraint by the king, however, meant suffering of an altogether different degree. Armed with a writ from the exchequer, royal agents would move in to an offender's manors and confiscate goods to the value of any outstanding debts to the Crown. Such debts, which might accumulate from one generation to the next, could be huge. Along with the earldom of Arundel, for example, Richard fitz Alan had inherited debts to the Crown in excess of £5,000.[60]

Whether distraint would solve anything in this instance remained to be seen. Within a week of the confrontation, parliament had broken up, Edward had left Westminster and nothing had been agreed on how to help Gascony. The king remained furious at the men who had refused him – on 3 September he repeated the order to distrain them in even harsher terms – but at the same time he could not afford to allow their opposition to provoke a wider crisis.[61] Things were already threatening to spiral out of control as the summer drew to a close. Before leaving London Edward had instituted new measures to protect the country's coast. His new galleys – fighting ships with 120 oars a piece – were now ready, under the command of William Leybourne, who was duly accorded the newly coined title 'admiral of the sea'. They were to be backed up by teams of paid men patrolling the shoreline. Even as orders were going out for their recruitment, however, the French – once again, with impeccable timing – launched attacks on the south coast, striking at Winchelsea and Hythe. These assaults were even less successful than the last, but, taken with the king's new orders, they seemed to confirm that a French invasion was an imminent prospect. By mid-September, from Land's End to Lincolnshire, men stood watch in their thousands, scanning the horizon for French sails.[62] In this tense atmosphere mad rumours started to circulate. In Essex the people of Harwich went into a panic, believing that an invasion was already under way. In Huntingdonshire the prior of St Neots was said to have raised the standard of the king of France above the belfry of his church – a completely malicious rumour, it later turned out, but one that at the time was given credence even by the councillors around the king. These men, above all, had good reason to feel jumpy and suspicious, having just discovered a traitor in their midst. Thomas Turbeville, a knight of the royal household, had been one of those men captured by the French earlier in the year, but had since returned to England, claiming to have escaped. In truth he had been turned, and had come back with the intention of provoking rebellion to coincide with a French landing, and even of kidnapping the king. His treason was uncovered – a messenger betrayed him – and Turbeville was sent to be executed in London. But the episode can only have served to emphasise a crucial point: in this time of great crisis, Edward could not afford to lose the loyalty of his leading men.[63]

Having left London in anger at the start of September, Edward was in danger of becoming isolated. But in the weeks that followed, he backed down on the issue of tax. As the king and his advisers moved into Kent, pardons began to be issued to dozens of magnates, excusing them from payment of the tenth, irrespective of whether they were serving in Gascony or not.[64] He also settled with the men who had refused to fight, though it is not clear on precisely what terms. Some of them had already crumpled under the force of his distraint, and may have agreed to go to the duchy merely in return for the release of their goods. At least four of their number, however, including the earl of Arundel, were also pardoned their tax, suggesting that Edward was ready to conciliate, even if he did not wish to seem conciliatory. When these men, along with several others, were ordered on 3 October to fight for a second time, the primary emphasis was on their duty ('you should omit nothing, just as you love the king and his honour'). But the writs informed their recipients that they would be accompanied by the steward of the royal household, who would not only pay their wages, but would also value their horses (for the purposes of compensation), and 'do other things that might arise during the voyage'. If men were willing to fight for him, Edward was willing to ensure that they did not end up out of pocket.[65]

The breach with his magnates repaired and the preparations for a new army at last in train, the king called another parliament. It was to be an exceptionally large assembly, with the usual array of earls, barons, bishops, abbots and priors joined by a wide range of representatives: knights of the shire, men of the towns and cities and members of the lower clergy. The Victorian historian William Stubbs, impressed by the scope of consultation on display, dubbed this 'the Model Parliament', rather ignoring the fact that it was an emergency session. The aim, naturally, was to obtain more money, but the difficulties during the summer had shown that to do so Edward would have to make a more convincing case for war. Not since the conquest of Wales had the king sought such a wide audience, and his writs of summons recaptured the same propagandist tone used on that earlier occasion. 'The king of France,' Edward warned, 'not satisfied with the treacherous invasion of Gascony, has prepared a mighty fleet and army, for the purpose of invading England and wiping the English tongue from the face of the earth.'[66]

Originally summoned for mid-November 1295, this giant parliament did not begin until the end of the month – Edward, as he explained in his letters proroguing the meeting, was detained at Winchelsea, 'assembling his fleet and making other preparations for the defence of the kingdom'. When the session finally started, the king was probably relieved to find that there was little opposition to his demands among the laity, who granted a tax of an eleventh after only a few days of debate. It may have helped Edward's case that the earl of Gloucester was absent, lying sick at his castle of Monmouth, where he died in early December.[67]

While the laity had lost their leader, however, the clergy had found their champion. Robert Winchelsea, the new archbishop of Canterbury, had returned to England from Rome at the start of the year, and been enthroned as recently as October. Winchelsea – he seems to have hailed from the town that Edward had saved from the sea – was described by chroniclers as well-mannered, affable, and more than a little overweight. But he was also formidably clever, and fierce in his determination to defend the rights of the Church. When the king sought from the clergy another punitive tax – he was hoping on this occasion for a quarter, perhaps even a third of their goods – the new archbishop led the opposition. While agreeing with Edward that the realm did indeed face grave danger, the assembled churchmen indicated that they were prepared to pay a tax of only 10 per cent. All the king managed to secure beyond this was a promise that more money would be forthcoming if the threat from France persisted.[68]

Edward was doubtless disappointed by the clergy's response, but now was not the time to risk another showdown with his subjects in England, because, as the king must have explained to those present in parliament, he now needed to lead an army against the Scots.

The Scots, much like the Welsh, had observed their self-appointed overlord struggling to cope with his Continental crisis and decided that they too were witnessing a moment of opportunity that was not to be missed. Their response had differed from that of their Celtic cousins only in being more carefully considered, more closely co-ordinated, and hence somewhat slower to make itself manifest. By the summer of 1295, however, the signs were unmistakable: the Scots had found the courage that had failed their unfortunate king. In July that year the great men of Scotland had taken steps to impose their corporate will on John Balliol, depriving him of executive initiative in much the same way that the English baronage had ultimately constrained Henry III. At the same time, they dispatched representatives across the sea to seek assistance from the king of France, who had already signified some two months earlier that he now regarded the Scots 'not as our enemies, but rather as our friends'. On 23 October this new-found friendship had been cemented in the form of a firm alliance: together, Scotsmen and Frenchmen would wage war against the king of England.[69]

That Edward I was aware of these manoeuvres is hardly open to doubt. When the traitor Thomas Turbeville was taken in September, his letters indicated that part of his plan was to foment rebellion not only in Wales but also in Scotland.[70] In October the king ordered the seizure of all property held by Scotsmen in England. Edward being Edward, however, he moved against Scotland using the deliberate, legalistic steps that he believed gave his actions their legitimacy. John Balliol had already been sentenced in Westminster to lose three of his towns and castles. When, therefore, the Scots king failed to respond to subsequent summonses in 1295, Edward dispatched two senior churchmen to demand the surrender of these sureties. And, when this demand met with an inevitable refusal, it gave the English king his mandate. On 16 December Edward declared his intention 'of marching against John, king of Scots, who has violated the fealty he owes the Crown of England'.[71]

The fact that Edward intended to apply his hand destructively rather than correctively can be reasonably surmised from the scale of his military preparations. In January 1296 the king advised the officials of his exchequer that he would need £5,000 a week for his trip to Scotland, since he intended to recruit 1,000 mounted men and 60,000 foot soldiers. Even if this infantry figure was an exaggeration, it implies that Edward wished his army to be large, perhaps the largest he had ever assembled. This is also suggested by the king's extraordinary efforts to secure military support from his magnates in Ireland.[72]

Like the rest of his domains, Ireland had been engulfed by trouble since 1294. Disorder there, however, was not so much due to increased disaffection among the natives (there was hardly room for increase) as the development of new attitudes among the English settlers. Absenteeism on the part of many of Ireland's greatest landlords (for example, the earls of Gloucester, Norfolk and Pembroke); lax and parasitic lordship on the part of the Crown: these had combined to leave those who remained in Ireland more or less free to chart their own course. And for some men – especially those magnates living on the frontiers – the key to survival and self-betterment had turned out to be the adoption of the methods, morals and manners of their Irish neighbours. The immediate cause of disorder in 1294 had been the sudden and violent re-eruption of an ancient feud between the settler community's two most powerful men: Richard de Burgh, earl of Ulster, and John fitz Thomas, last of the Geraldine dynasty. In December that year, fitz Thomas had rampaged through de Burgh's lands, captured the earl and cast him into prison, and as a result, said a contemporary, 'all Ireland was disturbed'.[73]

From a long-term perspective, however, the dispute's most disturbing feature was that, in raiding his rival's lordships, fitz Thomas had allied himself with the native Irish. This was hardly very surprising, given that fitz Thomas, although born of settler stock, had apparently been raised in an Irish household. But that simply served to make him the prime example of the phenomenon that the settler community feared most: degeneracy. Fitz Thomas and others like him had literally parted company with their own people (Latin, *gens*), fallen from the acceptable standards of civilised English society.[74]

Edward had been concerned about the feud between fitz Thomas and de Burgh – apart from anything else, such infighting among the settlers encouraged risings among the natives, as was the case in 1295. That summer the king had summoned fitz Thomas to Westminster to explain himself and bound both men to keep the peace on pain of forfeiting their estates. In real terms, however, Edward did nothing to stop the rot in Ireland, and plenty to encourage its spread. From 1294 his officials had shipped hundreds of tons of grain and other foodstuffs out of the lordship, in spite of the famine caused by poor harvests. He had also continued to drain money from Ireland, on top of the taxes he had introduced there in the early 1290s. And, ever since the French crisis had broken, the king had been trying to get men from Ireland, infantry and cavalry, to fight on his behalf in other theatres. Down to the start of 1296 he had met with no success, which explains the extraordinary offers he was willing by this point to make to his Irish magnates. In exchange for their agreement to serve in Scotland, Edward not only agreed to pay these men handsomely – Richard de Burgh received the highest rate of pay of any earl during the campaign – he also offered to pardon any crimes they had committed, and to cancel any debts they owed the Crown. In return for this generosity, the king managed to secure some 3,000 men (mostly infantry), the biggest force to set sail from Ireland up to that time. The cost to his own authority there, however, and the health of the lordship in general, would be disproportionately large in comparison.[75]

Edward arrived in Newcastle on 1 March 1296 to meet the giant English army he had summoned. The Scots, who had been ordered to present themselves on the same date, unsurprisingly failed to appear. The king therefore marched his host along the Northumbrian coast and drew it up at Wark, a castle on the River Tweed, where the English lord had decided to join the Scots on account of his love for a Scottish lady – a nice reminder, at this critical moment, that the Tweed was a political boundary between the two countries, not a cultural one. Edward's arrival at the Border coincided with the start of Holy Week, and so, with proper respect for Christian piety, the English army sat and waited. During this time, the Scots made an attack on nearby Carham, and on Easter Monday they tried, unsuccessfully, to take Carlisle. When the festivities at Wark were over, therefore, the English king had all the justification he needed for his invasion. As the end of March approached, he crossed the Tweed and led his army in the direction of Berwick.[76]

Berwick was one of the three towns whose surrender Edward had demanded by proxy the previous year, and that demand was now repeated in person. The citizens again rejected it, throwing back insults, taunts and gibes at the king, and even – according to one English chronicler – baring their buttocks at him. Such bravado was quite surprising, given the size of the English army, and the fact that Berwick's defences at this time amounted to no more than an insubstantial wooden palisade. The assault that followed, however, seems to have caught both sides unprepared. The king had drawn his forces up in front of the town and was engaged in the pre-battle ritual of creating new knights – a display perhaps intended to persuade the Scots to reconsider their position. But to the English navy lurking offshore, this military activity looked like a cry to arms, and they duly began their attack. When the sailors in turn got into difficulty and several ships were set on fire, Edward was obliged to sound a general advance. His troops rapidly breached Berwick's flimsy defences and poured into the town, putting many of its stupefied citizens to the sword.[77]

The king has often been criticised for his behaviour at Berwick, and stands accused of having ordered the indiscriminate massacre of the townspeople. In fact, Edward's tactics and the killing that took place – however reprehensible they may seem to modern sensibilities – were entirely in keeping with the conventions of medieval warfare. A town or city that refused to surrender left itself liable to be sacked in just this way. That Edward was operating squarely within the usual chivalric norms at Berwick is emphasised by his treatment of the 200-strong garrison who holed themselves up in the town's castle. To these men the king offered generous terms of surrender: safety of life and limb, the right to retain their lands and possessions, and even the right to go free, provided they swore never again to bear arms against him. It was a most magnanimous package, which the garrison wisely chose to accept.[78]

The mistake of the Scots, arguably, was to behave with the same kind of chivalric propriety in response. Having taken Berwick, Edward remained in its smoking ruins for a full four weeks, improving the town's defences with a great new ditch, reportedly eighty feet wide and forty feet deep. (The king, demonstrating his sureness of touch when it came to popular gestures, wheeled the first barrow of earth himself.) How long he could have remained there though, holding his expensive army together, is an open question. As it was, within days of Berwick's fall, Edward received a formal message of defiance from John Balliol, in which the Scottish king renounced his homage and fealty ('extorted by your violent pressure'). Then, as the end of April approached, the Scottish army abandoned its raids in northern England and offered the English battle. The setting for their encounter was Dunbar, some thirty miles further along the coast from Berwick. Edward had sent some troops under the earl of Surrey to capture the castle there, and the Scottish host soon materialised with the intention of raising the siege. The result was a total disaster for the Scots, whose inexperienced and undisciplined ranks collapsed in the face of a well co-ordinated English assault. Scottish foot soldiers perished in their hundreds, and several Scottish nobles were taken captive. The next day Edward himself arrived, Dunbar Castle was surrendered, and more prestigious prisoners – including three Scottish earls – were taken. The war was barely one month old, with just one city and one castle conceded, but already the Scottish resistance was in tatters.[79]

What followed was therefore more like a victory parade than a military campaign. From Dunbar Edward marched back to the Border, where he swiftly secured the submission of Roxburgh and Jedburgh – the two towns besides Berwick demanded in 1295 – and where he finally joined forces with the Irish magnates, who had arrived two months too late. Then it was north to Edinburgh, which surrendered after a siege of just five days. Stirling, the king's next target, put up no resistance at all. By the time the English army arrived, the castle's garrison had already fled.[80]

It was now mid-June and those Scottish leaders still at large were looking for a way to come in. John Balliol, a man bullied from above and bullied from below, had long since come to rue his promotion to ranks of royalty, and pined for the days when he had been a mere English magnate. He had also been in London and had no doubt seen the severed head of Llywelyn ap Gruffudd on its spike. Hence, when the bishop of Durham, acting on Edward's behalf, proposed to him the kind of deal that the late prince of Wales had proudly scorned, Balliol leapt at the chance. He would resign the Scottish kingship and become an English earl. 'Then he would go out of the realm of Scotland, to England, to dwell there in the ways that used to be his, and would hunt in his parks, and do what he wished for his solace and his pleasure.'

This idyllic vision, alas, proved to be fleeting. For reasons that remain unclear, Edward himself soon decided that the deal was off. Possibly the English, having taken Edinburgh, unearthed documentary evidence of the Franco-Scottish alliance to suggest that Balliol was more culpable than he had claimed. Whatever the case, by the time the king of England caught up with his disobedient vassal, he had devised for him a different fate. On 8 July Balliol and his supporters, having already confessed their crime of rebellion by letters, gave themselves up at Montrose, a town on Scotland's eastern seaboard. And there the Scottish king, created by Edward less than four years earlier, was ceremoniously and humiliatingly unmade. Balliol resigned his regalia, and suffered the personal indignity of having the royal coat-of-arms ripped from the tabard he was wearing (hence his popular nickname, Toom Tabard). Together with the other Scottish leaders, the demoted king was then dispatched into England, not to enjoy an earldom, but to endure a period of captivity at the Tower. Later he was conceded a less strict confinement in Hertfordshire, where he was at least allowed to do a bit of hunting.[81]

Edward, meanwhile, was completing his tour of Scotland, taking hostages and homages, and travelling – as in Wales – further than any English king before him. By the end of July he had reached Elgin, the northernmost limit of his progress, and by the end of August he was back at Berwick, where his campaign had begun just five months earlier. A parliament was held there, to which the Scots came in their thousands to swear fealty to their new, direct overlord, and Edward sat to decide the future governance of the country he had conquered.[82]

One thing was certain: Scotland was to have no new king, at least not for the time being. At the outset of the campaign, the Bruces had been optimistic at the prospect of belated promotion. The elderly Robert Bruce, erstwhile competitor for the Scottish throne, had died the previous year; but his namesake son had kept up the family tradition of collaborating with the English, and had joined Edward's army in the hope of supplanting Balliol. Once expressed, however, the hope had been immediately crushed. 'Do you think we have nothing better to do,' the English king had asked him, 'than to win kingdoms for you?' It was a put-down so withering that the poor man retired to his estates in Essex and never set foot in Scotland again.[83]

There remained, of course, the possibility that other disappointed candidates might be tempted to try their luck, so Edward had taken the trouble to remove temptation from their path. In the course of his victory tour, the king had confiscated the ancient Stone of Scone, the seat on which Scottish monarchs had been made since time imme-morial. Like the relics and regalia of Wales (and, indeed, like the other regalia of Scotland), the Stone was dispatched into England, the latest addition to Edward's now impressive collection at Westminster. The king even had a special cabinet made in which to display this new trophy, the so-called Coronation Chair.[84]

For the time being, Edward decided, he would rule Scotland directly. A new, English-style administration would be set up, based at Berwick – the ruined town would be rebuilt, like a bastide, with the help of experts like Henry le Waleys. From there, the country would be governed by a team of English officials, in charge of a new, nationwide network of sheriffs, soldiers and constables, overwhelmingly English in their origins. In charge of the whole operation would be the earl of Surrey, who had led the English to victory at Dunbar. In September, as Edward returned to England, he formally handed over the seal of Scotland to its new colonial governor. 'A man does good business,' he exclaimed, jokingly, 'when he rids himself of a turd.'[85]

As their conquering king returned south, his English subjects sang in praise of his astonishing victory. Soldiers made up ribald rhymes mocking the incompetence of their enemies at Dunbar. Monastic chroniclers composed more stately eulogies to celebrate so great a triumph. The reaction of Peter Langtoft is worth quoting in full:

Ah God! how often Merlin said the truth
In his prophecies, if you read them!
Now are the two waters united in one
Which have been separated by great mountains;
And one realm made of two different kingdoms
Which used to be governed by two kings.
Now are the islanders all joined together

And Albany (Scotland) reunited to the regalities
Of which king Edward is proclaimed lord.
Cornwall and Wales are in his power
And Ireland the great at his will.
There is neither king nor prince of all the countries
Except king Edward, who has thus united them
Arthur never held the fiefs so fully.
Henceforward there is nothing to do but provide his expedition
Against the king of France, to conquer his inheritances
And then bear the cross where Jesus Christ was born.[86]

In these last lines, at least, Langtoft was entirely right. The war with France was once again at the top of Edward's agenda and, more than ever, Gascony stood in need of his help.

The second force sent to the duchy had fared no better than the first. By the autumn of 1295, when Edward had twisted enough aristocratic arms to elicit the necessary enthusiasm, the main expedition was already a year behind schedule – and even then it had not left on time. Edmund of Lancaster, the king's appointed captain, had fallen ill, and had not recovered until after Christmas. It was not until January 1296 that the much-delayed fleet had finally set sail. Once arrived in Gascony, their luck had not improved. The French, having been left unmolested for so long, were found to be well entrenched. English attempts to retake Bordeaux, and even the smaller towns along the Garonne, came to nothing. Eventually, as his money had started to run out, Lancaster had been forced to abandon his efforts and had retired to Bayonne. There he had once again fallen sick, and died on 5 June. Henry de Lacy, the ultra-loyal earl of Lincoln, had taken command of the demoralised English forces.[87]

News of his brother's death had reached Edward while he was still in Scotland, just days after he had received John Balliol's resignation. Orders had been sent out immediately for masses to be said for Edmund's soul. The king spoke of his devastation, and enjoined his churchmen to pray for 'our dearest and only brother, who was always devoted and faithful to us, and to the affairs of our realm, and in whom valour and many gifts of grace shone forth'. It was almost certainly with Edmund's eternal salvation in mind that Edward had summoned his next English parliament to meet, not around the feast of St Edward (13 October), as was usual, but one month later, around the feast of St Edmund (20 November). For the same reason, the venue was not to be Westminster, but Bury St Edmunds, where his brother's saintly namesake was interred. The local chronicler confirms that, when the king arrived in the town in November, he and his great men solemnly kept St Edmund's feast.[88]

The principal reason for calling the parliament, however, was financial. War on all fronts was forcing Edward to disgorge unheard-of sums of money. Even before he had set out for Scotland, the king had spent something in the region of £250,000 – that is, considerably more than the cost of his crusade and the conquest of Wales combined. In January, as a damage-limitation exercise, all royal building projects had been cancelled, with the exception of Caernarfon, Beaumaris and the murals in the Painted Chamber (an indication that, in Edward's mind, the crusade was still a priority). The conquest of Scotland had demanded tens of thousands of pounds in addition; the recovery of Gascony would require a sum many times greater. Somewhere, somehow, more funds must be found.[89]

But by this point the country was groaning under the weight of Edward's wartime exactions. It was not just that his subjects had already paid two heavy taxes in as many years. They were also suffering from the new, impossibly heavy customs rate that the king had slapped on the export of wool. The merchants had simply absorbed this blow by slashing the prices they paid to their suppliers, and that included just about everyone, whether they owned ten sheep or ten thousand. It was no wonder that the new duty had become known as the maltote – the 'evil tax'.[90]

More aggravating still was the phenomenon known as purveyance, or prise. Since ancient times the royal household had claimed the right to seize goods – principally food, but sometimes horses, carts, boats and so on – without contradiction, and in return for only the promise of later compensation. Irritating enough in peacetime, prise had become the most controversial issue since the outbreak of war. Royal agents everywhere, whether they were with the household or not, had started to seize whatever they needed, whenever they felt like it, in the name of the king. Predictably, this had led in some instances to accusations of robbery by those being dispossessed, and even violent clashes. What was worse, however, was the fact that Edward was using prise to feed whole armies. Since 1294 orders had gone out for the seizure of grain in ever larger quantities. By the autumn of 1296 even the king's collecting officials had begun to object that the amounts being demanded were impossible.[91]

Unsurprisingly, therefore, it took time to wrangle yet another tax out of the laity. The parliament at Bury was under way by 6 November, but it was not until the end of the month that the assembled knights and burgesses agreed to a grant. The fact that the rate – a twelfth – was the lowest since 1294 was another sign of mounting opposition. There is no sign that any concession had been offered in return. One chronicler complained that the tax had been extorted.[92]

Altogether more surprising to Edward was the resistance he encountered from the clergy. They too, of course, were suffering from the same economic burdens. But, as the king had been pleased to recall in his writs of summons, the Church had nevertheless promised him further financial aid should France refuse a truce. One year on, and it was fair to say that all talk of truce had been firmly rejected. When, in January, Edward had sent his aged uncle, William de Valence, to meet with French negotiators at Cambrai, the result had been an out-and-out fight – Valence had returned wounded and died soon afterwards. The king, therefore, was quite clear: it was time for the clergy to honour their promise and pay up.[93]

That promise, however, now had to be balanced against a new proclamation from the pope. *Clericis Laicos*, as this bull was known, forbade the Church from granting taxes to secular rulers without prior permission from Rome. Ostensibly addressed to all of Christendom, its specific denunciation of rulers who extorted taxes of 'a half' suggests that the pope's particular target was the king of England; quite possibly the document had been drafted after a secret appeal by Robert Winchelsea. After days of debate in November, the archbishop approached the king and asked if the clergy could postpone their decision. Edward was not at all pleased, but allowed them until January to give him a definite answer. To focus their minds in the meantime, he began calling in the debts to the Crown of eminent churchmen. Winchelsea himself was advised he would have to pay £3,500 by mid-December.[94]

There was apparently no demand for military service in parliament. Such discussions as occurred took place behind closed doors, informed by English ambassadors who had just returned from the Continent. Ever since the outbreak of war, Edward had been endeavouring to construct a grand alliance against Philip IV. The English king had spent enormous sums – at least £75,000 – to secure the support of the dukes and counts on France's northern and eastern borders. For the first two years the results had been decidedly mixed. Some allies, such as the duke of Brabant (Edward's son-in-law), had signed up and remained loyal. Others, like the count of Holland (sometime claimant of the Scottish throne), had taken the king's money, only to turn against him. But, as 1296 drew to a close, the balance was at last tipping in England's favour. In June, the count of Holland met with an unfortunate accident – English involvement cannot be entirely ruled out – and his twelve-year-old son and successor had indicated that Holland was ready to revert to Edward's allegiance. So too, more importantly, was the count of Flanders, who had grown tired of being bullied by Philip IV. Early in the new year, when the court was at Ipswich, the alliances were sealed. On 7 January the young count of Holland was married to Edward's daughter Elizabeth. The same day the treaty with the count of Flanders was ratified. At last, the king's grand strategy was coming to fruition. He now had landing grounds in the Low Countries; a new northern front against France could be opened up.[95]

But not without the money to pay for these new allies and the necessary English troops. A week after the royal wedding at Ipswich, the clergy assembled in London to formulate their final answer to the royal demand for tax. As before, Edward sent thuggish knights to intimidate them, with the warning that, if they did not pay, their goods would be seized anyway. The clergy debated for several days but, by 26 January, the king had heard of their decision. They said no.[96]

Edward's anger was predictably great, as all the chroniclers attest. What must have infuriated him more than anything was the clergy's failure to honour their earlier promise. As the royalist Peter Langtoft commented, 'promise is debt due, if faith be not forgotten'. The king, in response, certainly kept his word, and made good his earlier threat. On 30 January 1297 the clergy were outlawed. Royal agents moved in at once to seize ecclesiastical estates and all the food and livestock they contained. Other laymen, understanding that it was effectively open season on the Church, began to rob clergymen of their horses. Edward made it known that the Church could easily buy back his protection: the price would be the same as the tax they had denied him.[97]

According to one chronicler, Edward's intention was that the laity should pass judgement on the Church. As soon as he had heard of the clergy's refusal, the king had summoned a parliament to meet at Salisbury in one month's time. It was to be an entirely secular assembly – only the earls, barons and knights were invited.[98]

In the few weeks that followed, however, two crucial things happened. First, news arrived in England of a fresh military catastrophe in Gascony. The earl of Lincoln had led an army from Bayonne to the new bastide at Bonnegarde, but had been ambushed en route by the French. Large numbers of infantry had been killed and several knights taken prisoner, including John of St John. This defeat, English monks noted with grim satisfaction, had taken place on 30 January – the same day that the king had outlawed the clergy.[99]

The second occurrence was a sudden and dramatic spike in the incidence of prise. Once the November parliament had ended, Edward had reiterated his mandate for a mammoth seizure of goods. In readiness for the renewed effort against France, royal agents were told to grab supplies of grain totalling 60,000 tons.[100]

When Edward met with his magnates at Salisbury, therefore, the question of the outlawed clergy was no longer the only item on the agenda, nor even the main one. Even the greatest men who came to the assembly – men who could normally bribe royal officials to go away – were feeling the full weight of the war burden. Taxes were being exacted, with no talk of special pardons; profits from wool had plummeted to less than half their pre-war levels; royal officials were moving into aristocratic estates, arbitrarily seizing corn, oats and barley by the ton.[101]

The king realised all of this, but reckoned that the recovery of his Continental inheritance mattered more. News of the disaster at Bonnegarde had convinced him that, in addition to the army he intended to lead into northern France, more men would have to be sent to Gascony. After his arrival in Salisbury, in the closing days of February, he therefore asked his magnates, for what was now the third time, to go and fight in the duchy.

The magnates, like the clergy, now said no. 'One after the other,' explains Walter of Guisborough, 'they began to excuse themselves.' The protest at overseas service, a rumble in 1294, marginal in 1295, had finally become general, and spread to the highest echelons of the aristocracy. The earl of Arundel was once again among those who refused the king's order, but was now joined by his peers. The earl of Warwick, normally so loyal, was one such. With the earl of Lincoln pinned down in Gascony and the earl of Surrey preoccupied in Scotland, Edward found himself without any major support. In hopeful expectation, he turned to Roger Bigod, the earl of Norfolk, the most powerful figure present besides the king himself, and the man who had been so demonstrably willing to help when war had first been declared.

But Bigod too now said no. Like the other magnates, he had been hit hard by almost three years of continuous warfare – serving at his own expense in Wales and Scotland, while back in England his wool could not be sold and his grain was being seized. Like the others, however, he couched his objection in terms of non-obligation. As well as being earl of Norfolk, Bigod also bore the ancient title 'marshal of England': by hereditary right, it fell to him, along with the constable, to muster the king's armies and maintain their discipline. As such, he accepted that it was his responsibility to fight – but only with the king. The suggestion that he could be sent elsewhere to perform his duty he denied.

'I am not bound,' he told Edward, 'nor is it my will, to march without you.'

At this, says Guisborough, the king became enraged.

'By God, Earl,' he exclaimed, 'either you will go, or you will hang!'

'By the same oath,' replied Bigod, 'I will neither go, nor hang!'

And, to prove his point, the earl quit the court without leave. The other earls, Arundel and Warwick, followed in his wake, and were soon joined by Humphrey de Bohun, earl of Hereford and constable of England, who was apparently absent at the time of parliament. Their numbers, says Guisborough, grew into a multitude, and the king began to fear them.[102]

But, the chronicler added, he did not show it. In fact, as royal records attest, Edward reacted to the desertion of his earls with swift retaliation. On 1 March he attempted to limit the political fall-out from the row by denouncing as 'rumour-mongers' those who were trying to create discord between the king, his clergy and his barons. Around the same time he resurrected the abandoned, draconian scheme of 1294 and ordered the seizure of all the country's wool. Then, on 12 March, the gloves really came off, with an order for the immediate investigation of all debts to the Crown. Edward had broken Arundel before by calling in his debts; now, it seems, he was out to break all his earls in the same way. In the last week of March, royal officials arrived at Roger Bigod's manors, demanding hundreds of pounds in unpaid money. Obligation, the king's opponents were being forcibly reminded, could cut both ways.[103]

Throughout Lent, therefore, and for several weeks thereafter, the country was plunged into a state of high tension. Edward pressed on to Plymouth, where he remained for most of April, declaring to his officials that he would not leave until he had dispatched some help to Gascony. The earls, according to Walter of Guisborough, 'went off to their own lands, where they would not allow the king's servants to take either wool or hides, or anything whatsoever out of the ordinary'. Both sides, in other words, went to ground, waiting to see who would break first.[104]

During this time, the clergy crumpled. A month and more of hunger, humiliation and robbery had already taken its toll, and in February Edward had raised the stakes further, promising his churchmen that their outlawry and loss of land would be made permanent if they failed to settle by Easter. Accordingly, when the prelates, abbots and priors assembled in London at the end of March, they collectively petitioned their archbishop for a change of course. Winchelsea responded by allowing that each could follow his own conscience, at which point the stream of submissions to the king turned into a flood. Only the archbishop himself and a few diehard supporters continued to hold out, retiring to their dioceses and remaining quietly defiant.[105]

Even as the clergy collapsed, however, the magnates were reassembling and reaffirming their determination to resist. Around Eastertime, the four recalcitrant earls – Norfolk, Hereford, Arundel and Warwick – met in the woods near Montgomery and declared that they would not cross overseas with the king on account of the innumerable taxes that he had extorted from them. Economic hardship was, no doubt, their chief complaint, and would have played well with both the other men present, as well as the wider public. But it is also significant that the earls should have chosen to congregate in the March of Wales. To a greater or lesser degree, each of them was a Marcher lord and, in this capacity, had run up against Edward's increasingly masterful behaviour in recent years. This was most obviously true of Hereford, who cannot have forgotten his humiliating treatment at the king's hands in 1291. But Arundel, too, had latterly been forced to surrender part of his lordship of Clun, and charged with refusing to admit royal officials there. The same was true of Edmund Mortimer, son and successor of the famous Roger, who was also present at the Montgomery meeting. All these men shared the sense that the liberties won by their ancestors were being eroded for the benefit of an overbearing Crown. Now the government's grip was weakening, they saw an opportunity to restore things to their proper order.[106]

In the second week of May, aware of his opponents' machinations, Edward seized the initiative. Having said goodbye to whatever troops he had sent to Gascony, the king summoned a parliament to meet at Westminster in June. At the same time, orders went out for a muster in London the following month. No concessions were made: the controversial attempt to link service with landed wealth was resumed, and in even starker terms: now all men worth just £20 a year were enjoined to attend. Nor was there any indication of where they would be going, beyond the fact that it was 'overseas'. As he issued these orders, however, Edward was heading east along the Channel coast, towards Canterbury, almost certainly for talks with Winchelsea. Whatever else happened, the king did not want his clerical and lay opponents making common cause. The archbishop was accordingly conciliated: on 12 June his confiscated houses were restored.[107]

One week later and Edward was back in Westminster. It was his first appearance there since the conquest of Scotland, and the king marked his arrival by ostentatiously presenting the regalia of the vanquished kingdom before the shrine of the Confessor. The audience for this act, however, was considerably smaller than it had been for the parallel performance that had followed the conquest of Wales. Those men with Edward in June were his remaining royalist supporters. It was not until 7 July, the day of the controversial muster, that the opposition arrived.[108]

Both camps were cagey and cautious, communicating by messengers and exchange of letters, but it did not take long to get to the point. Would Norfolk and Hereford, in their capacities as marshal and constable, draw up the muster lists for the coming campaign? No, the earls replied, they would not: the king's summons had been both irregular and inadequate. Talks immediately broke down. Edward summarily deprived the two men of their hereditary posts and appointed others in their stead. He then made ready to arrest his opponents but, before he could do so, they once again withdrew from his court.[109]

Or at least some of them did. As opposition began to resemble out-and-out rebellion, resolve among the opposition began to crack. The earl of Warwick was probably the first to desert, allegedly bought off by the king, with whom he was in any case friends. John de Hastings, a Marcher lord who had attended the Montgomery meeting, soon went the same way. Arundel, too, was starting to waver, to judge from an undated letter he sent to Edward, pleading his case. The king, no doubt, was sending messages of his own to these men, making them individual offers, and working on their private fears.[110]

Edward's bid for support culminated with a public performance on Sunday, 14 July, when he appeared on a stage outside Westminster Hall and addressed the assembled crowds. Admitting that he had made mistakes and acknowledging his subjects' suffering, the king nevertheless asserted that he was acting for the good of the realm and the defence of his people. 'I am castle for you, and wall, and house,' Peter Langtoft has him say. It was powerful stuff, and well contrived: beside Edward on the stage stood a tearful Archbishop Winchelsea, to all appearances reconciled. The speech was also effectively an ultimatum, for the king, on the grounds that he might not return from France, went on to ask all those present to swear fealty to his son, the thirteen-year-old Edward of Caernarfon. The fact that Norfolk and Hereford could only do so two days later, and from a distance, left them looking isolated, their loyalty open to doubt.[111]

For two more weeks, the stand-off continued. The clergy, led by Winchelsea, tried to mediate. Edward's agents, more provocatively, invited the earls to submit to the king's grace. Norfolk and Hereford hit back with their own propaganda, denouncing the summons to serve overseas, the maltote, the heavy taxes, and the general arbitrary turn that royal government had recently taken.[112] Edward himself clearly hoped for reconciliation. Towards the end of July he left London for St Albans, in a last-ditch attempt to meet with his opponents. But, when it came down to it, the king was not prepared to compromise, and was running out of time. His allies on the Continent, bought at immense cost, were waiting. On 28 July he gave up, and sent out new writs, merely inviting men to serve him in return for wages. Two days later, back in London, orders went out for yet another seizure of wool. With a candour born of his growing desperation, Edward explained he needed £50,000 to pay his allies, and that grabbing 8,000 woolsacks from his subjects was the only way to get it. Payment would be made later, he promised, from the proceeds of a new tax – an eighth – that parliament had approved the same day. This, of course, was a nonsense. Parliament by this time was just the rump of royalists whom the king still had with him – 'the people stood about in his chamber,' as one chronicler contemptuously put it.[113]

As soon as these orders had been issued, Edward left London, heading for the coast. His destination was the new town of Winchelsea, where the fleet to transport his army was waiting to sail. But as he rode south, the fragile consensus around him began to collapse, splintering under the weight of this last load of arbitrary measures. On 10 August, as the king reached Winchelsea, the town's most famous son was holding an ecclesiastical council in London. The new tax was rejected as being incompatible with the pope's proclamation, and the archbishop ordered the excommunication of anyone who laid hands on Church property. A few days later messengers from the lay opposition rode to meet Edward, but he refused to hear their petitions. Instead, the king elected to fight fire with fire. On 20 August he decreed that the Church was to be taxed 'by royal authority'. The same day he prepared an answer for his opposition earls, ordering 170 armed knights to Rochester, a day's ride from the capital. The earls, however, struck first. On 22 August they burst into the exchequer at Westminster and forbade the seizure of wool and the collection of the eighth, saying they would not suffer to be tallaged like serfs.[114]

Two days later, and more than three years since the start of his war with France, Edward finally set sail for Flanders. He left behind him a country teetering on the brink. As the end of August approached, the regency government ordered more knights to muster at Rochester. In the March of Wales Hereford's men went about saying openly that their lord was against the king's peace. On Sunday, 1 September, Winchelsea began preaching the excommunication of royal officials from the pulpit of Canterbury Cathedral; as he did so, he was shouted down by royalist knights sent to stop him. The regents summoned a parliament to meet in London; the earls called a rival assembly to Northampton. Civil war seemed all but inevitable.[115]

Then news came out of the north. The English forces in Scotland had been defeated in open battle, with massive loss of life. The Devil had assumed a new guise, and his name was William Wallace.[116]

10

Uniting the Kingdom?

Few men living in the summer of 1297 were genuinely enthusiastic about the prospect of fighting in Flanders alongside Edward I, but John de Warenne, earl of Surrey, was a clear exception. All his life – and this year he would be sixty-six – the earl had been a staunch supporter of the Crown and the king's close friend.[1]

On this occasion, however, Warenne's anxiety to serve had less to do with his loyalism and more to do with avoiding the responsibility that had been foisted upon him the previous year. In 1296, true to form, he had marched with Edward against the Scots, and had led the English in their decisive victory at Dunbar. But the earl's reward for this feat had been his appointment as Scotland's new royal governor, and it was a role he clearly did not relish: within a few months he was actively offering the job to others. The king may have been well pleased to have rid himself of a turd, but his old friend was correspondingly dismayed to find himself charged with its custody. Warenne, in fact, behaved entirely as one might expect in such circumstances, and stayed as far away as possible, saying that the task was bad for his health. According to Walter of Guisborough, the earl found the Scottish weather so unbearably awful that he spent most of his time in the north of England.[2]

Inevitably, the absence of the governor had a deleterious effect on Scotland's new English government, which by 1297 was already struggling to cope with a host of additional problems. Imposed on the country against the will of its people, the regime was in any circumstances likely to have proved unpopular and been perceived as oppressive. As it was, thanks to the stream of emergency demands emanating from England, the administration was from the first a genuinely extortionate affair. The Scots, like the other peoples of Edward I's empire, were expected to supply the money and materials that would enable their overlord to prosecute his war against France. When, in May 1297, they were asked to supply the manpower as well, it proved to be the last straw: at that point unrest and resistance in Scotland boiled over into outright revolt. Trouble started in the west, at Lanark, where the English sheriff was killed.[3]

Behind this revolt, it seemed, lurked the usual suspects. One of the prime movers, for example, was Robert Wishart, the bulldog bishop of Glasgow, who six years earlier had stood up to Edward I at Norham. Also involved were several high-ranking members of the Scottish nobility, not all of whom had been captured or imprisoned during the English invasion the previous year. A surprising newcomer to their rebel ranks was the young earl of Carrick, Robert Bruce. Grandson of the late competitor for the throne, son of the disappointed collaborator of 1296, this third Robert might have been expected to toe the family line and aid the English, but instead he broke with ancestral tradition and threw his weight behind the patriotic cause. 'I must join my own people,' he reportedly told his father's knightly tenants, 'and the nation in which I was born.'[4]

Alas for the Scots, however, their aristocratic and ecclesiastical leaders once again proved stronger in their patriotism than they did in arms. Towards the end of June an English army crossed the Border from Cumbria, and within days the rebels were forced to surrender. On 7 July Wishart, Bruce and their allies submitted to terms at Irvine on Scotland's western seaboard. To the young English commanders who had obtained this easy victory, it seemed that was the end of the matter. They rode east to the government's base at Berwick, from where a letter was dispatched to the king a fortnight later. 'Sire,' it read, 'your enemies are dispersed and dismayed.'[5]

The author of this now-anonymous announcement was evidently not the new regime's treasurer, Hugh Cressingham. Unlike the military men fresh in from the field, or his boss, John de Warenne, who continued to linger in England, Cressingham worked in Berwick at the centre of the web. He could perceive the whole picture and, as he explained in his own letters to Edward, it was deeply alarming. 'By far the greater part of your counties in Scotland still have no keepers,' he said, 'because of death, sieges or imprisonment.' There were other rebels massing in the north, beyond the River Forth, and also in the south, in the Forest of Selkirk. Cressingham himself had wanted to march against them immediately – indeed, he had personally raised an army for this purpose – but had been out-voted. The consensus at Berwick was that they should wait for Warenne to arrive. 'And so,' the treasurer lamented as he drew to a close, 'matters have gone to sleep.'[6]

A picture of a king painted on the sedilia in Westminster Abbey in the early fourteenth century, and thus perhaps intended as a representation of Edward I.

ABOVE: Conwy Castle. On the hill in the distance, across the Conwy estuary,
are the ruins of Henry III's castle at Deganwy.
BELOW: Harlech Castle, and the mountains of Snowdonia.

ABOVE AND BELOW: Caernarfon, seen from across the River Seiont, and an aerial view of Beaumaris. Despite massive expenditure, neither castle was ever completed.

The Eleanor Cross at Geddington in Northamptonshire.

TOP: The gilded bronze effigy of Edward's beloved queen, Eleanor of Castile, in Westminster Abbey. LEFT: The Coronation Chair, before the Stone of Scone was removed in 1996.

ABOVE: The bastide of Monpazier in France, founded in 1285, was visited by Edward the following year, and is almost perfectly preserved, with many surviving medieval buildings and an arcaded marketplace at its centre. BELOW: Edward's new chamber at the Tower of London, recently restored to its original decorative scheme.

ABOVE: Caerlaverock Castle in Scotland (with a replica trebuchet), besieged by Edward in the summer of 1300. BELOW: Lanercost Priory in Cumbria, where an ailing Edward stayed for five months during the last year of his life.

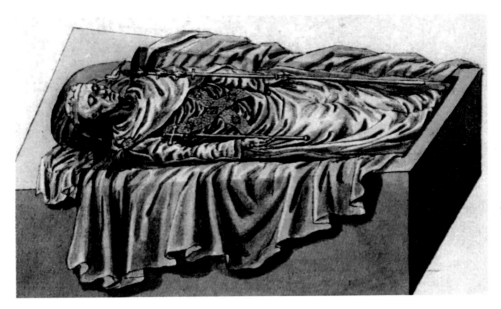

ABOVE: A drawing of Edward in his tomb at the time of its opening in 1774. He is wearing his coronation robes, but the crown on his head is a replica. BELOW: Edward's tomb in Westminster Abbey, showing its famous inscription, and the shrine of Edward the Confessor behind.

While the English slumbered, the Scots were indeed being roused. Those in the north were led by Andrew Murray, the son and heir of a prominent local lord. Captured the previous year at Dunbar, he had escaped during the winter and raised rebellion in the spring. By August a number of northern towns and castles were already in his hands.[7]

Meanwhile, in the south, leadership had been assumed by a certain William Wallace. Unlike Murray, Wallace was a virtual nobody – nothing at all is heard of him before this juncture, bar a possible reference in a court roll of 1296 which mentions 'William le Waleys, a thief'. When, the following year, he bursts unheralded into the picture, he is described by English chroniclers as 'a bloody man', 'a chief of brigands', 'a vagrant and a fugitive'. Most likely he was a younger son of Alan Wallace, a minor landowner in Ayrshire; such origins would account for the fact that his earliest activities were concentrated in western Scotland. The death of the sheriff of Lanark in May 1297 had been his handiwork, and thereafter he appears to have based himself in Selkirk Forest with his growing band of followers. 'The common folk of the land followed him as their leader and ruler,' wrote Walter of Guisborough, 'the retainers of great lords adhered to him.' By August 1297 Wallace and his popular army had moved into northern Scotland, where they linked arms with Murray's forces.[8]

By this point, finally, John de Warenne had arrived in Berwick and been convinced by a no doubt frantic Cressingham of the urgent need for military action. There was yet more delay while they waited for those Scots who had surrendered at Irvine to complete their submissions (a process that was deliberately drawn out by the likes of Wishart and Bruce). But at last, probably as the end of August approached, the English army and its reluctant captain set out to crush the Scottish rebels.[9]

To do so they had to enter northern Scotland, and that meant crossing the River Forth – a feat easier said than done. The Forth rises in the west, near Loch Lomond, and flows east to meet the sea, thus effectively cutting the country in half. Moreover, for much of its eastern length it forms a broad tidal estuary, or firth, which could not be crossed except by boat. In fact, in the thirteenth century the Forth was referred to as 'the Scottish Sea', and on contemporary maps, northern Scotland was designated as *Scotia ultra Marina* – Scotland beyond the Sea.[10]

Warenne therefore marched his army towards the first place that the Forth could be bridged, which at that time was the royal burgh at Stirling. As the principal gateway between northern and southern Scotland, Stirling had a unique strategic importance (indeed, on one thirteenth-century map, the town's bridge is shown as the *only* link between the two halves of the country). It was also a brilliantly defended gateway: half a mile from the bridge, on the river's southern shore, stood Stirling Castle. Nothing survives of the original medieval fortress, but it was almost certainly built of stone, and (like its latter-day replacement) rendered all but impregnable from its situation atop a great outcrop of volcanic rock.

When the earl arrived at Stirling in early September he discovered that Wallace and Murray were waiting for him on the opposite side of the Forth. By all accounts the Scots were greatly outnumbered, and thus the English commanders naturally assumed that, as at Irvine, their enemies would wish to negotiate. On this occasion, however, the negotiators were turned away with a celebrated rebuke. 'Go back and tell your people that we have not come for the benefit of peace,' said Wallace, 'but are ready to fight, to avenge ourselves, and to free our kingdom.'

According to Walter of Guisborough, who preserved these attributed words, this was invitation enough for the more hot-headed in the English camp. But wiser heads, the chronicler added, had surveyed the surrounding terrain and foreseen the danger. The bridge, their only way forward, was also their major obstacle, for it was only wide enough for men to cross in two-by-two formation. In addition, there was not much room to manoeuvre once they reached the other side. At Stirling the Forth meanders in large, lazy loops, and consequently the northern end of the bridge connects not to an open plain but to a narrow tongue of land. 'There was no better place in the kingdom of Scotland,' Guisborough was later told, 'to put the English into the hands of the Scots – the many into the hands of the few.'

Nevertheless, in the final council of war, the voices of caution were overruled. Cressingham, conscious of the enormous daily cost of fielding the army, argued for an immediate advance. Warenne, once woken from a long lie-in, agreed, and the order was duly given. It was late in the morning of 11 September 1297, and events that day unfolded with all the inevitability that had been predicted. The English began to cross the bridge and array themselves on the northern shore, but were attacked while their host was only half-formed. The Scots rushed towards the river, seized the bridgehead and so divided their enemies. Those English who had already crossed – Cressingham was among their number – were surrounded and killed. Those stranded on the southern shore – who included Warenne – could only watch the slaughter as it happened. Eventually the earl came to his senses, ordered the bridge to be destroyed, and rode hard in the direction of England. From Stirling to Berwick it is nearly a hundred miles. The old man, says Guisborough, did not rest until he reached the Border.[11]

As Warenne's forces were being wiped out by Wallace and the Scots, the greatest political crisis that England had faced for thirty years was also fast approaching its apparently unavoidable climax. A parliament had been summoned for the end of September, but it seemed that the time for talking had already passed. Royalist knights were assembling at Rochester in Kent to strengthen the hand of the regency government, and the regents themselves, nominally led by the thirteen-year-old Edward of Caernarfon, had moved from Westminster to within the walls of London, 'on account of the danger of sedition'. Their fear was readily understandable. On 21 September, the aggrieved earls of Norfolk and Hereford, Roger Bigod and Humphrey de Bohun, met with their supporters at Northampton, and found that they were many. Guisborough, with some exaggeration, estimated that they had 1,500 horse, and also added that they had a large force of foot.[12]

But by this date, if not before, news of Stirling Bridge had arrived in London, and immediately the situation was transformed. A disaster on this scale demanded a united response and made it imperative that the government settle with the opposition. Obtaining a settlement still took some time: the earls, fearing a trap, refused to enter the capital until their own guards had been posted on the gates. At length, however, thanks to the mediation of Archbishop Winchelsea, an agreement was reached, and the threat of civil war was averted.[13]

The basis of the agreement was Magna Carta, the 'great charter' famously wrung from King John over eight decades before. That the earls and the regents should have turned to such an apparently distant precedent might seem surprising, but in fact their response was entirely to be expected. For one thing, the political situation in 1297 was in many respects similar to that of 1215. King John had fought an unpopular war against France and made intolerable demands on his subjects in order to pay for it. Taxation had been heavy and unreasonably frequent; military service had been demanded overseas; political opponents had been broken by distraining them for debt. The circumstances that had produced Magna Carta, in short, were almost identical to those that had produced the current crisis.[14]

There was, however, a more obvious reason why men in 1297 should regard the ancient charter as the answer to their present woes, which was that, during those eight intervening decades, it had become the touchstone of good government. Throughout the reign of Henry III the rebel manifesto of 1215, revised somewhat in favour of the Crown, had been repeatedly confirmed and reissued. The same was true of a subsidiary document developed to deal with the highly contentious jurisdiction known as the Royal Forest. Together, the Great Charter and the Forest Charter had become the best known and most totemic of all royal promises, and hence the usual first recourse at times of political contention. Whenever folk felt that their rights and liberties were under threat, the cry would go up for 'the Charters'. For the same reason, if the government could see no other way out of a crisis, a regrant of 'the Charters' could be offered as a popular panacea.[15]

This, indeed, had been the scenario earlier in 1297. When, in July, the earls had drawn up a written statement of their grievances (the so-called Remonstrances), they had complained that Magna Carta was being neglected 'to the great loss of the people' and that the Forest Charter was 'not kept as it used to be in the past'. Edward, around the same time, had offered to confirm both Charters in return for a new grant of taxation.[16]

On this occasion, however, the king's opponents clearly felt that the Charters, while important, would not by themselves be enough. The Remonstrances also complained about the extortionate levels of prise, and the punitive 'maltote' on wool – matters for which Magna Carta, because of its age, offered no remedy. Nor did the Charter have anything helpful to say about taxation. For decades it had been assumed – and Edward I had done much to encourage the assumption – that tax could be collected by the Crown only if consent had been given by parliament. But in 1297, much to the anger of his opponents, the king had imposed a levy of an eighth, having obtained nothing more than the approval of 'the people who stood about in his chamber'.[17]

When, therefore, they sat down to negotiate in the autumn, the earls demanded – and received – more up-to-date assurances. Although the agreement they reached with the regents became known as 'the Confirmation of the Charters' (*Confirmatio Cartarum*), it actually included several new clauses, which promised that the maltote would be abolished altogether, and accepted that any future prise or taxation could be taken only 'with the common assent of the realm'. These were major concessions, and met most of the opposition's demands. The government's only victory lay in having moderated some of the language, and in having kept the new clauses separate and distinct from Magna Carta itself. Nevertheless, the regents could also feel pleased with the deal they had struck, for it re-established the much-needed political consensus. When the Confirmation of the Charters was sealed on 10 October, the mutual feeling was one of immense relief. Soon afterwards parliament gave the necessary 'common assent' for a new tax, and the magnates agreed that together they would set out against the Scots. 'Everyone was glad that day,' wrote Walter of Guisborough, adding that Edward of Caernarfon and his counsellors 'remitted to the earls and their followers all rancour of spirit and ill will'.[18]

But all of this, of course, depended on the approval of their absent king.

Edward had landed safely in Flanders six weeks earlier, but thereafter his fortunes had resumed their familiar downward trajectory. Soon after their landing his troops had fallen to fighting among themselves, further reducing the strength of an already inadequate army. Some of his allies, he discovered, had been defeated by the French the previous week; others meanwhile, despite the enormous sums they had been paid, had not yet materialised. The count of Flanders himself had turned out, and had escorted the English to Bruges, but the locals there had proved altogether less welcoming, and the threat of insurrection had forced the king and his host to flee to the more defensible city of Ghent, where they had remained ever since. Edward, it is true, had succeeded in putting some pressure on Philip IV: his ally and son-in-law, the count of Bar, had led some Welsh troops on plundering raids into French territory. As one chronicler attests, however, 'the king was surrounded by perils'. It must have come as a considerable relief when, on 9 October, the French agreed to a two-month truce.[19]

Nevertheless, Edward was not about to abandon his Continental campaign, nor was he going to be distracted by events back home. By the time the truce was sealed, for example, he must have known of Warenne's defeat at Stirling Bridge, yet when he wrote to the regents a week later, it was to urge them to send more money to Flanders, so that his still-absent German allies might be induced to appear. Soon after this (for news could travel between London and Flanders in under a week) he must have been presented with the deal that had been reached in England. It can hardly have pleased him. Before leaving for Flanders his own attitude towards his opponents had been uncompromising; now, it seemed, he was expected not only to bow to their demands but also to forgive them their trespasses. According to Walter of Guisborough, the king hesitated for three days before eventually making his decision, but in reality there was only one viable option. The Scots, he knew from experience, could easily be subdued at some later date; similarly, he could revisit the debate with his English subjects when circumstances were more propitious. But for the time being, it was imperative that he should keep up the pressure on Philip IV, for otherwise Gascony might be lost forever. The truce with France had only one month left to run. On 5 November, therefore, Edward did what expediency dictated and ratified the Confirmation of the Charters. As his messengers departed to carry his sealed approval back to England, the king looked expectantly to the east for the arrival of his German allies.[20]

While the political leaders of England laboured to resolve their differences, their countrymen in the north had been left exposed to unaccustomed suffering and terror. The Scots had followed up their victory at Stirling Bridge with assaults on every town and stronghold in southern Scotland; by early October only a few embattled outposts, such as the castles at Berwick and Roxburgh, still remained in English hands. By this date, too, the people of northern England had already been sent into a panic by sporadic Scottish raids. Yet worse was still to come. In early November William Wallace – now in sole command following the death of Andrew Murray from wounds sustained at Stirling – led his army across the Border and subjected the populations of Cumbria and Northumbria to a harrying on a scale they had not experienced in living memory. 'In all the monasteries and churches between Newcastle and Carlisle,' wrote Walter of Guisborough, 'the service of God totally ceased, for all the canons, monks and priests fled before the Scots, as did nearly all the people.' Carlisle itself came under siege, and at the nearby priory of Lanercost the chronicler accused the invaders of indulging in 'arson, pillage and murder'. The fury of the Scots was soon spent – by the end of November they had returned home, laden with spoil – but the devastation they had caused was long remembered, and served to cement Wallace's reputation in England as a bloodthirsty bogeyman.[21]

As the north burned, significant developments were occurring on other fronts. Back in Westminster, the regents had received the king's ratification, and the earls had resolved to march against the Scots. In Flanders, meanwhile, there had been a discreet but dramatic shift away from the idea of military action. Edward had now learned that his principal ally, the king of Germany, would definitely not be joining him, and this intelligence dashed any hopes of mounting a major campaign against France. As he explained in his letters home, the truce had lately been extended for three more months, and the plan now was to push for a permanent peace. This, however, meant it was even more imperative that he should *seem* strong in the coming weeks, and the king therefore concluded by instructing his regents to send additional troops over from England in advance of the final negotiations.[22]

Thus, as the tumultuous year 1297 drew to a close, the atmosphere everywhere was one of anxious anticipation. The earls and barons of England readied themselves to ride north, and the Scots steeled themselves for the oncoming assault. In Wales large numbers of men were recruited to provide the English with the necessary infantry, and in Flanders their king waited to see whether the essential diplomatic breakthrough could be achieved.[23]

For Edward, the anxiety ended on 28 January 1298, when an agreement with France was finally reached. Under its terms, both sides agreed to suspend hostilities for a further two years, and to put their quarrel over Gascony to the judgement of the pope. If this was not the permanent peace that the English king had hoped for, it was nevertheless about as good a deal as he could reasonably expect in the circumstances. His legal and moral case for retaining the duchy was likely to be far more persuasive than the distinctly limited military pressure he had been struggling to apply for the past three-and-a-half years. In the immediate term, moreover, the new truce meant that he could stand down his forces in Flanders and return home: a week after it was sealed, the king ordered a hundred ships to come and carry him back to England.[24]

A ceasefire with France also meant a rethink for Scotland. As soon as the truce was in place, Edward sent letters postponing the planned invasion until his return. On the face of it this was a terrible waste of resources: by the time the royal messengers arrived, the English army, 16,000 men strong, had already relieved Roxburgh and Berwick, and was just about to advance into the Scottish interior. From the king's point of view, however, it was more important that he should lead the assault in person. An under-resourced or ill-commanded effort (and, though Edward can hardly have known it, the earls' army was already facing shortages) ran the risk of another failure and that was a completely unconscionable prospect. By the same token, the thought of victory being achieved in his absence was not an altogether happy one either. The diminished army now paused on the Border was composed in large part of men who had opposed him the previous year, and he did not wish to hand these individuals any further political advantage. When Edward returned from Flanders – he landed at Sandwich on 14 March 1298 – it was with a determination to reassert his authority not only in Scotland, but in England as well.[25]

But Scotland had to come first, which meant that for the time being the king had to continue to appease his English critics. Roger Bigod and Humphrey de Bohun were equally determined to defend the guarantees of good government they had obtained the previous year, and so the parliament that was summoned for York at the end of May could well have proved contentious. (It would be the first occasion that Bigod and Edward had stood face to face since their row at Salisbury fifteen months earlier.) In the event, though, the meeting seems to have passed without incident; it may have helped that, immediately after his return, as was his wont, the king had launched a major inquiry into ministerial abuse. Soon the assembly at York was over, and an ostensibly united English army rode out from the city to deal with the Scots. Some suspicion still lingered within their ranks. As they rode north, Bigod and Bohun heard it whispered that Edward was secretly planning to disregard the Confirmation of the Charters on the grounds that his ratification had been given overseas; when they reached the Border, the earls refused to go further without reassurances that this was not the case. Once again, the king adopted a conciliatory line, and induced four other magnates to swear on his soul that, once the Scots had been defeated, he would address his critics' concerns. Bigod and Bohun declared themselves satisfied, and the army began its advance.[26]

It was massive. The infantry alone, as their pay rolls attest, amounted to almost 26,000 men; the cavalry, numbering perhaps as many as 3,000, was also mightily impressive. Clearly, Edward had been wise to postpone: the French truce had not only allowed him to redeploy his forces from Flanders; the spring had also witnessed the return of the English veterans from Gascony, led by the earl of Lincoln, who now rejoined the king. Patriotism, too, goes some way to explaining the large cavalry numbers, for the English military classes burned to avenge Stirling Bridge. The main reason, however, for the exceptionally high turnout probably lay in the nature of the campaign, as confirmed in the recent parliament. The Scottish nobility – many of whom had been released in return for fighting in Flanders – had also been summoned to appear at York. But inevitably they had failed to do so, and as a result had been declared disinherited. The English were setting out, said Peter Langtoft, 'to take vengeance, and to deprive the Scots of land and tenement'. This, in other words, was not a punitive campaign like that of 1296, intended to bring errant vassals back into line: it was a new war of conquest, of the kind that had led to the carve-up of Wales. Victory in Scotland now held out to the English aristocracy the enticing prospect of rich and (to judge from Dunbar) easy pickings. They had been summoned to fight by virtue of their fealty, but they turned out in great numbers in expectation of gain.[27]

Before this redistribution of wealth could occur, however, there was a dragon to be slain in the form of the Scottish army and its undisputed leader, William Wallace (or rather *Sir* William Wallace, for the people's champion had since been knighted and named as his country's sole Guardian until John Balliol could be restored). The only problem lay in locating the beast. As the English advanced into Scotland, burning and wasting as they went, no sign of the enemy was seen, and no intelligence could be had. After a week of fruitless provocation they paused at Kirkliston, a few miles west of Edinburgh, where supplies were expected by sea. But another week passed with no word of Wallace and, worse still, no food from England. Contrary winds prevented the majority of ships from getting through; those that did arrive were mostly carrying wine. Drunken fighting soon broke out between the English and Welsh infantry, and the latter withdrew, threatening to side with the Scots. According to Guisborough, Edward showed only cool disdain, saying, 'Who cares if our enemies joined together? We shall beat them both in a day.' But there could be no disguising the fact that his campaign had run into serious difficulty.

Then, suddenly, on the morning of 21 July, the longed-for news arrived. The king was about to retire to Edinburgh to reconsider his strategy when a spy reported that the Scots were just twenty miles to the west, readying themselves to attack the English army as it retreated. 'Praise God, who up to now has delivered me from all difficulties,' said Edward. 'They shan't have to follow me, for I shall go to meet them this very day.'[28]

It was not, in fact, until the dawn of the next day that the king finally caught up with his quarry, whose spears were spotted on high ground close to the town of Falkirk. For the English this brought a welcome end to weeks of uncertainty, and an especially restless twenty-four hours. They had spent the previous night camped at nearby Linlithgow in fearful expectation of a Scottish ambush: every rider – including Edward himself – had slept on the ground next to his standing horse ('with their shields as pillows,' said Guisborough, 'and their armour as bedclothes'). For one fraught moment it had seemed that their foes were indeed upon them; a rumour that the king had been wounded had caused an abortive rush to arms. Edward, it turned out, *had* been hurt in the night, but by rather more prosaic means. His horse, carelessly kept by its groom, had trodden on him.[29]

Now, in the clear light of day, it was apparent that the Scots had abandoned all thought of ambush; in the distance they could be seen arraying themselves ready for battle. To compensate for his inferior numbers, Wallace had adopted a defensive strategy. His army was drawn up on the side of a small hill, at the foot of which ran an insubstantial stream. His greatest asset, the massed pikemen of his infantry, were arranged in four great circular brigades, or 'schiltroms', as the Scots called them. With their bristling spears turned outwards, these giant hedgehogs would give the foot soldiers a fighting chance against a cavalry charge. Nestled between them for protection were the archers of Selkirk Forest, while the Scottish cavalry were stationed at the rear. Both these contingents, however, were tiny in comparison with their English counterparts.[30]

The strength of Wallace's formation is well attested by the reaction of his opponent. Edward, when advised of it, was inclined to be cautious: superiority in numbers only counted for so much. The last time he had charged uphill at a supposedly inferior foe, the result had been a disastrous defeat. That, of course, had been at Lewes, well over three decades earlier, and was, to be fair, his first taste of battle. But when one remembers that the king's most recent battlefield experience was the almost equally distant engagement at Evesham, the reason for his caution becomes even more apparent. Edward was now in his sixtieth year; his hair, once blond, had turned to snowy white. In general terms he was in remarkably robust health, but on this particular morning, thanks to his night-time mishap, he was nursing two broken ribs. Having arrived at Falkirk, he proposed pitching camp, and allowing his tired and hungry troops to feed themselves and their horses. His commanders, however, would have none of it: hesitation, they argued, would leave them once again exposed to attack. The king in due course agreed. The order to advance was given, and the Battle of Falkirk began.[31]

At first, Wallace's strategy seemed as if it might well work. The first line of the English cavalry, led by the earls of Norfolk, Hereford and Lincoln, thundered towards the Scots, but immediately ran into difficulty. The little stream they had dismissed as an insubstantial obstacle in fact fed a much larger area of boggy marsh, which halted their headlong charge and sent them veering to the left. The second line, commanded by the bishop of Durham, swerved right to avoid the same pitfall. It soon became apparent, however, that these initial diversions had done the Scots no favours. The marsh, while protecting them from a frontal assault, had merely forced their opponents to attack from the sides, and the Scots now found themselves caught in a pincer. Their schiltroms, as expected, were highly successful in deterring the English cavalry, but this simply meant that the cavalry concentrated on the softer target presented by the Scottish archers. Eventually the schiltroms stood alone, at which point the English infantry unleashed a hail of stones and arrows, which ultimately caused so many casualties among the spearmen that they broke ranks. Seeing that their enemies had lost their defensive advantage, the English cavalry rode back in, and the Scottish slaughter was complete.[32]

The Scottish cavalry – that is, the Scottish nobility – had fled at the start of the battle. ('Without a sword's blow,' said Guisborough, derisively.) This has given rise to the pernicious but persistent myth that they secretly despised Wallace as a common upstart, and were actually in league with Edward I. As we have already seen, nothing could be further from the truth. The nobles of Scotland had from the first defied the English king and were quite ready to resist him. What separated them from the unfortunate archers and infantry at Falkirk was not their commitment to the patriotic cause, but their ability to flee when they realised that defeat was inevitable. We should not be too quick to condemn as cowards men who faced such overwhelming odds: it was massive numbers and superior firepower, not treachery, that led to the English victory. Nor should we pretend that the behaviour of the Scottish cavalry in any way divided them from their general. Wallace too escaped from Falkirk – presumably on the back of a horse.[33]

The decision of the Scottish nobles to flee the field, far from condemning their country to defeat, in fact proved to be its saving grace. Had they been captured at Falkirk, as they had been at Dunbar two years before, resistance would have come to a swift end. As it was, their flight meant that the recent battle, although extremely bloody, was quite indecisive. Edward had succeeded only in killing a lot of Scottish commoners (and, to judge from the sudden drop in his infantry wages, a lot of English ones as well). Irritatingly, he now had no choice but to conduct a massive manhunt. The king therefore dismissed his surviving foot soldiers and set out with his cavalry to catch the Scottish fugitives.[34]

His first target (after the castle at Stirling, which fell in a fortnight) was Robert Bruce. It is not known whether the young earl was among the Scottish nobles at Falkirk (frustratingly, very few of their names are known), but certainly Edward's decision to pursue Bruce destroys the fanciful notion that he had fought on the English side. When, in August, the king and his men rode west into Bruce's earldom of Carrick, it was with the clear hope of capturing a man whom they regarded as one of the main leaders of Scottish resistance. Once again, however, their quarry eluded them. By the time they reached the west-coast town of Ayr, Bruce had burned his castle there and disappeared. Once again, the English ran into difficulties when their fleet failed to make the appointed rendezvous. After a week of waiting in vain, the king was forced to cut short his operations. Plans to move into Galloway were abandoned, and the cavalry instead rode down Annandale, seizing the Bruce castle of Lochmaben, but heading in the direction of England.[35]

The flight of his enemies, the lack of supplies – these were both serious problems. But what finally crippled Edward's campaign was an argument with his earls over the spoils of war. The English magnates had set out for Scotland excited at the prospect of acquiring new estates, but at the same time anxious to ensure that the redistribution was equitable. After the conquest of Wales the king had given a lot of land to his closest friends (for example, the earls of Surrey and Lincoln), but to others (notably Norfolk and Hereford) he had given nothing at all. For this reason, it seems, Bigod and Bohun had obtained a royal guarantee that, on this occasion, no grants would be made without their prior approval. As the army retreated from Ayrshire, however, Edward revealed how little store he set by this promise when he spontaneously awarded the Isle of Arran to an Irish adventurer called Hugh Bisset. Bigod and Bohun were stunned, and seem to have concluded that, although they had fought in the first line at Falkirk, they were once again going to be last in line for reward. At the start of September, when the army reached Carlisle, they made their excuses and left for home.[36]

Realising his mistake, Edward endeavoured to repair the damage. A few days after the departure of the earls and their followers, he began doling out Scottish estates to those men who still remained with him. Naturally, loyalists such as Lincoln were generously rewarded. But, says Guisborough, the king kept some land in reserve lest he should anger those who had already left, and the chronicler's comments find echo in royal letters sent out a week or so later, in which Edward tactfully promised to put his magnates in possession of the property he had granted 'or had intended to grant them'. But all of this smacked of closing the stable door after the horse had bolted. For years afterwards, to judge from comments made by Peter Langtoft, men would go about saying that the redistribution of estates in Scotland had been unfair. An opportunity had existed to give a large number of Englishmen a vested interest in completing the conquest of Scotland, but the king had foolishly squandered it.[37]

The campaign of 1298 was clearly at an end, but Scotland was nowhere near subjugated. With the country's native leaders still at large, there was no hope of re-imposing the kind of civilian administration that had temporarily held sway in 1296 and 1297. English power in Scotland was now limited to the castles captured during the summer – Edward's last action in the autumn on 1298 was to march the remaining rump of his army along the Border to take the castle at Jedburgh. When the king quit Scotland in October, he left behind him a military occupation of isolated garrisons, with all the danger and expense that that implies. It was his hope that this fragile structure would survive until the following summer, but within just a few weeks he was advised that his positions in Scotland were coming under renewed attack. A frustrating fortnight spent at Newcastle in November failed to get any help to the beleaguered English troops at Stirling. At the end of the year Edward rode south knowing that only another full-scale invasion would suffice.[38]

The king's return to England, however, refocused attention on the solemn promise he had made at the start of the summer: namely, that he would satisfy his subjects that he was sincere in his wish to uphold Magna Carta, the Forest Charter and the other concessions he had granted the previous year. Edward might well have argued that, having ratified them in Flanders, he had already given his word. Unfortunately, though, on one particular issue, his subjects felt that he had already broken it.

The issue in question concerned the Royal Forest, which, as we have already noted, was a deeply resented institution. The term itself is misleading to modern ears, for it suggests little more than a few areas of woodland set aside for the king's personal use: such indeed, had been the Forest's original function. But in the twelfth century the scope of the Forest had been massively extended, to include vast swathes of the English countryside, both wooded and unwooded. It is an oft-repeated but nonetheless impressive fact that almost all of Essex was officially designated as 'Forest'.

The reason for this expansion was financial. The Royal Forest was governed by its own law, and anyone caught breaking it – by killing a deer, for example, or by cutting down a tree – was liable to be fined. It did not matter that such infringements might be committed by individuals on their own lands within the Forest. Nor did transgressors have much in the way of legal recourse if caught. The Forest was an arbitrary jurisdiction that stood completely apart from the rest of the judicial system. The king and his foresters could impose fines, and even death, entirely at will.[39]

It is easy to understand, therefore, why people would wish to have the running of the Royal Forest regulated – hence the Forest Charter – and easier still to see why they would wish to escape it altogether. The very first clause of the Charter held out just such a tantalising prospect, for it promised that the extent of the Forest would be reviewed. 'Good and law-worthy men,' to use the Charter's own words, would walk or ride through the Forest to determine what its original bounds had been prior to the later expansions. Contemporaries coined a name for this inspection process: they called it a perambulation.[40]

Having regranted the Forest Charter in 1297, Edward could reasonably be regarded as bound by the same promise. Indeed, during his absence in Flanders, his regents had gone so far as to order a perambulation of the Forest soon after they had confirmed the Charters. The king himself, on the other hand, had been suspiciously noncommittal. According to Walter of Guisborough, he had promised a new perambulation to his critics in May 1298 as part of his wider effort to quell public concerns on the eve of his march to Scotland. Since then, however, there had been a notable silence. The closest Edward had come to addressing the issue had been his appointment in November of commissioners to look into the offences committed by his Forest officials – an act that fell far short of public expectations.[41]

This royal procrastination was not entirely capricious. As far as the king was concerned, there was simply no need for a perambulation to take place, for the good reason that it had already happened when the Forest Charter had first been issued. In 1225 the teams of 'good and law-worthy men' had carried out their task, and Henry III had duly conceded that large areas of Royal Forest should no longer be classed as such. Edward was therefore happy to confirm the Forest Charter, but he regarded its opening clauses – that is, those promising a peram- bulation – as redundant.

Unfortunately for the king, the issue was not quite so cut-and-dried as he believed (or pretended). A perambulation had indeed been performed in 1225, and the extent of the Forest had been reduced in line with the perambulators' findings. But, just two years later, Henry III had arbitrarily reclaimed certain areas as Forest. It was all a long time in the past, but local communities tended to have elephantine memories when it came to such executive injustices, and now believed that the moment had come to settle a long-standing score with the king's government.[42] Moreover, it was not just the inhabitants of debat- able areas of Forest that viewed the issue as important. Edward's failure to proceed with a new perambulation by the end of 1298 raised serious questions about his general trustworthiness, and this touched everyone. The king had solemnly sworn to uphold Magna Carta and the Forest Charter – documents that, seventy years after their original publica- tion, had attained the status of semi-sacred texts. Any attempt to re- interpret their contents in the Crown's favour, no matter how cogently argued, was bound to create a world of trouble.

Edward appears to have been blithely unaware of the storm that was brewing. When, in early February 1299, he summoned a parliament to Westminster, it was professedly in order to obtain advice about Gascony. (Happily, the pope had ruled that the duchy should be returned to English control, but the French had as yet to agree to the details.) The king might perhaps have imagined that the opposition would have been diminished by the death of Humphrey de Bohun. The outspoken earl had died on the last day of December, to be succeeded by his name-sake son, but only in the tenurial sense: there is no good evidence to suggest that the new, twenty-two-year-old earl of Hereford adopted his father's confrontational political stance.[43]

If Edward was counting on quiet, however, then he was quickly dis-appointed. When parliament met in March there was, in Guisborough's words, 'great contention'. The opposition, now led solely by Roger Bigod, remained strong in voice and in number, and demanded that the king honour his much-repeated promise to confirm the Charters. Edward's unpreparedness is suggested by his uncharacteristically flustered response. After several days of fruitless debate, he guaranteed his critics an answer on the morrow, but then slipped out of the city in secret at dawn the next day. When his exasperated opponents caught up with him at Harrow, the king blamed his sudden exit on Westminster's noxious air and again assured them of an answer if they would return to London.[44]

The response, when it finally came, provoked outrage. Edward re-issued the Charters, but it soon transpired that he had tampered with their contents. Not only had he added a catch-all reservation, 'saving the rights of our Crown', he had also deliberately omitted the first five clauses of the Forest Charter – those that promised a perambulation and the reduction of the Royal Forest. At this, says Guisborough, parlia-ment broke up, and the king's critics returned to their own parts un-pacified. Meanwhile, in the streets of the capital, Edward's revisions came close to provoking a riot. On 2 April the city's governors were ordered 'to arrest, try and punish persons congregating by day and night, and speaking ill of the king'.[45]

Realising that he still had a major struggle on his hands, Edward ordered parliament to reassemble the following month, and in the meantime took steps to counter his critics. From the first the oppo-sition had enjoyed the support of the citizens of London, who still resented the king's decision in 1285 to strip them of their ancient rights of self-government. This support had been mutual: while Edward had been in Flanders, Bigod and Bohun had presumed to relax the Crown's control of the city, and had ordered the royal warden 'to bear himself in all things as if he were mayor'. Now, a fortnight before parliament was due to resume, the king made his own bid for London's support. On 17 April – Good Friday – he formally restored the city's ancient liberties. Even then, he took no chances. Although parliament had been summoned to Westminster, its deliberations in the event took place at Stepney, to the east of the city – an attempt, perhaps, to avoid a repetition of the earlier civic unrest.[46]

But the dissension continued. Bigod returned to London, said one chronicler, accompanied by a thousand horse, evidently determined to hold Edward to account. The king, though, still refused to give ground, and the opposition were again 'exasperated by his irritable and empty words and prevarications'. When the session ended a fortnight later, it seems clear that nothing had been resolved. Edward left for Dover, in order to oversee the dispatch of ambassadors to France. Bigod, meanwhile, went west to the Welsh Marches, and his great castle at Chepstow, where engineers had been working through the winter to add giant crossbows to the top of the main tower. Others evidently returned home from parliament and began to voice their discontent. Now it was not just London but the whole country that was speaking ill of the king, saying openly that he did not intend to keep the Charters.[47]

With his subjects everywhere railing against him, Edward had no choice but to cave in to his critics' demands. On 25 June he issued an extraordinary propaganda letter, promising that a new perambulation of the Forest would begin in the autumn, and announcing that men had already been appointed to perform the task. Disingenuously, he blamed his opponents for the delays to date, and begged people not to believe the rumours that were circulating about his attitude towards the Charters. It was a remarkable declaration, not least for the efforts taken to publicise it, which in turn reveal the extent to which the royal credibility was felt to have collapsed. The king's officials were told not only to proclaim the letters in towns and villages, but also to take with them 'some worthy person of religion' for the purpose. In Worcester, at least, the proclamation was made in English – 'the mother tongue', as the local chronicler called it.[48]

A few days later Edward's fortunes were notably improved, albeit on a different front. By the end of June his ambassadors were back from France with the news of a diplomatic breakthrough. A treaty had been agreed with Philip IV that would lead to a permanent peace and the restoration of Gascony, and it was to be cemented in the conventional manner. Edward's son, the fifteen-year-old Edward of Caernarfon, was to be married to Philip's daughter, Isabella. Since, however, the princess was only three years old, their wedding would have to wait for some years. In the meantime, there was to be a more immediate match. Edward himself would marry Philip's sister, Margaret – sufficiently mature at seventeen, though perhaps not thrilled at the thought of being led to the altar to a man more than three times her age.[49]

But with the possible exception of Margaret, everyone was much happier at the end of the summer than they had been at the start. The king's climbdown on the perambulation, the joyous event of his marriage, the prospect of a lasting French peace: all this combined to cool the political temperature at the English court. When the bride-to-be arrived at Dover on 8 September, the welcome party that met her off the boat was led not only by Edward of Caernarfon, but also by Roger Bigod, recently returned from his two-month sojourn in the March. Similarly, when the wedding ceremony took place two days later, it was performed at the door of the Canterbury Cathedral by the king's other long-standing critic, Archbishop Winchelsea. The nuptials were followed by several days of feasting and chivalric celebration, and a glance at the guest list reveals the extent to which good relations between Edward and his earls had been restored.[50]

In part this was due to the rapid rate of renewal among the higher aristocracy in recent years. Besides Bigod, the only other veterans at Canterbury were Surrey and Lincoln, who in any case were arch-loyalists. As for the rest, they had all succeeded to their father's titles in the past three years. The new earls of Hereford, Warwick and Lancaster were all young men in their twenties, as was Aymer de Valence, son and heir of the king's late half-uncle, and de facto earl of Pembroke. As such, they must have had a different relationship with Edward – one that, given the king's already legendary reputation, was likely to have been more unquestioningly devoted than that of their predecessors. Such men were in addition keen to prove their prowess, not only in the tournament that took place at Canterbury, but also in war.[51]

And war was now back at the top of the agenda. Throughout the summer, domestic politics and diplomacy had repeatedly delayed Edward's intention to lead a new army against the Scots. With these problems now seemingly behind him, the king was once again ready to march north. A week after his wedding the order went out to muster at York on 12 November. Edward had conquered Wales in the depths of winter; he would do the same with Scotland.[52]

Scotland itself had become a land of confusion. Defeat at Falkirk had severely dented the credibility of William Wallace and obliged him to stand down as his country's sole Guardian. Leadership of the Scottish political community had now passed to two other young men, both in their twenties. One of them, as might be expected, was Robert Bruce, whose importance to the patriotic cause had received indirect acknowledgement from English efforts to apprehend him the previous year. The other was John Comyn, the son and heir of the man of the same name who had backed John Balliol during the Great Cause (which, for the record, made him Balliol's nephew).

Authority among the Scots, in other words, had passed to a new generation, but was split between the representatives of two traditionally hostile factions.[53]

For those charged with the task of defending Scottish independence, Edward's recent marriage had come as a bitter blow. 'The people of Scotland are aware of the alliance between our king and the king of France,' wrote the English constable of Lochmaben in October, 'and they are greatly depressed about it.' Since the Scots had been allied with France since 1295, they had hoped, not unreasonably, to be a party to the peace. But, in spite of French and papal pressure, Edward had adamantly refused to countenance their inclusion. To him Scotland was not a rival sovereign power, as France was, but a subordinate adjunct of his own kingdom. Those Scots who challenged him he regarded as nothing more than rebels, whom in due course he would chastise into submission.[54]

Nevertheless, in order to get the peace he desired, Edward had been obliged to make one substantial concession. At the insistence of papal and French negotiators, John Balliol had been freed from English captivity. In July the deposed king of Scots had been escorted across the Channel and handed over to the pope's representatives. To some Scots – John Comyn and his allies – this gave heart, for Balliol's release was an essential first step on the road to his restoration. But for those who had always been opposed to Balliol's kingship – that is, for Robert Bruce and his supporters – it was most unwelcome news. Within weeks of the prisoner's transfer, the tension between the two sides boiled over. When they met at Peebles on 19 August, an argument broke out, then a fight. 'John Comyn leaped at the earl of Carrick [i.e. Bruce]', reported an English spy, 'and seized him by the throat.'[55]

And yet, despite the fact that their spies were able to report such dissension among the Scottish leaders, English commanders in Scotland generally had very little to smile about. Supplies were constantly running low, wages were in arrears, and garrisons were threatening to desert or mutiny. Everything was exacerbated by the attitude of the natives, who continually seized crops and horses. For all their political differences, one thing still united the Scots: the desire to resist their English occupiers.[56]

Edward intended to pick up in Scotland precisely where he had left off the previous year. According to Walter of Guisborough, the king set out in November 1299 'wishing to break the Scottish siege of Stirling Castle'. Remarkably, the great fortress, so crucial for controlling the northern kingdom, was still in English hands despite a whole year of enemy assaults.[57]

The prospect of success seemed very good. Although the long delay had been frustrating, it meant that the main supply depots at Carlisle and Berwick were now well stocked. Moreover, Edward now had the support of his leading subjects. When he rode north to York, all the earls who had attended his wedding rode with him. Even Roger Bigod, whose poor health prevented him from riding in person, sent his army of followers under the captaincy of his most senior household knight, John de Seagrave.[58]

But by the time he arrived in York, the king was aware of a serious problem with infantry recruitment. Because of the winter weather, and because of a perceived diminution in the quality of the coinage (forged foreign pennies of low silver content had recently flooded the market), men were unwilling to serve. In response, Edward told his recruiting officers to be more persuasive, and permitted them to offer higher rates of pay. He also postponed the infantry muster, which had been due in a week, and moved it from Newcastle to Berwick.[59]

When the king reached Berwick in mid-December, however, it was obvious that these extra inducements had not been nearly enough. Of the 16,000 foot soldiers he had ordered, only 2,500 had materialised. Worse still, it was now equally clear that there was virtually no support for the campaign among England's knightly class. The earls may have accompanied the king with their retinues, but few other magnates had bothered to turn out (royal pay rolls reveal fewer than forty additional names). The cavalry's absence, moreover, had nothing to do with bad weather or bad money. This was a deliberate, political boycott.[60]

The king's mistake, once again, had been his signal failure to deliver on the Charters. Unbelievably, despite his elaborate and heavily publicised promise of the summer, no perambulation of the Forest had taken place. Edward might have realised the danger this posed to his Scottish plans had he taken proper consultation during the autumn, but it seems that the artificial gaiety and harmony occasioned by his wedding had convinced him that this would not be necessary. The 'parliament' he had held the following month had actually been nothing more than a council of senior magnates, and as such had completely failed to gauge the mood of the country. The north-country chronicler Peter Langtoft was in no doubt that the king had gone to Scotland 'ill-advised', and blamed the low turnout on one reason above all. 'Know for certain,' he wrote, 'that it was caused by the perambulation, which was not performed as was granted.'[61]

The only solution, as Edward himself now belatedly realised, was to have a full and frank discussion with his subjects of the kind he had consistently avoided since his return from the Continent. On 29 December writs went out summoning the biggest parliament England had seen since 1296. Earls, barons, knights and burgesses; bishops, priests, abbots and friars: all were instructed to assemble in London at the start of Lent 'for the safety of the Crown and the welfare of the people'. Three days later, having seen in the new century at Berwick in what we may reasonably assume was an impotent rage, the king started out on his return. His mood during the journey south can hardly have been improved by the news that reached him en route. Stirling had finally surrendered to the Scots.[62]

With patience wearing thin on both sides, the parliament that met in March was predictably lively. 'Do you think I am a child, or a deceiver?' asked Edward angrily when, according to one chronicler, his critics not only asked him to confirm the Charters but also required that their own seals be applied to the documents for greater security. In spite of Roger Bigod's reassurances to the contrary ('we know you to be a good and prudent prince,' the earl reportedly told the king), most of Edward's subjects must by now have felt that 'deceiver' was a fairly accurate description. Certainly, after three years of evasion and broken promises, they considered that the Charters, even with the extra concessions of 1297, were insufficient. In 1300 both the laity and the clergy (still lined up between Bigod and Winchelsea respectively) came to parliament armed with long lists of additional demands. In the clergy's case the king simply turned a deaf ear. The Church had made it plain from the outset that it would offer the Crown no financial assistance, so why should the Crown offer the Church any redress?[63]

Financial assistance, however, was something that Edward desperately needed, so some form of settlement with the laity had to be found. In the end, after three weeks of 'long and exhausting' argument, the king agreed to a new set of articles ('The Articles upon the Charters' is their modern label). For the most part they were concerned with the regulation of prise – still a very contentious issue because of the ongoing wartime demands – but they also created a new enforcement system for the Charters, whereby local worthies would be appointed in every county to ensure their upkeep. Taken in conjunction with the Charters themselves – now finally reissued on 28 March – this amounted to a substantial package of concessions. As Edward made clear in the preamble, he had granted it in expectation that henceforth his subjects would 'be readier in his service, and more willingly helpful'.[64]

But for most people the king had still not gone far enough. For all their length, the new articles had nothing to say about the most contentious issue of all, namely the Royal Forest. As parliament drew to a close, Edward appointed men to carry out the perambulation, but only on conditional terms. He continued to insist that, whatever the investigation's findings, the 'rights of the Crown' must be protected – a proviso that would effectively render the whole exercise pointless. His critics therefore responded by upping their demands, and making their consent to the much-needed tax similarly conditional. A perambulation, promised or even performed, was now no longer enough: the Forest must actually be reduced in extent before any funds were collected. 'When we have secure possession of our woods,' they told the king, 'we will willingly grant a twentieth, so that the folly of the Scots may be dealt with.'[65]

It is extremely doubtful whether, in any circumstances, Edward would have agreed to such large demands in exchange for so small a subsidy. As it was, he could not afford to wait for months while the Forest was surveyed. His garrisons in Scotland were under attack and awaiting deliverance; a campaign was scheduled for the summer and must proceed as planned. If the knights of the shires would not grant him taxation, so be it: he would find another way to finance the coming expedition. But they could not deny that they owed him military service.[66]

Or could they? As Edward left Westminster in April to spend the spring making his usual round of spiritual preparations in East Anglia, military service was once again being vigorously debated. The argument between the king and the knightly class had died down after his departure for Flanders, but in 1300 it had flared back into life. At the start of the year, no doubt greatly piqued by the boycott of his winter campaign, Edward had revived his earlier attempts to link military obligation to landed wealth: all men worth £40 a year had been instructed to turn out in the summer. This had provoked an immediate protest in the recent parliament and, although nothing had been conceded in writing, the king evidently decided to let the idea drop. On Easter Monday, when he was at St Albans, his earlier orders were revised. Sheriffs were now told merely to *invite* the £40 landowners to come to the muster (although, ominously, they were to note the names of those who refused).[67]

But the debate did not end there. Such was the mood in the country, and so unpopular had the Scottish war become, that even traditional service obligations based on tenure were beginning to be contested. At some point in the spring of 1300, for example, the local gentry in County Durham turned out in support of foot soldiers who had been imprisoned by their bishop for deserting the winter campaign. The people of Durham, they declared, were 'St Cutherbert's Folk', and as such not bound to provide any military service at all beyond the Rivers Tyne and Tees. Later, in early June, there were similarly extraordinary scenes in Yorkshire, when knights from all counties assembled to tell Edward that they owed him no service in Scotland. In this case the knights lost the argument: the king, as was his wont, resorted to the written record, and proved from a number of twelfth-century chronicles that there was a long tradition of service north of the Border. Nevertheless, the fact that Edward was having to go to such lengths to persuade his knightly subjects to fight flies in the face of Peter Langtoft's assertion that men marched to Scotland in 1300 'well-willing'. Only for those who had been granted or promised lands in Scotland can that comment have held true. Many others clearly had to be argued into fighting, and this could produce distinctly limited results. The muster roll for the 1300 campaign noted that Hugh fitz Heyr, a Shropshire landowner of little consequence, was obliged by the terms of his tenure to serve in the king's war 'with bow and arrow'. It also noted that 'as soon as he saw the enemy he shot his arrow, then went home'.[68]

When the army eventually mustered in Carlisle at midsummer, the cavalry numbered around 1,700 mounted men – much better, that is, than the previous year, but not nearly as impressive as the 3,000 horse that had ridden into battle in 1298. The infantry situation was one of similar half-measures, in part due to the parlous state of royal finances. Having failed to obtain a grant of taxation, Edward knew he could not afford to field 26,000 foot soldiers as he had done at Falkirk. The Welsh, who had contributed 40 per cent of that impressive figure, were told on this occasion to stay at home. Officially this was their reward for 'all the great work they have done in our service in the past'; in reality it was an ambitious experiment to balance the books. Wales, unlike England, was not subject to the niceties of parliamentary taxation, and in place of men from the valleys the king now wanted money. As Edward rode north, his commissioners were instructed to extract a subsidy from various Welsh districts, which would pay for an army of English foot soldiers – 16,000 had been ordered, though in the end only 9,000 turned up.[69]

Nevertheless, the king's 10,000-strong host looked impressive enough when it set out from Carlisle in early July. A poet in their midst captured something of the splendour of the scene: the colourful banners, the beautiful pennons hanging from the knights' lances, the horses richly caparisoned with embroidered silks and satins. Looking behind him, he saw that 'mountains and valleys were everywhere covered with sumpter horses, and wagons with provisions, and the train of tents and pavilions. The days', he added, 'were fine and long'.[70]

As the army's assembly in Carlisle implies, Edward's strategy in 1300 was new. Eschewing the eastern route of his earlier campaigns, the king had chosen to concentrate on south-western Scotland, where the garrisons he had established in 1298 had latterly been subjected to repeated attack. Once his hold on this area – modern Dumfries and Galloway – had been consolidated, he would then be able to strike north into Ayrshire, and lay waste the lands of Robert Bruce.

His first target was the castle of Caerlaverock, which lay just a few miles across the Border on the opposite shore of the Solway Firth. Probably captured in the course of the Falkirk campaign, but subsequently retaken by the Scots, this castle and its small Scottish garrison had been making life miserable for their English neighbours at Dumfries and Lochmaben ever since. Their ability to resist a large army, however, was limited: Caerlaverock (which still stands today) is no Stirling. The newly built home of a prosperous local knight, it had been designed with the intention of keeping out local raiders, not repelling a wrathful English king. For a few days in July 1300 its defenders manfully withstood some showy assaults by the English chivalry, but once Edward's fleet arrived with his heavy siege equipment, they recognised that the game was up. By the middle of the month, in exchange for life and limb, the garrison had surrendered.[71]

Yet even before this minor victory had been obtained, the wheels of the English war machine had started to wobble. Although only days had elapsed since their departure from Carlisle, the infantry were already beginning to desert in droves. On 15 July, as he moved from Caerlaverock to Dumfries, the king gave orders that all such fugitive foot should be arrested. But as he moved further west, the haemorrhage continued: on 27 July, orders were sent out to raise replacement contingents. The Scots, who on this occasion had wisely decided to avoid battle, were able to watch from a distance as their enemies evaporated. By the time Edward finally caught up with them on 8 August, half his army was gone. All that followed was a brief, botched skirmish on the banks of the River Cree near Wigtown, which saw the Scots running for the hills and the English, as in the past, left with nothing to do. After a week of pointless waiting, the king turned around and headed back in the direction of Dumfries.[72]

As the end of August approached, Edward drew up his depleted forces just south of Dumfries and encamped them in the once-serene surroundings of Sweetheart Abbey. Like nearby Caerlaverock, Sweetheart was another recent addition to the local landscape – it had been founded by John Balliol's mother – and it bespoke a similar, sadly misplaced confidence that Border warfare would remain a thing of the distant past. Now, as a frustrated English king paused in its precinct and considered his diminishing range of military options, the abbey found itself in the middle of a war zone – a situation that made the unannounced appearance of the archbishop of Canterbury all the more surprising. Winchelsea, rather shaken from a perilous journey across the quicksands of the Solway Firth, came bearing a letter from the pope.[73]

Edward might well have anticipated news to lift his spirits. Boniface VIII, elected in 1294, was not only the broker of the slowly progressing Anglo-French peace but an old personal friend. The two men had met over thirty years earlier, during the last stages of the Montfortian civil war, when the then-young papal notary had been among those trapped in the Tower of London, until the then-young Lord Edward had secured his deliverance. The episode had apparently had a lasting impression on Boniface: even now, as the king was sat in Sweetheart Abbey, the pope was in his palace at Anagni, recalling it for the benefit of English ambassadors. 'It was then,' he said, 'that we gave this king our particular affection, and formed the opinion . . . that he would be the finest prince in the world.'[74]

But Boniface's fond memories of Edward in 1300 only made the content of the letter that Winchelsea now read out all the more ironic. The pope had written it the previous year, after discussions with an especially persuasive Scottish embassy. Although it started in affectionate terms, it soon moved on to take the king to task over his intervention in Scotland, rehearsing in the process many of the Scots' historical arguments for their independence. Edward was accused of having ignored these arguments; of having longed to occupy 'a realm which was then destitute of the help of a king'; and, as a consequence, of having committed numerous 'outrages of justice': causing heavy losses to Scotland's inhabitants; imprisoning Scottish clergymen until they died; occupying Scottish castles and monasteries (this last charge being especially pertinent, given the king's current location). The pope concluded by telling Edward that 'out of reverence of God, the Apostolic See and ourselves' he should leave Scotland alone.[75]

Such an unequivocal admonition from God's representative on Earth could not be ignored, and would require a carefully considered response. In the immediate term, however, it made no great difference. The cold weather was already starting to set in, and the king's army had crumbled away to nothing, leaving his campaign dead in the water. At the start of September, Edward dismissed those troops still with him and took ship across the Solway Firth to England.[76]

Outwardly, he blamed everybody but himself for this latest military failure. In an undated letter to his new chief minister, Walter Langton, the king ordered the punishment of both the deserters themselves and the officials responsible for their recruitment. He also demanded the names of any lords who had obstructed the recruitment process, and insisted that any sheriffs who had failed to provide supplies should be chastised 'so that they may be an example for the future'. As this list of scapegoats suggests, however, the real reason for the expedition's collapse was a lack of resources and, above all, a lack of money. The cavalry, obliged to serve at their own expense, had on this occasion stayed the course; it was the infantry, starved of food and wages, that had deserted right from the start – an exodus that, as the best-informed chroniclers attest, had ultimately scuppered the English campaign.[77]

Privately, of course, Edward appreciated that scarcity had been the root of his failure. He had gone to war knowing his treasury was short of funds, and embracing the desperate (not to say deluded) notion that this deficit could somehow be made good by tapping the wealth of Wales. As a result, he had succeeded merely in proving an obvious point, namely that the Welsh were insufficiently well-off to subsidise an English conquest of Scotland. What was needed, as the king had known all along, was a sum of money such as could proceed from only one source. Towards the end of September he bowed to the inevitable. Parliament was ordered to reassemble in January.[78]

In the meantime, Edward remained in Cumbria, where he was rejoined by his new queen, Margaret. This reunion must have brought him some cheer, not least because Margaret had recently been safely delivered of her first child, a boy, born at Brotherton in Yorkshire and christened Thomas. Yet even this event, happy as it was, highlighted the contrast between the king's current situation and his fortunes of old. His previous son had been born in the wake of a successful conquest, rather than in the middle of a seemingly endless war. In the autumn of 1300 Edward's last act before returning south was to recross the Border for talks with the Scots. His distaste at having to compromise with men whom he considered to be rebels and traitors was clear, and he scoffed at their offer of a permanent peace. 'Every one of you has done homage to me as chief lord of Scotland,' he reminded them. 'Now you set aside your allegiance and make a fool of me as if I were a weakling.' In the end, all the king would grant was a six-month truce, and his promise that he would return in the spring to lay Scotland waste from sea to sea.[79]

When parliament reconvened at the start of 1301 – in Lincoln, unaccountably – Edward made no bones about the reason for the recall. 'I am without money,' he reportedly told the assembly. 'I must have aid of my land if I am to recommence the war with Scotland.' Such was his poverty, in fact, that the king now proposed that the knights and burgesses should grant him a fifteenth of their goods, rather than the twentieth they had offered the previous year. At this, says one chronicler, there was much disgruntled muttering.[80]

Edward, of course, knew what parliament's price would be. The perambulation of the Forest, so long postponed, had finally been performed during the past summer, and the results were now in the king's possession. As he had feared, they weighed heavily against the Crown. Roughly half of the Royal Forest, it had been found, was an unjust extension; thousands of acres all over England were earmarked to be returned to 'the community'.[81]

Lately, by dint of necessity, Edward had started to take the demands of his subjects seriously. In the autumn of 1300, for example, he had quietly instructed his officials to ensure that Magna Carta and the Forest Charter were kept in all their points. The perambulation of the Forest, however, he continued to regard as a ludicrous affair, and not without reason. The men appointed to determine the extent of the Forest had to rely in practice on the testimony of local juries, yet the very fact that these juries were local inevitably affected the nature of their testimony. Those who lived within the bounds of the Forest were only too happy to swear – as, for instance, they had just done in Warwickshire – that once upon a time their region had contained no Royal Forest at all. And 'once upon a time' was the perambulation's second laughable aspect. The Forest Charter asked jurors to recall what the extent of the Forest had been at the start of the reign of Henry II – that is, in the year 1154. Even in 1225, when the Charter had first been published, this was a question that set great store by the collective memory of local communities. By 1300, to anyone even slightly bothered about the burden of proof, it must have made the entire exercise seem invalid.[82]

That was certainly the way that the king saw it, and he came to parliament prepared to argue his case. Edward had never trusted the flexible collective memory of his subjects. His first recourse had always been to the written record, and it was to the written record that he now once again turned. In the months leading up to the Lincoln assembly, royal clerks had been ferreting through their rolls, and even leafing through the venerable pages of the Domesday Book, in a quest for evidence with which the findings of the perambulation could be challenged.[83]

On this occasion, however, the king's resort to the documents had come too late; the time for negotiation had passed. Edward's continual evasiveness and demonstrable bad faith in recent years had eroded his subjects' goodwill and trust, and with it their willingness to compromise. It was now politically unrealistic for him to imagine that the country would accept anything less than a full endorsement of the perambulators' findings. The fact that he may have had a strong case for contesting them was as irrelevant as it was ironic. The king had finally been backed into a corner, and faced a stark choice: approve the perambulation in its entirety, or forego the much-needed tax.

In desperation, Edward threw the challenge back into the face of his opponents. They too, he reminded them, were bound by their oaths of homage to uphold the rights of the Crown, just as he was bound to uphold them by his coronation oath. He would let the perambulation stand, but only if his critics advised him to do so; the responsibility for forcing his hand would thus be theirs. A committee of twenty-six men (its membership unknown, but presumably including Bigod and Winchelsea, both of whom were present) agonised, afraid they might one day be accused of treachery for their actions, and begged the king to take the decision himself. But Edward remained stubborn to the last, saying 'he had no desire to ease his people with what was his'. In the end, therefore, the decision was left to the committee, and they chose the Charters over the Crown. On 14 February 1301 the king issued a new confirmation, and ordered that Magna Carta and the Forest Charter should stand 'in all their points'. The findings of the perambulation, it was announced, would become effective without delay; 'the community' would be put in possession of what had become their Forest.[84]

It is important to keep the scale of Edward's defeat in perspective. What had happened to him in 1301 was nothing like what had happened to his father in 1258. During the great crisis of his reign Henry III had been reduced to a mere cipher, and executive power had been seized by his barons. Edward, by contrast, had been beaten only on a single issue; in all other respects he remained very much the imperious master of his own affairs. Indeed, when the Lincoln parliament had dared to complain about Walter Langton, the king's palpably corrupt chief minister, and called for his dismissal, Edward had flown into an indignant rage, and silenced his critics with an impromptu lecture on the proper nature of lordship. 'Perhaps everyone should have a crown,' had been his sarcastic suggestion.[85]

Nevertheless, defeat on the Charters, and in particular on the issue of the Forest, was painful and humiliating for a king who attached such overriding importance to the Crown's rights and the sacred oath he had sworn to uphold them. Edward would never forget how 'the stress of great necessity' in 1301 had led to 'the surrender of his hereditary right'. Nor would he forgive those whom he regarded as having forced this surrender upon him.[86]

Although Edward considered the Lincoln parliament to be the lowest point in his political fortunes, it did at least solve his financial crisis – a new tax was set for collection in the autumn – and silence his domestic critics. His international affairs, on the other hand – the threefold problem posed by France, Scotland and the papacy – remained in seemingly insoluble disarray. It was now well over two years since the pope had ruled in favour of Gascony's return, yet the French had still not surrendered possession. That left Edward reliant on continued papal pressure but, given his recently declared support for the Scots, Boniface now seemed an uncertain advocate for English interests. What if he were to insist on the Scots' inclusion in the Anglo-French peace? The French had been arguing in favour of such a move for the past two years, almost certainly as a cynical tactic to frustrate the whole process. Even now, in the spring of 1301, French and Scottish ambassadors were meeting at Canterbury to put the suggestion of a three-way peace to Edward's own representatives.[87]

Edward, naturally, had no intention of accepting their proposal, nor even of renewing his truce with the Scots, which was set to expire in May. It had been expressly for the purpose of subduing his northern enemies that he had compromised his coronation oath; the first writs of summons for a new campaign had been sent out on the very day that the unpalatable deal with parliament had been struck. The king's utter antipathy towards further negotiation is evident from his absence. At the time of the Canterbury talks Edward was in the west Midlands, having gone to Gloucestershire for the funeral of his cousin, Edmund of Cornwall – a black event more in keeping with his general mood.[88]

Having reached its lowest point, however, the wheel of fortune began to turn slowly but perceptibly in the king's favour. Soon after the Canterbury talks had ended, Edward was joined in the Severn Valley by several old and loyal friends, chief among whom was the earl of Lincoln, Henry de Lacy. Some six months earlier Lacy and his colleagues had been dispatched to the papal court, partly to fortify the existing English embassy there, and partly to offer a preliminary response to Boniface's censorious letter. They now returned with glad tidings. Although nothing decisive had been achieved in relation to either Gascony or Scotland, the earl and his party had received a far more favourable reception from the pope than his letter had led them to expect, and this goodwill had translated into an immediate and tangible advantage. Boniface had lately joined Edward in his desire to subjugate a small but troublesome neighbour – in this case, the ever-tumultuous kingdom of Sicily – and to this end he had been trying for several months to levy a 10 per cent tax on all the churches of Europe. The ambassadors had therefore been able to strike a deal. It had been agreed that the pope could raise his tax in England for the next three years – and that half the profits would go to the king.[89]

Here was excellent news! For the past five years the English Church, guided by Winchelsea, had refused to vote Edward any financial aid at all, on the grounds that such grants required prior papal approval. Now, on the pope's express authority, the clergy would be obliged to furnish the Crown with a three-year tax of 10 per cent. This was definitely one in the eye for the stiff-necked archbishop and his supporters. Moreover, gloating apart, it meant a huge and unforeseen addition to the royal war-chest, already about to be replenished by the recent parliamentary subsidy. Together, these taxes would provide the king with the funds for a decisive Scottish campaign.

It only remained to wait for the return of his son. Edward of Caernarfon, lately turned seventeen, had grown to be tall, good-looking and physically accomplished, and his father – fast approaching sixty-three – had evidently decided that a transfer of authority would be timely. During the controversial Lincoln parliament the king had endowed his eldest boy with a substantial appanage, much as his own father had done almost half a century earlier. The grant included the earldom of Chester, but its principal component was the royal estate in Wales, and as such it came with a new title. 'Prince of Wales', used in the past only by the rulers of Gwynedd, was now revived for the heir to the English throne (in which capacity it has been used ever since). Young Edward, of course, born in Caernarfon, had been predestined for some kind of role in Wales, but he had not been back to the land of his birth until this moment. In April 1301 he returned to the principality, there to receive the homages of the Welsh themselves and also of the lords of the March. One month later he rejoined his father, who had been occupying himself in the Severn Valley with pilgrimages and hunting. They met at Kenilworth Castle, where the queen and other members of the royal family were also in residence. A fortnight later they rode north. Edward of Caernarfon had participated in the previous campaign, but his role, as nominal commander of one battalion, had been only a minor one. Now, as prince, his responsibility was greatly enlarged. As the king himself had explained in a letter to the earl of

Lincoln, he hoped that his son would have 'the chief honour of taming the pride of the Scots'.[90]

Edward's plan, revealed by his letters, was ambitious. Two separate armies, one led by the newly invested prince, the other by the king himself, would advance into Scotland from both ends of the Border, taking the south of the country in a pincer that would close at Stirling. From there they would march together into the north, leaving the rebels with nowhere left to run. This was to be the decisive campaign.[91]

The forces were accordingly formidable. For his own army Edward individually summoned over a thousand English landowners to provide cavalry service (a request that, now that the king had answered their criticisms, would be difficult to refuse). Royal recruiting officers, meanwhile, eventually rounded up some 7,500 foot soldiers – a figure not terribly impressive by itself, perhaps, but on this occasion the English were not fighting alone. Edward of Caernarfon's army was mostly drawn from his new dominions in Wales and the March, and it was considerably larger than that commanded by his father; total expenditure suggests that the prince had almost twice as many infantry. Nor, moreover, was it just the Welsh who were rejoining the fray. For the first time since 1296, the justiciar of Ireland had been ordered to assemble an army, and the magnates of Ireland had been induced to participate by the pardon of their debts to the Crown. Some 650 additional horse and 1,600 extra foot were as a result ready to cross the Irish Sea. From every obedient quarter of Edward's 'British' empire, men and *matériel* were being marshalled in great quantities so that the one remaining rebel province should finally be subjugated.[92]

The prince's army, mustered in Carlisle at midsummer, got off to an impressive start. Avoiding the route through Galloway that had proved problematic the previous year, they marched straight across country to the western seaboard, where they linked arms with their Irish allies. By the end of July Robert Bruce's castle at Ayr, unmolested since 1298, had fallen in the face of their combined onslaught, and, within four further weeks, the neighbouring castle at Turnberry – Bruce's birthplace – had also surrendered.[93]

The king's army, by contrast, was making somewhat slower progress. From his base at Berwick, Edward had set out on a similar inland route, obliging his host to hack its way through the vastness of Selkirk Forest, wherein Wallace and his fellow brigands had for a long time lurked. Nonetheless, by 21 August the English had reached Glasgow, and Edward was thus only thirty miles from his son's army. Indeed, the two forces were close enough to communicate: on 2 September, the king heard news of Turnberry's fall, and gave thanks for it in Glasgow Cathedral.[94]

The pincer, however, was never fully closed. On 7 September a Scottish army appeared outside Lochmaben and began besieging the English garrison there. This, it seems, halted the northern advance of Edward of Caernarfon's army and drew it back south – they could hardly push on with hostile forces attacking positions to their rear. A fortnight later and Lochmaben had been made secure again, but by this time the prince himself was heading further south, reportedly on pilgrimage to the shrine of St Ninian at Whithorn. This was not necessarily as dilatory as it sounds: the process of subjugating Scotland involved the appropriation of its regalia and relics, and such symbolic larceny was clearly feared by the Scots on this occasion. But it did mean that there was now no hope of the two hosts uniting.[95]

The king's men, meanwhile, were beset by the more familiar problem of dwindling resources. Even before Edward had reached Glasgow, various English sheriffs had been ordered, in menacing terms, to see that more merchants brought their wares north of the Border. At the same time, in every other theatre, supplies were being squeezed in a desperate attempt to shore up the king's army. On 28 August the crossbowmen and archers at Berwick mutinied, having received no pay for a month. Yet by early September, when Edward began besieging Bothwell – a mighty stone fortress near Glasgow, seized by the Scots at the start of the year – two-thirds of his infantry had deserted.[96]

Once Bothwell had surrendered, therefore – and the castle's reduction took a further fortnight – the king decided to go for broke, and marched what remained of his army straight for Stirling. Elsewhere in Scotland, at Edinburgh and at Berwick, his officials strained to procure the engines and other equipment necessary to mount an effective siege. But in the end shortage of funds forced Edward to stop in October at Dunipace, some six miles short of his target. For three weeks he waited for fresh supplies to arrive, his mounting anger brilliantly illuminated by a series of increasingly irate letters to the exchequer. He is astonished, he says, that they have sent so little money; every time they have sent some it has been too little; they should ensure that their inefficiency does not cause him to withdraw; he has been unable to keep his promises to pay his men; every day more of them desert. The tirade concludes on 16 October with Edward in full King Lear mode, speculating in his impotence about what might have been. 'But for lack of money,' he blustered, 'we would have bridged the Forth', and had the river been crossed, 'we are sure that we would have done such exploits against our enemies that our business would have reached an honourable and satisfactory conclusion.'[97]

The king's frustration, with the walls of Stirling in sight, is understandable, but his inclination to blame his officials was (as before) quite
unfair. In one of his letters, dated 11 October, Edward informed the
exchequer that he thought they should be well supplied with funds
from the new parliamentary and papal taxes. Yet the collection of both
these levies, as he must have known, had not been scheduled to begin
until this point in the autumn; indeed, the king's orders to assess the
fifteenth had been issued only three days earlier, on 8 October. The
failure to reach 'an honourable and satisfactory conclusion' in 1301 lay
not with bureaucratic inefficiency, but with executive impatience. Edward
had tried to deliver a knock-out punch but had only had time to draw
his fist halfway back.[98]

It remained to be seen whether anything could be salvaged from
the campaign's wreckage. In October the prospect seemed extremely
bleak. As the king candidly admitted in his last letter to the exchequer,
the desertion of his army left him 'in danger of losing' what he had
won. Already the Scots were regrouping in Selkirk Forest and around
Glasgow, while elsewhere newly established English positions were
coming under direct attack. At Turnberry, the castle lately captured by
Edward of Caernarfon was being besieged by a Scottish army, and the
new garrison at nearby Ayr feared that they would be next. As for the
prince himself, he could offer no assistance. His own army was now
also dissipated, and his Irish allies had long since sailed for home. By
this point he was back in Carlisle, unable to contribute anything beyond
the news that 'the castles of Lochmaben and Dumfries are feebly
garrisoned, with troops lacking in victuals and other provisions'. Moreover, in addition to all these discouraging reports coming in from the
field, Edward received intelligence in October from abroad. John Balliol,
it transpired, had been released from papal custody and was at large in
northern France. Rumour had it he was raising an army and was coming
to reclaim his kingdom.[99]

Given that Balliol had been detained at the pope's pleasure, his release
might naturally be interpreted as the pope's own handiwork – a fresh
and provocative expression by Boniface VIII of the unequivocal support
for the Scots he had first voiced some two years earlier. In fact, however,
this was almost certainly not the case. Boniface was by this point endeavouring to remain neutral on the subject of Anglo-Scottish relations.
Although Scottish ambassadors to Rome were encouraged by the audience they received during the summer of 1301, so too were their English
counterparts. The pope, for example, had declared himself much
impressed with Edward's historical justification of his position in

Scotland (composed with the aid of the scholars of Oxford and Cambridge, this celebrated letter had cited, among other proofs, the well-known fact of King Arthur's superior lordship). Genuinely impressed or not, Boniface was certainly aware that his new and mutually beneficial financial arrangement with England was just about to take effect. He was not, therefore, going to rock the boat by taking any firm action in favour of the Scots.[100]

Balliol owed his liberty in 1301 not to papal partiality, but to French pressure; which is to say that, while the pope no longer posed a problem for Edward, the king of France continued to be a major pain. Philip IV was still playing the Scottish card for all it was worth, insisting that he could not agree to a permanent peace without his allies, knowing that Edward would never agree to this, and calculating that in this way France's grip on Gascony could be maintained indefinitely. No sooner had the English advanced into Scotland in 1301 than French ambassadors had arrived on the scene, trying to broker yet another truce. Balliol's release, procured more or less simultaneously, was part of the same cynical ploy. The army that was reportedly going to restore the former king was to be provided by his French backer.[101]

The only conceivable way to read Edward's reaction to this persistent interference is that he decided to play the French at their own game and call Philip's bluff. In late October the king moved from Dunipace to Linlithgow, established a new headquarters and announced that it was his intention to remain in Scotland during the coming winter ('to annoy his enemies,' as he explained in letters sent out a short while later). At the same time, he sent his wily chief minister, Walter Langton, to France, in order to negotiate[102]

As the year drew to a close Langton proceeded to arrange a remarkable treaty, the essential feature of which was that it invited the king of France to put his money where his mouth was. Under its terms, Edward agreed to a nine-month ceasefire with the Scots, and Philip agreed to enforce it. All the territory that the English king had captured in Scotland during his current campaign was to be handed over to French agents for the truce's duration. Of course, for this to happen, Philip would have to do what to date he had not, and actually deploy some troops in aid of his Scottish allies. The English were obviously banking on the assumption that he would ultimately balk at this commitment. It is certainly impossible to believe, bearing in mind Philip's previous form over the 'temporary' custody of Gascony, that Edward had any real intention of placing so much as an inch of territory into French hands.[103]

Nevertheless, in Scotland this cynical exercise was taken seriously, with deeply damaging consequences for the patriotic cause. The fact of Balliol's release lent credence to the far-fetched idea that Philip IV was about to sponsor the former king's return and thereby effect the Scots' salvation. In some quarters, of course, this was a cause for celebration – the Comyns imagined they were about to regain the lost leader in whose name they were fighting – but for Robert Bruce and his supporters, it marked the end of the road. Bruce had already seen his fortunes decline of late. The previous year he had been nudged out of office as a Guardian; the past summer he had seen his lands once again wasted by English armies and his castles occupied by English troops. The prospect of Balliol's restoration, which could only increase his grief, proved too much to bear. At some point during the winter of 1301–2, Bruce rode to Lochmaben Castle and turned himself in.[104]

At the start of the new year, therefore, Edward's decision to sit out the winter in Scotland had been almost entirely vindicated. In spite of the ongoing shortages, he had managed to sustain an impressive show of strength at Linlithgow, being joined there for Christmas by his eldest son, the prince of Wales, and also by his queen (lately delivered of another baby boy, named Edmund). Now there was much more to celebrate besides. News arrived from France of the truce's successful conclusion, which meant he could leave Scotland knowing his recent gains would remain secure. News arrived from Lochmaben of Bruce's surrender: at last his enemies were beginning to weaken and acknowledge his authority. The king was clearly in a jubilant mood as he prepared to leave Linlithgow. On 20 January, a 'Round Table' tournament was held at nearby Falkirk – another brazen display of power, staged on the field of his earlier victory.[105]

The best news of all, however, came a few weeks later, when Edward was paused on the Border at Roxburgh. On 16 February, according to the recent treaty, the French were supposed to take possession of the recent English gains in Scotland; as predicted, the date passed without a Frenchman in sight. The king's bluff had worked, and the essential emptiness of the Franco-Scottish alliance had been duly exposed. Edward was left completely free to tighten his grip on his newly won territories. Even before the king had re-entered England, Master James of St George had set out for the north.[106]

Of course, exposing the emptiness of the Franco-Scottish alliance was one thing; persuading the king of France to abandon it was another. Although he had signally failed to assist the Scots, Philip IV was unembarrassed about continuing to use them as his excuse for retaining Gascony. When French negotiators reappeared in England in the spring, they still insisted, much to Edward's annoyance, that no final peace between England and France could proceed unless Scotland was also included.[107]

What eventually solved this seemingly intractable diplomatic problem for the English king was an unexpected and dramatic turn of events in Flanders. Four years earlier, when he had cut short his Continental campaign, Edward had left his Flemish allies to their fate. Philip IV had soon moved in with his forces, occupying Flanders and removing its ruler in much the same manner that Edward had subjugated Scotland. Now, in the summer of 1302, the French king was to suffer a similar patriotic backlash. When the citizens of Bruges rose up and killed their French occupiers, Philip dispatched a large French army to quell their rebellion. On 11 July it met with an opposing force of Flemings outside the town of Kortrijk (Courtrai) and was completely annihilated. This was no ambush, of the kind that humiliated the English at Stirling Bridge. It was rather as if the Scots had won the day at Falkirk. At Kortrijk, the elite cavalry of France were wiped out by an infantry army of Flemish townsmen. Hundreds of French lords fell, including several counts, and the king's chief minister, Pierre Flote. So many rich trophies were stripped from their bodies that the encounter became known as the Battle of the Golden Spurs. It was a victory so worthy of remembrance that it is still commemorated in Flanders today.[108]

In England news of the French defeat, which happened to coincide with a parliament in Westminster, was received with ill-disguised glee. 'Much was the weeping and sorrow/In all of France, both young and old,' crowed one English songwriter in a ballad celebrating the battle. The news seemed all the more propitious in that it coincided with an almighty row that had recently erupted between Philip IV and Boniface VIII. In response to Philip's maltreatment of a French bishop, Boniface had delivered a damning indictment of the king and his government; Philip had retaliated with his own poisonous propaganda, publicly denouncing Boniface and questioning his fitness to hold office. As their quarrel escalated into one of the greatest Church–State conflicts of the Middle Ages, each side became increasingly anxious to ensure their stance had sufficient international backing. Suddenly, everyone wanted to be friends with the king of England.[109]

Edward, therefore, having done very little since his return south beyond hunting, spending time with his family and visiting his favourite shrines, found that the tectonic plates of European diplomacy had shifted decisively in his favour. In an effort to win English support for his struggle with France, Boniface dropped the Scots like a stone. In August he wrote to the bishop of Glasgow, Robert Wishart, chastising him for encouraging the patriotic cause, and at the same time sent letters to all the other bishops in Scotland, enjoining them to be obedient to the English king.[110]

Similarly, when talks with France resumed in the autumn, the English negotiators found that their French counterparts now spoke with an unaccustomed sincerity about their desire for a permanent peace: Edward was actually invited to visit France so that a treaty could be finalised. This suggestion, however, was rejected. The king of England would be staying at home, it was explained, to crush the rebels in Scotland; for the time being, France would have to settle for another truce. Nevertheless, that a decisive shift in French policy had taken place was plain for all to see and Edward made sure that it was seen by giving it widespread publicity, especially north of the Border. When the truce was renewed at the end of November, it was an exclusive, two-way affair: of the Scots there was no mention.[111]

With the papacy now actively condemning the Scots for their rebellion, and the French having forsaken them as allies, Edward's chances of succeeding in Scotland looked stronger than ever before. In other directions too, circumstances seemed auspicious. England remained politically quiescent; parliamentary and papal taxes approved the previous year had now been harvested; for the first time since the war's outbreak, royal receipts exceeded expenditure.[112]

Success, however, was by no means a foregone conclusion. The apparently ceaseless conflict had ground down the goodwill of the king's subjects in England, who were resisting royal demands for prise and the provision of ships. As a result, English resources in Scotland were stretched perilously thin. Nothing illustrates the weakness of Edward's grip better than the sorry predicament of Master James of St George, who had been charged with the construction of new fortresses at Selkirk and Linlithgow. To cement the conquest of Wales, James had been allowed virtually unlimited funds, and had, in consequence, created some of the greatest castles in the world: even during the crisis years of the mid-1290s, the exchequer had found him £250 a week to build Beaumaris. Now, by contrast, he was expected to make do with just a twelfth of that sum – a mere £20 a week. Such budgetary constraints explain why there is no Conwy or Caernarfon to be found in Scotland today. At the end of his career, the king's great master mason was reduced to the ignominy of working in wood.[113]

The extreme fragility of the English hold was exposed early in the new year 1303, when the Scots began attacking and re-occupying castles and towns. Linlithgow, the most strategically important of the two new timber fortresses, held out, but Selkirk, the more expensive, fell in January. There was more bad news for the English the following month, when a force of their cavalry was ambushed at Roslin, near Edinburgh, by a Scottish army commanded by John Comyn. Ralph Manton, the king's chief financial official in Scotland, was among those killed, and other high-ranking Englishmen were taken prisoner. The Scots were demonstrating to their enemies that denying them a truce had a definite downside.[114]

Edward therefore left no stone unturned in preparing for his spring offensive. Debtors to the Crown were hit with demands for repayment; foreign merchants were granted new privileges in exchange for a hike in customs. The king even called in the aid for the marriage of his daughter, approved but not collected thirteen years before.[115] Every available fiscal resource was squeezed, and every ounce of manpower summoned. Ten thousand infantry were demanded from northern England; unknown quantities were required from Wales. On Ireland, in particular, great hopes were pinned, and in the end some 3,500 men were assembled to embark in 173 ships, the largest naval force the island had ever seen. Many of them were provided by the earl of Ulster, whose debts to the Dublin exchequer, totalling more than £11,000, were written off in return.[116] And above and beyond this, of course, Edward now expected service from his newly obedient Scottish subjects: Robert Bruce was instructed to turn out with 2,000 foot and as many cavalry as he could muster. Bring all you owe and more besides: such was the common refrain in every royal writ. The king's lieges were exhorted 'to attend so powerfully accompanied that the contumacious resistance of the enemy may be overcome'.[117]

No single aspect of this furious preparation concerned Edward more than the work of fifty carpenters at King's Lynn, upon whose skill and diligence his whole strategy hinged. The king's plan in 1303 was simple. He intended to penetrate northern Scotland – that part of the country in which he had not set foot since 1296, and where Comyn power was strongest. This, of course, entailed crossing the Forth, which in turn explains the sudden burst of industry in Norfolk. Rather than waste time winning control of Stirling, Edward proposed to create a new crossing further down the river – a pontoon bridge, of the kind that had been used to conquer Wales two decades earlier. Great efforts were taken to ensure that the finished product would be both viable and defensible – the Welsh prototype, after all, had worked only on the second attempt, and memories were still fresh of the disastrous attempt to cross the Forth in 1297. Three separate bridges of differing size were built, each of them equipped with drawbridges and giant crossbows.

The scale of the enterprise, needless to say, was enormous. Preparing the bridges took almost four months, and cost almost £1,000. It took a fleet of thirty ships to ferry the completed parts into theatre.[118]

It is consequently disappointing to discover that this massive feat of medieval engineering was apparently never used. 'By chance there was no need of it,' said Peter Langtoft, and it looks as if he was right. Edward and his army mustered on the Border in late May and by 6 June had reached Linlithgow. As the king's writs show, however, he subsequently moved to Stirling, which suggests that in the event he crossed the Forth by the conventional route. Stirling Castle was still in Scottish hands, but its garrison was too small to trouble the English host as it swept past their walls and marched unopposed into the north.[119]

The reason for Edward's unimpeded progress soon became apparent. Within days his officials at Carlisle were writing panicked letters, reporting the arrival in south-west Scotland of 'a great multitude of armed men'. The Scots, knowing that 'almost all of the cavalry and infantry were with the king', were attacking the depleted garrisons of Dumfries and Galloway. Worse still, on 18 June they crossed the Border and began laying waste to northern England.[120]

Thus the nature of the conflict was established. It would not be decided in open confrontation, as at Stirling Bridge or Falkirk, but by attrition. Victory would go to whichever side could mete out the most pain and suffering in the territory of the other, while simultaneously enduring the misery inflicted in their own. Edward in due course heard the news from Carlisle and dispatched a relief force under Aymer de Valence and Robert Bruce. But the king himself pressed on northwards with the bulk of his host, razing everything in his path. 'Hamlets and towns, granges and barns/Both full and empty, he everywhere burns,' wrote Peter Langtoft. 'He advanced taking much plunder,' added Walter of Guisborough, 'burning and destroying almost everything.'[121]

If Edward hit hard, it was because his chances in a war of endurance were weak. From Stirling he advanced quickly to Perth, but there he was forced to wait for over a month while his supplies were replenished. As in previous campaigns, provisioning was perilously hand to mouth. Even in June, ships and crews were having to be arrested in southern England in order to ferry the requisite grain to the Firth of Tay. When the king finally struck out along Scotland's north-eastern coast in late July, he continued to be dependent on this naval lifeline. A successful rendezvous with more ships at Montrose delivered him the necessary artillery to reduce the castle at nearby Brechin in early August. But when he reached Aberdeen on 23 August, the ships full of coin he had expected to find were not there. By this point Edward had already lost half his infantry; he could not afford to lose more. After waiting five days with no sight of a sail, he wrote an exasperated letter to the exchequer. 'If we cannot make these payments,' he said, referring to the wages of his men, 'they will go back to their own parts, as they are already doing from day to day.'[122]

Meanwhile, in south-western Scotland the situation had been transformed by the arrival of the Irish, who landed in the middle of August and began capturing castles along the west coast. The creation of this new front, combined with the simultaneous appearance in the region of forces under Valence and Bruce, seems to have succeeded in drawing the Scots' fire. Certainly the English garrisons in Dumfries and Galloway, which a few weeks earlier had been on the verge of disintegration, were given succour enough that they managed to hold out.[123]

The king, too, scraped through by the skin of his teeth. On 28 August, the very day his desperate letter was sent, ships arrived in Aberdeen with the much-needed money, and the reimbursed royal host was able to push on into the heart of enemy territory. By the middle of September Edward had reached the shores of the Moray Firth, and the abbey of Kinloss, which marked the furthest point of his devastating progress. A week later he was laying siege to John Comyn's castle at nearby Lochindorb. By early October the fortress had fallen.[124]

Comyn himself, however, showed no signs of flagging. At this time the Scots' sole Guardian was still active in central Scotland, reportedly raiding English positions with a force of a hundred horse and 1,000 foot. To him and his allies it seemed impossible that their opponent could last much longer. In late September Aymer de Valence had written of his hope that some Scottish leaders might be about to come in, but within a few days he was obliged to eat his words. The Scots in question had approached the English camp at Linlithgow, taken one look at the sorry state of its starving Irish garrison, and concluded that their enemies were on the point of collapse.[125]

And yet, in spite of its apparent exhaustion, English power prevailed. When Edward returned from harrying Comyn's north-eastern heartlands, his forces were too weak to carry through his intention of reducing Stirling Castle, but the king nevertheless made it clear that he was not about to retire any further south. In November he ensconced his army on the north bank of the Forth at Dunfermline Abbey, while his son, the prince of Wales, established a separate camp on the Tay at Perth. It became evident that, once again, Edward was preparing to winter in the midst of his enemies.[126]

If the continued presence of their oppressor in a part of Scotland that had previously offered them safe refuge was an ominous development for the Scots, the location of his new winter quarters must have been more dispiriting still. Dunfermline was the burial place of Scotland's kings and queens – Edward's own sister, Margaret, was buried there, alongside her husband, Alexander III. Perth, meanwhile, stood adjacent to the abbey of Scone, long since robbed of its ancient Stone. The English occupation of these two symbolic sites, once the sacred centres of Scottish royal power, served to emphasise the same fundamental point. For more than seven years, Scotland had been a kingdom without a king. For all that time the Scots, and the Comyn faction in particular, had fought doggedly and hopefully in the name of John Balliol. It was now certain, however, that Balliol would not be coming back. On 20 May England and France had at last sealed their long-postponed peace, and the Scots had not been included. 'For God's sake, do not despair,' the Scottish negotiators in Paris had written to their compatriots back home. 'If ever you have done brave deeds, do braver ones now.' That summer the Scots had done their utmost to heed this exhortation, but, as the winter began to set in, so too did despair, and with it the painful realisation that the cause for which they had been fighting was now irredeemably lost.[127]

Comyn and his allies surrendered early in the new year, having spent several weeks negotiating the best possible deal for themselves and the Scottish people. The terms they eventually secured, if not quite the total amnesty that they had hoped for, were nevertheless remarkably generous. In return for their submission, Edward guaranteed that there would be no loss of life or limb, lands or liberty. Some of those who came in were obliged to accept a period of temporary exile, the duration determined by the perceived scale of their offence.[128]

In truth, Edward could hardly have acted otherwise. What was presented to the Scots as magnanimity was in reality a tacit acknowledgement of their persisting power. Once upon a time, he had regarded the Scots as little more than a joke; a people he might conquer in a single summer, and whose affairs he might reorder at his whim. But since then it had taken him seven long years and every last ounce of strength to persuade them to accept surrender for a second time. The king may not have cared to admit it, but these were men who had earned the right to his respect.

Comyn knelt before Edward in February; some 130 other landowners similarly swore allegiance to the king in a specially convened parliament at St Andrews in March. Thereafter, all that remained was to deal with those few Scots who had refused to attend the meeting and who continued to bear arms against their rightful overlord.[129]

The first target – in the most literal sense – was Stirling Castle. The small Scottish garrison there had long been a thorn in Edward's side; now their continued obstinacy gave the king the opportunity to conclude his conquest with an appropriately majestic display of royal might. From every quarter of Scotland, English artillery was shipped, trundled and reassembled in order to batter the fortress into submission.[130] As far away as Perth and St Andrews, lead was stripped from the roofs of churches to make the counterweights that would give the trebuchets their tremendous hurling power. Inevitably, given Stirling's virtually impregnable situation, the task of reducing it took weeks, but the spectacle was awesome. This was one of the earliest recorded occasions that gunpowder – 'Greek Fire', as contemporaries called it – was used in Britain. To distinguish them, possibly even to jollify them, the throwing machines were given names, and proceedings outside the castle soon assumed the air of a chivalric entertainment. Edward thoughtfully had a large new window inserted into the queen's chambers, so that she and her ladies could observe their gallant menfolk in action.

Eventually, after twelve weeks of bombardment and pyrotechnics, the garrison indicated their willingness to surrender – a decision probably encouraged by the sight of a truly giant trebuchet, the work of more than fifty men for two whole months, approaching the point of completion. Unfortunately, Edward had by this time developed a personal interest in the Warwolf, as the beast had become known, and insisted that no surrender would be accepted until his new toy had been tested. Some modern historians have condemned him for this, though at the time nobody seemed to think his behaviour so very unreasonable: the defenders, after all, had been targeting the king throughout the siege and, indeed, had on two occasions come within a whisker of killing him. At length, on 24 July – presumably after the Warwolf had scored a few hits – a surrender was accepted. The garrison presented themselves, as ritual recommended, barefoot and with ashes on their heads, in the hope that Edward would show them mercy; the king, with equal respect for convention, allowed that their lives would be spared. Thus the siege, and the war, ended in such a way that chivalric expectations were satisfied. There was even a tournament to mark the conflict's final conclusion.[131]

Only one individual of consequence was wholly exempted from the general clemency, and Edward did not intend to waste any more time tracking him down: the Scots themselves could do that as proof of their newly professed loyalty, and in due course they did. William Wallace was captured by his own countrymen in August the following year, led to London in chains, and charged with the crime of treason. This was somewhat ironic, for Wallace was probably the only Scottish leader who had *not* sworn allegiance to the English king – a fact that the prisoner himself pointed out at his hearing in Westminster Hall. Needless to say, it availed him nothing. On 23 August 1305, while Edward amused himself in the forests of Essex, his sometime adversary was dragged from Westminster to Smithfield, hanged on a gallows, cut down while still alive, disembowelled and beheaded. His entrails were then burned, his body quartered, and the quarters dispatched for public display in Newcastle, Berwick, Stirling and Perth. His head was mounted on a spike above London Bridge. Thus were the Scots made aware of treason's terrible reward, and the slaughter at Stirling Bridge was avenged.[132]

11

A Lasting Vengeance

For several months after the siege of Stirling, Edward I did little except recover his strength and savour his victory. Having left Scotland in the last week of August, he spent two months travelling slowly through the north of England, and a further seven weeks resting at the royal manor of Burstwick in Yorkshire – a stop that Peter Langtoft described as a 'sojourn awhile for his health'. At length the court crossed the Humber in December and arrived in Lincoln, where Christmas was kept in exceptionally lavish style. As one annalist explained, the buyers of the royal household had been ordered to prepare a feast worthy of a man who was now 'the king and lord of the monarchy of two realms'. Edward was also unusually lavish in his distribution of rewards, handing out valuable gifts as well as compliments to the earls and knights who had helped him obtain what the same writer referred to as 'his triumphant peace'.[1]

There was ample reason for feeling triumphant. With Scotland finally surrendered, Edward exercised a direct lordship in the British Isles far greater than that enjoyed by any of his ancestors. From the far north of Britain to the far west of Ireland, across the liberties of the March of Wales, the writ of the king of England now ran without challenge or contradiction. Nor was victory to be measured merely in insular terms. Gascony was also back in English hands as a result of the recently ratified peace with France. In June 1303, while Edward had been decisively harrying the Scots into submission, the duchy had been ceremoniously restored to his representatives in the church at St Emilion. At home and abroad, the king's rights were at last respected and acknowledged.[2]

Obtaining that acknowledgement, however, had come at an exceedingly heavy price. In order to recover Gascony, and especially to subjugate Scotland, Edward had placed an enormous, almost intolerable

345

strain on the rest of his empire. The peoples of England, Wales and
Ireland had been asked repeatedly, year in year out, to provide the men
to fight in these wars, the food to feed them and the money to pay
them. In financial terms alone the costs were staggering. During the
decade between the seizure of Gascony in 1294 and the surrender of
Scotland in 1304, Edward had spent a sum well in excess of a million
pounds. To raise it he had resorted to terrible expedients – visiting
violence on the clergy, seizing the goods of his subjects without their
consent, and even trying to impose taxation against the will of parliament. In consequence he had faced censure from the pope, provoked
rebellion in Wales and very nearly sparked a new civil war in England.[3]

As this brief list of repercussions implies, the costs had been more
than financial. The overall consequence of Edward's wars was massive
dislocation and disarray. In England, for example, the prolonged non-
residence of the king and his magnates had led directly to a dramatic
rise in lawlessness, far worse than the temporary crime waves occasioned by their earlier absences in Wales and Gascony. The remarkable
robbery of the Crown jewels from the treasury at Westminster Abbey
in the spring of 1303 was but one manifestation of the increase; across
the country as a whole its effects were far more serious and endemic.
Crime, in a word, had become organised. Every town and county had
witnessed the appearance of bands of armed men, popularly known as
'trailbastons' on account of the clubs they habitually dragged around
with them. Through threat of violence these thugs held local society
in their thrall. Langtoft explains how they would openly offer their
services on market days, undertaking to beat people up in return for
a fee. Other evidence shows how they indulged in racketeering,
the intimidation of juries, robbery and murder. It was all highly embarrassing for a king who earlier in his reign had issued so much legislation with the aim of reducing crime, yet it was hardly unexpected, for
Edward's contribution to the problem amounted to more than just
negligence. At the start of his war with France, such had been his
desperate need, the king had handed out pardons to all who were
willing to fight, emptying his prisons in the process. The problem he
now faced was partly the result of these former jailbirds coming home
to roost.[4]

Bad as things were in England, they were worse in Ireland, where
the same combination of pressure and neglect had brought an already
troubled lordship to a point of more or less perpetual crisis. Edward's
war effort had several times emptied Ireland of its English military
tenants, leaving the colony's less martial members at the mercy of their
native Irish neighbours. At the same time, his willingness to pervert the

course of justice in pursuit of his rights in Scotland had made it ridiculously easy to secure pardons for murder, which meant that homicides among the settler community had risen as a result. The extent of the problem had already been apparent in 1297, when a celebrated parliament had assembled in Ireland and drawn up a set of emergency measures 'to establish the peace more firmly'. As these measures indicated, lawlessness was seen to be increasing in line with absenteeism of English landlords and the degeneracy of those who remained. Profits at the Dublin exchequer were diminishing, and the area of the country under English control was contracting.[5]

In Gascony, meanwhile, the disarray was equally great, albeit for different reasons. Although the rule of law was now slowly returning to the duchy, for the past decade its inhabitants had known little besides disorder and destruction. French occupation had led to many Gascons being dislocated and disinherited; English military efforts to reverse the situation had merely added to the devastation. According to the terms of the recent peace, Gascony was to be returned to its *status quo ante bellum*. But naturally this was proving impossible in practice, partly because of the chaos the conflict had created, and partly because the duchy's legal relationship with France was now more hopelessly confused than ever.[6]

Nowhere, of course, was the confusion greater than in Scotland. It was not just that the country had been invaded and laid waste time and again by English armies, with the result that so many churches, castles, abbeys, towns and villages now lay in ruin. It was also that, for a whole generation, Scotland had been a nation divided against itself, with Robert Bruce and his adherents almost always ranged against the supporters of the absent John Balliol. Healing this rift was going to be a time-consuming and nigh-on impossible task; so too was the job of reconciling the rights of Englishmen who had been rewarded with lands north of the Border with the competing claims of Scotsmen who had latterly been guaranteed the restoration of their estates. For the moment Scotland had been left in the care of an ad hoc regime of military governors; for the future, some new form of civilian government would have to be found.[7]

Thus, while Edward rested and gave thanks, it fell to others to begin the business of restoring order on his behalf. Towards the end of November 1304, before he had left Burstwick, measures were put in place to deal with the trailbaston gangs. In three northern counties, commissioners were appointed with wide powers to identify, arrest and detain any individuals suspected of involvement, and the authority to raise posses for pursuit should the need arise. As the king moved into East Anglia in January to visit the holy sites of Norfolk and Suffolk the operation was extended into these areas too, and by the time he arrived in Westminster at the start of March it had evidently become nationwide. A few weeks later the first justices of trailbaston were appointed to hear cases up and down the country against the numerous individuals who were already in gaol awaiting trial. The crackdown had clearly been effective, though in some quarters it was regarded as disproportionate. A contemporary songsmith who purported to be a war veteran complained that, as a result of the new measures, good men like himself were being falsely accused and unjustly imprisoned, simply because they had knocked their servants about a bit.[8]

Parliament, naturally, was the forum in which such new remedies were discussed, and Edward's return to Westminster after an absence of over two years coincided with the start of a new session. With both knights and burgesses in attendance it was as large an assembly as could be, perhaps for no other reason than to celebrate the victory over the Scots. Towards its end, on the feast of the Annunciation (25 March), the king held a special service in Westminster Abbey to thank God and St Edward for his triumph.[9]

Scotland, however, was also the subject of much businesslike discussion. Several leading Scots were present for the purpose, and three of them were called upon to advise how their country might best be governed in the future. Their involvement indicates the extent to which Edward had learned from his earlier mistake of disregarding Scottish opinion, and their identities reveal the quite considerable lengths to which he was now ready to go in order to retain Scotland's loyalty. Robert Bruce was admittedly an unsurprising choice, as arguably was John Mowbray, a close confidant of John Comyn. But it must have required a very dispassionate state of mind on the king's part to accept advice from Robert Wishart, the bishop of Glasgow, who just a few months earlier had been accused of committing 'great evils'. Nevertheless, on the recommendation of this trio, it was decided to give the Scottish political community time to hold a parliament of their own, and to choose a ten-man delegation to treat for a final settlement later in the year.[10]

Because of the length of time since the last parliament there was plenty of other business to deal with besides Scotland, and the many petitions that poured into Westminster from England, Ireland and Gascony provide a further reminder of the scope of Edward's authority. Petitions came from Wales too, though in this case they were heard at nearby Kennington – a reminder that part of the king's authority had lately been delegated, for Kennington was the London residence of his eldest son.[11]

Wales was arguably the territory that had suffered least as a result of the Scottish wars, for it had not been required to supply money or provisions on the same scale as England or Ireland. If anything, Wales had been a beneficiary of the conflict, for the wealth extracted from these other regions had provided the wages for the Welsh armies that had been so frequently called upon to fight.

Nevertheless, the reason Wales had been such a reliable source of manpower was because, in the wake of their own conquest, its people needed all the money they could get. As many of the petitions presented at Kennington attest, everyday life in Wales had become much more onerous under English rule. Tolls were heavier than they had been under the native princes, as were the labour services extracted in order to build the king's new castles (construction at Caernarfon, abandoned during the Scottish wars, had recently been resumed). The Welsh looked to their new prince to put these and other matters right, 'esteeming him their rightful lord, because he derived his origins in those parts' (the words, admittedly, of an English chronicler). In practice, however, Edward of Caernarfon could do little to provide redress; he too was bound by the settlement that had been imposed on Wales in the weeks leading up to his birth.[12]

In any case, it is to be doubted whether the prince possessed the inclination to improve the lot of his Welsh subjects. His true attitude towards them is perhaps better indicated by a letter he sent to Philip IV's half-brother, Louis of Evreux, just a few weeks after the hearings at Kennington. 'If you want anything from our land of Wales,' he joked, 'we can send you plenty of wild men, who will know well how to teach breeding to the young heirs and heiresses of great lords.' As this comment suggests, part of the prince's problem was his frivolity. Other evidence – particularly the entry in his wardrobe book that shows he had gone swimming in February 1303 with Robert the Fool – points to the same conclusion. Of course, at that time he had still been a teenager, and in 1305 he was only just turned twenty-one; his father, at a similar age, had exhibited a similar irresponsible streak. But the older Edward was not a man to indulge his offspring as Henry III had been, as events soon showed.[13]

In June 1305, as the king was making his way to Chichester in Sussex, a row erupted between his son and his chief minister, Walter Langton. It arose, said one annalist, because the prince had earlier been trespassing in the minister's woods. The rights and wrongs of their argument, however, were irrelevant; what caused uproar, according to an official record, was young Edward's use of 'certain gross and harsh words' to Langton's face. This was more than his father was willing to stand – to insult his chief servant was to disrespect the peace of his court – and he reacted by banishing the prince from his presence. During the month that followed he continued to tour the cathedrals and castles of south-eastern England, while Edward of Caernarfon followed at a distance, trying to effect a reconciliation. Eventually the king, still greatly annoyed, commanded his son to wait at Windsor until the start of the next parliament.[14]

That parliament, when it assembled in September, saw reconciliation on several fronts. Most importantly, the business of providing a government for Scotland was finally resolved. Despite the execution of William Wallace the previous month, the reception afforded the Scottish delegates in London was welcoming, and after a spate of tournaments they sat down with the English council to devise a settlement. Unsurprisingly, there was no talk this time round of reviving Scotland's kingship. As the records of the meeting make clear, Scotland was no longer regarded as a kingdom (*regnum*), but had been demoted to the status of a land (*terra*). As such, it was to be governed in future by the king of England's lieutenant, and that role was set to be filled by Edward's nephew, John of Brittany. Beyond this, however, the scheme of government agreed that September testified to the ongoing desire in England to appease Scottish feelings. Of the nineteen sheriffs appointed in Scotland, for example, only two were English, while the rest were natives. Similarly, the council nominated to advise the new lieutenant was almost entirely Scottish in its composition, and the four Englishmen chosen to act as judges in Scotland were each paired with a Caledonian counterpart. All of this stood in marked contrast to the overwhelmingly English, 'colonial' administration that Edward had attempted to impose on Scotland nine years earlier.[15]

This willingness to draw a line under the past was equally apparent at the start of October, when the committee visited the king at Sheen in Surrey to present him with their conclusions. Once Edward had approved the new governmental scheme and the Scots, touching holy relics, had sworn to uphold it, more concessions were forthcoming. The conflict between English and Scottish claims to land was resolved by means of a process akin to that used to end the civil war in England almost four decades earlier. The Scots, it was allowed, could redeem their estates in return for cash, and the English would in turn be compensated for their losses. As these measures were announced, many of the sentences of exile imposed on the Scots the previous year were also declared lifted. The king, said one chronicler, rejoiced at the hope of firm and lasting peace in Scotland, and the Scots themselves were said to have returned home happy. The spirit of reconciliation, moreover, was also manifest on the domestic front. Edward subsequently moved from Sheen to Westminster and made peace with his eldest son. On 13 October – the feast of the Confessor – the prince of Wales celebrated his restoration to favour by holding a feast in his father's palace.[16]

Edward I was coming close to achieving the peaceful disposition of his empire that he craved. Only one crucial matter arising from the struggle of recent years remained to rectified, and that was the damage that had been done to the rights of the Crown. At his coronation the king had sworn to preserve these rights unimpaired, yet in 1301 he had been forced to compromise on the issue of the Royal Forest, which had been reduced in size as a result. These injuries, therefore, would have to be mended. And, at the same time, the men who had inflicted them must be called to account.

One might imagine – as some contemporaries certainly did – that Roger Bigod, earl of Norfolk and long-time leader of the lay opposition, would be first in line for an interview. Bigod, however, had seen this day coming and had already taken steps to avoid it. More than three years earlier, in the spring of 1302, he had cut a face-saving deal, and – in return for a generous annuity – nominated Edward as his heir. From the earl's point of view this had solved several pressing problems, not only restoring him to the king's good graces but also plugging the gaping hole that a private army of followers had created in his finances. At the same time, it had cost him very little in personal terms, for he had no children to disinherit. By the same token, the deal had also been an excellent one as far as Edward was concerned, for it promised eventually to bring a vast amount of land to the Crown for a comparatively modest outlay, and such land would soon be needed. Unlike Bigod, the king had many children to provide for, not least the two new sons from his second marriage. Thus, by dint of a mutually beneficial agreement, the relationship between the two men had been repaired. In 1305 Edward had further eased the earl's financial worries by cancelling his debts to the Crown – a gesture, as the king explained in his letters, inspired by the 'great affection' he now felt towards his former critic.[17]

This was not a phrase that he would readily have used about Bigod's erstwhile ally, Robert Winchelsea. While the earl had quickly made his peace with Edward, the archbishop had continued to act as the king's principal antagonist, and not just in parliament. In addition – and far more provocatively – Winchelsea had been backing the cause of a young man called John de Ferrers. Readers with very retentive memories may recall how, at the end of his struggle with Simon de Montfort, Edward and his friends had compelled Robert de Ferrers, earl of Derby, to surrender his estates to Edmund of Lancaster. John de Ferrers, as the son of the dispossessed and long-deceased victim, had lately begun a campaign to recover his lost inheritance, and Winchelsea had decided to act as his champion. In 1301, having secured permission from the pope, the archbishop had actually begun to judge the case in his own court, and had summoned the new earl of Lancaster to answer Ferrers' accusation of unlawful disseisin. Needless to say, the king, already deeply embittered, must have been enraged by Winchelsea's efforts to revisit this discreditable episode from his distant past. The archbishop had soon found himself being countersued in the king's courts, charged with trying to disinherit the Crown and subvert the realm.[18]

In 1305 the gloves really came off. During the spring, as Bigod was being pardoned his debts, Winchelsea was hit with a demand for £4,000 of unpaid taxes. Then, in the summer, a new pope was elected and the archbishop's fate was sealed. Boniface VIII, who would have defended Winchelsea, had died in 1303, shamefully hounded to death by the king of France's thugs. Clement V, a Gascon by birth and a former archbishop of Bordeaux, was more inclined to oblige the English king. In October, apparently after a stormy interview with Winchelsea himself, Edward dispatched a high-ranking embassy to the Curia, charged with a two-fold task: to undo the concessions that had diminished his Crown, and to secure the archbishop of Canterbury's deposition.[19]

Having spent a quiet Christmas in the West Country, Edward received his answer early in the New Year. On 11 February 1306, while he was hunting in Dorset, a papal bull arrived, reciting the royalist version of events since 1297, and absolving the king from his oath to all the concessions that his opponents had compelled him to grant. The following day – though Edward would not learn of it for several weeks – the pope suspended Winchelsea from office.[20]

With the arrival of this letter of absolution, the king's work was effectively complete. His many territories were at peace, his authority was supreme and uncontested, and the rights of his Crown had been restored. Moreover, though Edward himself may not have known it, he had also smashed another record. By February 1306 he was sixty-six years and eight months old, which meant that he had lived longer than any previous king of England (his great-great-great-grandfather, Henry I, had lived to a similar age, but was no more than sixty-six years and seven months at his death). And yet, in spite of his advanced years, Edward remained fit and healthy. The conquest of Scotland, it is true, had left him feeling drained and in need of a lengthy convalescence, but since that time he had rallied and recovered his strength. The past twelve months had seen him hunting and going on pilgrimages, travelling at the same rate as of old. During the summer of 1305, perhaps during a stay at Leeds Castle in July, he had clearly been feeling particularly energetic. In February 1306 Queen Margaret was once again heavily pregnant.[21]

Was there a reason, beyond luck and the law of averages, for this extraordinary longevity and potency? Could it be that Edward had been spared to serve some higher purpose? With conflict at home now finally concluded, it was possible to consider again the idea of renewing the fight overseas. Almost two years earlier, in a letter to the Master of the Knights Templar, the king had noted that he had 'long been hindered by diverse wars . . . from going to Jerusalem as he had vowed'. But, he had added hopefully, he still intended to go there 'at all speed' once those wars were over. 'Upon this journey,' he said, 'we have fixed our whole heart.' The recent embassy to the pope had raised the prospect of a new crusade in earnest, and Edward had been granted a crusading tax in return. Perhaps, at last, it was time for the king's long-delayed vow to be fulfilled.[22]

But then, just a week or so after receiving the pope's letter, other news arrived. Apparently, there had been a murder.

By any standards, the crime was appalling. It had been committed on 10 February, in the town of Dumfries, within the hallowed walls of the Franciscan church, right in front of the altar. Two men had come there in order to talk, but their conversation had quickly become a quarrel, and the quarrel had ended in bloodshed, with one man drawing his dagger and stabbing the other. It was, it seems, an impulsive, unpremeditated act, yet there was little room for mitigation. As the injured man had lain stricken on the altar steps, the friends of his assailant had weighed in and finished him off with their swords. What made this case especially appalling, however, were the identities of the two individuals involved. The victim was John Comyn, lord of Badenoch and erstwhile Guardian of Scotland. The killer was his long-time rival, Robert Bruce.

Precisely what passed between the two men that day in Dumfries must forever remain a mystery. It certainly mystified Edward I, who heard of the killing within a week or so and dispatched agents to investigate. Yet with hindsight there can be no doubt about the motive for the meeting, and ultimately for Comyn's murder, for the seeds had been sown almost two years earlier. In the summer of 1304, while the king of England had been laying siege to Stirling Castle, Bruce had met with the bishop of St Andrews and entered into a secret alliance.

Here too the details are vague, and deliberately so, for the purpose of the pact was clearly treasonable. A few months before it was sealed, Bruce's father, the nondescript collaborator of the 1290s, had died, and his claim to the Scottish throne, dormant for over a decade, had passed to his son. Bruce was evidently preparing to reactivate it, and the bishop, although a long-time backer of Balliol, was evidently ready to assist him. What had happened in Dumfries, it seems certain, is that Comyn had been invited to join the conspiracy but had refused. Bruce had reacted angrily, but also decisively, knowing that if his rival opposed him, his bid for the throne must fail.[23]

With the plot now public, Bruce was forced to move fast. He and his supporters rapidly secured control of the castles of south-west Scotland, then rode to Glasgow, where they met with the city's bishop, Robert Wishart. The stalwart upholder of the patriotic cause absolved the earl of his crime and urged him on, producing from his cathedral treasury certain regalia he had long ago secreted: a banner bearing the Scottish royal arms, and vestments suitable for the making of a king. As an anonymous letter from Berwick reveals, the English in Scotland were aware of the direction in which Bruce was moving, but his swiftness took them by surprise. By the last week of March the earl had arrived at Scone Abbey, where a sizeable number of other Scottish nobles and churchmen had also assembled to witness and approve a revolution. It was 25 March, the feast of the Annunciation. Precisely one year earlier Bruce had been in Westminster, watching Edward I celebrate his final victory over the Scots before the shrine of the Confessor. Now, one year on, the earl was crowned as King Robert I. Scotland, recently relegated to the status of a land, was defiantly declared to be a kingdom once more.[24]

'And when bold Edward was told how Bruce, who was so bold, had finished off the Comyn, and then made himself king, he went nearly out of his mind.' Although written some seven decades later, these lines by the Scottish poet John Barbour may come very close to the truth. Edward's wrath when he finally understood what was happening in Scotland was truly terrible, and probably contributed to a sharp and sudden decline in his health. In January and February 1306, as we have seen, the king was itinerating at much the same rate as usual. But by early March he was confined to Winchester, from where he did not stir for the next two months. When, at length, he left the city in the middle of May, he was being carried in a litter.[25]

As his strength finally began to fail him, Edward knew that he must look to others to take up the struggle. His contemporaries were almost all gone. John de Warenne, the ancient earl of Surrey, had died soon after returning from Scotland in 1304. Roger Bigod still lived but was himself too ill to campaign. Only Henry de Lacy, the fifty-six-year-old earl of Lincoln, was conceivably fit enough to fight. The conclusion was inescapable. Command must pass to a new generation. It was Aymer de Valence, the son and successor of his late uncle William, whom the king sent north in April to lead an immediate counter-attack.[26]

Above all, though, the burden of leadership must now fall to his own son and heir. The arguments of the previous year would have to be forgotten. Edward of Caernarfon, it was announced, would be commanding the main royal army that was ordered to assemble at Carlisle in July. Before then, it would be necessary to enhance his authority. On 7 April, the prince was granted Gascony by his father. Around the same time, word went out that there was to be a great ceremony in Westminster at Whitsun. The king would be knighting his eldest son, and all those who wished to receive the same accolade were invited to attend.[27]

Part of Edward's motivation for promoting the prince was financial. Custom entitled a lord to levy a tax in such circumstances, and the king was quick to do so on this occasion. But the ceremony was also intended to serve a higher purpose. The young noblemen of England – 'tyros', as one chronicler termed them – were to be bound together in a new cause, much as their fathers and grandfathers had been united by their oaths to liberate the Holy Land. When the day itself arrived, Edward knighted his son in the palace chapel, and they then proceeded to the abbey, where the prince performed the repetitive task of knighting around 300 others. The choice of date was probably significant: it was at Whitsun that Arthur was supposed to have held his celebrated 'plenary' court at Caerleon. Certainly, once the dubbing ritual was over and the newly ennobled company had repaired to the palace, their feast assumed an unmistakably Arthurian air. The king himself vowed revenge against Bruce, and promised that once his enemy had been vanquished he would head straight for the Holy Land. The prince followed suit, swearing that he would not sleep two nights in the same place until the Scots had been defeated, a vow clearly modelled on Perceval's declaration in the story of the Holy Grail. The feast was evidently magnificent, with a multitude of minstrels paid to perform, and each knight uttering his vow over two specially prepared golden swans. These, it seems, were an innovation, but one that set a fashion for swearing oaths on birds for the next two centuries.[28]

Assuming his vow was genuine, Edward of Caernarfon must have set out for Scotland more or less immediately. Two days after the feast, the king wrote to Aymer de Valence, saying that he was sending his son north with a strong force. He also added – perhaps surprisingly, given his condition – that he would follow in person as soon as possible.[29]

By the time these letters reached him, Valence was already well ahead with his advanced operations and scoring notable victories. In early June, having crossed the Forth, he captured both the bishop of St Andrews and the bishop of Glasgow – the latter was found holding the castle at Cupar in Fife 'as a man of war'. A week or so later, the lieutenant came close to apprehending his principal target. On 18 June, after the English had reoccupied Perth, the new king of Scotland approached with his host, hoping to provoke battle. Valence declined to respond immediately, but the next day advanced his own army to nearby Methven and fell upon his enemy's camp in the pre-dawn light. Many Scots were killed or captured, though Bruce himself escaped, fleeing west into the mountains with only a few hundred men.[30]

The king of England, meanwhile, had set out to join the fray but was heading nowhere fast. Ten days after leaving Westminster, Edward had travelled no further than Dunstable, a distance of only thirty miles. In the weeks that followed his progress continued at the same laborious rate, suggesting that he was in considerable pain. The agonies he suffered, both physical and mental, are also reflected in the remarkable preamble to an ordinance about the Royal Forest issued in the days before his departure. 'While we behold the imperfection of human weakness,' the king began, 'and weigh with attentive consideration the widespread burdens that lie upon our shoulders, we are indeed inwardly tormented . . . tossed about by the waves of diverse thoughts, and are frequently troubled, passing sleepless nights, dwelling in our inmost soul about what ought to be done.' His chief concern, he explained, was the ease of his subjects, 'in whose quiet we have rest', and he trusted that God, 'in the clemency of his goodness, will mercifully look upon and supply our deficiency'.[31]

Edward's own reserves of clemency and mercy were by this point entirely exhausted. It had taken six expeditions across eight years, countless expenditure and bitter compromises to subjugate the Scots, and it was only a matter of months since they had sworn to uphold his new scheme of government – a scheme that he considered to have been very generous and accommodating. Now his generosity had been thrown back in his face. The king was at the end of his tether, and his only thoughts were of vengeance. Valence had been told to take no prisoners, but seems to have interpreted his brief leniently: at least some of the knights taken at Methven had been subsequently dispatched into England to await sentence. In early August, however, on Edward's express orders, the killings began, and the aristocratic status of the captives availed them nothing. 'They bore arms against their liege lord the king and are prisoners of war,' read the royal writ that condemned these men to be drawn through the streets of Newcastle and hanged.[32]

Nor did the status of the clerical captives count for much on this occasion. Edward, though pleased by the early arrest of the bishop of Glasgow, had instructed Valence 'not to have any regard for his estate of prelate', and Wishart can have anticipated little sympathy, for he presented the very model of rebellious ingratitude. A recent royal gift of timber, intended for the repair of his cathedral, had been used by the firebrand bishop to build siege-engines. On 10 August he was brought before the king, by this point in County Durham, along with the bishop of St Andrews and the abbot of Scone. Their tonsures were sufficient to save them from the scaffold, but at Edward's command all three were sent south in chains, to be kept in castle dungeons.[33]

In Scotland the fortunes of King Robert had continued to deteriorate. Support for his rebellion, slight from the start, was waning visibly in the wake of his defeat at Methven. In July Bruce had been beaten for a second time at Dalrigh, near Tyndrum, and by a force of his own countrymen. Again he had escaped, but the net around him was drawing ever tighter. By mid-July the prince of Wales and his army of young tyros had left Carlisle and retaken south-western Scotland, closing off one set of escape routes, and by early August they had moved up to Perth to link arms with Valence. In desperation, therefore, Bruce decided to split his party in two. His wife, daughter and the other womenfolk were sent north-east, with the hope that they might make it to Orkney or even Norway. Meanwhile, Bruce himself fled in the opposite direction, and hid among the lochs and islands of Scotland's western seaboard.[34]

During the second half of August King Edward was in Northumberland but evidently very ill. In the middle of the month, while he rested at Hexham Abbey, one of the monks was paid a pound for his medical efforts, and for the next fortnight the king remained motionless at nearby Newbrough. Most ominously, at the end of August Edward made assignments of land to his youngest children, including his new baby daughter, Eleanor. Thereafter, however, he appears to have rallied, and the court resumed its slow progress in the direction of Carlisle. 'He is hearty and strong enough, considering his age,' wrote an unnamed courtier on 21 September, and at the same time Edward himself sent letters to the king of Castile, indicating that he had now recovered from his recent infirmity. Yet one week later, with their destination just ten miles in the distance, it was once again decided that the king should move no further. The court had reached Lanercost Priory, which was close enough, and would make a comfortable headquarters for the time being.[35]

In any case, the war was all but over. Everywhere in Scotland was back under English control, or in the hands of non-rebellious Scots. In September military efforts were concentrated on just two castles: Dunaverty, on the southern tip of the Mull of Kintyre, where Bruce was believed to be hiding, and Kildrummy in Aberdeenshire, where his female relatives had sought refuge. When the former fortress finally fell, the besiegers were disappointed. The king of Scots was already gone, escaped across the sea to Ireland. The women, however, were not so fortunate. Before Kildrummy was captured they made a last dash for freedom, escorted by the earl of Atholl and Bruce's brother, Neil. Having reached the far north of Scotland, they were taken at Tain by adherents of the Balliol–Comyn cause, and sent south to face Edward I.[36]

Despite pleas for clemency from Queen Margaret and several English magnates, the killings continued. Neil Bruce was dispatched to die in Berwick, where he was drawn, hanged and beheaded. Atholl was condemned to a similar death in London, regardless of the fact that English royal blood flowed in his veins (he was a great-great-grandson of King John). This was a true watershed moment: no earl had been executed in England for 230 years, and Edward acknowledged it by having Atholl hanged on a gallows built thirty feet higher than that of his fellows, then beheaded and burned. Even the women prisoners, if reckoned to be complicit in the revolt, were subjected to cruel and unusual punishments. Isabella, countess of Buchan, who had participated in Bruce's coronation, and Mary, the new king's sister, were imprisoned in specially constructed cages, set high in the towers of the castles at Roxburgh and Berwick. As living spectacles, they sent out the same message as the mutilated remains of their menfolk. This was the new and terrible price of rebellion against the king of England.[37]

The execution of rebels was now officially proclaimed policy. After Edward's arrival at Lanercost, it was announced that all those involved in Comyn's murder would themselves be killed, as would anyone who had assisted Bruce or who was taken fighting in his name. Only those who surrendered would escape the noose, and even they faced an uncertain future of indefinite imprisonment at the king's pleasure. The men carrying out these orders, of course, had a vested interest in seeing to the immediate dispatch of their enemies, for the rebellion had led to the territorial settlement of the previous year being torn up. Rich estates had once again been declared forfeit and were being regranted to the loyal. The result has been described as a 'reign of terror'. 'Alas, the noble blood that was thus spilt!' lamented Peter Langtoft, a man not normally given to expressions of sympathy for the Scots.[38]

But besides the butchering of Scotsmen there seemed little left to do, and so, in a bout of self-congratulatory jubilation, some of the younger English nobles took themselves off to tourney, even going overseas. The king was enraged, and ordered the arrest of twenty-two named individuals, even demanding that they be imprisoned in the Tower. Many of them were associates of Edward of Caernarfon, though whether the prince had personally absconded is unclear. In December he was certainly staying by the Kentish coast, but this was probably in order to welcome Cardinal Peter 'the Spaniard', come to England to help finalise the French peace. When, in the new year, young Edward and his friends returned to Carlisle in time for the parliament that was being held there, all was forgiven. Thanks to the intercession of the queen, most of the errant knights were pardoned or had their presumptuous behaviour overlooked.[39]

In February 1307, however, a fresh and furious row erupted between the two Edwards over the treatment of one of these men. According to a London chronicler, the king 'saw that his son, the prince of Wales, had an inordinate love for a certain Gascon knight'. The knight in question was Piers Gaveston, a young man of similar age to the prince and a member of his household for several years. Conventionally, and probably correctly, their relationship has been construed as homosexual; other chroniclers wrote of the 'undue intimacy' between the pair. Whatever the case, it was certainly regarded by contemporaries as wholly inappropriate, and the cause of the king's wrath in 1307 was an inappropriate attempt on the part of his son to promote Gaveston far beyond his comparatively humble station. Walter of Guisborough describes the scene in dramatic terms, and explains how the prince first asked Walter Langton, the treasurer, to put a request to his father on his behalf. When Langton in due course did so, Edward was incredulous, and angrily ordered his son to be summoned.

'On what business did you send this man?' he demanded.

'That I might, with your assent, give the county of Ponthieu to Sir Piers Gaveston,' the prince replied.

At this the king exploded.

'You bastard son of a bitch! Now you want to give lands away – you who never gained any? As the Lord lives, were it not for fear of breaking up the kingdom, you should never enjoy your inheritance!'

As these words were spoken, says Guisborough, the old man seized his son's hair in both hands and tore out as much as he could until, at length exhausted, he threw him out.[40]

Edward's readiness to lash out was not merely a result of his son's provocation, nor simply a rage against the dying of the light. His fury was also fuelled by the knowledge that Robert Bruce had returned. At the start of February the fugitive king had re-crossed the Irish Sea and was understood to be at large 'in the isles off the Scottish coast'. Thanks to the ongoing collaboration of certain clans in that region, his initial moves had met with disaster. A force led by his brothers, Thomas and Alexander Bruce, had been captured in Galloway, and both men were subsequently hanged and beheaded. Yet Bruce himself continued to evade capture, to the immeasurable frustration of his incapacitated opponent, still stranded at Lanercost after five months. In the second week of February Edward had sent withering letters to Aymer de Valence and his other young commanders, expressing utter amazement at their inability to apprehend Bruce, chastising them for their failure to furnish him with news, and suspecting from their silence that they were being excessively cautious.[41]

In fact, as Edward was beginning to realise, it was not the caution of his lieutenants that was causing difficulty, but the total lack of restraint to which he had urged them up to this point. The king's savage policy of revenge had driven many Scots, whom in other circumstances might have submitted to English justice, into supporting the cause of his enemy. In mid-March, having finally managed to complete his journey to Carlisle, Edward sent out new orders. Apparently, he said, some people had interpreted his recent ordinance for the settlement of Scotland too rigorously; his commanders were now to have it proclaimed that all those who had been 'compelled' to rise to rebellion could come in without fear of reprisal. This sudden and wholesale volte-face suggests that the English in the field were experiencing grave difficulties, reaping the whirlwind they had sown by their earlier severity. Bruce had left Scotland the previous year as an unpopular rebel; in 1307 he returned as a potential redeemer.[42]

In April news came of the first English reversal. Valence, having learned that Bruce was lurking near Loch Trool in Galloway, and no doubt with the accusation of laxity still ringing in his ears, elected to mount an attack. On this occasion, however, his troops were repulsed by those of the Scottish king and, though their material losses were minor, their credibility was cracked. In the month that followed Bruce cemented his success with two further victories, first beating Valence himself at Loudon Hill on 10 May, and then roundly defeating one of his deputies in Ayrshire a few days later. In each case the English commanders escaped, but the myth of their invincibility had now been shattered. On 15 May a Scottish lord on the English side penned a vivid and alarming summary of the new situation. 'I hear that Bruce never had the goodwill of his own followers or of the people in general so much as now. It appears that God is with him, for he has destroyed King Edward's power both among the English and the Scots . . . May it please God to prolong King Edward's life, for men say openly that when he is gone the victory will go to Bruce.'[43]

This plea to the Almighty to preserve the king, as well as indicating a belief in his almost superhuman ability, also betrays a total absence of faith in his successor. Edward of Caernarfon by this stage had long since left the north-west. In early May he was at Dover, bidding farewell to Piers Gaveston, who was preparing to sail into exile on the king's orders. The prince had evidently accompanied his favourite with his father's leave, for he was expected to lead an embassy to France in order to further the peace process. But when, in early June, the command came to abort this mission – no doubt in light of the worsening situation in Scotland – the king's son showed himself in no hurry to return to the war zone, and remained in the south of England.[44]

King Edward had reacted to the defeats in Scotland, inevitably, with orders for more troops: a new army was to muster at Carlisle in the middle of July. In the meantime, however, his health again went into decline. According to Walter of Guisborough, the king was now suffering from dysentery, an affliction that all the electuaries, cordials and ointments prepared by his doctors in the past months can have done nothing to alleviate. There can thus have been little celebration in mid-June when Edward passed his sixty-eighth birthday. So grave was his condition that he had become all but invisible, and his seclusion gave rise to the rumour that he was in fact already dead.[45]

When, at length, these murmurs reached the king's own ears, they stirred that part of his spirit that was indubitably great. Around 24 June the order was given to prepare for an immediate advance. With the muster date still three weeks into the future, whatever army had assembled in Carlisle can only have been half-formed at best. But leadership was required at once, and Edward had now abandoned the notion that it could be provided by others, least of all by his feckless and still-absent son. Instead, the ailing king rose from his bed to lead his men to war in person. The litter that had borne him on his agonising journey to the Border he rejected, and it was ceremoniously surrendered in Carlisle Cathedral. Edward now mounted his war-horse, as of old, and rode out from the city at the head of his host.[46]

It was all, of course, a magnificent act, undertaken in defiance – of the rumours, of the Scots, of pain and illness, and thus even of death itself. As such it was unsustainable. The king had headed west out of Carlisle, evidently with the intention of sailing to Scotland across the Solway Firth. But after ten days he had advanced only six miles, and on 6 July he was forced to stop at Burgh by Sands, an isolated settlement close to the Cumbrian coast. In this windswept wilderness Edward spent his last night on Earth. The following day – Friday, the feast of St Thomas – around mid-afternoon, his attendants appeared to help him to eat, but as they lifted the king from his bed, he died in their arms.[47]

12

A Great and Terrible King

For almost a fortnight Edward's death remained a closely guarded secret. According to Walter of Guisborough, anyone who spoke of it during this time was imprisoned. Only three letters are known to have been dispatched the following day: one to the queen, one to the earl of Lincoln and one to the prince of Wales. This last was received on 11 July, and Edward of Caernarfon set out at once for the north-west, arriving a week later to mourn over the body. It was not until 20 July that his rule was proclaimed in Carlisle Castle, and the veil of secrecy surrounding his father's death was lifted.[1]

As the news spread throughout England, it elicited a chorus of despair. 'Death has taken him, alas!' cried Peter Langtoft. 'My heart is in desolation,' wrote another Englishman in French. 'Me thuncheth that deth hath don us wrong,' said yet another in his native tongue. When messengers found the pope in Poitiers he was reportedly unable to stand on account of his grief. During the last days of July prayers and sermons were recited in Poitiers Cathedral – the first of their kind to be said for any king at the Curia – and across the city the bells rang out. Back in England Edward's body began its long journey southwards from Burgh by Sands, led by the bishop of Coventry, and slowed by a crowd of lamenting subjects.[2]

Edward of Caernarfon was able to accompany this procession only during its opening stages; after a few days he had to return to Carlisle in order to lead the abandoned host. Their expedition, however, proved short lived and uneventful, and no doubt the English troops were deeply dispirited. They advanced into south-western Scotland, but Bruce wisely chose to remain hidden, and less than a month had elapsed before the campaign was called to a halt. The new king returned to the Border, where he paused to receive the homages of loyalist Scots, and then continued south to attend his father's funeral.[3]

Since the start of August Edward's corpse had lain embalmed in Waltham Abbey in Essex, not far from London. Around 18 October it began the final stage of its journey. On entering the capital it was received with maximum honour, resting for consecutive nights in the priory of Holy Trinity and St Paul's Cathedral, as well as being taken to other city churches besides. At length it was brought to Westminster Abbey, where the funeral was held on Friday, 27 October. The service, says Guisborough, was attended by magnates of all lands and diverse regions, and Edward was laid to rest amongst his fathers.[4]

Contemporaries were in no doubt: this was a farewell to a truly great king. *Edwardus Magnus* was a phrase that sprang readily and naturally to the minds of men from Westminster to the far west of Ireland. Some went further still. Peter Langtoft averred that there had been no greater king since the time of Arthur, and in Poitiers one of the pope's preachers ventured that his subject had been no less and perhaps more worthy of praise than Alexander. In Westminster itself, meanwhile, there was no such hesitation. According to the local writer who composed the longest lament of all, Edward had been entirely without equal, outshining not only Arthur and Alexander but also Brutus, Solomon and Richard the Lionheart. 'We should perceive him to surpass all the kings of the earth who came before him,' was this author's unstinting conclusion.[5]

On what basis did this conclusion rest? Several obituarists went on to justify their superlative assessment and, unsurprisingly, one reason stood out above all others. Edward, as Guisborough put it, had been a king 'most strong'. 'The most renowned combatant on steed,' opined Peter Langtoft, 'he had no equal as a knight in armour.' 'King Edward was an outstanding warrior from his adolescence,' added the Westminster eulogist, 'in tournaments most mighty, in war most pugnacious.' That these and other authors were right to remember their former leader as a valiant fighter is hardly open to doubt. Evidence of Edward's courage and prowess in arms is abundant across his entire career. His personal participation in tournaments appears to have ended in 1273, after an especially bloody encounter at Chalon-sur-Saône in France drew condemnation from the pope. But the king had continued to throw himself into the even deadlier business of war regardless of the risks involved. As late as 1304, as his Westminster obituary recalled, he had very nearly been killed by crossbow bolts and other projectiles during the siege of Stirling. It is especially noteworthy that in respect of his valour Edward's reputation was not simply the work of flatterers. After the Battle of Lewes in 1264, even his enemies had acknowledged that 'he was not slow to attack in the strongest places, fearing the onslaught of none'.[6]

Of course, physical strength, and even valour, while crucial, were by themselves insufficient: tyrants could also be strong and courageous. To be truly useful these qualities had to be combined with wisdom, and here too the obituarists were in agreement. Edward was the wisest and most prudent king, said Guisborough; 'full of understanding', added Langtoft, while another author affirmed that 'all the things he did, he wisely brought them to an end'.[7] Again, it is difficult in general terms to disagree with this assessment. Wisdom is clearly a more subjective quality than valour; what seems wise to one person at a particular time may seem less wise to another, or in retrospect. The fundamental measure of Edward's wisdom, however, is that he was a good judge of other people. He could spot frauds (such as the knight who claimed to have been cured of blindness at the tomb of Henry III), and he had a talent for selecting men of outstanding ability to serve him. As one of the preachers in Poitiers put it: 'He did not rule in a frivolous state of mind, nor under the influence of flatterers . . . but with the prudent counsel of good and wise men.' Certain names spring immediately to mind. Robert Burnell, the longest serving chancellor until the eighteenth century; Otto de Grandson, a brave soldier and a brilliant statesman. Both had served Edward since his youth, at a time when his faculty for recruiting the right people was already demonstrably superior to that of his father. Roger Leybourne, Roger Clifford, Roger Mortimer – many of those whom he bound to his side were men of his own warlike stamp. Yet Edward also proved adept at choosing the best lawyers and clerics to serve at his court. His wisdom was such that he could channel their differing talents and satisfy their considerable (and often competing) ambitions.[8]

The corollary of this – contrary to what some historians have asserted – is that Edward's lordship was emphatically good. A king who shared their longing for feats of arms, adventure and the pursuit of noble causes – this was a king worth serving for his own sake. Unlike his father, Edward had no need to buy loyalty with lavish grants of land or money. He had friends but not favourites. As his Westminster obituarist explained, men would come from all over the king's dominions simply in the hope of joining the company of his knights. But those who served him well Edward did reward generously. The extensive new lordships given to Henry de Lacy, Reginald de Grey and John de Warenne in Wales, or to Thomas de Clare in Ireland, are a standing argument against the spurious notion that Edward was somehow lacking in largesse.[9]

Masterful in the management of his own household, Edward was no less competent in managing the wider political community. He took care, for example, to involve his greatest magnates in the running of the realm, consulting them in council on matters of importance. He proved able to handle the prickliest of characters, placating them where possible, overruling them when necessary. Thus Gilbert de Clare was allowed to lead armies in south Wales and to marry the king's daughter, but given a severe dressing-down when he failed to respect the Crown's authority.

An important part of Edward's success as a leader, also mentioned by his Westminster obituarist, was his ready eloquence. According to a later writer, the king had some form of mild speech impediment – possibly a lisp. If this was so, it clearly did not affect his powers of persuasion. One thinks of his success in talking round former Montfortians in the wake of a bitter civil war – men like John de Vescy, who went on to follow Edward for the rest of his days. One also recollects the broad Christian coalition he built in the Holy Land, and his speech outside Westminster Hall that moved an archbishop to tears. It is a pity that no one preserved any of the pre-battle harangues that the king must surely have delivered, for he was clearly an orator of considerable skill.[10]

Eloquence, of course, had been held against him by his Montfortian enemies. Edward was said to 'cloak himself in pleasant speech' but then go back on his word. This, the author of *The Song of Lewes* opined, showed that he thought himself above the law, and prompted the lament, 'O Edward, thou dost wish to become a king without law; verily, they would be wretched who were ruled by such a king'. But to judge from his obituaries, these fears had been unfounded. Edward was lauded in 1307 as a rigorous ruler who loved the law. 'Truly,' said one preacher, 'in our times no king's kingdom was made firm and strong with so much justice and so much mercy.' In terms of lawgiving this was certainly true: Edward's reign, especially during its first half, had witnessed an unprecedented volume of legislation – a stream of wide-ranging statutes that led seventeenth-century commentators to dub the king 'the English Justinian'. Recent research has put Edward's contribution to this process in perspective. It is now appreciated that he had little personal interest or involvement in the practical business of lawmaking, or even in passing judgement. Nevertheless, that so much regulation was introduced during Edward's reign was significant, and shows that the king was anxious that justice should be maintained. In this respect his attitude had not altered since, at the age of twenty, he had instructed his bailiffs to exhibit 'common justice' to all, lest he lose the favour of God and man, and his lordship was belittled.[11]

Modern historians have found fault with Edward's justice, identifying several occasions when the king departed from such high ideals for his own or his family's advantage. The most notorious example, the disinheritance of Robert de Ferrers, has already been discussed. Another incident, wherein royal ministers persuaded the dying countess of Devon to sell her lands to the king, thereby disinheriting her distant relatives, also looks highly suspect. There can be no denying that, in his desire to increase the Crown's estate, Edward occasionally indulged in quite low skulduggery. Here too, however, it is important to retain a sense of proportion. It would have been a rare medieval monarch indeed who never manipulated the law to suit his own purposes. What mattered in Edward's case was that, in spite of the odd lapse, his rule was generally perceived to be equitable. People could feel confident about approaching him for justice in a way they could not have done during the reigns of his father and grandfather. The king's own attitude is well illustrated by a private letter he sent to the chancellor in 1304 concerning a royal ward called Thomas Bardolf. This young man had given offence by refusing to go through with a marriage that Edward had arranged for him, and the chancellor was therefore instructed 'to be as stiff and harsh towards Thomas in this business as can be, without offending the law'. Were such a letter leaked from the heart of government today it would be enough to generate resignations, but thirteenth-century kings did not have to be so careful in their correspondence. What is more striking in this instance is that, even as he instructed his chancellor to be partial, Edward reminded him to stay within the limits of what was legal.[12]

Another quality that the eulogists singled out for praise was Edward's piety. He was, in the opinion of one writer, 'the most Christian king of England'. This description probably rested more on his reputation as a crusader rather than the kind of piety for which his father had been famous. 'O Jerusalem, thou hast lost the flower of thy chivalry,' was one poet's response to the news of his passing, and the general emphasis on crusading in the obituaries seems to have been encouraged by the rumour that, in his dying moments, Edward had willed his heart to the Holy Land, along with a fighting company of eighty knights. (The story that he commanded his body be carried at the head of future armies until Scotland was conquered was only told later, and is palpably nonsense.)[13]

In many respects, however, the king's piety was very similar to the kind practised by his father. Like Henry, Edward distributed alms to the poor on a grand scale, feeding (or at least paying) hundreds of paupers at his court every week. He also undertook the unpleasant business of touching people suffering from 'the king's evil' – scrofula, or tuberculosis of the neck – and was apparently more sought out for this reason than any of his successors. Like his father, Edward was a frequent visitor to cathedrals and other places of worship, and he made rich offerings of gold, jewels and money at their shrines and tombs. He did not share Henry's inordinate devotion to Edward the Confessor – that much was clear from the fact that Westminster Abbey, half-built at the time of his coronation, was still in much the same state at the time of his funeral. Nor did he indulge in ostentatious displays of piety in order to compensate for political and military failure. Edward's pilgrimages were often undertaken in advance of military campaigns, and his ecclesiastical patronage was more eclectic. When his armies advanced, they carried with them the banners of a host of English saints. For Edward, pious conduct was a necessary buttress to military success. An inventory drawn up after his death reveals that the king possessed a veritable arsenal of ornamented relics, including an arm of St David, a nail from Christ's cross, and even a saint's tooth 'effective against lightning and thunder'.[14]

It was small wonder that Edward believed in the efficacy of these and other relics. As another of his obituarists observed, he was an exceedingly fortunate king, at least to the extent that he survived numerous near misses. Many have been mentioned in the preceding pages: the storm at sea that prompted him to found Vale Royal Abbey, the chamber that collapsed beneath his feet in Gascony, the two battles from which he emerged unscathed and, most famously, the unsuccessful attempt on his life at Acre. The list could easily be extended. Nicholas Trivet, a later chronicler whose patrons included Edward's daughter Mary, preserved two episodes that would otherwise be unknown. In 1297, while the king was at Winchelsea waiting to sail to Flanders, his horse was startled by a windmill and leapt clean over the town's lofty ramparts, along with its royal rider. Miraculously both survived. On another, earlier occasion, a youthful Edward was reportedly playing chess in a certain chamber and, for no apparent reason, got up to stretch his legs, only to have a stone crash down from the vaulting in the place where he had been seated. This escape was said to be the source of his devotion to the shrine of the Virgin at Walsingham.[15]

Trivet also told a story of how Edward, out hunting one day, rode his horse through a river to pursue a man who had mistakenly presumed he could disregard royal orders with impunity. The chronicler's intention was to demonstrate that the king was 'heedless of danger when he wanted revenge', but his tale has recently been taken to indicate that Edward also possessed 'a violent temper'. Given the story's suspiciously allegorical appearance, its value as evidence in this last respect is open to debate. Edward could undoubtedly get angry on occasion: financial records show that in 1290 he paid twenty marks' compensation to an esquire whom he had assaulted with a stick, while in 1297 repairs were necessary to a coronet, the property of his daughter Elizabeth, after the king had thrown it into the fire. Beyond this, however, evidence of genuine royal wrath seems rather thin on the ground: there are certainly no stories of Edward falling to the floor and biting the rushes after the fashion of his Angevin ancestors. By the thirteenth century, as the murals in the Painted Chamber make clear, it was important that *ira* (anger) should be vanquished by *débonaireté* (urbanity, literally 'having a fine air'). Naturally, that did not mean that the chamber's occupants were always capable of similar self-restraint. But there is far more evidence of debonair activity at Edward's court than there is for explosions of ire. His financial accounts show frequent payments to jesters, acrobats, minstrels and dancers (including, in the last instance, a certain Matilda Makejoy). They also record the charming fact that every year on Easter Monday the queen's ladies-in-waiting would try to catch the king in bed, and he rewarded them with a ransom if they were successful.[16]

Of the remaining observations made by writers at the time of Edward's death, most are bland or commonplace – he was 'illustrious', for example, or 'noble'. One of the sermons preached before the pope, however, contained some words that were clearly well considered and that ring especially true. More than any other ruler, it was claimed, Edward 'wished to know much about the changes and variations of the world . . . he never knew how to be at rest'. The preacher went on to substantiate his point by listing some of the places the king had visited in his lifetime: Spain, Wales, Flanders, Scotland, Gascony and the Holy Land. He could have also added France, Italy, Sicily, Sardinia, Savoy, North Africa and Cyprus: Edward was the most widely travelled English monarch until well into the modern age. And yet the king's restlessness was never more apparent than when circumstances forced him to remain in one place. It tended to manifest itself in building work: his tower in Acre, his new towns at Bonnegarde and Burgus Reginae. There can be little doubt that Edward loved building, and the regularity of bastides must have appealed to his orderly mind. But it was military architecture above all that gave him the greatest delight. In spite of the lack of direct evidence, historians have inevitably wondered about how involved he was in the design of his great Welsh castles, but the answer must surely be: intimately. When, in 1302, the king wanted a new fortress in Scotland at Linlithgow, he entered into detailed discussions with Master James of St George, concerning himself with such matters as the construction of the towers and the depth of the ditch. If Edward took this much interest in a wooden pele that cost less than £1,000, it presupposes that he was equally if not more involved in the planning of castles that cost ten to twenty times as much.[17]

Edward, then, had the character of a great king – brave, wise, eloquent, just, pious – combined with an abundance of good fortune and a restless, venturesome nature. But what of his actions, and what of his motives? Were these also adjudged great by his contemporaries, or indeed by posterity? With regard to his youth the answer in both cases has generally been a resounding no. Matthew Paris, commenting on Edward's alleged attack on another young man in 1256, had been deeply concerned. 'If he does such things when the wood is green,' the chronicler worried, 'what can be hoped for when it is seasoned?' Modern writers have also been unimpressed with Edward's apparent juvenile delinquency. One twentieth-century historian called him 'an irresponsible, arrogant and headstrong boy' and labelled him treacherous, self-indulgent and incapable of self-discipline.[18] Both judgements, however, seem unduly harsh if not wholly unfounded. There is no doubt that Edward was a pushy teenager, and that, like most teenagers, what he craved was greater independence. Given his notions about the way kings and knights ought to conduct themselves, it was almost inevitable that he should clash with his father, who, as well as being unwilling to cede authority, espoused a radically different idea of what kingship entailed. But when Henry's government was overthrown, and father and son were shackled, Edward's struggle to control his own destiny suddenly became far more serious, and so did his own conduct. That Edward tried to throw off the restraints that had been placed upon him does not automatically render his behaviour ignoble. Nor do his actions during a period of kaleidoscopic change seem particularly inconstant. What he wanted, and what he endeavoured to obtain, was the free disposition of his lands and castles. To do this he perceived it was necessary to ally himself with those demanding reform, but he soon found that this placed him in an impossible situation, caught between two sides in an increasingly bitter family feud. He may, perhaps, have regretted his decision to desert Simon de Montfort in the spring of 1261, as for a time it cost him many friends. But by the end of 1263 Edward's decision was vindicated. Montfort in power proved to be a disaster. From that moment onwards, all but a minority of diehards saw that the surer guarantee of good government lay in supporting the king's eldest son.

Having won the struggle for power with Montfort, Edward had two main motives that would occupy him for the rest of his life. One was the recovery of Jerusalem; the other was the recovery of the rights of the Crown. The former, however misguided it may seem today, was regarded as the highest ideal of Edward's age, and by pursuing it he won lasting international fame. The latter was made manifest at the moment of his coronation, and prosecuted with vigour in the months and years that followed. In England, the effort was cleverly handled. By presenting the Crown as the friend of the oppressed, the new king won widespread popular support, and this enabled him to begin recouping his father's losses. Magnates who had usurped royal rights were made to answer for their actions; smaller landowners, meanwhile, thanks to the development of parliament, were given a greater voice, and in turn became Edward's most consistent allies. For the first time since the Norman Conquest, England had a government that was perceived to be working in the interests of the majority of its subjects.

The consequence was that a minority of subjects suffered. In his effort to appease his Christian taxpayers in parliament, Edward stripped away the traditional protections that earlier kings of England had extended towards the country's Jewish community. During his rule the Jews were forbidden to lend money at interest, stigmatised as infidels and ultimately expelled. Modern commentators have naturally judged Edward harshly for this, though they often err in presenting him as a pioneer. He was, it is true, the first European leader to carry out an expulsion on a nationwide scale, but this only goes to show that he was a powerful ruler of a precociously united kingdom. Other kings, earls and counts before him had expelled Jews to the furthest extent of their more limited authority. To say this much is not to deny that Edward was a thorough-going anti-Semite: he was, as his pogrom of 1279 proves all too clearly. It is merely to emphasise that, in his anti-Semitism, Edward was altogether conventional. A bigoted man, he lived in a bigoted age, and was king of a bigoted people. Abhorrent as it seems to us today, the fact that 'he expelled the faithless multitude of Jews and unbelievers from England' was regarded by his Westminster obituarist as one of Edward's most commendable achievements.[19]

Chief among his achievements in contemporary eyes, however, was his success in war – and war, of course, was another consequence of Edward's determination to recover his rights. 'The most victorious king', 'the conqueror of lands and the flower of chivalry' – Edward was, as one poet put it, 'a king who knew much of war', and in war all his talents – bravery, strong leadership, eloquence, strategic sense, organisational ability – came to the fore. The result, as we can appreciate in retrospect, was conflict on an uncommonly awesome scale: the largest armies seen in Britain until the seventeenth century, and the most spectacular chain of castles ever constructed.[20]

With the possible exception of historians, who tend to get swept along by all the excitement, modern observers would probably be less ready in their praise. But to thirteenth-century Englishmen, who perceived themselves to be surrounded by many perils, it was more important to have a warlike king than a peaceable one. Edward, said one preacher admiringly, 'tried to war down and subdue all those who wished to throw his people into confusion'. As the author of *The Song of Caerlaverock* explained poetically, the king confronting his enemies was like the three lions embroidered in gold on the red of his banner – dreadful, fierce and cruel. The Westminster obituarist put it in even more telegraphic terms. Edward, he said, was peaceable to the obedient, but to the sons of pride he was indeed 'a terrible king'.[21]

The sons of pride in the first instance were the princes of Wales, Llywelyn ap Gruffudd and his brother Dafydd, whose dynasty Edward warred down to the point of extinction. Whether he was justified in doing so has been a much-debated question in modern times. Contemporary Englishmen, as we have already seen, entertained no such doubts. To them the Welsh did not seem to be an oppressed people; rather they were considered to be an immoral, lazy, anarchic, turbulent and faithless race – 'that domestic enemy', as one vitriolic cleric put it, 'the disturber of English peace'. In view of such hostile attitudes, one is bound to wonder just how important the king's own contribution really was. It is doubtful whether Wales would have been conquered so thoroughly, so ruthlessly, so swiftly and so successfully had Edward I died in the Holy Land. It is equally doubtful that it would have survived as an independent power even had that been the case. By the time Edward arrived home in 1274, his peace with Llywelyn was already compromised by clashes in the March, and the March itself was a reminder that the English and the Welsh had been at loggerheads for more than two centuries. To this extent, both the king of England and the princes of Wales were representatives of their respective peoples. The Welsh, in truth, had too far to travel, economically and socially, for the English to cease regarding them as barbarians. Consequently, it is hard to imagine circumstances in which native power in Wales could have endured. Whether by sudden conquest or slow erosion, English domination seems a foregone conclusion.[22]

It seems equally certain that England would have eventually gone to war with France, though here too the historian has the advantage of hindsight. To Edward himself it seemed more natural that the two kingdoms should get along well. Their courts shared a common chivalric culture, and the royal families had been happily intermarried for two generations. In retrospect, however, the four decades of peace from 1254 to 1294 seem like a remarkable but brief interruption to long centuries of hostility. Edward certainly did not want a war with France; he worked hard in the first half of his reign to try to minimise friction with his Continental overlord, and gave Gascony the best government it had experienced for over a hundred years. But the same forces of nationalism and bigotry that were making the English increasingly intolerant of the Welsh and the Jews were also growing apace in France, and by the early 1290s they had infected the French court. This happened in secret, of course, so Edward's failure to foresee the coming conflict should not be held too strongly against him. His only mistake was to negotiate without consulting his councillors, and for this his subjects chastised him accordingly (up to this point, said one chronicler, he had seemed like another Solomon). Yet when they too realised that the seizure of Gascony was the result of French trickery, they soon forgave him. 'King of France, thou hadst sin,' said one English poet in 1307, 'to hinder the will of King Edward to go to the Holy Land', and there can be no doubt that this was a fair judgement.[23]

The expulsion of the Jews, the conquest of Wales, the resumption of war with France: all required Edward I in order to occur precisely how and when they did, but all might easily have happened without him. What would have been almost impossible to foresee in, say, 1272, and what might well not have happened had, for example, Edward died in Acre that summer, was that England should go to war with Scotland. It was not just that the English and Scottish royal families had been intermarrying for several generations, nor even that similarly convivial cross-border relations had been maintained by their respective aristocracies. For a century and more before Edward's day, Scotland had been busily approximating itself to England: welcoming English settlers and adopting English customs. Here the trend was not one of growing intolerance, but of increasing convergence.

For this reason alone, the mid-point of Edward's reign stands to be regarded as a watershed moment in British history. The year 1290 was eventful in so many ways. It saw the king's compromise over his Quo Warranto campaign, the finalisation of his plans for a second crusade, and the total expulsion of all England's Jews. At a more personal level, it also witnessed the marriage of two of his daughters and the death of his beloved queen. All of these events, however, paled in significance compared to the death in September that year of Margaret, the Maid of Norway, heiress to the Scottish throne and intended bride of Edward of Caernarfon.

Had the Maid lived, and had this marriage taken place, the ramifications would have been far-reaching: a union of the Crowns, three centuries before the eventual union of 1603, only far more natural and amicable; Robert Bruce and John Balliol fighting alongside Edward I in a future war against France, just as their fathers and brothers had fought alongside him at Lewes and in the Holy Land; the French war resolved more swiftly as a result, and Edward travelling east for a second time, again with Scotsmen in his company. Nor is it unrealistic to imagine a more distant future, in which nobles from both nations, cousins in spirit as well as in blood, went on to tackle together the problematic peoples to the west whom both regarded as barbarians. In Edward I's own day, his friend John de Vescy had participated not only in the conquest of Wales but also in the Scottish conquest of the Isle of Man, fighting under the banner of Alexander III. A future king of an Anglo-Scottish realm, leading an integrated Anglo-Scottish aristocracy, might well have dealt decisively with the 'wild Irish' or 'wild Scots' of the Western Isles, resulting in a British Isles that was precociously united.[24]

But none of this was to be. It happened that the Maid died, and Edward decided to lord it over the Scots, with fatal consequences. It meant that his war with France was far more protracted and expensive than it otherwise need have been, and it meant that he was committed to a war of conquest in Scotland that he lacked the resources to win. The combination of these two conflicts, moreover, had a disastrous impact on his other dominions, undoing much of the constructive work the king had carried out earlier in his reign. Criminals were pardoned in return for military service; Ireland was bled dry in the quest for supplies; England was taxed more heavily in the space of four years than it had been in the previous two decades, as well as being made to bear other oppressive burdens besides. Edward argued bitterly with the Church and with his magnates, and brought his people to the brink of rebellion, while in Wales rebellion actually occurred. Throughout this time, the king himself began to act in an unrestrained manner, bullying when persuasion failed, going back on his word, and becoming massively angry in the face of mounting opposition. 'Either you will go or you will hang!' he told Roger Bigod in front of a stunned parliament at Salisbury.

Eventually, in England, much of Edward's behaviour was excused. 'We know you to be a good and prudent prince,' said Bigod in 1300, presumably remembering the king's earlier record as a consensus builder rather than his more recent arbitrary acts. It was precisely because he had been such an excellent ruler before the crisis that Edward retained or recovered the loyalty of most of his subjects. Moreover, as he entered his seventh decade, he found that his contemporaries were dying out, and the new generation at his court had less desire to contradict a king who had already attained legendary status. The prime example in this category is provided by Humphrey de Bohun, earl of Hereford and namesake son of Roger Bigod's erstwhile ally. The old earl had died in 1298 apparently urging his offspring not to abandon the struggle for the Charters, but Humphrey junior did nothing of the sort. Instead he moved swiftly to ingratiate himself with Edward, supporting the king in war and marrying his widowed daughter, Elizabeth, in 1302. By 1306 he had acquired the status of favourite son-in-law; in the spring of that year he was rewarded with Robert Bruce's forfeited estates.[25]

Men like Humphrey de Bohun, or for that matter Roger Bigod, did not doubt that Edward had been right to act as he did in Scotland. They too had read their copies of Geoffrey of Monmouth and knew that the kings of England had the right to rule the whole of Britain (indeed, they argued as much in a collective letter to the pope in 1301).[26] They shared in Edward's triumph in 1304 and did not doubt his greatness because war in the north subsequently re-erupted. Success seemed all but secured at the time of the king's death in 1307. It only remained to take out Bruce and the two kingdoms that he had briefly ruled would once again be united.

But Edward's legacy, largely because of his action in Scotland, was not one of unity but of profound and lasting division. In Ireland English power was already in retreat by 1307, such was the damage that the Scottish wars had caused to the colony, and in the decades that followed the lordship there went into steep decline. Crown revenues fell sharply. Within a year of the king's death it was deemed necessary to bring the rolls of the Dublin exchequer inside the castle at night on account of the threat of war. Ultimately royal government would contract to a small area confined by 'the Pale', and although some English settlers continued to live beyond it, they found a settled English way of life impossible to maintain. Those dwelling in towns developed a permanent siege mentality, living in constant fear of attack from 'the wild Irish, our enemies'. Meanwhile, those English magnates who remained in Ireland survived only by compromising with the natives, adopting Irish political customs and an overtly Irish way of life. They sported Gaelic names and learned to speak the language; some even found fame as composers of Gaelic poetry.[27]

In Wales, by contrast, there was no such compromise, and the result was a society in some respects even more bitterly divided. At a political level, English power prevailed: there could be no arguing with the wholesale nature of the conquest that Edward had inflicted. Welsh lords who wished to do so could play subordinate roles, serving as sheriffs in the new colonial administration, or even as knights in the royal household. But at a popular level there was no such mutual understanding; culturally, Wales and England remained worlds apart. As in Ireland, the English settlers locked themselves away in the new Edwardian boroughs, always suspicious of native intentions. The people of Caernarfon complained in 1345 that they suffered daily from 'the malevolence and enmity of the Welsh'. When uprisings occurred, as they did in 1316 and more famously in 1400, the English were always able to crush and contain them. But the Crown had no interest in Wales beyond maintaining the divided status quo. Nothing symbolises the revised limits of royal ambition in the principality better than the fate of its two principal castles. Caernarfon and Beaumaris, incomplete at the time of Edward's death, were left in that state by his successors. In 1330 building work on both sites was abandoned forever.[28]

Naturally, though, it was in Scotland that the English failure proved most dramatic and the legacy of bitterness most lasting. The final, devastating decade of Edward's reign had not merely halted the trend towards convergence but thrown it into reverse. Englishmen, remembering the raids of William Wallace, resurrected the hostile stereotypes of the previous century: the Scots were once again lumped with the Welsh and the Irish as faithless and barbaric Celts. Scotsmen, for their part, responded in kind. Before 1290 they had been pleased to christen their sons Edward – Bruce's sole surviving brother and Balliol's eldest son both bore the name. By 1307, however, Edward was regarded in Scotland as 'the Covetous king' of Merlin's prophecy: after his death, the soothsayers foretold, the Celtic peoples would 'band together, and have full lordship, and live in peace until the end of the world'.[29]

Fortunately for the English, the Bruces' attempts to construct such a pan-Celtic alliance proved short lived. Yet in Scotland itself the tide was turned decisively. King Robert overcame his domestic opponents and consolidated his rule; English garrisons fell one by one before the onslaught of his forces. When, in 1314, an English army appeared north of the Border with the intention of saving Stirling, it was wiped out at nearby Bannockburn; Edward of Caernarfon – Edward II, as he then was – was lucky to escape with his life. Their enemies might not care to admit it, but the Scots had vindicated their right to independence. Yet because the English could not admit it, there could be no return to the days before 1290. Scotland, which had once seemed nothing less than England's double, now defined itself against its southern neighbour. 'As long as a hundred of us remain alive,' its leaders wrote to the pope in 1320, 'we will never on any conditions submit to the dominion of the English.'[30]

Not all of these failures and reverses, of course, can be blamed on Edward I alone. The ideas that drove him had been developing for generations before his own birth, and were the accepted commonplaces of his age. Moreover, the swiftness with which English power in the British Isles contracted after his death was due in large part to the incompetence of his successor, whose behaviour as king was causing alarm in England even before his coronation. Edward II possessed almost none of the attributes that had made his father great, and from the first his rule was hopelessly compromised by his relationship with Piers Gaveston. The favourite had been recalled from exile as soon as the old king's authority had expired; before the funeral had taken place he had been invested as earl of Cornwall.[31]

Part of Edward's legacy, however, from which neither his son nor his successors could escape, was the use of extreme violence to solve intractable political problems. The shift is often dated to the new reign, as if to lay responsibility at the door of a degenerate younger generation, but in fact it had begun far earlier. It was first manifest in the summer of 1265, which witnessed 'the murder of Evesham'; it was seen again at Shrewsbury in 1283, when the law of treason was twisted to justify the killing of a prince. And so inexorably on, with the executions of Rhys ap Maredudd, Thomas Turbeville and William Wallace, culminating in the orgy of blood-letting that had attended the final campaign in Scotland. In the last instance, the perpetrators were Edward II and his contemporaries. It was thus unsurprising that, when these men eventually fell out, they should use the same methods against each other. Gaveston was murdered in 1312; his killer, Thomas of Lancaster, in 1322. Few English magnates died happily in their beds in a reign that would end with the murder of the king himself.[32]

It is appropriate, therefore, that even in death Edward I should exhort men to vengeance. After his funeral rites had been performed in 1307, the king's body, dressed in his coronation robes, was entombed near the altar of Westminster Abbey. As is well known, his tomb bears a famous inscription. The letters as they appear today were evidently painted in the sixteenth century, but the sentiments they express are almost certainly earlier. *EDWARDUS PRIMUS SCOTTORUM MALLEUS HIC EST*, the legend reads. *PACTUM SERVA*.

The first part is easy enough to translate. *Scottorum malleus* means 'Hammer of the Scots', which is certainly an appropriate epithet. It is also the principal reason for believing that the motto was concocted soon after Edward's death; as early as 1320, a visitor to the tomb described him as 'the most Maccabean king', and the Hebrew word *makabeh* translates as 'hammer'.[33]

This being the case, the second part of the inscription may have a more specific meaning than is usually allowed. *Pactum Serva* is commonly mistranslated as 'Keep the Faith'; a more accurate rendering would be 'Keep the Vow'. In the early years of the fourteenth century there was only one vow that the nobility of England could have understood in this context: the vow they had all sworn at Whitsun 1306, when the legendary king had gathered them together for a feast in Westminster Hall, and committed them to avenge the rebellion of Robert Bruce.[34]

The real mystery of Edward's tomb lies not so much in its inscription but in its uncompromising severity. One every side, the king is surrounded by the most elaborate funerary displays imaginable: the gilt-bronze effigies of his wife and his father; the brightly coloured, canopied confection that holds the bones of his brother. Yet Edward, inscrutable to the last, lies hidden in an unadorned box of black Purbeck marble. Once this was assumed to be a sin of omission on the part of his son, but that argument cannot be sustained. In the 1320s Edward II commissioned a new set of murals for the Palace of Westminster celebrating his father's victories. If Edward I lacks an effigy, it was not for lack of filial devotion. The simplicity of his tomb, we are forced to conclude, was deliberate.

There are few parallels for such austerity in medieval Europe. The kings of Sicily are interred in similarly simple style, and so it is not impossible that Edward, as a sometime visitor to the island, may have drawn his inspiration from that direction. There was, however, another parallel closer to home, and that was the tomb that the king himself had constructed at Glastonbury for the bones of King Arthur. This too, according to seventeenth-century observers, had been a black marble box.[35] In the final analysis, therefore, the tomb of Edward I may stand, like the unfinished castle at Caernarfon, not only as a monument to the past, but also as a warning to the future: a final reminder of the power of myth to shape men's minds and motives, and thus to alter the fate of nations.

Abbreviations

AM	*Annales Monastici*, ed. H. R. Luard (5 vols., Rolls Series, 1864–69).
Ann. Lond.	'Annales Londonienses', *Chronicles of the Reigns of Edward I and Edward II*, ed. W. Stubbs, vol. 1 (Rolls Series, 1882).
AWR	*The Acts of Welsh Rulers, 1120–1283*, ed. H. Pryce (Cardiff, 2005).
Barrow, *Bruce*	G. W. S. Barrow, *Robert Bruce and the Community of the Realm of Scotland* (3rd edn, Edinburgh, 1988).
BIHR	*Bulletin of the Institute of Historical Research*
Bury	*The Chronicle of Bury St Edmunds, 1212–1301*, ed. A. Gransden (London, 1964).
CACW	*Calendar of Ancient Correspondence Concerning Wales*, ed. J. G. Edwards (Cardiff, 1935).
Carpenter, *Struggle*	D. A. Carpenter, *The Struggle for Mastery: Britain 1066–1284* (London, 2003).
CCR	*Calendar of Close Rolls* (HMSO, 1892–).
CDS	*Calendar of Documents Relating to Scotland*, ed. J. Bain et al. (5 vols., Edinburgh, 1881–1988).
CLR	*Calendar of Liberate Rolls* (HMSO, 1916–64).
Commendatio	'Commendatio Lamentabilis in Transitu Magni Regis Edwardi', *Chronicles of the Reigns of Edward I and Edward II*, ed. W. Stubbs, vol. 1 (Rolls Series, 1882).

Cotton	*Bartholomaei de Cotton, Historia Anglicana (A.D. 449–1298)*, ed. H. R. Luard (Rolls Series, 1859).
CPR	*Calendar of Patent Rolls* (HMSO, 1906–).
CR	*Close Rolls, Henry III* (HMSO, 1902–38).
Cron. Maior.	*De Antiquis Legibus Liber. Cronica Maiorum et Vicecomitum Londoniarum*, ed. T. Stapleton (Camden Society, 1846).
CRV	*Calendar of Various Chancery Rolls, 1277–1326* (HMSO, 1912).
Davies, *Empire*	R. R. Davies, *The First English Empire: Power and Identities in the British Isles 1093–1343* (Oxford, 2000).
Denton, *Winchelsey*	J. H. Denton, *Robert Winchelsey and the Crown, 1294–1313* (Cambridge, 1980).
DNB	*Oxford Dictionary of National Biography*, ed. H. C. G. Matthew and B. Harrison (60 vols., Oxford, 2004).
Documents 1297	*Documents Illustrating the Crisis of 1297–98 in England*, ed. M. Prestwich (Camden Society, 4th Series, xxiv, 1980).
Duncan, *Kingship*	A. A. M. Duncan, *The Kingship of the Scots, 842–1292* (Edinburgh, 2002).
EHD	*English Historical Documents 1189–1327*, ed. H. Rothwell (London, 1975).
EHR	*English Historical Review*
Evesham	J. H. Denton, 'The Crisis of 1297 from the Evesham Chronicle', *EHR*, xciii (1978).
Flores	*Flores Historiarum*, ed. H. R. Luard (3 vols., Rolls Series, 1890).
Foedera	*Foedera, Conventiones, Litterae et Acta Publica*, ed. T. Rymer, amended edn by A. Clarke and F. Hólbrooke (4 vols. in 7, Record Commission, 1816–69).
Guisborough	*The Chronicle of Walter of Guisborough*, ed. H. Rothwell (Camden Society, lxxxix, 1957).
HBC	*Handbook of British Chronology*, ed. E. B. Fryde, D. E. Greenway, S. Porter and I. Roy (3rd edn, London, 1986).

HMSO	Her Majesty's Stationery Office
Ibn al-Furāt	*Ayyubids, Mamlukes and Crusaders: selections from the Tārikh al Duwal wa'l Mulūk of Ibn al-Furāt*, ed. U. and M. C. Lyons, introduction by J. S. C. Riley-Smith, vol. 2 (Cambridge, 1971).
Itinerary	*Itinerary of Edward I*, ed. E. W. Safford (3 vols., List and Index Society, 103, 132, 135, 1974–77).
Kaeuper, *Bankers*	R. W. Kaeuper, *Bankers to the Crown: the Riccardi of Lucca and Edward I* (Princeton, 1973).
KW	R. A. Brown, H. M. Colvin and A. J. Taylor, *The History of the King's Works*, vols. 1 and 2 (HMSO, 1963).
Lanercost	*Chronicon de Lanercost*, ed. J. Stevenson (Edinburgh, 1839).
Langtoft	*The Chronicle of Pierre de Langtoft*, ed. T. Wright, ii (Rolls Series, 1868).
Maddicott, *Montfort*	J. R. Maddicott, *Simon de Montfort* (Cambridge, 1994).
Morris, *Bigod Earls*	M. Morris, *The Bigod Earls of Norfolk in the Thirteenth Century* (Woodbridge, 2005).
Morris, *Welsh Wars*	J. E. Morris, *The Welsh Wars of Edward I* (Oxford, 1901).
NA	National Archives
NHI	*A New History of Ireland, vol. II: Medieval Ireland, 1169–1534*, ed. A. Cosgrove (Oxford, 1987).
Paris	*Matthaei Parisiensis, Monachi Sancti Albani, Chronica Majora*, ed. H. R. Luard (7 vols., Rolls Series, 1872–83).
Political Songs	*Thomas Wright's Political Songs of England*, ed. P. Coss (Cambridge, 1996).
Powicke, *Henry III*	F. M. Powicke, *King Henry III and the Lord Edward* (Oxford, 1947).
Prests	*Book of Prests, 1294–5*, ed. E. B. Fryde (Oxford, 1962).
PROME	*The Parliament Rolls of Medieval England, 1275–1504*, vol. 1, ed. P. Brand and C. Given-Wilson (Woodbridge, 2005).

PW
Parliamentary Writs and Writs of Military Summons, ed. F. Palgrave, vol. 1 (Record Commission, 1827).

RCWL
The Royal Charter Witness Lists of Edward I, ed. R. Huscroft (List and Index Society, 2000).

Rishanger
Willelmi Rishanger, Chronica et Annales, ed. H. T. Riley (Rolls Series, 1865).

RWH
Records of the Wardrobe and Household, 1286–1289, ed. B. F. and C. R. Byerly (HMSO, 1986).

Smith, Llywelyn
J. B. Smith, Llywelyn ap Gruffudd, Prince of Wales (Cardiff, 1998).

Stacey, 'Expulsion'
R. C. Stacey, 'Parliamentary Negotiation and the Expulsion of the Jews from England', TCE, vi (1997).

Stevenson, Documents
Documents Illustrative of the History of Scotland, ed. J. Stevenson (2 vols., Edinburgh, 1870).

Studd, Itinerary
An Itinerary of the Lord Edward, ed. R. Studd (List and Index Society, 284, 2000).

SR
The Statutes of the Realm, ed. A. Luders, T. E. Tomlins, J. France, W. E. Taunton and J. Raithby, vol. 1 (Record Commission, 1810).

TCE
Thirteenth Century England

Trabut-Cussac, L'Administration
J.-P. Trabut-Cussac, L'Administration Anglaise en Gascogne sous Henry III et Edouard I (Paris, 1972).

Trivet
Nicholai Triveti . . . Annales Sex Regum Angliae, ed. T. Hog (London, 1845).

Watson, Hammer
F. Watson, Under the Hammer: Edward I and Scotland, 1286–1306 (East Linton, 1998).

WPF
M. Prestwich, War, Politics and Finance under Edward I (London, 1972).

Notes

CHAPTER I: A SAINT IN NAME

[1] M. Howell, *Eleanor of Provence* (Oxford, 1998), 1, 5, 14–16, 22–7; Powicke, *Henry III*, 751–4.

[2] Paris, iii, 539–40; *CLR, 1226–40*, 406; Carpenter, *Struggle*, 340.

[3] R. Bartlett, *The Making of Europe* (London, 1993), 271–3; D. A. Carpenter, 'King Henry III and Saint Edward the Confessor: the Origins of the Cult', *EHR*, 122 (2007), 865–91; Paris, iii, 539–40.

[4] *The Royal Charter Witness Lists of Henry III*, ed. M. Morris, vol. 1 (List and Index Society, 291, 2001), 172–3.

[5] *KW*, i, 120–30; ii, 864–9.

[6] Carpenter, *Struggle*, 340; M. Prestwich, *Edward I* (London, 1988), 5–6; Howell, *Eleanor of Provence*, 28, 76, 78, 100.

[7] Ibid., 29, 35–7, 76, 99.

[8] Ibid., 30, 35, 45; Prestwich, *Edward I*, 5.

[9] Howell, *Eleanor of Provence*, 27, 32; Prestwich, *Edward I*, 5.

[10] Ibid.; Howell, *Eleanor of Provence*, 24–6, 30–2; *CR, 1237–42*, 308 (with thanks to David Carpenter).

[11] Paris, iv, 553; N. Orme, *From Childhood to Chivalry* (London, 1984), 5–7.

[12] Ibid., 16; M. T. Clanchy, *From Memory to Written Record* (2nd edn, Oxford, 1993), 2.

[13] Howell, *Eleanor of Provence*, 6; Carpenter, *Struggle*, 9; Orme, *From Childhood to Chivalry*, 124–5.

[14] Carpenter, 'King Henry III and Saint Edward the Confessor', 885–6

[15] Howell, *Eleanor of Provence*, 7, 82–4.

[16] M. Keen, *Chivalry* (New Haven and London, 1984), 2, 11, 37, 52, 99, 104, 158–9.

[17] Howell, *Eleanor of Provence*, 71–4, 76; Prestwich, *Edward I*, 6; Paris, iv, 639. See also *CLR, 1240–45*, 286.

18 Prestwich, *Edward I*, 6–7; *DNB*, xxvi, 470.
19 Carpenter, *Struggle*, 27–8, 31–4, 42–3; Davies, *Empire*, 120.
20 P. D. A. Harvey, *Mappa Mundi: The Hereford World Map* (London, 1996), *passim*; J. Gillingham, *1215: The Year of Magna Carta* (London, 2003), 233–54.
21 Keen, *Chivalry*, 44–63; Tyerman, *England and the Crusades, 1095–1588* (Chicago and London, 1988), 8–14; S. Lloyd, *English Society and the Crusade, 1216–1307* (Oxford, 1988), 9, 245.
22 *DNB*, xlvi, 705; N. Denholm-Young, *Richard of Cornwall* (Oxford, 1947), 22, 39, 44; Paris, iv, 147, 166–7.
23 Tyerman, *England and the Crusades*, 111–17.
24 Carpenter, *Struggle*, 106–16, 137–8, 213–23.
25 Ibid., 191–5, 263–70, 307, 345.
26 Howell, *Eleanor of Provence*, 9–14, 32–6, 38, 55–6, 61–2; Prestwich, *Edward I*, 7–8.
27 Maddicott, *Montfort*, 9–10, 21–9, 107–10.
28 Ibid., 29–31, 78–9, 105, 110–12, 348.
29 Ibid., 112–19.
30 Tyerman, *England and the Crusades*, 113; Maddicott, *Montfort*, 114–16.
31 Carpenter, *Struggle*, 310, 348–50; D. Crook, 'The Sheriff of Nottingham and Robin Hood: the Genesis of the Legend?', *TCE*, ii (1988), 59–68.
32 Carpenter, *Struggle*, 260, 272, 292; Kaeuper, *Bankers*, 259; J. R. Maddicott, '"An Infinite Multitude of Nobles": Quality, Quantity and Politics in the Pre-Reform Parliaments of Henry III', *TCE*, vii (1999), 17–46.
33 Paris, v, 335.
34 Ibid., 313–14; Powicke, *Henry III*, 231.
35 Maddicott, *Montfort*, 120; Paris, v, 383.
36 J. C. Parsons, *Eleanor of Castile* (New York, 1995), 12–14.
37 Ibid.; Prestwich, *Edward I*, 11; Howell, *Eleanor of Provence*, 126.
38 Trabut-Cussac, *L'Administration*, 3–4; M. Howell, 'Royal Women of England and France in the Mid-Thirteenth Century: A Gendered Perspective', *England and Europe in the Reign of Henry III (1216–1272)*, ed. B. K. U. Weiler and I. W. Rowlands (Aldershot, 2002), 167.
39 Parsons, *Eleanor of Castile*, 9, 15–16.
40 Studd, *Itinerary*, 8; Trabut-Cussac, *L'Administration*, 8.
41 Ibid., 11.
42 Ibid., 8–11.
43 J. R. Studd, 'The Lord Edward and King Henry III', *BIHR*, 50 (1977), 4–19.
44 Trabut-Cussac, *L'Administration*, 12; *CR, 1254–56*, 219–20.
45 *CR, 1254–56*, 128; J. C. Parsons, 'The Year of Eleanor of Castile's Birth

and her Children by Edward I', *Mediaeval Studies*, xlvi (1984), 257; *RWH*, 167–8 (nos. 1618–19).

[46] Paris, v, 513–14; *Rôles Gascons*, ed. Francisque-Michel and C. Bémont (4 vols., Paris, 1885–1906), i (suppl.), 38–9 (no. 4554).

[47] E. L. G. Stones, *Edward I* (Oxford, 1968), 2 (a translation of Trivet, 281–2); J. Ayloffe, 'An Account of the Body of King Edward the First', *Archaeologia*, iii (1786), 385; *EHD*, iii, 236; *Political Songs*, 223; *Commendatio*, 5.

[48] Studd, *Itinerary*, 27–9; Paris, v, 527.

[49] Ibid., 538–9.

[50] Ibid., 513–15.

[51] *DNB*, xxix, 418; Howell, *Eleanor of Provence*, 54–5.

[52] Ibid., 55, 57–8, 66–70, 141.

[53] H. W. Ridgeway, 'Foreign Favourites and Henry III's Problems of Patronage, 1247–1258', *EHR* 104 (1989), 601–2; idem, 'The Lord Edward and the Provisions of Oxford (1258): A Study in Faction', *TCE*, i (1986), 90.

[54] Paris, v, 557, 609; N. Denholm-Young, 'The Tournament in the Thirteenth Century', *Collected Papers* (Cardiff, 1969), 95–120. In general, see D. Crouch, *Tournament* (London, 2005).

[55] Studd, *Itinerary*, 30.

[56] K. Staniland, 'The Nuptials of Alexander III of Scotland and Margaret Plantagenet', *Nottingham Medieval Studies*, 30 (1986), 20–45.

[57] R. R. Davies, *Domination and Conquest* (Cambridge, 1990), 51; idem, *Empire*, 156–7 (cf. Duncan, *Kingship*, 173–4).

[58] Studd, *Itinerary*, 30; R. R. Davies, *The Age of Conquest: Wales 1063–1415* (new edn, Oxford, 2000), 17; idem, 'The Peoples of Britain and Ireland, 1100–1400: IV. Language and Historical Mythology', *Transactions of the Royal Historical Society*, 6th series, vii (1997), 1–24.

[59] Davies, *Age of Conquest*, 58–9, 70–1, 120–1, 230–1, 267–8.

[60] Carpenter, *Struggle*, 106–9; Davies, *Age of Conquest*, 12–15, 267–70.

[61] King John, however, did marry his bastard daughter Joan to Llywelyn the Great. Ibid., 249.

[62] Davies, *Age of Conquest*, 236–51, 300–7; Smith, *Llywelyn*, 58–9, 77–84; Howell, *Eleanor of Provence*, 145–6.

[63] Studd, *Itinerary*, 30–1; Paris, v, 574–5.

[64] Prestwich, *Edward I*, 15–16; Paris, v, 593–4, 598; Studd, *Itinerary*, 32.

[65] R. C. Stacey, 'Crusades, Crusaders and the Baronial *Gravamina* of 1263–1264', *TCE*, iii (1991), 143–8; D. A. Carpenter, 'The Gold Treasure of King Henry III', *The Reign of Henry III* (London, 1996), 120; Howell, *Eleanor of Provence*, 130–4, 138–45.

[66] Ibid., 49–54, 140, 274–5.

CHAPTER 2: THE FAMILY FEUD

[1] Smith, *Llywelyn*, 77–85.

[2] Ibid., 56–77, 85–91.

[3] Studd, *Itinerary*, 31–2; Smith, *Llywelyn*, 88; Paris, v, 592–4.

[4] Ibid., 593, 613–14; *DNB*, xxvi, 462.

[5] Smith, *Llywelyn*, 90–5.

[6] Ibid., 97–101.

[7] Ibid., 101–6.

[8] Ibid., 108–9.

[9] Howell, *Eleanor of Provence*, 145–8.

[10] R. R. Davies, *Lordship and Society in the March of Wales, 1282–1400* (Oxford, 1978), *passim*, and esp. 3, 73–9, 217.

[11] Smith, *Llywelyn*, 94–7, 102–3; Howell, *Eleanor of Provence*, 146–7; *DNB*, xii, 109; Paris, v, 95; J. F. Lydon, 'Three Exchequer Documents from the reign of Henry III', *Proceedings of the Royal Irish Academy*, 65 (1966–67), 26–7.

[12] Howell, *Eleanor of Provence*, 148.

[13] Ibid., 148–9.

[14] D. A. Carpenter, 'What Happened in 1258?', *Reign of Henry III*, 187–8, 194; Morris, *Bigod Earls*, 184–5; Maddicott, *Montfort*, 109.

[15] Carpenter, 'What Happened in 1258?', 188; Howell, *Eleanor of Provence*, 154; *EHD*, iii, 119.

[16] Carpenter, 'What Happened in 1258?', 195–6; *EHD*, iii, 123; Morris, *Bigod Earls*, 73, 218–19.

[17] Maddicott, *Montfort*, 156–8, 160; *EHD*, iii, 124, 155, 361–7.

[18] *EHD*, iii, 155–6; Ridgeway, 'The Lord Edward and the Provisions of Oxford', 89; Prestwich, *Edward I*, 25–6.

[19] Maddicott, *Montfort*, 151, 158–9.

[20] *EHD*, iii, 156, 363.

[21] *DNB*, xxvi, 463; M. A. Hennings, *England Under Henry III* (London, 1924), 93.

[22] Davies, *Age of Conquest*, 310; *AM*, i, 166; iv, 445; *CPR, 1258–66*, 5; *CLR, 1251–60*, 441; Studd, *Itinerary*, 43–4.

[23] D. A. Carpenter, 'The Lord Edward's Oath to Aid and Counsel Simon de Montfort, 15 October 1259', *Reign of Henry III*, 250–2.

[24] Morris, *Bigod Earls*, 75–80.

[25] Maddicott, *Montfort*, 50–3, 122–3, 129–51.

[26] *EHD*, iii, 157–8; T. F. Tout, 'The "Communitas Bacheleriae Angliae"', *EHR*, 17 (1902), 89–95.

[27] Carpenter, 'The Lord Edward's Oath', 242, 248, 251.

[28] R. F. Treharne, *The Baronial Plan of Reform, 1258–63* (Manchester, 1932) is the most complete expression of this view.

29 Maddicott, *Montfort*, 155–6, 181–8.
30 Ibid., 192–3; Howell, *Eleanor of Provence*, 163–4, 170; Studd, *Itinerary*, 46–7.
31 Maddicott, *Montfort*, 193–4.
32 *Documents of the Baronial Movement of Reform and Rebellion, 1258–1267*, ed. R. F. Treharne and I. J. Sanders (Oxford, 1973), 175–7; Howell, *Eleanor of Provence*, 162, 166–70.
33 *EHD*, iii, 160–1, 197; *Flores*, ii, 448–9; *DNB*, xxvi, 464.
34 *EHD*, iii, 197–8; Howell, *Eleanor of Provence*, 170–1; Treharne, *Baronial Plan*, 232–4. Reconciliation clearly occurred in mid-May: on 13 May Edward was still with Montfort, and on 15 May he was ordered to remove his castellans; not until 16 May did Henry III leave London for Westminster. Maddicott, *Montfort*, 197; *CR, 1259–61*, 42; *EHD*, iii, 161.
35 Maddicott, *Montfort*, 197–9.
36 Davies, *Age of Conquest*, 311; Smith, *Llywelyn*, 116–27; Prestwich, *Edward I*, 11.
37 Smith, *Llywelyn*, 127–31.
38 Maddicott, *Montfort*, 199; Morris, *Bigod Earls*, 83.
39 Maddicott, *Montfort*, 200–3.
40 Ibid.; Morris, *Bigod Earls*, 83.
41 Howell, *Eleanor of Provence*, 175–6; *The Historical Works of Gervase of Canterbury*, ed. W. Stubbs (2 vols., Rolls Series, 1879–80), ii, 211; cf. *EHD*, iii, 198.
42 Studd, *Itinerary*, 56; Howell, *Eleanor of Provence*, 177–9; D. A. Carpenter, 'King Henry III and the Tower of London', *Reign of Henry III*, 199–206; H. Ridgeway, 'King Henry III's Grievances against the Council in 1261: a New Version and a Letter describing Political Events', *Historical Research*, 61 (1988), 229, 235–6, 240.
43 *DNB*, lvi, 47; Howell, *Eleanor of Provence*, 179–80; Maddicott, *Montfort*, 196, 200.
44 Ibid., 208.
45 *EHD*, iii, 198 (where it is also stated that Edward did badly in the tournaments and sustained heavy losses); Howell, *Eleanor of Provence*, 180.
46 Maddicott, *Montfort*, 207, 209.
47 *Flores*, ii, 466–7.
48 Howell, *Eleanor of Provence*, 180–1; Morris, *Bigod Earls*, 84–5; Studd, *Itinerary*, 57–8.
49 Howell, *Eleanor of Provence*, 183–4; Studd, *Itinerary*, 58–60.
50 Maddicott, *Montfort*, 213–14; *EHD*, iii, 199.
51 D. A. Carpenter, 'Simon de Montfort: The First Leader of a Political Movement in English History', *Reign of Henry III*, 232–3.

52 Ridgeway, 'The Lord Edward', 98; D. A. Carpenter, 'King Henry III's "Statute" against Aliens: July 1263', *Reign of Henry III*, 271n.

53 Howell, *Eleanor of Provence*, 181, 187–8; Prestwich, *Edward I*, 37.

54 Studd, *Itinerary*, 62, 64; Howell, *Eleanor of Provence*, 186, 189; Prestwich, *Edward I*, 38.

55 Carpenter, 'King Henry III's "Statute"', 271; Howell, *Eleanor of Provence*, 181.

56 *EHD*, iii, 199; Studd, *Itinerary*, 65; Maddicott, *Montfort*, 215–21; *CCR, 1261–64*, 272–3.

57 Davies, *Age of Conquest*, 312; Smith, *Llywelyn*, 137–48.

58 Ibid., 148; Howell, *Eleanor of Provence*, 190–1; Studd, *Itinerary*, 66.

59 Maddicott, *Montfort*, 216–17; Howell, *Eleanor of Provence*, 193–4.

60 Ibid., 188.

61 Maddicott, *Montfort*, 222–3.

62 Ibid., 225–7; Howell, *Eleanor of Provence*, 193.

63 Studd, *Itinerary*, 69; Carpenter, 'King Henry III and the Tower', 206; *EHD*, iii, 201; G. A. Williams, *Medieval London: From Commune to Capital* (London, 1963), 218.

64 *EHD*, iii, 167–8; Maddicott, *Montfort*, 228–9.

65 *EHD*, iii, 201; Maddicott, *Montfort*, 230.

66 Ibid., 229–30, 234; Howell, *Eleanor of Provence*, 196.

67 Ibid.

68 Maddicott, *Montfort*, 229; Studd, *Itinerary*, 70; *Flores*, ii, 482; *EHD*, iii, 170; Howell, *Eleanor of Provence*, 197–8.

69 Maddicott, *Montfort*, 231–2, 239, 242–4.

70 Ibid., 237–8, 241–2; Howell, *Eleanor of Provence*, 200–1.

71 Maddicott, *Montfort*, 244.

72 Ibid., 228; Smith, *Llywelyn*, 154; Howell, *Eleanor of Provence*, 197.

73 Maddicott, *Montfort*, 237, 244–5; *EHD*, iii, 171, 203.

74 Maddicott, *Montfort*, 247–65; Howell, *Eleanor of Provence*, 202–5.

75 D. A. Carpenter, 'A Noble in Politics: Roger Mortimer in the Period of Baronial Reform and Rebellion, 1258–1265, *Nobles and Nobility in Medieval Europe*, ed. A. J. Duggan (Woodbridge, 2000), 183–203; Maddicott, *Montfort*, 263–4.

76 Ibid., 265–8.

77 Ibid., 269.

78 D. A. Carpenter, *The Battles of Lewes and Evesham 1264/65* (Keele, 1987), 18, 20, 22–3; *EHD*, iii, 175.

79 Carpenter, *Battles of Lewes and Evesham*, 24–7, 30–1.

80 Ibid., 27, 30.

81 Ibid., 31–2; *EHD*, iii, 905.

82 Carpenter, *Battles of Lewes and Evesham*, 32–4; *Political Songs*, 69–70.

83 *EHD*, iii, 900; Carpenter, *Battles of Lewes and Evesham*, 26–7.

[84] Ibid., 34–5; Carpenter, *Struggle*, 126–7.

[85] Maddicott, *Montfort*, 272–3.

[86] Ibid., 280–2; *EHD*, iii, 174, 207.

[87] Maddicott, *Montfort*, 289–91, 306–8; Prestwich, *Edward I*, 47.

[88] Maddicott, *Montfort*, 220, 264, 285, 288, 302–3, 307, 312.

[89] Ibid., 318–22, 338, 364; *EHD*, iii, 180–1.

[90] Maddicott, *Montfort*, 329–33.

[91] Ibid., 333–4; Prestwich, *Edward I*, 49.

[92] Maddicott, *Montfort*, 334–9.

[93] Ibid., 339.

[94] Ibid., 339–40; O. de Laborderie, J. R. Maddicott and D. A. Carpenter, 'The Last Hours of Simon de Montfort: A New Account', *EHR*, 115 (2000), 396.

[95] Carpenter, *Battles of Lewes and Evesham*, 50–4.

[96] Ibid., 58–9.

[97] Laborderie, Maddicott and Carpenter, 'Last Hours of Simon de Montfort', 395–406 is the most accurate reconstruction of these events.

[98] Ibid., 391, 400, 404; Carpenter, *Battles of Lewes and Evesham*, 59.

[99] Ibid., 58, 63–4.

[100] Ibid., 65–6; Laborderie, Maddicott and Carpenter, 'Last Hours of Simon de Montfort', 403, 405, 411.

[101] Ibid., 406; Powicke, *Henry III*, 502; Carpenter, *Battles of Lewes and Evesham*, 64.

[102] Laborderie, Maddicott and Carpenter, 'Last Hours of Simon de Montfort', 403, 411–12.

CHAPTER 3: CIVIL PEACE AND HOLY WAR

[1] Maddicott, *Montfort*, 346–7, 367–8.

[2] Ibid., 336–7, 342; Powicke, *Henry III*, 505; *EHD*, iii, 183.

[3] Trivet, 266; *Royal and Other Historical Letters Illustrative of the Reign of Henry III*, ed. W. W. Shirley (2 vols., Rolls Series, 1862–66), ii, 291; *CR, 1264–68*, 131; Maddicott, *Montfort*, 67–8.

[4] C. H. Knowles, 'The Resettlement of England after the Barons' War, 1264–67', *Transactions of the Royal Historical Society*, 5th series, 32 (1982), 25–6.

[5] Studd, *Itinerary*, 85–6; *Royal and Other Historical Letters*, ed. Shirley, ii, 289–90.

[6] Powicke, *Henry III*, 505–8; Maddicott, *Montfort*, 335.

[7] *The Chronicle of William de Rishanger of the Barons' Wars*, ed. J. O. Halliwell (Camden Society, 1st series, xv, 1840), 49; Knowles, 'Resettlement of England', 26.

[8] *EHD*, iii, 181n, 184.

9 Ibid., 184–5; Powicke, *Henry III*, 517–18; Prestwich, *Edward I*, 54.

10 Howell, *Eleanor of Provence*, 199–205, 211–17, 232–4, 241.

11 Parsons, *Eleanor of Castile*, 24–5; idem, 'The Year of Eleanor of Castile's Birth', 258.

12 Powicke, *Henry III*, 518.

13 Ibid., 518, 526–7; Howell, *Eleanor of Provence*, 229, 232.

14 Powicke, *Henry III*, 518–19, 529–30.

15 *EHD*, iii, 904–5.

16 Powicke, *Henry III*, 519, 521.

17 Ibid., 521–2; *EHD*, iii, 186–8.

18 Ibid., 189; *AM*, iv, 187; Powicke, *Henry III*, 520–2, 531.

19 Ibid., 522–3; *EHD*, iii, 190–1; Howell, *Eleanor of Provence*, 234–5.

20 Powicke, *Henry III*, 531.

21 *EHD*, iii, 191; Studd, *Itinerary*, 97.

22 Ibid.; Powicke, *Henry III*, 532; *EHD*, iii, 193.

23 Powicke, *Henry III*, 532–8; *EHD*, iii, 192.

24 Powicke, *Henry III*, 538–9; *EHD*, iii, 193.

25 Powicke, *Henry III*, 539–41; Studd, *Itinerary*, 100.

26 *AM*, iv, 197; *DNB*, lvi, 387.

27 Edward was at Pontefract on 21 March: Studd, *Itinerary*, 100. *AM*, iv, 197–8; *DNB*, lvi, 387.

28 *AM*, iv, 196.

29 *EHD*, iii, 193–4.

30 *Flores*, iii, 15; Powicke, *Henry III*, 543–4; Howell, *Eleanor of Provence*, 238–40.

31 *EHD*, iii 194–6; Powicke, *Henry III*, 545–6.

32 *EHD*, iii, 121–2, 194, 197; *AM*, iv, 211.

33 Prestwich, *Edward I*, 60; Smith, *Llywelyn*, 178.

34 *AM*, iv, 212.

35 Tyerman, *England and the Crusades*, 144–51.

36 Lloyd, *English Society and the Crusade*, 113; Powicke, *Henry III*, 562.

37 Ibid., 541, 562. In general, the number of former Montfortians that took the cross was minimal. Lloyd, *English Society and the Crusade*, 126–32.

38 Ibid., 115, 201–7.

39 Ibid., 146–7, 232; Powicke, 562n.

40 H. A. Wait, 'The Household and Resources of the Lord Edward' (D. Phil. thesis, Oxford, 1988), ch. 8, v; Lloyd, *English Society and the Crusade*, 115.

41 Ibid., 114, 147; Powicke, *Henry III*, 557, 562.

42 Parsons, 'Year of Eleanor of Castile's Birth', 259; Lloyd, *English Society and the Crusade*, 77–8.

43 J. Riley-Smith, *The Crusades: A Short History* (New Haven and London, 1987), 12–13.

44 Lloyd, *English Society and the Crusade*, 16–23.
45 R. Graham, 'Letters of Cardinal Ottoboni', *EHR*, 15 (1900), no. 26; F. M. Powicke, *The Thirteenth Century, 1216–1307* (2nd edn, Oxford, 1962), 231.
46 J. R. Maddicott, 'The Crusade Taxation of 1268–1270 and the Development of Parliament', *TCE*, ii (1988), 93–5, 101–2.
47 R. Huscroft, *Expulsion: England's Jewish Solution* (Stroud, 2006), 11, 63–5.
48 Ibid., 43–6, 68.
49 Ibid., 46–8, 54–6, 60.
50 Ibid., 83–5, 90.
51 R. C. Stacey, '1240–60: A Watershed in Anglo-Jewish Relations?', *Historical Research*, 61 (1988), 135–150.
52 Huscroft, *Expulsion*, 91–2; Stacey, 'Expulsion', 93–4; idem, '1240–60: A Watershed', 142–3.
53 R. C. Stacey, 'The English Jews under Henry III', *The Jews in Medieval Britain: Historical, Literary and Archaeological Perspectives*, ed. P. Skinner (Woodbridge, 2003), 51. Note, however, that Edward and Montfort are not themselves named in the evidence for the raid on the exchequer: NA E159/33, m. 10.
54 Maddicott, 'Crusade Taxation', 101–2, 109–10 and n.
55 Prestwich, *Edward I*, 62; *DNB*, xxvi, 468; Powicke, *Henry III*, 523–5, 709; K. B. McFarlane, 'Had Edward I a "Policy" towards the Earls?', *The Nobility of Later Medieval England* (Oxford, 1973), 254–7.
56 Maddicott, 'Crusade Taxation', 103; Tyerman, *England and the Crusades*, 127–9.
57 *KW*, i, 130, 150; D. A. Carpenter, 'Westminster Abbey in Politics, 1258–1269', *TCE*, viii (2001), 54–5.
58 Powicke, *Henry III*, 575–6; *AM*, iv, 227; Maddicott, 'Crusade Taxation', 105–6 (only permission to assess was granted).
59 S. Lloyd, 'Gilbert de Clare, Richard of Cornwall and the Lord Edward's Crusade', *Nottingham Medieval Studies*, xxx (1986), 46–53.
60 *EHD*, iii, 204; J. R. Studd, 'The Lord Edward's Lordship of Chester, 1254–72', *Transactions of the Historic Society of Lancashire and Cheshire*, 128 (1979), 16–17.
61 Powicke, *Henry III*, 579. But it seems unlikely, given the chronicler's silence, that Edward also went to France.
62 Lloyd, 'Gilbert de Clare', 54; Maddicott, 'Crusade Taxation', 108–10.
63 Lloyd, 'Gilbert de Clare', 55–62.
64 Lloyd, *English Society and the Crusade*, 116–24; Tyerman, *England and the Crusades*, 125.
65 R. Huscroft, 'Should I Stay or Should I Go? Robert Burnell, the Lord Edward's Crusade and the Canterbury Vacancy of 1270–3',

Nottingham Medieval Studies, xlv (2001), 97, 102–5; Powicke, *Henry III*, 582; Parsons, *Eleanor of Castile*, 28.

66 Lloyd, *English Society and the Crusade*, 139, 142n; Studd, *Itinerary*, 130.

67 Powicke, *Henry III*, 597–8.

68 J. Dunbabin, *Charles I of Anjou: Power, Kingship and State-Making in Thirteenth-Century Europe* (Harlow, 1998), 3–5, 57, 194–7.

69 Studd, *Itinerary*, 131.

70 Ibid.; Prestwich, *Edward I*, 73–4.

71 Ibid., 74; *A History of the Crusades*, ed. K. M. Setton (6 vols., Philadelphia and Madison, 1955–89), ii, 517.

72 *Cron. Maior*, 131; *AM*, iv, 239–40; Prestwich, *Edward I*, 74–5.

73 Riley-Smith, *The Crusades*, xvi, 40–5, 56–60, 61–4, 77–8.

74 Ibid., 84–7, 156–7; *The Atlas of the Crusades*, ed. J. Riley-Smith (London, 1991), 98–9, 102–3.

75 Riley-Smith, *The Crusades* 200–3; R. Irwin, *The Middle East in the Middle Ages: The Early Mamluk Sultanate, 1250–1382* (London, 1986), 42–56.

76 *AM*, iv, 245. See also *Political Songs*, 132.

77 Ibn al-Furāt, 150.

78 'Annales de Terre Sainte', ed. R. Röhricht, *Archives de l'Orient Latin*, ii (1884), 455; Ibn al-Furāt, 151–2; 'Gestes des Chiprois', *Receuil des Historiens des Croisades: Documents Arméniens*, ed. C. Kohler, vol. 2 (Paris, 1906), 778.

79 D. Nicolle and A. McBride, *The Mamluks, 1250–1517* (London, 1993), 15; 'Gestes des Chiprois', 778.

80 Ibid.; 'L'Estoire de Eracles Empereur', *Receuil des Historiens des Croisades: Historiens Occidentaux*, ed. A. Beugnot et al., vol. 2 (Paris, 1859), 461; Ibn al-Furāt, 150.

81 'Gestes des Chiprois', 777–8; Prestwich, *Edward I*, 76–7.

82 *Cron. Maior.*, 143.

83 D. Morgan, *The Mongols* (Oxford, 1986), provides a good short survey.

84 Powicke, *Henry III*, 600–1.

85 *Cron. Maior.*, 143; Powicke, *Henry III*, 600, 602.

86 'L'Estoire de Eracles Empereur', 461; Ibn al-Furāt, xi.

87 'L'Estoire de Eracles Empereur', 461; 'Gestes des Chiprois', 778–9; Ibn al-Furāt, 155. For a description of Qaqun, see H. Kennedy, *Crusader Castles* (Cambridge, 1994), 35–7, 99.

88 'L'Estoire de Eracles Empereur', 461.

89 Ibn al-Furāt, xi–xii, 156.

90 Prestwich, *Edward I*, 75–6; Parsons, *Eleanor of Castile*, 29; Tyerman, *England and the Crusades*, 125; Ibn al-Furāt, 157–9.

91 Ibid., 159; 'Gestes des Chiprois', 779; Guisborough, 208–10.

92 Parsons, *Eleanor of Castile*, 29–30.

93 *Foedera*, I, i, 495; Guisborough, 209–10.

94 'L'Estoire de Eracles Empereur', 462; J. H. Pryor, *Commerce, Shipping and Naval Warfare in the Medieval Mediterranean* (London, 1987), 378–83; Parsons, *Eleanor of Castile*, 29–30.

CHAPTER 4: THE RETURN OF THE KING

1 Howell, *Eleanor of Provence*, 252–3.
2 Ibid.; D. A. Carpenter, 'The Burial of King Henry III, the Regalia and Royal Ideology', *Reign of Henry III*, 429; *AM*, iv, 252.
3 Prestwich, *Edward I*, 74, but it took two months for messages to travel between England and Sicily. *Cron. Maior.*, 158; Trivet, 284.
4 R. Bartlett, *England under the Norman and Angevin Kings* (Oxford, 2000), 123–7, provides an excellent short summary.
5 *Foedera*, I, ii, 497; *HBC*, 30–1.
6 *Cron. Maior.*, 158.
7 Wait, 'The Household and Resources of the Lord Edward', 136–53.
8 *DNB*, xlvi, 710; *Cron. Maior.*, 158. The other conciliar casualty was Philip Basset. Powicke, *Henry III*, 532, 583, 586.
9 *AM*, iv, 239–40.
10 Maddicott, *Montfort*, 370–1; R. Studd, 'The Marriage of Henry of Almain and Constance of Béarn', *TCE*, iii (1991), 176–7; Powicke, *Henry III*, 606–12.
11 L. F. Salzman, *Edward I* (London, 1968), 34–5; T. F. Tout, *Edward the First* (London, 1893), 86; Parsons, *Eleanor of Castile*, 30–1; R. Huscroft, 'Robert Burnell and the Government of England', *TCE*, viii (2001), 66.
12 Powicke, *Thirteenth Century*, 280.
13 Parsons, *Eleanor of Castile*, 31; Maddicott, *Montfort*, 188; M. Bloch, *Feudal Society* (2nd edn, 1962), 145–7.
14 Carpenter, *Struggle*, 346. The assertion that Louis afterwards said to his barons, 'He is my man now, and he was not before' was not made until half a century later, by which time it looks like mere wish-fulfilment on the part of the French. *Jean de Joinville, Histoire de St Louis*, ed. N. de Wailly (Paris, 1874), 65.
15 *EHD*, iii, 376–9.
16 Prestwich, *Edward I*, 314.
17 *Itinerary*, i, 16–17; Trabut-Cussac, *L'Administration*, 42; M. W. Labarge, *Gascony, England's First Colony, 1204–1453* (London, 1980), 43, citing *Receuil d'actes relatifs à l'administration des Rois d'Angleterre en Guyenne au XIIIe siècle: Recogniciones feodorum in Aquitania*, ed. C. Bémont (Paris, 1914), 52 (no. 174); S. Raban, *A Second Domesday? The Hundred Rolls of 1279–80* (Oxford, 2004), 28–33.
18 Trabut-Cussac, *L'Administration*, 42–4; J. B. Smith, 'Adversaries of Edward I: Gaston de Béarn and Llywelyn ap Gruffudd', *Recognitions:*

essays presented to Edmund Fryde, ed. C. Richmond and I. M. W. Harvey (Aberystwyth, 1996), 68–70.

19 Raban, *Second Domesday*, 30–2; Trabut-Cussac, *L'Administration*, 46–7.

20 Parsons, *Eleanor of Castile*, 31; *Cron. Maior*, 170.

21 *Itinerary*, i, 31; *Political Songs*, 128.

22 *AM*, iv, 259–60; NA SC1/7/46 (from *KW*, ii, 715). Cf. R. Strong, *Coronation: A History of Kingship and the British Monarchy* (London, 2005), 133.

23 *The Cambridge Urban History of Britain, vol. 1: 600–1540*, ed. D. M. Palliser (Cambridge, 2000), 215.

24 P. Binski, *The Painted Chamber at Westminster* (London, 1986), 33–69; idem, *Westminster Abbey and the Plantagenets: Kingship and the Representation of Power 1200–1400* (New Haven and London, 1995), 130.

25 Binski, *Westminster Abbey*, 130–2; *KW*, ii, 1044.

26 Binski, *Westminster Abbey*, 130, 134.

27 H. G. Richardson, 'The Coronation in Medieval England', *Traditio*, 16 (1960), 151–61, 171–3.

28 D. A. Carpenter, 'King Henry III and the Cosmati Work at Westminster Abbey', and idem, 'Burial of King Henry III', *Reign of Henry III*, 409–26, 435–7; Binski, *Westminster Abbey*, 130.

29 Strong, *Coronation*, 87–8; Carpenter, 'Burial of King Henry III', 443–54.

30 J. R. Maddicott, 'Edward I and the Lessons of Baronial Reform', *TCE*, i (1986), 10; W. Stubbs, *The Constitutional History of England* (3rd edn, Oxford, 1887), ii, 109n.

31 Prestwich, *Edward I*, 103–5; below, 366–7.

32 Guisborough, 216, exhibits a similar confusion reporting the baronial reaction.

33 D. A. Carpenter, 'King, Magnates and Society: The Personal Rule of King Henry III, 1234–1258', *Reign of Henry III*, 85–8, 99–106.

34 Maddicott, 'Edward I and the Lessons of Baronial Reform', 1–10. For a more positive assessment, cf. Huscroft, 'Robert Burnell and the Government of England', *passim*.

35 *DNB*, viii, 898–900. For the fullest treatment, see R. Huscroft, 'The Political and Personal Life of Robert Burnell, Chancellor of Edward I' (Ph.D. thesis, London, 2000).

36 Huscroft, 'Should I Stay or Should I Go?', *passim*; idem, 'Robert Burnell and the Government of England', 65–6.

37 Carpenter, *Struggle*, 64–5, 199, 475, 479; *HBC*, 85, 228.

38 Maddicott, 'Edward I and the Lessons of Baronial Reform', 19; Carpenter, *Struggle*, 63–4, 92–3.

39 *EHD*, iii, 392–6; Maddicott, 'Edward I and the Lessons of Baronial Reform', 19.

[40] Ibid., 12–14.

[41] Ibid., 19.

[42] Ibid., 11, 14; *EHD*, iii, 397–410.

[43] Prestwich, *Edward I*, 96; Huscroft, 'Robert Burnell and the Government of England', 69–70.

[44] Maddicott, 'Edward I and the Lessons of Baronial Reform', 14–16; *EHD*, iii, 397, 409–10.

[45] Above, 16–17.

[46] Maddicott, 'Edward I and the Lessons of Baronial Reform', 23–5; Carpenter, *Struggle*, 479.

[47] Ibid., 31, 33–4, 37, 40, 42–3, 45–6.

[48] Kaeuper, *Bankers*, 135–51; *EHD*, iii, 410; Carpenter, *Struggle*, 40; Davies, *Lordship and Society*, 119.

[49] Kaeuper, *Bankers*, 1–4, 75–86, 118–21, 164–5. Cf. Prestwich, *Edward I*, 240–1.

[50] Ibid., 79–81; Lloyd, *English Society and the Crusade*, 144–7; Powicke, *Henry III*, 568–9; *AM*, iv, 265. Edward had also obtained £4,000 from the Jewry. His other debts, beyond those owed to the Riccardi, amounted to at least £14,000. Prestwich, *Edward I*, 80–1.

[51] Stacey, 'Expulsion', 96–7.

[52] Ibid., 95–6; Huscroft, *Expulsion*, 110–11.

[53] *EHD*, iii, 411–12; Maddicott, 'Edward I and the Lessons of Baronial Reform', 17; Prestwich, *Edward I*, 102.

[54] *EHD*, iii, 411–12. Huscroft, *Expulsion*, 119–21.

[55] Maddicott, *Montfort*, 15–16, 268, 315; Howell, *Eleanor of Provence*, 277–9, 299; Huscroft, *Expulsion*, 86, 102.

[56] *EHD*, iii, 411–12; Huscroft, *Expulsion*, 69, 84.

[57] *EHD*, iii, 412–13.

[58] *Itinerary*, i, 53; *KW*, ii, 715–23.

[59] Ibid., i, 150.

[60] Salzman, *Edward I*, 44; *Flores*, iii, 44–5.

[61] Maddicott, 'Edward I and the Lessons of Baronial Reform', 16; *The Brut*, ed. F. W. D. Brie, *Early English Text Society*, 131 (1906), 179; Prestwich, *Edward I*, 89. Note, however, that the food orders were for a coronation on 8 April.

[62] *DNB*, xxxviii, 809; xlvi, 710; xlix, 136, 139.

[63] *HBC*, 456, 463, 465, 468, 470, 473, 476, 479, 484, 486.

[64] *The Brut*, ed. Brie, 179–80.

CHAPTER 5: THE DISOBEDIENT PRINCE

[1] *AWR*, 555–6.

[2] Davies, *Age of Conquest*, 312.

3 Maddicott, *Montfort*, 212–13, 228, 263, 289, 307, 337–8. Llywelyn did, however, send some Welsh troops to fight at Evesham. Ibid., 340.

4 *AWR*, 538, 541, 549; *CACW*, 11.

5 *AWR*, 536–42; Smith, *Llywelyn*, 1–2, 177–86.

6 *AWR*, 537, 539.

7 Smith, *Llywelyn*, 175–6, 340–3.

8 Ibid., 344–7; Lloyd, 'Gilbert de Clare', 53, 55–6.

9 Smith, *Llywelyn*, 351–4.

10 Ibid., 355–9; *CACW*, 57, 109–10.

11 Smith, *Llywelyn*, 360–3; *AWR*, 553–4.

12 *Oxford Book of Welsh Verse in English*, ed. G. Jones (Oxford, 1977), 22.

13 *Gerald of Wales, The Journey through Wales and The Description of Wales*, ed. L. Thorpe (London, 1978), 220.

14 *AWR*, 627–8; Davies, *Age of Conquest*, 160–5; idem, *Empire*, 162; T. Jones-Pierce, 'The Growth of Commutation in Gwynedd in the Thirteenth Century', *Bulletin of the Board of Celtic Studies*, 10 (1941), 329.

15 *AWR*, 497–8, 506–7 (figures incorrectly given as marks), 536–42; Davies, *Age of Conquest*, 256, 267.

16 Smith, *Llywelyn*, 255–9, 363–6, 586; *AWR*, 557.

17 *CCR, 1272–79*, 2; *CACW*, 57.

18 Morris, *Bigod Earls*, 114–16; Smith, *Llywelyn*, 367–9.

19 Ibid., 369–72.

20 Ibid., 72–3, 86–7, 154, 180–1.

21 Ibid., 372–3.

22 *AWR*, 537–8, 540, 562–4.

23 Paris, iv, 324.

24 Smith, *Llywelyn*, 385.

25 Ibid., 388; *AWR*, 568–70.

26 *AWR*, 568–70.

27 *Itinerary*, i, 49; *Brut y Tywysogyon, or The Chronicle of the Princes (Red Book of Hergest Version)*, ed. and trans. T. Jones (Cardiff, 1952), 263; Davies, *Age of Conquest*, 327.

28 Smith, *Llywelyn*, 388n.

29 *CPR, 1272–81*, 126.

30 Maddicott, *Montfort*, 325; Smith, *Llywelyn*, 390.

31 Ibid., 391, 399–401, 403; *AWR*, 574; *CCR, 1272–79*, 266; *CPR, 1272–81*, 131.

32 Smith, *Llywelyn*, 389, 402.

33 *AWR*, 568–70, 575–6; *CACW*, 53, 162.

34 *AWR*, 574.

35 Smith, *Llywelyn*, 404, 406; *PW*, 5.

36 *AWR*, 579–88; Smith, *Llywelyn*, 407–14.

37 *Itinerary*, i, 71–2.

[38] Prestwich, *Edward I*, 136.

[39] Ibid., 147–8; Morris, *Welsh Wars*, 115.

[40] Ibid., 115, 118–21; *DNB*, iv, 604; xii, 109; xxxii, 181; Howell, *Eleanor of Provence*, 80.

[41] *RCWL*, 9; *Itinerary*, i, 72.

[42] Smith, *Llywelyn*, 414–25.

[43] *Itinerary*, i, 74–5; Prestwich, *Edward I*, 177–9.

[44] Smith, *Llywelyn*, 422–5; *RCWL*, 9–10. See also *AWR*, 231–4, 238–9 for the surrenders of Rhys ap Maredudd and Rhys Wyndod.

[45] *Itinerary*, i, 79; *PW*, 193–6.

[46] Carpenter, *Struggle*, 84; M. Prestwich, *Armies and Warfare in the Middle Ages: The English Experience* (New Haven and London, 1996), 68–71; Morris, *Welsh Wars*, 60.

[47] Ibid., 60, 62–5.

[48] Ibid., 126, 136–7.

[49] Ibid., 127, 137.

[50] Ibid., 127–8.

[51] Ibid., 88, 128; Prestwich, *Armies and Warfare*, 121–3.

[52] Ibid., 123–4, 133–4.

[53] Morris, *Welsh Wars*, 119; Prestwich, *Edward I*, 179; *WPF*, 119; D. S. Bachrach, 'Military Logistics during the Reign of Edward I of England, 1272–1307', *War in History*, 13 (2006), 423.

[54] Morris, *Welsh Wars*, 38, 106, 128; Prestwich, *Armies and Warfare*, 62–3.

[55] *Itinerary*, i, 80.

[56] Prestwich, *Edward I*, 180.

[57] Paris, v, 639.

[58] *Gerald of Wales*, ed. Thorpe, 233–4.

[59] *KW*, i, 309; A. J. Taylor, 'Castle-Building in the Later Thirteenth Century: the Prelude to Construction', *Studies in Castles and Castle-Building* (London, 1985), 124–5n.

[60] *KW*, i, 309–10.

[61] Ibid., 310; *Itinerary*, i, 80–1.

[62] *KW*, i, 299–300; Morris, *Welsh Wars*, 136–8.

[63] *KW*, i, 310; Morris, *Welsh Wars*, 128.

[64] *Itinerary*, i, 80–1.

[65] Powicke, *Henry III*, 722; *KW*, i, 248–57; *The Ledger Book of Vale Royal Abbey*, ed. J. Brownhill (Record Society of Lancashire and Cheshire, 68, 1914), 4–5. The conventional foundation date is 13 August, but by then Edward was back in the Wirral: *Itinerary*, i, 81.

[66] *KW*, i, 310–11; Morris, *Welsh Wars*, 130, 138–9; *EHD*, iii, 461.

[67] *Foedera*, I, ii, 544; Smith, *Llywelyn*, 425–6.

[68] Morris, *Welsh Wars*, 130–2; Smith, *Llywelyn*, 428; *KW*, i, 318–19.

[69] Morris, *Welsh Wars*, 134.

70 Smith, *Llywelyn*, 104–5; Morris, *Welsh Wars*, 132.

71 Ibid., 134–5; *Gerald of Wales*, ed. Thorpe (London, 1978), 187, 230; Cotton, 155.

72 *Itinerary*, i, 82; Morris, *Welsh Wars*, 136–8; Morris, *Bigod Earls*, 118.

73 Smith, *Llywelyn*, 434–6, 438–9, 443.

74 Ibid., 444–5; *Itinerary*, i, 86.

75 *AM*, iv, 274; Smith, *Llywelyn*, 445.

CHAPTER 6: ARTHUR'S CROWN

1 Davies, *Age of Conquest*, 333, and 333–42 for this section.

2 *KW*, i, 319.

3 Ibid., 295, 329; Smith, *Llywelyn*, 125–7, 421.

4 A. J. Taylor, 'Master James of St George', *Studies in Castles and Castle-Building*, 63–97.

5 Davies, *Age of Conquest*, 339–41.

6 *KW*, i, 301–4, 310–11, 322; Davies, *Age of Conquest*, 371–2.

7 *AWR*, 590. Smith, *Llywelyn*, 446–7.

8 *CCR*, 1272–79, 493; Smith, *Llywelyn*, 448–50; Davies, *Empire*, 22–3.

9 Prestwich, *Edward I*, 120. Cf. Powicke, *Henry III*, 724.

10 For a comprehensive debunking of the Arthur myth, see N. J. Higham, *King Arthur: Myth-Making and History* (London, 2002), *passim*. For a good short treatment, see M. Wood, *In Search of England: Journeys into the English Past* (London, 1999), 23–42.

11 *Geoffrey of Monmouth, History of the Kings of Britain*, ed. L. Thorpe (London, 1966), 9.

12 Ibid., 17; Davies, *Empire*, 39.

13 *King Arthur in Legend and History*, ed. R. White (London, 1997), 517–19; Higham, *King Arthur*, 230.

14 *DNB*, xlvi, 711; Howell, *Eleanor of Provence*, 7; Crouch, *Tournament*, 116–21; R. S. Loomis, 'Edward I, Arthurian Enthusiast', *Speculum*, 28 (1953), 116–17. *Pace* Loomis, Edward himself does not appear to have attended Mortimer's tournament: cf. *Itinerary*, i, 116.

15 *King Arthur in Legend and History*, ed. White, 520–3.

16 Loomis, 'Arthurian Enthusiast', 115; Stevenson, *Documents*, ii, 468; Prestwich, *Edward I*, 118, 120–2.

17 *King Arthur in Legend and History*, ed. White, 529; Loomis, 'Arthurian Enthusiast', 116; C. Shenton, 'Royal Interest in Glastonbury and Cadbury: Two Arthurian Itineraries, 1278 and 1331', *EHR*, 114 (1999), 1249–55. Cf. J. C. Parsons, 'The Second Exhumation of King Arthur's Remains at Glastonbury, 19 April 1278', *Arthurian Literature*, 12 (1993), 173–7.

18 *Geoffrey of Monmouth*, ed. Thorpe, 17.

[19] See J. Gillingham, 'The Context and Purposes of Geoffrey of Monmouth's *History of the Kings of Britain*', and 'The Beginnings of English Imperialism', in idem, *The English in the Twelfth Century* (Woodbridge, 2000), 3–39, for this section.

[20] *Geoffrey of Monmouth*, ed. Thorpe, 54–5, 66, 72, 74–5, 80, 131, 207.

[21] *Chrétien de Troyes, Arthurian Romances*, ed. and trans. W. W. Kibler and C. W. Carroll (London, 1991), 384; *AM*, iv, 168; Paris, iii, 202; Smith, *Llywelyn*, 480–1.

[22] Kaeuper, *Bankers*, 177–80; Davies, *Age of Conquest*, 339. The castles at Builth, Aberystwyth, Flint and Rhuddlan together came to £22,500: *KW*, i, 298, 307, 317, 324.

[23] *PW*, 214–16, 218, 220–1; *EHD*, iii, 413. Edward also imposed an old-fashioned levy called a scutage, but not until February 1279. H. M. Chew, 'Scutage under Edward I', *EHR*, 37 (1922), 326–7.

[24] Prestwich, *Edward I*, 244–5; Huscroft, *Expulsion*, 124.

[25] Prestwich, *Edward I*, 245; Huscroft, *Expulsion*, 124–8.

[26] Ibid., 124–6, 140. Confiscated goods raised £11,000 and the remint a further £25,000: Prestwich, *Edward I*, 245, 247.

[27] Powicke, *Thirteenth Century*, 288; *CCR, 1272–79*, 493.

[28] Powicke, *Thirteenth Century*, 285–9; Smith, 'Adversaries of Edward I', 55–88.

[29] Powicke, *Thirteenth Century*, 289–93; H. Johnstone, 'The County of Ponthieu, 1279–1307', *EHR*, 29 (1914), 437; Crouch, *Tournament*, 37, 45–6, 77.

[30] Maddicott, 'Edward I and the Lessons of Baronial Reform', 27–30.

[31] *PROME*, 32–40; Prestwich, *Edward I*, 238 (cf. 569), 249–55.

[32] Ibid., 258–64; *RCWL*, 12–43.

[33] *Itinerary*, i, 93, 114–16, 121–2, 129–33, 136–8, 147–8; *KW*, i, 550–1; ii, 944, 984, 1002; *AM*, ii, 393; Prestwich, *Edward I*, 115–17.

[34] Trivet, 281–2; Parsons, *Eleanor of Castile*, 53–5; *Itinerary*, i, 127, 129, 133, 138, 142–4; *KW*, ii, 695–7, 970–1; J. Ashbee, '"The Chamber called *Gloriette*": Living at Leisure in Thirteenth and Fourteenth-Century Castles', *Journal of the British Archaeological Association*, 157 (2004), 17–40.

[35] Parsons, 'Year of Eleanor of Castile's Birth', 262–4.

[36] *Itinerary*, i, 90–1, 108, 123–4, 139–40, 155–6. The delights of this area appear to have been discovered in 1276. Ibid., 56.

[37] *AWR*, 600–1, 615–16, 622, 624; Davies, *Age of Conquest*, 344–7.

[38] *AWR*, 627–8.

[39] Smith, *Llywelyn*, 455–7, 505–6.

[40] Ibid., 460–3; *AWR*, 651–3.

[41] Ibid., 240–1; 648–9.

[42] Smith, *Llywelyn*, 451; *KW*, i, 329–30.

[43] Ibid., 304, 322–3; *PW*, 222. That some burgesses escaped from

Aberystwyth is suggested by the order to the earl of Gloucester in May to see to their resettlement. Morris, *Welsh Wars*, 165.

44 Smith, *Llywelyn*, 451–2.

45 Ibid., 465–7, 506–10.

46 Ibid., 460; *PW*, 222.

47 Ibid., 222–4; Morris, *Welsh Wars*, 155; *KW*, i, 323n, 331; Prestwich, *Edward I*, 189, 198.

48 *PW*, 222–5; *RCWL*, 44; Morris, *Welsh Wars*, 155–8; Prestwich, *Edward I*, 196.

49 *Itinerary*, i, 159; *RCWL*, 44; *PW*, 222.

50 Morris, *Welsh Wars*, 160.

51 Ibid., 160–2; *KW*, i, 331.

52 Morris, *Welsh Wars*, 165–6. *Pace* Morris, the date of the attack was 16 June. *Annales Cambrie*, ed. J. Williams ab Ithel (Rolls Series, 1860), 106.

53 *PW*, 227; *RCWL*, 45.

54 *Itinerary*, i, 159a; *KW*, i, 322–3; Morris, *Welsh Wars*, 173.

55 Ibid., 174.

56 Ibid., 176–7; *KW*, i, 355–6; Smith, *Llywelyn*, 526.

57 *Itinerary*, i, 162–3; *KW*, i, 328; Morris, *Welsh Wars*, 177–8.

58 *Itinerary*, i, 163–4; Morris, *Welsh Wars*, 168–9, 178; *KW*, i, 333; Smith, *Llywelyn*, 527, 529–30.

59 Ibid., 530.

60 *AWR*, 617–25; Smith, *Llywelyn*, 532–4.

61 Ibid., 534–5.

62 Ibid., 535–6, 542–3. It is inconceivable that this offer could have been made after 6 November.

63 Ibid., 233–4, 536–43; Guisborough, 219–20; *AM*, iv, 290.

64 *AWR*, 626–8.

65 *Itinerary*, i, 165; Morris, *Welsh Wars*, 180–1; *PW*, 10; *CRV*, 275–6.

66 *PW*, 244–5; Morris, *Welsh Wars*, 181; Prestwich, *Edward I*, 238.

67 Morris, *Welsh Wars*, 181; Smith, *Llywelyn*, 550; *DNB*, xxxix, 394; *CRV*, 257; Prestwich, *Edward I*, 190–1.

68 *CACW*, 83–4; Smith, *Llywelyn*, 550–68; Davies, *Empire*, 40, 45; Bury, 75–6; *Flores*, iii, 57; *Ann. Lond.*, 90; *AM*, iv, 291.

69 Smith, *Llywelyn*, 570; *AWR*, 653–5; Prestwich, *Edward I*, 194.

70 Morris, *Welsh Wars*, 185–9; Morris, *Bigod Earls*, 126; *PW*, 244–5.

71 A. J. Taylor, 'The Death of Llywelyn ap Gruffydd', *Studies in Castles and Castle-Building*, 230; NA E101/351/9 (from November 1282).

72 Morris, *Welsh Wars*, 185, 190–1; *KW*, i, 336; *Itinerary*, i, 169.

73 Morris, *Welsh Wars*, 191; *PW*, 12–13.

74 *Itinerary*, i, 170; *KW*, i, 337; *PW*, 246–8.

[75] Morris, *Welsh Wars*, 192–5; *Itinerary*, i, 173–4.

[76] Ibid., 174–8; *KW*, i, 323; *PW*, 15–16; Smith, *Llywelyn*, 576, 578; Prestwich, *Edward I*, 196.

[77] Prestwich, *Edward I*, 200, 569; Kaeuper, *Bankers*, 182–91; Smith, *Llywelyn*, 529.

[78] Smith, *Llywelyn*, 570. See also F. G. Cowley, *The Monastic Order in South Wales, 1066–1349* (Cardiff, 1977), 214–15.

[79] *AM*, iv, 294; J. G. Bellamy, *The Law of Treason in the Middle Ages* (Cambridge, 1970), 23–6.

[80] *Itinerary*, i, 181–6; *AM*, iv, 488; A. J. Taylor, 'Royal Alms and Oblations', *Studies in Castles and Castle-Building*, 257–90.

[81] *EHD*, iii, 422–7.

[82] *KW*, i, 337–54, 357–65. Cf. N. Coldstream, 'Architects, Advisers and Design at Edward I's Castles in Wales', *Architectural History*, 46 (2003), 19–36; R. K. Morris, 'The Architecture of Arthurian Enthusiasm: Castle Symbolism in the Reigns of Edward I and his Successors', *Armies, Chivalry and Warfare in Medieval Britain and France: Proceedings of the 1995 Harlaxton Symposium*, ed. M. Strickland (Stamford, 1998), 72–3.

[83] *KW*, i, 369–95, and specifically 370; Morris, 'Architecture of Arthurian Enthusiasm', 65–6. Cf. A. Wheatley, *The Idea of the Castle in Medieval England* (Woodbridge, 2004), 112–21.

[84] *Itinerary*, i, 188; *KW*, i, 372; *AM*, iv, 490; *Ann. Lond.*, 91; D. Powel, *The Historie of Cambria* (London, 1584), 76–7. The birth of another daughter, Elizabeth, at Rhuddlan in August 1282 may represent an earlier attempt to the same end. Parsons, 'Year of Eleanor of Castile's Birth', 265.

[85] Davies, *Empire*, 27n, 32; *Flores*, iii, 59; NA E101/372/11, m. 1; *Ann. Lond.*, 92.

[86] *Itinerary*, i, 190–4; J. G. Frazer, *The Golden Bough* (London, 1922), 76; see also Taylor, 'Royal Alms', 288–9; Davies, *Empire*, 31–2; *Flores*, iii, 62; *AM*, iii, 313; iv, 489.

CHAPTER 7: PEACEFUL ENDEAVOURS

[1] *AM*, iv, 298.

[2] *KW*, i, 202n; Salzman, *Edward I*, 78–9; Prestwich, *Edward I*, 127.

[3] *AM*, iv, 298; Howell, *Eleanor of Provence*, 101–2 (cf. idem, 'The Children of King Henry III and Eleanor of Provence', *TCE*, iv (1992), 57–72); Prestwich, *Edward I*, 128–9; Parsons, *Eleanor of Castile*, 38–9.

[4] A. J. Taylor, 'A Fragment of a *Dona* Account of 1284', *Studies in Castles and Castle-Building*, 196–201; idem, 'Royal Alms', 281–2; *Itinerary*, i, 195–200; *KW*, i, 306; *RCWL*, 57–8.

[5] Lloyd, *English Society and the Crusade*, 234.

[6] *Calendar of Papal Registers, Papal Letters, 1198–1304* (London, 1893), 473–4.

[7] Powicke, *Thirteenth Century*, 264–5. About £110,000 of the £130,000 had been collected by 1283, of which Edward seized about £40,000. W. E. Lunt, *Financial Relations of the Papacy with England to 1327* (Cambridge, Mass.,1939), 332–3; Kaeuper, *Bankers*, 200–1.

[8] Dunbabin, *Charles I of Anjou*, 4–6, 90, 99–108.

[9] Ibid., 113.

[10] Powicke, *Thirteenth Century*, 252–3.

[11] J. R. Strayer, 'The Crusade against Aragon', *Speculum*, 28 (1953), 104–8.

[12] Powicke, *Thirteenth Century*, 241–3, 257–8, 271, 311n; Strayer, 'Crusade against Aragon', 105.

[13] *AM*, iv, 300. See also *RCWL*, 58–61.

[14] *AM*, iv, 300 (cf. *Itinerary*, i, 201); *CPR, 1281–92*, 149–52.

[15] *Itinerary*, i, 202–5; *AM*, iv, 301; P. Chaplais, 'Le Duche-Pairie de Guyenne', *Essays in Medieval Diplomacy and Administration* (London, 1981), iii, 22; Trivet, 310, is probably relying on the confused memories of his patron (Edward's daughter), Mary, who was travelling with the court at this time (cf. *Itinerary*, i, 209–10; *Bury*, 83). See A. Gransden, *Historical Writing in England c. 550 to c. 1307* (London, 1974), 504, and below, n. 24.

[16] Cotton, 166; *Ann. Lond.*, 93–4; *Flores*, iii, 63; *AM*, ii, 402; *Chronica Johannis de Oxenedes*, ed. H. Ellis (Rolls Series, 1859), 243; Taylor, 'Royal Alms', 283–4.

[17] Chaplais, 'Duche-Pairie de Guyenne', 22–4.

[18] *EHD*, iii, 428–60; Cotton, 166.

[19] Williams, *Medieval London*, 208, 232–5, 242.

[20] *KW*, i, 715–22.

[21] Williams, *Medieval London*, 245–52. For more on Ruxley and Waleys, see *DNB*, xlviii, 427–8; lvi, 799–800.

[22] Williams, *Medieval London*, 249–50, 252–4. For approximate population levels, see Carpenter, *Struggle*, 44.

[23] Williams, *Medieval London*, 254–5; Prestwich, *Edward I*, 265.

[24] A. J. Taylor, 'Edward I and the Shrine of St Thomas of Canterbury', *Studies in Castles and Castle-Building*, 291–7; *Itinerary*, i, 209–10; Howell, *Eleanor of Provence*, 300.

[25] *EHD*, iii, 460–2; M. Morris, 'King Edward I and the Knights of the Round Table', *Foundations of Medieval Scholarship: records edited in honour of David Crook*, ed. P. Brand and S. Cunningham (York, 2008).

[26] John de Vaux, one of the three ambassadors sent in May, was back with the king by 10 September: *RCWL*, 74; Powicke, *Thirteenth Century*, 252; Chaplais, 'Duche-Pairie de Guyenne', 24.

[27] Ibid., 24n; Strayer, 'Crusade against Aragon', 102; Powicke, *Thirteenth Century*, 255.

[28] Edward's presence in Exeter was probably occasioned by the recent scandal there. D. Douie, *Archbishop Pecham* (Oxford, 1952), 302–4.

[29] *AM*, ii, 403; *PROME*, 46; Prestwich, *Edward I*, 323.

[30] Ibid.; E. Gemmill, 'The King's Companions: The Evidence of Royal Charter Witness Lists from the Reign of Edward I', *Bulletin of the John Rylands University Library*, 83 (2001), 145.

[31] J. R. Strayer, *The Reign of Philip the Fair* (Princeton, 1980), 3, 5–6, 12.

[32] Powicke, *Thirteenth Century*, 255–6; Prestwich, *Edward I*, 323.

[33] Ibid.; Powicke, *Thirteenth Century*, 290–1. For *ardua negocia*, see *PROME*, 45; also Guisborough, 223 (*quibusdam arduis corrigendis*).

[34] Strayer, *Reign of Philip the Fair*, 6, 10–11; Powicke, *Thirteenth Century*, 256–7.

[35] Ibid., 253.

[36] Crouch, *Tournament*, 37, 45, 77; Powicke, *Thirteenth Century*, 248.

[37] *Foedera*, I, ii, 668–70.

[38] Ibid., 672–3; Powicke, *Thirteenth Century*, 291.

[39] Lunt, *Financial Relations*, 338.

[40] J.-P. Trabut-Cussac, 'Itinéraire d'Édouard Ier en France, 1286–89', *BIHR*, 25 (1952), 166–73.

[41] Ibid., 174–5; *Rôles Gascons*, ed. Francisque-Michel and C. Bémont, iii, xlv; *RWH*, nos. 73, 853.

[42] Ibid., nos. 575, 824–6.

[43] *Chronica Johannis de Oxenedes*, ed. Ellis, 246–7, gives the date as 'the first week in Lent', but Edward is too mobile down to Easter for this to have been the case. For the true date, see *RWH*, no. 255.

[44] Unless 1287 was a bumper year for indoor near-death experiences, Trivet, 313, is probably describing the same incident. For other vague reports, see *AM*, ii, 404; *Flores*, iii, 65–6.

[45] *RWH*, nos. 827–9; Lunt, *Financial Relations*, 338.

[46] Trabut-Cussac, 'Itinéraire', 177–9; For Blanquefort's acquisition, see idem, *L'Administration*, 15, 38. Two English chroniclers say Edward took the cross there: *Flores*, iii, 65–6; Trivet, 314. Another says he recovered there and took the cross at Bordeaux: *AM*, ii, 404. See also R. R. Mundill, *England's Jewish Solution: Experiment and Expulsion, 1262–1290* (Cambridge, 1998), 85–6.

[47] Lunt, *Financial Relations*, 338–9n; Tyerman, *England and the Crusades*, 235.

[48] *RWH*, nos. 289, 341, 575.

[49] Ibid., nos. 429, 958, 967–8, 979, 987.

[50] Powicke, *Thirteenth Century*, 259.

[51] Ibid., 259–60.

[52] Trabut-Cussac, 'Itinéraire', 181–4; *RWH*, no. 543, 1082; Prestwich, *Edward I*, 330.

[53] Ibid., 324; Powicke, *Thirteenth Century*, 259n; Trabut-Cussac, 'Itinéraire', 185.

[54] Ibid., 187–9.

[55] M. W. Beresford, *New Towns of the Middle Ages: Town Plantation in England, Wales and Gascony* (London, 1967), 351–9.

[56] Ibid., 8–9, 149–50, 166–7, 584.

[57] Ibid., 359–62.

[58] Ibid., 191, 234–6.

[59] Ibid., 30, 99–102, 362, 584.

[60] Ibid., 29, 79, 83–5, 363–72.

[61] Ibid., 35–51.

[62] Ibid., 51, 58–60, 96, 427–8, 445–6. For Edward's other unsuccessful urban initiatives, ibid., 83.

[63] Ibid., 6, 14–15, 19, 28–9; *EHD*, iii, 799–800. For the fullest treatment, see D. and B. Martin, *New Winchelsea, Sussex* (2004).

[64] Beresford, *New Towns of the Middle Ages*, 270, 338, 593–4, 597.

[65] Powicke, *Thirteenth Century*, 260.

[66] Trabut-Cussac, 'Itinéraire', 191–3.

[67] Powicke, *Thirteenth Century*, 260, 282–3; Trabut-Cussac, 'Itinéraire', 193–4.

[68] Powicke, *Thirteenth Century*, 284. J.-L. Blanc and J.-F. Massie, 'Le Castera de Bonnegarde', *Extrait du Bulletin de la Société de Borda* (1977), 1–22; Beresford, *New Towns of the Middle Ages*, 187.

[69] Powicke, *Thirteenth Century*, 284; *RWH*, nos. 1730, 1757–8, 1779, 2012, 2665–71, 2774, 3229.

[70] Powicke, *Thirteenth Century*, 261, 263, 298–304; Trabut-Cussac, 'Itinéraire', 201.

[71] Davies, *Age of Conquest*, 380–1, Morris, *Welsh Wars*, 205–19; Kaeuper, *Bankers*, 195–9; *RWH*, 423–98.

[72] *DNB*, xlvi, 618.

[73] *CCR, 1272–79*, 493.

[74] Prestwich, *Edward I*, 13.

[75] *NHI*, 67–141, 241–3, 441–4.

[76] Ibid., 156–75.

[77] Ibid., 179–84, 244–51.

[78] S. Duffy, *Ireland in the Middle Ages* (Basingstoke, 1996), 129.

[79] Powicke, *Henry III*, 700–1; Davies, *Empire*, 101–2, 146, 148.

[80] Ibid., 108; *NHI*, 242, 271, 346, 394.

[81] *DNB*, xi, 768; R. Frame, 'The Justiciar and the Murder of the MacMurroughs in 1282', *Irish Historical Studies*, xviii (1972), 223–30.

[82] *DNB*, xi, 768; Duffy, *Ireland in the Middle Ages*, 129; *NHI*, 259.

83 Salzman, *Edward I*, 87.
84 Stacey, 'Expulsion', 78–9. The remainder of this chapter draws heavily on Prof. Stacey's reconstruction of events.
85 Ibid., 79–80; *CCR, 1279–88*, 547.
86 In general, see D. W. Sutherland, *Quo Warranto Proceedings in the Reign of Edward I, 1278–1294* (Oxford, 1963).
87 Guisborough, 216; Prestwich, *Edward I*, 262.
88 Stacey, 'Expulsion', 81.
89 *The Mirror of Justices*, ed. W. J. Whittaker (Selden Society, vii, 1895), 6–8; Powicke, *Thirteenth Century*, 520–1; Powicke, *Henry III*, 701–2; M. Morris, 'The King's Companions', *History Today*, 55 (December 2005), 55; Guisborough, 216.
90 Stacey, 'Expulsion', 81–2; *AM*, iv, 316.
91 Stacey, 'Expulsion', 83–4; *EHD*, iii, 463; P. A. Brand, 'Edward I and the Judges: the "State Trials" of 1289–93', *TCE*, i (1986), 31–40.
92 Stacey, 'Expulsion', 86–7; *EHD*, iii, 464–6.
93 Salzman, *Edward I*, 92; below, 234.
94 Stacey, 'Expulsion', 88, 90.
95 Ibid., 95–9; cf. Mundill, *England's Jewish Solution, passim*.
96 Parsons, *Eleanor of Castile*, 61, 119–20, 176, 252.
97 Ibid., 120–1.
98 Huscroft, *Expulsion*, 131–2, 154.
99 Ibid., 133, 144–7.
100 Ibid., 146.
101 Stacey, 'Expulsion', 89–90.
102 Huscroft, *Expulsion*, 147–8; Mundill, *England's Jewish Solution*, 299–301.
103 Stacey, 'Expulsion', 90–1.
104 Ibid., 91–3.
105 Huscroft, *Expulsion*, 151–2, 155–7.
106 *DNB*, xxxii, 497; Tyerman, *England and the Crusades*, 236–8; Powicke, *Henry III*, 733; idem, *Thirteenth Century*, 261–3, 266–8; Lunt, *Financial Relations*, 339–40.

CHAPTER 8: THE GREAT CAUSE

1 D. Crook, 'The Last Days of Eleanor of Castile', *Transactions of the Thoroton Society of Nottinghamshire*, xciv (1990), 17–28.
2 Parsons, *Eleanor of Castile*, 4–5, 58–60, 64, 102–13, 120, 122.
3 N. Coldstream, 'The Commissioning and Design of the Eleanor Crosses', *Eleanor of Castile 1290–1990*, ed. D. Parsons (Stamford, 1991), 55–67; P. Lindley, 'Romanticizing Reality: The Sculptural Memorials of Queen Eleanor and their Context', ibid., 69–92; Parsons, *Eleanor*

of Castile, 60, 209. Henry III had been quietly translated to a new tomb earlier in 1290. Carpenter, 'King Henry III and the Cosmati Work', 423–4.

4 Prestwich, *Edward I*, 131–2; Parsons, *Eleanor of Castile*, 50; Powicke, *Henry III*, 734–5.

5 Tyerman, *England and the Crusades*, 237–8.

6 *DNB*, i, 653–5; M. Morris, *Castle: A History of the Buildings that Shaped Medieval Britain* (London, 2003), 203.

7 *DNB*, i, 655; Barrow, *Bruce*, 1–2; Duncan, *Kingship*, 171.

8 Ibid., 175–7.

9 Ibid., 178–9.

10 *Eleanor of Provence*, 293–300, 305.

11 Powicke, *Henry III*, 732–3, 788–90.

12 Duncan, *Kingship*, 165–6, 169–70, 175–9.

13 Ibid., 171, 179–82.

14 Ibid., 182–4.

15 Ibid., 185, 187–91, 196.

16 Ibid., 156–8, 191–3, 196; Powicke, *Thirteenth Century*, 592–3.

17 Duncan, *Kingship*, 190, 192, 194; *EHD*, iii, 467–8.

18 Duncan, *Kingship*, 195–7.

19 *DNB*, xxx, 170.

20 *DNB*, iii, 605–6; xxx, 170.

21 *DNB*, xii, 904.

22 *DNB*, viii, 373–4.

23 Duncan, *Kingship*, 178, 197–9.

24 Ibid., 199, 202, 208; *AM*, ii, 409.

25 G. W. S. Barrow, *Kingship and Unity: Scotland 1000–1306* (London, 1981), 3, 10–14.

26 Ibid., 25, 33, 105–21; Carpenter, *Struggle*, 13–14; Duncan, *Kingship*, 336.

27 Carpenter, *Struggle*, 11–14.

28 Bartlett, *Making of Europe*, 274–7.

29 Ibid., 78–81; Barrow, *Bruce*, 20–1; Carpenter, *Struggle*, 142–3, 178–82.

30 Davies, *Domination and Conquest*, 13–14; idem, *Empire*, 151–2, 156–8, 160–6; Carpenter, *Struggle*, 179–80; J. Campbell, 'The United Kingdom of England', *Uniting the Kingdom?*, ed. A. Grant and K. J. Stringer (London, 1995), 47.

31 J. Gillingham, 'Conquering the Barbarians: War and Chivalry in Twelfth-Century Britain and Ireland', *The English in the Twelfth Century*, 41–58; Davies, *Domination and Conquest*, 51.

32 Morris, *Bigod Earls*, 5, 13n, 48; Barrow, *Bruce*, 23, 26.

33 Davies, *Empire*, 11–14, 64–5.

34 Duncan, *Kingship*, 154–5.

35 *Geoffrey of Monmouth*, ed. Thorpe, 90, 218–21, 227–8.

[36] Davies, *Empire*, 47.
[37] Duncan, *Kingship*, 127–53; Powicke, *Thirteenth Century*, 593–4.
[38] Above, 25; Howell, *Eleanor of Provence*, 102–3; *Lanercost*, 81 (the summer of 1268 is the likeliest context: see Maddicott, 'Crusade Taxation', 96, and cf. Studd, *Itinerary*, 111); A. A. M. Duncan, *Scotland: The Making of the Kingdom* (Edinburgh, 1975), 577; M. Penman, *The Scottish Civil War: The Bruces and the Balliols and the War for Control of Scotland* (Stroud, 2002), 26.
[39] Duncan, *Kingship*, 159; cf. Prestwich, *Edward I*, 90n.
[40] Duncan, *Kingship*, 160.
[41] Ibid., 161–4.
[42] Ibid., 205–9.
[43] Ibid., 213–15.
[44] Ibid., 215–16.
[45] Ibid., 206, 211–13, 216.
[46] Ibid., 199–203, 218–19, 232.
[47] Ibid., 179, 237–8.
[48] Ibid., 245–6.
[49] Ibid., 218; *RCWL*, 100; Prestwich, *Edward I*, 365.
[50] Duncan, *Kingship*, 245–54.
[51] *Edward I and the Throne of Scotland, 1290–1296: an Edition of the Record Sources for the Great Cause*, ed. E. L. G. Stones and G. G. Simpson (2 vols., Oxford, 1977), i, 1; Duncan, *Kingship*, 259, 261, 264; *Itinerary*, ii, 10; Prestwich, *Edward I*, 366.
[52] Duncan, *Kingship*, 257–61.
[53] Ibid., 265.
[54] Ibid., 346–7.
[55] Ibid., 184–5, 240, 265–6.
[56] Howell, *Eleanor of Provence*, 307–12.
[57] Morris, *Welsh Wars*, 224–30.
[58] Ibid., 231–5; *PROME*, 57.
[59] Morris, *Welsh Wars*, 235–7; *DNB*, xlvi, 618–19.
[60] *Itinerary*, ii, 24; Duncan, *Kingship*, 267.
[61] Ibid., 267–9.
[62] Ibid., 270, 346.
[63] Ibid., 269.
[64] Ibid., 272–4, 277–8.
[65] *Itinerary*, ii, 26–30; Duncan, *Kingship*, 309–10.
[66] Ibid., 274–5, 277, 284, 291.
[67] Ibid., 268, 297–9.
[68] Ibid., 300–6.
[69] Ibid., 306–7.
[70] Ibid., 316–20; Barrow, *Bruce*, 50–2.

CHAPTER 9: THE STRUGGLE FOR MASTERY

[1] Riley-Smith, *The Crusades*, 206–7; Tyerman, *England and the Crusades*, 235–40.

[2] Prestwich, *Edward I*, 313, 331; *CPR, 1281–92*, 435; Tyerman, *England and the Crusades*, 235.

[3] *KW*, i, 252, 510; Binski, *Painted Chamber*, 1–7; M. Reeve, 'The Painted Chamber at Westminster, Edward I, and the Crusade', *Viator*, 37 (2006), 189–221. Some surviving fragments of the Chamber can be seen in the British Museum.

[4] Lunt, *Financial Relations*, 340–1; Tyerman, *England and the Crusades*, 236, 240; *Itinerary*, ii, 34–9.

[5] Guisborough, 240; *CPR, 1292–1301*, 15 (the writ is vacated because the embassy was cancelled: see Trabut-Cussac, *L'Administration*, 108n).

[6] Powicke, *Thirteenth Century*, 644; Guisborough, 241.

[7] Powicke, *Thirteenth Century*, 645–6; P. Chaplais, 'Réglement des Conflits Internationaux Franco-Anglais au 14e Siècle, 1293–1377', *Essays in Medieval Diplomacy*, ix, 271–2; idem, *English Medieval Diplomatic Practice, Part I* (2 vols., HMSO, 1982), i, 394–5; *Itinerary*, ii, 43–6; *AM*, iv, 513.

[8] M. Vale, *The Angevin Legacy and the Hundred Years War, 1250–1340* (Oxford, 1990), 183; Chaplais, 'Réglement des Conflits', 272–3.

[9] Duncan, *Kingship*, 320–1; Barrow, *Bruce*, 58–9, 62.

[10] Vale, *Angevin Legacy*, 184–7, 196; Howell, *Eleanor of Provence*, 136–7.

[11] *DNB*, xvii, 759.

[12] *CPR, 1292–1301*, 33. The failure of the legal ambassadors by November is inferred from the reappearance of one of their number (Roger Brabazon) in England. *RCWL*, 117.

[13] *Foedera*, I, ii, 794; Chaplais, *English Medieval Diplomatic Practice*, ii, 428n.

[14] Ibid.

[15] Vale, *Angevin Legacy*, 196–7; Strayer, *Reign of Philip the Fair*, 369.

[16] Vale, *Angevin Legacy*, 179, 196–200.

[17] *DNB*, viii, 901; xxxii, 512; *AM*, iv, 515; Cotton, 232.

[18] *Foedera*, I, ii, 794; Vale, *Angevin Legacy*, 190.

[19] *Itinerary*, ii, 52–4; Cotton, 233.

[20] Salzman, *Edward I*, 111; *Evesham*, 573.

[21] Powicke, *Thirteenth Century*, 648; Chaplais, *English Medieval Diplomatic Practice*, ii, 428n; *Foedera*, I, ii, 800.

[22] *Bury*, 118; W. M. Ormrod, 'Love and War in 1294', *TCE*, viii (2001), 148–50.

[23] *Evesham*, 573; Guisborough, 243; Langtoft, ii, 202–3.

[24] J. R. Strayer, 'The Costs and Profits of War: The Anglo-French Conflict of 1294–1303', *The Medieval City*, ed. H. A. Miskimin, D. Herlihy and

A. J. Udovich (New Haven and London, 1977), 273; Trabut-Cussac, *L'Administration*, 108.

25 Tyerman, *England and the Crusades*, 236.

26 Kaeuper, *Bankers*, 209, 218–21 (although 12 June given wrongly as 2 June); Denton, *Winchelsey*, 61, 63.

27 Morris, *Bigod Earls*, 118, 125–6, 155; *PW*, 259–62.

28 *Itinerary*, ii, 58; J. Gillingham, 'Richard I, Galley Warfare and Portsmouth: The Beginnings of a Royal Navy', *TCE*, vi (1997), 1–15; M. K. Vaughn, '"Mount the War-Horses, Take your Lance in your Grip...": Logistics Preparations for the Gascon Campaign of 1294', *TCE*, viii (2001), 97–111.

29 *PW*, 25; *Evesham*, 573–4; *Rôles Gascons*, ed. Francisque-Michel and Bémont, iii, no. 2934.

30 *NHI*, 260; *Bury*, 123.

31 *AM*, iv, 515–17; *Evesham*, 574; *PW*, 262–3.

32 Prestwich, *Edward I*, 402–3; *EHD*, iii, 469; *PW*, 25–6.

33 *PW*, 263–4.

34 *Itinerary*, ii, 62; *Evesham*, 574; Guisborough, 244.

35 Carpenter, *Struggle*, 268; *Select Pleas in Manorial and Other Seignorial Courts*, ed. F. W. Maitland (Selden Society, ii, 1889), 76–9; Morris, *Welsh Wars*, 241–2.

36 Denton, *Winchelsey*, 67–75; Powicke, *Thirteenth Century*, 484.

37 Morris, *Welsh Wars*, 242; *PW*, 26–7.

38 Morris, *Welsh Wars*, 242; *Prests*, xxvii–xxviii; *KW*, i, 364, 377.

39 Guisborough, 251; Davies, *Age of Conquest*, 382–3; Prestwich, *Edward I*, 219.

40 Langtoft, ii, 220–1; Morris, *Welsh Wars*, 242, 244; Guisborough, 244, says the delayed fleet left around 9 October.

41 *EHD*, iii, 469; Prestwich, *Edward I*, 404; *Itinerary*, ii, 64–5.

42 Davies, *Age of Conquest*, 383; *Prests*, xxix–xxx.

43 *KW*, i, 348–50, 364; *Prests*, xxx.

44 Ibid., xxxii–xxxiv.

45 *Bury*, 125; Cotton, 256; Guisborough, 251–2.

46 Robert Winchelsea had reached the king and sworn fealty before 4 February: *Prests*, xxxii, n.

47 Ibid., xxxiv; R. F. Walker, 'The Hagnaby Chronicle and the Battle of Maes Moydog', *Welsh History Review*, 8 (1976), 127.

48 Ibid., 127–38; *Prests*, xxxviii; Prestwich, *Edward I*, 223.

49 *Prests*, xxviii, xxxix–xl; Beresford, *New Towns of the Middle Ages*, 49–50.

50 *Prests*, xxxv, xxxix–xliv.

51 On his journey south in May he had travelled via Llanrug: *Itinerary*, ii, 72.

52 *Prests*, xliv–xlvi.

53 Prestwich, *Edward I*, 382–3.

54 *Calendar of Documents relating to Ireland, 1293–1301* (HMSO, 1881), 88 (no. 204); *AM*, iv, 521; *PW*, i. 28–9.

55 *Flores*, iii, 94; *Itinerary*, ii, 64; R. C. Anderson, 'English Galleys in 1295', *Mariners' Mirror*, 14 (1928), 221; *PROME*, 77.

56 *PW*, 226, 267; Cotton, 299; above, 178–9.

57 NA E159/68, mm. 73–5. Cf. F. J. Willard, *Parliamentary Taxes on Personal Property, 1290 to 1334* (Cambridge Mass., 1934), 111–12.

58 Denton, *Winchelsey*, 72; *HBC*, 104; *CCR, 1288–96*, 422.

59 E. B. Fryde, 'Magnate Debts to Edward I and Edward III: A Study of Common Problems and Contrasting Royal Reactions to Them', *National Library of Wales Journal*, 27 (1992), 263–7.

60 Ibid., 262–3; *Prests*, xlviii; *WPF*, 236n.

61 Fryde, 'Magnate Debts', 262.

62 A. Z. Freeman, 'A Moat Defensive: The Coast Defense Scheme of 1295', *Speculum*, 42 (1967), 442–62; R. J. Whitwell and C. Johnson, 'The "Newcastle" Galley, A.D. 1294', *Archaeologia Aeliana*, 4th series, 2 (1926), 143; *HBC*, 135.

63 *Prests*, xlvii; *Select Cases in the Court of King's Bench*, vol. 3, ed. G. O. Sayles (Selden Society, lviii, 1939), xlv, 50–1; J. G. Edwards, 'The Treason of Thomas Turbeville', *Studies in Medieval History Presented to F. M. Powicke* (Oxford, 1948), 296–309; *EHD*, iii, 918–19.

64 *RCWL*, 125; *PW*, 391–2. These pardons were not simultaneous, but spread over several weeks: NA E159/68, m. 76.

65 NA E159/68, m. 46v (Fryde, 'Magnate Debts', 263). The four pardoned their tax were Arundel, William de Vescy, Henry de Grey and Peter de Mauley: *PW*, 391–2.

66 *PW*, 29–31; D. A. Carpenter, 'The Beginnings of Parliament', *Reign of Henry III*, 381, 406–8.

67 *PW*, 32–3, 45–6; Cotton, 299; *DNB*, xi, 749.

68 Denton, *Winchelsey*, 7–12, 86–8.

69 Barrow, *Bruce*, 63–4.

70 Edwards, 'Treason of Thomas Turbeville', 298–9. Cf. Duncan, *Kingship*, 321–4.

71 Prestwich, *Edward I*, 373–4; Barrow, *Bruce*, 59, 68; Duncan, *Kingship*, 321.

72 Prestwich, *Edward I*, 470.

73 *NHI*, 169, 268–70; Duffy, *Ireland in the Middle Ages*, 126–7; *DNB*, viii, 786.

74 S. Duffy, 'The Problem of Degeneracy', *Law and Disorder in Thirteenth-Century Ireland*, ed. J. Lydon (Dublin, 1997), 98; idem, *Ireland in the Middle Ages*, 127.

75 *DNB*, xix, 827; *NHI*, 260; *PW*, 262; J. Lydon, 'Ireland in 1297: "At Peace after its manner"', *Law and Disorder in Thirteenth-Century Ireland*, ed. Lydon, 21–2; idem, 'An Irish Army in Scotland, 1296', *Irish Sword*, 5 (1961–62), 184–9.

76 *Itinerary*, ii, 85–6; Prestwich, *Edward I*, 469–70; Duncan, *Kingship*, 322.
77 M. Strickland, 'A Law of Arms or a Law of Treason? Conduct in War in Edward I's Campaigns in Scotland, 1296–1307', *Violence in Medieval Society*, ed. R. W. Kaeuper (Woodbridge, 2000), 64–6; Guisborough, 274–5.
78 Strickland, 'Law of Arms', 64, 67.
79 *KW*, ii, 563; Duncan, *Kingship*, 323; Prestwich, *Edward I*, 471–2; Barrow, *Bruce*, 71–2.
80 *Itinerary*, ii, 88–90; Barrow, *Bruce*, 73; Lydon, 'Irish Army in Scotland', 186 (cf. Guisborough, 279–80).
81 E. L. G. Stones and M. N. Blount, 'The Surrender of King John of Scotland to Edward I in 1296: some new evidence', *BIHR*, 48 (1975), 94–106; Prestwich, *Edward I*, 473–4.
82 *Itinerary*, ii, 90–3; D. B. Tyson, 'A Royal Itinerary: the Journey of Edward I to Scotland in 1296', *Nottingham Medieval Studies*, 45 (2001), 127–44; Barrow, *Bruce*, 75–7.
83 *DNB*, viii, 375–6.
84 Binski, *Westminster Abbey*, 135–40. Guisborough, 281, says the Stone was seized on the way back from Elgin.
85 Watson, *Hammer*, 30–7; *Scalacronica*, ed. J. Stevenson (Edinburgh, 1836), 123.
86 Prestwich, *Edward I*, 474–5; Davies, *Empire*, 33, 43; *EHD*, iii, 230–1. See similar comments in *Bury*, 133, and *Lanercost*, 182.
87 Guisborough, 261–2 (cf. *AM*, iv, 525–6); *DNB*, xvii, 759.
88 *Foedera*, I, ii, 842; *PW*, 47–8; *EHD*, iii, 220.
89 *Prests*, lii; *KW*, i, 379–80.
90 *EHD*, iii, 469; Prestwich, *Edward I*, 402.
91 *WPF*, 118–21; D. Crook, '"Thieves and Plunderers": an Anti-Ministerial Protest of 1296', *Historical Research*, 67 (1994), 327–36.
92 *PROME*, 83; *Flores*, iii, 98.
93 *PW*, 47–8; *DNB*, lvi, 48.
94 Denton, *Winchelsey*, 89–92, 95–6.
95 *EHD*, iii, 233; *Prests*, l; Prestwich, *Edward I*, 386–91; *Documents 1297*, 34; *Foedera*, I, ii, 850–1.
96 Denton, *Winchelsey*, 101–7.
97 Ibid., 107–12; *EHD*, iii, 232.
98 *Evesham*, 568; *PW*, 51–2.
99 Prestwich, *Edward I*, 385; *EHD*, iii, 212, 235–6.
100 *WPF*, 121, 128.
101 Morris, *Bigod Earls*, 162–3.
102 Ibid., 163–4; *EHD*, iii, 226–7. The whereabouts of the earl of Cornwall, who would almost certainly have supported Edward, is unknown. *Pace* Prestwich, *Edward I*, 413, he was not in Gascony.

[103] *EHD*, iii, 227; Denton, *Winchelsey*, 116; G. O. Sayles, 'The Seizure of Wool at Easter 1297', *EHR*, 67 (1952), 543–7; Morris, *Bigod Earls*, 164.

[104] *Documents 1297*, 4; *EHD*, iii, 213, 227.

[105] Denton, *Winchelsey*, 118, 126–30.

[106] *Evesham*, 576; Davies, *Lordship*, 261; *Documents 1297*, 14.

[107] *PROME*, 85; *PW*, 282; *EHD*, iii, 214; *Itinerary*, ii, 105–6; Denton, *Winchelsey*, 131.

[108] *Flores*, iii, 101; *RCWL*, 131.

[109] Morris, *Bigod Earls*, 165.

[110] Ibid., 165–6; *Evesham*, 576; *Documents 1297*, 105–6, 141–2.

[111] Denton, *Winchelsey*, 132; *EHD*, iii, 237; Morris, *Bigod Earls*, 166.

[112] Ibid.; *Evesham*, 577; *EHD*, iii, 469, 472.

[113] *Itinerary*, ii, 109; *Documents 1297*, 5, 8; *EHD*, iii, 473–6.

[114] *Itinerary*, ii, 109; *EHD*, iii, 216, 228, 480–1; Denton, *Winchelsey*, 144–7; Morris, *Bigod Earls*, 166–7.

[115] *EHD*, iii, 218, 223, 483; Denton, *Winchelsey*, 154–5; *PW*, 55–6, 297; *CACW*, 101 (for true date see Davies, *Lordship and Society*, 269).

[116] *Political Songs*, 169–70.

CHAPTER 10: UNITING THE KINGDOM?

[1] *DNB*, lvii, 395–8.

[2] Watson, *Hammer*, 31, 39–41.

[3] Prestwich, *Edward I*, 476–7.

[4] Guisborough, 295–6; cf. Barrow, *Bruce*, 332, n. 30.

[5] Watson, *Hammer*, 45, 48; Stevenson, *Documents*, ii, 204–5.

[6] Ibid., 200–3, 206–7.

[7] A. Fisher, *William Wallace* (2nd edn, Edinburgh, 2002), 68–70.

[8] *DNB*, lvi, 947–8.

[9] Stevenson, *Documents*, ii, 216–17; Watson, *Hammer*, 45–6.

[10] e.g. Stevenson, *Documents*, ii, 202.

[11] Guisborough, 298–303.

[12] *PW*, 55–6; *EHD*, iii, 223, 228–9.

[13] *CDS*, ii, 244 (no. 950); *EHD*, iii, 229.

[14] Carpenter, *Struggle*, 269–73.

[15] Ibid., 301–2, 307–9, 348; above, 92.

[16] *EHD*, iii, 469, 472, 474; Denton, *Winchelsey*, 136.

[17] *EHD*, iii, 472; *Flores*, iii, 296.

[18] *EHD*, iii, 229, 485–6 (cf. the demands in *De Tallagio*, ibid., 486–7); *PW*, 62–3.

[19] Prestwich, *Edward I*, 392; *EHD*, iii, 218, 223 (where 'Portuguese' should read 'men of the Cinque Ports'), 238–9; *Bury*, 143–4; *Foedera*, I, ii, 878–80.

20 *Documents 1297*, 162–4 (no. 159); M. Prestwich, 'Edward I and Adolf of Nassau', *TCE*, iii (1991), 132–3; *EHD*, iii, 230, 486.

21 C. J. McNamee, 'William Wallace's Invasion of Northern England in 1297', *Northern History*, 26 (1990), 40–58; Guisborough, 304; *Lanercost*, 190; Barrow, *Bruce*, 98–9.

22 *EHD*, iii, 219–20, 242; *Documents 1297*, 33, 174–5 (no. 176).

23 *CDS*, ii, 267 (no. 1044); *PW*, 306–7.

24 *Foedera*, I, ii, 885–6; *Documents 1297*, 183–4 (no. 193).

25 Watson, *Hammer*, 53, 56; *Itinerary*, ii, 119.

26 Morris, *Bigod Earls*, 168; *PW*, 65; Prestwich, *Edward I*, 431–2; Guisborough, 324.

27 Prestwich, *Edward I*, 479; *AM*, iv, 536; *RCWL*, 133; *EHD*, iii, 244.

28 Fisher, *William Wallace*, 119, 126; Guisborough, 324–6.

29 Guisborough, 326–7.

30 Ibid., 327–8. Barrow, *Bruce*, 101, 345n.

31 Trivet, 281–2, 372; Guisborough, 327–8.

32 Ibid., 327–8.

33 Ibid., 328. Barrow, *Bruce*, 102. The myth of noble treachery began with Fordun in the fourteenth century, and was, of course, massively reinforced by *Braveheart*.

34 Watson, *Hammer*, 67.

35 Ibid.; Barrow, *Bruce*, 101–3; Guisborough, 328–9; *Itinerary*, ii, 126.

36 Prestwich, *Edward I*, 191, 204; Guisborough, 329 (cf. Watson, *Hammer*, 68, 95 and *NHI*, 199):

37 Watson, *Hammer*, 68; Guisborough, 329; *PW*, 317; *EHD*, iii, 248.

38 Watson, *Hammer*, 69–70, 77; Guisborough, 329; *Itinerary*, ii, 127–30.

39 Carpenter, *Struggle*, 92, 197–8.

40 *EHD*, iii, 338, 347.

41 *PROME*, 87; Guisborough, 324; *PW*, 397.

42 D. A. Carpenter, *The Minority of Henry III* (London, 1990), 384–5, 392–3.

43 *PW*, 78–9; Powicke, *Thirteenth Century*, 650–2; *DNB*, vi, 444. Guisborough, 329, thought that the earl of Hereford supported the opposition in 1299, but was probably as confused as Langtoft (*EHD*, iii, 245–6). Cf. below, 375.

44 Guisborough, 329–30; *Bury*, 151; *Itinerary*, ii, 135.

45 *EHD*, 491–4; Guisborough, 330; *CPR, 1292–1301*, 403.

46 *PW*, 80; Williams, *Medieval London*, 260–2; *PROME*, 92.

47 *Bury*, 152 (cf. Guisborough, 330); *Itinerary*, ii, 138; *Foedera*, I, ii, 904–5; *RCWL*, 137; NA SC6/922/6; *Chepstow Castle: Its History and Buildings*, ed. R. Turner and A. Johnson (Logaston, 2006), 168, 285.

48 *CPR, 1292–1301*, 424; *AM*, iv, 541.

49 Salzman, *Edward I*, 147; *Foedera*, I, ii, 906–7; E. H. Hallam, *English*

Royal Marriages: The French Marriages of Edward I and Edward II: 1299 and 1307 (HMSO, 1982).

50 *Bury*, 153 (Bigod had returned to East Anglia in August: NA SC6/1000/20); Prestwich, *Edward I*, 521.

51 *HBC*, 465, 468, 477, 486.

52 *PW*, 321–4.

53 Barrow, *Bruce*, 103–4, 145.

54 *CDS*, ii, 279 (no. 1101); Powicke, *Thirteenth Century*, 651.

55 *Foedera*, I, ii, 906; *DNB*, xxx, 172; Barrow, *Bruce*, 107.

56 Watson, *Hammer*, 80–90.

57 Guisborough, 332.

58 Watson, *Hammer*, 88–9; *RCWL*, 138–9; *Bury*, 154.

59 *PW*, 325–6; Prestwich, *Edward I*, 530–1.

60 Ibid., 483–4.

61 *PROME*, 93; *EHD*, iii, 246, 248. See also Guisborough, 332. Rishanger, 402–3, is rendered suspect by idem, 445–6, and vice versa (see below, n. 77).

62 *PW*, 82–4; Watson, 92–3.

63 Rishanger, 404–5; Prestwich, *Edward I*, 522–3.

64 *Bury*, 154; *EHD*, iii, 495–501.

65 *PW*, 397; *CPR, 1292–1301*, 506; *AM*, iv, 544.

66 *PW*, 327–8.

67 *PW*, 330–9, 341–2; Prestwich, *Edward I*, 523.

68 *PW*, 326, 329; C. M. Fraser, *A History of Antony Bek* (Oxford, 1957), 139–40; *Bury*, 156; *EHD*, iii, 247; *Documents and Records illustrating the History of Scotland*, ed. F. Palgrave (HMSO, 1837), 218–19.

69 Watson, *Hammer*, 104 (extrapolated from Prestwich, *Edward I*, 484–5); Prestwich, *Edward I*, 479, 485–6; *PW*, 343; *CPR, 1292–1301*, 526, 534; Davies, *Age of Conquest*, 386, says the subsidy was £2,400.

70 *Roll of Arms…Caerlaverock*, ed. T. Wright (London, 1864), 1.

71 Watson, *Hammer*, 68, 74, 81, 87, 107–8; D. Grove, *Caerlaverock Castle* (2nd edn, Edinburgh, 2004), 18–19, 23–5; Strickland, 'Law of Arms', 71.

72 *PW*, 344–5; Prestwich, *Edward I*, 486, 489; *Itinerary*, ii, 160.

73 Ibid., 160–1; J. S. Richardson, *Sweetheart Abbey* (2nd edn, Edinburgh, 1995), 2–4, 8; Prestwich, *Edward I*, 491.

74 Ibid., 332, 395; *EHD*, iii, 504.

75 Denton, *Winchelsey*, 179; Barrow, *Bruce*, 116; *Anglo-Scottish Relations, 1174–1328*, ed. E. L. G. Stones (2nd edn, Oxford, 1970), 162–75.

76 *AM*, iv, 547; *WPF*, 96; Prestwich, *Edward I*, 490; *Itinerary*, ii, 161. For a much later report of Edward's reaction to the pope's letter, see *Thomae Walsingham, quondam monachi Sancti Albani, Historia Anglicana*, ed. H. T. Riley (2 vols., Rolls Series, 1863–66), i, 82.

77 *CDS*, v, 162 (no. 226); *AM*, iv, 547; cf. Rishanger, 445–6, dubious because repeated from idem, 402–3 (see above, n. 61).

78 *PW*, 88–91.

79 K. Staniland, 'Welcome, Royal Babe! The Birth of Thomas of Brotherton in 1300', *Costume*, 19, (1985), 1–13; Barrow, *Bruce*, 114; *Foedera*, I, ii, 924–5.

80 *EHD*, iii, 249; Prestwich, *Edward I*, 525.

81 Ibid., 527.

82 *CCR, 1296–1302*, 410; Prestwich, *Edward I*, 527; *EHD*, iii, 347.

83 *PROME*, 98.

84 *EHD*, iii, 249–50, 510–12.

85 Rishanger, 460; J. R. Maddicott, '"1258" and "1297": Some Comparisons and Contrasts', *TCE*, ix (2003), 1–14.

86 Ibid., 13.

87 *EHD*, iii, 250; Watson, *Hammer*, 114–15.

88 Ibid.; *PW*, 347–8; *Itinerary*, ii, 170–2; *DNB*, xvii, 772.

89 *RCWL*, 147; *Foedera*, I, ii, 922, 928 (for more details see M. C. L. Salt, 'List of English Embassies to France, 1272–1307', *EHR*, 44 (1929), 274); T. S. R. Boase, *Boniface VIII* (London, 1933), 211, 271; Denton, *Winchelsey*, 200–1.

90 H. Johnstone, *Edward of Carnarvon, 1284–1307* (Manchester, 1946), 13, 51, 55–63, 73; Salzman, *Edward I*, 157–8; *CDS*, ii, 305 (no. 1191).

91 *PW*, 347–8; *CDS*, v, 168–9 (no. 262).

92 *PW*, 347–56; *WPF*, 96–7; J. F. Lydon, 'Irish Levies in the Scottish Wars, 1296–1302', *Irish Sword*, 5 (1961–62), 214. Some troops from Ireland had been used in 1298 and 1300: *NHI*, 199.

93 Prestwich, *Edward I*, 494; Barrow, *Bruce*, 26.

94 Ibid., 96, 120; *Itinerary*, ii, 178; Prestwich, *Edward I*, 494.

95 Watson, *Hammer*, 123–5.

96 Ibid., 98, 126; *WPF*, 97.

97 Prestwich, *Edward I*, 493; Watson, *Hammer*, 129–31; *CDS*, v, 168–9 (nos. 260–2).

98 Ibid., no. 260; *PW*, 106.

99 Watson, *Hammer*, 129, 132, 138–9; *CDS*, v, 168 (no. 259).

100 R. J. Goldstein, 'The Scottish Mission to Boniface VIII in 1301', *Scottish Historical Review*, 70 (1991), 1–15; E. L. G. Stones, 'The Mission of Thomas Wale and Thomas Delisle from Edward I to Pope Boniface VIII in 1301', *Nottingham Medieval Studies*, 26 (1982), 8–28 and esp. 18–19; *Anglo-Scottish Relations*, ed. Stones, 192–219.

101 *EHD*, iii, 251; *CDS*, v, 168 (no. 259).

102 Watson, *Hammer*, 151–2; *Itinerary*, ii, 180; *PW*, 400–1; Salt, 'English Embassies', 274.

[103] *Treaty Rolls*, i, 149–52. The truce, drawn up at Asnières-sur-Oise on an unknown date, was ratified by Philip IV at St Benoît-sur-Loire on 25 December 1301.

[104] Barrow, *Bruce*, 109–12, 121–4.

[105] Guisborough, 351; Johnstone, *Edward of Carnarvon*, 80; Salzman, *Edward I*, 158; *Ann. Lond.*, 104.

[106] *KW*, i, 412–13.

[107] Salt, 'English Embassies', 274–5.

[108] *EHD*, iii, 252; J. F. Verbruggen, *The Battle of the Golden Spurs (Courtrai, 11 July 1302)*, trans. D. R. Fergusson, ed. K. DeVries (Woodbridge, 2002), *passim*.

[109] *PROME*, 107; *Political Songs*, 193; Strayer, *Reign of Philip the Fair*, 260–79.

[110] *Foedera*, I, ii, 942; *CDS*, v, 173 (nos. 286–7).

[111] Salt, 'English Embassies', 275; *Flores*, iii, 111; Watson, *Hammer*, 168.

[112] Prestwich, *Edward I*, 529.

[113] Watson, *Hammer*, 172–3; *KW*, i, 400, 413–16.

[114] Watson, *Hammer*, 169–71.

[115] Ibid., 167; *EHD*, iii, 515–18; Prestwich, *Edward I*, 529.

[116] *PW*, 370–1, 406; J. F. Lydon, 'Edward I, Ireland and the War in Scotland, 1303–1304', *England and Ireland in the Later Middle Ages*, ed. idem (Dublin, 1981), 46, 48, 52; *NHI*, 200.

[117] Stevenson, *Documents*, ii, 178–9 (misdated to 1297); *CDS*, ii, 348–9 (no. 1356); *PW*, 366–7.

[118] *KW*, i, 416–17; M. Haskell, 'Breaking the Stalemate: The Scottish Campaign of Edward I, 1303–4', *TCE*, vii (1999), 226.

[119] *EHD*, iii, 254; *Itinerary*, ii, 209–10.

[120] Watson, *Hammer*, 175–6.

[121] Ibid., 180; *EHD*, iii, 255; Guisborough, 357.

[122] *Itinerary*, ii, 210–14; Watson, *Hammer*, 174–5, 178–9; *WPF*, 97–8.

[123] Lydon, 'Edward I, Ireland and the War in Scotland', 48–9; Watson, *Hammer*, 177, 180.

[124] Ibid., 179–80; Guisborough, 357; *Itinerary*, ii, 214–16.

[125] Barrow, *Bruce*, 127; Watson, *Hammer*, 180–1.

[126] Ibid., 181–2.

[127] *DNB*, xxxvi, 635; Barrow, *Bruce*, 127–8.

[128] Watson, *Hammer*, 182, 185–7.

[129] Ibid., 187–9.

[130] Prestwich, *Edward I*, 501; *KW*, i, 417–18.

[131] Haskell, 'Breaking the Stalemate', 235–7; Strickland, 'Law of Arms', 71–4; Watson, *Hammer*, 191.

[132] Strickland, 'Law of Arms', 64; Barrow, *Bruce*, 136–7; *Itinerary*, ii, 250.

CHAPTER 11: A LASTING VENGEANCE

1 *Itinerary*, ii, 230–7; *EHD*, iii, 258; *KW*, ii, 903–4; *Flores*, iii, 120–1; Davies, *Empire*, 172.

2 Vale, *Angevin Legacy*, 224.

3 Prestwich, *Edward I*, 400, 570.

4 T. F. Tout, 'A Medieval Burglary', *Bulletin of the John Rylands Library*, 2 (1915), 348–69; *EHD*, iii, 258; Prestwich, *Edward I*, 283–6.

5 Lydon, 'Ireland in 1297', and P. Connolly, 'The Enactments of the 1297 Parliament', *Law and Disorder in Thirteenth-Century Ireland*, ed. Lydon, 17–20, 23–4, 149–61.

6 Vale, *Angevin Legacy*, 224–5; J. Gardelles, *Les Châteaux du Moyen Age dans la France du Sud-ouest: la Gascogne Anglaise de 1216 à 1327* (Geneva, 1972), 34–6.

7 Watson, *Hammer*, 197–200; M. Prestwich, 'Colonial Scotland: The English in Scotland under Edward I', *Scotland and England 1286–1815*, ed. R. A. Mason (Edinburgh, 1987), 9–10.

8 *PW*, 407–8; *EHD*, iii, 519–22, 919–21.

9 *PROME*, 114; *Flores*, iii, 120–1.

10 Watson, *Hammer*, 187, 214.

11 Davies, *Empire*, 28, 172–3.

12 Johnstone, *Edward of Carnarvon*, 63–4, 97; J. Given, 'The Economic Consequences of the English Conquest of Gwynedd', *Speculum*, 64 (1989), 28, 39, 41.

13 Johnstone, *Edward of Carnarvon*, 64, 86.

14 Ibid., 97–100; *Itinerary*, ii, 246–8.

15 *Ann. Lond.*, 138–9, 142; *PW*, 161–3; Davies, *Empire*, 173; Watson, *Hammer*, 214–18; Barrow, *Bruce*, 134–5.

16 Watson, *Hammer*, 218–19; *Flores*, iii, 124; *Ann. Lond.*, 143.

17 Morris, *Bigod Earls*, 171–83.

18 Denton, *Winchelsey*, 170, 201–6.

19 Ibid., 212–13, 218–27.

20 Ibid., 229–32; Trivet, 408; Salzman, *Edward I*, 169–70.

21 C. W. Hollister, *Henry I* (New Haven and London, 2001), 31; *Commendatio*, xiv, 5–6; *Itinerary*, ii, 248.

22 *CCR, 1302–7*, 208; *CPR 1301–7*, 387; Prestwich, *Edward I*, 532–3; Denton, *Winchelsey*, 220; cf. Johnstone, *Edward of Carnarvon*, 104: 'Edward I's crusading zeal may well have been both warm and sincere'.

23 Barrow, *Bruce*, 131, 142–3, 145–8, 150; Prestwich, *Edward I*, 505.

24 Barrow, *Bruce*, 148–51.

25 Strickland, 'Law of Arms', 40; *Itinerary*, ii, 259–65; Trivet, 408.

26 *Ann. Lond.*, 133; Morris, *Bigod Earls*, 182; *PW*, 374.

27 *CCR, 1302–7*, 438; Prestwich, *Edward I*, 553; *PW*, 374–5.

[28] *PW*, 164; Johnstone, *Edward of Carnarvon*, 106–9; Loomis, 'Arthurian Enthusiast', 122–5; *Geoffrey of Monmouth*, ed. Thorpe, 225–30; *EHD*, iii, 260–1; Trivet, 408; C. Bullock-Davies, *Menestrellorum Multitudine: Minstrels at a Royal Feast* (Cardiff, 1978), *passim*.

[29] *CDS*, ii, 476–7 (no. 1773); cf. *Ann. Lond.*, 146.

[30] Barrow, *Bruce*, 153–4; Strickland, 'Law of Arms', 42.

[31] *Itinerary*, ii, 266–70; *SR*, 147.

[32] *CDS*, ii, 480 (no. 1790), 485–7 (no. 1811).

[33] Ibid., 478–80 (nos. 1780, 1786), 487–8 (nos. 1812–15); Strickland, 'Law of Arms', 42; *EHD*, iii, 261.

[34] Barrow, *Bruce*, 160–1, 163; *CDS*, ii, 483 (no. 1803), 485 (no. 1809).

[35] *Itinerary*, ii, 270–3; Prestwich, *Edward I*, 507; *CPR, 1301–7*, 460; *CDS*, ii, 491 (no. 1832); *CCR, 1302–7*, 458.

[36] Barrow, *Bruce*, 161, 163–4.

[37] Ibid., 161–2; Strickland, 'Law of Arms', 40; *DNB*, liii, 35.

[38] Prestwich, *Edward I*, 509; idem, 'Colonial Scotland', 10–11; Barrow, *Bruce*, 161; *EHD*, iii, 262.

[39] *PW*, 377–9; Johnstone, *Edward of Carnarvon*, 115–16.

[40] *Chronicles of the Reigns of Edward I and Edward II*, ed. W. Stubbs (2 vols., Rolls Series, 1882–83), ii, 255; *Lanercost*, 210; Guisborough, 382–3. Cf. P. Chaplais, *Piers Gaveston: Edward II's Adoptive Brother* (Oxford, 1994), *passim*.

[41] Barrow, *Bruce*, 166, 169–72; *CDS*, ii, 504 (no. 1896).

[42] *Itinerary*, ii, 280–1; *CDS*, ii, 508 (no. 1909); Barrow, *Bruce*, 173.

[43] Ibid., 172.

[44] Johnstone, *Edward of Carnavon*, 124–5.

[45] *PW*, 380; Guisborough, 378–9; H. Moorman, 'Edward I at Lanercost Priory, 1306–7', *EHR*, 67 (1952), 167–8.

[46] Guisborough, 379; Trivet, 413–14; NA E101/370/15, m. 6, shows Edward leaving Carlisle on 26 June (my thanks to Henry Summerson for this reference).

[47] Guisborough, 379.

CHAPTER 12: A GREAT AND TERRIBLE KING

[1] Guisborough, 379; Prestwich, *Edward I*, 557; Chaplais, *Piers Gaveston*, 23–4; R. M. Haines, *King Edward II* (Montreal and London, 2003), 49.

[2] *EHD*, iii, 264; *Political Songs*, 244–6; W. Ullmann, 'The Curial Exequies for Edward I and Edward III', *Journal of Ecclesiastical History*, vi (1955), 26, 30; Guisborough, 379; Haines, *King Edward II*, 49.

[3] Ibid.; Barrow, *Bruce*, 173; Guisborough, 379.

[4] Ibid.; Prestwich, *Edward I*, 558.

5 Davies, *Empire*, 29; *EHD*, iii, 264; D. D'Avray, *Death and the Prince: Memorial Preaching before 1350* (Oxford, 1994), 71; *Commendatio*, xvi–xvii, 7, 11, 13–15.

6 Guisborough, 379; *EHD*, iii, 264, 905; *Commendatio*, 12–13, 16; Powicke, *Thirteenth Century*, 226, 233; Prestwich, *Edward I*, 84–5. For the one discordant (but deeply suspect) note, see ibid., 50, 110, 354.

7 Guisborough, 379; *EHD*, iii, 265; *Political Songs*, 242.

8 Trivet, 302; Howell, *Eleanor of Provence*, 298; D'Avray, *Death and the Prince*, 72; Powicke, *Thirteenth Century*, 338, 469–70.

9 *Commendatio*, 16.

10 Ibid., 6; Trivet, 281.

11 *EHD*, iii, 905; D'Avray, *Death and the Prince*, 71; *Flores*, iii, 137–8; P. Brand, 'Edward I and Justice' (read 2007, as yet unpublished); above, 40.

12 Above, 89, 351–2; McFarlane, 'Had Edward I a "Policy" towards the Earls', 257–9; Powicke, *Henry III*, 706–7.

13 *Flores*, iii, 327; *Political Songs*, 242, 249; D'Avray, *Death and the Prince*, 72; *Commendatio*, 7; Trivet, 413–14; *Adami Murimuthensis, Chronica sui temporis*, ed. T. Hog (London, 1846), 8–9.

14 M. Prestwich, 'The Piety of Edward I', *England in the Thirteenth Century: Proceedings of the 1984 Harlaxton Symposium*, ed. M. W. Ormrod (Woodbridge, 1985), 120–8. For the saints and their relics, see the forthcoming article by H. Summerson, originally entitled 'The End of the Reign: Edward I at Carlisle'.

15 *Commendatio*, 13; Parsons, *Eleanor of Castile*, 33; Gransden, *Historical Writing in England*, 504; Trivet, 282, 359.

16 Ibid., 281–3; Prestwich, *Edward I*, 111, 117; Howell, *Eleanor of Provence*, 84.

17 *Flores*, iii, 329; D'Avray, *Death and the Prince*, 75–6; Prestwich, *Edward I*, 208, 498; *KW*, i, 413.

18 Prestwich, *Edward I*, 3, 63.

19 *Commendatio*, 14.

20 *Flores*, iii, 137–8; M. D. Legge, 'La Piere D'Escoce', *Scottish Historical Review*, 38 (1959), 110–11; *Political Songs*, 242.

21 D'Avray, *Death and the Prince*, 72; *Roll of Arms...Caerlaverock*, ed. Wright, 9; *Commendatio*, 9–10.

22 Taylor, 'Death of Llywelyn ap Gruffydd', 230; Davies, *Domination and Conquest*, 85–7, 108. For a contrary view, see Carpenter, *Struggle*, 19–24.

23 Vale, *Angevin Legacy*, 21–47; *Bury*, 118; *Political Songs*, 247.

24 Powicke, *Thirteenth Century*, 583; K. Stringer, 'Scottish Foundations: Thirteenth-Century Perspectives', *Uniting the Kingdom?*, ed. A. Grant and K. J. Stringer (London, 1995), 88–90.

25 *Johannis de Trokelowe et Henrici de Blaneforde, Chronica et Annales*, ed.

H. T. Riley (Rolls Series, 1866), 74; Prestwich, *Edward I*, 128–9, 437, 489, 502, 521, 538; idem, 'Colonial Scotland', 10.

26 Prestwich, *Edward I*, 492. Around the time of his investiture as prince of Wales, Edward of Caernarfon was given a book 'concerning the deeds of the kings of England'. The earls of Lincoln (d. 1311) and Warwick (d. 1315) both owned copies of the Brut. *DNB*, xvii, 825; L. M. Matheson, *The Prose Brut* (Tempe, Arizona, 1998), 9–10.

27 Lydon, 'Edward I, Ireland and the War in Scotland', 55–7; idem, 'Ireland in 1297', 23; Duffy, *Ireland in the Middle Ages*, 168; Davies, *Age of Conquest*, 425; idem, *Empire*, 181–2.

28 Davies, *Age of Conquest*, 385–8, 419–21, 443–59; M. Prestwich, *Plantagenet England, 1225–1360* (Oxford, 2005), 164; *KW*, i, 389, 405–6.

29 Davies, *Empire*, 22, 185; Carpenter, *Struggle*, 19; Barrow, *Bruce*, 172–3.

30 Ibid., 174–232, 307.

31 *DNB*, xvii, 827.

32 Prestwich, *Plantagenet England*, 188, 201–2, 219–20.

33 It is also, of course, a reference to Judas Maccabeus, whose exploits were depicted on the walls of the Painted Chamber. Reeve, 'The Painted Chamber', 20–1.

34 Salzman, *Edward I*, 176; *EHD*, iii, 264.

35 Binski, *Westminster Abbey*, 120, 198; Morris, 'Architecture of Arthurian Enthusiasm', 67–8.

Bibliography

PRIMARY SOURCES

The Acts of Welsh Rulers, 1120–1283, ed. H. Pryce (Cardiff, 2005).

Adami Murimuthensis, Chronica sui temporis, ed. T. Hog (London, 1846).

Anglo-Scottish Relations, 1174–1328, ed. E. L. G. Stones (2nd edn, Oxford, 1970).

Annales Cambrie, ed. J. Williams ab Ithel (Rolls Series, 1860).

'Annales de Terre Sainte', ed. R. Röhricht, *Archives de l'Orient Latin*, ii (1884).

'Annales Londonienses', *Chronicles of the Reigns of Edward I and Edward II*, ed. W. Stubbs, vol. 1 (Rolls Series, 1882).

Annales Monastici, ed. H. R. Luard (5 vols., Rolls Series, 1864–69).

Ayyubids, Mamlukes and Crusaders: selections from the Tārikh al Duwal wa'l Mulūk of Ibn al-Furāt, ed. U. and M. C. Lyons, introduction by J. S. C. Riley-Smith, vol. 2 (Cambridge, 1971).

Bartholomaei de Cotton, Historia Anglicana (A.D. 449–1298), ed. H. R. Luard (Rolls Series, 1859).

Book of Prests, 1294–5, ed. E. B. Fryde (Oxford, 1962).

The Brut, ed. F. W. D. Brie, (Early English Text Society, 131, 1906).

Brut y Tywysogyon, or The Chronicle of the Princes (Red Book of Hergest Version), ed. and trans. T. Jones (Cardiff, 1952).

Calendar of Ancient Correspondence Concerning Wales, ed. J. G. Edwards (Cardiff, 1935).

Calendar of Close Rolls (HMSO, 1892–).

Calendar of Documents relating to Ireland, 1293–1301 (HMSO, 1881).

Calendar of Documents relating to Scotland, ed. J. Bain et al. (5 vols., Edinburgh, 1881–1988).

Calendar of Liberate Rolls (HMSO, 1916–64).

Calendar of Papal Registers, Papal Letters, 1198–1304 (London, 1893).

Calendar of Patent Rolls (HMSO, 1906–).

Calendar of Various Chancery Rolls, 1277–1326 (HMSO, 1912).

Chrétien de Troyes, Arthurian Romances, ed. and trans. W. W. Kibler and C. W. Carroll (London, 1991).

Chronica Johannis de Oxenedes, ed. H. Ellis (Rolls Series, 1859).

The Chronicle of Bury St. Edmunds, 1212–1301, ed. A. Gransden (London, 1964).

The Chronicle of Pierre de Langtoft, ed. T. Wright, ii (Rolls Series, 1868).

The Chronicle of Walter of Guisborough, ed. H. Rothwell (Camden Society, 3rd series, lxxxix, 1957).

The Chronicle of William de Rishanger of the Barons' Wars, ed. J. O. Halliwell (Camden Society, 1st series, xv, 1840).

Chronicles of the Reigns of Edward I and Edward II, ed. W. Stubbs, (2 vols., Rolls Series, 1882–83).

Chronicon de Lanercost, ed. J. Stevenson (Edinburgh, 1839).

Close Rolls, Henry III (HMSO, 1902–38).

'Commendatio Lamentabilis in Transitu Magni Regis Edwardi', *Chronicles of the Reigns of Edward I and Edward II*, ed. W. Stubbs, vol. 1 (Rolls Series, 1882).

De Antiquis Legibus Liber. Chronica Maiorum et Vicecomitum Londoniarum, ed. T. Stapleton (Camden Society, 1st series, xxxiv, 1846).

Documents and Records Illustrating the History of Scotland, ed. F. Palgrave (HMSO, 1837).

Documents Illustrating the Crisis of 1297–98 in England, ed. M. Prestwich (Camden Society, 4th series, xxiv, 1980).

Documents Illustrative of the History of Scotland, ed. J. Stevenson (2 vols., Edinburgh, 1870).

Documents of the Baronial Movement of Reform and Rebellion, 1258–1267, ed. R. F. Treharne and I. J. Sanders (Oxford, 1973).

Edward I and the Throne of Scotland, 1290–1296. An Edition of the Record Sources for the Great Cause, ed. E. L. G. Stones and G. G. Simpson (2 vols., Oxford, 1977).

English Historical Documents 1189–1327, ed. H. Rothwell (London, 1975).

'L'Estoire de Eracles Empereur', *Recueil des Historiens des Croisades: Historiens Occidentaux*, ed. A. Beugnot et al., vol. 2 (Paris, 1859).

Flores Historiarum, ed. H. R. Luard, (3 vols., Rolls Series, 1890).

Foedera, Conventiones, Litterae et Acta Publica, ed. T. Rymer, amended edn by A. Clarke and F. Holbrooke (4 vols. in 7, Record Commission, 1816–69).

Geoffrey of Monmouth, History of the Kings of Britain, ed. L. Thorpe (London, 1966).

Gerald of Wales, The Journey through Wales and The Description of Wales, ed. L. Thorpe (London, 1978).

'Gestes des Chiprois', *Receuil des Historiens des Croisades: Documents Arméniens*, ed. C. Kohler, vol. 2 (Paris, 1906).

The Historical Works of Gervase of Canterbury, ed. W. Stubbs (2 vols., Rolls Series, 1879–80).

Jean de Joinville, Histoire de St Louis, ed. N. de Wailly (Paris, 1874).

Johannis de Trokelowe et Henrici de Blaneforde, Chronica et Annales, ed. H. T. Riley (Rolls Series, 1866).

King Arthur in Legend and History, ed. R. White (London, 1997).

The Ledger Book of Vale Royal Abbey, ed. J. Brownhill (Record Society of Lancashire and Cheshire, 68, 1914).

Matthaei Parisiensis, Monachi Sancti Albani, Chronica Majora, ed. H. R. Luard (7 vols., Rolls Series, 1872–83).

The Mirror of Justices, ed. W. J. Whittaker (Selden Society, vii, 1895).

Nicholai Triveti . . . Annales Sex Regum Angliae, ed. T. Hog (London, 1845).

Oxford Book of Welsh Verse in English, ed. G. Jones (Oxford, 1977).

Parliamentary Writs and Writs of Military Summons, ed. F. Palgrave (2 vols. in 4, Record Commission, 1827–34).

The Parliament Rolls of Medieval England, 1275–1504, vol. 1, ed. P. Brand and C. Given-Wilson (Woodbridge, 2005).

Receuil d'actes relatifs à l'administration des Rois d'Angleterre en Guyenne au XIIIe siècle: Recogniciones feodorum in Aquitania, ed. C. Bémont (Paris, 1914).

Records of the Wardrobe and Household, 1286–1289, ed. B. F. and C. R. Byerly (HMSO, 1986).

Rôles Gascons, ed. Francisque-Michel and C. Bémont (4 vols., Paris, 1885–1906).

Roll of Arms . . . Caerlaverock, ed. T. Wright (London, 1864).

Royal and Other Historical Letters Illustrative of the Reign of King Henry III, ed. W. W. Shirley (2 vols., Rolls Series, 1862–86).

The Royal Charter Witness Lists of Edward I, ed. R. Huscroft (List and Index Society, 279, 2000).

The Royal Charter Witness Lists of Henry III, ed. M. Morris (2 vols., List and Index Society, 291-2, 2001).

Scalacronica by Sir Thomas Grey of Heton, Knight, ed. J. Stevenson (Edinburgh, 1836).

Select Cases in the Court of King's Bench, vol. 3, ed. G. O. Sayles (Selden Society, lviii, 1939).

Select Pleas in Manorial and Other Seignorial Courts, ed. F. W. Maitland (Selden Society, ii, 1889).

The Statutes of the Realm, ed. A. Luders, T. E. Tomlins, J. France, W. E. Taunton and J. Raithby, i (Record Commission, 1810).

Thomae Walsingham, quondam monachi Sancti Albani, Historia Anglicana, ed. H. T. Riley (2 vols., Rolls Series, 1863–66).

Thomas Wright's Political Songs of England, ed. P. Coss (Cambridge, 1996).

Willelmi Rishanger, Chronica et Annales, ed. H. T. Riley (Rolls Series, 1865).

SECONDARY SOURCES

Anderson, R. C., 'English Galleys in 1295', *Mariners' Mirror*, 14 (1928).

Ashbee, J., '"The Chamber called *Gloriette*": Living at Leisure in Thirteenth and Fourteenth-Century Castles', *Journal of the British Archaeological Association*, 157 (2004).

The Atlas of the Crusades, ed. J. Riley-Smith (London, 1991).

Ayloffe, J., 'An Account of the Body of King Edward the First', *Archaeologia*, iii (1786).

Bachrach, D. S., 'Military Logistics during the Reign of Edward I of England, 1272–1307', *War in History*, 13 (2006).

Barrow, G. W. S., *Kingship and Unity: Scotland 1000–1306* (London, 1981).

—— *Robert Bruce and the Community of the Realm of Scotland* (3rd edn, Edinburgh, 1988).

Bartlett, R., *The Making of Europe* (London, 1993).

—— *England under the Norman and Angevin Kings* (Oxford, 2000).

Bellamy, J. G., *The Law of Treason in the Middle Ages* (Cambridge, 1970).

Beresford, M. W., *New Towns of the Middle Ages: Town Plantation in England, Wales and Gascony* (London, 1967).

Binski, P., *The Painted Chamber at Westminster* (London, 1986).

—— *Westminster Abbey and the Plantagenets: Kingship and the Representation of Power 1200–1400* (New Haven and London, 1995).

Blanc, J.-L. and Massie, J.-F., 'Le Castera de Bonnegarde', *Extrait du Bulletin de la Société de Borda* (1977).

Bloch, M., *Feudal Society* (2nd edn, 1962).

Boase, T. S. R., *Boniface VIII* (London, 1933).

Brand, P. A., 'Edward I and the Judges: the "State Trials" of 1289–93', *TCE*, i (1986).

—— 'Edward I and Justice', (read 2007, as yet unpublished).

Brown, R. A., Colvin, H. M., and Taylor, A. J., *The History of the King's Works*, vols. 1 and 2 (HMSO, 1963).

Bullock-Davies, C., *Menestrellorum Multitudine: Minstrels at a Royal Feast* (Cardiff, 1978).

Campbell, J., 'The United Kingdom of England', *Uniting the Kingdom?*, ed. A. Grant and K. J. Stringer (London, 1995).

The Cambridge Urban History of Britain , vol. 1: 600–1540, ed. D. M. Palliser (Cambridge, 2000).

Carpenter, D. A., *The Battles of Lewes and Evesham, 1264/65* (Keele, 1987).

—— *The Minority of Henry III* (London, 1990).

—— *The Reign of Henry III* (London, 1996), which includes all the essays below published up to and including that date. Original places of publication are noted, but my references follow the pagination in the book.

—— 'What Happened in 1258?', *War and Government in the Middle Ages*, ed. J. Gillingham and J. C. Holt (Woodbridge, 1984).

—— 'King, Magnates and Society: the Personal Rule of King Henry III, 1234–58', *Speculum*, 60 (1985).

—— 'The Lord Edward's Oath to Aid and Counsel Simon de Montfort, 15 October 1259', *BIHR*, 58 (1985).

—— 'The Gold Treasure of King Henry III', *TCE*, i (1986).

—— 'Simon de Montfort: The First Leader of a Political Movement in English History', *History*, 76 (1991).

—— 'King Henry III's "Statute" against Aliens: July 1263', *EHR*, 107 (1992).

—— 'King Henry III and the Tower of London', *The London Journal*, 19 (1995).

—— 'The Burial of King Henry III, the Regalia and Royal Ideology', *Reign of Henry III* (London, 1996).

—— 'King Henry III and the Cosmati Work at Westminster Abbey', *The Cloister and the World: Essays in Medieval History in Honour of Barbara Harvey*, ed. J. Blair and B. Golding (Oxford, 1996).

—— 'The Beginnings of Parliament', *The House of Commons: 700 Years of British Tradition*, ed. J. S. Moore and R. Smith (London, 1996).

—— 'A Noble in Politics: Roger Mortimer in the Period of Baronial Reform and Rebellion, 1258–1265, *Nobles and Nobility in Medieval Europe*, ed. A. J. Duggan (Woodbridge, 2000).

—— 'Westminster Abbey in Politics, 1258–1269', *TCE*, viii (2001).

—— *The Struggle for Mastery: Britain 1066–1284* (London, 2003).

—— 'King Henry III and Saint Edward the Confessor: the Origins of the Cult', *EHR*, 122 (2007).

Chaplais, P., 'Le Duche-Pairie de Guyenne', *Essays in Medieval Diplomacy and Administration* (London, 1981).

—— 'Réglement des Conflits Internationaux Franco-Anglais au 14e Siècle, 1293–1377', *Essays in Medieval Diplomacy and Administration* (London, 1981).

—— *English Medieval Diplomatic Practice, Part I* (2 vols., HMSO, 1982).

—— *Piers Gaveston: Edward II's Adoptive Brother* (Oxford, 1994).

Chepstow Castle: Its History and Buildings, ed. R. Turner and A. Johnson (Logaston, 2006).

Chew, H. M., 'Scutage under Edward I', *EHR*, 37 (1922).

Clanchy, M. T., *From Memory to Written Record* (2nd edn, Oxford, 1993).

Coldstream, N., 'The Commissioning and Design of the Eleanor Crosses', *Eleanor of Castile 1290–1990*, ed. D. Parsons (Stamford, 1991).

—— 'Architects, Advisers and Design at Edward I's Castles in Wales', *Architectural History*, 46 (2003).

Connolly, P., 'The Enactments of the 1297 Parliament', *Law and Disorder in Thirteenth-Century Ireland*, ed. J. Lydon (Dublin, 1997).

Cowley, F. G., The Monastic Order in South Wales, 1066–1349 (Cardiff, 1977).

Crook, D., 'The Sheriff of Nottingham and Robin Hood: the Genesis of the Legend?', *TCE*, ii (1988).

—— 'The Last Days of Eleanor of Castile', *Transactions of the Thoroton Society of Nottinghamshire*, xciv (1990).

—— '"Thieves and Plunderers": an Anti-Ministerial Protest of 1296', *Historical Research*, 67 (1994).

Crouch, D., *Tournament* (London, 2005).

Davies, R. R., *Lordship and Society in the March of Wales, 1282–1400* (Oxford, 1978).

—— *Domination and Conquest* (Cambridge, 1990).

—— 'The Peoples of Britain and Ireland, 1100–1400: IV. Language and Historical Mythology', *Transactions of the Royal Historical Society*, 6th series, 7 (1997).

—— *The Age of Conquest: Wales 1063–1415* (new edn, Oxford, 2000).

—— *The First English Empire: Power and Identities in the British Isles 1093–1343* (Oxford, 2000).

D'Avray, D., *Death and the Prince: Memorial Preaching before 1350* (Oxford, 1994).

De Laborderie, O., Maddicott, J. R., and Carpenter, D. A., 'The Last Hours of Simon de Montfort: A New Account', *EHR*, 115 (2000).

Denholm-Young, N., *Richard of Cornwall* (Oxford, 1947).

—— 'The Tournament in the Thirteenth Century', *Collected Papers* (Cardiff, 1969).

Denton, J. H., 'The Crisis of 1297 from the Evesham Chronicle', *EHR*, 93 (1978).

—— *Robert Winchelsey and the Crown, 1294–1313* (Cambridge, 1980).

Douie, D., *Archbishop Pecham* (Oxford, 1952).

Duffy, S., *Ireland in the Middle Ages* (Basingstoke, 1996).

—— 'The Problem of Degeneracy', *Law and Disorder in Thirteenth-Century Ireland*, ed. J. Lydon (Dublin, 1997).

Dunbabin, J., *Charles I of Anjou: Power, Kingship and State-Making in Thirteenth-Century Europe* (Harlow, 1998).

Duncan, A. A. M., *Scotland: The Making of the Kingdom* (Edinburgh, 1975).

—— *The Kingship of the Scots, 842–1292* (Edinburgh, 2002).

Edwards, J. G., 'The Treason of Thomas Turbeville', *Studies in Medieval History Presented to F. M. Powicke* (Oxford, 1948).

Fisher, A., *William Wallace* (2nd edn, Edinburgh, 2002).

Frame, R., 'The Justiciar and the Murder of the MacMurroughs in 1282', *Irish Historical Studies*, xviii (1972).

Fraser, C. M., *A History of Antony Bek* (Oxford, 1957).

Frazer, J. G., *The Golden Bough* (London, 1922).

Freeman, A. Z., 'A Moat Defensive: The Coast Defense Scheme of 1295', *Speculum*, 42 (1967).

Fryde, E. B., 'Magnate Debts to Edward I and Edward III: A Study of Common Problems and Contrasting Royal Reactions to Them', *National Library of Wales Journal*, 27 (1992).

Gardelles, J., *Les Châteaux du Moyen Age dans la France du Sud-ouest: la Gascogne Anglaise de 1216 à 1327* (Geneva, 1972).

Gemmill, E., 'The King's Companions: The Evidence of Royal Charter Witness Lists from the Reign of Edward I', *Bulletin of the John Rylands University Library*, 83 (2001).

Gillingham, J., 'Richard I, Galley Warfare and Portsmouth: The Beginnings of a Royal Navy', *TCE*, vi (1997).

—— 'Conquering the Barbarians: War and Chivalry in Twelfth-Century Britain and Ireland', *The English in the Twelfth Century* (Woodbridge, 2000).

—— 'The Context and Purposes of Geoffrey of Monmouth's *History of the Kings of Britain*', *The English in the Twelfth Century* (Woodbridge, 2000).

—— 'The Beginnings of English Imperialism', *The English in the Twelfth Century* (Woodbridge, 2000).

—— *1215: The Year of Magna Carta* (London, 2003).

Given, J., 'The Economic Consequences of the English Conquest of Gwynedd', *Speculum*, 64 (1989).

Goldstein, R. J., 'The Scottish Mission to Boniface VIII in 1301', *Scottish Historical Review*, 70 (1991).

Graham, R., 'Letters of Cardinal Ottoboni', *EHR*, 15 (1900).

Gransden, A., *Historical Writing in England c. 550 to c. 1307* (London, 1974).

Grove, D., *Caerlaverock Castle* (2nd edn, Edinburgh, 2004).

Haines, R. M., *King Edward II* (Montreal and London, 2003).

Hallam, E. H., *English Royal Marriages: The French Marriages of Edward I and Edward II: 1299 and 1307* (HMSO, 1982).

Handbook of British Chronology, ed. E. B. Fryde, D. E. Greenway, S. Porter and I. Roy (3rd edn, London, 1986).

Harvey, P. D. A., *Mappa Mundi: The Hereford World Map* (London, 1996).

Haskell, M., 'Breaking the Stalemate: The Scottish Campaign of Edward I, 1303–4', *TCE*, vii (1999).

Hennings, M. A., *England Under Henry III* (London, 1924).

Higham, N. J., *King Arthur: Myth-Making and History* (London, 2002).

A History of the Crusades, ed. K. M. Setton (6 vols., Philadelphia and Madison, 1955–89).

Hollister, C. W., *Henry I* (New Haven and London, 2001).

Howell, M., 'The Children of King Henry III and Eleanor of Provence', *TCE*, iv (1992).

—— *Eleanor of Provence* (Oxford, 1998).

—— 'Royal Women of England and France in the Mid-Thirteenth Century: A Gendered Perspective', *England and Europe in the Reign of Henry III (1216–1272)*, ed. B. K. U. Weiler and I. W. Rowlands (Aldershot, 2002).

Huscroft, R., 'The Political and Personal Life of Robert Burnell, Chancellor of Edward I' (Ph.D. thesis, London, 2000).

—— 'Robert Burnell and the Government of England', *TCE*, viii (2001).

—— 'Should I Stay or Should I Go? Robert Burnell, the Lord Edward's Crusade and the Canterbury Vacancy of 1270–3', *Nottingham Medieval Studies*, xlv (2001).

—— *Expulsion: England's Jewish Solution* (Stroud, 2006).

Irwin, R., *The Middle East in the Middle Ages: The Early Mamluk Sultanate, 1250–1382* (London, 1986).

Itinerary of Edward I, ed. E. W. Safford (3 vols., List and Index Society, 103, 132, 135, 1974–77).

Itinerary of the Lord Edward, ed. R. Studd (List and Index Society, 284, 2000).

Johnstone, H., 'The County of Ponthieu, 1279–1307', *EHR*, 29 (1914).

—— *Edward of Carnarvon, 1284–1307* (Manchester, 1946).

Jones-Pierce, T., 'The Growth of Commutation in Gwynedd in the Thirteenth Century', *Bulletin of the Board of Celtic Studies*, 10 (1941).

Kaeuper, R. W., *Bankers to the Crown: the Riccardi of Lucca and Edward I* (Princeton, 1973).

Keen, M., *Chivalry* (New Haven and London, 1984).

Kennedy, H., *Crusader Castles* (Cambridge, 1994).

Knowles, C. H., 'The Resettlement of England after the Barons' War, 1264–67', *Transactions of the Royal Historical Society*, 5th series, 32 (1982).

Legge, M. D., 'La Piere D'Escoce', *Scottish Historical Review*, 38 (1959).

Lindley, P., 'Romanticizing Reality: The Sculptural Memorials of Queen Eleanor and their Context', *Eleanor of Castile 1290–1990*, ed. D. Parsons (Stamford, 1991).

Lloyd, S., 'Gilbert de Clare, Richard of Cornwall and the Lord Edward's Crusade', *Nottingham Medieval Studies*, xxx (1986).

—— *English Society and the Crusade, 1216–1307* (Oxford, 1988).

Loomis, R. S., 'Edward I, Arthurian Enthusiast', *Speculum*, 28 (1953).

Lunt, W. E., *Financial Relations of the Papacy with England to 1327* (Cambridge, Mass., 1939).

Lydon, J. F., 'An Irish Army in Scotland, 1296', *Irish Sword*, 5 (1961–62).

—— 'Irish Levies in the Scottish Wars, 1296–1302', *Irish Sword*, 5 (1961–62).

—— 'Three Exchequer Documents from the reign of Henry III', *Proceedings of the Royal Irish Academy*, 65 (1966–67).

—— 'Edward I, Ireland and the War in Scotland, 1303–1304', *England and Ireland in the Later Middle Ages*, ed. idem (Dublin, 1981).

—— 'Ireland in 1297: "At Peace after its manner"', *Law and Disorder in Thirteenth-Century Ireland,* ed. J. Lydon (Dublin, 1997).

Maddicott, J. R., 'Edward I and the Lessons of Baronial Reform', *TCE*, i (1986).

—— 'The Crusade Taxation of 1268–1270 and the Development of Parliament', *TCE*, ii (1988).

—— *Simon de Montfort* (Cambridge, 1994).

—— '"An Infinite Multitude of Nobles": Quality, Quantity and Politics in the Pre-Reform Parliaments of Henry III', *TCE*, vii (1999).

—— '"1258" and "1297": Some Comparisons and Contrasts', *TCE*, ix (2003).

Martin, D. and B., *New Winchelsea, Sussex* (2004).

Matheson, L. M., *The Prose Brut* (Tempe, Arizona, 1998).

McFarlane, K. B., 'Had Edward I a "Policy" towards the Earls?', *The Nobility of Later Medieval England* (Oxford, 1973).

McNamee, C. J., 'William Wallace's Invasion of Northern England in 1297', *Northern History*, 26 (1990).

Moorman, H., 'Edward I at Lanercost Priory, 1306–7', *EHR*, 67 (1952).

Morgan, D., *The Mongols* (Oxford, 1986).

Morris, J. E., *The Welsh Wars of Edward I* (Oxford, 1901).

Morris, M., *Castle: A History of the Buildings that Shaped Medieval Britain* (London, 2003).

—— *The Bigod Earls of Norfolk in the Thirteenth Century* (Woodbridge, 2005).

—— 'The King's Companions', *History Today*, 55 (December 2005).

—— 'King Edward I and the Knights of the Round Table', *Foundations of Medieval Scholarship: records edited in honour of David Crook,* ed. P. Brand and S. Cunningham (York, 2008).

Morris, R. K., 'The Architecture of Arthurian Enthusiasm: Castle Symbolism in the Reigns of Edward I and his Successors', *Armies, Chivalry and Warfare in Medieval Britain and France: Proceedings of the 1995 Harlaxton Symposium,* ed. M. Strickland (Stamford, 1998).

Mundill, R. R., *England's Jewish Solution: Experiment and Expulsion, 1262–1290* (Cambridge, 1998).

A New History of Ireland, vol. II: Medieval Ireland, 1169–1534, ed. A. Cosgrove (Oxford, 1987).
Nicolle, D., and McBride, A., *The Mamluks, 1250–1517* (London, 1993).

Orme, N., *From Childhood to Chivalry* (London, 1984).
Ormrod, M. W., 'Love and War in 1294', *TCE*, viii (2001).
Oxford Dictionary of National Biography, ed. H. C. G. Matthew and B. Harrison (60 vols., Oxford, 2004).

Parsons, J. C., 'The Year of Eleanor of Castile's Birth and her Children by Edward I', *Mediaeval Studies*, xlvi (1984).
—— 'The Second Exhumation of King Arthur's Remains at Glastonbury, 19 April 1278', *Arthurian Literature*, 12 (1993).
—— *Eleanor of Castile* (New York, 1995).
Penman, M., *The Scottish Civil War: The Bruces and the Balliols and the War for Control of Scotland* (Stroud, 2002).
Powel, D., *The Historie of Cambria* (London, 1584).
Powicke, F. M., *King Henry III and the Lord Edward* (Oxford, 1947).
—— *The Thirteenth Century, 1216–1307* (2nd edn, Oxford, 1962).
Prestwich, M., *War, Politics and Finance under Edward I* (London, 1972).
—— 'The Piety of Edward I', *England in the Thirteenth Century: Proceedings of the 1984 Harlaxton Symposium*, ed. M. W. Ormrod (Woodbridge, 1985).
—— 'Colonial Scotland: The English in Scotland under Edward I', *Scotland and England 1286–1815*, ed. R. A. Mason (Edinburgh, 1987).
—— *Edward I* (London, 1988).
—— 'Edward I and Adolf of Nassau', *TCE*, iii (1991).
—— *Armies and Warfare in the Middle Ages: The English Experience* (New Haven and London, 1996).
—— *Plantagenet England, 1225–1360* (Oxford, 2005).
Pryor, J. H., *Commerce, Shipping and Naval Warfare in the Medieval Mediterranean* (London, 1987).

Raban, S., *A Second Domesday? The Hundred Rolls of 1279–80* (Oxford, 2004).
Reeve, M., 'The Painted Chamber at Westminster, Edward I, and the Crusade', *Viator*, 37 (2006).
Richardson, H. G., 'The Coronation in Medieval England', *Traditio*, 16 (1960).

Richardson, J. S., *Sweetheart Abbey* (2nd edn, Edinburgh, 1995).

Ridgeway, H. W., 'The Lord Edward and the Provisions of Oxford (1258): A Study in Faction', *TCE*, i (1986).

—— 'King Henry III's Grievances against the Council in 1261: a New Version and a Letter describing Political Events', *Historical Research*, 61 (1988).

—— 'Foreign Favourites and Henry III's Problems of Patronage, 1247–1258', *EHR*, 104, (1989).

Riley-Smith, J., *The Crusades: A Short History* (New Haven and London, 1987).

Salt, M. C. L., 'List of English Embassies to France, 1272–1307', *EHR*, 44 (1929).

Salzman, L. F., *Edward I* (London, 1968).

Sayles, G. O., 'The Seizure of Wool at Easter 1297', *EHR*, 67 (1952).

Shenton, C., 'Royal Interest in Glastonbury and Cadbury: Two Arthurian Itineraries, 1278 and 1331', *EHR*, 114 (1999).

Smith, J. B., 'Adversaries of Edward I: Gaston de Béarn and Llywelyn ap Gruffudd', *Recognitions: essays presented to Edmund Fryde*, ed. C. Richmond and I. M. W. Harvey (Aberystwyth, 1996).

—— *Llywelyn ap Gruffudd, Prince of Wales* (Cardiff, 1998).

Stacey, R. C., '1240–60: A Watershed in Anglo-Jewish Relations?', *Historical Research*, 61 (1988).

—— 'Crusades, Crusaders and the Baronial *Gravamina* of 1263–1264', *TCE*, iii (1991).

—— 'Parliamentary Negotiation and the Expulsion of the Jews from England', *TCE*, vi (1997).

—— 'The English Jews under Henry III', *The Jews in Medieval Britain: Historical, Literary and Archaeological Perspectives*, ed. P. Skinner (Woodbridge, 2003).

Staniland, K., 'Welcome, Royal Babe! The Birth of Thomas of Brotherton in 1300', *Costume*, 19, (1985).

—— 'The Nuptials of Alexander III of Scotland and Margaret Plantagenet', *Nottingham Medieval Studies*, 30 (1986).

Stones, E. L. G., *Edward I* (Oxford, 1968).

—— 'The Mission of Thomas Wale and Thomas Delisle from Edward I to Pope Boniface VIII in 1301', *Nottingham Medieval Studies*, 26 (1982).

—— and Blount, M. N., 'The Surrender of King John of Scotland to Edward I in 1296: some new evidence', *BIHR*, 48 (1975).

Strayer, J. R., 'The Crusade against Aragon', *Speculum*, 28 (1953).

—— 'The Costs and Profits of War: The Anglo-French Conflict of 1294–1303', *The Medieval City*, ed. H. A. Miskimin, D. Herlihy and A. J. Udovich (New Haven and London, 1977).

—— *The Reign of Philip the Fair* (Princeton, 1980).

Strickland, M., 'A Law of Arms or a Law of Treason? Conduct in War in Edward I's Campaigns in Scotland, 1296–1307', *Violence in Medieval Society*, ed. R. W. Kaeuper (Woodbridge, 2000).

Stringer, K. J. 'Scottish Foundations: Thirteenth-Century Perspectives', *Uniting the Kingdom?*, ed. A. Grant and Stringer (London, 1995).

Strong, R., *Coronation: A History of Kingship and the British Monarchy* (London, 2005).

Stubbs, W., *The Constitutional History of England* (3rd edn, Oxford, 1887).

Studd, J. R., 'The Lord Edward and King Henry III', *BIHR*, 50 (1977).

—— 'The Lord Edward's Lordship of Chester, 1254–72', *Transactions of the Historic Society of Lancashire and Cheshire*, 128 (1979).

—— 'The Marriage of Henry of Almain and Constance of Béarn', *TCE*, iii (1991).

Summerson, H., 'The End of the Reign: Edward I at Carlisle' (forthcoming).

Sutherland, D. W., *Quo Warranto Proceedings in the Reign of Edward I, 1278–1294* (Oxford, 1963).

Taylor, A. J., *Studies in Castles and Castle-Building* (London, 1985), for all the following essays (original places of publication given, but pagination as in book):

—— 'Master James of St George', *EHR*, 65 (1950).

—— 'The Death of Llywelyn ap Gruffydd', *Bulletin of the Board of Celtic Studies*, 15 (1953).

—— 'Castle-Building in the Later Thirteenth Century: the Prelude to Construction', *Studies in Building History*, ed. E. M. Jope (London, 1961).

—— 'Royal Alms and Oblations', *Tribute to an Antiquary*, ed. F. G. Emmison and R. Stephens (London, 1976).

—— 'A Fragment of a *Dona* Account of 1284', *Bulletin of the Board of Celtic Studies*, 27 (1977).

—— 'Edward I and the Shrine of St Thomas of Canterbury', *Journal of the British Archaeological Association*, 132 (1979).

Tout, T. F., *Edward the First* (London, 1893).

—— 'The "Communitas Bacheleriae Angliae"', *EHR*, 17 (1902).

—— 'A Medieval Burglary', *Bulletin of the John Rylands Library*, 2 (1915).

Trabut-Cussac, J.-P., 'Itinéraire d'Édouard Ier en France, 1286–89', *BIHR*, 25 (1952).

—— *L'Administration Anglaise en Gascogne sous Henry III et Edouard I de 1254 à 1307* (Geneva, 1972).

Treharne, R. F., *The Baronial Plan of Reform, 1258–63* (Manchester, 1932).

Tyerman, C., *England and the Crusades, 1095–1588* (Chicago and London, 1988).

Tyson, D. B., 'A Royal Itinerary: the Journey of Edward I to Scotland in 1296', *Nottingham Medieval Studies*, 45 (2001).

Ullmann, W., 'The Curial Exequies for Edward I and Edward III', *Journal of Ecclesiastical History*, vi (1955).

Vale, M., *The Angevin Legacy and the Hundred Years War, 1250–1340* (Oxford, 1990).

Vaughn, M. K., '"Mount the War-Horses, Take your Lance in your Grip . . . ": Logistics Preparations for the Gascon Campaign of 1294', *TCE*, viii (2001).

Verbruggen, J. F., *The Battle of the Golden Spurs (Courtrai, 11 July 1302)*, trans. D. R. Fergusson, ed. K. DeVries (Woodbridge, 2002).

Wait, H. A., 'The Household and Resources of the Lord Edward' (D. Phil. thesis, Oxford, 1988).

Walker, R. F., 'The Hagnaby Chronicle and the Battle of Maes Moydog', *Welsh History Review*, 8 (1976).

Watson, F., *Under the Hammer: Edward I and Scotland, 1286–1306* (East Linton, 1998).

Wheatley, A., *The Idea of the Castle in Medieval England* (Woodbridge, 2004).

Whitwell, R. J., and Johnson, C., 'The "Newcastle" Galley, A.D. 1294', *Archaeologia Aeliana*, 4th series, 2 (1926).

Willard, F. J., *Parliamentary Taxes on Personal Property, 1290 to 1334* (Cambridge Mass., 1934).

Williams, G. A., *Medieval London: From Commune to Capital* (London, 1963).

Wood, M., *In Search of England: Journeys into the English Past* (London, 1999).

Family Trees

The English Royal Family

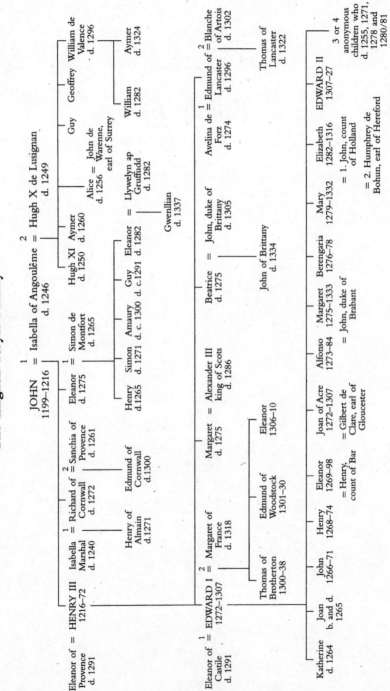

Scotland

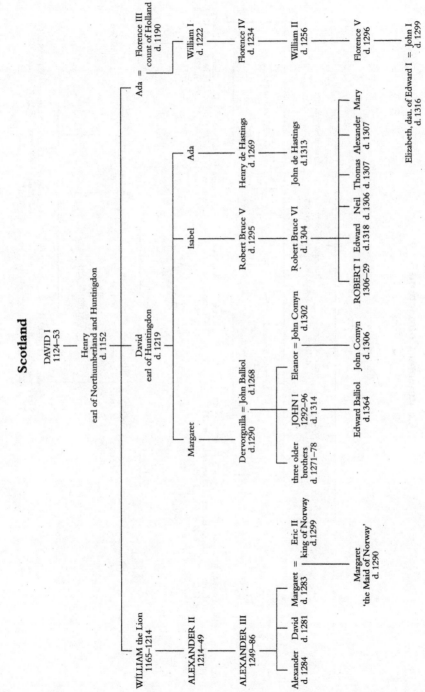

DAVID I
1124–53

Henry
earl of Northumberland and Huntingdon
d. 1152

Ada = Florence III
count of Holland
d. 1190

William I
d. 1222

Florence IV
d. 1234

William II
d. 1256

Florence V
d. 1296

Elizabeth, dau. of Edward I = John I
d. 1316   d. 1299

David
earl of Huntingdon
d. 1219

WILLIAM the Lion
1165–1214

Margaret

Isabel

Ada

ALEXANDER II
1214–49

Dervorguilla = John Balliol
d.1290   d.1268

Robert Bruce V
d. 1295

Henry de Hastings
d. 1269

ALEXANDER III
1249–86

three older
brothers
d. 1271–78

JOHN I
1292–96
d. 1314

Eleanor = John Comyn
d.1302

Robert Bruce VI
d. 1304

John de Hastings
d.1313

Alexander
d. 1284

David
d. 1281

Margaret =
d. 1283

Eric II
king of Norway
d.1299

Edward Balliol
d.1364

John Comyn
d. 1306

ROBERT I
1306–29

Edward
d.1318

Neil
d. 1306

Thomas
d. 1307

Alexander
d. 1307

Mary

Margaret
'the Maid of Norway'
d. 1290

Continental Connections

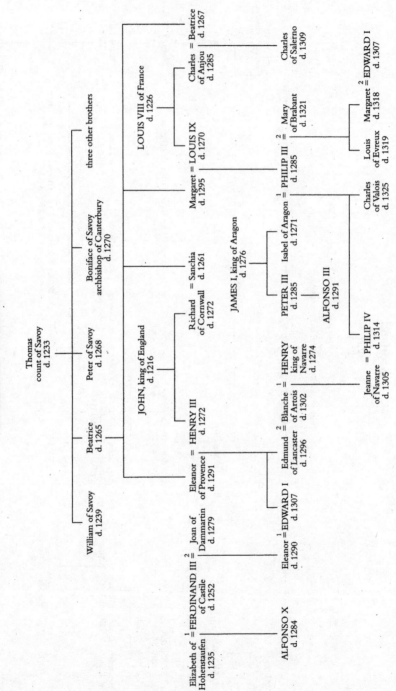

Index

Abbreviations: archbp (archbishop); bp (bishop); dau. (daughter); Ed (Edward I)

Abagha, il-khan of Persia (1265–82), 97–8, 211

Aberdeen, 340–1

Abergavenny (Gwent), 256, 278

Aberystwyth (Ceredigion), castle, 152, 157, 159–61, 177, 181, 187, 191, 195, 399; town, 161, 175, 177, 214, 279, 400

Abingdon, Edmund of, archbp of Canterbury (1233–40), 207

Achaea (Greece), prince of, 270

Acre (Akko), 95–101, 106, 124, 127, 262–3, 368–9, 373

Ada, countess of Holland, sister of William the Lion, 254

Africa, 93–4

Agen (Lot-et-Garonne), 172, 207

Agenais, 172, 207, 212, 265

Aigues Mortes (Gard), 93

Ain Julat, battle of (1260), 98

Albania, kingdom of, 197

Aleppo, 98–9

Alexander the Great, king of Ancient Greece, 364; romance of, 9

Alexander (d. 1284), son of Alexander III

Alexander II, king of Scotland (1214–49), 243

Alexander III, king of Scotland (1249–86), 235–7, 251, 253–4, 342, 374; his enthronement (1249), 245–6; his successful rule, 232; his marriages (1251 and 1285), 25–6, 232, 243–6; visits England (1256 and 1260), 28, 246; visited in Scotland by Ed (1256 and 1268), 25, 246; attends Ed's coronation, 128–30, 247; attends Llywelyn's wedding (1278), 247; does homage to Ed (1278), 247–9; death, 232–3

Alfonso (d. 1284), son of Ed, 110, 128, 153, 174, 192–5, 230

Alfonso III, king of Aragon (1285–91), 210, 215–17

Alfonso X, king of Castile (1252–84), 17–18, 110

Alice, nurse to Ed, 6–8

Almain, Henry of (d. 1271), Ed's cousin, 6, 34, 51, 76–7, 83, 88–9, 94, 116; imprisoned with Ed (1264–65), 63–4; his murder (1271), 105–7, 141

Alnwick Castle (Northumb), 78, 83

Alton Wood (Hants), 76

Amesbury Priory (Wiltshire), 202, 234, 255

Amiens (Somme), 60, 172, 204, 267, 269; Mise of, 59

Anagni (Italy), 326

Anglesey, 156–8, 181, 183–4, 186, 188, 278–9

439

Anglo-Saxons, 4, 162, 164, 166, 223, 241

Anjou, 43, 108, 198, 227–8; counts of, *see* Charles

Annandale (Dumf and Gall), 240, 313

Antioch, 95

Aquitaine *see* Gascony

Aragon, 198, 200, 203, 205, 208–11, 215, 228, 268; kings of, *see* James I; Peter III; Alfonso III

Arghun, il-khan of Persia (1284–91), 211, 263

Arran, isle of, 314

Arthur, legendary king of Britain, 9, 162–6, 168, 192–3, 222, 245, 247, 291, 335, 355, 364; tomb of, 162–6, 192, 378; crown of, 192, 194; *see also* Winchester

Articles upon the Charters (*Articuli super Cartas*), 322

Artois *see* Blanche

Arundel, earl of, *see* fitz Alan, Richard

Arwystli, 175–6

Ashridge (Herts), 231, 240

Asnières-sur-Oise (Val-d'Oise), 416; treaty of, 335–6

Atholl, earl of, *see* Strathbogie, John of

Auguselus, legendary king of Scotland, 245, 247

Aumale, earldom of, 88–9

Auxerre (Yonne)

Avon, river, 67

Axholme, Isle of, 74, 77

Ayr, town, 313; castle, 313, 332, 334

Ayrshire, 303, 314, 325, 360

Baa (Gironde), 215

bachelors of England, community of the, 41–2

Balliol, Dervorguilla (d. 1290), 239, 243, 326

Balliol, Edward (d. 1364), 376

Balliol, Eleanor, 239

Balliol, John (d. 1268), 239, 243

Balliol, John (d. 1314), king of Scotland (1292–96), 290–1, 311, 326, 342, 347, 354, 374, 376; birth, parentage and early years, 239, 243; brothers, 239, 246; connection with Comyns, 239, 319; claimant of Scottish throne, 239–40, 249, 251–4; basis of his claim, 257–8; made king, 258–9; his fealty and homage to Ed, 260; acquits Ed of earlier promises, 261; summoned to Westminster (1293), 266; deprived of executive initiative by Scots (1295), 285; defies Ed (1296); stripped of kingship and imprisoned, 289; transferred to papal custody (1299), 320; released and rumoured to be returning (1301), 334–6

Balliol College, Oxford, 239

Bangor (Gwynedd), 183

Bannockburn, battle of (1314), 376

Barbour, John (d. 1395), 354

Bardolf, Thomas, 367

Barnard Castle (Durham), 239

Bar Sauma, Rabban, 211

Basset, Philip (d. 1271), 393

Bastide, La, *see* Burgus Reginae

bastides, 212–16, 290, 294, 369; and *paréage*, 213; *see also* towns

Baybars, al-Zahir, sultan of Egypt (1260–77), 95–101, 262

Bayonne (Pyrénées-Atlantiques), 110, 265, 280, 291, 294

Béarn, Gaston de (d. 1290), 109–10, 171, 216

Beatrice (d. 1275), sister of Ed, 6, 84, 128

Beatrice of Provence (d. 1267), wife of Charles of Anjou, 266

Beauchamp, Guy de, earl of Warwick (d. 1315), 319, 420

Beauchamp, William de, earl of

Warwick (d. 1298), 145–6, 148–9,
153–4, 157, 278–9, 295–8
Beaulieu Abbey (Hants), 10
Beaumaris Castle (Anglesey), 279,
292, 338, 376
Bek, Anthony, bp of Durham (1283–
1311), 237, 270, 289, 312, 323
Belinus and Brennius, legendary
Britons, 245
Bere (Gwynedd), castle, 188; town,
214
Berkhamsted (Herts), 71
Berkshire, 5
Berwick (Northumb), 248, 251–3,
255–6, 258, 260, 269, 287–90,
302–4, 308–9, 321–2, 332–3, 344,
354, 358; castle, 288
Bigod, Hugh (d. 1266), 41, 43, 45,
47, 50
Bigod, Roger, earl of Norfolk
(d. 1270), 36–8, 41, 43, 45, 47, 50,
243
Bigod, Roger, earl of Norfolk (d.
1306), 157, 195, 286, 321, 355,
374–5; marshal of England, 295,
298; prepared to go to Gascony
(1294), 271; refuses to go (1297),
295–6; leader of opposition,
297–8, 305, 309–10, 314, 317–19,
322, 329; fights at Falkirk, 312,
314; strikes a deal with Ed (1302),
351–2
Birgham (Borders), 236–7
Biron (Dordogne), 213
Bisset, Hugh, 314
Blackfriars (London), 230
Blanche of Artois (d. 1302), countess
of Champagne, wife of Edmund
of Lancaster, 267–8
Blanquefort (Gironde), 209, 403
Blaye (Gironde), 280
Blyth (Notts), 25
Bohun, Humphrey de, earl of
Hereford (d. 1275), 129
Bohun, Humphrey de, earl of

Hereford (d. 1298), 129, 195, 278;
constable of England, 179, 295–6,
298; reoccupies Brecon (1273),
134–5, 137; clash with Gloucester
(1291), 255–6; leader of opposition
(1297–98), 296–9, 305, 309–10;
fights at Falkirk, 312, 314; death,
317, 375
Bohun, Humphrey de, earl of
Hereford (d. 1322), 317, 319, 375,
413
Bologna (Italy), 107
Boniface VIII, pope (1294–1303),
293, 299, 309, 316, 320, 326,
330–1, 334–5, 337, 346, 352, 375
Bonnegarde (Landes), 216, 294–5,
369
Bordeaux (Gironde), 6, 17, 19, 28,
51, 89, 109–10, 124, 171, 208–9,
211–13, 265, 267, 280, 291, 403;
archbp of, *see* Clement V
Boston (Lincs), 221
Botetourt, John de (d. 1324), 280
Bothwell Castle (Lanark), 333
Boulogne (Pas-de-Calais), 57
Bourg (Gironde), 280
Brabant, duke of, *see* John II; *see also*
Mary
Brabazon, Roger (d. 1317), 249, 408
Brechin (Angus), 340
Brecon, 134–5, 255
Bristol, 57, 88, 152, 196, 199, 265,
278; castle, 18, 43–4
British Empire, 97
British Isles, Britain, 11, 14, 101,
134, 153, 214, 228, 246, 332, 343,
345, 372, 374–5, 377; ancient
history and legends of, 9, 162–8,
184, 223, 241, 245; *see also* Arthur;
Geoffrey of Monmouth
Brittany, 264; duke of, 226; *see also*
John
Brittany, John of, earl of Richmond
(d. 1334), 272, 280, 350
Brix (Manche), 242

Bromholm (Norfolk), 146

Brotherton (Yorks), 327; *see also* Thomas

Bruce, Alexander (d. 1307), 360

Bruce, Edward (d. 1318), 376

Bruce, Mary, 357–8

Bruce, Neil (d. 1306), 358

Bruce, Robert (d. 1295), 239–40, 242–3, 246, 249–54, 257–9, 289, 302

Bruce, Robert (d. 1304), 290, 302, 354

Bruce, Robert, earl of Carrick, king of Scotland (1306–29), 325, 332, 339–41, 347–8, 363, 374–6, 378; joins rebels (1296), 302–3; pursued after Falkirk, 313; appointed Guardian, 319–20; surrenders (1301/2), 336; seizes Scottish throne but driven into exile (1306), 353–8; returns and scores victories (1307), 360–1

Bruce, Thomas (d. 1307), 360

Bruges (Belgium), 307, 337

Brus, Robert de (d. 1142), 242

Brutus, legendary British leader, 168, 184, 245, 364

Buchan, countess of, *see* Isabel of Fife

Builth (Powys), castle and lordship, 46, 132, 159, 185, 399

Bunratty Castle (Co. Clare), 220

Burgh, Richard de, earl of Ulster (d. 1326), 286, 339

Burgh by Sands (Cumbria), 362–3

Burgos (Castile), 19, 112

Burgundy, 53

Burgus Reginae (Gironde), 212, 215, 369

Burnell, Robert, bp of Bath and Wells (1275–92), chancellor, 120, 129, 153, 158, 161, 195, 204, 215, 365; origins, offices and character, 117–18; regent (1270–74), 117, 135; sent to France (1278), 171–2;

children, 117, 183, 188; speech in Paris (1286), 205, 269; death, 269

Burstwick (Yorks), 345, 347

Bury St Edmunds (Suffolk), 78–9, 272, 291–2

Cadair Idris, 188

Cadbury (Somerset), hill fort, 166

Caerlaverock (Dumf and Gall), castle, 325; song of, 324, 372

Caerleon (Gwent), 355

Caernarfon (Gwynedd), castle, 191–3, 195, 275, 277, 279, 292, 331, 338, 349, 376, 378; town, 214, 275, 376; Edward of, *see* Edward II

Caerphilly Castle, 134

Caeserea, 95

Caldicot Castle (Gwent), 195

Camber, son of Brutus, 168, 184

Cambrai (Nord), 293

Cambridge, 79, 335

Cambridgeshire, 273

Camelot, 163, 166

Canfranc (Aragon), 216

Canterbury (Kent), 73, 88, 202, 217, 297, 319, 330; cathedral, 299, 319

Cardiff Castle (Glamorgan), 195

Cardigan Castle, 33, 181, 195

Carham (Northumb), 287

Carlisle (Cumbria), town, 168, 173, 287, 308, 314, 321, 324–5, 332, 334, 340, 355, 357, 359–63, 418; castle, 244, 363; cathedral, 361

Carmarthen, castle and lordship, 33, 35, 146, 148, 152, 160, 180–1, 186–7

Carreg Cennen (Carmarthen), 160, 177, 180

Castile, 17, 19–20, 174; kings of, *see* Alfonso X; Ferdinand

castles and castle-building: England, 38–40, 42–3, 45, 57, 88, 105, 174; Wales, 28, 33, 133–5, 151–3, 155, 157, 159–61, 169, 191, 275–9, 349, 369–70, 376; Scotland, 236–7,

251–2, 259, 338; Gascony, 15, 17, 20, 109, 209; Ireland, 219–20; Holy Land; 95; *see also individual castle names*

Chalon-sur-Saône (Saône-et-Loire), 364

Champagne, 53; countess of, *see* Blanche

chancellor, 47, 367; *see also* Burnell, Robert; Langton, John

chancery, 117–18, 178, 199, 269

Charing (London), 173, 231

Charlemagne, romance of, 9

Charles of Anjou, king of Sicily (1266–85), 93–4, 101–2, 105–6, 197–8, 203, 205, 266; king of Jerusalem, 197

Charles of Salerno (Charles II of Anjou, 1284–1309), 205, 210–11, 216–17, 223, 227, 267

Charles of Valois (d. 1325), 268–9, 280

Charters *see* Magna Carta; Forest Charter; Confirmation; Articles

Chaworth, Payn de (d. 1278), 145–8

Cheapside (London), 112, 128, 231

Chepstow Castle (Gwent), 195, 318

Chester, or Cheshire, lordship of, 18, 26, 40, 46, 71, 76, 91, 160, 331; city of, 28, 33, 46, 140, 142, 146, 148–53, 175–7, 179–81, 278

Chesterfield (Derby), 76

Cheviot Hills, 244

Chichester (Sussex), 349

China, 97

Church (as international body), 2, 19, 84–5, 126–7, 187, 239, 262, 293, 337; *see also* papacy

Church (English), clergy, 74, 79, 82, 88, 90, 113–14, 124, 184, 221, 281, 283; grievances of (1280s), 221; and taxation (–1290), 124, 173, 197, 228; scrutiny of funds of (1294), 271–3; arguments with Ed about taxation (1294–), 274–6,

284, 293–9, 322, 331, 374; outlawed (1297), 294–7, 346

Cilmeri (Powys), 186

Cinque Ports, 75–6, 149–50, 153, 156–7, 178, 181, 264, 412

Cirencester (Glos), 174

Clare, Gilbert de, earl of Gloucester (d. 1230), 243

Clare, Gilbert de, earl of Gloucester (d. 1295), 129, 153, 195, 204, 219, 223, 286, 366, 400; during civil war (1264–65), 64–8; occupies London (1267), 79–80; takes cross, 83, 227; disaffected (1269–70), 90–2; struggle with Llywelyn (1267–73), 133–4, 137; defeated by Welsh (1282), 179–81; marries Joan of Acre (1290), 224, 234; clash with Hereford (1291), 255–6; during Welsh revolt (1294), 275–7, 279; death, 284

Clare, Richard de, earl of Gloucester (d. 1262), 37–8, 40–1, 43–51, 64

Clare, Thomas de (d. 1288), 66, 219–21, 365

Clarendon (Wilts), palace of, 9

Clement V, pope (1305–14), 352–3, 363–4, 369

clergy *see* Church

Clericis Laicos, 293, 299

Clerkenwell, 45

Clifford Castle (Hereford), 35

Clifford, Roger (d. c. 1286), 35, 43, 51–2, 54–5, 58, 63, 66, 83, 145, 147, 177, 183, 186

Clifford, Roger (d. 1282), 183, 188

Clipstone (Notts), 228–9

Clun (Salop), lordship of, 297

Cluny, abbot of, 231

Clwyd, river, 155, 159, 181

coinage, 14, 122, 136, 167, 169–71, 226, 243, 321, 399

Colchester (Essex), 168

Columbus, Christopher, 11

Comyn, Alexander (d. 1289), 239

Comyn, John (d. 1302), 239, 251
Comyn, John (d. 1306), 319–20, 336,
    339, 341–2, 348, 353–4, 358
Confirmation of the Charters
    (*Confirmatio Cartarum*), 306, 308,
    310, 316
Constantine, Roman emperor, 191,
    200
Constantinople, 191, 197; emperor
    of, 98, 198
Conwy, river, 27, 31–2, 155–6, 176,
    181, 187–8, 277; castle, 191–2,
    195, 275, 277–9, 281, 338; town,
    188, 214; abbey, 158, 189
Corfe Castle (Dorset), 141, 214, 265
Cornwall, 168, 291; earls of *see*
    Richard; Edmund; Gaveston, Piers
coronation, English, 104, 111–17,
    121, 128–32, 135, 138, 140, 194,
    201, 219, 221, 224, 245, 247, 263,
    351, 368, 371, 377, 395; Scottish,
    246, 354, 358; French, 204
Coronation Chair, 290
coronation oath, 113–14, 116, 329–30
council, royal, 170, 178–9, 247, 256,
    258–9, 321, 350, 366, 373; as
    reconstituted by reformers (1258–
    60), 38–48, 50, 54, 63, 119, 237;
    during regencies, 103, 217
Courtrai *see* Kortrijk
Crac des Chevaliers (Syria), 95
Cree, river, 325
Cressingham, Hugh (d. 1297),
    treasurer of Scotland, 302–4
Criccieth (Gwynedd), 214, 275, 279
Croes Naid, 200
Crown, English, 14, 34, 58, 70, 74,
    82–3, 85–6, 128, 133, 139–40, 145,
    161, 201–2, 217, 220–1, 255, 267,
    274, 281, 297, 301, 305–6, 316,
    322, 328, 352, 366, 371, 376; lands
    acquired for, 28, 115, 157, 159,
    177, 367; rights of, 114, 116, 176,
    224, 256, 317, 323, 329, 351; debts
    to, 138, 282, 286, 293, 296, 332,

339, 351; finances of, 122–4,
    127, 170, 172, 223–4, 331, 375;
    relationship with Scottish Crown,
    26, 246, 250, 285, 374; jewels, 346
crusades and crusaders, 3, 56, 110–11,
    250, 262, 274, 367; First Crusade;
    12–13, 82–4, 95; Third Crusade,
    12, 244; of the 1240s, 12–13, 95,
    226, 263; Henry III's plans, 13–17,
    26, 29; political, 81–2, 187, 198,
    203, 270; Ed's first, 81–3, 90–102,
    104–6, 109, 116–7, 123, 131, 134,
    145, 153, 160, 195, 197, 219, 223,
    231, 246, 292; Ed's intended
    second, 196–7, 203, 205, 211, 226,
    228, 231, 263–4, 270, 292, 353,
    373; funding, 20, 84–5, 88–90, 92,
    124–5, 209, 264, 271–2, 274–5
Cumbria, 244, 302, 308, 327, 362
Cupar Castle (Fife), 356
customs, 23, 89, 123–4, 136, 169,
    171, 271, 273, 292, 339
Cyprus, 97–8; king of, *see* Lusignan,
    Hugh de

Dafydd ap Gruffudd (d. 1283), 185,
    195, 200, 372; reputation for
    treachery, 138; covets share of
    Snowdonia, 139, 154–5; flees to
    England (1274), 139, 141; fights
    against Llywelyn (1277), 146;
    signs of disaffection, 154; receives
    two of Four Cantrefs, 157;
    complains of English oppression,
    176; instigator of Welsh rebellion
    (1282), 177–8; resists from
    Denbigh, 179–81; succeeds
    Llywelyn, 186; captured and
    killed, 188–90, 377
Dalrigh (Stirling), 357
Dante, 107
Darnhall (Cheshire), 91–2, 153
David, biblical king, 114
David (d. 1281), son of Alexander
    III, 232

David, earl of Huntingdon, younger
  brother of William the Lion (d.
  1219), 254
David I, king of Scotland (1124–53),
  242–4
Dax (Landes), 211
Dean, forest of (Glos), 146
Dee, river, 27, 152, 195
Deganwy Castle (Conwy), 28, 32–4,
  54, 58, 81, 131, 151, 155–7
Deheubarth, 33
Denbigh Castle, 180–1, 184
De re militari, 100, 150
Devon, countess of, *see* Forz, Isabella
  de; earldom of, 88–9
Deyville, John, 77–9
Dinas Brân, castle, 146
Dinefwr (Carmarthen), 160, 180
Disinherited, The, 71–2, 74, 76–80
distraint, 273, 282–3, 305; of
  knighthood, 169
Divine Comedy, 107
Dolforwyn Castle, 135, 137, 146–7,
  150
Dolwyddelan Castle (Conwy), 187–8
Domesday Book, 119, 328
Dordogne, river, 207, 212
Dorset, 214, 278, 352
Dover (Kent), 22, 39, 51, 54, 59–60,
  73–4, 79, 92, 110, 172, 199, 204,
  221, 233, 265, 280, 318–19, 361;
  castle at, 56–7, 60, 64, 172
Down Ampney (Glos), 174
Dryslwyn (Carmarthen), town and
  castle, 217
Dublin, 218, 221, 339, 347, 375
Dumfries, castle, 325, 334; town,
  325, 353–4; Franciscan church,
  353
Dumfries and Galloway, 325, 340–1
Dunaverty Castle (Argyll and Bute),
  358
Dunbar (East Lothian), castle, 288;
  battle of, 288, 290, 301, 303, 310,
  313

Dunfermline (Fife), town, 253;
  abbey, 341–2
Dunipace (Falkirk), 333, 335
Dunstable (Beds), 356; annalist, 229–
  30
Durham, 173, 239, 323; bps of, 248;
  see also Bek, Anthony
Dyserth Castle (Denbigh), 28, 32–4,
  54, 58, 81, 131, 151, 155

East Anglia, 40, 55, 76–7, 146, 173,
  199, 269, 323, 348; *see also*
  Norfolk; Suffolk; Essex
Edessa, 95
Edinburgh, 232, 253, 288–9, 311,
  333, 338
Edmund, earl of Cornwall (d. 1300),
  153, 203, 217, 330, 411
Edmund, earl of Lancaster (d. 1296),
  Ed's younger brother, 90, 129,
  162, 204, 234, 255; birth (1245), 6;
  and Sicily, 29, 32; his lands and
  titles, 73, 76, 81, 89, 352; his
  marriages, 88, 267; and the
  crusade, 83, 97, 101, 196; and the
  first Welsh war, 148, 152, 157;
  diplomacy with France (1293–94),
  267–9; captain of forces for
  Gascony (1294–96), 272, 276;
  illness and death, 291; his tomb,
  378
Edmund of Woodstock (d. 1330),
  son of Ed, 336, 351, 357
Edward the Confessor, saint, king of
  England (1043–66), 4, 5, 8–9, 19,
  72, 89–90, 103, 112–15, 162, 192,
  202, 263, 291, 298, 348, 351, 354,
  368
Edward I, king of England (1272–
  1307):
  character, qualities and interests:
    physical appearance, 22, 312;
    dress, 22; literacy and languages,
    7–8, 165; understanding of
    history, 9, 12, 191–2, 200, 245,

334–5; juvenile delinquency,
28–9, 370; courage and
prowess, 10, 25, 61–2, 80–1,
361–2, 364–5; military
expertise, strategic sense, 25,
66–8, 150, 156–7, 371; bullying
tactics, 175, 249–50, 260–2,
266, 274–5, 282, 294, 296, 374;
use of extreme violence, 68,
189, 256, 283, 343–4, 356–9, 377;
piety, 190, 367–8; pilgrimages,
25, 146, 199, 207, 272–3, 337;
wisdom, 270, 365; political
ability, 365–6; eloquence, 366;
clemency, 71, 75–6, 78, 158,
189, 288, 342; belief in justice,
40, 117, 366–7; injustices, 89,
351–2, 367; deceitfulness, 58,
60, 75, 80, 254, 260–1, 315–18,
322, 329, 367; temper, 140,
274–5, 282–3, 294, 296, 333,
350, 354, 359–60, 368–9, 374;
restlessness, 216, 369;
indomitability, 116, 224, 329;
Arthurian enthusiasm, 165,
192–3, 202–3, 222, 334, 355,
378; hunting and hawking, 10,
173, 202, 208, 231, 331, 337,
352–3, 368 (*see also* tournaments); building, 100, 127, 174,
211–12, 214, 369–70; luck, 105,
208, 233, 353, 368; attitude
towards Welsh, Irish and Scots,
175, 220, 240, 245–7, 290,
342–3; anti–Semitism, 171–1,
228, 371; friendships, 34–5, 52,
58, 78, 81, 101, 116, 145–6,
171, 185, 195, 374
household: before accession, 7, 28,
34, 47–8, 51–3, 64, 83, 97, 117,
124; as king, 111–12, 124, 144–7,
154, 178, 180, 183, 199, 204,
208–9, 215–16, 223, 229, 252,
269, 272, 280, 283, 292, 345,
365, 376

family relationships: with father,
21–3, 32, 45, 90, 103–4; with
mother, 6–9, 45, 58, 234, 255;
with brother, 291; with sisters,
6, 25, 128; with wife, Eleanor,
20, 22, 73, 230–1; with children,
174, 194–5, 349–51, 359–60;
with Lusignan half-uncles, 24,
35, 38, 48–9; with Simon de
Montfort, 42, 49–50, 58; with
Richard of Cornwall, 13, 92
selective chronological survey: birth
and baptism, 2–5; upbringing,
5–13; granted Gascony (1249
and 1252), 15, 17; given a great
appanage (1254), 18–19, 21;
knighted and married to
Eleanor (1254), 18–20; first stay
in Gascony (1254–55), 20–2;
returns to England (1255), 23;
first tournament (1256), 24–5;
first visits to Scotland and
Wales (1256), 25–8, 246; bad
behaviour (1255–56), 28–9;
unable to counter Welsh
rebellion (1256–57), 32–3; allies
with Marchers and Lusignans
(1258), 34–5; opposes revolution
but embraces reform (1258),
37–42; allied with Montfort
(1259), 42–6, and Clare (1260),
46–9; returns to parents' side
(1261), 50; in Gascony and
France (1261–63), 50–3; at
war with Montfort (1263–64),
54–61; defeated at Lewes
(1264), 61–3; imprisoned
(1264–65), 63–5; escapes and
triumphs at Evesham (1265),
66–8; settles with Montfortians
(1265–67), 71–80; settles with
Llywelyn (1267), 81, 131–2;
prepares for crusade (1268–70),
81–92; his first crusade (1270–
72), 93–102; accession (1272),

102–5; on Continent (1273–74), 105–10; return and coronation (1274), 110–15, 128–30; institutes wide–ranging reforms (1274–75), 115–27; rebuilds Tower of London (1275–85), 127–8; dealings with Llywelyn (1274–76), 137–43; first war against Llywelyn (1277), 143–58; settlement of Wales (1278), 159–166; demands Alexander III's homage (1278), 246–8; visits France (1279), 171–2; tours northern England (1280); 173; conquers Wales (1282–83), 178–90; settlement of Wales (1284), 190–5; prepares for second crusade (1284–91), 196–9, 209, 211, 228, 231–2, 263; subjugates London (1285), 200–2; on Continent (1286–89), 204–17; returns to England, conciliates (1289–90), 221–5; plans Scottish marriage for son (1289–90), 235–7; fixes English succession (1290), 234–5; expels the Jews (1290), 225–8; dealings at Norham (1291), 248–52; hears Great Cause (1291–92), 252–9; intervenes in March (1291–92), 255–6; receives Balliol's homage, annuls earlier concessions (1292–93), 259–61; appeases France (1293–94), 264–9; engulfed by crises (1294), 269–75; reconquers Wales (1294–95), 275–9; troubles in England (1295), 280–4; conquers Scotland (1296), 284–91; provokes opposition in England (1296–97), 292–300, 305–6; expedition to Flanders (1297–98), 307–9; invasion of Scotland (1298), 309–15;

appeases opposition in England, marries Margaret (1299), 315–19; intransigence on Forest scuppers Scottish campaigns (1299–1300), 320–7; forced to compromise at Lincoln (1301), 327–30; reconquers Scotland in two campaigns (1301–4), 331–44; attempts to restore order to his domains (1304–5), 345–51; deals with former critics (1302–6), 351–2; last campaign against Scotland (1306–7), 354–61; death and burial, 362–4, 377–8

Edward II (Edward of Caernarfon), prince of Wales (1301–), king of England (1307–27), 202, 221, 319, 378, 420; appearance and character, 331, 349, 377; household, 359; birth (1284), 192; and the succession, 234–5; and the Maid of Norway, 235–6, 373; as nominal regent (1297–98), 298, 305, 307; betrothal to Isabella of France (1299), 318; invested as prince of Wales (1301), 331; attitude towards Welsh, 349; campaigns in Scotland, 331–4, 336, 341, 355–7, 363, 376; arguments with Ed, 349–50, 359; invested with Gascony and knighted (1306), 355; and Piers Gaveston, 359, 361, 377; accession (1307), 363; death, 377

Eleanor (d. c. 1298), dau. of Ed, 92, 174, 202, 210, 221, 265, 269

Eleanor (d. 1310), dau. of Ed, 357

Eleanor Crosses, 231

Eleanor of Castile (d. 1290), queen of England, Ed's wife, 25, 58, 112, 113, 129, 153, 165, 171, 187, 204, 212, 216; appearance, character and interests, 19–20, 23, 173–4, 225–6, 229–31; marriage (1254),

18–20, 246; attachment to Ed, 22, 101, 231; marginal political role, 225, 234; children, 22, 73, 76–7, 84, 101, 107, 110, 192, 194–6, 202; and the crusade, 84, 92; gives *De re militari* to Ed, 100; inherits Ponthieu (1279), 172; illness and death, 228–30, 373; tombs, 230, 232, 255, 378

Eleanor of Provence (d. 1291), queen of England, Ed's mother, 5, 10, 13, 50–1, 55, 57, 79, 103, 129, 145, 164–5, 202, 226; marriage and coronation (1236), 1, 14, 111; birth of Ed (1239), 2, 4; births of other children, 6, 194–5; her uncles, 6–7; her household, 145; role in Ed's upbringing, 7–9; wants Gascony for Ed, 15; regent (1253–54), 18; accompanies Ed to Gascony (1254), 19; meets her sisters in Paris (1254), 266; head of Savoyard faction, 23–4, 29, 34–6; in contention with Ed (1258–61), 42–5, 48–9; harasses Ed's former associates (1261–2), 52, 54; attacked at London Bridge (1263), 56, 58, 62, 201; in France (1263–65), 59, 64; returns to England (1265), 73–4; attitude towards Jews, 126, 226; retires to Amesbury (1286), 234; death and burial, 255

Elgin (Moray), 289, 411

Elizabeth (d. 1316), dau. of Ed, 202, 221, 254, 294, 369, 375, 401

Ely (Cambs), 77–80, 82

England: landscape and economy, 10, 16, 122–3, 136, 151, 167, 214; population, 10, 26, 85–6, 161; aristocracy, 37, 129; military service, 147–50, 178–9, 273–4, 281–2, 295–8, 305, 321, 323–4, 339, 374

English language, 8, 26, 184, 243, 284, 318

Essex, 173, 178, 282, 290, 315, 344

Evesham, town and abbey, 67–9, 129; battle of, 68–70, 71, 73–5, 78, 80, 82, 89, 106, 131, 133, 246, 312, 377, 396

Ewloe Castle (Flint), 180

exchequer: of England, 92, 282, 285, 299, 333–4, 338, 341; of Ireland, 219, 221, 339; of the Jews, 88

Exeter (Devon), 203, 403

Falkirk, battle of, 311–14, 319, 324–5, 336–7, 340

Feast of the Swans, 355, 378

Ferdinand III, king of Castile (1217–52), 84

Ferdinand IV, king of Castile (1295–1312), 357

Ferrers, John de (d. 1312), 351–2

Ferrers, Robert de, earl of Derby (d. 1279), 89–90, 352, 367

Fieschi, Ottobuono de, *see* Ottobuono

fitz Alan, Richard, earl of Arundel (d. 1302), 282–3, 295–8, 410

fitz Heyr, Hugh, 324

fitz Thomas, John (d. 1316), 286

Flanders, 53, 122–3, 242, 294, 299, 301, 307–310, 315–17, 323, 337, 368–9; count of, 294, 307

Flint, castle, 152–5, 157, 159–61, 177, 191, 399; town, 161, 177, 214

Florence V, count of Holland (d. 1296), 253–9, 293

Flote, Pierre (d. 1302), 337

Fontevrault Abbey (Maine-et-Loire), 207

Forest, as a royal jurisdiction, 306, 315–17, 323, 328–9, 351, 356; perambulations of, 315–17, 319, 321, 323, 328–9

Forest Charter, 306, 315–18, 321–2, 328–9, 375

Forth, river and firth of, 232, 253, 302–4, 333, 339–41, 350, 356

Forz, Avelina de (d. 1274), wife of Edmund of Lancaster, 89, 267

Forz, Isabella de, countess of Devon (d. 1293), 367

Fountains Abbey (Yorkshire), 153

Four Cantrefs (or Perfeddwlad), 27–8, 31–4, 58, 131–2, 138, 154, 157, 175–6, 179, 181, 184

France, 1, 3, 9, 14, 51, 73, 94, 141, 146, 164, 178 ,198–200, 211, 217, 226, 228, 231, 239, 242, 247; Henry III's visits to, 6, 15, 21, 43–4, 53, 57, 59, 108, 266; Ed's visits to, 23, 47–8, 52–3, 57, 59, 89–90, 92–3, 107–10, 171–2, 203–7, 233–4, 267, 364; war with, 264–5, 267–70, 272, 275, 281, 291, 293–5, 298–9, 302, 305, 346, 369, 372–4; truces with, 307–9, 318; peace with, 342, 345, 347, 361; allied with Scotland, 285, 320, 330, 334–8; kings of, *see* Louis IX; Philip III; Philip IV

Francheville *see* Newtown

Fraser, William, bp of St Andrews (1279–97), 240

French language, 3, 8, 9, 26

friars, 226, 263, 322

galleys, 270, 280, 282

Galloway, 239, 313, 332, 360; *see also* Dumfries and Galloway

Garonne, river, 208, 212, 280, 291

Garth Celyn (Gwynedd), 183

Gascony, 14, 16, 24, 29, 41, 43, 52–3, 93–4, 105, 118, 164, 196, 219, 221, 229, 277, 292, 307, 355; landscape and economy of, 213, 218; granted to Ed, 15, 17–18; Ed's visits to, 19–23, 48, 51, 109–10, 208–17, 223, 225–6, 233–4, 246, 368–9; resources from, 149, 151, 178, 186, 189, 278; seneschals of,

38, 181, 269, 272; legal relationship with France, 107–9, 171–2, 198, 200, 203–5, 207, 247, 265–7; French seizure of, 268–9, 284, 309, 330, 335–6, 346, 373; forces for recovery of, 271–3, 275–6, 280–3, 291, 294–7, 310; restoration of, 316, 318, 345, 347

Gaveston, Piers, earl of Cornwall (d. 1312), 359, 361, 377

Geddington (Northants), 231

Geoffrey of Monmouth, 163–4, 166–8, 192, 245, 375; his *History of the Kings of Britain*, 163–4, 166–8, 245

Gerald of Wales (d. 1223), 136, 156, 163, 165

Germans, Germany, 93, 164, 307; king of, 308

Ghengis Khan (d. 1227), 97–8

Ghent (Belgium), 307

Giffard, Hugh, teacher of Ed, 6–8, 10

Giffard, Sybil, nurse of Ed, 6–8

Gironde, 212

Glamorgan, 133–4, 255, 279

Glasgow, 332–4, 354; cathedral, 333, 354, 357; bp of, *see* Wishart, Robert

Glastonbury Abbey (Somerset), 162–6, 378

Gloucester, 60, 75; earls of, *see* Clare, Gilbert de; Clare, Richard de

Gloucestershire, 129, 174, 190, 330

Golden Spurs, battle of the, *see* Kortrijk

Gower, 33

Grandson, Otto de (d. 1328), friend and advisor of Ed, 171, 195, 204, 365; crusader, 101, 228, 232, 262; warrior, 145, 156, 183, 188, 365; diplomat, 171–2, 365; hostage (1288–89), 216

Great Cause proceedings, 253–9, 269, 319

Gregory X, pope (1271–76), 106–7, 124, 142, 352

Grey, Henry de, 410

Grey, Reginald de (d. 1308), justiciar of Chester, 176, 180–1, 279, 365

Grilly, John de (d. c. 1301), 171, 208

Grosseteste, Robert, bp of Lincoln, 126

Gruffudd ap Gwenwynwyn (d. 1286), 138–9, 146, 175

Guardians of Scotland, 233, 236, 239–40, 248, 250–2, 260, 311, 319, 336, 341, 353; *see also* Bruce; Comyn; Fraser; Wishart; Wallace

Guinevere, legendary queen, 163, 165–6

Guisborough, Walter of, 275, 278, 295–6, 301, 303–5, 307–8, 311, 313–14, 316–17, 320, 340, 359, 361, 363–5

Gurdon, Adam, 76

Gwenllian (d. 1337), dau. of Llywelyn ap Gruffudd, 178

Gwynedd (or Snowdonia), 27, 31, 138–9, 147–8, 152, 154, 156–8, 175–6, 178, 180–2, 184–5, 187–9, 190–1, 331

Haddington (East Lothian), 253

Hailes Abbey (Glos), 129

Hampshire, 10, 76, 178, 202, 273

Harby (Notts), 229–30

Hardingstone (Northants), 231

Harlech (Gwynedd), castle, 191, 195, 275, 277, 279; town, 214

Harrow (Middx), 317

Harwich (Essex), 282

Hastings, John de (d. 1313), 259, 298

Hawarden Castle (Flint), 177, 180

Henry (d. 1274), son of Ed, 84, 92, 128, 195

Henry, count of Bar (d. 1302), 265, 269, 307

Henry, king of Navarre (1271–74), 110

Henry I, king of England (1100–35), 3, 104, 235, 242, 244, 352

Henry II, king of England, (1154–89), 3, 14, 23, 165, 207, 218, 244

Henry III, king of England (1216–72), Ed's father, 1–29, 31–66, 70–6, 78–90, 92–3, 111–17, 119, 123, 126, 128–9, 131, 134, 136, 144–7, 153, 155–6, 164, 169, 172–3, 175, 197, 202, 239, 243, 285, 305, 316, 349; character, abilities and interests, 1–4, 36; attachment to Edward the Confessor, 3–4, 8–9, 112–14; luxurious tastes, 5–6; love of ceremony, 26, 112; love for his children, 5–6, 45, 104, 194–5; lack of martial skill, 4, 10, 13, 15, 25, 39; problems with parliament, 16–17, 29, 121–2; his household, 63, 78, 144–5

selective chronological survey: marries Eleanor (1236), 1; favours her relatives, 1, 6–7, 23; tallages Jews without mercy (1240–), 86–7; invades and confiscates north–east Wales (1241, 1245), 27–8, 31; welcomes and indulges Lusignans (1247–), 24, 29; takes the cross (1250), 13, 15; demands homage of Alexander III (1251), 244–6; policy towards Gascony, 14–15, 17; goes to Gascony (1253–54), 18–19; grants lands to Ed (1254), 18–19; befriends Louis IX (1254), 266–7; overrules Ed in Gascony, orders him to Ireland (1255), 20–2, 218; quarrels with Ed over authority, 23, 28; response to Welsh revolt (1256–57), 32–3; oppressive government of, 16, 29, 36; deprived of power (1258), 36–9, 329; seals Treaty of Paris (1259), 43, 108; returns

from France (1260), 45;
occupies Tower of London
(1261), 48; overthrows
Provisions of Oxford, 50–1, 54;
argues with Montfort in
France (1262), 53; flees to
Tower but forced to surrender
(1263), 55–7; sets Mortimer
against Montfort, 59–60;
defeated at Lewes (1264), 60–3;
in Montfort's power (1264–65),
63, 65–6; wounded at Evesham
(1265), 68; restored to power,
70; disinherits Montfortians,
71–2; punishes London, 72, 75,
201; reunited with Eleanor, 73;
fails to take Ely (1267), 79;
proclaims peace in London, 80;
grants peace to Llywelyn
(1267), 81, 132–3, 139; grants
certain revenues to Ed (1269),
88; dedicates Westminster
Abbey (1269), 89–90; transfers
counties and castles to Ed
(1270), 105; death and burial
(1272), 103–4, 112, 134, 234, 263;
tomb, 230, 255, 365, 378, 406
Hereford, 65–6, 184; cathedral, 11;
earls of, *see* Bohun, Humphrey de
Herefordshire, 35, 53, 60, 190
Hertfordshire, 174, 231, 289
Hexham Abbey (Northumb), 357
Holland, count of, *see* Florence; John
Holy City *see* Jerusalem
Holy Land, 12–13, 29, 81–2, 93,
94–6, 98–101, 103, 105, 124, 127,
145, 160, 164, 196, 205, 209, 228,
232–3, 262–3, 275, 355, 366–7,
369, 372–4
Holy Trinity Priory (London), 364
Honorious IV, pope (1285–87), 207,
209, 211
Hope (Caergwrle) Castle (Flint),
180
Hopton Commission, 160–1

Hospitallers, 95, 97–8
households, 8, 148, 177, 243, 286,
321; *see also* Henry III; Eleanor of
Provence; Edward I; Edward II
Humber, river, 245, 345
Hundred Rolls inquiry, 118–20, 122
Huntingdonshire, 282
Hythe (Kent), 282
Hywel ab Owain Gwynedd (d.
1170), 136

Ipswich (Suffolk), 294
Ireland, 14, 21–3, 25, 52, 64–5, 196,
241, 271–2, 291, 345, 348–9, 358,
364–5, 376; given to Ed (1254),
18; native Irish, 218–19, 285–6,
374–5; English attitudes towards,
22, 218, 220, 243; English settlers
in, 218–20, 285, 375; degeneracy
of settlers, 285–6, 347, 375;
absenteeism of English lords, 219,
285–6, 347; repressive policy in
(1274–89), 219–21; supplies from,
20, 33, 150, 178, 186, 189, 271,
278–9, 374; neglect of, 219, 286,
346, 374; disturbed state of
(1294–), 285–7 346, 375; military
service from, 286–8, 332, 334, 339,
341, 346; justiciar of, 220, 332
Irish Sea, 218, 332, 360
Irvine (Ayr), 302–4
Isabel of Aragon (d. 1271), wife of
Philip III, 84, 205
Isabel of Fife, countess of Buchan,
358
Isabella of Angoulême (d. 1246),
mother of Henry III, 3, 24
Isabella of France (d. 1358), queen
of England, wife of Edward II,
318
Italy, 94, 106–7, 160, 164, 197, 369

Jaca (Aragon), 215
James I, king of Aragon (1213–76),
110

Jeanne of Navarre (d. 1305), queen of France, 267–8

Jedburgh (Borders), town, 288; castle, 314

Jerusalem, 12–13, 83, 94–5, 98, 100, 197, 209, 262, 264, 275, 353, 367, 371; king of, *see* Charles of Anjou; Lusignan, Hugh de; kingdom of, 95, 99, 262

Jewry, statute of, *see* statutes

Jews, 85–8, 92, 125–8, 225, 230, 371, 395; badges for, 127; and coin–clipping, 170–1; expulsion of, 226–8, 276, 373

Joan (d. 1237), bastard dau. of King John, 385

Joan (d. 1238), legitimate dau. of King John, queen of Scotland, 243

Joan (d. 1265), dau. of Ed, 73, 195

Joan of Acre (d. 1307), dau. of Ed, 101, 174, 202, 221, 224, 227, 234, 373

Joan of Dammartin (d. 1279), mother of Eleanor of Castile, 172

John (d. 1271), son of Ed, 77, 92, 105, 195

John, brother of the Order of St Thomas of Acre, 127

John, king of England (1199–1216), 3, 8, 14, 16, 218, 305, 358

John I, count of Holland (d. 1299), 254, 294

John II, duke of Brabant (1294–1312), 227, 293

John II, duke of Brittany (1286–1306), 84, 128

justice 23, 40, 114–15, 117–18, 160–1, 189, 265, 326, 347, 360, 366–7

justices, royal, 16, 29, 36, 85, 116–17, 222–4, 249, 260, 348

Katherine (d. 1257), dau. of Henry III, 195

Katherine (d. 1264), dau. of Ed, 73, 195

Kenilworth (Warwick), castle, 66–7, 70–2, 74, 76–8, 164, 184, 331; town, 67; Dictum of, 77–9, 89

Kennington (London), 348–9

Kent, 56, 60, 64, 73, 75, 174, 178, 199, 269, 283; earl of, 243

Khalil, al-Ashraf, sultan of Egypt (d. 1293), 262

Kidwelly (Carmarthen), 33, 145

Kildrummy Castle (Aberdeen), 358

Kilwardby, Robert, archbp of Canterbury (1272–78), 114, 142–3, 155, 173

Kinghorn (Fife), 232

king's evil, 368

King's Langley (Herts), 174

King's Lynn (Norfolk), 339

Kinloss Abbey (Moray), 341

Kirkliston (Midlothian), 311

knights of the shires *see* parliament

Kortrijk, Courtrai (Belgium), town and battle, 337

Lacy, Henry de, earl of Lincoln (d. 1311), Ed's close friend, 145, 157, 204, 319, 330, 332, 355, 363, 420; in Wales, 145, 157–8; in Scotland, 310, 312; rewarded with lands in Wales and Scotland, 314, 365; leader of army sent to Gascony (1294–98), 272, 276, 294–5; diplomat (1300–1), 330–1

Lamberton, William, bp of St Andrews (1297–1328), 353, 356–7

Lanark, 302; sheriff of, 302–3

Lancashire, 278

Lancaster, earls of, *see* Edmund; Thomas

Lanercost Priory (Cumbria), 308, 358, 360

Langtoft, Peter, 276, 290–1, 294, 298, 310, 314, 321, 324, 340, 345–6, 359, 363–5

Langton, John, bp of Chichester (1305–37), chancellor, 269

Langton, Walter, bp of Coventry and Lichfield (1296–1321), treasurer, 327, 329, 335, 349–50, 359, 363
La Réole (Gascony), 21
La Rochelle (Charente-Maritime), 265
Las Huelgas, monastery of, 20
Latimer, William (d. 1304), 183
Latin, 8
law, laws: English, 4, 66, 88, 114, 118–20, 124–5, 127, 149, 160–1, 175, 184, 190, 200, 202, 220, 257–9, 366–7; Welsh, 160, 168, 175–6, 182, 190, 220; Irish, 220; Scotland, 252, 257–60, Marcher, 160; of the Sea, 265; imperial, 257–8; *see also* Forest; justice; statutes; treason
Leeds Castle (Kent), 174, 191, 202, 225, 353
Leicester, 126; earl of, *see* Montfort, Simon de
Lescar (Pyrénées-Atlantiques), 215
Lestrange, Roger (d. 1311), 186, 188
Lewes (Sussex) town and castle, 61–2; priory, 61–3; battle of (1264), 61–4, 68, 80, 133, 201, 239, 312, 364, 374
Leybourne, Roger (d. 1271), 52, 54–5, 58, 63, 66, 68, 75, 79, 83, 109, 215, 225
Leybourne, William (d. 1310), 225, 282
Libourne (Gironde), 215
Limoges (Haute-Vienne), 110
Lincoln, 88, 173, 229–31, 327–31, 345; cathedral, 229–30; earl of, *see* Lacy, Henry de; bp of, *see* Grosseteste, Robert
Lincolnshire, 11, 74, 154, 190, 221, 282
Lindisfarne (Northumb), 252
Linlithgow (West Lothian), town, 253, 311, 335 6, 340 1; pele, 338, 369 70
Llanberis (Gwynedd), 188

Llandovery (Carmarthen), 160, 177
Llanfaes (Anglesey), 279
Llangernyw (Conwy), 18
Llanrug (Gwynedd), 409
Llwn (Gwynedd), 192
Llyn Cwm Dulyn (Gwynedd), 192
Llywelyn ap Gruffudd, prince of Wales (d. 1282), 35, 171–2, 275, 289, 372; early career and victories, 31–3; adopts title 'prince of Wales' (1258), 34, 219; granted truces (1258–60), 40, 46; destroys Builth (1260), 45–6, 132; destroys Dyserth and Deganwy (1263), 58, 81, 131; Montfort's ally (1263–65), 131, 396; granted Treaty of Montgomery (1267), 81, 131–3; struggles with Marchers (1267–73), 90, 133–5, 137; absent from coronation (1274), 130–2, 140; financial difficulties (1270–), 136–7; plot against (1274), 138–9; fails to do homage, 139–40, 142–3, 244; first war against (1276–77), 145–156, 247; submits (1277), 157–9, 165–6; marriage, 141, 161–2, 168, 247; grievances (1277–), 174–6; belatedly rebels (1282), 177–8; second war against (1282), 178–9, 182–6; death, 186–7, 189; regalia and relics, 192, 195, 200
Llywelyn ap Iorwerth, 'the Great' (d. 1240), 27, 31, 132, 187, 385
Lochindorb Castle (Highland), 341
Loch Lomond, 303
Lochmaben Castle (Dumf and Gall), 313, 325, 333–4, 336; constable of, 320
Loch Trool (Dumf and Gall), 360
Loire, river, 207
London, 2, 17, 23, 28, 38, 44–5, 50, 53, 55–7, 59–60, 63, 72–3, 75, 77, 79–80, 82, 86, 88, 111–12, 146, 168, 186, 199–202, 230–1, 272, 274, 280, 282–3, 289, 294, 296–7,

299–300, 305, 307, 317, 318, 322,
343, 349–50, 358, 364, 387; mayor
of, 72, 111–12, 201, 214, 317 (*see
also* Ruxley, Gregory of; Waleys,
Henry le); citizens of, 2, 23, 55–8,
62–3, 72, 79, 80, 90, 110, 127–8,
190, 201–2, 221, 227, 281, 317;
Tower of, 48, 55–6, 70, 79, 111–12,
127, 134, 186, 200–2, 280, 289,
326, 359
London Bridge, 56, 58, 344
Loudon Hill (Ayr), 360
Louis IX, king of France (1226–70),
73–4, 91, 126; marriage, 14, 266;
warm relations with Henry III
(1254–), 21, 172, 266–7; agrees to
Treaty of Paris (1259), 108, 393;
rules in Montfort's favour (1263),
57; rules in Henry's favour (1264),
59; loans money to Ed (1269), 89,
124; his first crusade (1248–52),
13, 95, 226, 263; his second
crusade (1270), 82–3, 93; death,
94, 105, 203; memorials crosses
for, 231
Louis of Evreux (d. 1319), 349
Louvre, Palace of, 204
Ludlow (Salop), 66
Lusignan, Alice de, 24
Lusignan, Geoffrey de, 24, 38
Lusignan, Guy de, 24, 38, 48
Lusignan, Hugh de, king of Cyprus,
king of Jerusalem (d. 1284), 97–8
Lusignans, 24, 28–9, 35–42, 48–9; *see
also* Valence, William de; Valence,
Aymer de
Luy, river, 216
Lyon (Rhône), 47, 160

Maccabees, Book of, *and* Maccabeus,
Judas, 263, 378, 420
MacMurrough, Art and Murchertach
(d. 1282), 220
Madog ap Llywelyn, 275–6, 278
Maes Moydog, battle of, 278

Magna Carta, 92, 305–6, 315–18,
321–2, 328–9, 375; *see also* Forest
Charter.
Magnus Maximus, 191 2
Maine, 43, 108, 227
Makejoy, Matilda, 369
Malmesbury, William of, 167
maltote, 292, 298, 306
Mamluks, Mamluk Empire, 95 99
Man, Isle of, 374
Manton, Ralph (d. 1303), 339
Mappa Mundi, 11 12
Margheh (Iran), 98
March of Wales, 34–5, 46, 53–5, 60,
90, 133, 137, 140–2, 147, 160, 241,
255–6, 297, 299, 319, 331–2, 345,
372
Marcher lords, 34–5, 40, 51, 53, 59,
62–6, 68, 133–5, 137, 142, 160,
241, 255–6, 297–8
Margaret (d. 1275), Ed's eldest sister,
queen of Scotland, wife of
Alexander III, 6, 9, 25–6, 28, 128,
232, 237, 243–4, 246–7, 342
Margaret (d. 1283), dau. of
Alexander III, 232, 235
Margaret (d. 1290), 'the Maid of
Norway', 232, 235–7, 240, 373–4
Margaret (d. 1318), queen of
England, wife of Ed, 267, 318,
327, 331, 336, 343, 353, 358–9,
363
Margaret (d. c. 1333), dau. of Ed,
174, 202, 221, 227, 373
Margaret of Provence (d. 1295),
queen of France, 14, 84, 266
Marlborough (Wilts), palace of, 9
Marshal, Gilbert, earl of Pembroke
(1234–41), 243
Martin IV, pope (1281–85), 197–8,
203
Mary (d. 1332), dau. of Ed, 174, 202,
221, 234, 368, 402
Mary of Brabant (d. 1321), queen of
France, 267–8

Mauley, Peter de, 410
Mediterranean Sea, 11, 93, 95, 99,
    197–8
Médoc (Gironde), 208
Meirionnydd, 188
Menai Strait, 156, 191
Mersey, river, 153
Methven (Perth), 356–7
Mews, Royal, 173
Milan, 107
Mirror of Justices, 223
Mongols, Mongol Empire, 97–9,
    211, 228, 263
Monmouth, castle, 284; Geoffrey of,
    see Geoffrey
Monpazier (Dordogne), 212–13
Montfort, castle of, 96
Montfort, Eleanor de, countess of
    Leicester (d. 1275), sister of
    Henry III, 15, 41, 43, 73, 84
Montfort, Eleanor de (d. 1282), wife
    of Llywelyn ap Gruffudd, 141,
    143, 161–2, 168, 178, 195
Montfort, Guy de (d. c. 1291), 74,
    105–7
Montfort, Henry de (d. 1265), 47,
    71
Montfort, Simon de, earl of
    Leicester (d. 1265), 71–4, 76, 78–
    82, 85, 88, 105, 115–16, 119, 201,
    219, 226, 351, 370–1, 387, 391;
    character and abilities, 15, 41,
    126; royal lieutenant in Gascony
    (1248–52), 15, 21, 109; leading
    reformer (1258–59), 37–8, 41;
    allies with Ed and opposes
    French peace (1259), 42–3;
    unsuccessful rising and trial
    (1260), 44–5; allies with
    Gloucester and takes over
    government, 46–8; deserted by
    Ed (1261), 49–50; leaves England
    for France, 51, 53; returns to
    England and takes over
    government (1263), 54–8; alliance
    with Llywelyn (1263–), 131, 141,
    168; feud with Mortimer (1263–),
    59–60; wins Battle of Lewes, 60–3;
    rules England (1264–65), 63–5;
    strategic errors, 65–7; killed at
    Evesham, 68, 70, 189; burial, 129;
    posthumous cult, 70, 78
Montfort, Simon de (d. 1271), 47,
    60, 66–7, 70, 74–5, 105–6
Montfortians, 59–62, 67–8, 71–2,
    74–5, 77, 88–90, 366, 390
Montgomery, 133–5, 139, 145–6,
    180, 187, 278, 297–8; treaty of,
    132–6, 138–9, 141, 143
Montrose (Angus), 289, 340
Moray Firth, 341
Morgan ap Maredudd, 275–6, 279
Morlais (Glamorgan), 255
Mortimer, Edmund (d. 1304), 185,
    297
Mortimer, Roger (d. 1282), 59–60,
    63, 66, 68, 72, 77, 134–5, 145–7,
    159, 164, 179, 185, 297, 365
Mortimer, Roger (d. 1326) of Chirk,
    185
Mowbray, John, 348
Murray, Andrew (d. 1297), 303–4, 308

Naples, 205
Navarre, king of, *see* Henry
Nefyn (Gwynedd), 192, 202, 278
Nennius, 162, 164
Newborough (Anglesey), 279
Newbrough (Northumb), 357
Newburgh, William of, 163, 166
Newcastle (Northumb), 173, 260,
    287, 308, 315, 321, 344, 357
New Forest, 173
Newgate Prison, 202
Newtown, or Francheville (Isle of
    Wight), 214
Nicholas IV, pope (1288–92), 215,
    228, 263–4
Norfolk, 199, 339, 348; earls of, *see*
    Bigod, Roger

Norham (Northumb), town and castle, 248–53, 260, 302

Norman Conquest, 3–4, 34, 86, 104, 147, 241, 371

Normandy, 14, 43, 108, 242, 264

Northampton, 60, 74, 83, 90–1, 185, 237, 300, 305; church of the Holy Sepulchre, 83

Northamptonshire, 173

Northumbria, 241, 244, 287, 308, 357

Northwich (Cheshire), 153

Norway, 235, 237, 241, 357; kings of, 232, 235; ambassadors of, 236; Maid of, *see* Margaret

Norwich, bp of, 248

Nottingham, 88

Nottinghamshire, 25

O Brian, Brian (d. 1277), 220

Offa's Dyke, 30, 167

Oléron, Isle of, 38

Oloron (Pyrénées-Atlantiques), 209–11, 215, 217; Treaty of, 210–11, 215

Orkney, 232, 237, 357

Orvieto, 107

Oswestry (Salop), 177

Ottobuono de Fieschi (d. 1276), cardinal and legate, 74, 77, 79, 82–4, 106

Outremer *see* Holy Land

Overton (Wrexham), 195

Owain ap Gruffudd (d. 1282), 31, 138, 155

Oxford, 37–9, 49, 54, 59, 60, 85, 163, 166, 239, 335; *see also* Provisions of Oxford

Painted Chamber, 112, 247, 263–4, 292, 369, 408, 420

Palermo (Sicily), 94, 198

papacy, 8, 29, 50, 81–6, 106, 142, 196, 198–9, 205, 207, 210–11, 246, 264–5, 270, 274, 330, 338, 377; *see also* Church; Gregory X; Martin IV; Honorious IV; Nicholas IV; Boniface VIII

Paris, 21, 48, 53, 89, 91, 107, 109, 200, 202–5, 207, 258, 263, 265–7, 269, 342; treaty of (1259), 43, 108, 110, 172, 205

Paris, Matthew (d. 1259), 1, 2, 7, 9, 13, 15, 17, 18, 21, 23, 25, 28, 32, 37, 80, 139, 168, 370

parliament: 29, 155, 169, 185, 346, 351; origins and development of, 16, 39, 85–6, 121–2, 306, 371; petitions in, 122, 348–9; Model parliament, 283–4

individual sessions (at Westminster unless stated otherwise): (1252), 17; (1258), 35–6; Oxford (1258), 38, 85; (1259), 41; (1260), 44–5, 47; (1261), 48, 50; (1263), 57–8; Winchester (1265), 71; Kenilworth (1266), 77; Northampton (1268), 83; (1269), 88, 90; (1270), 91–2, 124; (1273), 107; (1275), 121–5, 127, 169; (1276), 142–3; (1277), 146–7; (1278–81), 172–3; Shrewsbury (1283), 190; (1285), 199–200, 202, 222; (1286), 203; (1290), 224–5, 227; Clipstone (1290), 228–9; Norham (1291), 248; (1292), 256; (1293), 264–5; (1294), 270–1; (1295), 280–4; Bury St Edmunds (1296), 291–3, 295, 322; Salisbury (1297), 294–6, 374; (1297), 297–300, 305–6; York (1298), 310; (1299), 316–18, 321; (1300), 322–3, Lincoln (1301), 327–31; (1302), 337; (1305), 348, 350; Carlisle (1307), 359

outside of England: Bordeaux (1274), 110; Berwick (1296), 289; St Andrews (1304), 342; Dublin (1297), 347

Parliament, Houses of, 2
Parma, 107
Pecche, Bartholomew, 10, 19
Pecham, John, archbp of Canterbury
     (1279–92), 168, 173, 176, 182–4,
     186, 194, 200, 225–7, 230, 234,
     275
Peebles (Borders), 320
Pembroke, earls of, *see* Marshal,
     Gilbert; Valence, William de;
     Valence, Aymer de
Pembrokeshire, 65
Pennines, 190
Penrith (Cumbria), 247
perambulations *see* Forest
Perceval, 168
Perfeddwlad *see* Four Cantrefs
Perth, 237, 340–2, 343–4, 356–7
Peter III, king of Aragon (1276–85),
     198, 203, 210, 268
Peter 'the Spaniard', cardinal, 359
Peyrenère (Pyrénées-Atlantiques),
     216
Philip III, king of France (1270–85),
     84, 94, 107–10, 171–2, 198–200,
     203–4, 267,
Philip IV, king of France (1285–
     1314), 204–5, 207, 211, 265–70,
     274, 283–5, 291, 293–4, 307, 318,
     320, 335–7, 349, 352, 373, 416
Plymouth (Devon), 273, 275–6, 296
Poitiers (Vienne), 363–5; cathedral,
     363
Poitou, 24, 43, 108
Ponthieu, 172, 178, 189, 359
Pontigny Abbey (Yonne), 207
Portsmouth (Hants), 18, 19, 92, 271–4,
     276
Powys, 33, 138, 146
prise, 292, 295, 306, 322, 338
Provence, 1, 9, 210–11
Provisions of Oxford, 38–41, 44, 49–
     50, 54–5, 58–9, 63
Provisions of Westminster, 42, 120
purveyance *see* prise

Pyrenees, 14, 17, 51 109, 198, 203,
     208–9, 215–16, 218

Qaqun, 98–9
Queen Camel (Somerset), 166
Queensferry (Midlothian), 232
Quenington (Glos), 174
Quercy, 206–7
Quo Warranto campaign, 173, 221–4,
     227, 276, 373

Ramsey (Cambs), abbey of, 274;
     abbot of, 273–4, 282
Ravenna, archbp of, 209
Red Sea, 95
Remonstrances (1297), 298, 306
Rhuddlan (Denbigh), castle, 155,
     157–61, 177–81, 184–92, 278–9,
     399, 401; town, 161, 177, 214;
     statute of, *see* statutes
Rhys ap Maredudd (d. 1292), 217–18,
     222, 256, 377, 397
Rhys Wyndod (d. 1302), 159–60,
     176–7, 397
Riccardi of Lucca, 123–4, 169, 178,
     188, 197, 201, 223, 270–1, 395
Richard I, 'the Lionheart', king of
     England (1189–99), 3, 8, 12, 16,
     97, 101, 110–11, 207, 224, 244,
     250, 271, 364
Richard, earl of Cornwall (d. 1272),
     15, 32, 34, 87, 90, 115, 164, 204,
     266; crusader (1240–41), 12–13,
     95; quells discord in London
     (1260), 44–5; captured and
     imprisoned (1264), 61–4;
     condemns policy of disinheri-
     tance (1265), 71–2; brokers lasting
     peace (1267), 79; arbitrates
     between Ed and Gloucester
     (1270), 91–2; guardian of Ed's
     lands and children (1270–72), 92,
     105; death, 105, 116; burial, 129
Richmond, earl of, *see* Brittany, John
     of

Robert the Fool, 349

Robin Hood, 16

Rochester (Kent), 299, 305; castle at, 60

Rome, 9, 74, 86, 106, 187, 189, 196–8, 208–9, 215, 228, 253, 275, 284, 293, 334; *see also* papacy

Roslin (Midlothian), 339

Round Table *see* Winchester

Roxburgh (Borders), town, 288, 309, 336; castle, 308, 358

Russia, 97

Ruthin (Denbigh), 181

Ruxley, Gregory of (d. 1291), 201–2

St Albans (Herts), 1, 299, 323

St Andrews (Fife), 253, 342–3; bps of, *see* Fraser, William; Lamberton, William

St Asaph (Denbigh), town and bp of, 155

St Benoît-sur-Loire (Loiret), 416

St Briavel's Castle (Glos), 146

St David's Cathedral (Pembrokeshire), 195

St Emilion (Gironde), 345

St Faiths (Norfolk), 146

St George, 187, 192, 202

St George, Master James of (d. c. 1309), 160, 191, 277–9, 336, 338, 370

St Georges de Espéranche (Isère), castle, 160

St Georges Lebeyne (al-Bi'na), 96–7

St Germain-des-Prés, monastery of, Paris, 204

St Helena, priory of, Bishopsgate, 200

St John, hospital of, Clerkenwell, 45

St John, John de (d. 1302), 269, 272, 280, 294

St Macaire (Gironde), 208

St Neots (Hunts), prior of, 282

St Ninian, shrine of, 25, 333

St Omer (Pas-de-Calais), 44

St Paul's Cathedral, 45, 364; churchyard of, 202; dean of, 274

St Sever (Landes), 211

St Stephen's Chapel, Westminster, 263–4

Sainte Chapelle, Paris, 263

Saintes, Saintonge (Charente-Maritime), 206–7

Salisbury (Wilts), 236, 272, 294–5, 310, 374

Sanchia of Provence (d. 1261), wife of Richard of Cornwall, 266

Sandwich (Kent), 75, 309

Sarah, nurse to Ed, 6–8

Sardinia, 369

Savoy, county of, 6

Savoy, palace and hotel, 7

Savoy, Bernard of, 7

Savoy, Boniface of, archbp of Canterbury (1241–70), 6–7, 23, 24, 35, 57, 92, 117, 129

Savoy, Peter of (d. 1268), 7, 15, 21–3, 43, 129

Savoy, Philip of (d. 1285), 160

Savoy, William of (d. 1239), 6

Savoyards, 7, 23, 29, 34–7, 42, 48, 54–5, 57

Scone (Perth), abbey, 237, 246, 259–60, 342, 354; abbot of, 357; stone of, 246, 259, 290, 342, 411

Scota, legendary Scottish princess, 245

Scotland, 25–8, 79, 164, 178, 232–61, 264, 271, 284–92, 295, 308, 367, 369, 377; landscape and economy, 26, 240–1; ethnic mix, 241–2; anglicisation, 242–3, 373, 376; English attitudes towards, 26, 243, 246, 290, 342, 374–6; political relationship with England (to 1290), 243–8; surrender of custody to Ed (1291), 248–52; Great Cause (1291–92), 253–9; objections to English overlordship (1292–95), 260–1, 266; alliance with France (1295), 285; English conquest (1296), 287–91; rebellion (1297), 300–5, 308; war with England (1298–1304), 309–15, 319–28, 330–42; surrender to Ed (1304), 342–6, 352; settlement (1305), 347–8, 350–1; rebellion (1306), 353–4; war with England (1306–), 355–63; regalia of, 289, 297; kings of, *see* Alexander; Balliol, John; Bruce, Robert; David; William

Scott, Walter, 232

scutage, 399

Seagrave, John de (d. 1325), 321

Segontium (Gwynedd), Roman fort, 191

Seiont, river, 191

Selkirk (Borders), forest, 302–3, 312, 332, 334; pele, 338–9

Severn, river, 66–7, 133, 196, 330

Shannon, river, 220

Sheen (Surrey), 350–1

sheriffs: in England, 16, 29, 36, 50, 85, 116–21, 126, 137, 149, 185, 190, 281, 323, 327, 333; in Scotland, 290, 302–3, 350; in Wales, 279, 376; of London, 201

Sherwood Forest, 228

Shrewsbury (Salop), 138, 179, 190, 273, 275, 377

Shropshire, 117, 137, 185, 190, 324

Sicilian Vespers, 197–8

Sicily, kingdom of, 29, 32, 36, 81, 93–4, 101, 103, 164, 197–8, 205, 211, 270, 331, 369, 378, 393

Smithfield (London), 344

Snowdon, Mount, 188–9

Snowdonia *see* Gwynedd

Solomon, king, 112, 114, 129, 270, 364, 373

Solway Firth, 325–6, 362

Somerset, 162

Song of Antioch, 13

Song of Lewes, 63, 75, 366

South Downs, 61

Southwark (Surrey), 45, 79

Spain *see* Aragon; Castile

statutes, 366; Westminster I (1275), 120–1, 124–5; Jewry (1275), 125–7; Rhuddlan *or* Wales (1284), 190; Westminster II (1285), 200; Merchants (1285), 200; Winchester (1285), 202

Stepney (Middx), 317

Stirling, town, 253, 303–4, 332–3, 339–40, 344; castle, 288, 304, 313, 315, 320, 322, 325, 334, 340–1, 343, 345, 353, 364, 376

Stirling Bridge, battle of, 300, 305, 307–8, 310, 337, 340, 344

Stone of Destiny *see* Scone

Strathbogie, John of, earl of Atholl (d. 1306), 358

Stubbs, William, 283

Suffolk, 199, 348

Surrey, 178, 350; earl of, *see* Warenne, John de

Sussex, 44, 60, 75

Swansea Castle, 33

Sweetheart Abbey (Dumf and Gall), 325–6

Tabriz (Iran), 98

Tain (Highland), 358

Tany, Luke de (d. 1282), 109, 171, 181, 183, 212

taxation: 16–18, 20, 36, 85, 88, 90, 122, 170, 286, 294–5, 297–8, 305, 324, 346, 352, 371, 374

lay: twentieth (1270), 91–2, 124; fifteenth (1275), 124–5, 169; thirtieth (1283), 185, 187–8; fifteen (1290), 223, 225, 227–8; tenth (1294), 275–7, 281, 283; eleventh (1295), 284; twelfth (1296), 292–3; eighth (1297), 299, 306; ninth (1297), 306; twentieth (1300), 323, 328; fifteenth (1301), 328–30, 334, 338; thirtieth (1306), 355

clerical: fifteenth and tenth (1279 and 1280), 173; half (1294), 274–5, 293; tenth (1295), 284
papal: 196–7, 207, 228, 270–1, 331, 334, 338, 353
other: aid for Ed's knighting (1253), 18; aid for marriage (1290), 224–5, 339; scutage, 399; tallages of Jews, 86–7, 227; taxes in Gascony, 20, 213
Tay, river and firth, 241, 340–1
Tees, river, 324
Templars, 56, 95, 97–8, 262, 353
Temple, New (London), 56, 274
Thames, river, 2, 5, 56, 127
Thomas, earl of Lancaster (d. 1322), 319, 352, 377
Thomas of Brotherton (d. 1338), son of Ed, 327, 351, 357
Thomond, 220
Tintagel Castle (Cornwall), 164
Tiptoft, Robert (d. 1298), 179
Toulouse, counts of, 212
tournaments, 9, 20, 24–5, 40–1, 47, 49, 51, 53–4, 62, 81, 145, 164, 172, 192, 202, 205, 319, 336, 343, 350, 359, 364, 387, 398
towns, new: in England, 10, 214, 299; in Wales, 161, 177, 213–14, 217, 276, 279; in Ireland, 219; in Scotland, 242–3, 290; in Gascony, 369; *see also* bastides
trailbaston, 346–8
Trapani (Sicily), 94
treason, 190, 276, 283, 343–4, 354, 377
treasurer: in England, 47, 281 and *see* Langton, Walter; in Scotland, *see* Cressingham, Hugh
Trent, river, 229
Tripoli, 95–6
Trivet, Nicholas (d. c. 1334), 368
Tunis, 93–4
Turbeville, Thomas (d. 1295), 283, 285, 377

Turnberry Castle (Ayr), 332–4
Tuscany, 106
Tweed, river, 244, 248–9, 251–2, 287
Tyne, river, 324
Tynedale (Northumb), 247
Tywi, river, 160, 256

Ulster, earl of, *see* Burgh, Richard de
Upsettlington (Borders), 252

Valence, Aymer de, bp–elect of Winchester (1250–60), 24, 35–6, 48
Valence, Aymer de, earl of Pembroke (d. 1324), 319, 340–1, 355–7, 360
Valence, William de, *de facto* earl of Pembroke (d. 1296), 87, 89, 115, 129, 204, 234, 286, 293, 319, 355; arrival in England (1247), 24; allies with Ed and quarrels with English magnates (1258), 35–6; exiled, 38–9; returns to England (1261), 48–50; joins Ed (1265), 65; crusader, 83; captain in south Wales (1282–83), 180–1, 186–7; death, 293
Valence, William de (d. 1282), 180, 188
Vale Royal Abbey (Cheshire), 153–4, 195, 263, 368, 397
Valois *see* Charles
Vaux, John de, 402
Vegetius, 100, 150
Venice, Venetians, 99–100
Vescy, John de (d. 1289), 78, 83, 101, 145, 147, 156, 195, 204, 209, 366, 374
Vescy, William de, 410
Viterbo, 106

Wales, 14, 40, 46, 65–6, 131–62, 169, 172, 174–93, 195–9, 202, 221–3, 232, 242, 245, 256, 270–1, 282, 284–5, 289–91, 295, 331, 346, 348,

365–6, 369; landscape and economy of, 26, 135–6, 151–2, 156, 167, 240–1; political divisions within, 27, 138–9, 147, 241, 376; relationship with England, 139–40, 243–4; ancient and legendary history of, 164–8, 184, 191–2, 218; Welsh language, 26, 241; distinctive customs of, 26–7, 139, 167, 184; English attitudes towards, 26–8, 31, 166–8, 175, 187, 243, 349, 372; lands in, granted to Ed (1254), 18, 25; rebellion in (1256–58), 31–6, 219; war with (1262–63), 52–4; English losses in (1263), 58, 81, 131; peace with (1267), 132–3; war with (1276–77), 142–57, 247; settlement (1277–78), 157–62; grievances in (1277–82), 174–6, 182; rebellion in (1282), 177–84; conquest of (1282–83), 184–90, 281, 292, 298, 310, 314, 319, 338–9, 372–4, 376; rebellion in (1287), 217; rebellion and reconquest of (1294–95), 275–80, 374; monetary demands made on (1293–1304), 276, 324, 327, 349; military demands (1294–1304), 273–6, 307, 309, 311, 324, 332, 339, 349; *see also* castles; towns

Wales, princes of, *see* Dafydd; Llywelyn

Waleys, Henry le (d. 1302), 201, 214, 290

Wallace, Alan, 303

Wallace, William (d. 1305): obscure and humble origins, 303; based in Selkirk Forest, 303, 332; defeats English at Stirling Bridge (1297), 300, 304–5; raids northern England, 308, 377; diabolical reputation in England, 300, 308; knighted and made Guardian, 310–11; defeated at Falkirk but

escapes (1298), 311–13; resigns as Guardian, 319; captured and executed, 343–4, 350, 377

Wallingford (Berks), castle, 64, 71

Walsingham (Norfolk), 146, 368

Waltham (Essex), 231, 364

Warenne, John de, earl of Surrey (d. 1304), friend of Ed, 129, 153, 301, 319; marriage, 24; and Quo Warranto, 223; victor of Dunbar (1296), 288, 301; governor of Scotland (1296–97), 288, 290, 295, 301–5; defeated at Stirling Bridge (1297), 304, 307; rewarded with lands in Wales, 314, 365; death, 355

Wark Castle (Northumb), 287

Warwick, 40; earls of, *see* Beauchamp, William de; Guy de

Warwickshire, 328

Warwolf, 343

Weaver, river, 153

Welsh *see* Wales

Westminster, 4, 5, 8, 9, 10, 28, 33, 35, 44, 46–7, 48, 58, 91, 104–5, 111, 120, 127–8, 140, 142, 146, 155, 158, 173, 195, 202–3, 218, 227, 230, 241, 246–7, 256, 264–5, 273–6, 280, 282, 285–6, 290–1, 297, 299, 305, 308, 316–17, 323, 337, 344, 348, 351, 354–6, 364, 387

Westminster, palace of, 2, 4, 11, 36–7, 48, 65, 80, 103–4, 112–13, 129, 263–4, 298, 344, 351, 355, 366, 378; *see also* Painted Chamber; St Stephen's Chapel

Westminster, statutes of, *see* statutes

Westminster Abbey, 4, 72, 89–90, 103–4, 113–14, 128, 153, 192, 194, 200, 227, 230, 255, 346, 348, 364, 368, 377

Weston, Richard, 229

Weyland, Thomas (d. 1298), 224

Whithorn (Dumf and Gall), 25–6, 333

Wight, Isle of, 89, 203, 214
Wigtown (Dumf and Gall), 325
William I, the Conqueror, king of England (1066–87), 3, 5, 14, 48, 104, 223
William II, king of England (1087–99), 104
William the Lion, king of Scotland (1165–1214), 244, 250, 254, 257
Wiltshire, 9, 202, 234, 255
Winchelsea (Sussex), 75, 214, 282, 284, 299, 368
Winchelsea, Robert, archbp of Canterbury (1293–1313), 366, 409; his character, 284; opposes Ed on tax; 284, 293, 296–9, 331; mediates between regency and opposition (1297), 305; officiates at Ed's wedding (1299), 319; delivers *Scimus Fili* (1300), 326; supports John de Ferrers, 351–2; suspended from office (1306), 352
Winchester (Hants), 9, 11, 37, 39, 50, 59, 71–2, 74, 88, 90, 92, 202–3, 265, 274, 354; Round Table at,

203; statute of, *see* statutes; bp of, 214; *see also* Valence, Aymer de
Windsor (Berks), castle at, 5–7, 9, 10, 32, 34, 56–9, 70, 72, 76–7, 141, 174, 265, 350; forest of, 10
Winsford (Cheshire), 91
Wirral, 153, 397
Wishart, Robert, bp of Glasgow (1271–1316), 250–1, 302, 337, 348, 354, 356–7
Wolvesey Castle, 39
Woodstock (Oxon), palace of, 9, 174
wool: trade in, 122–3, 292, 295; seizures of, 271, 273, 296, 299; *see also* customs; maltote
Worcester, 66–7, 88, 144, 147–8, 161, 168, 178, 247, 272–3, 276, 280, 318
Worcestershire, 190

Yolande of Dreux (d. 1330), 232–3, 240
York, 26, 173, 185, 244, 256, 310, 319, 321; archbp of, 90
Yorkshire, 89, 153, 190, 324, 327, 345